Macroeconomics

Macroeconomics
Theories and Applications for Emerging Economies

Sreejata Banerjee

Visiting Professor, Madras School of Economics, Chennai;
Adjunct Professor, Chennai Mathematical Institute, Chennai

P. Nandakumar Warrier

Visiting Professor, School of Business Economics,
Södertörn University, Stockholm;
Professor Emeritus, Indian Institute of Management, Kozhikode

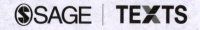

Los Angeles | London | New Delhi
Singapore | Washington DC | Melbourne

First published in 2018

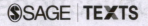

SAGE Publications India Pvt Ltd
B1/I-1 Mohan Cooperative Industrial Area
Mathura Road, New Delhi 110 044, India
www.sagepub.in

SAGE Publications Inc
2455 Teller Road
Thousand Oaks, California 91320, USA

SAGE Publications Ltd
1 Oliver's Yard, 55 City Road
London EC1Y 1SP, United Kingdom

SAGE Publications Asia-Pacific Pte Ltd
3 Church Street
#10-04 Samsung Hub
Singapore 049483

Published by Vivek Mehra for SAGE Publications India Pvt Ltd, typeset in 10.5/12.5 pt Adobe Garamond Pro by Diligent Typesetter India Pvt Ltd, Delhi and printed at Sai Printo Packs Pvt. Ltd., A-102/4, Okhla Industrial Area, Phase-II, New Delhi-110 020.

Library of Congress Cataloging-in-Publication Data

Names: Banerjee, Sreejata, author. | Warrier, P. Nandakumar, author.
Title: Macroeconomics : theories and applications for emerging economies/Sreejata Banerjee and P. Nandakumar Warrier.
Description: Thousand Oaks, California : SAGE Publications Inc., 2017. | Includes index.
Identifiers: LCCN 2017024045 | ISBN 9789386602091 (pbk)
Subjects: LCSH: Macroeconomics.
Classification: LCC HB172.5 .B354 2017 | DDC 339—dc23 LC record available at https://lccn.loc.gov/2017024045

ISBN: 978-93-866-0209-1 (PB)

SAGE Team: Amit Kumar, Indrani Dutta, Apoorva Mathur and Ritu Chopra

To my family: Ashok, Ishan, Siddhika, Mou and Deep

To my family: Sheela, Sitara and Nirupama

Thank you for choosing a SAGE product!
If you have any comment, observation or feedback,
I would like to personally hear from you.

Please write to me at **contactceo@sagepub.in**

Vivek Mehra, Managing Director and CEO, SAGE India.

Bulk Sales

SAGE India offers special discounts
for bulk institutional purchases.

For queries/orders/inspection copy requests
write to **textbooksales@sagepub.in**

Publishing

Would you like to publish a textbook with SAGE?
Please send your proposal to **publishtextbook@sagepub.in**

Get to know more about SAGE

Be invited to SAGE events, get on our mailing list.
Write today to **marketing@sagepub.in**

Contents

Foreword   xvii
Preface and Acknowledgements   xix
About the Authors   xxi

Chapter 1
Introduction to Macroeconomics   1

Chapter 2
National Income Accounts: The Toolbox for Macroeconomics   22

Chapter 3
The Basic Keynesian Demand Model and the Hidden Cross   52

Chapter 4
Economic Growth   75

Chapter 5
Introduction to the Financial Sector: Bonds and Interest Rates   112

Chapter 6
Money, Money Supply and the Banking System   129

Chapter 7
The Demand for Money   157

Chapter 8
The IS–LM Model: The Demand Side of the Economy   178

Chapter 9
The IS–LM Model: Fiscal Policy and Compatibility with the Keynesian Model   196

Chapter 10
Monetary Policy, the Policy Mix and Constraints on Policy-making   218

Chapter 11
Consumption and Investment Demand   242

Chapter 12
The Role of the Government and the Government Budget Balance   265

Chapter 13
The Supply Side: A Complete Macroeconomic Model of the Economy   286

Chapter 14
The Budget: Links to Unemployment, Inflation and the Debt Burden   315

Chapter 15
The Open Economy   337

Chapter 16
Capital Mobility   362

Chapter 17
Determination of Exchange Rates in an Open Economy   386

Chapter 18
Business Cycle Theory   411

Chapter 19
The Labour Market as the Kingpin: The Various Schools of
Macroeconomic Thought   434

Chapter 20
Disaggregated Multi-sector Models for Industrial Nations and
Developing Countries   466

Index   I–1

Detailed Contents

Foreword xvii
Preface and Acknowledgements xix
About the Authors xxi

Chapter 1
Introduction to Macroeconomics 1
  1.1. Introduction: What is Macroeconomics? 1
  1.2. What Exactly Constitutes the Field of Study of Macroeconomics? 2
  1.3. Myopic and Long-run Views: Supply Side Specifications and the Time Horizon for Macroeconomic Analysis 4
  1.4. Macroeconomic Models for Industrial Nations and for Developing Countries: Stabilization and Growth 5
  1.5. Why Study Macroeconomics? 6
  1.6. Macroeconomic Aggregates 9
  1.7. What is New in This Book? 17
  1.8. Conclusion 18
  Summary 18
  Keywords 20
  Concept Check 20
  Discussion Questions 21

Chapter 2
National Income Accounts: The Toolbox for Macroeconomics 22
  2.1. Introduction: The National Income Accounts 23
  2.2. Measuring GDP 24
  2.3. Real GDP, Nominal GDP and the Price Indices 31
  2.4. Looking at GDP from the Production and Demand Sides 34
  2.5. Problems and Issues in GDP Measurement 37
  2.6. The Circular Flow of Income and the Macroeconomic Model 40
  2.7. Conclusion 44
  Summary 46
  Keywords 48
  Concept Check 49
  Discussion Questions 50

Chapter 3
The Basic Keynesian Demand Model and the Hidden Cross 5
  3.1. Introduction: The Basic Keynesian Model
  3.2. Explaining the Multiplier: Cascading Effects on Consumer Spendi

3.3.   A Diagrammatic Representation of Consumption and Aggregate
       Demand: The 45 Degree Representation of the Keynesian Model   57
3.4.   A New Diagrammatic Approach: The Hidden Cross in
       the Basic Keynesian Model   60
3.5.   The Government Budget   62
3.6.   Conclusion   69
Summary   69
Keywords   72
Concept Check   73
Discussion Questions   73

Chapter 4
Economic Growth   **75**
4.1.   Introduction: Growth Theory   75
4.2.   What Drives Growth?   77
4.3.   Measuring Growth   77
4.4.   The Solow Growth Model in a Closed Economy   83
4.5.   The Cobb Douglas Production Function   84
4.6.   The Solow Residual   85
4.7.   The Divergence Between Countries across the World   98
4.8.   The Endogenous Growth Model   100
4.9.   Conclusion   104
Summary   105
Keywords   110
Concept Check   110
Discussion Questions   111

Chapter 5
Introduction to the Financial Sector: Bonds and Interest Rates   **112**
5.1.   Introduction: The Financial Sector   112
5.2.   The Bond Market: Bond Prices and Interest Rates   113
5.3.   The Bond Market: Supply and Demand   115
5.4.   The Bond Market: The Interest–Quantity Diagram   119
5.5.   The Interest Rate and the Market for Money   120
5.6.   The Term Structure of Interest Rates and the Yield Curve   120
5.7.   Conclusion   125
Summary   125
Keywords   127
Concept Check   127
Discussion Questions   128

Chapter 6
Money, Money Supply and the Banking System   **129**
6.1.   Introduction   129
6.2.   Money Supply   133
6.3.   The Money Multiplier Approach   137

6.4.   Credit Creation by Commercial Banks   139
6.5.   The Determinants of Money Supply   145
6.6.   Government Behaviour: Budget Deficit and the Money Supply   148
6.7.   Conclusion   152
Summary   153
Keywords   155
Concept Check   155
Discussion Questions   155

Chapter 7
The Demand for Money   **157**
7.1.   Introduction: The Demand for Money   157
7.2.   The Quantity Theory of Money   165
7.3.   The Demand for Money as Behaviour Towards Risk   170
7.4.   Conclusion   172
Summary   173
Keywords   176
Concept Check   176
Discussion Questions   176

Chapter 8
The IS–LM Model: The Demand Side of the Economy   **178**
8.1.   Introduction to the IS–LM Model   178
8.2.   Elements of the IS–LM model   179
8.3.   Output and Interest Rate Determination in the IS–LM Model   188
8.4.   Construction of the Aggregate Demand Curve from the
       IS–LM Curves   189
8.5.   The LM Curve: The Balance of Payments and Adjustments over Time   191
8.6.   Conclusion   193
Summary   193
Keywords   194
Concept Check   194
Discussion Questions   195

Chapter 9
The IS–LM Model: Fiscal Policies and Compatibility with the
Keynesian Model   **196**
9.1.   Introduction: The IS–LM Model and Fiscal Policy   197
9.2.   Deriving the Basic Keynesian Model as a Special
       Case of the IS–LM Model   208
9.3.   Effects of Changes in Taxes on Autonomous Income and Spending   210
9.4.   Conclusion   213
Summary   213
Keywords
Concept Check
Discussion Questions

Chapter 10
Monetary Policy, the Policy Mix and Constraints on Policy-making   218
10.1. Introduction   218
10.2. Monetary Expansion in the IS–LM Model   219
10.3. What Decides the Effectiveness of Monetary Policy?   223
10.4. Monetary Policy and the State of the Economy   226
10.5. Policies, Policy Effects and Political Colour   228
10.6. The Multiplier with Price Changes   231
10.7. The Policy Mix in Action   233
10.8. Constraints on Government Policy   234
10.9. Conclusion   237
Summary   238
Keywords   240
Concept Check   240
Discussion Questions   241

Chapter 11
Consumption and Investment Demand   242
11.1. Introduction to Consumption and Investment   242
11.2. Consumption Based on the Present Value of Income   248
11.3. The Modigliani Life Cycle Theory   249
11.4. The Permanent Income Hypothesis   253
11.5. Investment Demand   255
11.6. The User Cost of Capital   257
11.7. The Extended Investment Function and the IS–LM Model Results   259
11.8. Tobin's 'q'   259
11.9. Conclusion   260
Summary   260
Keywords   263
Concept Check   263
Discussion Questions   263

Chapter 12
The Role of the Government and the Government Budget Balance   265
12.1. Introduction   265
12.2. The Size and Reach of the Public Sector in Different Types of
      National Economies   266
12.3. The Mixed Economy   267
12.4. Market Failures and Corrective Government Action   269
12.5. The Economies of Scale   274
12.6. Market Power   274
12.7. Automatic Stabilizers   275
12.8. The Government Budget Balance   275
12.9. The Fiscal Deficit   277
12.10. Conclusion   280

Summary   281
Keywords   283
Concept Check   283
Discussion Questions   284

Chapter 13
The Supply Side: A Complete Macroeconomic Model of the Economy   **286**
13.1. Introduction   287
13.2. The Slope of the Supply Curve   287
13.3. Policy Effects   291
13.4. The Keynesian Income Multiplier with an Upward-sloping
        Supply Curve: The Crowding-out Effect of a Price Rise   293
13.5. Inflation and Output   293
13.6. The Aggregate Supply Curve in the Long-run   304
13.7. The Complete IS–LM Model with the Supply Side Included   305
13.8. The Complete Macroeconomic Model with Labour Market Clearing   309
13.9. Conclusion   309
Summary   310
Keywords   313
Concept Check   313
Discussion Questions   314

Chapter 14
The Budget: Links to Unemployment, Inflation and the Debt Burden   **315**
14.1. Introduction   315
14.2. Unemployment and the Government Budget   316
14.3. Unemployment and Full Employment: Frictional, Structural and
        Cyclical Unemployment   320
14.4. The Costs of Unemployment   320
14.5. Government Budget Balance and Its Macroeconomic Impacts   321
14.6. Stopping High Inflation   326
14.7. The Costs of Inflation and Disinflation   326
14.8. Government Budget Deficits and the Public Debt Burden   328
14.9. Derivation of the Debt Burden Stability Condition   328
14.10. Conclusion   332
Summary   333
Keywords   334
Concept Check   335
Discussion Questions   335

Chapter 15
The Open Economy   **337**
15.1. Introduction to the Open Economy   337
15.2. The Balance of Payments   338
15.3. Trade and Capital Flows in an Open Economy   346

15.4. The Openness of an Economy   348
15.5. Conclusion   354
Summary   355
Keywords   356
Concept Check   357
Discussion Questions   357
Appendix   359

Chapter 16
Capital Mobility   **362**
16.1. Introduction   362
16.2. The Open Economy Model   364
16.3. Internal and External Balance in an Open Economy   365
16.4. Devaluation and the Trade Balance   368
16.5. Monetary and Fiscal Policies in Open Economies   373
16.6. Macroeconomic Policy with Imperfect Capital Mobility   377
16.7. Conclusion   380
Summary   380
Keywords   383
Concept Check   383
Discussion Questions   384
Appendix   384

Chapter 17
The Determination of Exchange Rates in an Open Economy   **386**
17.1. Introduction to Exchange Rates   386
17.2. The Gold Standard, Bretton Woods and After: A Brief History of
      the Exchange Rate Regimes   387
17.3. Determinants of the Exchange Rate   388
17.4. The Time Frame   393
17.5. Exchange Rate Dynamics: The Short-run to the Long-run in
      Dornbusch's 'Overshooting Model'   396
17.6. The Portfolio Balance Model: Short-run Exchange Rate Determination
      and Overshooting   401
17.7. Fixed Exchange Rates and Managed Floats   403
17.8. The Pros and Cons of Fixed and Floating Exchange Rates   404
17.9. Conclusion   406
Summary   407
Keywords   409
Concept Check   409
Discussion Questions   410

Chapter 18
Business Cycle Theory   **411**
18.1. Introduction   411
18.2. The Simple Income Determination Model   413

18.3. The Monetarist Theory of Business Cycles   420
18.4. The Real Business Cycle Theory   422
18.5. Dating Business Cycles   423
18.6. Conclusion   427
Summary   428
Keywords   432
Concept Check   432
Discussion Questions   433

Chapter 19
The Labour Market as the Kingpin: The Various Schools of
Macroeconomic Thought   **434**
19.1. Introduction   435
19.2. The Classical Model   436
19.3. The Monetarist Model   442
19.4. A Synthesis of the Keynesian, Classical and Monetarist Approaches 448
19.5. The Future's Ours' To See: New Classical Economics and Rational
      Expectations by the Labour Market Participants   451
19.6. New Keynesian Economics and Other Labour Market Theories   453
19.7. Real Business Cycle Models with Exogenous Labour Productivity Shocks 455
19.8. The Natural Rate of Unemployment and Labour Market Equilibrium   457
19.9. Conclusion   461
Summary   462
Keywords   463
Concept Check   463
Discussion Questions   464

Chapter 20
Disaggregated Multi-sector Models for Industrial Nations and
Developing Countries   **466**
20.1. Introduction: Multi-sector Models   467
20.2. Policy Results in the Aggregated Models   467
20.3. Two Sector Models   468
20.4. The Small Open Economy Model for Industrialized Nations   468
20.5. The Bose Model: A Model for Developing Nations   472
20.6. Conclusion   476
Summary   477
Keywords   481
Concept Check   481
Discussion Questions   482

Index   I–1

Dr. C. Rangarajan

**Former Chairman, Economic Advisory Council
to the Prime Minister
Former Governor, Reserve Bank of India**

**Chairman
Madras School of Economics
Gandhi Mandapam Road, Kottur
Chennai 600025**

Foreword

Sreejata Banerjee and Nandakumar Warrier have written a very useful textbook on macroeconomics. The narrative is straight and simple, and suitable examples drawn from Indian experiences illustrate the concepts and enhance the understanding.

Macroeconomics is in a flux. Neither the classical theory nor Keynesian analysis provide adequate explanation of the behaviour of the economy. With the enormous expansion of the financial sector, the interlinks between the financial sector and the real sector have become more complex, as the recent 2008 crisis has shown. Increasingly, economies are becoming more and more open, even though, of late, some retreat from globalization has also been seen. However, for understanding the current trends, some knowledge of the basic concepts of macroeconomics is a prerequisite. This book by Banerjee and Warrier will not only enable students to understand the fundamental concepts of macroeconomics but also help them to explore further. I have no doubt that students will benefit greatly from this book, which is a good combination of theory and application.

**Place: Chennai
Date: July 10, 2017**

C. RANGARAJAN

Preface and Acknowledgements

This book on macroeconomic theory will, we hope, fill a vacuum in the offerings in this area for the students of economics. Standard textbooks in this field present macroeconomic theory and empirical examples, and information is presented in a manner designed for the students of North America and other developed nations. It is, of course, true that fundamental economic theory is the same for developing countries too, but certain assumptions, especially those made about the structure of the economy including the labour market, make these standard books more appropriate for students and readers in industrialized countries.

It needs to be emphasized that in this book, no effort has been spared to present the main models the workhorses of macroeconomic theory. Thus, the basic Keynesian model, the Hicksian IS–LM model, the Mundell Fleming model of the open economy, the supply side specifications and the Phillips Curve are all presented in painstaking detail. A novel feature of the book is that the Keynesian model is derived as a special case of the IS–LM model in a later chapter in the book. A new diagrammatic representation of the Keynesian model, as a regular cross, is also provided. As each model is discussed, the assumptions which will make the model applicable to developing and emerging market nations are laid down.

Other novel features of the book include a chapter on the different schools of macroeconomic thought, one on international capital movements and, lastly a chapter devoted to a comparison of disaggregated models for developed industrial nations and developing countries (and emerging market nations). To our knowledge, no other book has dealt with this topic in detail.

In the chapter on schools of macroeconomic thought, the common, important role of the labour market as the kingpin is highlighted, something usually ignored in such comparisons. The chapter on international capital movements deals with issues of major concern for developing nations, such as the determinants and the role of foreign direct investment and the relationship between macroeconomic policy and the external debt burden. It may be recalled in this context that John Maynard Keynes had, at the time of the negotiations leading to the establishment of the World Bank and the International Monetary Fund, put forward the proposal for an assured flow of adequate capital funds to developing nations, but to no avail.

The chapter dealing with comparisons of macroeconomic models for industrial nations and developing countries does so against the background of past crises, such as the Dutch disease problem and the perceived pattern of 'unbalanced' growth in industrial nations, which stand in stark contrast to balanced growth in developing and emerging market nations, with sectors often expanding in tandem.

Finally, from a pedagogical view, the theoretical content of each chapter is illustrated and supplemented by examples and case studies based on developments and policies undertaken in the Indian economy. Illustrations in boxes with topical discussions that help the reader to connect the theoretical content of the chapter with the real world are inserted to highlight the relevance of macroeconomics and its implications. Perhaps this may be the book feature which will sow the seeds of fascination with the subject of macroeconomics in the mind of the students.

The book is suitable for rigorous introductory courses in universities and management institutions, in economics and MBA programmes and also for those aspiring to join administrative and civil services or writing professional examinations such as those for chartered accountancy and cost accountancy. It would also be quite suited to an advance course, when more advanced topics or materials identified by double asterisks (**) are included at the beginning of relevant sections.

Sreejata Banerjee would like to thank the MBA students of DG Vaishanav College, Chennai, who first inspired her to write this book, motivating her with the argument that macroeconomics books used for teaching in Indian colleges and universities are written for a foreign audience. She would also like to acknowledge her students Dhruv Mehrotra, Vinod Kumar and Abhinandan Ghosh for their contribution in Chapters 5 and 14, respectively.

Nandakumar Warrier, would like to thank Södertörn University Business School, especially Professor Cheick Wague, for the hospitality extended to him during various stages of this work.

They are grateful to their respective families who have supported them through this journey and tolerated their consistent preoccupation with the project. They would like to thank SAGE Publications for their exceptional professionalism in supporting this book and sparing no effort to launch it in time for the academic sessions.

But their acknowledgement will not be complete without mentioning the names of the pioneering giants in this field such as Keynes and Friedman, on whose shoulders we stand.

About the Authors

Sreejata Banerjee began her teaching career from Stella Maris College after completing her PhD from the University of Madras. She taught at postgraduate level from 1993 in various colleges and institutes in Chennai. She taught economics and finance at the Edinburgh Business School of the Herriot-Watt University. She was a visiting faculty at Loyola Business School and Great Lakes Institute of Management, teaching macroeconomics, international finance and capital markets. Since 2000, she has been associated with Madras School of Economics (MSE) where she was the Union Bank Chair until 2013. She is a visiting professor at MSE where she teaches derivatives, financial economics and financial regulation. Currently, she teaches financial mathematics in the Master in Application of Mathematics programme at Chennai Mathematical Institute as an adjunct professor. Her research articles have been published in national and international journals, and she has contributed to edited volumes; she is also a reviewer for Taylor and Francis Publications, SAGE Publications, Oxford University Press and National Council of Applied Economic Research (NCAER) among others. She has also organized training programmes for bank managers, corporate executives and entrepreneurs. She is an adapted volume author of *Managerial Economics: Economic Tools for Today's Managers*, 7th edition, which is forthcoming. She has presented research papers at several national and international conferences in India and abroad.

P. Nandakumar Warrier received an MBA degree from Case Western Reserve University, Cleveland, Ohio and a PhD from Stockholm University, Stockholm and has been associated with several research organizations in India and abroad. He has worked at the Institute for International Economic Studies, Stockholm University; the Department of Economics at Stockholm University; the National Institute of Economic Research, Stockholm; the School of Business Economics, Södertörns Högskola, Stockholm; Sultan Qaboos University, Muscat, Oman; Centre for Development Studies (CDS), Trivandrum; Indira Gandhi Institute of Development Research (IGIDR), Mumbai; Madras School of Economics; and the Indian Institute of Management Kozhikode (IIMK). After retiring from regular service at IIMK, he has been a regular visitor at the School of Business Economics, Södertörns Högskola, Stockholm. His research articles have appeared in journals published from India, the USA, the UK, Germany and Greece.

CHAPTER

Introduction to Macroeconomics

LEARNING OBJECTIVES

Upon completion of this chapter, the reader will be able to:

- Answer the question: 'What is macroeconomics?'
- Explain the concepts of economic aggregates that are the components of a country's macroeconomic environment and their relationship to microeconomics.
- Comprehend the reason why there is a need to study macroeconomics, in view of the impacts of government policy and exogenous developments on all aspects of our lives.
- Understand the methods of using economic models of the short, medium and long-terms, and the behaviour of macroeconomic aggregate variables and their interactions with each other in the real and financial markets.

1.1. INTRODUCTION: WHAT IS MACROECONOMICS?

This book is devoted to the subject of what has come to be known as *macroeconomics*. The discussions you read in newspapers about the trajectory and future of the economy, the pressing problem of unemployment and the burning issue of inflation, all come under the realm of this subject. The man on the street, your hairdresser with whom you have intense discussions on the state of the economy (and with whom you always wisely agree!) are all interested in such issues but are unequipped with the tools required to analyse them. This book intends to provide the reader with a theoretical

Macroeconomics is the study of the economy as a whole, so it is concerned with the determinants of the level of aggregate output, inflation and related aggregate economic variables.

foundation and the analytical apparatus to make it possible to conduct a logical and consistent enquiry into the present state and prospects of the economy as well as the means to evaluate alternate possible policies to achieve desired goals.

A theoretical foundation is absolutely essential to understand such issues, explain past developments and—to some extent—forecast future trends, because the relationships involved are not static and independent of causality. Thus, while interest rates and prices may move together during one period, the relationship may be reversed at another time. It may all depend upon the initial change or shock that has taken place. To discern such differences and nuances, a proper founding in macroeconomic theory is indispensable.

In this chapter, Section 1.1.1 introduces the reader to what macroeconomics is, as well as its connection to microeconomics, the aggregate markets and their equilibrium. Sections 1.1.2 and 1.1.3 discuss the interlinkages with the political economy, the structure of the economy and the global economy. The canvas for macroeconomics lies in the time dimension of the study and that is elaborated upon in Section 1.1.4. Section 1.1.5 explains the concerns of policy-makers in developed, developing and emerging economies, and in Section 1.1.6 we answer the question why study macroeconomics? The various macroeconomic aggregates are explained in Section 1.1.7, while Section 1.1.8 elaborates what is new in this book followed by the conclusion.

1.2. WHAT EXACTLY CONSTITUTES THE FIELD OF STUDY OF MACROECONOMICS?

The Gross National Product measures the total value of goods and services that any country's citizens produce within and outside the country in a year.

This question can be best answered if one reverts back to the scope of what is known as microeconomics. Microeconomics, as a field of study actually provides the foundation on which macroeconomic theory is built. Microeconomics deals with the economic activities of individual units or agents in the economy, the production of a typical firm, or the consumption of a representative consumer. Here, the demand and supply of goods and services in the market place is analysed to provide solutions at the individual level.

On the other hand in macroeconomics, the major topics of interest are national output or *gross national product* (GNP), total exports and the balance of payments, *inflation* or the rate of increase in the aggregate price level and the total employment and unemployment levels. Also, the concern here is with aggregate variables as described in the next section and not with levels of variables at the individual unit.

Inflation is an increase in the general price levels in the economy.

1.2.1. Individual Markets and Agents Versus the Aggregate Economy

Microeconomics is concerned with the behaviour of individual agents and units in the economy. In macroeconomics, the field of study includes all agents and markets, for it is the aggregate, national economy, which is in the spotlight.

While, in microeconomics the concern is with consumption, production, exports, imports, borrowing, lending, etc., of individual units and their underlying behavioural determinants, in macroeconomics the concern is with aggregates such as total consumption, total production, total exports, etc., that is, national aggregates. So macroeconomics is concerned with factors like aggregate demand and supply and the relationships between different aggregates. It is not just macro variables but also their interactions and such concerns are reflected in the market equilibrium analysis discussed in the next section.

1.2.2. Aggregate Economic or General Equilibrium with Feedbacks Across Markets

Microeconomics looks at equilibrium situations in individual markets, assuming no feedback effects from changes in other markets. An equilibrium situation is one in which the demand for say tickets for a football game matches with the number of seats in the stadium or supply in the market. All those who want to see the game are satisfied and all the tickets are sold. So no extra chairs are put in the stadium to accommodate any additional requirements by spectators and there is no tendency for a change in this situation. In macroeconomics, the analysis necessarily covers all markets, because changes in one market equilibrium situation affects all the other markets, thereby changing the value of variables describing such markets.

For example, in a country, the central bank's *monetary policy* brings about changes in the interest rate, as will be discussed in detail in chapters on money and monetary policy. The effect of such a policy is not confined to one or more of the financial markets, such as the bond market alone. Rather, the goods market, part of what is called 'the real economy' (as opposed to the financial economy) also gets affected. Such changes influence a businessman when he borrows for his firm or the householder when he/she saves. This in turn influences the labour market, which is part of the real economy. The prevailing equilibrium in all these markets thereby changes. Macroeconomic analysis is concerned with what happens, in both the financial and the real markets of the economy.

> Monetary policy is any central bank's policy of managing the country's financial system through controlling the money supply by adjusting interest rates and open market operations of purchasing or selling Government Debts and thereby regulating the banking sector.

Therefore, macroeconomics is concerned with general equilibrium, meaning a simultaneous equilibrium in all the markets since a change in the equilibrium in one market will change the prevailing equilibria in all the other markets as well. Microeconomic analysis, on the other hand, typically studies equilibrium and changes in equilibrium in only a single market.

From the foregoing discussion it is clear that macroeconomic analysis traces the links and feedbacks between different markets, including those between the financial and real goods and labour markets.

1.2.3. Macroeconomics, Political Economy and the Structure of the Economy

The structure of any economy can be affected by government policies, as well as the behaviour of economic agents such as trade unions and firms. By the structure of the economy, we mean the relative sizes of the government and the private sectors, the share of consumption, investment, exports, etc. in national output. As we cruise through the various chapters in this book, we will study how the decisions made by individual entities and government policy-makers, affect the structure of the economy. In this sense, macroeconomics

> The full employment level of output is when all factors are fully employed to produce the potential level of output.

is the rightful inheritor of the traditions of a field of study originally known as 'political economy', which later on has come to be known as 'economics'. Indeed, we will see how the political 'colour' of the government in power can have strong implications for the structure of the economy.

One example of the interplay between decisions of entities and the economic structure is the effect of unionized real wage setting in the Swedish economy that is a European welfare state committed to maintaining almost *full employment* levels. With the government functioning as an 'employer of last resort', to mop up unemployed labour, real wage increases in the labour market have led to a steady growth of the public sector, often at the expense of the private sector that had to reduce employment with shrinking profitability.

1.2.4. Macroeconomics and a Country's Place in the Global Economy

No country is an isolated island in the economic sense, perhaps the only exceptions being Albania, Cuba, Myanmar and North Korea sometime back, before these countries, too, opened up cautiously. Passenger air travel between the USA and Cuba is a landmark event marking the opening up of Cuba. Macroeconomic theory takes this reality into consideration, and the interactions between the domestic economy and the global economy are an integral part of this subject. It will be seen in Chapters 15 to 17, dealing with open economics, that developments abroad, such as changes in the prevailing global economic environment, can on the one hand offer opportunities for growth to an individual nation, but on the other can also pose major problems. Similarly, it will be shown that macroeconomic policies and events in the domestic economy can affect a country's global competitive position and the external or foreign debt burden that a country has accumulated over the years. The scope of macroeconomic theory, which includes the exchange rate theory and trade competitiveness, sometimes distinguishing between traded goods and non-traded goods, does tend to overlap into the fields of international finance and international trade.

1.3. MYOPIC AND LONG-RUN VIEWS: SUPPLY SIDE SPECIFICATIONS AND THE TIME HORIZON FOR MACROECONOMIC ANALYSIS

Macroeconomic analysis can be conducted for three different time horizons: the short-run, the medium run and the long-run. These definitions stem from conditions in the production or supply side of the economy. As the first course in microeconomics would have instructed, the basic production factors are labour, capital, natural resources (including oil and gas), management and technology. In this book, the spotlight will be on three factors, namely labour, capital and technology.

The myopic and longer run models differ in their specifications as follows.

The *short-run* is a time period during which the wage rates of labour are not revised, since existing contracts have to run out. So, basically, the costs of production do not change and output can be increased to meet increases in demand. This scenario implies

The short-run is a time period during which the costs of production do not change and output can be increased to match increases in demand.

that prices of goods also do not change. The model discussed in Chapter 3, a very important one, the benchmark model for all other models, corresponds to this description. The models in Chapters 8–10, which include financial markets, also fall into the category of short-run models.

The medium run is a time horizon within which the wage rates of labour can be revised, as wage contracts do not typically last for more than a year. So, as the demand for goods increases, thereby increasing the labour demand for added output, the wage rates will rise, as is evident from the traditional demand–supply diagram for the labour market. This also implies that the price level will not be fixed in the model. Such a specification is needed to study the trade-off that policy-makers need to address when posed with the twin problems of unemployment and inflation.

The *long-run* horizon: so far, we have not mentioned anything about the other major factor of production, namely capital. In both the short- and medium-run models discussed previously, capital accumulation does not occur, so the stock of capital is fixed in the economy. However, investment takes place in these models, laying the ground for increased capital stock in terms of new roads, bridges, airports, hospitals, schools, factories and so on which are built in the economy in the next period, or the longer run. Investment demand adds to total demand in the economy, leading to an increased output in the short and the medium run, without any price increases in the short-run, but with a higher price in the medium run.

> The long-run is the time period when all factors of production change, new capital is invested and new technology is adopted, so that the production potential of the economy changes.

The long-run contrasts starkly with the scenario depicted in the short and medium run as in the long-run, the *capital stock* increases due to investments carried out in the past (periods). Thus, the production potential of the economy (remember the production potential curve in the basic microeconomics course!) is enhanced, since there is an increase in one of the factors of production. Note here that in both the short and the medium run, there is no increase in the production potential, since the capital stock is fixed, and there is no specific assumption about population increases that add to labour supply (which will be discussed in later chapters). So, in terms of which of these approaches are utilized, which time horizons are adopted, in this book, the following section provides an answer.

> An economy's capital stock is the amount of physical capital available for use in terms of equipment, machinery and infrastructure.

1.4. MACROECONOMIC MODELS FOR INDUSTRIAL NATIONS AND FOR DEVELOPING COUNTRIES: STABILIZATION AND GROWTH

In the summer of 2013, there was widespread dismay among policy-makers, industrialists, economists and even the informed general public because the growth rate of the Indian economy had slipped from 9% to less than 5% on a year-on-year basis. This concern was nothing unusual, because India as well as other developing nations were striving desperately to improve the standard of living of their people as fast as possible, while the global financial crisis (GFC) created havoc. And, while a faster aggregate growth offers no panacea for all economic problems (such as poor income distribution), it does make solutions easier. It is heartening that by the first quarter of 2016, the gross domestic product (GDP) growth rate rose to 7.9% and appears to be on an upward path.

Per capita income is the total national income earned per head in a country.

To illustrate this, consider, the useful 'Rule of 70' and the concept of *per capita income*. Per capita income is the national income per resident, which is the total national income divided by the population. The Rule of 70 says that if the growth rate of per capita income is 'n', the per capita income doubles in 70/n years. To take an example, if the growth rate of per capita income is 10% (as has been the case in China sometimes), it takes only 70/10, or 7 years for a doubling of per capita income. If the growth rate of per capita income is 2%, it will take 70/2, or 35 years for a doubling of per capita income. In this context, note that the growth rate of per capita income is the growth rate of national output GDP growth rate minus the population growth rate. Applying the rule of 70 and taking a borderline of 12,000 dollars per capita income as the entry threshold to the club of developed nations, a developing country with a per capita income of 1,500 dollars today, which has a growth rate in per capita income of 7%, can become a developed nation within 30 years.

Foreign direct investment is the net inflow of capital investments from abroad to acquire management control or ownership of companies operating in the home country.

Thus, growth is a vital concern for developing countries and even for the so-called emerging market nations, including the BRICS countries (Brazil, Russia, India, China and South Africa). Reflecting this importance, Chapter 4 is devoted to growth theory. We have also included Chapter 15 with a detailed discussion on *foreign direct investment*—and other types of capital flows that affect the balance of payments. Chapter 16 looks at the effects of international capital flows in determining government policy outcomes under fixed as well as flexible exchange rates. However, the formal macroeconomic models presented in this book, do not incorporate additions to the capital stock, as a full-scale long-run model would necessitate. Rather, only changes in investments, which would add to the capital stock in the future are modelled, as is the case in all macroeconomic textbooks.

In the case of industrialized, high-income countries, it would be fair to say that the major concerns for policy-makers and even the general public include macroeconomic stabilization, a stable internal balance with close to full employment and low inflation and a stable external balance, namely the export–import scenario. Growth itself is not a major issue, with the growth rates, in any case, not expected to be more than a couple of percentage points.

Now, for developing nations, while growth is of vital concern, macroeconomic stabilization, with low inflation, high employment and good trade performance is also important. Thus, the models presented in this book, which pertain to the short and the medium run, are applicable to industrial nations as well as to developing countries. However, specific conditions which would make the models more appropriate to the case of *emerging economies or* developing nations are pointed out as and when the models are presented.

1.5. WHY STUDY MACROECONOMICS?

Macroeconomics affects our daily life in innumerable ways, because it involves the study of the various factors which influence our consumption and investment or savings decisions. It is closely associated with government policy, as it is the branch of economics, which examines 'that part of individual and social action which is most closely connected with the attainment of and with the use of material requisites of well-being'.[1] The news media abounds with stories of rapid income growth in some countries and extreme poverty in others, of escalating prices in some countries and a slowdown in some others. The problems of inflation and unemployment are of vital concern for government policy-makers and lie at the heart of macroeconomics, as it examines and analyses these key factors in the aggregate.

Since the state of the economy affects all citizens, macroeconomic issues play a pivotal role in political debates and hence government policy-making. The 21st century is witnessing volatile fuel prices, the evolution of a common currency in Europe, financial turbulence in Asia and large trade deficits in different countries across the world, as well as the ongoing global financial crisis. The wide economic disparity among nations also leads to different issues of focus in different regions. While most governments in the developed world are primarily concerned with economic stability, leaders in developing countries look at growth as the central theme of policy-making. However, the integration of the world economy as a consequence of globalization and liberalization pose new challenges for governments and macroeconomists alike. In the last five decades, until the end of the 20th century, the Indian government, like those of other emerging countries, aimed at growth and development. But today, the problems of stability and business cycles are looming large.

Macroeconomics is a young social science, tracing its origin in its present version to John Maynard Keynes. However, notwithstanding its antiquity, its scope is wide. While the ability of macroeconomists to predict the future course of economic events may be limited, a sound grasp of the subject is indispensable for explaining economic events and formulating policy. One key issue confronting policy-makers is whether policies should concentrate on long-term growth or short-term stability. The dilemma has heightened as developed economies face slower growth while developing nations experience periodic economic fluctuations. This book on macroeconomics aims to address these problems at the theoretical level, while providing illustrations and real-life country experiences.

Macroeconomics touches almost every aspect of our lives. Households are impacted by the prices of goods and services consumed. The frequent increases in petrol and diesel prices and LPG gas for domestic cooking, has caused much hardship to the average Indian. For a businessman the corporate tax rate and income taxes are key parameters, affecting any firm's investment and sales decisions. The politician knows only too well that the political party's manifesto has to contain a range of issues from unemployment benefits, to the generation of nuclear power, to defence expenditure, to keep him/her in power. The worker in the factory is affected by minimum wage legislations, as well as by inflation. The rate of interest influences the government budget balance and the firm's decisions. The minimum support price for crops affect farmers' lives and livelihoods. However, the layman does not make any effort to study the subject of macroeconomics and it is given serious attention only in the hallowed class rooms of business schools and in universities. Sometimes even business journalists are found to be uninformed about the implications of macroeconomics.

---

[1] Alfred Marshall, *Principles of Economics*, 8th ed. (New York, NY: Macmillan, 1920), 1.

BOX 1.1   Reflections on the Journey of India's Economy since Independence

India became independent in 1947 and marched ahead into the planned era. More than six decades later, it is time to reflect. A time to look back on the path trodden and the lessons learnt. Is the road ahead in the 21st century as rough and fraught with obstacles? The views of some eminent authors over the last 65 years are reproduced as follows.

From the Approach Papers of the First Five Year Plan,

> [I]n the early 1950s it was believed that the state could play a significant role both in raising the domestic rate of savings and in putting it to more productive use.... Apart from its role in maintaining law and order, defining and protecting property rights, enforcement of contracts and the like, the State has to take the responsibility for providing elementary education, basic health care, safe drinking water, road networks, major irrigation, steel plants, railways which call for investment on a scale far beyond the capacity of individual investors and/or are in the nature of natural monopolies as public utilities.[2]

In 1983, an astute civil servant and economist S. Boothalingam wrote,

> The first prerequisite for such planning is that it should proceed from the basic proposition that the standard of living can be raised only to the extent that the growth of national income permits.... This naturally takes us to the question, what are the essentials for securing and sustaining growth: First comes the development in human beings of the knowledge and skills necessary for production of all kinds. Secondly, society must be so ordered that people also develop and cherish the willingness and the desire to work. In practical terms, this means that the system of payment for work should be such that people have an incentive to work and to improve the range of their capacity to work still further. Thirdly, for different types and qualities of production, whether of goods and services, the forms of organisations chosen should contain inbuilt provisions for prompt and adequate response to changing conditions such as new developments in ideas or materials.... Production is meaningful when what is produced is wanted.[3]

Jean Dreze and Amartya Sen wrote in 1995,

> In India a form of market mania is the common notion that radical deregulation is all it would take to 'kick start the economy' ... this is naïve. There is urgent need not only for more efficient and equitable economic institutions, but also for uprooting corruption, protecting the environment, eradicating caste inequalities, preventing human rights violations and restoring credibility to the legal system to name a few....[4]

In 2011, Y. V. Reddy, the former Governor of the Reserve Bank of India wrote,

> Macroeconomic management in India is by large reasonably balanced ... there is however, vulnerability of the macro-economy due to potential for shocks on four fronts: fuel, food,

---

[2] Uma Kapila, ed., *Indian Economy Since Independence*, 17th ed. (New Delhi: Academic Foundation, 2006), 36.

[3] S. Boothalingam, 'Indian Planning: What's Gone Wrong with Planning?' in *Plain Speaking* (1983) (Affiliated East West Press, 1993), 42 (copyright Boothalingam family 2009).

[4] Amartya Sen, Jean Dreze and Athar Hussein, eds., *The Political Economy of Hunger: Selected Essays* (Oxford: Oxford University Press, 1995), Available at http://EconPapers.repec.org/RePEc:oxp:obooks:9780198288831

fiscal and external finance. The vulnerability of the economy on account of fuel is due to the significant dependence on imported fuel. The impact of drought or floods on the availability of food items, their prices and the import bill is well known. On the fiscal front, the quality of fiscal compulsions continues to be of concern. In external finance the volatility in such flows due to heavy dependence on portfolio flows and the quality of such capital continue to be of concern.[5]

The challenges ahead are formidable, especially with the ongoing global financial crisis and the turmoil in the Euro area as well as the Brexit, all of which impact India, a country with tremendous dependence on the export-promoted growth model adopted when the economic reforms were launched in the early 1990s.

1.6. MACROECONOMIC AGGREGATES

Governments in developing countries are more concerned with economic growth which is synonymous with increases in the GDP. That is why development economists and politicians quote GDP growth rates in their discussions. Over the years, there has evolved a distinct discipline called Growth Economics, which is closely associated with macroeconomics. If governments focus on growth, the two vital tools in their hands are *fiscal policy* and monetary policy.

The governments of developed economies also face challenges of growth as these countries are facing a saturation on their growth front, but being more prone to cyclical fluctuations, they need to maintain economic stability. Coming to the case of the developing countries, today many of them have attained a reasonably high growth rate and their citizens enjoy a better quality of life; however, business cycles (discussed in Chapter 18) have become more prominent and are a cause of serious concern here. The governments of these countries, now popularly called the emerging economies, face the instabilities associated with rapid growth.

Thus, in the 21st century, most countries face the conflicting dilemmas of growth and instability. Can the two issues be synchronized? Macroeconomists today are busy researching these crucial issues. In this book, we put forward the different views of macroeconomic theory on these vital concerns, as well as some current research findings.

From an economic perspective a government has two broad objectives a) to promote economic growth and development and b) to maintain price stability. To perform these two tasks it has two instruments: fiscal policy and monetary policy. The tools of fiscal policy include taxes and government expenditures, discussed in Chapter 3. Both of these reflect the revenue and spending activities of the government. Monetary policy refers to the management of the money supply and interest rates and is discussed in Chapters 5–7. We initially assume that the economy is a closed one and hence there are no transactions with other countries. In Chapter 15, we proceed to introduce the open economy, with

> Fiscal policy is a government policy with respect to government purchases, transfer payments and tax structure.

[5] Y. V. Reddy, *Global Crisis, Recession and Uneven Recovery* (Hyderabad: Orient Blackswan, 2011), 338.

international trade in goods and services and with mobility of capital across national borders. In such a widened context, exchange rate developments and policy also assume an important role in influencing macroeconomic outcomes.

In the next section, we glance at some macroeconomic aggregates that form the building blocks of macroeconomic theory namely, real GDP, inflation, unemployment.

1.6.1. Gross Domestic Product or the Real GDP

Gross domestic product measures all final goods and services produced within a country in one year.

The *gross domestic product (GDP)*, in real terms, or fixed prices, measures the value of the total goods and services produced in a country during a given year at constant prices. Figure 1.1 shows the real GDP of India from 1952 to 2014. Measuring GDP in real terms implies that the price of the total product is reported without taking into account the effect of inflation. Figure 1.2 shows the rate of growth of output of India for the years 1952–53 to 2013–14. We see that there is wide dispersion in the GDP growth rates in last 50 years. Until 1960, the growth remained less than 6%, hovering around 2.3%. In 1959, the country actually experienced a negative growth rate. The same phenomenon was observed again in 1967–68 and 1981–82. After that the country enjoyed positive growth rates touching 10% in 1990–91. In 1991, the country shifted away from the planned era of command and control to gradual liberalization and reforms. The impact of the new policy initiatives is visible in the upward movement in the growth rates.

The annual growth rate of real GDP in India averaged 5.8% reaching an all-time high of 10.2% in 1988 and a record low of –5.99% in 1979. In 2010–11, it grew at 9.3%.

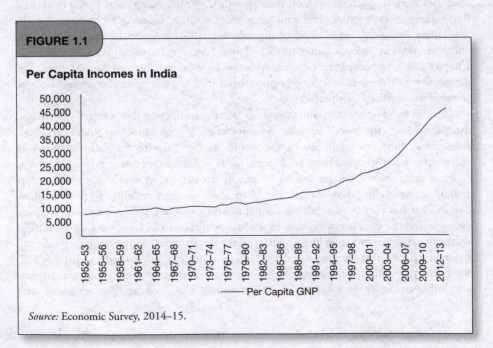

FIGURE 1.1

Per Capita Incomes in India

—— Per Capita GNP

Source: Economic Survey, 2014–15.

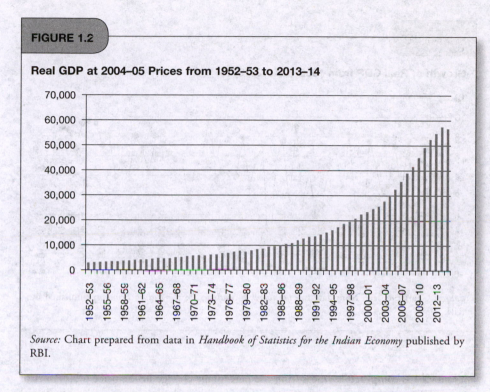

FIGURE 1.2

Real GDP at 2004–05 Prices from 1952–53 to 2013–14

Source: Chart prepared from data in *Handbook of Statistics for the Indian Economy* published by RBI.

After the GFC, India as almost all the countries across the globe experienced severe declines in growth, but recent data shows that India and many others have started to recover, including even the USA which bore the brunt of the financial crisis of 2008. Figure 1.3 shows the GDP growth rate of India over the last six decades. It is interesting to note how the country experienced a 10% growth rate in 1990 and subsequently a growth rate on an average of above 8% in the second decade of the 21st century. Also, it is observed that on at least on two occasions, the growth rate fell in the negative territory in the 1960s and later 1970s.

1.6.2. Inflation

To understand how the economy is performing, we measure the value of the country's total output or the GDP for different years. GDP can be measured by the nominal price or real price. The *nominal price* is the absolute or current market price unadjusted for inflation. The real price, on the other hand, refers to the price relative to an aggregate measure adjusted for inflation. The *rate of inflation* is defined as the percentage rate of change in the overall price level from one year to the next. Inflation is generally computed by using the consumer price index (CPI).

The nominal price is the absolute or current market price that has not been adjusted for inflation.

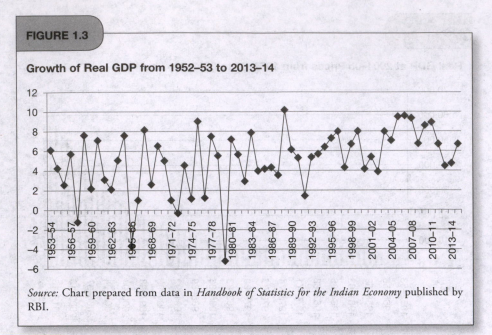

FIGURE 1.3

Growth of Real GDP from 1952–53 to 2013–14

Source: Chart prepared from data in *Handbook of Statistics for the Indian Economy* published by RBI.

The CPI is computed by measuring the percentage change in the price of a basket of consumption goods in a particular year with reference to the price for the same basket of goods in a base year when the price is assumed to be 100. The Bureau of Labour in the USA computes the CPI by considering the retail price of a large range of 'fixed basket' of goods and services purchased by a household. In India, inflation is measured by the *Wholesale Price Index* (WPI). The annual rate of inflation measured by the WPI over the past five decades averaged at 6%. In the 1950s, it was 1.7% but was quite volatile ranging between 12.5% and 13.8%. Since 2010, the RBI has been moving towards applying the CPI as measure of inflation which has now become a more widely used index for estimating inflation.

The most comprehensive measure of inflation on annual basis is the implicit GDP deflator at market prices, which is defined as the ratio of GDP at current prices to GDP at constant prices. Unlike the WPI, the GDP deflator also covers prices in the services sector which now accounts for well over 55% of the GDP. Overall inflation, as measured by the aggregate deflator for GDP at market prices, increased from 4.7% in 2005–06 to 5.6% in 2006–07 and then declined to 5.3% in 2007–08, before rising again to 7.2% in 2008–09. It has been estimated at 3.6% in 2009–10.

Similarly, in the absence of an economy-wide CPI, it is useful to look at the deflator for private final consumption expenditure (PFCE) as a more comprehensive measure of consumer inflation on an annual basis. It is defined as the ratio of PFCE at current prices to PFCE at constant prices. Consumer inflation, as measured by the deflator for

> The Wholesale Price Index is an index of the price of a representative basket of goods which is used as a measure of inflation especially in India.

the PFCE, increased from 2.9% in 2005–06 to 5.9% in 2006–07, followed by a decline in 2007–08 to 4%, before rising again to 7% in 2008–09 and was estimated at 6.4% in 2009–10.[6] India has experienced an average of more than 9% inflation between 2006 and 2013.[7] The central bank's policy is to curb inflation within a range which is known as 'inflation targeting'. The other key concern of the policy-makers is unemployment, discussed in the next section. Figure 1.4 reports inflation in the years 1997 to 2016 using the WPI. It shows how high inflation shot up during the financial crisis years and then subsequently fell sharply after 2013 remaining well below 6%. Part of this decline has been attributed to the decrease in fuel prices caused by reductions in global crude oil prices.

FIGURE 1.4

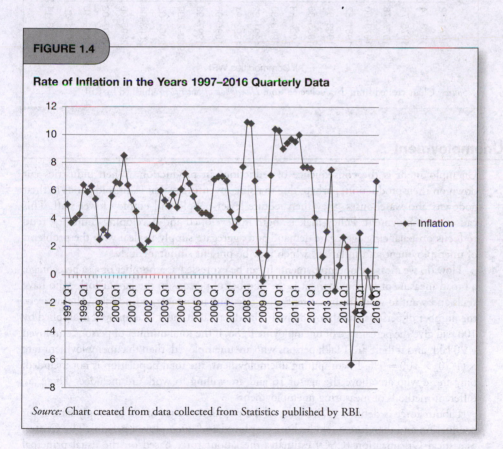

Rate of Inflation in the Years 1997–2016 Quarterly Data

Source: Chart created from data collected from Statistics published by RBI.

[6] Ministry of Finance Government of India, 'State of the Economy and Prospects', in *Economic Survey 2010*, 13. Available at: http://indiabudget.nic.in/es2010-11/estat1.pdf

[7] Raghuram G. Rajan, 'The Fight Against Inflation: A Measure of Our Institutional Development', Foundation Day Lecture at Tata Institute of Fundamental Research, Mumbai, 20 June 2016.

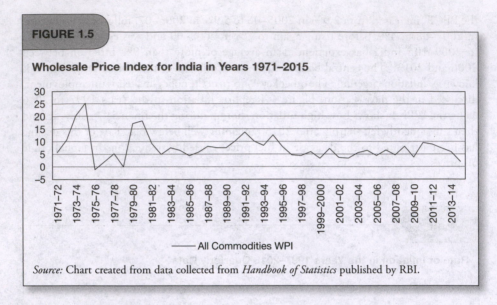

FIGURE 1.5

Wholesale Price Index for India in Years 1971–2015

——— All Commodities WPI

Source: Chart created from data collected from *Handbook of Statistics* published by RBI.

1.6.3. Unemployment

Unemployment is the consequence of reductions in production. When industries cut down on their production, perhaps due to rising inventories, that is, unsold goods in their godowns and warehouses, they then require lesser people and employ fewer staff. This causes unemployment. Policy-makers, both in developed and developing countries, tend to focus on balancing aggregate demand and aggregate supply to deal with the problems of unemployment and inflation, which may be present simultaneously.

How do we measure unemployment? It can be expressed as a number or as a percentage: a broad measure of unemployment is the number of persons in the labour force who have skills and want to work at the current wage rate, but are unable to find jobs. Alternatively, the number of persons unemployed divided by the total number of employed multiplied by 100 will give the percentage of unemployment. So, if the total number of persons employed is 20 lakh and if there are 1 lakh persons who are unemployed, then the unemployment rate is $(1/20) \times 100 = 5\%$. In computing unemployment, the total population is not included; only those who are above the age of 16 and are willing to work are included. There are different methods of measuring unemployment.

Labour force is defined as that part of the population that offers to supply labour for production and therefore, includes both employed and unemployed persons. The Central Statistical Organization (CSO) estimates the labour force based on the usual principal status approach. They consider the number of persons who either worked or were looking for work for a reference period, usually one year. The labour force participation rate (LFPR) is defined as the number of persons in the labour force per 1,000 persons.

$$\text{LFPR} = \frac{[\text{Number of employed} + \text{Number of unemployed persons}] \times 1,000}{\text{Total population}}$$

Worker–population ratio (WPR) is defined as the number of persons employed per 1,000 persons.

$$WPR = \frac{[\text{Number of employed persons}]}{\text{Total population}} \times 1,000$$

Proportion Unemployed (PU) is defined as the number of persons unemployed per 1,000 persons.

$$UR = \frac{\text{Number of unemployed persons}}{\text{Total population}} \times 1,000$$

Comprehensive data on employment and unemployment for India as a whole is available with large lags. The survey in January–July 2014 by the Labour Bureau reported that the LFPR was 52.5%, while it was higher for rural areas at 54.7% vis-à-vis urban areas at 47.2%. It was also substantially low for women both in rural and urban regions (see Table 1.1).

In developed countries, especially those with strong welfare policies such as Sweden and other Scandinavian countries, the measure of unemployment is based on claimant unemployment. This means that all those who claim unemployment benefits are counted as unemployed. There is, however, some debate as to who should be entitled to such benefits and there have been revisions of the eligibility criteria. In that sense, some people believe that the claimant methods underestimate unemployment.

In India, unemployment is inextricably interlinked to poverty. There have been, even during the early 1990s, a large number of educated unemployed young people—until the technology upsurge following the economic reforms created jobs for software engineers. In that new milieu, economic reforms bestowed unanticipated job opportunities to Indians across the urban new milieu landscape. The export of software pushed the Indian economy to the so-called 'kick off point'. The rural poor however continued to remain in poverty; the frequent reports of farmers' suicide are a grim testimony. To fight the curse of rural poverty, the Mahatma Gandhi National Rural Employment Guarantee Act (MGNREGA) was passed in 2005. It is an Indian job-guarantee scheme, which provides

TABLE 1.1

LFPR, WPR and UR for Persons Aged 15 Years (in %)

	Rural			*Urban*			*Total*		
	Male	*Female*	*Persons*	*Male*	*Female*	*Persons*	*Male*	*Female*	*Persons*
LFPR	74.7	29.1	54.7	73.8	18.5	47.2	74.4	25.8	52.5
WPR	71.6	27.2	52.1	70.9	16.2	44.6	71.4	23.8	44.9
UR	4.2	6.4	4.7	3.9	12.4	5.5	4.1	7.7	4.9

Source: Fourth Annual Employment–Unemployment Survey 2013–14, Labour Bureau.

a legal guarantee for 100 days of wage employment in every financial year to adult members of any rural household willing to do public work-related unskilled manual work at the statutory minimum wage of ₹120 per day, it was launched in 2006 across 200 districts, later the rural areas of the entire country came under its purview.[8]

The Economic Survey of 2010 reports that under the MGNREGA, 4.34 crore households were provided employment during the year 2009–10. Out of the 182.88 crore person days created under the scheme during this period, 29% and 22% were in favour of the Scheduled Caste and Scheduled Tribe population respectively and 50% in favour of women. The Figure 1.6 depicts the overall rural and urban unemployment rate in percentage between the years 1978 and 2012. Unemployment is measured per 1,000 persons. The legislation to guarantee jobs in rural areas through the MGNREGA is evidence of the reality of unemployment and rural poverty that plagues India. In 2013, the unemployment rate fell to 4.9% from 5.2% in 2012. On an average, unemployment was 7.32% between 1983 and 2013, reaching an all-time high in 2009. The Centre for Monitoring Indian Economy (CMIE) and the Bombay Stock Exchange (BSE) have analysed unemployment data and they report that unemployment in India was 5.98% in 2016 with 7.63% in urban and 5.17% in rural areas.

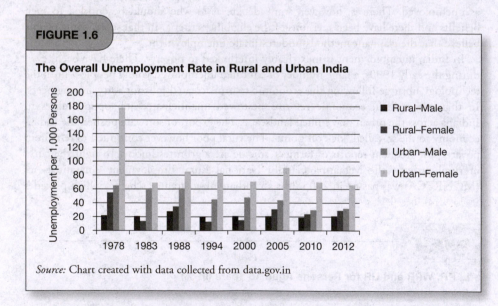

FIGURE 1.6

The Overall Unemployment Rate in Rural and Urban India

- ■ Rural–Male
- ■ Rural–Female
- ■ Urban–Male
- ■ Urban–Female

Source: Chart created with data collected from data.gov.in

---

[8] In 2016, the remuneration under MGNREGA was raised. It varied in different states; in Kerala it became ₹240 from ₹229, in Karnataka it was raised to ₹224 from ₹204, in Tamil Nadu to ₹203 from ₹183 and ₹194 in Andhra Pradesh from ₹180. (*Source:* Indian Express, April 2016. Available at http://indianexpress.com/article/india/india-news-india/mgnrega-wages-states-in-a-quandary-over-new/)

The marked difference in urban and rural unemployment—with urban jobs often taken up by migrating males from rural areas, and requiring more skills and training even for informal sector jobs in the 1970s (see Figure 1.6) is a clear indication of the gender bias experienced by women in India and is currently debated in various forums.[9]

1.7. WHAT IS NEW IN THIS BOOK?

The course material covered in macroeconomics is vast, almost all-pervading. It can be challenging to any reader who embarks on a journey of investigating the analytical apparatus that exists for understanding the mechanics of macroeconomics. It is a dynamic subject that is evolving as we speak. The role of policy-makers in any country is an exigent one, for which a sound knowledge of macroeconomics can be undoubtedly handy. For politicians, given the constraints that political parties in and out of power face, hands-on exposure to macroeconomics could be invaluable. Therefore, this book is intended not only for use in classrooms, but even for practitioners in the real world.

In the aftermath of the global financial crisis, the widespread turbulence in every part of the world has made life more difficult for decision makers and the designers of policy measures. There are innumerable factors outside the control of policy-makers and therefore the globalized, integrated world that we live in today needs many tools, often to be designed afresh, to assess the problems faced. We attempt to address issues that are discussed in drawing rooms and offices and in the chambers of leaders, business tycoons and financiers. The harsh truth is that the 'one size fits all' philosophy does not work.

We have included in this book several research findings that could be useful in understanding the many conundrums that face us. The problems faced by a developed economy are quite different from those of a developing one. Chapter 20 concentrates on comparisons between macroeconomic models for industrial nations and those which reflect realities in developing nations in a more befitting way. The comparison is facilitated by taking into consideration structural differences in the economies of high-income and low-income countries, in terms of demand and labour market conditions, to name a few.

Thus, this book incorporates a number of new elements, not seen in other macroeconomic textbooks. Importantly, the relationships between the standard macroeconomic models in use are explained and explicitly derived, as perhaps, in no other textbooks. The new elements in this book include a chapter on the different schools of macroeconomic thought highlighting the role of the labour market as 'the kingpin' of all macroeconomic models; a chapter comparing macroeconomic models for industrial nations with models

---

[9] The World Bank report titled, 'Reassessing Female Labour Force Participation in India' March 2017, writes 'our estimates show that the magnitude of the drop in Female Labour Force Participation (FLFP) for 2004–05 to 2011–12 was quite substantial, amounting to 19.6 million women and girls no longer actively participated in labour force'. 53% of this was in the rural areas. Decomposition of the factors contributing to low FLFP is the stability in household/family income indicated by increase in regular wage earners and decline in casual labour. With reference to the rural urban divide, implicitly assuming that urban women have greater access to schools and higher education, it is observed that rise in educational qualification is correlated with decline in work force. Higher literacy does not lead to greater decision-making power for women in India.

suitable for developing nations and emerging market economies; and a chapter on international capital movements and financial integration.

A new diagrammatic (cross-shaped) representation of the basic Keynesian model is also developed in the book as is the derivation of the basic Keynesian model presented in all textbooks as a special case of the so-called IS–LM model, an important workhorse of macroeconomic theory. We believe that with all these additions and innovations this book can bridge a gap that exists in this field of study.

1.8. CONCLUSION

Macroeconomics is actually what is on the lips of the man in the street when the problems of the national economy and of daily economic life are discussed. For example, the concerns of citizens centre around employment opportunities, inflation, availability of goods in shops and markets, adequate foreign exchange for personal needs, etc. All these issues form part of the subject of macroeconomics.

We have discussed in this chapter how macroeconomics diverges sharply from microeconomics in a number of ways, though the latter provides the foundations for macroeconomic theory. One main difference between the two lies in the fundamental nature of macroeconomic analysis, namely the general equilibrium approach, which simultaneously considers all markets in the economy. The policy-maker has to be necessarily informed and concerned about developments in all markets, since the markets are all interlinked. Thus, any change in financial markets has an echo in the goods and labour markets (and vice versa). This unique feature of macroeconomic analysis (when compared to other branches of economics) will become clear as the reader progresses through this book.

Before one engages in building models that capture economic relationships, the variables entering such relationships have to be defined in a measurable way. Only then can policies be formulated to affect the economy in a desired fashion. A system of national accounts is imperative for fulfilling these requirements. The next chapter presents the system and methods currently in vogue of national income accounts (NIA) that need in-depth understanding.

SUMMARY

- Macroeconomics is concerned with total consumption, total production and total exports and the relationship between the different aggregates of all these variables, not just the aggregate of one or some of these variables.
- Microeconomics provides the foundation on which macroeconomic theory is built. It deals with consumption, production, exports, imports, borrowing, lending activities of individual units and their underlying behavioural determinants.

- Again, microeconomics looks at equilibrium situations in individual markets, assuming no feedback from changes in other markets. On the other hand in macroeconomics, the analysis covers all markets.
- General equilibrium in all the markets is the keystone in macroeconomics.
- An integral part of macroeconomic theory is the interaction between the domestic economy and the global economy.
- The scope of macroeconomic theory therefore includes exchange rate theory and trade competitiveness, overlapping the fields of international finance and international trade.
- The structure of the economy relates to the relative sizes of the government and the private sectors.
- Macroeconomic analysis is conducted for three different time horizons: the short-run, the medium run and the long-run.
- In the short-run, the wage rates of labour are not revised, but production can be increased to meet higher demand.
- In the medium run, wage rates of labour can be revised, as wage contracts do not exceed one year. So, as the demand for goods increases, wage rates can rise with increasing demand for labour.
- The long-run contrasts vastly differently from the short and medium runs as not only wages but even the capital stock can increase due to investments made in the past. Thus, the production potential of the economy is enhanced.
- According to the useful 'Rule of 70' and the concept of per capita income, the latter is national income per resident. So, if the growth rate of per capita income is 'n', the per capita income doubles in 70/n years.
- Growth is a vital concern for developing countries and even for the so-called emerging market nations, such as the BRICS countries.
- The major concern for policy-makers in industrialized, high-income countries is macroeconomic stabilization, which encompasses a stable internal balance with close-to-full employment and low inflation and a stable external balance.
- Governments in developing countries are more concerned with economic growth and development. Economic growth is synonymous with increases in GDP.
- Governments have two instruments, namely fiscal policy and monetary policy. The tools of fiscal policy are broadly two items, namely taxes and government expenditure. Both of these reflect the revenue and spending activities of the government. Monetary policy refers to the management of money supply and interest rates.
- The real GDP measures the total value of goods and services produced in that country for that particular year, at constant price. Such measurement of output implies that the price of the total product is reported without the effect of inflation.
- The rate of inflation is defined as the percentage rate of change in the overall price level from one year to the next. It is computed as the CPI.
- In India, while inflation is measured by the WPI but it is on the way to adopting the CPI.

- Unemployment can be expressed as a number or as a percentage: it is the number of persons in the labour force who have skills and want to work at the current wage rate, but are unable to find jobs.

KEYWORDS

Macroeconomics	Capital stock
Unemployment	Per capita income
Gross national product	Foreign direct investment
Inflation	Fiscal policy
Monetary policy	Gross domestic product
Full employment	Nominal price
Short-run	Wholesale Price Index
Long-run	

CONCEPT CHECK

State if the following statements are true or false:

1. Macroeconomics is concerned with general equilibrium, meaning simultaneous equilibrium in all markets because a change in equilibrium in one market will change the prevailing equilibrium in the other markets as well.
2. In microeconomics, the field of study includes all agents and markets, for it is the aggregate economy, but macroeconomics is concerned with the behaviour of individual agents and units in the economy.
3. The short-run is a time period during which the wage rates of labour are not revised, since existing contracts have to run out.
4. Investment demand adds to total demand in the economy, leading to increased output in the short and the medium run, without any price increase in the short-run, but with a higher price in the medium run.
5. The 'Rule of 70' says that if the growth rate of per capita income is 'n', the per capita income doubles in 70/n years. Therefore if the per capita income grows at 10% like it did in China for some time, then it will take 7 years for that country to double its per capita income.
6. In the industrialized, high-income countries, the major concern for policy-makers and even for the general public, is macroeconomic stabilization, a stable internal balance with close to full employment and low inflation and a stable external balance.
7. The governments of developing economies face challenges of growth as these countries are facing saturation on their growth front.
8. Monetary policy refers to the management of money supply and interest rates by the central bank of the country.

9. The CPI computed by measuring the percentage change in the price of a basket of consumption goods in a particular year, with reference to the price for the same basket of goods in a base year when the price is assumed to be 100.

10. The National Rural Employment Guarantee Act is an Indian job guarantee scheme, which provides a legal guarantee for 100 days of employment in each year to adult members of any rural household to do public work-related unskilled manual work at a minimum wage.

DISCUSSION QUESTIONS

1. What are the main differences between microeconomic analysis and macroeconomic analysis?

2. Mention some variables usually figuring in microeconomic analysis. Are these variables spotlighted in macroeconomic analysis?

3. What do think are the economic issues most affecting the average citizen? Is he/she equipped to analyse these issues? How would training in macroeconomic theory help in this effort?

4. What are the main concerns of economic policy-makers in developing nations? And of those in the industrial nations?

5. Do you think that the same models can capture economic realities in developing countries and in developed countries?

6. Has macroeconomics anything to do with a country's relation with the external world, the global economy?

7. How does macroeconomic analysis for the short-run differ from that for the longer time horizon?

8. Why is inflation important in the life of an average citizen of a country? How is inflation calculated? Are there different ways to measure it?

2
CHAPTER

National Income Accounts: The Toolbox for Macroeconomics

LEARNING OBJECTIVES

Upon completion of this chapter, the reader will be able to:

- Understand how macroeconomic aggregates in the national income accounts are computed and their role in assessing an economy's performance.
- Understand how national output is computed using three different approaches, that is, the production, income and expenditure approaches.
- Comprehend the relevance and method of computing the real GDP vis-à-vis the nominal GDP and the manner in which the rate of inflation is computed.
- Understand how the unemployment rate is measured and distinguish between different types of unemployment.
- Be able to present the demand and supply side of economies through the national income accounts and appreciate the dilemma of the twin deficits of fiscal conditions and trade.
- Comprehend how the macro-economy functions through the circular flow of income with the help of a basic macroeconomic model.

2.1. INTRODUCTION: THE NATIONAL INCOME ACCOUNTS

In Chapter 1 you read about what is macroeconomics and why one needs to study it. To go any further, we need to be equipped with the tools of national income accounts (NIA) to understand how the economy of a country is moving and measure the factors that influence its path. The NIA are computed to assess the economic performance of the aggregate output of an economy. It provides a comprehensive, conceptual and accounting framework for analysing and evaluating the performance of an economy.

But why do we need to study about the NIA? In macroeconomics, a formal structure is required for building any theory that explains the macroeconomic behaviour of the different sectors of the economy. Secondly it helps us to understand how the economy of a given country is growing in relation to other countries' economies. Thus, one is able to trace the path of the given economy over time and make development and growth plans for it. The NIA provides the framework on which analytical models are built. It also creates the foundation for understanding behavioural relationships of different players in the economy.

The GDP at market prices is the value of output less indirect taxes plus subsidies.

The GDP is the most important measure of how the economy of a country is performing. It measures the value of the total goods and services that a country produces in a year by multiplying the current price of all the goods produced with the total volume or amount produced.

The GDP for India can be described as the total rupee value of everything that was made in the country in the past three months, that is, in the last quarter, or in the past twelve months, that is, in the last one year. We can also look at GDP from the consumer's point of view, as the output consumed by all those belonging to the three sectors in the economy: the household sector, the private business sector (by which we mean business or firms) and the public sector (the government). Output is invested when the resources are used in the physical production of equipment capital like plants, equipment, machinery, or infrastructure like roads, bridges, railways, etc. which would be used in the future. So, consumption and investment demand adds up to total output. When the rest of the world or the foreign sector is included, it becomes an open economy and in that case the fourth sector is included. From the production side, the measure of the nation's total output is the sum of the value added to total product during one quarter or one year at different stages of production.

On the other hand, when the output is produced, it leads to payments made to labour in the form of wages and to capital in the form of interest, profits and dividends. So, output is also income. Thus, payment made to all the factors of production is the income earned by all those who participated in the production process. So, the output calculated from the demand side equals that which is calculated from the production or supply side. From another point of view can be that the income that is earned is spent and that relates to the expenditure of all the members in the three sectors and this is known as the expenditure method. How money flows from one sector to another is illustrated in the circular flow of income which is discussed in Section 2.6 of this chapter. All these three values should be the same.

In Section 2.2, the three methods of accounting for the national income are discussed, followed by a discussion of the real GDP and the deflator. Section 2.3 analyses some of the drawbacks of the national income accounting approaches, while Section 2.4 of this chapter looks at the national income from the production and consumption sides, that is, the supply and the demand sides. In Section 2.5, problems and issues in GDP measurement are discussed. In Section 2.6, we explore the circular flow of income between different sectors. This is followed by the conclusion in the last section. A data section with the NIA of India from 1952–53 to 2013–14 has been included for illustration.

2.2. MEASURING GDP

The GDP which indicates the value of a country's total output can be measured in three different ways, namely

- The national product
- Total national expenditure
- Total national income

2.2.1. The National Product

The national product measures the output of all goods and services arising out of economic activity, while the national income is the sum of all incomes earned as a result of the economic activity. The production process generates a given amount of money income which is distributed by the productive units to the factors of production, namely, capital and labour. The measure of income this way indicates the share of the national product distributed to the factors of production, or in other words, the national income by factor shares.

The three methods look at the economic activities of a country from three different angles. In the product method, GDP is computed by aggregating or summing up the value of all goods and services produced in the different industries and agricultural sector. In the expenditure method we compute the sum of all the expenditure of the four different sectors of the economy to arrive at the gross national expenditure. In the income method we aggregate the earnings of all the factors of production or the factor incomes to arrive at the gross national income. Theoretically, if there is no error, we should arrive at the same value for GDP, Gross Domestic Expenditure and Gross Domestic Income. Each of these methods is discussed in the next section.

2.2.1.1. Final Goods and Services

The GDP is the basic measure of output. It is the value of all *final*, not intermediate, used in production of any other good. If we include the *intermediate goods* as well as the final good, it will lead to double counting of the goods and services produced in the economy, in the accounting period which is usually one year.

Intermediate goods are goods used to produce other goods or services; like cement for the construction of buildings.

With two goods A and B only,

GDP = Output of A × Price of A + Output of B × Price of B.

This can be illustrated as follows: many industries specialize in producing intermediate goods, for instance the car tyre industry. These are used in the production process of the final good, the car. For the automobile manufacturer, say the Tata Motors Company, its final good is the Tata car. To get the value added by the company, we have to deduct the value of tyres purchased from, say the MRF tyre company and used in the Tata car. This is because the tyre value is already a part of the value added by MRF; so, including it in the value added at Tata will result in double counting when the national output being is calculated.

Thus, in the computation of the GDP, only final goods and services are included. If we count the intermediate goods like tyres, wheels, windshields, etc., separately then it will lead to double counting. Hence, the GDP is the sum of all the *value added* by all the firms located in a particular country.

> Value-added GDP is the value of all the final goods and services produced in an economy in a year.

To take an example, assume that the Indian economy consists of only three companies, the Tata Motors company, the MRF tyre company and a company supplying rubber to MRF tyres. Assume also the following:

Value of Tata company output = 100 lakh (₹)

Value of tyres bought from MRF = 8 lakh

Value of MRF company output (sold entirely to Tata) = 8 lakh

Value of rubber bought = 1 lakh

Output of rubber firm = 1 lakh

Now, the GDP is calculated as the sum of the value added by any firm:

Value added by Tata Company = (100 − 8) = 92 lakh

Value added by MRF = (8 − 1) = 7 lakh

Value addition by rubber company = 1 lakh

So, GDP = 92 + 7 + 1 = 100 lakh.

Thus, GDP = Sum of value added = Value of final goods sold. (The final good here is only the Tata automobile.)

> Capital goods are those goods which are used in the production process, like plants equipment and infrastructure.

If intermediate inputs were not taken out, GDP would have been calculated as = 100 + 8 + 1 = 109 lakh. This would have been double counting!

There are however, two types of goods involved in the production process that are included in the GDP; they are *capital goods* currently produced and inventory investments. The plants, equipment, buildings, work sheds, etc. are capital goods which are ultimately used in the production process, but only a part of such capital goods are used in the current year. That part is known as *depreciation*. So, although we include the entire value of the capital good in the current year, double counting is avoided as these goods are embodied into the production process in the coming years, by assuming that they depreciate in value in the life time of that capital good. *Capital stock* increases from year to year, it also gets

> Depreciation is the decline in the value of capital equipment due to wear and tear.

> Capital stock is the amount of physical capital available for use in terms of equipment, machinery and infrastructure.

constantly worn out due to wear and tear. So, every year a part of new investment is set aside for replacing worn out capital, without increasing capital stock. In GDP accounting, investment is reported, but the loss to capital stock is accounted for by an estimate of depreciation.

Net investment = Gross investment – Depreciation

So Capital stock in y_t = Capital stock in y_{t-1} – Depreciation + Gross investment in y_t

We can write, Net investment = $Ky_t - Ky_{t-1}$

Where, K = Capital stock

To obtain the *net domestic product* (NDP) we deduct depreciation of capital (the amount of the country's stock of plants, equipment, residential structures that wear out during that year) from the GDP.

Net Domestic Product is the GDP less depreciation.

Net Domestic Product = Gross domestic product – Depreciation

2.2.1.2. Inventory Investment

Inventory investment is the increase in the stock of goods on hands.

Inventory investment is the net change in fixed goods at the end of year t awaiting sales or of material used in the production process.

Inventory investment = Stock of inventory in Y_t – Stock of inventory in Y_{t-1}

Suppose the number of cars produced by Tata India was 12,000 in the year 2014, then the entire batch of cars would be included in the GDP, even if one was not sold. As and when cars are sold the inventory investment starts to decrease by that amount. When 250 cars are bought by a dealer, the Tata India's inventory comes down by 250 and the dealer's inventory increases by 250. Total investment does not change, nor does the GDP for that year. Inventory investment is positive when production is more than sales and negative when sales is higher than production. In recession years, inventory investment is negative indicating the mood and expectation of the business sector, therefore the production has exceeded sales/consumption.

The product method of computing national output involves valuing all the final goods and services produced during the given accounting period. Alternatively, it is calculated by aggregating the values imparted by the intermediate products at each stage of production by the industries or service providers in the economy. The sum of all these values gives the GDP at factor cost. If the net factor income from abroad is included in it, we get the GNP (see Table 2.1).

2.2.2. The Income Method

The national income measures how much everyone in the economy has earned in the year. Income payments can be viewed as accruing to different factors of production. However, income receipts can be organized according to the sector that ends up with the

TABLE 2.1

The Value Added Method in ₹1,000 crores

	Agriculture and mining industries	10
Plus	Manufacturing industries	35
Plus	Services, construction and infrastructure	45
Equals	GDP at factor cost	90
Plus	Net factor income from abroad (which is income received from abroad minus income paid abroad)	10
Equals	GNP	100
Less	Capital consumption or depreciation	−20
Equals	Net national product	80

Source: Authors.

Gross national product is the value of all final goods and services produced by factors of production owned by citizens of the country inside and outside the domestic borders.

income. After computing the total GNP, various deductions and adjustments as well as additions are made in order to arrive at the income that is finally available to the household sector to spend or save as it chooses. To derive the *personal disposable income*, income tax has to be deducted.

National income is categorized into five components based on the way income is earned. Compensation to employees which is the wages, salaries and other fringe benefits earned by workers, proprietor's income; income earned by non-corporate businesses, for example, those in small sector business like small retail *kirana*[1] shops, income from self-employment earned by professionals like doctors, accountants, lawyers and also others like carpenters, beauticians, actors and sports persons. Rental income; earned by owners of houses, commercial buildings, etc. Here, the rental income is imputed for homeowners living in their own accommodation. Corporate profits; the income earned by corporate bodies after payment of taxes and to creditors. Net interest is the domestic interest paid by business minus interest received, to which the interest earned from foreigners is added.

Personal disposable income is the national income less corporate taxes less social security contributions less net interest plus dividends, plus government transfer plus personal interest income.

Some adjustments are made for accounting in the income method. For instance, depreciation is adjusted for indirect taxes like sales tax; excise duty, etc. National income of the country is obtained after indirect taxes are deducted from net national income. To compute personal disposable income, another set of adjustments are required.

First, corporate bodies do not pay out their entire profits to the shareholders, they keep a part of it as retained earnings. Hence, retained earnings and corporate taxes and dividends to shareholders are deducted from corporate profits and then dividends are added back. Second, *transfer payments* by the government are added to the national

Transfer payments are those made by the government to people without their providing any service in the current year such as social security benefits, retirement benefits, unemployment benefits.

[1] *Kirana* refers to small grocery retailer.

income and the social security contributions paid to the government are deducted. Third, the national income is adjusted for interest earned by the household sector rather than the interest paid by the business sector and this is done by adding personal interest and subtracting net interest. So the personal disposable income can be denoted by Equation (2.1).

Personal income = National income – Corporate taxes – Social insurance contributions – Net interest + Dividends + Government transfer to individuals + Personal interest income.

Personal disposable income Y_d is obtained after deducting tax payments on income received and adding transfers from the government (assumed to be non-taxed):

$$Y_d = Y - T + T_r \tag{2.1}$$

Where, Y is personal income and T is the tax paid on income—which would equal $Y(1 - t)$, where 't' is the tax rate. For simplicity, here we assume lump sum taxes, T. Government transfer payments that add to disposable income are denoted by T_r. In what follows, we consider only government transfer payments that are not taxed, so that these payments do not appear in the gross, pre-tax personal income.

National income includes only the flow of incomes and products associated with current productive activity. On the other hand, some receipts go to the personal sector, which are not a part of national income because they are incomes not earned in the current year. But, individuals do receive some part of their total income in the form of transfer payments such as unemployment compensation, pensions, disability benefits and the like. Since these receipts are not earned in the current year, they are excluded from the national income but as they are a part of the personal income they must be added to compute the personal income. After these deductions and additions are made, the resultant figure is the income of the personal sector or the household sector prior to the deduction of income tax. This is the final amount that the household sector has at its disposal to spend or to save.

The income method for measuring national income does not merely aggregate all incomes; rather, it aggregates only incomes of the residents of the nation, corporate and individual, who earn incomes directly from the productive activities during the current year. This approach excludes all earnings which have not been accrued to the factors for current services or production. In other words, transfer payments such as disability pensions or student study grants, or even old age pensions, etc. are not included. Thus, wages and salaries, interest and profits are included, giving total domestic income which is then adjusted for stock appreciation to give GDP at factor cost. Corporate bodies earn profits and so, retained earnings after tax and surpluses dividends are also included. In terms of the open economy, addition of the net factor income from abroad gives the GNP.

The GNP equals national income plus capital depreciation provided transfer payments to corporate bodies and government subsidies to business and indirect business taxes are zero. The GDP and GNP computed for our hypothetical economy are illustrated in Table 2.2.

TABLE 2.2

The Income Method

	Income from employment (wages and salaries)	45
Plus	Income from self-employment	15
Plus	Gross trading profits of companies	10
Plus	Gross trading surplus of public corporations	5
Plus	Rent	15
Equals	GDP at factor cost	90
Plus	Net factor income from abroad	10
Equals	GDP at factor cost	100

Source: Authors.

2.2.3. The Expenditure Method

The expenditure method or the spending method accounts for GDP from the consumption side, from the point of view of each sector, namely the household, business government and external sectors. The consumption of durable goods and non-durable goods by the household, business and government sectors, when aggregated, give the value of the GDP in the expenditure method, to which net exports are added to compute GNP (the gross national product).

Durable goods are all those goods which have a life of more than one year, like household appliances, machinery, equipment, etc.

$$Y = C + I + G + (X - M) \qquad (2.2)$$

Or

$$Y = C + I + G + NX \qquad (2.3)$$

Where, C is private consumption spending, I is private investment by households and business, G is total government purchases of goods and services (even salaries of government servants) and NX is total net exports = X – M (M is imports).

2.2.3.1. The Household Sector

Households purchase food, clothing, petrol, etc. which are non-durables. They also buy durables like refrigerators, televisions, computers, cars, cycles, etc. Thirdly, they buy services like health care, education, transport, entertainment, etc. The sum of all these purchases are added to depict C, consumption, in the aforementioned equation.

Expenditure on the construction of dwellings by households constitutes gross fixed capital formation. When dwellings are rented by their owners, rentals are recorded as the

TABLE 2.3

The Expenditure Method

	Consumer's expenditure (C)	70
Plus	Government current expenditure on goods and services (G)	20
Plus	Gross domestic fixed capital formation (I)	20
Plus	Value of physical increase in stocks and work in progress	10
Equals	Total domestic expenditure at market price	120
Plus	Exports and factor income from abroad (E)	20
Minus	Imports and factor income paid abroad (M)	−30
Equals	GNP_{mp}	110
Less	Indirect taxes	−20
Plus	Subsidies	10
Equals	GNP at factor cost	100

Source: Authors.

output of housing services by owners and as final consumption expenditure by tenants. When residential houses are occupied by their owners, the imputed value of the housing services enters into both the output and final consumption expenditure of the owners.

Valuables are expensive durable goods that do not deteriorate over time, are not used up in consumption or production and are acquired primarily as stores of value. They consist mainly of works of art, precious stones and metals and jewellery fashioned out of such stones and metals. Valuables are held in the expectation that their prices, relative to those of other goods and services, will tend to increase over time, or at least not decline. The expenditure approach to national income accounting is illustrated in Table 2.3.

2.2.3.2. The Business Sector

Investment spending is an expenditure made by the business sector. Plant equipment and inventories form the bulk of the expenditure of business sector, besides raw materials and research and technology. The household sector's expenditure on housing is also called investment. We compute the total investment as the sum of the expenditure on fixed investment and inventory investment. Fixed investment refers to expenditure on new factories, machinery, houses, plant equipment. This is represented by 'I' in the aforementioned equation.

2.2.3.3. Government Expenditure

The government purchases goods and services that are part of the current product, which is utilized by the government, the state as well as the central government. When the government builds roads, bridges, schools, hospitals, etc., they are all included in *government expenditure*. Moreover, salaries for the judiciary, police and government administration are also part of government expenditure. But not all government expenditure represents a demand for currently produced goods and services. Transfer payments such as unemployment benefits, soldiers' disability payments, old age pension, etc. are excluded from the GDP.

> Government expenditure is the total amount of goods and services purchased by the government, including transfer payments.

2.2.3.4. The Open Economy

If a country has trade and financial relations with the rest of the world, it is called an *open economy*. While the GDP measures the total product produced domestically, the GNP measures the total income earned by the nationals (citizens of a country). For example, if an Indian national owns an apartment in London, the rental income earned by him is part of the British GDP because it is earned in the UK. However, since rental income is a factor payment abroad it is not a part of the British GNP. Similarly, the profits/dividends and interest earned by say Microsoft India that are repatriated to the USA are counted among factor incomes received by the citizens of USA and is accounted for as payments in India's Balance of Payments, but is excluded in the Indian GNP.

> An open economy is an economy that trades goods and services and has financial interactions also with the rest of the world.

In the expenditure method of GDP accounting, *net exports* are total exports minus total imports. This item in the GDP account represents the direct contribution of the foreign sector or the rest of the world sector. Gross exports are currently produced goods and services sold to foreigners. Imports are purchases made by domestic buyers of goods and services produced outside the country and these have to be excluded from the GDP. So net exports = X – M where X is gross exports and M is gross imports.

> Net exports is the difference between a country's exports and imports.

In the expenditure approach, all money spent by private citizens, firms and the government within a year are aggregated to obtain total domestic expenditure at market prices. Total domestic spending of consumers and investors excludes all expenditures on intermediate goods. The final total expenditure at market prices also incorporates the effect of taxes and subsidies.

2.3. REAL GDP, NOMINAL GDP AND THE PRICE INDICES

National income is measured at current prices. When calculated over a number of years, the changes in national income include implicitly not only the effect of the changes in production but also the changes in prices. This estimate compared over the period would not, therefore, give a proper measure of the overall real increase in production of the country or the economic welfare of the people or the growth of the economy. This is because it does not reflect the true picture of the value of the country's output because prices change over time. Therefore, it is necessary to eliminate the effect of prices, or in other words to re-compute the whole series at given prices for one particular base year. To capture the impact of changes in prices of goods and services and also to capture its influence on the purchasing power of the domestic currency, different index numbers are used. The CPI, the WPI and the Index of Industrial Production (IIP) are usually utilized as measures of inflation.

The CPI takes a representative group's basket of consumption goods and services, that of a typical household belonging to a specific group such as 'urban industrial worker', 'agricultural labourer' or 'urban non-manual worker'. The index is constructed by using the following information:

1. consumption basket in the base year
2. prices of items in the basket in the base year
3. prices of items in the given year

In USA, the CPIs for various population groups are computed and published by the Bureau of Labour. In India, the Office of the Economic Adviser in the Ministry of Commerce and Industry, Government of India (GOI) does the same.

The WPI includes items such as minerals, fertilizers, industrial raw materials, semi-finished goods like machinery and equipment and also items from the food, fuel and light, etc. It is an index of prices paid by producers at the whole sale level. Altogether 676 items have been included in the advanced WPI in the 2004–05 base year series. The weights are based on the value of transaction in the various items, for example, ex-factory prices are used for manufactured goods and the value of marketable surplus is used for agricultural commodities. The indicator tracks the price movement of each commodity individually. It is the weighted arithmetic mean based on the fixed value-based weights for the base period. For the WPI, the Laspeyres Index is used. Its formula is

$$\frac{\sum X_{ni} W_{oi}}{\sum X_{oi} W_{oi}}$$

where X_{ni} is the value of the variable in the ith item in the current year and X_{oi} is the value of the variable in the base year and W_{oi} is the weight assigned to the ith item for the base year. The IIP shows the growth rate of the industrial sector and is not a comprehensive reflection of the whole economy, since a separate indicator for the index of agricultural production is required.

However, the GDP deflator is found to be the best indicator to compute the real GDP, because, unlike the CPI, it includes investment goods and, unlike the WPI, it excludes raw materials and intermediate goods. The basket of goods entering the GDP deflator are those which are produced in the current year.

Real GDP is the value of the total output of an economy at constant prices, or prices in a base year.

Nominal GDP is the value of the economy's total output production in a year in current market prices.

National income computed at constant prices is also called the *real GDP*. Suppose we need to compare the changes in the GDP of a country across different years, then the *nominal GDP* will not serve the purpose, because current prices in different years include the inflation rate. Inflation is the rate of change in prices and the price level is the accumulation of past inflation. Thus

$$\text{The inflation rate} = \frac{(P_t - P_{t-1}) \times 100}{P_{t-1}}$$

The existence of inflation implies that the purchasing power of money does not remain constant throughout. In some years, the inflation rate will be low, so the purchasing power of the country's currency will be higher than in years when inflation is high. To account for this discrepancy, we use real GDP as the benchmark as against the nominal GDP. The *GDP deflator*, which is a price index like the CPI, but includes all produced goods, links nominal (current) and real GDP:

$$\text{GDP deflator} = \frac{\text{Current nominal GDP}}{\text{Real GDP}}$$

The GDP deflator measures the changes in the price level or inflation. It is the ratio of nominal GDP to real GDP.

Real GDP is the current nominal GDP measured at *fixed prices* of the base year. So, in 2005, with only two produced goods A and B, real GDP at 2000 prices = Nominal output A in 2005 × (price of A in 2000 divided by price of A in 2005) + Nominal output B in 2005 × (price of B in 2000 divided by price of B in 2005).

To compare the GDP of 2000 with that of 2005, we have to take account of the changes in prices. Table 2.4 provides a simple example, for an economy producing only three goods.

Real GDP can be used to measure changes in the physical output of the economy across different time periods by valuing all goods and services produced in the two periods at the same price, that is, at constant prices. So to calculate real GDP, today's physical output is multiplied by prices in the earlier period, which we call the base year and here the year 2000 in our example. This shows what would be the worth of 2005's output if it had been sold at year 2000 prices.

Nominal GDP measures the value of the output in a given year in the prices of the same year. It is sometimes called GDP at current prices. The hypothetical economy's nominal GDP, at current prices and real GDP at base year prices are shown in Table 2.4. The last row shows from left to right the nominal GDP in the years 2000 and 2005 and the real GDP.

The GDP deflator is based on the computation of all the goods produced in the economy, is a widely based price index and is used to measure inflation. If we divide the nominal GDP of 2005 with the real GDP of the same year we get the GDP deflator.

TABLE 2.4

Illustration of Real and Nominal GDP

	Nominal GDP 2000			Nominal GDP 2005			Real GDP 2005*		
	Price (₹)	Quantity	$P_0 \times Q_0$	Price (₹)	Quantity	$P_1 \times Q_1$	Price (₹)	Quantity	$P_0 \times Q_1$
Rice	40	35	1,400	42	38	1,596	40	38	1,520
Sugar	12	20	240	14	22	308	12	22	264
Tea	150	10	1,500	154	11	1,694	150	11	1,650
Total			3,140			3,598			3,434

Source: Authors.
* At 2000 prices in Indian Rupees.

In our example, the deflator is $3,598/3,433 = 1.0478$. We can attribute the 4.7% increase in price to inflation over the five years from 2000 to 2005. In reality, the inflation in India between the same years was around 31.7%.[2]

In most countries, inflation is measured using the rate of change of the CPI, usually measured annually—which means that it is the price increase relative to the same date in the previous year. The CPI includes all the items consumed and weights are assigned according to their respective shares in the consumption basket. It also includes prices of imported goods. One drawback of the CPI is that the composition of the basket is not changed year to year while in reality, consumption patterns change as do fashion and technology. For example, the type of mobile phones used in the early nineties were vastly different from those in use today. Thus, prices of the same item are not strictly comparable either. Moreover, another problem of the price index is that it does not capture changes in quality—which may make the new good of better quality actually a different good altogether.

Another price index is the producer price Index (PPI) and it does not include many items as in the CPI. In contrast, raw materials used in production and construction like cement, steel, etc. are included in the PPI. Changes in the PPI can give advance signals about changes in inflation due to the inclusion of basic intermediate goods.

In India, the WPI is generally used as a measure for computing inflation. The WPI refers to a mix of agricultural and industrial goods at various stages of production and distribution and includes import duties.[3] The value of the WPI (2005 = 100) in India over the past 50 years reached a maximum value of 133.88 in 2010 and a minimum value of 4.15 in 1960. Since the beginning of this century the RBI has been gradually adopting the CPI as an alternative measure of inflation in line with the central banking policies of developed economies.

2.4. LOOKING AT GDP FROM THE PRODUCTION AND DEMAND SIDES

In the previous sections, we have discussed the three different methods of computing the national income. We now proceed to note how these different approaches give comparable estimates, with some required adjustments.

We have seen that the national product (GDP) from the production side is given as: wages and salaries income + capital income (interest and rental income, proprietors' income) + profits. Then, deducting depreciation from the GDP gives the NDP. Inclusion of the rest of the world sector into our accounts leads to the gross national product or the GNP. So the GNP includes incomes received by the home country's production factors, labour and capital, abroad. But we have to subtract the income received by foreign factors of production in the home country and thus, GNP = GDP + Net factor income received from abroad.

---

[2] 2004–05 as base year.
[3] *Source:* Index mundi, IMF International Financial Statistics data files.

Now, if we look at GDP from the demand side, we find that the GDP from the demand and production sides are not exactly equal. This is because GDP from the demand side will be equal to GDP from the production side after indirect taxes are added at the factory level and sales taxes are added on when sold at the retail level. So what are the components of aggregate demand? It includes 'C' which is spending on food, clothes, etc., and also on durable goods such as TVs and cars; 'G' government expenditure excluding transfer payments such as unemployment benefits, as this may lead to double counting and 'I' business spending to increase physical capital, including inventories. Spending on bonds or stocks, or on 'human capital' by way of educational spending are not included. So we re-visit Equation (2.2):

$$Y = C + I + G + (X - M) \qquad (2.2)$$

Using the notation 'S' for savings, we may also write (with the left hand side expression standing for disposable income Y_d):

$$Y - T + T_r = C + S + (X - M) \qquad (2.4)$$

In Equation (2.4), 'T' denotes total taxes paid on income received and T_r represents transfer payments from the government. Equation (2.4) indicates that disposable income (after taxes and transfer receipts) must be either consumed or saved.

By manipulating Equations (2.2) and (2.4), equating the expressions for Y from both equations and replacing (X – M) by NX (Net Exports) we get

$$C + I + G + NX = C + S + T - T_r \qquad (2.5)$$

Or

$$(G + T_r - T) = (S - I) - NX \qquad (2.6)$$

In Equation (2.6), the term on the left hand side is nothing but the *government budget deficit*, that is, the excess of government spending on goods and services and transfer payments over tax revenues received. The first bracketed term on the right hand side is the excess of private saving over investments, while the second term is the *trade deficit*, –NX, equal to (M – X), that is, the excess of imports over exports.

> The government budget deficit is the shortfall of revenue compared to the government's expenditure, or excess of expenditure above its revenue.

From Equation (2.6), it can be seen that when private savings are less than or equal to investment, a government budget deficit implies a trade deficit. And, when private saving matches private investment, the government budget deficit will exactly equal the trade deficit.

Thus, there are important relationships linking the government budget and the external sector. An imbalance in the government budget has a ready reflection, a definite impact, on the country's trade account. In other words a governments' budget deficit will move the BOP into a deficit.

> Trade deficit occurs when a country's imports exceed its exports.

The dilemma here is that an economy can suffer a dual deficit or twin deficit syndrome at any point of time. On the one hand its government's total expenditure can exceed its revenue causing a budget deficit and on the other, the households and business sector can consume excess amounts of goods and services in relation to what is produced domestically by importing more than what the country is exporting, creating a trade deficit.

This dual deficit conundrum may be resolved in one of two ways: firstly, if there is a government budget deficit, the private sector's savings have to rise in excess of its investments to prevent a spill-over of the government disequilibrium on to the external sector, creating a trade deficit. Secondly, if there is a trade deficit, which is a current reality in almost all countries across the world, then external equilibrium may be obtained by the elimination of the trade deficit through either a reduction in government spending, or an increase in taxation—or by the business sector reducing investment, something that would negatively affect economic growth of the country. In major oil importing countries like India, a perpetual trade deficit is a harsh reality that cannot be ameliorated by reducing private and government investments. Increasing the compliance of taxes to mop up higher tax revenues and preventing leakages in government expenditures through corrupt practices would be significant policy initiatives for ensuring equilibrium in the system.

2.4.1. Unemployment

A person is said to be unemployed when he/she is able and desirous to work but does not find a job; that is, a state of joblessness. The unemployment rate is defined as the fraction of the total labour force that is unemployed; so, here the total population is not considered. Those who are physically and mentally capable of undertaking productive activity above 14 years of age are supposed to be in the labour force. Hence, anyone actively looking for work is counted as unemployed.

Then, if no one is unemployed, is the economy in a state of full employment? No. Why? Full employment does not mean zero unemployment.

At any point of time, there are people who are migrating or moving from one region to another looking for jobs at a new place or for a different type of job. These persons are part of the workforce in a condition that is known as *frictional* unemployment.

On the other hand and this is quite common nowadays, persons are also without jobs since they have been rendered unemployed because of technological advancements in their work place. Such persons may begin to enhance their skills or upgrade their knowledge of technology to become employable; this situation is termed as *structural* unemployment. There are also those who are out of work due to the seasonal nature of their work, as in the agricultural sector. This is referred to as *seasonal* unemployment. In India, agricultural activity being seasonal, there is substantial seasonal unemployment and it is not uncommon for those persons to seek work in urban areas.

Finally, people also lose jobs during economic downturns or in a recessionary situation as most of the world is in today and this phenomenon is termed as *cyclical* unemployment. In this scenario, cyclical unemployment can be removed by the government by creating new jobs through launching short-run expansionary policies. Such unemployment occurs because of a shortfall in aggregate demand, primarily due to inadequate investments by the business sector, if it finds that their inventory is accumulating at a steady rate. Thus the government has to step in to ameliorate such adverse outcomes of insufficient demand on cyclical unemployment. In any event, life is hard for those who are without jobs; it obviously becomes more difficult to get a job when the unemployment rates are high. Thus, the unemployment rate is an important indicator of how an economy is performing.

2.4.2. The Interest Rate

The interest rate is an important instrument in the hands of the central bank of a country. In percentage form, it is the rate of payment made to the lender over and above the principal amount on a loan. The payment a bank makes on a savings bank account is an interest rate. For the sake of simplification, we can refer to a single rate of interest, but in reality there are a wide range of interest rates that depend on the time of repayment of the loan or maturity, the riskiness of the borrower and even the purpose for which a loan is being given. A more detailed description of interest rates and their significance in relation to the *monetary policy* of a central bank is provided in Chapter 5.

> Monetary policy is the management of the money supply and interest rate to ensure economic stability by the central bank of any country.

The *real interest rate* is a concept similar to the real GDP. The real interest rate is different from the nominal rate, as seen in the following equation:

The real interest rate = nominal rate – expected inflation.

When the government takes a loan, the financial instruments or bills issued are called treasury bills, or government debt-bearing bonds. Some of these bonds are indexed, meaning that the interest rate paid is adjusted to inflation; they are called inflation adjustable rate bonds which adjust the returns according to inflation and protects the value of (return from) your investment. They are also called Treasury Inflation Protected Securities (TIPS).

> The real interest rate is the difference between the nominal interest rate and the rate of inflation.

When inflation rate is high, the value of money falls in terms of it purchasing power. So, then what happens to the lender whose interest payment is not adjusted to inflation? He or she is a loser if the inflation rate is higher than the interest rate. Suppose you buy a bond (become a lender) for ₹5,000 with maturity of one year and an interest rate of 10%. After one year you should get ₹5,000 + 100 = ₹5,100. If the inflation rate this year is 2% then after one year the real return on your bond will be 10% – 2% = 8%. Therefore the real interest is nominal minus inflation. In India, the inflation rate has risen steadily, so that if the interest rate earned on an investment is lower than the inflation rate, then the investor is the loser.

But if the inflation rate exceeds the nominal interest rate, then real interest minus inflation will be negative, so that lenders will be the losers.

We have now taken a bird's eye view of the macroeconomic scenario from the NIA's perspective, looking at the national income from the production and consumption sides. Then we took a peek into the Pandora's box of twin deficits. A brief overview of the key macroeconomic aggregates, unemployment and the interest rate, was also undertaken. The extremely difficult terrain that policy-makers tread in managing the economy is a challenge that will unfold as we proceed in this book. A taste of this is provided as early as in the next section, where we take up the problems associated with the computation of national income.

2.5. PROBLEMS AND ISSUES IN GDP MEASUREMENT

The estimation of national income, while seemingly straightforward, is vulnerable to certain conceptual and statistical problems. While some items which should be included are not, sometimes certain items may be included twice, leading to double counting. In what follows, we focus on the chief constraints that the national income estimation procedures run up against.

2.5.1. Non-market Production

Non-market production relates to goods produced, or services given outside the market, such as home-made goods consumed within a household, or housewives' contribution to the family.

The national product does not include household work—simply because it is not involved in a market transaction. So the household services of millions of people are not accounted for in the national accounts. On the other hand, the same work done by hired help gets counted. In countries like India, it would be correct to include imputed wages for household work. For instance, the services provided by day-care centres for children are accounted for, but the valuable service done by mothers or grandmothers taking care of their own children or grandchildren at home goes unaccounted. This anomaly needs to be addressed.

2.5.2. The Imputation of Values

Self-supplied goods are given an imputed value for inclusion in the national product. There is a strong possibility of these values being overestimated or underestimated. To reduce the tax burden, companies may state higher values of imputed rental accommodation for owned office space. Again, households may report lower values from self-occupied dwellings or imputed rent.

2.5.3. The Quality of Goods

The quality of goods and services is not considered in GDP measurement. This is particularly important in the case of computers. Information technology has vastly improved in terms of the products' speed of delivery and the range of services that computers can achieve. Although national income accountants are trying to incorporate these improvements in quality, it is not an inbuilt mechanism in the accounting system.

2.5.4. The Underground Economy

There are many transactions that go unreported either because they are illegal, or are carried out for tax evasion. Underground activities produce goods like illicit liquor that are valued by their consumers, but they are not accounted for. The same is true for addictive drugs, for which a large active market prevails, but it remains outside the national accounting system.

In India, another serious problem is that of black money, the income earned by individuals and companies that is under-reported to evade taxes. This creates black money. Some reports claim that an amount exceeding US$1.4 trillion of black money belonging to Indian nationals is stashed in Switzerland.[4]

---

[4] According to the White Paper on Black Money in India report in May 2012, Swiss National Bank estimates that the total amount of deposits in all Swiss banks, at the end of 2010, by Indians was ₹9,295 crore, or US$2.1 billion Available at: http://en.wikipedia.org/wiki/Indian_black_money

2.5.5. Economic 'Bads' and Side Effects

NIA do not adjust for side effects or the 'bads' in the production process if they do not involve market transactions, for example, the environmental damage caused by the production of certain goods. As private property rights over air and water are not properly defined, their adverse impacts on future production possibilities and the quality of life remain unaccounted for.

2.5.6. Leisure and Human Costs

Simon Kuznets, one of the pioneers in national income accounting, pointed out the failure of the system to include leisure and human costs. When leisure increases productivity, it should be included as a valuable commodity. The human costs associated with many jobs such as physical and mental stress and the dangers linked to them are also not included. And, while increased development of technology has rendered many jobs much less strenuous and exhausting than they were forty years ago, their impact on productively is excluded.

2.5.7. The Environmental Cost

Environmental damage due to production and the consequent reduction in non-renewable resources and degradation of the ecology is not accounted for in the current

---

BOX 2.1 **Stocks and Flows of Economic Variables**

In economics, there are two measures for economic variables, which are distinguished as stocks or flows. When an economic variable is measured at one point in time it is called a *stock;* for instance, the supply of money is a stock, which amounted to around ₹500,000 crore in the first quarter of 2012; similarly, the capital stock of some ₹258,756 crore in India is also a stock. From a lay man's point of view, the amount of petrol in a car at the beginning of the week is a stock. But when petrol is filled into the tank it is a *flow,* so the litres of petrol pumped into the tank is a flow, that is, a change in the quantity of the good per unit of time. Remember that the measures of stocks and flows are in different units. A flow measures a rate per unit of time. The national income of a nation is an example of a flow and the GDP is a significant flow variable in economics.

So, when the GDP of a country if expressed in US dollars as 760 billion, it really means that it is $760 billion per year. The increase in investment and hence the increase in the plants and equipment in a country is a flow. We can compare a stock to a still photograph and a flow to a video which changes over time. Thus, in measuring the GDP, we need to make a distinction between the two concepts; the stock and the flow.

Source: Authors.

format of NIA. The loss of livelihoods due to major infrastructure developments like dams and nuclear power plants is also yet to be incorporated into the national accounting systems.

2.6. THE CIRCULAR FLOW OF INCOME AND THE MACROECONOMIC MODEL

We have explored so far the methods and intricacies of calculating the national income of an economy and some technical impediments to the definitions and measurements. In this section, we proceed to build a rudimentary model for macroeconomic analysis.

In Chapter 1, we outlined the key objectives of macroeconomic policy, namely, full employment, price stability and growth. No doubt there are difficulties to cope with, such as budget and trade deficits and mismatches between savings and investment that have been explained in the previous section. In the first decade of the 21st century, food and energy shocks pushed the Indian economy into a recessionary spell, which has been further aggravated by the global meltdown. If you follow the news headlines you will be also aware of the struggle that the government and the central bank is facing in initiating recoveries and keeping inflation in check.

For an understanding of the way an economy operates, macroeconomic theory can be a systematic guide. The initial step in that direction is to develop a model, which is a simplifying device to comprehend macroeconomic problems, so that the relationships and processes of economic system are highlighted. A model can consist of mathematical equations or a set of diagrams, or even a schema like a flowchart. The circular flow of income model gives an insight into the mechanisms of the macro-economy and for which the concepts of stocks and flows described in Box 2.1 have to be kept in mind.

2.6.1. The Circular Flow of Income

At the outset, we start with a basic hypothetical economy where there are only two types of economic agents: producers and consumers. The producers are those who produce output and sell them in the market; they are bundled together in the 'business sector'. The consumers are those agents who purchase the producers' output for their consumption; this group is called the 'household sector'. While, the producers' work is to produce output for sale, the consumers' activity is to consume. In this model the household sector is assumed to possess all the factors of production (land, labour and capital), the household sector's income comprising of wages, salaries, rent, dividends, interest are derived from sales to the business sector.

The economy is not a closed one; rather, it is similar to a hydraulic mechanism where the water level falls if it is drained through outlets or rises when fresh inflow comes in through inlets. In Figure 2.1 the household sector is assumed to earn ₹10,000 per year by

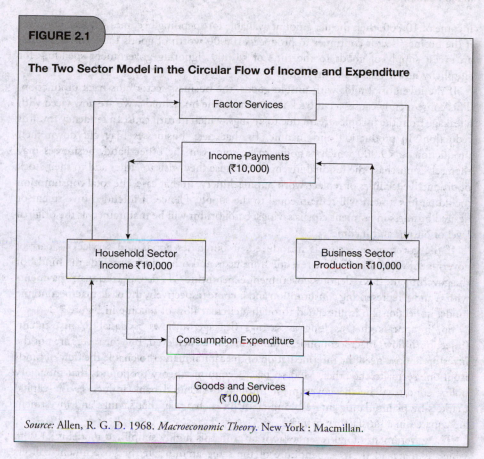

FIGURE 2.1

The Two Sector Model in the Circular Flow of Income and Expenditure

Source: Allen, R. G. D. 1968. *Macroeconomic Theory.* New York : Macmillan.

selling its factor services and the business sector is assumed to produce ₹10,000 worth of goods and services by utilization of the factors of production provided by the household sector. The members of the households sector are assumed to consume all the goods produced by spending the entire amount of the income. This amount now goes back to the business sector. As long as the income payments by the business sector for factor services go back to it because of the purchases made by the household sector, the circular flow of income between the two sectors tends to perpetuate itself. This is a macroeconomic equilibrium, since the demand for goods and services is exactly met by the supply and production and there will be a tendency to continue at the same level.

This structure of flows can be self-perpetuating, but it is not a closed system. Rather, it resembles a plumbing system of liquid flows with inlets and outlets. We can refer to these outlets and inlets as leakages and injections to the system. One source of outflow from the system is savings. Suppose the households wish to save ₹1,000 out of a disposable income of 10,000, then the net amount available for spending becomes ₹9,000. However if the business sector continues to produce ₹10,000 worth of goods there will now exist an excess supply of goods to the tune of ₹1,000 (ignoring government spending for simplicity now). This is the inventory.

If the inventory builds with unsold goods, the business sector cuts back production. This consequently causes a cut back in income to the households. We are now faced with a leakage from the income stream due to savings, which in turn causes a tendency towards reductions in production and income. In that case, businesses may cut down their production to ₹9,000 which is going to be sold. On the other hand, businesses may themselves purchase the residual inventory, because they wish to either add to their stock of productive facilities or replace worn out machinery; in that case, the total consumption including investment will remain equal to the supply. Hence, if intended investment or desired business investment equals savings, equilibrium will be maintained at the original level of output and income.

If the government sector is introduced, it purchases goods and services as part of government expenditures. The revenue from taxes and other duties provide the funds for the government. If 'G' denotes government expenditure, 'T' taxes, 'Tr' transfer payments with C and Y representing consumption and income respectively, the basic macroeconomic model in Section 2.6 is illustrated through a circular flow of income in Figure 2.2.

So, it appears that as long as savings (leakage/outflow) is equal to investment, (injection/inflow) macroeconomic equilibrium can be achieved. But the savers are not the investors and we need the intermediation of the capital market to enable the flow of funds from one sector to the other. Modern macroeconomic theory propounds that monetary policy conducted by the government through the central bank influences the capital markets by manipulating interests and credit in such a way that savings and investment are equated in a satisfactory manner.

The government's total revenue from taxes in this highly simplified model is ₹1,000, which is matched by its expenditure of the same amount. If the government collects ₹1,000 from the household sector's income in the form of taxes, it will decrease both household consumption and savings. Since consumption comes down, business sales will fall and incomes will in turn shrink. To offset the leakage of taxes, if the government spends an equivalent to the amount of tax revenue then total production and sales of the business sector will equal total consumption of the household and government sectors and the circular flow of income will continue to be in equilibrium. In this system there are two identities I=S and T=G.

When the foreign trade sector or the rest of the world is introduced into this hypothetical economy, the household sector purchases goods from abroad and hence imports those goods. Then this expenditure represents an outflow out of the circular flow. The offsetting transaction would be when foreigners purchase goods from this country and hence we have exports. This transaction will represent an inflow or injection into the circular flow. These flows pass through the *balance of payments* accounts, which are influenced by foreign policies of various kinds. So in the circular flow of income, we have savings, taxes and imports as leakages and investment, government expenditure and exports as injections.

The Balance of Payments is the record of the transactions between the residents of a country with the rest of the world, with two components: the current account and the capital account.

FIGURE 2.2

The Circular Flow of Income and Expenditure with Savings and Investment

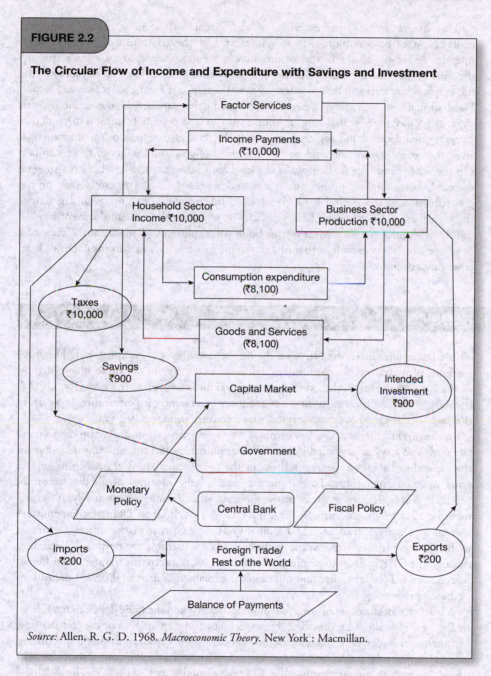

Source: Allen, R. G. D. 1968. *Macroeconomic Theory*. New York : Macmillan.

The diagrammatic representation of the circular flow is a highly simplified explanation of how economic factors interact and the relationships between them operate. As long as all the factors of production are used or employed in an economy, the total output that is produced is its potential level of output. Then an economy at the full employment level will be one where its actual output is the same as its *potential output.* Fixed capital and technology determine the productive capacity of the economy, this capacity is called the potential output. Another way to view potential output is through that of aggregated demand and aggregate supply. If the level of output is below the potential level, then there is very little tendency for the prices of goods and wages of factors to fall. On the other hand, if actual output is at a level above the potential level, then aggregate demand, being higher, pushes up prices and wages. It is the onerous task of the government and the central bank to be watchful, providing incentives and penalties through fiscal policies and monetary policies to maintain the full employment level of output with price stability. Most of this book will explore this issue from the view of a developed economy as well as that of a developing one, which in current parlance is an emerging economy.

> Potential output is the maximum feasible output that a country can produce given its factor endowments and productive capacity.

2.7. CONCLUSION

This chapter introduced the NIA and the different methods of computing it. The three methods of measuring the economic activities of a country are the value added method or the product approach, the expenditure method and the income method. The GDP is the most important measure of how the economy of a country is performing. It measures the value of the total goods and services that a country produces in a year.

In the product method, GDP is computed by aggregating or summing up the value of all goods and services produced in the different industries and the agricultural sector. In the expenditure method the expenditure of the four sectors are summed up to get the gross national expenditure. In the income method the earnings of all the factors of production is aggregated to arrive at the gross national income. Theoretically, if there is no error, then we should arrive at the same value for GDP, Gross Domestic Expenditure and Gross Domestic Income. The nominal GDP is at current market prices and is not useful for comparisons across years; so the real GDP is used for the purpose by scaling it through the GDP deflator to eliminate the effect of inflation. In this chapter, the different methods or indices for estimating inflation are explained as are the different definitions of unemployment.

A brief view of the issues of government budget deficit and the trade deficit in the foreign trade sector have also been provided. That was followed by an analysis of the circular flow of income to understand macroeconomic models. This exploration of the producers' side or supply side and consumers' side or the demand side for connecting the NIA paves the way for understanding the Keynesian model in Chapter 3. The National Income of India data in the post-independence for 60 years 1952–53 to 2013–14 are reported in Table 2.5.

TABLE 2.5

National Income of India 1952–53 to 2013–14 (Figures in ₹ Billion)

Year	1952–53	1962–63	1972–73	1982–83	1992–93	2002–03	2012–13	2013–14
Base: 2004–05	1	2	3	4	5	6	7	8
GDP at Factor Cost	2,942.67	4,319.60	5,938.43	8,680.91	14,405.03	25,709.35	54,821.11	57,417.91
Consumption of Fixed Capital	222.49	254.75	474.52	791.54	1,458.47	2,733.67	6,878.84	7,536.74
NDP at Factor Cost	2,720.18	4,064.85	5,463.91	7,889.37	12,946.56	22,975.68	47,942.27	49,881.16
Indirect Tax less subsidies	162.77	335.67	575.09	822.03	1,452.52	2,143.23	4,177.36	4,540.51
GDP at Market Prices	3,105.44	4,655.27	6,513.52	9,502.94	15,857.55	27,852.58	58,998.47	61,958.42
NDP at Market Prices	2,882.95	4,281.61	6,039.00	8,711.40	14,399.08	25,118.91	52,119.63	54,421.67
Net Factor income from Abroad	–4.76	–23.66	–37.05	–38.02	–178.12	–189.60	–654.52	–679.34
GNP at Factor Cost	2,937.91	4,295.94	5,901.38	8,642.88	14,226.92	25,519.75	54,166.59	56,738.57
NNP at Factor Cost	2,715.41	4,014.19	5,426.86	7,851.34	12,768.45	22,789.08	47,287.75	49,201.83
GNP at Market Prices	3,100.68	4,631.61	6,476.47	9,464.91	15,679.44	27,662.98	58,343.95	61,279.08
NNP at Market Prices	2,878.18	4,376.86	6,001.95	8,673.37	14,220.97	24,929.31	51,465.11	53,742.34
GDP of Public Sector	NA	446.62	893.73	1,750.98	3,516.56	6,384.05	12,450.10	NA
NDP of Public Sector	NA	358.10	717.91	1,409.13	2,769.01	5,407.12	NA	NA
Gross Domestic Capital Formation	345.69	804.65	1,244.04	1,800.32	3,577.10	7,086.37	22,978.07	NA
Net Domestic Capital Formation	123.20	549.90	786.78	1,051.89	2,118.62	4,352.70	16,099.25	NA
Per Capita GNP at FC	7,898	9,462	10,681	12,172	16,315	24,166	44,508	46,017
Per Capita NNP at FC	7,299	8,901	9,855	11,091	14,643	21,578	38,856	39,904

Source: Reserve Bank of India's Handbook of Statistics, 2014.

SUMMARY

- NIA are indispensable in assessing the economic performance of an economy.
- The GDP is the value of the total goods and services produced in a year. It is measured in three ways: the product, expenditure and income methods
- The national product measures the value of all goods and services and national income is the sum of all incomes earned in an open economy.
- Capital goods and inventory investment are used in the production process. Inventory investment is the net change in fixed goods at the end of the year. Depreciation is the wear and tear of the country's capital stock.
- National income is categorized as wages, salaries, proprietor's income, non-corporate business, self-employment income, rental income. Personal Income = National Income − Corporate Taxes − Social Insurance Contributions − Net interest + Dividends + Government Transfers to individuals + Personal Interest Income.
- In the expenditure method, GNP is the sum of consumption by households, businesses, the government and net exports, $Y = C + I + G + (X − M)$.
- Nominal GDP measures the value of the output at current prices. Real GDP is the value of output in the economy at constant prices. To eliminate the impact of inflation, real GDP is a better measure, which is computed by using the GDP deflator.
- The GDP from the demand side is equal to GDP from the production side after indirect taxes and sales taxes are added.
- A government budget deficit occurs when the government's expenditure 'G' exceeds the receipts from tax revenue. A trade deficit occurs when imports exceed exports, that is, net exports is negative and a surplus occurs if exports exceed imports.
- This dual deficit dilemma can be resolved through either eliminating the government budget deficit, or by the private sector saving more than its investments. However, reducing investments will negatively affect economic growth.
- A person is unemployed when he/she is able and desirous to work but does not find a job. The unemployment rate is the fraction of the total labour force that is unemployed,
- Unemployment can be due to (a) change in technology: *structural* unemployment, (b) migration or desire for a change in the type of work: *frictional* unemployment or (c) due to recessionary conditions, that is, *cyclical* unemployment.
- The interest rate is in percentage form. It is the rate of payment made to the lender. It is an important tool in the hands of the central bank of a country in managing the financial sector. Real interest rate = nominal rate − expected inflation.
- Problems of double counting, the underground economy or black money and non-marketed goods pose difficulties in any rigorous computation of national accounts.

- The circular flow of income is a simplified depiction of how the economic factors interact and operate.
- When income payments by the business sector for factor services return through purchases by the household sector, the circular flow of income between two sectors tend to perpetuate it and there is macroeconomic equilibrium.
- The potential output is the productive capacity of the economy, determined by the fixed capital and technology.

CASE STUDY

Real GDP and the National Income Accounts

In the tables below, the estimates of national income for the financial year 2010–13 and the quarterly estimates of GDP) for the fourth quarter (January–March) both at constant (2004–05) and current prices are reported, based on the press note of the Central Statistics Office, Ministry of Statistics and Programme Implementation. The 2012–13 data are Quick Estimates.

TABLE CS 2.1

Quarterly Estimate of Expenditures of GDP at Market Prices in Q1 (April–June) of 2012–13 (At 2004–05 Prices)

Industry	₹ *Crores Expenditures of Gross Domestic Product for Q1*			*Rates of GDP at Market Prices (%)*	
	2010–11	*2011–12*	*2012–13*	*2011–12*	*2012–13*
1. Private Final Consumption Expenditure (PFCE)	747,741	784,113	815,319	59.5	59.5
2. Government Final Consumption Expenditure	132,685	139,179	151,747	10.6	11.1
3. Gross Fixed Capital Formation (GFCF)	389,641	446,754	449,701	33.9	32.8
4. Change in Stocks	45,184	48,411	47,813	3.7	3.5
5. Valuables	31,673	34,792	15,522	2.6	1.1
6. Exports	264,394	311,908	343,335	23.7	25.1
7. Less Imports	356,700	425,661	459,422	32.3	33.6
8. Discrepancies	–45,905	–22,118	5,248	–1.7	0.4
GDP at Market Prices	1,208,714	1,317,379	1,369,263	100	100

Source: Press Information Bureau Government of India, Press Note Estimates of Gross Domestic Product 9 Bhadra, 1934 Saka 31 August 2012.

TABLE CS 2.2

Quarterly Estimate of Expenditures of GDP at Market Prices in Q1 (April–June) of 2012–13 (At Current Prices)

Industry	₹ Crores Expenditures of Gross Domestic Product for Q1			Rates of GDP at Market Prices (%)	
	2010–11	2011–12	2012–13	2011–12	2012–13
1. Private Final Consumption Expenditure (PFCE)	996,858	1,138,337	1,281,799	55.8	56
2. Government Final Consumption Expenditure	196,255	224,124	267,337	11	11.7
3. Gross Fixed Capital Formation (GFCF)	526,832	636,371	684,893	31.2	29.9
4. Change in Stocks	59,155	69,063	74,019	3.4	3.2
5. Valuables	43,676	67,553	39,239	3.3	1.7
6. Exports	364,171	470,527	559,298	23	24.4
7. Less Imports	466,263	601,758	705,197	29.5	30.8
8. Discrepancies	–3,482	37,331	89,193	1.8	3.9
GDP at Market Prices	1,717,201	2,041,548	2,290,582	100	100

Source: Press Information Bureau Government of India, Press Note Estimates of Gross Domestic Product 9 Bhadra, 1934 Saka 31 August 2012.

After examining the data given in the tables in this case study, answer the following questions:

1. Compute the GDP deflators for the years 2012–13 and 2011–12.
2. What is the net exports of the country in the years 2010–11, 2011–12, 2012–13?
3. What is the meaning of valuables?

KEYWORDS

Gross domestic product
Intermediate goods
Value-added GDP

Open economy
Net exports
Real GDP

Capital goods	Nominal GDP
Depreciation	GDP deflator
Capital stock	Government budget deficit
Net domestic product	Trade deficit
Inventory investment	Monetary policy
Gross national product	Real interest
Personal income	Non-market production
Durable goods	Balance of payments
Government expenditure	Potential output

CONCEPT CHECK

State if the following statements are true or false:

1. In the income method the gross national income is the aggregate earnings of all the factors of production.
2. GDP is the value of all final and intermediate goods, used in production processes in an economy.
3. Inventory investment is the net change in fixed goods at the end of the year.
4. Real GDP is the value of physical output in the economy produced during a given time period at current prices.
5. Nominal GDP is the value of output produced at constant prices.
6. Underground activities produce goods that are valued by their consumers, like illicit liquor, which are not accounted for in the GDP.
7. The net export is negative when the imports are more than the exports of a country.
8. The unemployment rate is the fraction of the total labour force that is unemployed in an economy.
9. Personal disposable income is equal to personal income minus income tax and non-tax payments.
10. GDP from the demand side is exactly equal to GDP from the production side.
11. The nominal GDP takes current market prices and is not useful for comparison across years.
12. The GNP includes incomes received by the country's production factors at home and abroad after the income received by foreign factors of production in the home country is subtracted.
13. Government deficit can be reduced either by increasing government expenditure or by reducing taxation.
14. The circular flow of income is a simplified depiction of how the economic factors interact and operate.
15. The net national product is computed by deducting depreciation of capital from the GDP.

DISCUSSION QUESTIONS

1. CemCo, a cement company, manufactures 10,000 tonnes of cement whose price was ₹2,500 in 2008. If ConsCo, a construction company, buys 3,000 tonnes of cement at ₹37,500,000 and construct buildings and sells them for ₹55,500,000, what will be the value added to GDP by these transactions? Does the GDP computation take the value of CemCo and ConsCo together? If not, then why? How will you describe an intermediate good?

2. If in 2002 the government pays out ₹90 crore transfer payment to disabled persons to provide them support for their consumption expenditure, then would this government expenditure be included in the current year's GDP? If not, then why?

3. In what way is GDP different from GNP?

4. How is personal income computed? Does an individual's contribution to employees' provident fund get included? If not, then why? What is the difference between personal income and personal disposable income?

5. How can the GDP calculated from the product method be equated with GDP from the income method?

6. How is nominal GDP computed? Why is real GDP a better measure for comparing an economy's growth rate in different time periods?

7. Suppose you buy a 5-year indexed bond with a coupon rate (interest rate) of 10%. After one year if the inflation rate increases by 2% what will be the rate of return on your bond? Are you better off than your neighbour who bought a non-indexed bond with the same coupon rate? How do you define the real interest rate?

8. The following information is extracted from the NIA of a country Alarek for the year 2009–10.

	In lakhs of Alarekan (name of currency)
GNP at factor prices	95,000
Indirect taxes	14,000
NDP at market prices	100,422
NNP at market prices	100,000
GNP at market prices	1,007,000
Personal income taxes	10,000
Corporate profit taxes	6,500
Retained profits	30,000

Compute the values of
  i.   Depreciation
  ii. Net factor income from abroad
  iii. Subsidies

    iv. NDP at factor cost*

    v. National income

    vi. Personal income

    vii. Personal disposable income

* Hint NDP at factor cost = NDP at market price – Indirect taxes + Subsidies.

9. Calculate the following using the following data collected from the UK National Income Accounts 1996

    i.   GDP at market prices

    ii. GDP at factor cost

    iii. Total domestic expenditure

    iv. Total final Expenditure

GDP at market prices by expenditure method for the UK in 1996

	£ lakhs
Consumption expenditure	547,247
Government final expenditure	249,474
Gross Fixed capital formation	205,385
Value of physical increase in stocks and work in progress	4,851
Exports of goods and services	197,600
Imports of goods and services	−203,086
Statistical discrepancy	419
Taxes on expenditure	−103,597
Subsidies	6,966

CHAPTER

The Basic Keynesian Demand Model and the Hidden Cross

LEARNING OBJECTIVES

Upon completion of this chapter, the reader will be able to:

- Understand the principles of the basic Keynesian model of income determination using a simple mathematical as well as geometrical formulation.
- Comprehend how the multiplier process works.
- See how the Keynesian model can be represented in a novel fashion in a perfectly straight, vertical cross and derive policy results from such a diagram.
- Understand the role of the government budget in stabilizing the economy and how the automatic stabilizer operates.
- Appreciate the implications of the fiscal, primary and revenue deficits in terms of fiscal policy.
- Explain how a fiscal stimulus package helps the economy to recover from a downturn.

3.1. INTRODUCTION: THE BASIC KEYNESIAN MODEL

The basic Keynesian model presented in this chapter is perhaps the most popular and publicized one through the decades—and appealing for combating recessions, especially in developing nations. The model dates back to the years of the Great Depression of the 1930s and was first presented in John Maynard Keynes' most famous book that became renowned worldwide under the fondly shortened title, *The General Theory*. A brief background of the founder of macroeconomics is given in Box 3.1.

BOX 3.1   Who was John Maynard Keynes?[1]

Born in June 1883, John Maynard Keynes, a pioneer and brilliant thinker was the leading light in liberal economic theory. After joining the British Treasury during the First World War, he represented Britain in negotiations in the Versailles Treaty. He wrote abundantly on wide ranging issues from philosophy, probability to politics. His book *The Economic Consequences of the Peace* criticized the severe reparations on Germany and forecast the impending recession in Europe. Naturally this made him unpopular until the market crash of 1929, when Keynes' advice was sought after. In 1936, he published his masterpiece, *The General Theory of Employment, Interest and Money*, that deeply influenced economic thought and policy throughout the 20th century. He is regarded as the father of modern macroeconomics.

Rejecting the classical view of Adam Smith of laissez faire, Keynes argued that economic distress manifested by cyclical recessions and booms needed government interventions. Instead of keeping 'hands off' and maintaining a balance budget, the government should create jobs by investing in roads, bridges, etc. through public works. He argued that the proper response to economic slowdowns was to boost demand through government spending, if the private sector was not investing enough while inventories piled up, as was the case through the 1930s. Jobs would lead to income in the hands of people and demand for goods and services would therefore rise, propelling the economy forward.

Following the Great Depression, the American President Roosevelt pursued Keynes' policy. Unemployment gradually fell and their economy revived. Post Second World War, economists ardently followed Keynes, calling themselves the 'Keynesians'. His ideas were widely accepted and became the corner stone of government policy. But, in the 1970s, the global economic distress of high inflation and unemployment failed to respond to the Keynesian prescription. Keynes' view of emphasizing demand was replaced by the conservative policies of the monetarist economist Milton Friedman, who stressed adjustments in the interest rates and money supply. The monetarists prescribed lower taxes, lower interest rates and non-interference by the government. The monetarists had their way until the financial crisis in 2008.

Monetary policy has been pushed to its limits with a near zero interest rate, economic activity has slumped and unemployment has soared. With the global meltdown, the governments of almost all countries are increasing expenditures to boost aggregate demand, just as Keynes would have advised. The key goal is to push up consumer spending and counter the effect that Keynes called 'the paradox of thrift'. If everyone tries to save money in an economic downturn, the reduction in spending only accelerates the downward spiral. So the Keynesians are back.

Source: http://healthofmywealth.com/dividend-policies-companies-in-india/

---

[1] The idea presented in the Box 3.1 draws from *The Week*, 'Keynes Comeback', 5 March 2009. Available at: visit http://theweek.com/article/index/93913/Keynes_comeback (accessed on 13 July 2017).

The Keynesian model (hereafter referred to as the model) is still widely used in the developing world, but is applicable whenever the presence of—a considerable degree of—unemployment restrains increases in wage costs. Policy prescriptions based on this model would be, therefore, inappropriate under conditions of full employment and rising inflation.

This chapter is organized as follows: In Section 3.1.1, we present the basic features of the model in a non-technical fashion and clarify the important assumptions underlying its formulation. In Section 3.2, we proceed to present the model in mathematical terms, laying out the relationships between the variables and eliciting the all-important multiplier formula. Numerical examples are also provided to explain the concepts in Section 3.2. In Section 3.3 we move to the demand–supply diagrammatic analysis, presenting the traditional approach in this regard. Following this standard presentation, in Section 3.4, as a novelty, it is shown that the Keynesian model can be perfectly captured by a straight, vertical cross! This chapter also takes up the concept of the government budgetary balance, which enables a discussion of the costs associated with fiscal expansions to create income multiplier effects to address the problem of unemployment. The chapter ends with some thought-provoking remarks on the model, relating to the times we live in now.

3.1.1. Important Features of the Model

Multiplier effect is the increase in total output or GDP for each increase in ₹1 of autonomous investment or government expenditure.

The model links spending and output, specifically taking into account the mutual feedbacks between the two. Spending determines output, which, in turn, provides income for spending. Essentially, this implies that increased spending gets multiplied due to such a circular relationship, which translates into an income increase greater than that of the initial hike in spending.

Thus, when the government increases spending in a recession, output increases, which raises private incomes and consumer spending—leading to further increases in output, incomes and private spending.

So, there is a so-called a '*multiplier effect*' on national income and output of the initial spending increase. This provides the rationale for government spending stimuli during deep recessions when output and employment have hit a nadir.

The model builds on certain key assumptions. Firstly, there is an assumption of fixed prices, linked to the absence of wage cost pressures due to large-scale unemployment. This means that the supply curve is horizontal in the supply–demand diagram. Such a situation can be explained also in terms of the short-run model presented in Chapter 1, the time period being too short for wage renegotiations.

Aggregate demand is the sum of the values of all the final goods purchased in an economy.

Secondly, the model has no financial markets; it is a real model, with no financial sector. The financial sector plays no role in a deep recession with no rise in interest rates with increased private or government spending. So, the real financial sector feedbacks play no role. Before presenting the model in its totality and its resplendent form, some basic relationships have to be laid out clearly.

3.1.2. Some Basic Relationships and the Keynesian Multiplier

The following presentation uses the nomenclature of Chapter 2, which pertains to the national income accounts. To start with, the key identity from Chapter 2 is:

$$AD = C + I + G + NX \qquad (3.1)$$

where AD is *aggregate demand*, C is *private consumption*, I is *gross private investment* and NX is net exports. AD will equal output Y in equilibrium (since we have Chapter 2 behind us, we do not distinguish between GDP and national income).

$$Y = C + I + G + NX \qquad (3.2)$$

When Y is greater than AD, there is involuntary *inventory accumulation and* firms cut back on output. When Y is less than AD, inventories are run down and firms increase output. So there is always a tendency to move to equilibrium represented by (3.2).

We now come to the specification of the Keynesian consumption function, which drives the model, namely

$$C = C_0 + cYD \qquad (3.3)$$

where 'c' is the *marginal propensity of consumption* out of *disposable income*, C_0 is the autonomous level of consumption (subsistence or basic, not dependent on income) and YD is disposable income after taxes and transfers:

$$YD = Y - T + TR = Y - tY + TR \qquad (3.4)$$

where T is total income taxes, TR is total transfers from the government and 't' is the income tax rate.

Substituting (3.4) and (3.3) into (3.2),

$$Y(1 - t) = A_0, \qquad (3.5)$$

Where A_0 is total autonomous spending (not dependent on Y):

$$A_0 = C_0 + I + G + cTR + NX \qquad (3.6)$$

Net exports NX is kept endogenous for simplicity here. From Equation (3.6), the equilibrium level of national income is given by

$$Y = A_0/[1 - c(1 - t)] \qquad (3.7)$$

We also get, from Equation (3.7)

$$\Delta Y = \acute{\alpha} \times \Delta A_0, \qquad (3.8)$$

where $\acute{\alpha}$ is the Keynesian income multiplier given as

$$\acute{\alpha} = 1/1 - c(1 - t) \qquad (3.9)$$

Without taxes, $\acute{\alpha}$ reduces to

$$\acute{\alpha} = 1/(1 - c). \qquad (3.10)$$

Private consumption spending is total spending by households, excluding investment spending by firms and government spending, but including expenditure on imported goods and services.

Gross private investment is the total amount of investment spending by business and firms.

Inventory accumulation occurs when aggregate demand falls short of output and depletion when aggregate demand exceeds output.

The Marginal Propensity to Consume is the fraction of additional rupee income that will be consumed. Empirically it is found to be less than one.

Disposable Income is the income in hand after tax deduction.

Autonomous spending is expenditure that is not dependent on income.

Since the marginal propensity to consume, c, is less than 1, the Keynesian multiplier will be greater than 1, so that an increase in *autonomous spending*, such as a change in G or I, has a multiplier effect on income.

Clearly, the larger the value of c, the larger will be the Keynesian multiplier. In (3.10), the value of $\acute{\alpha}$ is 10 when c = 0.9. With c = 0.8, the value of the multiplier is 5. Similarly, the value of the tax rate *t* also influences the multiplier. It is easy to see that a larger *t*, denoting a larger drain from income, makes the multiplier smaller. The numerical example provided here illustrates these relationships.

Suppose there is an increase in government spending from ₹1,000 to 2,000 crore. In the same period, private investment falls by ₹500 crore and government transfers rise by ₹300 crore. The marginal propensity to consume is 0.9 and the tax rate is 0.1. What would be the impact on income 'Y'?

Using Equation (3.9), the value of $\acute{\alpha}$ is obtained as 3.57. The change in autonomous spending = −500 + 1,000 + 0.9 × 300 = 770. So, the increase in Y = 3.57 × 770 = 2,748.9. The underlying dynamics leading to this increase is explained in Section 3.2.

Note that a cut in the tax rate also constitutes an increase in autonomous spending (besides increasing the multiplier). With a cut in the tax rate of 0.1, disposable income increases by (0.1 × Y) and consumption increases by (c × 0.1 × Y). This is actually an increase in autonomous spending, since it is independent of Y. Note also that a cut in the tax rate that amounts to a reduction in the tax amount T by ₹100 crore, or a cut in transfers by ₹100 crore, will fall short of the autonomous spending impact of an increase in G of ₹100 crore. With a cut in transfers of ₹100, the increase in autonomous spending is c × 100. With a cut in the tax rate, so that dt × Y = 100, the increase in autonomous spending is again, c × dt × Y = c × 100.

When government expenditure is covered by revenues, there is a balanced budget prevailing.

It can be shown that for a policy of *balanced budget* spending, where the government increases spending, financing it entirely by taxes (so that ΔG = ΔT), the multiplier is unity. This problem is given as an exercise at the end of the chapter.

3.2. EXPLAINING THE MULTIPLIER: CASCADING EFFECTS ON CONSUMER SPENDING

For simplicity, let us ignore the tax rate for the time being. Assume now that there is an increase in private investment demand of ₹100 crore. ΔI = 100 is then an immediate addition to income Y. Out of this, c × 100 will be the immediate increase, in the first time period, in private consumption spending. But, this increase of c × 100 also represents an addition to Y, since it is received by some private participants in the economy. Out of this addition to income, they spend c (c × 100) crore. Tracing the increases in consumption spending in this fashion, we get the total addition to national income Y as:

$$\Delta Y = 100 + c \times 100 + c\,(c \times 100) + c\,(c \times c \times 100) \tag{3.11}$$

$$= 100\,(c \times 100 + c^2 \times 100 + c^3 \times 100 + c^4 \times 100$$

Note that in Equation (3.11), only the first 100 (=ΔI) is the increase in income due to the initial change in autonomous spending. The remaining terms represent 'induced' consumption, which give then rise to the multiplier effect.

TABLE 3.1

The Keynesian Multiplier in Stages

Stage	Change in Autonomous Spending	Induced Consumption Spending	Total Added Up Effect on National Income
Stage 1	$\Delta I = 100$		100
Stage 2		$c(1-t)\,100$	$100\,[1 + c(1-t)]$
Stage 2		$c(1-t) \times c(1-t)\,100$	$100\,[1 + c(1-t) + c^2(1-t)^2]$
Stage 3		$C(1-t) \times c^2(1-t)^2\,100$	$100\,[1 + c(1-t) + c^2(1-t)^2 + c^3(1-t)^3]$
Stage n			$100\,[1 + c(1-t) + c^2(1-t)^2 + c^3(1-t)^3 + \ldots + c^n(1-t)^n + \ldots]$
,,			
,,			
Last stage			$1/[1 - c(1-t)] \times 100$

Source: Authors.

Now, (3.11) represents a geometric progression such that we can write

$$\Delta Y = [1/(1-c)] \times 100 \tag{3.12}$$

Thus, we have the same expression for the multiplier as obtained in the mathematical treatment in the previous section.

Table 3.1 gives the different stages of the induced consumption process that adds up to the total multiplier effect, including the tax rate in the reckoning.

3.3. A DIAGRAMMATIC REPRESENTATION OF CONSUMPTION AND AGGREGATE DEMAND: THE 45 DEGREE REPRESENTATION OF THE KEYNESIAN MODEL

In this section, we will present the traditional diagrammatic approach used for income and output determination—and for the derivation of the Keynesian income multiplier. For simplicity, we will proceed in a step by step fashion, ignoring taxes and transfers (but see discussion question no. 4):

1. In Figure 3.1a, with income and output 'Y' on the X-axis and demand or expenditure (spending) on the Y-axis, draw a line at 45 degrees from the origin. This line represents equilibrium points, with demand equalling income and output. Points above the line in the figure will mean that there is inventory depletion going on, since demand exceeds output. Points below the line will

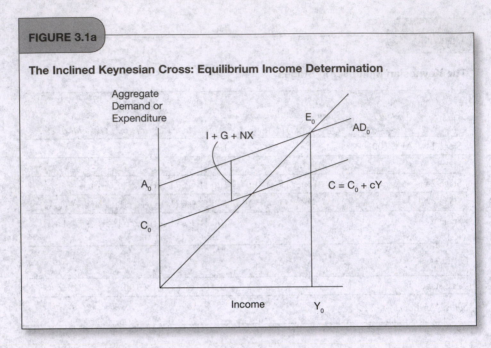

FIGURE 3.1a

The Inclined Keynesian Cross: Equilibrium Income Determination

mean that there is inventory accumulation going on since demand falls short of output. Such points will not represent a stable equilibrium situation since there will be output adjustments taking place to match demand.

2. Mark off a distance C_0 on the vertical axis from the origin, this is autonomous consumption.

3. Draw a line with a slope of 'c', the marginal propensity to consume (MPC) from the point C_0. This line represents the path (the values) of aggregate consumption as aggregate income changes (see note at the end of this section).

4. Mark off a distance along the vertical axis, above the point C_0, equal to $(I + G + NX)$, so that the distance C_0A_0 in the figure represents aggregate autonomous spending which is not dependent on income, as given in expression (3.6).

5. Now draw a line at a slope equal to the marginal propensity to consume, 'c', from the point A_0. This line represents the values taken by aggregate demand as income changes. Note that this line is parallel to the line drawn in a similar fashion from the point C_0. This is because the only part of aggregate demand changing as income changes is consumption spending, given the assumptions of exogenous investment and exports.

6. The point E_0 where the aggregate demand line AD_0 cuts the 45 degrees line represents an equilibrium situation where aggregate demand equals total income and output. The corresponding income level is marked off as Y_0 on the X-axis.

Figure 3.1a can be used to derive the income multiplier. The figure is reproduced as Figure 3.1b, omitting the consumption line.

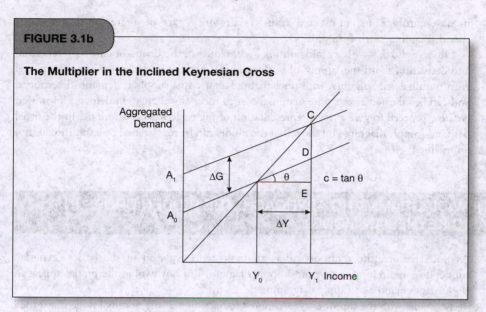

FIGURE 3.1b

The Multiplier in the Inclined Keynesian Cross

7. Consider now an increase in aggregate autonomous spending due to an increase in government spending by ΔG. An increase in exogenous investment or exports will give similar results for the multiplier effect.

8. The aggregate demand line shifts up from AD_0 to AD_1 by the vertical distance measured out on the vertical axis from the origin, the shift being parallel to the initial AD line. The new demand line AD_1 cuts the 45 degrees line at E_1, representing the new equilibrium situation. Y_1 then is the new equilibrium level of income and output.

9. In the figure now, the distance E_1C equals ΔG, while the distance E_1D equals the increase in income, $(Y_1 - Y_0)$, or ΔY. Thus, the distance CD is equal to $(\Delta Y - \Delta G)$.

10. Note now from the figure that the slope of the parallel lines, given by 'c' (equal to $\tan \theta$ in the Figure 3.3), the marginal propensity to consume, can be written as

$$c = (\Delta Y - \Delta G)/\Delta G \qquad (3.13a)$$

Simplifying,

$$(\Delta Y/\Delta G) = 1/(1 - c) \qquad (3.13b)$$

Equation (3.13b) is nothing but the multiplier expression (3.10) derived in the mathematical treatment earlier in this chapter!

Note: The approach including taxes and transfers is given as an exercise; see discussion question 3 as well as 4. (Hint: inclusion of taxes, introducing the tax rate 't', changes the slope of the consumption line to $c(1 - t)$; and, consumption cTR based on income-autonomous, non-taxed transfers becomes part of aggregate autonomous spending, along with I, G and NX).

Observe also that we have said nothing in the course of this diagrammatic representation and derivation about the 'supply' of output. This is because in the basic Keynesian model with nominal wage rigidity, with unchanging factor costs, supply is demand-determined and can be adjusted at the same marginal cost to meet any changes in demand. However, we now proceed to give a novel representation of the basic Keynesian model in the usual demand–supply diagram and show that the model can be represented by a traditional (not an inclined) cross.

3.4. A NEW DIAGRAMMATIC APPROACH: THE HIDDEN CROSS IN THE BASIC KEYNESIAN MODEL

As noted before, the traditional diagrammatic representation of the basic Keynesian model does not refer to a demand–supply diagram. But how would the model appear in the usual demand and supply diagrammatic set-up?

Let's start with the supply curve. As noted in Section 3.2, the nominal wage is assumed to be fixed, due to the prevalence of large-scale unemployment, or because the time period considered is too short for the renegotiation of wage contracts. This makes it a fixed price model, and the supply curve is therefore drawn appropriately as a horizontal line.

The demand curve: The demand curve will not slope down as in the models presented in Chapter 1. In those models, the demand curve has a negative slope because the financial sector is included (this is not really discussed in Chapter 1). Also note that the usual negative slope of the macro demand curve is not due to a substitution effect in demand of a price rise; having only one aggregate good in the model, there are no price substitution effects in demand! (However, we do present a disaggregated model with more goods in the last chapter).

The usual slope of the demand curve is seen also in the IS–LM model presented later. In the IS–LM model in Chapter 9, the financial sector is included. As seen in that chapter, with money in the model, a rise in the price level results in a rise in the interest rate and leads to a fall in investments and output. This result, working through the real-financial sector linkage, gives the negative slope of the demand curve.

However, there is no financial sector in the Keynesian model that we discuss here. A price rise has no effect on investments through changes in the interest rate. So, essentially, the demand curve is invariant with respect to price and can be drawn as a vertical line in the price-output space.

Keep in mind that this representation is also valid when there is a financial sector, but constrained in the sense that the interest rate is kept constant, usually by a central bank decree, as in many developing countries. In this case also, a price rise has no effect on interest rates and hence on investment demand and output.

We have, therefore, in front of us, the hidden cross in the Keynesian model! The supply curve is perfectly horizontal and the demand curve is vertical. As implied earlier,

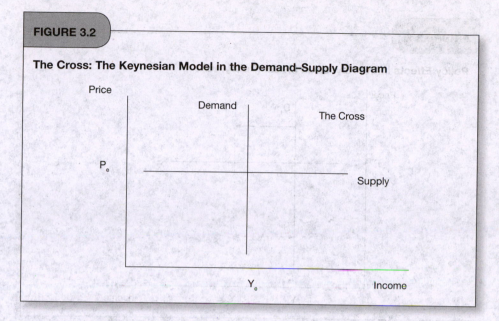

FIGURE 3.2

The Cross: The Keynesian Model in the Demand–Supply Diagram

the cross vanishes when the financial sector is introduced, since the demand curve is then no longer vertical.

Let us repeat the salient facts with respect to Figure 3.2. The supply curve is horizontal as costs do not rise and price rises are therefore not needed to increase supply as a rise in demand can be met by a supply increase at a given price.

In Figure 3.2, the supply curve is horizontal as costs do not rise and price rises are therefore not needed to increase supply. Rather, a rise in demand can be met by increases in supply at a given price.

3.4.1. Policy Effects in the Model: A Demand-determined Model

The basic Keynesian model is a demand-determined model, with the level of demand determining the equilibrium level of output. An increase in government spending of ΔG shifts the vertical demand curve to the right by more than ΔG, as the multiplier process comes into play (see Figure 3.3). The shift of the vertical demand curve will be equal to $\acute{\alpha}\Delta G$, which depicts the increase in output (from Y_1 to Y_2).

It will be seen later, in the IS–LM model of Chapter 9, that the rightward shift of the demand curve is less with a sloping demand curve. This follows from the fact that the multiplier $\acute{\alpha}$ is less in that model due to the crowding out of investment demand by an increase in the interest rate.

The basic Keynesian model is applicable even when the financial sector is included and when output levels are low, since then there is no perceptible rise in the interest rate with increases in demand. Then *fiscal policy*, as represented by an increase in G or

The term fiscal policy refers to government policy with respect to government purchases, transfer payments and tax structure.

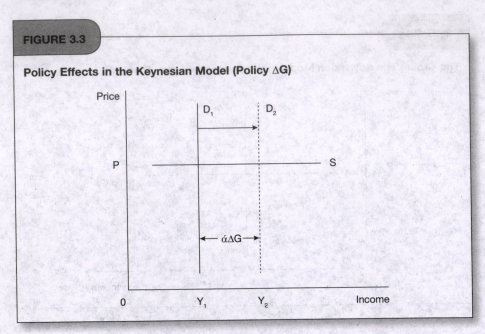

FIGURE 3.3

Policy Effects in the Keynesian Model (Policy ΔG)

a cut in the tax rate is highly effective, while monetary policy, as will be seen be later in Chapter 9, is ineffective.

3.5. THE GOVERNMENT BUDGET

We have seen that it is possible to increase output and reduce unemployment (since more output requires more employment) by increased government spending, that too with a multiplier effect. But it is important to keep in mind that there are costs and trade-offs, associated with such a policy. There are trade-offs with inflation and the external sector balance, but these may not be operative at low-output levels.

The budgetary balance of the government is negatively affected by a fiscal expansion, that is, by an increase in government spending or a reduction in taxes. To analyse this effect, let us first define the government budget balance (BS) as the excess of government revenue (here we limit it to tax revenue) over government spending on goods and services and on transfers:

$$BS = T - G - TR; \quad Or \quad BS = tY - G - TR \quad \quad (3.13c)$$

The budget deficit BD can be written as

$$BD = G + TR - TY \quad \quad (3.14)$$

Clearly, for a given G and TR, the budget surplus improves as output Y rises. See Figure 3.4

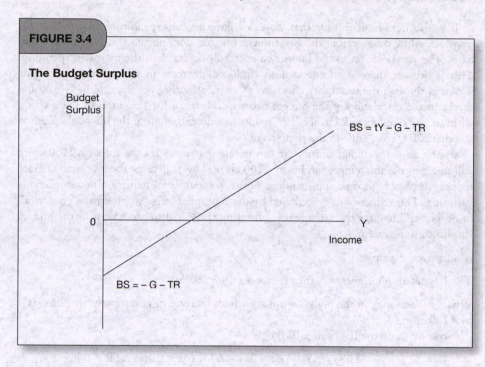

FIGURE 3.4

The Budget Surplus

In the Figure 3.4, BS and Y are positively related. So the budget tends to be in surplus during booms, as the tax revenue tY rises and in deficit during recessions.

3.5.1. The Role of Automatic Stabilizers

The so-called *automatic stabilizers* tend to dampen cyclical fluctuations in the economy, putting brakes during booms and inciting expansionary spending during recessions. Unemployment benefits function this way; these are paid out during a downturn and provide income for additional consumption spending through the multiplier effects. The income tax functions as a dampener during booms, siphoning away purchasing power, which is further reduced as people climb to higher tax brackets with a progressive tax system.

However, the effect on the budget surplus runs the other way! When unemployment benefits are paid out in a recession, they increase the budget deficit of the government. This will add to the woes of reduced tax revenue for the government in the downturn.

Notice, however, that government budgetary surplus may change even when G, t and TR are left unchanged, that is, with a passive government stance. For instance, an increase in private investment demand increases output, thereby the tax revenue and this improves the budget balance (for which the government in power may take unwarranted credit if it happens to be election time!).

Automatic stabilizers are policies that reduces the impact of economic shock without the need for step by step intervention.

It is also important to note that increased government expenditure on goods or on transfers, while deteriorating the government budget, does not do this on a one-to-one basis. The deterioration in the budget balance will be *less* than the increased spending. This is because there is an endogenous (induced) increase in tax revenues as output increases through the multiplier effect (so tY rises, offsetting the increase in G to some extent in the calculation of the budget balance). Thus, an increase in G of ₹100 crore, without any simultaneous change in 't' results in a deterioration of the budget balance of less than ₹100 crore (due to the effect $t\Delta Y$).

By the same reasoning, an increase in the rate that raises tax revenues by ₹100 crore will not improve the budget surplus by ₹100 crore. This is because the increased tax rate reduces disposable income and spending, which translates as a reduction in autonomous spending. This reduction is exacerbated by the multiplier effect to produce a greater fall in output and reduces the tax revenue, offsetting the initial improvement in the budget surplus to some extent.

A numerical example:

The Keynesian multiplier = 3, the tax rate 't' = 0.2 (20%).

What is the change in the budget surplus with an increase in government spending (G) by ₹100 crore?

Now, we can write the change in BS as

$$\Delta BS = t\Delta Y + Y\Delta t - \Delta G - \Delta TR \ (\Delta t = 0 \text{ and } \Delta TR = 0 \text{ here})$$

$$\Delta Y = \acute{\alpha}\Delta G = 3 \times 100 = 300.$$

$$\text{So, } \Delta BS = 0.2 \, (300) - 100 = -40.$$

Hence, the budget surplus deteriorates by less than the increase in government spending as Y and therefore tY rises.

3.5.2. The Ex-ante and Ex-post Budget Deficits

The government may undertake a policy targeting a certain level of budget surplus, say, by raising taxes. But the final outcome may be different; it may end up with a different level of BS due to interactions in the economy, specifically, due to the impact on income (and the induced changer in tax revenue). Thus, the ex-ante (the targeted) and the ex-post (the actual) budget deficits or surpluses may differ. In the aforementioned numerical example, the ex-ante budget deficit, starting from a balanced budget, is −100. But ex-post budget deficit turns out to be −40.

The difference between the ex-post and the ex-ante budget deficits become more obscure when the model of the economy is more complex, with the financial sector and the price level added in. But it is important not to be guided by the simple ex-post estimate of the budget deficit, as it is quite unrealistic.

3.5.3. Structural and Cyclical Budget Balances

The budget surplus at full employment can be represented as

$$BS_f = tY_f - G - TR$$

Here, the subscript f represents full employment, for the budget surplus as well as output levels. Then, the difference between the full employment budget surplus and the actual budget surplus is the cyclical component, namely

$$BS_f - BS_{actual} = \text{Cyclical budget surplus.}$$

The actual budget surplus can consequently be written as

$$BS = \text{structural budget surplus} + \text{cyclical budget surplus}$$

Here, the cyclical surplus reflects the deviation from the full employment surplus due to cyclical factors, the automatic (not affected by policy) components of government revenue and spending. Deterioration in the cyclical budget surplus is due to insufficient demand in the economy, due to short-term changes in economic conditions. Automatic stabilizers contribute to cyclical budget surpluses or deficits. A decrease in tax revenue and an increase in unemployment benefits in a downturn will worsen the cyclical budget surplus.

The cyclical component of the actual budget surplus is not influenced by fiscal policy via *discretionary* changes in spending or the tax rate. So, the measure of fiscal stimulation or restraint is embodied in the structural budget surplus. Actually, in a downturn, one could expect the structural deficit to *increase,* reflecting fiscal stimulus. But this often does not happen, reflecting a wrong policy stance. For instance, it has been noted that even in the Great Depression of the 1930s, the US structural budget deficit actually *decreased!* This was contrary to the spirit of the basic Keynesian model—which however was not in vogue at that time period.

3.5.4. The Fiscal and Revenue Deficits

The terms fiscal and revenue deficits are widely in use in the Indian context. Table 3.2, adapted from the Economic Survey of the Ministry of Finance, shows the fiscal and revenue deficits for recent years. The models of calculation are self-evident from the table.

More attention seems to be having been given to the *fiscal deficit*, even in Indian economic debates in terms of the need for reductions in its level from a high of 9% of GDP to 4%, etc. But lately, there has been some redressing; the *revenue deficit* has also come into the limelight and rightly so, as ought to become evident from the following discussion.

The fiscal deficit is defined as:

Fiscal deficit = Revenue on the revenue (current) account + repayment of loans on capital account – total spending.

The fiscal deficit is the excess of the government's expenditure over its tax revenue, excluding borrowings.

A revenue deficit exists when the government's current/revenue expenditure exceeds its revenue earnings.

TABLE 3.2

Receipts and Expenditures of the Central Government

	2008-09	2009-10	2010-11	2011-12	2012-13	2013-14 (BE)	2013-14 (RE)	2014-15 (BE)
1. Revenue receipts (a + b)	540,259	572,811	788,471	751,437	8,776,330	1,056,330	1,029,251	1,189,763
(a) Tax revenue (net of States' share)	443,319	456,536	569,869	629,765	740,256	884,078	836,025	977,258
(b) Non-tax revenue	96,940	116,275	218,602	121,672	137,357	172,252	193,226	212,505
2. Revenue expenditure	796,798	911,809	1,040,723	1,145,786	1,243,509	1,436,168	1,399,539	1,568,112
(a) Interest payment	192,204	213,093	234,022	273,150	313,169	370,684	380,066	427,011
(b) Major subsidies	123,206	134,658	164,516	211,319	247,493	220,972	245,451	251,397
(c) Defence expenditures	73,305	90,669	92,061	103,011	111,277	11,693	124,800	134,412
3. Revenue deficit	253,539	338,998	252,252	394,349	365,896	379,838	370,288	378,349
4. Capital receipts	343,697	451,676	408,857	552,928	532,754	608,967	561,183	605,129
(a) Recovery of loans	6,139	8,613	12,420	18,850	16,268	10,654	10,803	10,527
(b) Other receipts	566	24,581	22,846	18,088	25,890	55,814	25,841	63,425
(c) Borrowings and other liabilities	336,992	418,482	373,591	515,990	490,596	542,499	524,539	531,177
5. Capital expenditure	90,158	112,678	156,604	158,579	166,858	229,129	190,895	226,780
6. Non-debt receipts [1 + 4(a) + 4(b)]	546,964	606,005	823,737	788,375	919,771	1,122,798	1,065,895	1,263,715
7. Total expenditure [2 + 5 = 7(a) + 7(b)]	883,956	1,024,487	1,197,327	1,304,365	1,410,367	1,665,297	1,590,434	1,794,892
(a) Plan expenditure	275,235	303,391	379,029	412,375	413,625	555,322	475,532	575,000
(b) Non-plan expenditure	608,721	721,096	818,298	891,990	996,742	1,109,975	1,114,902	1,219,892
8. Fiscal deficit [7 − 1 − 4(b)]	336,992	418,482	373,590	515,990	490,596	542,499	524,539	531,177
9. Primary deficit [8 − 2(a)]	144,788	205,389	139,568	242,840	177,427	171,815	144,473	104,166

Source: Table prepared from data in The Economic Survey 2014–15.

Note: BE—Budget Estimates; RE—Revised Estimates.

TABLE 3.3

Fiscal, Revenue and Primary Deficits (2003–04 to 2014–15)

Year	Revenue Deficit	Fiscal Deficit	Primary Deficit	Revenue Deficit as % of Fiscal Deficit
		(As a % of GDP)		
2003–04	3.6	4.5	0	79.7
2004–05	2.4	3.9	0	62.3
2005–06	2.5	4	0.4	63
2006–07	1.9	3.3	–0.2	56.3
2007–08	1.1	2.6	–0.9	41.4
2008–09	4.4	5.9	2.5	74. 8
2009–10	4.6	6.5	2.8	70.5
2010–11	3.2	4.8	1.8	72.3
2011–12	4.4	5.7	2.7	77.2
2012–13	3.6	4.9	1.8	73.5
2013–14	3.3	4.8	1.5	68.8
2014–15	2.9	4.1	0.8	70.7

Source: The Handbook of Statistics, RBI.

The revenue deficit is defined as:

Revenue deficit = Revenue on revenue account – Spending on revenue account.

The key to the difference between the two concepts lies in the types of spending encompassed. While capital spending on infrastructure, etc., is included in the fiscal deficit, in the revenue deficit, only current spending such as on salaries, pensions and interest on government debt is included.

Table 3.3 reports the fiscal deficit, revenue deficit and primary deficit between 2003–04 and 2014–15.

Now, it is easy to see that a reduction in the fiscal deficit can be achieved by reducing capital spending, although this does not augur well for economic growth. On the other hand, reducing the revenue deficit does not touch capital spending and only outlays on the revenue account, such as on salaries and consumption goods, etc., have to be reduced (or tax collections enhanced). See the trends in government of India's deficit in Figure 3.5.

The *primary budget deficit*: It is also useful to consider the primary budget deficit, which is obtained by subtracting net interest payments from the revenue deficit. The advantage is then that we can narrow down on the components of the budget deficit which should be and can be reduced. Interest payments have been already contracted and nothing can

The Primary deficit is the revenue deficit excluding interest payments.

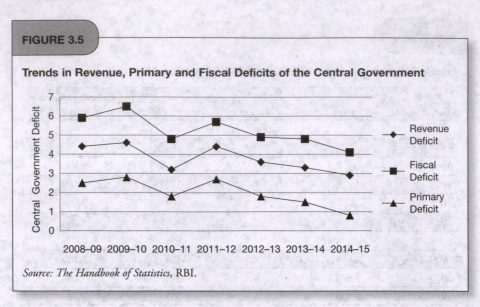

FIGURE 3.5

Trends in Revenue, Primary and Fiscal Deficits of the Central Government

Source: The Handbook of Statistics, RBI.

be done about those. Concentrating on the primary deficit will enable us to see if the possible reductions in revenue spending are actually being made. The primary deficit also has important implications for the stabilization of the government debt, as briefly discussed here.

3.5.5. The Budget Deficit and the Level of Government Debt**

The budget deficit is the shortfall in the government's expenditure relative to its tax revenue.

One of the problems with expansionary government fiscal policies that give rise to budget deficits is that these pile up as government debt. In fact, the existing level of government debt is nothing but the cumulated deficits of the past. So, if the debt burden has to be stopped from increasing any further, deficits have to be controlled as well. A simple measure of the debt burden is the debt to GDP ratio. Stabilizing the debt burden therefore, means stabilizing this ratio (rather than not taking any more debt at all). It can be shown that debt dynamics for reducing the debt–GDP ratio, or keeping it from rising could then imply balancing the primary account of the budget as otherwise a further increase in debt can be only halted by cutting down on capital spending.

A fiscal stimulus is the policy of increased government spending and tax cuts to stimulate the growth in economy during a downturn or recession.

The other trade-off that emerges in a dynamic scenario is the accumulation of government debt due to *fiscal stimulus* for greater output in the present. More government debt means burdening our future generations. In this chapter, we have outlined a strategy for the stabilization of government debt burden, linking it to the growth trajectory as well.

The rate of growth of real GDP should be greater than the average interest rate on debt. So, a country on a high growth trajectory can incur more government debt than one with a stagnant economy.

3.6. CONCLUSION

The Keynesian model is a powerful tool for combating deep recessions. At the trough of a downturn, there is no danger of cost hikes, or of a warning sign from the external sector—in the form of a sharp deterioration in the trade balance (which is usually not much in the red in a recession). Thus, the inflation and trade balance trade-offs with a domestic expansion will not be operative. Also, there will not be any crowding out of the private sector due to interest rate hikes that contract investment demand. For developing countries with large-scale unemployment and a poorly developed financial sector, the Keynesian model is something of a real boon.

The model in this chapter is very much of a short-run nature. When dynamic considerations are brought in, other trade-offs besides the immediate ones such as inflation and the trade deficit become apparent. In the treatment here, private consumption rules the roost; an increase in the marginal propensity to consume increases output and hence employment. But we will see in the growth chapter that follows that it is saving which drives economic growth. This points to a trade-off between more consumption today and more growth or consumption in the future. This trade-off is addressed in an optimizing fashion in the next chapter.

Finally, the nature of the exchange rate regime also has important implications for the impacts of fiscal policy, a topic addressed in the open economy chapter. The effects of fiscal stimuli in a disaggregated model, with attendant trade-offs, is taken up in the last chapter of this book.

SUMMARY

- The basic Keynesian model was presented by John Maynard Keynes. The model links spending and output; through mutual feedbacks between the two, while increased spending gets multiplied due to the circular relationship.
- When a government increases spending in a recession, output increases which raises private incomes and consumer spending—leading to further increases in output, incomes and private spending. This is called the 'multiplier effect'.
- Prices are assumed to be fixed, due to the absence of wage cost pressures and large-scale unemployment. So the supply curve is horizontal.
- Secondly, the model has no financial markets; so it plays no role in a deep recession with no increases in interest rates and private or government spending. Hence, the demand curve does not slope down.
- $AD = C + I + G + NX$ where AD is aggregate demand, C is private consumption, I is gross private investment and NX is net exports. AD will equal output Y in equilibrium.
- The economy is defined by $Y = C + I + G + NX$. When $Y > AD$, there is involuntary inventory accumulation and firms will cut back on output. When

Y < AD, inventories fall and firms increase output. So there is always a tendency to move towards equilibrium.

- The Keynesian model is driven by the consumption function: $C = C_0 + c \times Y_D$ where 'c' is disposable income, C_0 is autonomous consumption and Y_D is disposable income after taxes and transfers.

- $Y_D = Y - T + TR = Y - t \times Y + TR$ where T is total income taxes, TR is total transfers from the government and 't' is the income tax rate.

- A cut in the tax rate constitutes an increase in autonomous spending which is independent of Y.

- $\Delta Y = \acute{\alpha} \times \Delta A_0$, where $\acute{\alpha}$ is the Keynesian income multiplier given as $\acute{\alpha} = 1/1 - c (1 - t)$. The marginal propensity to consume, c, is less than 1, the Keynesian multiplier will be greater than 1, so that an increase in autonomous spending, such as a change in G or I, has a multiplier effect on income.

- The supply curve is horizontal as costs do not rise and price rises are therefore not needed to increase supply. A rise in demand can be met by a supply increase.

- From this we get the hidden cross in the Keynesian model! The supply curve is perfectly horizontal and the demand curve is vertical.

- The cross vanishes when the financial sector is introduced. The basic Keynesian model is applicable even when the financial sector is included while output levels are low.

- Though increased government spending increases output and lowers unemployment through the multiplier effect, there are costs and trade-offs associated with this policy with inflation and the external sector balance.

- Automatic stabilizers tend to dampen cyclical fluctuations in the economy, putting the brakes during booms and inciting expansionary spending during recessions. The income tax functions as a dampener during booms, siphoning away purchasing power.

- When unemployment benefits are paid out in a recession, they increase the budget deficit. This causes reductions in tax revenue in the downturn. Increased government expenditure, further deteriorates the budget deficit.

- The measure of fiscal stimulation or restraint (fiscal policy) is embodied in the structural budget surplus. In a downturn, the structural deficit should increase, reflecting fiscal stimulus.

- Fiscal deficit = Revenue on the revenue (current) account + repayment of loans on capital account − total spending.

- Revenue deficit = Revenue on revenue account − spending on revenue account.

- The key difference between the two deficits depends on the spending. Capital spending is included in the fiscal deficit. Revenue deficit, includes only current spending such as on salaries, pensions and interest debt.

- One of the problems with expansionary government fiscal policies is that they increase budget deficits that can pile up. The existing level of government debt is nothing but the cumulative deficits of the past. So, to curtail the debt burden, deficits have to be controlled as well.

CASE STUDY[2]

The Stimulus Package in the Aftermath of the Global Financial Crisis in the G20 Countries

The prompt, coordinated global response to the Great Recession was remarkable. Most countries introduced their stimulus packages in the last quarter of 2008, in the immediate aftermath of the Lehman collapse. But the time it took for countries to turn around in response to the stimulus and start their recovery varied widely. In Turkey and Italy, the response was sharper and recovery started within less than a quarter after the stimulus was applied. At the other extreme, Spain did not start recovering until 6 quarters after the stimulus was introduced and the lag was 5 quarters in Australia. The response lag was 4 quarters in India and Indonesia.

These differences in the time lag between the stimulus and the response were attributable to differences in the underlying economic environment and the size of the stimulus and the severity of the crisis in different G20 countries. The severity of the crisis, defined as the absolute difference between the average annual growth rate prior to deceleration and at the bottom of the trough in the country, varied a great deal. It ranged from as little as 31% and 41% in Indonesia and India respectively to over 500% in countries like Italy and Japan.

An assessment of the readiness of different G20 countries to initiate withdrawal of the stimulus is, therefore, critical. On assessing the performance of the G20 countries in terms of selected macroeconomic indicators, it turns out that there were large variations among them in their readiness for stimulus withdrawal. While interesting in itself, much of this discussion is of limited relevance for stimulus withdrawal in India and presumably also some of the other emerging G20 countries.

- First of all, growth is robust, making immediate stimulus withdrawal feasible and inflation is also high in countries like India making such withdrawal urgent.
- Second, at least in India, the financial sector is healthy, with well capitalized banks and there was no extraordinary asset acquisition by the central bank as part of its stimulus measures. This suggests that monetary tightening should be the policy of choice for curbing inflationary pressures. Indeed, the Reserve Bank of India has been tightening monetary policy and gradually raising nominal interest rates during the past few quarters.
- Third, the public debt: GDP ratio is high in India and the fiscal authorities have announced their commitment to a programme to meet the fiscal consolidation targets set by India's Thirteenth Finance Commission.

The Commission has recommended that the consolidated debt–GDP ratio should be reduced from 79% in 2009–10 to 68% in 2014–15. In the Commissions' scheme, this translates into a reduction of the combined fiscal deficit of the central and state governments from 9.5% of GDP to 5.4% over the same period. The essential logic of recommendations of the Finance Commission is to combine fiscal consolidation with high growth by reducing the fiscal deficit while preserving growth promoting capital expenditure. This is to be accomplished by a gradual compression of revenue expenditure. It is believed that in India public investment crowds in private investment. This is supported by evidence of a much strong multiplier effect of government capital expenditure compared to current or revenue expenditure.

[2] The idea for this case study has been drawn from S. Mundle, G. M. Rao, and N. R. Bhanumurthy, 'Stimulus, Recovery and Exit Policy G20 Experience and Indian Strategy' (working paper no. 2011-85, NIPFP, New Delhi, 2011).

TABLE CS 3.1

Stimulus Packages in Some Countries

Australia	1. A stimulus of A$10.4 billion in October 2008 to protect pensioners and parents
	2. A stimulus worth of A$42 billion in February 2009 through cash transfers (for workers and families to cope with crisis) and investments in infrastructure
India	1. December 2008, US$4.1 billion for enhancing development expenditures, cheaper credit to housing
Indonesia	1. December 2008, income tax relief to eight industries
	2. February 2009, US$6.5 billion
Italy	1. February 2009, US$2.56 billion through creating incentives for car makers and homes
Japan	1. First stimulus in August 2008 to mitigate the global food and fuel prices
	2. Second in December 2008 to protect job losses due to crises
	3. April 2009, US$150 billion package through subsidies and tax breaks
Spain	1. April 2008, a 18 billion Euros package through tax cuts and spending on housing
	2. November 2008, 11 billion Euros package for infrastructure and auto industry
Turkey	1. March 2009, US$9.84 billion for financial support to companies to curb lay-offs and for infrastructure spending

Source: The data for this table has been drawn from S. Mundle, G. M. Rao, and N. R. Bhanumurthy, 'Stimulus, Recovery and Exit Policy G20 Experience and Indian Strategy' (working paper no. 201185, NIPFP, New Delhi, 2011).

After reading the text in the case given above discuss the following questions:

1. What was the need for countries to introduce stimulus packages when the Great Recession began? Why has there been variations in the size and composition of the stimulus package across different G20 countries?
2. What factors influence the response and size of stimulus packages?
3. Why was there the need to withdraw the stimulus package in India?
4. What are the targets set by the Thirteenth Finance Commission? What is its justification?

KEYWORDS

Multiplier effect

Aggregate demand

Private consumption

Gross private investment

Balanced budget

Automatic stabilizers

Fiscal policy

Fiscal stimulus

Inventory	Revenue deficit
Disposable income	Fiscal deficit
Autonomous Spending	Primary deficit
Marginal propensity to consume	Budget deficit

CONCEPT CHECK

State if the following statements are true or false:

1. When the government increases spending in a recession, output increases, which raises private incomes and consumer spending and pushes the economy out of a slump.
2. When the marginal propensity to consume is less than 1, the Keynesian multiplier will be greater than 1, so that an increase in autonomous spending, such as a change in G or I, has a multiplier effect on income.
3. When the GDP is greater than aggregate demand, there is involuntary inventory accumulation and firms will cut back on output.
4. The debt to GDP ratio measures the government deficit, so to reduce government's fiscal deficit it should balance its primary account.
5. Fiscal deficit is the revenue on the revenue (current) account less repayment of loans on capital account plus total spending.

DISCUSSION QUESTIONS

1. Is the Keynesian model applicable for
   i. A long-time horizon?
   ii. A scenario with rising interest rates?

2. Does a reduction in the tax rate by 1% have any impact on the GDP? If yes, then what is the initial change in autonomous spending?

3. Will all the following developments have an equal impact on income? Explain in detail
   i. An increase in government spending by 100 crore
   ii. An increase in transfers by 100 crore
   iii. An increase in the tax rate thereby increasing the tax revenue by 100 crore

4. Using the inclined Keynesian cross diagram, show
   i. How a change in the marginal propensity to consume, 'c', affects equilibrium income and the income multiplier and
   ii. How a change in the tax rate affects equilibrium income and the multiplier.
   iii. Show these effects also for an increase in transfers that are not taxable.

5. If c = 0.7 and ΔG = 1,000 crore. Assume no taxes to begin with.
   i. How much will be ΔY?
   ii. If the tax rate is 20%, what is the answer to a)?
   iii. What is the answer if the tax rate is changed to 10%?

6. Derive the balanced budget multiplier. Assume that government spending and tax revenues increase by the same amount, so that ΔG = ΔT, or ΔG = tΔY.

$$C = 40 + 0.7 \, Y_D \quad I = 100 \quad G = 300 \quad TR = 200 \quad t = 20\%$$

   What is the budget surplus? What is the ex-ante budget surplus when the tax rate is raised to 30%? What is the ex-post budget surplus?

7. Is expansionary fiscal policy a panacea for all economic scenarios? Are there any costs or trade-offs?

CHAPTER

Economic Growth

LEARNING OBJECTIVES

Upon completion of this chapter, the reader will be able to:

- Understand what drives economic growth in a country.
- Explain how economic growth can be measured.
- Understand how factors like technical progress, the savings rate and population influence growth in Solow's exogenous growth model.
- Comprehend how the endogenous growth model explains the growth process and the importance of human capital formation.

4.1. INTRODUCTION: GROWTH THEORY

Newspaper and media reports inundate us with the latest news about the economy; whether the GDP has grown in the last quarter, whether unemployment has risen, if inflation has fallen, etc. News channels have discussions about retail sales, productivity, money supply, interest rates and market capitalization, business investments and a myriad of data that are collected, processed and published by government agencies. But what is at the centre of all these discussions? It is growth, economic growth.

Economic growth is the expansion of an economy's productive potential over the long-run. It is measured by the rate of change of an economy's GDP. When the GDP grows, people of the country earn higher incomes that enable them to enjoy more goods and services. After Independence, until 1960, the Indian economy grew at a rate of around 2.3% per annum, but after 1981–82 the growth rate improved steadily to reach 10% in

Economic growth is the expansion of an economy's productive potential over a long period.

1990. India's real GDP has grown by eight times since the 1950s. In the same period, the real GDP of the USA has grown three times and the per capita GDP has doubled. The two countries widely differ in the state of their economic growth. Different economies across the world exhibit great divergence in the rate of growth and standard of living of their citizens. But why do different countries grow at different rates? To understand why some economies grow more rapidly than others we have to study how their national incomes change over time.

In Chapter 2, we saw how national income is measured and in Chapter 1, we saw how the statistical aggregates of GDP, inflation, unemployment and foreign exchange reserves change over time. But merely measuring the movement of macroeconomic aggregates is not sufficient to gauge the performance to an economy. For that we must specify certain targets for economic activity, and then evaluate how far the economy has succeeded in achieving these goals. From the policy-maker's point of view, the macroeconomic targets for an economy are full employment and price stability accompanied by growth.

Economists of the early 19th century were concerned with economic growth following Adam Smith. Later, with the need to examine the day-to-day life of the common man, the focus shifted to microeconomics a la Alfred Marshall. In the post war years of the 20th century, interest in growth theory was renewed as reconstruction of war-ravaged economies took centre stage. Later, interest in economic growth revived in the last decade of the 20th century. In this chapter, we discuss the theory of growth that was developed by Robert Solow in 1956, also known as the neo-classical model. The Solow growth model shows how savings, population growth and technological progress affect the level of economic output and growth. The model takes the rate of savings and population growth as exogenous (i.e., outside the system) and shows how these two variables determine the steady state level of income per capita. The exogeneity of technical progress and the physical capital accumulation embedded in the model prove to be inadequate in explaining long-term economic growth. Although the model explained the dynamics of the economic growth process, there were no policy variables in it that could be used to trigger or slowdown growth since both the variables were exogenous. Hence, there were hardly any policy conclusions from the neo-classical theory. In 1986, Romer[1] developed the endogenous growth model as did Lucas,[2] laying emphasis on human capital accumulation as a significant determinant of growth. We look at these developments in the theory of growth as it has evolved. Current research provides evidence that education (e.g., years of schooling) contributes to the growth of income in an economy, India is no exception.

Therefore, to assess an economy's performance, we need to use the systematic guide of a macroeconomic model, to help us understand the real world and interpret its complexities. An economic model is a simplification of reality which suppresses details so that the relationships between different variables are accentuated to comprehend the problem at hand. A model represents reality using diagrams, or equations, which show how various variables interact.

[1] Paul M. Romer, 'Increasing Returns and Long Run Growth', *Journal of Political Economy* 94, no. 5 (1986): 1002–37.

[2] R. E. Lucas, 'On the Mechanics of Economic Development', *Journal of Monetary Economics* 22, no. 1 (1988): 3–42.

After the introduction in Section 4.1, this chapter unfolds with what is growth and how it can be measured in Sections 4.2 and 4.3. The Solow's growth model and its intricacies are exposed in Sections 4.4 to 4.6. In Section 4.7, convergence is explained followed by the endogenous model and its relevance for India in Section 4.8, and finally the conclusion is presented in Section 4.9.

4.2. WHAT DRIVES GROWTH?

Policy-makers are largely concerned with the long-run growth of GDP. Developing countries tend to have large unused resources and a large number of persons in the labour force who remain unemployed due to inadequate jobs. Low levels of income cause low consumption levels and a low savings rate which in turn lead to little or no capital formation. Such economies tend to remain at a low-level equilibrium.

To understand these issues we have to examine what drives the growth path of an economy. Growth in an economy takes place because of growth in the factors of production like labour and capital and technological progress. Growth theory helps in understanding how economic decisions determine the build-up of capital and improvements in factor productivity. It helps to understand, for instance, how the savings rate influences the future *capital stock*, or how new methods of production techniques raise labour output.

Capital stock is the amount or stock of equipment, machinery and structures used in the production process in an economy.

The growth in the GDP comes from rising incomes that enable people of a country to consume more goods and services and experience a better quality of life. Although people care about income, they also care about education, freedom, liberty, health and a host of other factors. Hence a proper measure of well-being, let us say living standard, needs to account for many factors. It is difficult to measure most of these factors and even more difficult to assign weights to each of them while calculating any index of well-being. Therefore, we use real per capita income as a rough measure of economic well-being.

So why do some countries grow faster than others? To understand that, we need to comprehend how the national income changes over time. We now proceed to examine how growth can be measured.

4.3. MEASURING GROWTH

Economists measure economic growth by the change in real GDP, which reflects how the total amount of goods and services produced increase over time. To compare the well-being of different countries, economists use real per capita income as a broad measure of long-term economic growth.

There are two issues in measuring output and productive potential: firstly, output can be measured over long periods of time or between periods of time when the resource utilization is similar. Suppose the Y-axis measures the growth in GDP and the X-axis measures time (see Figure 4.1). To measure the growth rate between two periods we can use the average

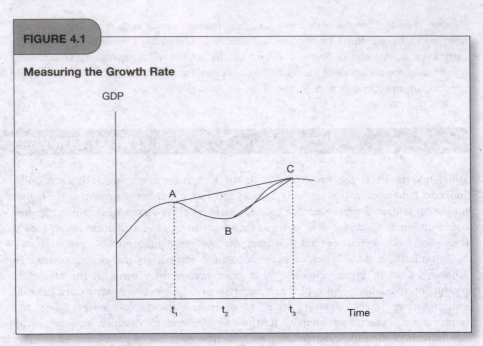

FIGURE 4.1

Measuring the Growth Rate

annual growth rate. But what should be the time period? If we measure growth between t_1 and t_3 it will be lower than the rate of growth between t_2 and t_3, since line AC is less steep than line BC. We must measure growth rate from the same point on the business cycle.

The second issue in the measurement of the growth rate is the concept of productive potential. A country's productive potential depends upon its resource endowments. Larger countries, possessing greater stock of resources, are likely to grow faster than smaller ones, with fewer resources. Hence, it is difficult to compare growth rates between countries of differing size. We can overcome this by using the *per capita GDP*, that is, if we divide a country's GDP by its population we get a per capita measure that eliminates the size effect. Table 4.1 shows per the capita GDP growth in some countries over the last seventy years.

While the USA tops the list of countries with $35,619 per capita GDP in year 2000, Bangladesh had $1,172 per capita which was 5% of that of the USA. Japan's per capita GDP has grown more than 100 times between the mid-20th century and 2015 and stands second only to the US. Sri Lanka's per capita GDP fell at the turn of the 21st century, the country being ravaged by civil war, but it then recovered well and its per capita GDP stands at double that of India in 2015. Chinese citizens are enjoying a more than 40 times increase in their per capita income in the last 55 years.

Real per-capita income in the developing world grew at an average rate of 2.3% per annum during the four decades between 1960 and 2000. This is a high growth rate by almost any standard. At this pace, incomes double every 30 years, allowing each generation to enjoy a level of living standards that is twice as high as the previous generations. To provide some historical perspective on this performance, it is worth noting that Britain's per capita GDP grew at a mere 1.3% per annum during its period of

TABLE 4.1

Per Capita Gross Domestic Product in US$ (Current Price)*

	1950	1960	1970	1980	1990	2000	2010	2015
USA	1,933	2,888	5,000	12,170	23,005	35,619	48,374	51,638
UK	1,350	2,264	3,640	8,204	15,931	24,252	38,709	41,188
Japan	412	1,103	3,579	8,903	19,431	25,924	42,935	44,657
India	127	199	322	670	1,484	2,684	1,346	1,751
Sri Lanka	262	332	470	984	2,158	3,841	2,820	3,638
Pakistan	181	196	391	757	1,528	2,158	1,043	1,143
China	NA	154	243	617	1,568	3,844	4,561	6,497
Argentina	1,182	1,734	2,771	6,111	6,188	11,729	10,332	10,515
Bangladesh	NA	247	330	532	1,104	1,772	760	973
Brazil	299	556	1,103	3,687	5,491	7,745	11,159	11,121

Source: Table prepared from data in Penn World Tables PWT 9.0 version.
* Chart 4.1 is the graphical representation of data in Table 4.1.

economic supremacy in the middle of the 19th century (1820–70) and that of the United States grew at only 1.8% during the half century before World War I when it overtook Britain as the world's economic leader (Table B-22, 265).[3] Figure 4.2 shows the per capita GDP growth of selected countries. Moreover, with a few exceptions, economic growth in the last few decades has been accompanied by significant improvements in social indicators such as literacy, infant mortality, life expectancy and the like. So on balance, the recent growth record looks quite impressive.

However, since the rich countries themselves grew at a very rapid pace of 2.7% during the period 1960–2000, few developing countries consistently managed to close the economic gap between them and the advanced nations. Figure 4.3 is a scatter diagram of real per capita GDP of 25 countries from 1960 to 2000. It demonstrates that countries of East and Southeast Asia constitute the sole exception. Excluding China, this region experienced per-capita GDP growth of 4.4% over 1960–2000. Despite the Asian financial crisis of 1997–98, countries such as South Korea, Thailand and Malaysia ended the century with productivity levels that stood significantly closer to those enjoyed in the advanced countries.[4] The Latin American countries experience is somewhat different as they experienced an economic crisis, political instability and social unrest around the same time, but as the globalization and financial integration progressed across the world, this began to change. We discuss the Latin American countries' source of growth in the next section.

[3] Maddison Angus, 'The World Economy: A Millennial Perspective' (Development Centre Studies, Luxembourg OECD, 2001).
[4] Dani Rodrik, 'Growth Strategies', *Handbook of Economic Growth* 1, part A, (2005): 967–1014.

FIGURE 4.2

Per Capita Gross Domestic Product in US$ of Selected Countries

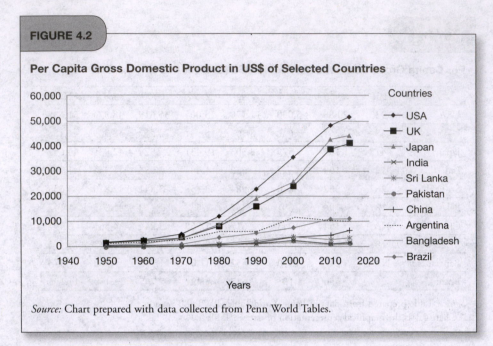

Source: Chart prepared with data collected from Penn World Tables.

FIGURE 4.3

Average Per Capita GDP

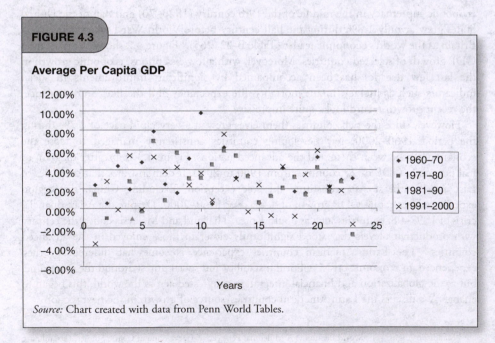

Source: Chart created with data from Penn World Tables.

Growth theory helps in understanding how economic decisions determine the build-up of capital and increases in productivity. For instance, it helps us better comprehend how savings rate influences future capital stock, or how new production techniques raise labour output, which is also referred to as *labour productivity*. In the long-run, the GDP level depends positively on the savings rate and negatively on the rate of growth of population.

Policy-makers are concerned mostly with the long-run. Growth is a long-term issue in the sense that its impact can be visible only in the medium or long-terms. While savings and investment promote the accumulation of capital, the increases in population raise the labour force in the longer horizon.

The Solow growth model explains how savings, population growth and technological progress affect the level of economic output and growth. Technological change is assumed not to affect the marginal productivities of the two factors. In other words, the change in technology is neutral. Solow's study of shifts in production finds that in the United States, the shifts in the aggregate production function had indeed been neutral.[5]

Not all countries keep growing at the same pace. Actually countries change their relative position in the international income distribution. To look at this effect we see for instance in 1970, that the per capita income of Singapore was 36% of the USA; in 2003 it became almost 75%. However, for Venezuela, it decreased from 37% in 1970 to 18% in 2003. There is also a pattern of groupings, so that some countries in the 1970s appear to have joined either the low-income or the high-income club. Thus, we find that not only is there diversity among countries in the rate of growth of per capita GDP but also wide differences between their growth paths. This is particularly visible from the experience of the Latin American countries in the four decades post 1965, which is discussed in Box 4.1.

> Labour productivity is the ratio of output to labour, Y/N.

| **BOX 4.1** | **The Diversity of Growth Experience in the Latin American Countries[6]** |

Since 1965, the Latin American countries have experienced episodes of economic crises, political instability and social unrest. In the interim period, they also embarked on economic stabilization programs, political re-organization and structural reforms. A quick review of the basic indicators suggests net positive results from these efforts because income per capita rose and health as well as education indicators improved. Earlier, the region had been insulated but over this period, there was greater integration with global trade and institutional quality improved[7] (see Table 4.2). The economic performance of the Latin American countries in this period was impressive but not really satisfactory. A closer examination of the data between 1960 and 1999, the last four decades of the 20th century indicates that on an average these countries experienced slower growth than the rest of the developing world. This produced a widening of the income gap between the Latin American countries and the rest of the world.

[5] Robert M. Solow, 'Technical Change and the Aggregate Production Function', *The Review of Economics and Statistics* 39, no. 3 (1957): 312–20.

[6] Blyde and Fernandez Arias 2005, 'Why Latin America Is Falling Behind?'

[7] Blyde and Arias, 'Why Latin America Is Falling Behind?'

Why was this gap widening? The key to this difference was not factor accumulation but total factor productivity (TFP). This is supported by Blyde and Fernandez Arias who have shown that the slower TFP growth accounts for slower growth relative to other regions.[8] Also, institutional quality, lack of openness and macroeconomic instability were important factors behind the difference in productivity growth in this region. Another explanation for the broad-based decline in growth is the decline in population, if we compare the population growth rate of 1960–75 to that of 1988–2003 (Table 4.2).

TABLE 4.2

Basic Growth Indicators of Latin American Countries, Other Regions and Rest of the World

Years/Regions	Real GDP Per Capita in 2005 US Dollars				Trade Volume % of GDP			
	1960s	1970s	1980s	1990s	1960s	1970s	1980s	1990s
Latin America	1,590	2,000	2,050	2,170	37	44	48	57
Rest of the World	2,380	3,350	4,100	4,800	55	67	72	78
Developed Countries	13,420	18,860	23,160	27,790	47	55	61	66
East Asia	1,860	3,360	5,590	9,480	112	131	166	193

Years/Regions	Life Expectancy at Birth				Years of Education of 15 Years and Above			
	1960s	1970s	1980s	1990s	1960s	1970s	1980s	1990s
Latin America	56	61	65	68	3.1	3.8	4.7	5.4
Rest of the World	58	61	65	67	3.1	4.3	5.3	6.3
Developed Countries	71	73	75	77	7.1	7.8	8.7	9.4
East Asia	60	65	70	73	4.5	5.3	6.5	7.6

Source: Juan Blyde and Fernandez Arias, 'Why Latin America Is Falling Behind?, in *Sources of Growth in Latin America: What is Missing?*, eds. Fernandes Arias, Roberto Manuelli, and Juan Blyde (Washington, DC: Inter-America Development Bank, 2005).
Notes: Latin American Countries—Argentina, Bolivia, Brazil, Chile, Columbia, Costa Rica, Dominican Republic, El Salvador, Guatemala, Haiti, Honduras, Jamaica, Nicaragua, Panama, Paraguay, Peru, Uruguay, Venezuela and Mexico.
Rest of the World—Botswana, Cameroon, Cote d'Ivore, Cyprus, Egypt, Fiji, France, Greece, Ghana, Hungary, Iceland, India, Israel, Kenya, Morocco, Pakistan, Papua New Guinea, the Philippines, Portugal, Senegal Sierra Leone, South Africa, Sri Lanka, Syria, Togo, Tunisia and Zimbabwe.
Developed Countries—Australia, Austria, Belgium, Canada, Denmark, Finland, Germany, Ireland, Italy, Japan, The Netherlands, New Zealand, Norway, Spain, Sweden, Switzerland, UK and the USA.
East Asia: Hong Kong, Korea, Malaysia, Singapore, Thailand.

[8] Blyde and Arias, 'Why Latin America Is Falling Behind?'

4.4. THE SOLOW GROWTH MODEL IN A CLOSED ECONOMY

The Solow growth model or the exogenous model assumes a closed economy so that there is no trade or government and hence in equilibrium, saving and investment are equal. This is the national income identity we saw in Chapter 2. At the heart of Solow's model lies the production function and new technology, exogenous to the system, driving the economy to higher levels of output. The capital stock is the crucial determinant of the economy's output, but capital stock changes over time through savings and investment and these changes cause the economy to grow.

4.4.1. The Production Function

The *production function* is a concise statement of the relationship between total inputs and total outputs given the state of technology. It provides a quantitative link between the inputs and the real output denoted by Y, and determines how much output is produced from a given quantity of inputs. Let us assume for the sake of simplicity that there are only two inputs, namely capital $\underline{K}$ and labour N. Equation (4.1) shows the level of production or output for each level of input

> The production function is a concise statement of the relationship between total inputs and total outputs, given the state of technology.

$$Y = F (\underline{K}, N) \qquad (4.1)$$

The short-run view of this production function specifies that capital remains constant; the state of technology and the labour force are also constant. In the long-run, both capital and labour are variable therefore, long-run capital changes so K replaces $\underline{K}$ in Equation (4.2).

$$Y = F (K, N) \qquad (4.2)$$

The model assumes that the production function has *constant returns to scale*; this simplifies the analysis but is believed to be realistic. The assumption of constant returns to scale implies that output increases by the same proportion as all inputs. The production function with constant returns to scale enables us to analyse all quantities relative to the size of the labour force. Hence per capita labour and per capita capital remains unchanged. If we multiply both capital and labour by any positive number z, we also multiply the output by z. Hence a production function with constant returns will function such that an increase of a certain proportion of both labour and capital will cause an increase in the output by the same proportion—see Equation (4.3).

> Constant returns to scale is the change in output resulting from a proportional change in inputs or change in inputs at a constant factor.

$$zY = F (zK, zN) \qquad (4.3)$$

If $z = 3$, then labour and capital inputs are tripled and output will also triple. So if we assume that z is equal to 1/N, then the production function can be written in per capita form as

$$Y/N = F (K/N, 1) = y = f(k) \qquad (4.4)$$

In Equation (4.4), we denote per capita output by y (which is Y/N, that is, output per worker) as a function of per capita capital k. In other words, per capita computation allows us to observe how these economic variables change over time, ignoring the size of the economy.

4.4.2. Growth Accounting

So far we have discussed the production function that relates output growth to inputs of labour and capital, given the state of technology. Let A reflect the current state of technology:

$$Y = AF (K, N) \qquad (4.5)$$

New technology changes the production function. In the long-run, technology, capital and the labour force change and we have another production function where a new term representing technology change is introduced (say A` instead of A). In the long-term, as technology changes with the same level of labour and capital, more output can be produced.

4.5. THE COBB DOUGLAS PRODUCTION FUNCTION

Solow's growth model assumes the Cobb Douglas constant returns-to-scale production function. In Equation (4.6), θ and $(1 - \theta)$ are weights equal to labour's share of income and capital's share of income respectively.

$$Y = A F (K^{\theta}, N^{1 - \theta}) \qquad (4.6)$$

The capital–labour ratio is the amount of capital or machinery used by one unit of labour.

The per capita production function in Figure 4.4 first slopes upwards and then slopes downwards. The marginal productivity of increasing the *capital–labour ratio* is positive,

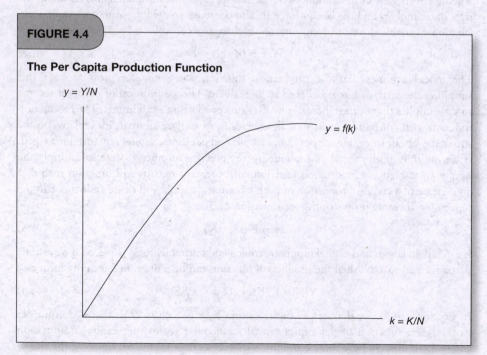

FIGURE 4.4

The Per Capita Production Function

$y = Y/N$

$y = f(k)$

$k = K/N$

but diminishing. That is $f'(k) > 0$ but $f''(k) < 0$. In the constant returns-to-scale Cobb Douglas production function, the weights of the factors sum to one. In per capita terms the production function denoted by Equation (4.6) can be written as

$$y = Y/N = A \, F \, (K/N)^\theta, \ N/N^{(1-\theta)} = AK^\theta/N^{(-\theta)} \tag{4.7}$$

The *marginal productivity* of k (MPK) is where the first derivative is given by MPK $= \delta y/\delta k = \theta AK^{9-1} > 0$ and the second derivative by $\delta MPK/\delta k = \delta^2 y/\delta k^2 = (1-\theta) < 0$ which is negative since $\theta < 1$. This explains the concave downward slope of the production function. However, it does not violate the constant returns to scale assumption because constant returns to scale requires factor proportions to be constant. Diminishing returns relate to an increase in capital intensity per worker, which is an increase in the amount of one factor (capital) per unit of another factor (labour).

> Marginal productivity is the change in output resulting from a change of one unit of labour or one unit of capital.

Therefore we can say that:

Output growth = labour share $(1 - \theta)$ × labour growth + capital share θ × capital growth + *technological progress,* which is shown in Equation (4.8)

$$\Delta Y/Y = (1-\theta) \times \Delta N/N + \theta \times \Delta K/K + \Delta A/A \tag{4.8}$$

> Technological progress is the improvement in the method of production, including changes in technical knowledge or methods of organizing business.

Labour's share indicates the fraction of total output that compensates labour, that is, wages, salaries divided by the GDP. The rate of growth of output is identically equal to the rate of change in technology (technical progress) called *total factor productivity (TFP)* plus the rate of growth of each of the factor inputs multiplied by their respective weights in total, that is θ for capital and $(1-\theta)$ for labour. Suppose θ is about 0.5 and $(1-\theta)$ is 0.5, if labour force grows at 1% and the capital stock at 3%, then from the growth accounting identity, the growth rate must be 2.6%. Since labour's share is greater, a 1% increase in labour force has a greater effect on output growth than a 1% increase in capital.

> Total factor productivity is the amount by which output would increase as a result of improvements in the methods of production, with all inputs unchanged.

4.6. THE SOLOW RESIDUAL

The technical identity allows the potential importance of TFP and labour and capital inputs to be computed. However, the growth in TFP cannot be measured directly. Solow derived an estimate of A.[9] This measure is referred to the Solow residual and is defined as

$$A = Y - [\theta K + (1-\theta)N] \tag{4.9}$$

Since outputs and inputs can be measured while changes in TFP cannot, we can re-arrange Equation (4.8) to get another definition of the Solow residual

$$\Delta A/A = \Delta Y/Y - (1-\theta) \times \Delta N/N + \theta \times \Delta K/K \tag{4.10}$$

[9] Solow, 'Technical Change and the Aggregate Production Function', 312–20.

where all the factors deducted from $\Delta Y/Y$ on the right hand side are attributed to changes in TFP.

In Solow's model, the key determinants of growth are in the following order:

1. Technical progress
2. Rising labour
3. Capital accumulation

Solow's estimates of US GDP growth between 1909 and 1949 show that the annual average growth rate per year was 2.9%, of which 0.32% was due to *capital accumulation*, 1.09% to increases in labour force and 1.49% due to technical progress. Denison's extension of Solow's work using US data for 1929 to 1982 shows that the average growth rate stood at 2.92% annually and 1.02% was attributed to technical progress, 66% of which was due to 'advances in knowledge'.[10] Does technological progress play an important role in explaining growth in other countries? To answer this question, let us look at the Table 4.3 where TFP and its contributions are shown.

All the three countries, namely Hong Kong, South Korea and Taiwan experienced high growth rates in GDP. We note that the percentage contribution of TFP growth in GDP growth is small. Therefore, capital accumulation and growth in labour force play a significant role in contributing to the high growth in GDP in these countries. In sum, we infer that countries with high growth experiences may not always register high growth in TFP. Mankiw, Romer and Weil have shown that investment in *human capital* through education and training is a significant source of economic growth.[12]

Capital accumulation is investment in real capital goods like machinery, equipment or infrastructure which help to raise productive potential.

Human capital is new education and training that increases or improves the skills of the labour force and in turn raises labour productivity. It is the skill or knowledge, stock of competencies and cognitive abilities of an individual or population that contributes to the growth of an organization or nation.

TABLE 4.3

The Contribution of TFP in GDP Growth in East Asian Countries[11] (in %)

Country	Growth in GDP	Growth in TFP Percentage	Contribution of TFP in GDP Growth
Hong Kong	7.3	2.2	30.1
South Korea	10.3	1.2	11.6
Taiwan	9.1	1.8	19.8

[10] Edward Denison, *Trends in American Economic Growth, 1929–1982* (Washington: Brookings Institution, 1985).

[11] A. Young, 'The Tyranny of Numbers: Confronting the Statistical Realities of the East Asian Growth Experience', *Quarterly Journal of Economics* 110, no. 3 (1995): 641–80.

[12] N. Gregory Mankiw, David Romer, David N. Weil, "A Contribution to the Empirics of Economic Growth," *The Quarterly Journal of Economics* 107, no. 2 (May, 1992): 407–37.

4.6.1. Accounting for Growth in Per Capita Output

Why are we interested in accounting for growth? The answer lies in the definition. Growth accounting exercise, which explains a country's growth by the following factors: (a) growth in labour force, (b) growth in capital accumulation and (c) growth in technological progress. Output grows as inputs are increased and with increases in productivity due to better technology and a larger labour force. Let us recall the production function already described. We can summarize growth accounting as follows which is the same as Equation (4.8),

$$\Delta Y/Y = (1 - \theta) \times \Delta N/N + \theta \times \Delta K/K + \Delta A/A \qquad (4.11)$$

Output growth = (Labour share × Labour growth) + (Capital share × Capital growth) + (Technological progress)

To compute growth '$\Delta y/y$' in per capita terms, subtract labour force growth $\Delta N/N$ from both sides:

Let us define $k = K/N$, then the capital–labour ratio

$$\Delta y/y = \theta \times \Delta k/k + \Delta A/A \qquad (4.12)$$

The capital–labour ratio is the amount of capital per unit of labour or the number of machines per worker. If θ is say 0.25 it means that a 1% increase in the amount of capital per worker will cause a rise in output that is one fourth of 1%. Per capita income growth depends on the change in the capital–labour ratio and on technical progress (see Figure 4.5).

FIGURE 4.5

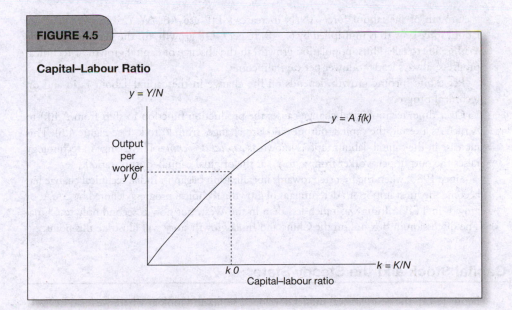

Capital–Labour Ratio

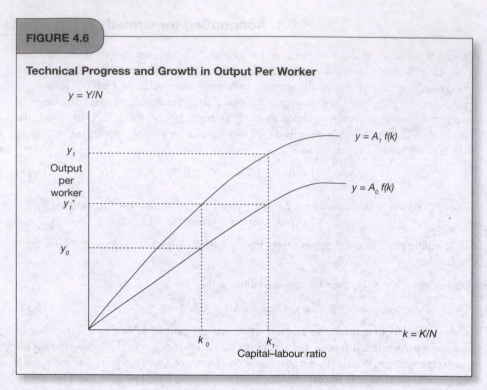

FIGURE 4.6

Technical Progress and Growth in Output Per Worker

Growth of the labour force $\Delta N/N$ increases GDP growth, $\Delta Y/Y$. But given that the labour force growth is multiplied by $(1 - \theta)$ to get GDP growth, for the per capita income Y/N, tends to fall. Thus, population growth, in the absence of capital growth or technical progress, always leads to lower per capita income.

Per capita income growth depends on the change in the capital–labour ratio and on technical progress.

Over time, technological change causes the production function to shift from $A_0 f(k)$ to $A_1 f(k)$. As a result, the capital–output ratio also changes from k_0 to k_1 (see Figure 4.6). This increase in the capital–labour ratio is known as *capital deepening*. The change in technology raises the output per worker from y_0 to $y_1`$ at the original capital–output ratio k_0.

Capital deepening is the increase in the capital stock per labour hour. Also known as an increase in capital intensity.

Since 1985, when the first step towards liberalization began in India, technical change has become the most important determinant of growth. Technical progress denoted by $\Delta A/A$, or growth in TFP in India was much less than in the West, but now is second only to China. The discussion in Box 4.2 on the China and India growth story will illustrate this point.

4.6.2. Capital Stock and the Steady State

Let us re-cap the neo-classical model developed so far and look at where we head next. At first, we assumed a closed economy so there was no trade or government. Hence at equilibrium, saving and investment were equal, hence $S = I$. This was the national income

BOX 4.2	Technical Progress in India and China[13]

'Can India surpass China?' is no longer a silly question, and if it turns out that India has indeed made the wiser bet, the implications—for China's future growth and for how policy experts think about economic development in general—are enormous.

—Huang and Khanna[14]

Economic theories acknowledge that capital accumulation is the most important ingredient of output growth.[15] There is a divergence in the pattern of capital accumulation and growth in India and China. They face different challenges in their quest for growth and prosperity. India must address impediments to investment whereas China has to face the question of whether the pace of their investment can maintain its steam.

Since 1992, India's GDP per capita grew by 4.2% while China's GDP rose by 6.7%. Therefore, while in 1992, their per capita GDP's were nearly identical at US$333 for India and US$332 for China, by 2003, China's per capita GDP at US$1,067 had nearly doubled that of India's at US$502. The question for consideration is 'Why India has lagged behind China?'

In 1978, China started a process of modernization in its industrial sector adopting greater openness to world trade. India too sought to modernize its industrial sector and relaxed controls and dismantled the license raj in the late 1980s. China attempted to move towards a market based structure and acquire new technology to compete with the rest of the world from the early 1990s. India embarked on unprecedented economic reforms in 1991. Felipe et al. provide empirical evidence to compare the performance of the two countries, by documenting and contrasting the evolving key economic variables that reflect the stylized facts of these two economies.[16] Particularly then, what is the main factor underlying the difference in the growth of China and India?

In China, the rapid rise in labour productivity was achieved through high rates of capital accumulation leading to an increased capital–labour ratio. On the other hand, in India, the labour productivity, wage rates, capital–labour ratio and profit rate, all increased relatively. In India growth in capital productivity and capital–labour ratio have been associated with modest growth in labour productivity.

The main difference between China and India lies in the relative importance given to investment. Investment has played a crucial role in propelling economic growth in China. The Gross Fixed Capital Formation in China as a share of GDP stood at 42.5% in 2003 while the comparable figure in India was merely 27.7%. Whereas investment grew at 11.7% in China

---

[13] Yasheng Huang and Khanna Tarun, 'Can India Overtake China?' *Foreign Policy no. 137 July*, (Harvard Faculty and Research, August 2003).

[14] Huang and Khanna, 'Can India Overtake China?', 2003.

[15] Maurice Scott, *A New View of Economic Growth* (Oxford: Oxford University Press, 1989).

[16] Jesus Felipe, Editha Lavina and E. F. Xiaoqin, 'The Divergent Pattern of Profitability, Investment and Growth of China and India during 1980–2003, *World Development* 36, no.5 (2008): 741–74.

between 1980 and 2003, in India the rate was 6.8%. Due to higher growth rate and larger proportion of investment in total output, the contribution of investment to overall growth in China far exceeded that of India.

Profitability: In China the profit rate declined from 13.5% in 1980 to 8.7% in 2003, while in India the profit rate increased from 11.5% in 1980 to 16.5% in 1999. China's profit rate averaged at 10.9% between 1978 and 2003 and India's was 14.3% between 1980 and 1999. It is not easy to explain why China's profit rate has declined while that of India has increased. Different theories provide different insights. One explanation for this trend in China and India is that from 1980 to 2003 capital share decreased in China by 7% from 36% to 29% and labour's share rose by approximately that much. In India on the other hand, the share of capital rose from 40% to 44% around the same period.

Capital Productivity: The other significant variable that explains the divergence in capital accumulation is capital productivity. During the two decades when both the countries made huge advances, the comparison of their capital productivity reveals a major difference. While capital productivity increased in India it declined in China. It fell by 10% in China but rose approximately by the same amount in India. This is a very important factor as it reveals that there has been poor utilization of capital in China vis-à-vis in India. A probable cause for this may be the recent industrialization effect in China leading to an over-supply of infrastructure. However, the difference in investment share between the two countries is so large that India's increasing capital productivity cannot compensate for its lower investment share, resulting in a much smaller growth rate of its capital stock.

Technical Progress: Felipe et al. show that in China capital productivity and labour productivity as well as capital–labour ratios were moving in opposite directions, while in India the three variables are moving in the same direction (see table).[17] During 1980–2003, China's labour productivity rose at an annual average rate of 8%, capital–labour ratio at 9.5% while capital productivity fell by 1.3%. In contrast, between 1981–99 India's labour productivity increased by an annual average rate of 4.1%, the capital–labour ratio by 2.6% and capital productivity by 1.5.

	China 1980–2003	India 1981–99
Labour Productivity (avg. annual rate)	↑ by 8%	↑ by 4.17%
Capital–Labour Ratio (avg. annual rate)	↑ by 9.5%	↑ by 2.6%
Capital Productivity (avg. annual rate)	↓ by 1.3%	↑ by 1.5%

Rodrik and Subramanian forecast India's growth rate to be 7.5% annually in the period 2000 to 2025, in a growth accounting exercise, using a Cobb Douglas Production function with constant returns to scale.[18] Capital's share was kept constant at 0.35 and the capital stock was assumed to grow at 8.3% annually. This was justified on the argument that India's dependency ratio[19] will decline, leading to higher savings and investment. They assumed that TFP to grow at 2.5% per annum.

[17] Felipe et al.

[18] Dani Rodrik and Arvind Subramanian, '"Hindu Growth" to Productivity Surge: The Mystery of the Indian Growth Transition' (IMF working paper no. 304, International Monetary Fund, Washington, DC, 2004).

[19] The dependency ratio is the proportion of children and old people to working adults. India has the best dependency ratio in the world and will remain so for at least one generation. *The Economist*, 2 October 2010.

China's spectacular growth story has dazzled the world and it is a miracle that many countries would love to emulate. India has plodded along, while China began earlier and pursued aggressive investments and macroeconomic policies conducive to growth. India despite a later start at a far lower level has several advantages says *The Economist*.[20] Firstly demography, in an ageing world there is a need for young workers. The proportion of Indian working age population will increase by 135 million by 2020 while that of China by 23 million. India's work force will stay young and keep growing with millions of them speaking English. India's economy will benefit from the demographic dividend, as the literacy rate is rising with new private schools proliferating across the country. Secondly, economic reforms have unleashed a massive flood of entrepreneurship. Indian capitalism is driven by millions of private businesses, many of whom are world class. Thirdly, India's growth initiative comes from individuals, while that of China is state sponsored. Therefore, India's brand of individualistic capitalism may be more robust than a state directed one. Finally, the global economy is moving towards knowledge intensive industries like software and India's advantage here is palpable. In 2005–06, India achieved impressive growth rates of 8.1% and 9.2% respectively. Huang (January 2006) wrote in an article in the *Financial Times* that 'India is achieving this result with just half of China's level of domestic investment only 10% of China's FDI. The evidence is clear as ever, China's growth stems from massive capital accumulation of resources, while India's growth comes from increasing efficiency'.[21]

identity we discussed in Chapter 2. Savings is a proportion of income S = sY, where s is the average marginal propensity to save and is less than one, s < 1. Saving = savings rate × income which is denoted as follows in Equation (4.13):

$$S = s \times y = s \times f(k) \tag{4.13}$$

The capital stock is the key determinant of an economy's output, but capital stock changes over time and these changes cause the economy to grow. Investment and *depreciation* are the two major factors that influence capital stock. Depreciation is required to replace wear and tear of older equipment. Change in capital stock is therefore assumed to be gross investment less depreciation.

$$\Delta k = I - \delta k, \tag{4.14}$$

Where Δk is the change in capital stock between one year and the next, 'I' is investment and δk is depreciation. The change over time of capital stock is investment less depreciation. In Figure 4.7, there is a single capital stock k^*, at which the amount of investment is equal to depreciation. When the economy is in such a state, the capital stock will neither increase nor decrease, as the two components depreciation and investment just balance each other. So at the point k^*, $\Delta k = 0$ and so capital stock as well as output $f(k)$ are steady over time. This is known as the *steady state*, it represents the long-run growth equilibrium. When the economy is in a steady state, the per capita income and capital are constant, denoted by y^* and k^* respectively.

Depreciation is the decline in the value of a capital asset due to wear and tear or obsolescence, for which replacement investment is required.

Steady state is the long-run equilibrium of the economy when investment is exactly equal to depreciation.

[20] *The Economist*, 2–8 October 2010, 9: 58–60.
[21] Yasheng Huang, 'China Could Learn from India's Slow and Quiet Rise', *Financial Times*, (24 January 2006): https://www.ft.com/content/e4462190-8c42-11da-9efb-0000779e2340

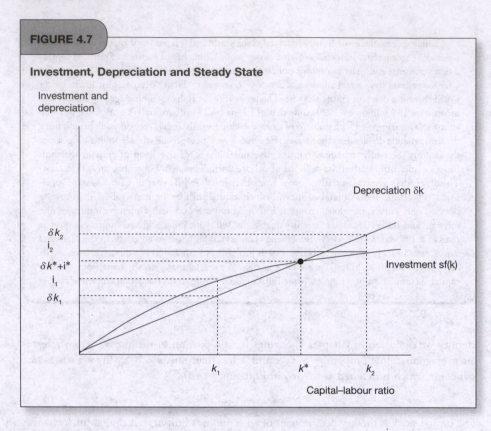

FIGURE 4.7

Investment, Depreciation and Steady State

The steady state is the point where depreciation (that replaces worn out equipment and machinery) and new investment just equal savings. If the economy is below the steady state, say at k_1 and in that situation, investment exceeds depreciation. With time the capital stock and output $f(k)$ continue to rise until it reaches the steady state k^*. On the other hand, if the economy is above the steady state k_2 in this situation the level of investment is less than depreciation so that capital equipment wears out more rapidly than being replaced. Capital stock falls until it reaches the steady state k^*. Once it reaches this state, there is no pressure to deviate from it.

4.6.3. A Numerical Illustration of the Steady State

Let us see how the neo-classical model developed by Solow operates using a numerical illustration. It will help us to understand how an economy approaches the steady state with the Cobb Douglas production function described above. We assume that the production function is:

$$Y = F(K^{\theta}, N^{1-\theta}), \tag{4.15}$$

If we assume that θ is half, that is, ½, then $(1 - \theta)$ is also ½ and the production function can be written as follows:

$$Y = F(K^{1/2}, N^{1/2})$$ (4.15a)

To obtain the per worker production function $f(k)$, we divide both sides by N

$$Y/N = \frac{K^{1/2}, N^{1/2}}{N}$$ (4.16)

Re-arranging and writing y for Y/N and k for K/N we get

$$y = \sqrt{k}$$ (4.17)

So Equation (4.17) states that the output per worker is the square root of the quantity of capital used per worker. For our numerical illustration let us assume that 25% of the total output is saved ($s = 0.25$), 75% of output is consumed and 25% is invested. Suppose depreciation of capital stock is to the tune of 10%, hence $\delta = 0.1$. If the stock of capital at the beginning is 2 units per worker we have $k = 2$. We can now observe how the economy moves towards the steady state over the years.

Table 4.4 shows how the economy progresses each year. Given the parameters of savings, depreciation, capital per worker, we can see how each year capital grows and how the economy moves towards the steady state. In year 2 the capital increases to 2.154.

TABLE 4.4

Numerical Illustration of How the Economy Moves Towards a Steady State

Year	$K = 2.0$	$y = \sqrt{k}$	$c = y - s$	$i = s = 0.25$	$\delta k = 0.1$	$\Delta k = 1 - \delta k$
1	2.000	1.414	1.061	0.354	0.200	0.154
2	2.154	1.467	1.101	0.367	0.215	0.152
3	2.305	1.518	1.139	0.380	0.231	0.149
4	2.454	1.567	1.175	0.392	0.245	0.146
5	2.600	1.613	1.209	0.403	0.260	0.143
6	2.743	1.656	1.242	0.414	0.274	0.140
7	2.883	1.698	1.273	0.424	0.288	0.136
8	3.019	1.738	1.303	0.434	0.302	0.132
9	3.152	1.775	1.332	0.444	0.315	0.129
10	3.281	1.811	1.358	0.453	0.328	0.125
—	—	—	—	—	—	—
	—	—	—	—	—	—
25	4.750	2.179	1.635	0.545	0.475	0.070

(continued)

Year	$K = 2.0$	$y = \sqrt{k}$	$c = y - s$	$i = s = 0.25$	$\delta k = 0.1$	$\Delta k = I - \delta k$
	—	—	—	—	—	—
	—	—	—	—	—	—
100	6.217	2.493	1.870	0.623	0.622	0.002
	—	—	—	—	—	—
	—	—	—	—	—	—
∞	6.250	2.500	1.875	0.625	0.625	0.000

Source: Table prepared by authors' computation.

With every passing year, the economy's output increases, as new capital is added. The economy approaches a steady state when the units of capital per worker becomes 6.25. The depreciation of 0.625 exactly offsets investment of 0.625, so that the output and capital stock stop growing and $\Delta k = 0$.

A simpler way of computing the steady state capital per worker can also be done. We know that

$$\Delta k = s\, f(k) - \delta k$$

which shows how k changes over time. The steady state capital per worker is by definition that value of k when it stops increasing so $\Delta k = 0$.

Hence,

$$s\, f(k^*) - \delta k^*$$

where k* is the capital per worker in the steady state. If we insert the values we have assumed for savings and depreciation that are 0.25 and 0.10 respectively, we can get k* as follows

$$k^*/\sqrt{k^*} = 0.25/0.1$$

By squaring on both sides we get k* = 6.25. The steady state capital per worker is 6.25 per worker and this result confirms the computation of the steady state in Table 4.4.

4.6.4. Growth with Exogenous Technological Change

In the analysis presented in the previous section technological change is assumed to be zero, that is, $\Delta A = 0$. This is a simplification to understand *steady state growth* behaviour. Over time, new technology causes labour and capital to increase their productivity, so now $\Delta A > 0$. If technology A_0 changes to A_1 then the production function $y_0 = f(k)$ becomes $y_1 = f_1(k)$ because technological changes happen and that drives the economy to move to a higher level of output represented by y_1. When technology changes to A_2 the production function becomes $y_2 = f_2(k)$, see Figure 4.8.

Technological change is labour augmenting, which implies that new technology increases the productivity of labour. In equilibrium both y and k grow at the rate of technical progress. We can modify Equation (4.12) to measure the rate of growth g as

$$g = \Delta y/y = \theta \times \Delta k/k + (1 - \theta)\Delta A/A \qquad (4.18)$$

Figure 4.8 shows how with technological progress, the production function and the savings curve shift upwards and the investment schedule intersects at different levels so that the economy moves from one steady state k^*_0 to a higher one k^*_1 and k^*_2.

The labour-augmenting technological progress analysis overcomes the issue of computing labour productivity. Labour productivity = output/labour input and TFP is obtained as a residual. Therefore, the increase in growth is not explained by labour and capital stock increases—see Equation (4.11), but by technological progress. It is also difficult to specify the causes of TFP increase. In contrast, capital stock increase is clearly due to increases in savings and investments.

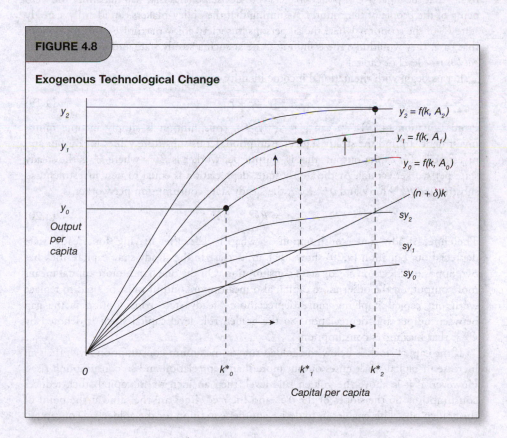

FIGURE 4.8

Exogenous Technological Change

4.6.5. The Dilemma: More Saving or More Consumption

So increase in capital stock from higher savings means there is more investment—which means more growth.

But as we have seen in Chapter 3, in the Keynesian Model, more consumption, that is, an increase in 'c', the marginal propensity to consume, increases the multiplier effect on current output. A higher 'c' means a lower 's' and lower marginal propensity to save. Basically, higher consumption gives greater current output, while higher savings gives more growth, more future output. The increase in per capita capital is the excess of savings over investment required to cover depreciation and capital for new workers. New entrants to the labour force are denoted by n = ΔN/N. Investment for depreciation = δ × k, where δ is the depreciation rate, for new workers = n × k, where n = ΔN/N.

The dilemma of whether to have more savings or more consumption is resolved by choosing the rate of saving (and consumption) that gives maximum long-run or steady state consumption.

Golden rule is the saving rate in the Solow growth model that leads to the steady state in which consumption per worker is maximized.

So far we have not introduced any policy-makers who will now enter the picture. Let us say that the objective of policy-makers is to devise policies that will maximize the well-being of the people of the country. Assuming that the policy-makers can identify a steady state $k*$ of the economy where the all persons in society enjoy maximize consumption. In that case, they would like the economy to be at such a steady state and this is called the *golden rule* level of capital.

Let us begin with the national income identity as follows:

$$y = c + i \qquad (4.19)$$

From Equation (4.19), we can get $c = y - i$, consumption is simply income minus investment. To find the steady state consumption, let us substitute values for output and investment. Per capita output, that is, output per worker is $f(k*)$ where $k*$ is the steady state per worker capital. At the steady state, depreciation is equal to new investment, so substituting $f(k*)$ for y and $\delta k*$ for i, the steady state consumption per worker is

$$c* = f(k*) - \delta k* \qquad (4.20)$$

Therefore, steady state consumption is what is left after paying for steady state depreciation. Equation (4.20) shows that an increase in the steady state capital stock has two opposing effects on steady state consumption. On the one hand, more capital means more output, on the other more capital also means more output must be used to replace worn out capital implying more depreciation. Steady state consumption is the gap between output and depreciation. So the golden rule level capital stock is denoted by $k*_{gold}$ that maximizes consumption.

If the capital stock is below the golden rule or maximum consumption level, then an increase in capital stock raises output more than depreciation and so consumption rises. However, if it is above the golden rule level, then an increase in capital stock reduces consumption. So the slopes of the $\delta k*$ and the $f(k*)$ lines are the same at the point of the golden rule. This enables us to derive another condition for the golden rule of capital.

FIGURE 4.9

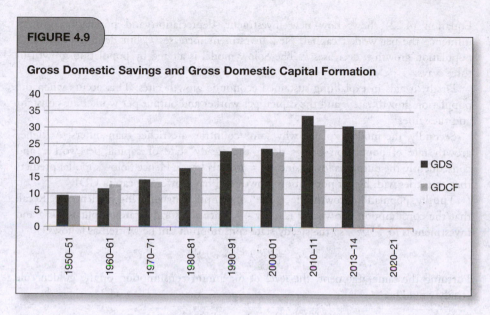

Gross Domestic Savings and Gross Domestic Capital Formation

We know that the slope of the production function is the marginal product of capital MPK. The slope of the steady state depreciation δk^* line is δ. Since the two slopes are equal at k^*_{gold} the golden rule can also be described by

$$MPK = \delta \qquad (4.21)$$

In other words Equation (4.21) shows that at the golden rule, the marginal product of capital equals the depreciation rate. Figure 4.9 shows the gross domestic savings and gross domestic capital formation in India as a percent of GDP at current market prices between 1950–51 and 2013–14.

Solow's model demonstrates that capital accumulation does not explain sustained economic growth. High saving rates cause high growth temporarily and eventually the economy arrives at the steady state in which capital and output are stable and constant. How does Solow's growth model explain the effect of population growth? That is discussed next.

4.6.6. Population Growth and the Steady State

We know that investment increases the capital stock and depreciation reduces it. However, if the labour force increases due to a rise in population, it causes a decline in the capital per worker. Let n denote the rate of change in population, k the per capita capital stock and δ the depreciation, then we can write the change in capital stock per worker as follows:

$$\Delta k = i - (\delta + n)k \qquad (4.22)$$

Equation (4.22) shows how new investment, depreciation and population growth influence the per worker capital. New investment increases k, but depreciation δ and population growth n decreases k. The Solow model is altered by population growth in three ways.

Firstly, it aids in explaining sustained economic growth rates. This occurs when the population growth rate n and the capital per worker and output per worker are constant and the same.

Secondly, the model explains why some countries are richer than others. A higher growth rate of population brings down the steady state of capital per worker and consequently the output is lower since $y^* = f(k^*)$ is lower. Hence Solow's model predicts that countries with higher population growth will have lower per capita GDP.

Thirdly, population growth affects the consumption maximizing golden rule. Recall that the consumption per worker is $c = y - i$, since the steady state output is $f(k^*)$ and investment is $(\delta + n)k^*$, so the steady state consumption can be written as follows:

$$c^* = f(k^*) + (\delta + n)k^*$$

Pursuing the same argument, the level of maximum consumption or the golden rule steady would be:

$$\text{MPK} = (\delta + n) \text{ or MPK} - \delta = n$$

The marginal product of capital less depreciation is the rate of growth of population. Solow's model illustrates that countries with higher population growth rates tend to have a lower steady state of capital stock and hence lower per capita incomes. With increasing population, it is difficult to maintain a higher level of capital per worker when n keeps ahead of δk. So larger population impoverishes the country, hence policy-makers in the developing world are advised by international finance agencies to reduce fertility. If Solow's model is correct, such policies should cause per capita incomes to rise in the long-run.

So what is Solow's model's answer to the question, 'What happens if there is growth in the labour force?' Will a $\Delta N/N$ rise lead to an increase GDP growth, $\Delta Y/Y$? If we look at the production function to get the GDP growth rate, we see that the increased labour force is multiplied by $(1 - \theta)$, resultantly Y/N per capita income comes down. Therefore, population growth, in the absence of capital growth or technical progress, always leads to lower per capita incomes. The Solow growth model demonstrates how growth in capital stock, growth in the labour force and development of new technology interact in an economy. It shows how these affect a country's total output through the TFP.

4.7. THE DIVERGENCE BETWEEN COUNTRIES ACROSS THE WORLD

The huge difference in per capita income across countries, as discussed earlier, can be attributed to differences in their rates of growth in the past. How does the neoclassical theory explain this divergence? Is the inequality of distribution of wealth of nations likely to diminish? Much of the discussion on convergence indicates that the per capita income across countries will converge over time with poorer countries growing faster to catch up, with the richer countries growing much more slowly. Solow's model supports the view of convergence such that economies that are below the steady state capital–labour ratio will have a relatively higher growth rate as they progress towards their steady state, long-run equilibrium.

The standard neoclassical growth model with exogenous technological progress and a closed economy predicts convergence. So the neoclassical model predicts absolute convergence for economies with the same rate of savings and population growth, provided the same technology is available. Therefore, different countries would converge to the same steady state if their production functions, savings rates and investments in human capital were the same and technology could be freely accessed across national boundaries. The divergence that we observe in inter-country per capita income at present would be in this case due to shocks like wars, natural calamities and colonial domination that in the past leading to the economies shifting away from their steady state long-run equilibrium. The discussion so far has focused on the hypothesis of absolute convergence.

Does empirical evidence support convergence? Research undertaken for 21 OECD (Organization for Economic Co-operation and Development) countries consisting of the most advanced countries for the period 1960–97 does support absolute convergence. In this study, economies that were at a higher initial GDP growth rate slowed down whereas those with lower rates speeded up. Similarly, a study of states within the USA included in another study for a much longer period from post 1880 also provides evidence for absolute convergence. But when a sample of 71 countries with a broader sample base including the OECD countries, middle income and poor countries was studied, the results did not support absolute convergence. In other words, these economies had different steady states, hence they were not moving to a particular capital–labour ratio. So those countries' capital output ratio and their per capita incomes were not likely to converge. In a larger and more divergent sample, we cannot assume that they exhibit similar economic infrastructure; naturally, this assumption is invalid.

Empirical studies[22] document the existence of convergence in the sense that economies tend to grow faster in per capital terms when they are further below the steady-state position. This phenomenon shows up clearly for the USA over various periods from 1840 to 1988. Over long samples, poor states tended to grow faster in per capita terms than rich states even if no variables were kept constant other than the initial per capita income or product. However, Barro et al. point out that there exists evidence of convergence for a sample of 98 countries from 1960 to 1985 only in a conditional sense.[23] We now see a weaker concept of *conditional convergence*.

Other studies have found evidence that conditional convergence does occur over many decades providing we hold variables such as initial school enrolment rates and the ratio of government consumption to GDP constant. We interpret these variables as proxies for the steady-state value of output per effective worker and the rate of technological progress. If we hold these additional variables constant, then the estimated rates of convergence are only slightly smaller than those found for the USA.

Conditional convergence happens for countries with different saving rates or population growth where the steady state incomes differ as predicted by Solow's model, but growth rates equalise.

[22] Robert J. Barro and Xavier Sala-i-Martin, 'Convergence', *Journal of Political Economy* 100, no. 2 (1992): 223–51.

[23] Barro et al., 'Convergence', 223–51.

Conditional convergence is forecast for countries with different rates of savings or population growth so that in the steady state, while their incomes differ, the rates of growth will eventually equalize. From the endogenous growth theory, Barro has shown that while economies that invest more tend to grow faster, they end up at their steady state with high per capita incomes but not high growth rates.[24] Therefore, his evidence indicates that conditional convergence takes place at a rate of 2% per year. Suppose Ghana's income level now is 5% that of the USA, in 35 years it would become 10% of the USA's GDP provided that the other variables that affect the level of income such as the savings rate between the two countries remain the same. Thus, convergence is a very slow process, taking several decades if not many more. In the next section we explore the endogenous growth theory where human capital accumulation is the engine for growth.

4.8. THE ENDOGENOUS GROWTH MODEL

Many economists have asserted that the exogenous Solow model cannot account for international differences in income, and this has stimulated research on endogenous-growth theory. While the neo-classical model forecasts the convergence of income per capita between rich and poor countries, empirical evidence does not fully support it. The alternative model of growth looks for an explanation as to why the rich get richer and the poor get poorer.

The pertinent question is why the supply of capital does not flow from rich countries to the poorer where the marginal product of capital is higher? Perhaps this is because the marginal product of capital does not fall in the rich countries despite a rising capital-labour ratio. Ultimately the new theory intends to eliminate the assumption of diminishing returns to reproducible factors of production such as capital. The neoclassical model theory postulates that technological progress drives economic growth but is silent on how technological progress occurs and so labour-augmenting progress is exogenous like 'manna from heaven'. However, the endogenous growth theories propose that labour-augmenting technical progress is endogenous and depends on the capital–labour ratio.

The Solow model predicts that countries that start with capital per worker much below the balanced growth path (i.e., the initially poor) grow faster along the transition path than do countries that are initially richer. Hence the model predicts convergence among countries with similar saving rates, depreciation rates and population growth rates. With the unconditional convergence hypothesis, we obtain no evidence for convergence for the entire set of countries or for the non-OECD countries. Is it in line with the predictions of the Solow Model?

The Solow model predicts that countries that are further away from their balanced growth path grow faster than countries that are closer to their balanced growth path (always assuming that the rate of technological progress is the same across countries). The predictions of the Solow model rely on transition dynamics that is, countries are not in

---

[24] Barro et al., 'Convergence', 223–51.

the balanced growth path and hence can grow at rates different from g; the rate of technological progress.

It is important to note that the major problem with the Solow Model is that it is not able to explain why countries have different balanced growth paths. And the model does not explain the reasons behind technological progress, the source of growth in the model.

Solow's model therefore, clearly explains the role of physical capital accumulation and emphasizes the importance of technological progress as the ultimate source of sustained economic growth. However, dissemination of technical knowledge linked through human capital is absent in the Solow model. Eminent economists like Romer,[25] Lucas,[26] Rebelo,[27] Barro and Salai Martin[28] and Mankiw[29] have embedded human capital into production function and evolved the endogenous growth model.

To construct economic models, the variables have to be observed over different periods. Time can be split into periods. In static analysis, the passage of time is ignored. Dynamic analysis helps to explain the actual process of adjustment. In this section, we introduce dynamic analysis t.[30]

The endogenous growth model can be derived from Solow's version of the exogenous model. The labour augmenting technology in Solow's model can be written as:

$$Y = F(K, N) = K^{\alpha}(AN)^{(1-\alpha)} \tag{4.23}$$

A is the labour augmenting technology. We assume that technology grows at a constant rate g. So,

$$dA/dt = Ag \tag{4.24}$$

And physical capital accumulation grows at a rate of

$$dK/dt = sY - \delta K \tag{4.25}$$

We can re-write Equation (4.23) in terms of output per worker that is

$$Y = k^{\alpha} A^{(1-\alpha)} \tag{4.26}$$

If we take the log on both sides and differentiate we have

$$[dy/dt]/y = \alpha \ [(dk/dt/k)] + (1-\alpha) \ [(dA/dt/A)] \tag{4.27}$$

If we define capital per worker to the technology ratio as $k' = K/N = k/A$, which is the capital technology ratio. Again let us re-write Equation (4.23) in terms of k' we get

$$Y' = (k')^{\alpha} \tag{4.28}$$

[25] Romer, 'Increasing Returns and Long Run Growth', 1986.

[26] Lucas, 'On the Mechanics of Economic Development'.

[27] Sergio Rebelo, 'Long-run Policy Analysis and Long-run Growth', *Journal of Political Economy* 99, no. 3 (1991): 500–21.

[28] Robert J. Barro and Xavier I. Sala-i-Martin, *Economic Growth Theory* (Cambridge, US: MIT Press, 1995).

[29] N. Gregory Mankiw, Edmund S. Phelps and Paul M. Romer, 'The Growth of Nations', *Brookings Papers on Economic Activity* 26, no. 1 (1995): 275–326.

[30] The problem with this kind of analysis is that the time is not real time as in calendar time but rather a model-based time. To gain knowledge about real world adjustment speeds, statistical estimations which are a non-trivial and difficult exercise are needed.

where $y' = Y/AN = y/A$ which represents the output technology ratio. Then the capital accumulation equation gives us:

$$dk'/dt = sy' - (n + g + \delta)k' \qquad (4.29)$$

In the steady state, $dk'/dt = 0$, so solving for y^* the steady state we get

$$y^*(t) = A(t).[s/(n + g + \delta)]^{\alpha/(1 - \alpha)} \qquad (4.30)$$

In the endogenous growth model developed by Lucas and Romer, a Cobb Douglas production function with constant returns to scale is used and we are now already familiar with it, but we now have a new variable H in

$$Y = K^\alpha - (AH)^{1 - \alpha} \qquad (4.31)$$

Here H is skilled labour. Individuals spend time acquiring new skills and so human capital is accumulated. Let 'u' represent the fraction of time learning new skills and N the total amount of unskilled labour. So if we assume that N spends time 'u' to learn new skills then

$$H = e^{\theta u} N \qquad (4.32)$$

If θ is a positive constant and $u = 0$, then from Equation (4.32), $H = N$ or in other words all the labour force is unskilled. Notice that Equation (4.31) is similar to Equation (4.23). We can re-write Equation (4.31) in terms of output per unskilled labour such that

$$y = k^\alpha (Ah)^{(1 - \alpha)} \qquad (4.33)$$

where $h = e^{\theta u}$ since $H/N = e^{\theta u}$

This reconciles Solow's model with human capital and the endogenous model developed by Lucas and Romer. Dividing Equation (4.33) by Ah, in the steady state, output per worker will grow at

$$y^*(t) = hA(t).[s/(n + g + \delta)]^{\alpha/(1 - \alpha)} \qquad (4.34)$$

Equation (4.34) summarizes the extended Solow model to explain why some countries are rich and others are poor. Rich countries continue to be rich as they have high investments in physical capital and they spend a substantial time accumulating skills and increasing their human capital. They have low population growth rates and have high levels of technology.

4.8.1. Human Capital Accumulation

Human capital accumulation led growth, which is known as the endogenous growth model as elaborated by Romer, represents an extension of Solow's neoclassical growth model incorporating externalities related to the accumulation of knowledge or ideas. Romer[31] and Lucas questioned the neoclassical model by emphasizing the role of

---

[31] P. M. Romer, 'What Determines the Rate of Growth and Technological Change?' (working paper series no. 279, Country Economics Department, The World Bank, Washington DC, September 1989).

human capital stock, scientific research and development activities of a country. Romer has identified three factors that make the distinction between physical capital and human capital (measured as knowledge accumulation or the stock of ideas). These factors are: first the expansion of new knowledge, which has a positive external effect on the production possibilities of a firm, because knowledge can never be perfectly patented and is non-trivial in nature. Second, the creation of new knowledge which exhibits diminishing returns. And third, new knowledge being more profitable when it leads to more efficient production.

The Lucas[32] model of endogenous growth is similar to the Romer model, except that he assumes human capital to evolve according to the time spent on accumulating skills. His focus is on policy, which he proposes will have a permanent increase in time that agents spend in obtaining skills like compulsory schooling till class 10 leads to an increase in the labour productivity that is output per worker. The production of human capital as a country wide policy is akin to a social activity when person's set aside time to improve their skills. In contrast, Romer emphasizes on advances in knowledge through research in science and technology as 'ideas'.

The other major contributor to the human capital led growth theory Mankiw defines knowledge as the sum total of technological and scientific discoveries and human capital is a stock of knowledge.[33] Going back to Lucas' model, we see that the 'H' term is externality effect of human capital which has a positive impact due to the government's role in investing in educational infrastructure. Government expenditure on building social infrastructure comprising education, health and nutrition within a legal framework of rules and regulations is the primary determinant of how much citizens are willing to invest in human capital as well as physical capital, both of which are associated with long-term economic growth.

4.8.2. Human Capital Accumulation: The Indian Scenario

Is the endogenous growth model valid for India? The challenges faced by policy-makers in India are enormous, the major impediments being dated data and estimation lags between policy implementation and impact. Does human capital accumulation drive growth in India? Yes, says Haldar.[34] He has explored the scope of human capital accumulation and export-led growth for 53 years in India to show that investment in human capitals such as education, health and nutrition as a percentage of GNP is crucial and positively and significantly affect per capita GNP. His findings support the endogenous growth model for India. He declares that only 4.3% of GNP was spent on education, although the target was 6% since 1968. Indian government has spent just 11% of GNP on education in comparison to 20% in some countries that included both poor

---

[32] Lucas, 'On the Mechanics of Economic Development'.
[33] Mankiw et al., 'The Growth of Nations', 275–326.
[34] S. K. Haldar, 'Economic Growth in India Revisited: An Application of Cointegration and Error Correction Mechanism', *South Asia Economic Journal* 10, no. 1 (2009): 105–26.

and rich ones (UNDP 2003).[35] Therefore, if India could spend 20% of total expenditure on education, the aggregate growth rate would increase substantially.

Again Haldar and Mallick[36] suggest that physical capital investment has neither long-run nor short-run effects, but human capital investments have significant long-run effects on per capita GNP. The primary gross enrolment rate and openness have major positive impacts on GNP growth per capita. They prove that GNP growth is positively and significantly influenced by the enrolment up to class eight, thus concluding that the opening up of the Indian economy in 1991 has significantly increased economic growth.

Good health and nutrition enhance workers' productivity because healthier people live longer have stronger incentives to invest in developing their skills, which increases workforce productivity by reducing incapacity, debility and loss of man days due to sick leave. Haldar's[37] findings are supported by Schultz's[38] study where the latter identifies scholastic performance to be significant. Zon and Muysken[39] argue that economic growth is driven by knowledge accumulation as in the traditional Lucas model[40] and as such is based on labour services supplied by healthy people. Obviously, investments in health and education work differently for different countries.

Despite the strong evidence of benefits from investments in education, health and nutrition the government of India's policies expenditures on human development are inconsistent and severely inadequate. While various policies and programmes have been initiated, the progress of human capital in India has remained slow. In 1968, the Government of India proposed to invest 6% of GNP in education until 1986. However, in 2005–06, it was merely 3.8% which is better than 0.6% in 1951–52. So there has been some progress but still it is well below the average of many developing countries. As governments realize the importance of economic growth and how it improves the quality of life of its citizens, they will become pro-active in their policies.

4.9. CONCLUSION

Economic growth is at the centre of many discussions of policy-makers, media and the public and has captured the attention of researchers since the late 18th century. The per capita GDP is a widely accepted measure of economic growth, as it avoids the issue of comparison between countries of different sizes and resource endowments. Investing

---

[35] UNDP 2003.

[36] S. K. Haldar and Girijasankar Mallik, 'Does Human Capital Cause Economic Growth? A Case Study of India', *International Journal of Economic Sciences and Applied Research* 3, no. 1 (2010): 7–25.

[37] Haldar, 'Economic Growth in India Revisited'.

[38] T. P. Schultz, 'Assessing the Productive Benefits of Nutrition and Health: An Integrated Human Capital Approach', *Journal of Econometrics* 77, no. 1 (1997): 141–58.

[39] Adriaan Van Zon and Joan Muysken, 'Health as Determinant of Economic Growth', *Health and Economic Growth: Findings and Policy Implications* (2005): 41, Availabe at *https://www.researchgate.net/publication/4869357_Health_as_a_Principal_Determinant_of_Economic_Growth* Accessed on 27 October 2017.

[40] Lucas, 'On the Mechanics of Economic Development'.

more on capital goods through higher savings and hence raising the productive potential of the economy is the prescription given by the neo-classical economists.

Solow, whose growth theory led economic thought for several decades of the second half of the 20th century, proposed the constant returns to scale Cobb Douglas production function. In his model, the savings rate, population and the state of technological progress are the drivers of economic output and growth. The capital stock of a country grows with savings and investments which are assumed to be identical as in a closed economy. All economies reach a point when their depreciation is exactly equal to new investments and this is the *steady state*. If policy-makers can identify a steady state for the economy where all persons enjoy maximized consumption, then that would be the economy at the *golden rule* level of capital.

According to Solow, although countries exhibit diversities in their rates of growth, eventually all of them converge towards their steady state. But empirical evidence does not support convergence, rather countries with different saving rates or population growth where the steady state incomes differ converge in their growth rates. The model is exogenous as all the factors including capital accumulation, population growth and technological progress are determined outside the system.

Despite the robustness of the Solow model, the exogeneity provides no leverage to policy-makers. In the 1990s, Lucas, Romer and Mankiw developed the endogenous growth model. They argued that human capital accumulation and the inclusion of technological progress in the model can explain the path of economic growth. Presently, many economists are focusing on alternative drivers of growth like exports, health, nutrition and education. In the next chapter, we explore how the market for money and the bond markets operate in the macro economy.

SUMMARY

- Growth is the expansion of an economy's productive potential over the long-run; it is measured by the rate of change of an economy's GDP.
- The Solow growth model explains how savings, population growth and technological progress are the drivers of economic output and growth. In the long-run, the GDP level depends positively on the savings rate and negatively on the rate of population growth.
- While savings and investment promote the accumulation of capital, increases in the population raise the labour force. Solow's model or the exogenous model assumes a closed economy hence there is no trade or government and therefore, at equilibrium, savings and investment are equal.
- Solow's model assumes the Cobb Douglas Production function with constant returns to scale.
- The rate of growth of output is equal to the rate of change in technology called TFP plus the rate of growth of each of the factor inputs multiplied by their respective weights.

- All changes are not due to changes in factor inputs but due to change in technical progress, Solow Residual A measures the change in TFP or technical progress.
- Growth accounting explains a country's growth by (a) growth in labour force, (b) growth in capital accumulation and (c) growth in technological progress. Output grows as the inputs are increased and by increases in productivity due to better technology and a larger labour force.
- The capital–labour ratio is the amount of capital per unit of labour. Per capita income growth depends on the change in the capital–labour ratio and on technical progress.
- The capital stock is the key determinant of an economy's output. Investment and depreciation are the two major factors that influence the capital stock. Depreciation is required to replace wear and tear of older equipment.
- When investment is exactly equal to depreciation, the economy reaches the steady state. Then capital stock as well as output become steady over time, and this represents the long-run growth equilibrium.
- If more savings means more investment, it leads to lower consumption. If policy-makers identify a steady state where everyone enjoys maximized consumption, then that economy is at the *golden rule* level of capital.
- Different countries have huge differences in per capita incomes. This can be attributed to differences in their past growth rates. But the neoclassical theory proposes that different countries would converge to the same steady state if the production function, the savings rate and investments in human capital were the same and technology moved freely across countries.
- Solow's exogenous model gives little leeway to policy-makers as all the factors are outside the model (that is exogenous), thus the scope for the government to influence the growth process is absent. Economists in the 1990s like Lucas and Romer proposed the endogenous model and the role of human capital accumulation.
- The new knowledge that has evolved from research and technology and improvements in labour productivity through the acquisition of skills, have been shown to be the drivers of growth and not capital accumulation alone.
- The human capital accumulation led growth, represents an extension of the Solow model, incorporating externalities related to the accumulation of knowledge or ideas.
- The current growth theory is focused on human capital accumulation and investments in social infrastructure.
- From the policy-makers' view, human capital formation can be increased by building more schools and colleges and pursuing government policies that encourage enrolments in higher education.
- The production of human capital is a country wide policy similar to a social activity where people set aside time to improve their skills.

CASE STUDY[41]

The State of Higher Education in India

The World Bank's India Country Summary of Higher Education, April 2007 states that India possesses a well-developed higher education system in all aspects of human, creative and intellectual endeavours. In its size and diversity, it has the third largest higher education system in the world, next only to China and the United States. However, before Independence, access to higher education was very limited. Although several universities and technology institutes were established, they remained inadequate. Realizing the need to raise both the enrolment rates and access to higher education, the government proposed to establish 30 new central universities, 8 new IITs, 20 new IIITs and 7 new IIMs and several high grade medical institutes during the 10th Plan 2002–07. Subsequently the gross enrolment rate[42] went up from 6% to 10% and the 11th Plan proposes to raise it 15%. Though the enrolment rate in higher education is increasing steadily, it remains low compared to many developing countries of Asia and Latin America.

TABLE CS 4.1

Enrolment Rate in Higher Education (Region Wise), 2001–02

Groups of Countries	*GER (in %)*
Countries in Transition	36.5
Developed Countries	54.6
Developing Countries	11.3
World	23.2
India (tentative)	About 10%

The Gross Enrolment Rate (GER) for higher education has risen from 0.7% in 1950–51, 1.4% in 1960–61 and 8% in early 2000, yet it is still very low compared to the world average of 23.2% (Table CS 4.1). Even the existing enrolment rate (ER) of 60% indicates that 40% of students who complete their high school do not enter tertiary education. If we increase the enrolment rate for higher education by 5% in every plan period, it would take 25 years more to come close to advanced countries' levels of enrolments.

The distribution of GER in terms of educational degrees is skewed towards undergraduate in humanities then on science or commerce. Of the total GER, 32% was in the UG

---

[41] The text for Case Study 4.1 was adopted from the following sources:

[1] http://www.business-standard.com/article/opinion/arvind-singhal-the-four-a-s-of-education-110031100007_1.html Accessed on 31 October 2017.

[2] http://siteresources.worldbank.org/EDUCATION/Resources/278200-1121703274255/1439264-1193249163062/India_CountrySummary.pdf

[42] The GER measures the access level by taking the ratio of persons in all age groups enrolled in various programmes to total population in age group of 18–23.

stream of humanities and 12% each in the science and commerce streams. Merely 2% of GER was in medicine, dentistry and related areas in 2004–05. Thus, it is quite clear that enrolments in postgraduate studies and research in science and technology need to be augmented with emphasis on medicine/pharmacology (Table CS 4.2).

TABLE CS 4.2

Enrolment by Stages in 2004–05

	Educational Degree Stage	Total Gross Enrolment	% of Total GER
1.	PhD/DSc/DPhil	55,352	0.47
2.	MA	469,291	3.98
3.	MSc	198,719	1.69
4.	MCom	122,257	1.04
5.	BA/BA Hons	3,772,216	32.03
6.	BSc/BSc Hons	1,490,785	12.66
7.	BCom/BCom Hons	1,465,028	12.44
8.	BE/BSc Engg/BArch	696,609	5.91
9.	Medicine/Dentistry/Pharmacy/Nursing/ Alternate Medicine	256,748	2.18
10.	BEd/BT	155,192	1.32
11.	Others*	3,095,099	26.28
12.	Total in Higher Education	11,777,296	0.47

Source: Selected Educational Statistics 2004–05, MHRD 2007.
* Others include data of Open & Distance Learning Institutions.

Government expenditure on technical education has actually declined as a percentage of GDP from 0.51 in 1990–92 to 0.42 of GNP in 2003–04. For higher education, public expenditure has actually declined from 0.46% of GNP to 0.37% (Table CS 4.3).

Arvind Singhal writes, 'It is very heartening to see the education sector getting its due attention'. The increase of 24% in the budgetary outlay for Ministry of Human Resource Development (MHRD) in 2011 reflects the government's greater emphasis on investments in education, taking the budget to about ₹52,000 crore (US$11 billion), to cater to the needs of the 25 million newly borns per year through primary to secondary education. Of course, the overall spending on education is much more on account of private spending because the government has—for decades—neglected this vital social sector. Annual spending by Indians going for studies abroad is now estimated to be in the region of ₹15,000–20,000 crore. Annual spending on private tuitions and coaching is estimated to be in the range of ₹35,000–40,000 crore.

TABLE CS 4.3

Public Expenditure on Higher and Technical Education as % of GDP

	Higher Education: Relative Priorities			
	Government Expenditure on Higher Education as		*Government Expenditure on Technical Education as*	
	% of GNP	*% of Total Government Revenue Expenditure*	*% of GNP*	*% of Total Government Revenue Expenditure*
1990–91	0.46	1.58	0.15	0.51
1991–92	0.42	1.43	0.14	0.48
1992–93	0.41	1.42	0.14	0.48
1993–94	0.40	1.42	0.13	1.47
1994–95	0.39	1.40	0.13	0.47
1995–96	0.37	1.35	0.12	0.45
1996–97	0.35	1.30	0.12	0.44
1997–98	0.35	1.31	0.12	0.44
1998–99	0.43	1.39	0.13	0.47
1999–2000	0.47	1.61	0.14	0.48
2000–01	0.49	1.61	1.13	0.44
2001–02	0.39	1.31	0.12	0.41
2002–03RE	0.40	1.28	0.13	0.41
2003–04BE	0.37	1.23	0.13	0.42

Source: Based on Analysis of Budget Expenditure on Education (Various Years).

Singhal points out that the education sector is itself a potential driver of growth for the Indian economy (and not only because a more educated population will make all the sectors of the economy more efficient and productive). The potential has to be seen in the context of the aging population in the major developed countries and India's potential to deliver, beyond IT and BPO and on-site/off-shore 'outsourced' services.

Referring to a journal report of Jaipur emerging as a dentistry centre, Singhal highlights the need to attract foreign visitors and create new business and employment opportunities in Jaipur in particular and in Rajasthan in general, from the tourism and medical viewpoints. In his vision of the need to exploit the potential for medical tourism he sees a proactive role by the Medical Council of India in promoting the same.

Moreover, with an aging population internationally, India can meet the increased global demand for healthcare-givers including doctors, nurses and technicians. It is very likely that governments overseas will have no option but to liberalize visa regimes to allow for a more liberal entry of such workers even if they do not get permanent residency in those countries. After reading the text given in the case study, answer the following questions:

1. Did the government of India give adequate attention to higher education after Independence? Has the trend changed? If not, how is the mismatch between the demand for educational infrastructure and its supply met in India?
2. What is the argument for improving the quality of education and access to it relevant for economic growth in India?
3. Is there sufficient emphasis on enrolments in research and development? What is the endogenous growth theory of human capital accumulation?
4. What is the potential for medical tourism in India? Can the country evolve as a major health care provider internationally?

KEYWORDS

Economic growth	Total factor productivity
Capital stock	Capital accumulation
Per capita GDP	Human capital
Labour productivity	Capital deepening
Production function	Depreciation
Constant returns to scale	Steady state
Capital–labour ratio	Golden rule
Marginal productivity	Conditional convergence
Technological progress	

CONCEPT CHECK

State if the following statements are true or false:

1. Using per capita GDP as a measure of growth eliminates the effect of size of different countries, when comparing the growth of countries.
2. The production function is a concise statement of the relationship between total inputs and total outputs given the state of technology.
3. The Solow growth model assumes that the Cobb Douglas production function is an increasing returns to scale.
4. The capital–labour ratio is the number of persons or labour using one unit of capital or one machine.
5. When the growth rate of two countries changes in the long-run so that they are the same, it is called absolute convergence.

6. We have to account for depreciation of capital as it is major factor that influences labour productivity.
7. When consumption per worker is maximized such that the saving rate leads the economy to its steady state, it is known as the Golden Rule.
8. Whereas the neoclassical growth theory emphasized the role of savings and investment, the current school of thought on growth theory identifies human capital formation as a key driving force of growth.

DISCUSSION QUESTIONS

1. What are the two issues in measuring the growth of output? How are the two issues resolved?
2. Suppose a country is characterized by the production function of the form:

$$Y = AK^{0.4} N^{0.6}$$

   We assume that the average annual growth rate of capital K is 1% and that of labour N is 2%.
   i. If the growth in total output is 3%, then what is the average growth rate in TFP?
   ii. Suppose the measure of the growth rate of capital is incorrect. So when the growth rate of N increases to 3%; the growth rate of capital really increases to 3% (instead of being constant at 1%). If the average growth rate of output was 5% a year, what should the growth rate of TFP have been?
3. Suppose in an economy the savings rate = 20% and population growth = 0, depreciation = 10% and the production function is given as $Y = K^{\frac{1}{2}} N^{\frac{1}{2}}$. If there is no technical progress then:
   i. What is the steady state capital stock and output?
   ii. What is the golden rate of saving?
4. Can the endogenous growth theory explain international differences in growth rates? If so how?
5. What is the difference between absolute convergence and conditional convergence?

CHAPTER

Introduction to
the Financial Sector:
Bonds and Interest Rates

LEARNING OBJECTIVES

Upon completion of this chapter, the reader will be able to:

- Distinguish between the interest rate, the rate of return and the yield to maturity of a bond.
- Understand how the bond market operates and how bond prices and interest rates are determined in the market.
- Explain the term 'structure of interest rates' in the money market.
- Comprehend the meaning of the yield curve and its function.
- Understand how the interest rate is arrived at through the supply of and demand for bonds in the market for money.

5.1. INTRODUCTION: THE FINANCIAL SECTOR

The interest rate is the opportunity cost of holding money, or the reward for foregoing current consumption.

In this chapter, we introduce the financial sector. In the basic Keynesian model of Chapter 3, there is no interaction between the financial and the real sides of the economy. In this and subsequent chapters, the link between the two sectors, driven by changes in the *interest rate* are exposed, reflecting its predominant position.

5.1.1. The Interest Rate

In this book, as in all macroeconomics textbooks, we deal with one aggregate interest rate for the economy. In fact, this is quite acceptable, as the various interest rates move together. Yet, we need to distinguish between the mutually related concepts of:

i. The interest rate
ii. The rate of return and
iii. The *yield to maturity* of a *bond*

> The yield to maturity is the rate of return anticipated on a bond if it is held until the maturity date.

The mechanism of equilibrium in the financial markets is modelled by considering either the bond market or the market for money. The aggregate interest rate can be obtained from either of these markets. Usually, the bond market is omitted, since equilibrium in the market for money implies equilibrium in the bond market as well. This is what will be done in the models that follow. However, in this chapter, we consider the *bond market* specifically, since we need to explain the impact of the bond markets on the financial sector as a whole, despite that fact that developments in the market for money do give a picture, a mirror image, of that in the bond market.

> Government securities are all fixed interest bearing debt instruments issued by the government including Treasury bills and Gilt.

The plan of this chapter is as follows. Firstly the concepts of interest rate, rate of return and yield to maturity are defined with appropriate examples. Next, the focus is on the bond market, namely the supply and the demand for bonds, which primarily consists of *government securities*/debt and show that the aggregate interest rate to be used in macroeconomic models can be derived from the bond market. The final section explains the structure of interest rates and the yield curve, which serve as indicators or signals for the expected levels of economic activity.

> Bond is a long-term debt instrument issued by the government to finance its deficit.

5.2. THE BOND MARKET: BOND PRICES AND INTEREST RATES

Let us now deal with the interest rate as derived from the bond market. The treatment of the market for money, from which we will derive the aggregate interest rate is discussed in a later chapter. We will now see how the concepts of yield, interest rate and rates of return are related and that they need not always be equal to each other.

5.2.1. Yield and Interest

The yield to maturity is the interest rate that equates the present value (PV) of all future payments with the face value of the bond as illustrated in the following numerical example:

A bank loan of ₹100 (this is the debt instrument) is to be paid back after one year with the stated market interest rate as 10%.

So, the payment due after one year is = 110.

That is, $PV = 100 = 110/(1 + i)$

Solving, i = 10%, is the yield of the debt instrument.

So, here, the yield = stated market interest rate.

Extending this example: consider a coupon bond giving a fixed coupon payment of 10% of the face value of 1,000 each year (equal to 100) and the face value at maturity. Here the stated interest rate is the coupon rate of 10% and the calculated yield will also equal this. So, yield = interest rate.

Now suppose, if the bond in the aforementioned example is bought in the secondary market at a price of 1,100. Then the yield for the buyer from holding the bond will be different from the interest rate. Now, the price of the bond = 1,100, which is equal to the present value PV, but greater than the face value. The PV calculations will give a yield of 8.5%, which is lower than the stated interest (coupon) rate.

So, as the price of the bond goes up, the yield goes down and vice versa. If the current price is 900, the yield is calculated as 11.75%.

This inverse relationship explains the impact of monetary policy: with an expansionary monetary policy, bonds are purchased by the central bank, driving up bond prices and lowering actual market interest rates as opposed to what we said earlier.

5.2.2. Rate of Return and Yield to Maturity

The actual rate of return obtained by holding a bond can differ from the yield to maturity, if the final price received is not equal to the face value. If the final price received is greater than the face value, an element of capital gain also enters the picture. Then,

The rate of return from holding the bond = current yield + capital gain,

where the capital gain = $(P_{t+1} - P_t)/P_t$,

with P_{t+1} being the selling price and P_t the buying price.

5.2.3. Interest Rate Risk and Period to Maturity

Interest rate risk is the risk by which an investment's value will change, due to a change in the absolute level of interest rates.

The discussion on capital gains and losses naturally extends its implications for *interest rate risk*. Which bonds have a greater interest rate risk, longer-term or short-term bonds?

To understand this, consider a risk in actual interest rates, which could be due to central bank policies. This would mean that the denominator in the present value calculations rises (note: the stated coupon rate is affecting the numerator only by deciding the coupon payments). When the denominator in the PV calculations rises, the PV, which is the current market price, falls more for longer term bonds, simply because there are more terms, with more numbers of years to maturity in the case of the longer-term bonds.

Thus, if you sell the bond now, after the interest rate rises, you suffer a greater loss with a longer-term bond, one of longer maturity. Hence, the interest rate risk is clearly higher for longer-term bonds. For an illustration, see Table 5.1.

In Table 5.1, the face value of the bond is 1,000 and the coupon rate = 10%. The market interest rate rises to 20%, as a result of the central bank policy.

TABLE 5.1

Capital Gain with Short- and Long-term Bonds

Holding Time	Price Next Year	Capital Gain	Rate of Return (in %)
1 year	1,000	0	10
5 years	741	−25.9	−15.9
30 years	503	−49.7	−39.7

Source: Authors.

The first column in the table shows maturity in years. The second shows the present value (PV) next year, calculated back from the maturity date, using 20% for 'i' in the expressions $(1 + i)^n$ in the denominator. The rate of return = the yield of 10% − capital loss in the second column. The rate of return thus calculated in the third column is least for the bond with a maturity of 30 years, because this bond will experience the largest capital loss when sold next year.

5.3. THE BOND MARKET: SUPPLY AND DEMAND

Now we proceed to see how the market interest rate can be determined from the market for bonds, first from a conventional demand–supply diagram and then from a representation where the interest rate, rather than the price, figures on the vertical axis. In fact, for the rest of the book, we will not make any distinction between the interest rate and the yield or the rate of return. We will also be dealing with just one aggregate interest rate that equilibrates the financial markets.

5.3.1. Demand for Bonds

We know from the theory of asset demand that the demand for an asset rises with its return and with an increase in total wealth. A rise in the expected return also increases demand for the asset, while a rise in the returns to other assets reduces the demand for this asset.

Thus, for a bond, a rise in the interest rate (representing the return on the bond), as well as a rise in wealth and liquidity, increases bond demand. Demand for the bond also rises if it becomes less risky compared to other assets. The expected return, which is the associated probability multiplied by the return then also rises relative to other assets. In the demand–supply diagram for bonds, Figure 5.1, the demand curve slopes down.

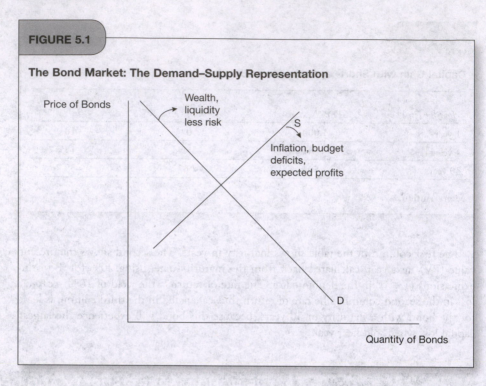

FIGURE 5.1

The Bond Market: The Demand–Supply Representation

An increase in wealth (W) and liquidity, less riskiness in holding the bond, or an increase in expected returns, shift the demand curve right. Given an upward sloping supply curve, such a shift in demand to the right raises the price—which means that the interest rate falls, given the inverse relation between the two. With a greater demand for bonds, lower interest induces the borrowers to borrow.

5.3.2. The Bond Market: The Supply Side

The supply curve for bonds slopes up in the demand–supply diagram, the supply of bonds increasing with the price (this means that the supply increases as the interest falls, given the negative relation between price and interest).

All 'other' factors shift the supply curve as follows:

The real interest rate is the nominal rate of interest minus the inflation rate.

- A rise in expected inflation reduces the *real interest rate* (= nominal interest rate – expected inflation) and increases the demand for investment funds, increasing the supply of bonds issued for borrowing funds.
- Government budget deficits financed by bonds increases the supply of bonds.
- An expected profit also leads to an increased supply of bonds by firms.

In Figure 5.1, the demand curve slopes down as usual, with a fall in price leading to increases in demand (which means that the demand increases with an increase in the interest rate, given the negative relation between the interest rate and the price).

All the following 'other' factors shift the demand curve as follows:

The effects of various shocks on the interest rate can be obtained from Figure 5.1 by looking at the shifts of the supply and the demand curves.

- Consider, for instance, a fall in the savings rate. This leads to reductions in wealth, which reduces the demand for bonds, shifting the demand curve left, thereby reducing the price, which means that the interest rate rises.
- An increase in wealth increases the demand for bonds, shifting the demand curve to the right, which tends to raise the price and lower the interest rate. However, typically, an increase in wealth is also seen to induce investment activity by firms, as investment opportunities present themselves. This leads to a rightward shift of the supply curve, which tends to reduce price and increase the interest rate. Empirically, an increase in wealth has been found to lead to an increase in the interest rate.
- A rise in expected inflation shifts the supply curve right, as discussed here, since the real interest rate falls and more investment funds are sought by issuing bonds. However, demand is also affected. Since the return on bonds falls in real terms, the demand curve also shifts, to the left. The effect on the price and interest rates are clear: the price falls, which translates as a rise in the interest rate.

| **BOX 5.1** | **Profile of India's Bond Market**[1] |

A well functioning liquid and resilient finance market help monetary policy transmission as well as in allocation and absorption of risks entailed in financing India's growth.

—Reserve Bank of India (RBI)[2]

Bonds are interest bearing debt certificates which are traded in the bond market. In India bonds are issued by large private organizations and public sector units. The single largest issuer of bonds in India is the government. In most countries in Asia, government securities dominate the market, while corporate sector bonds are relatively smaller except in South Korea where they constitute more than 70% of the debt market. In India, the corporate sector is a minority compared to government debt. In Malaysia, South Korea and Singapore, corporate debts play a significant role (see Figure 5.2).

---

[1] C. P. Chandrasekhar and Jayati Ghosh, *India's Elusive Bond Market*, http://www.thehindubusinessline.com/opinion/columns/indias-bond-market-is-in-crisis/article9262562.ece

[2] Reserve Bank of India. Availabe at https://www.rbi.org.in/scripts/FS_Notification.aspx?fn=6

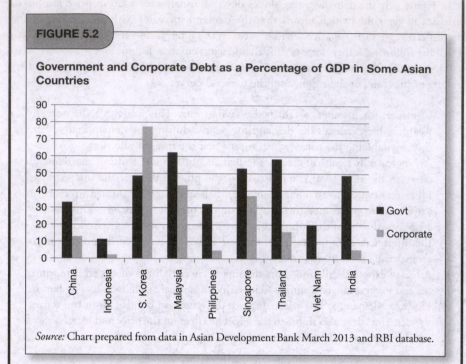

FIGURE 5.2

Government and Corporate Debt as a Percentage of GDP in Some Asian Countries

Source: Chart prepared from data in Asian Development Bank March 2013 and RBI database.

The bond market in India has huge opportunities for growth and depth but presently it is still quite shallow. A number of reforms to stimulate the market and provide incentives for the private sector to access the money market have been launched. These include:

1. To increase the appetite and liquidity for corporate bonds they have been permitted to register for repos with brokers engaged in market-making to enable price discovery.
2. Foreign Portfolio Investors (FPIs) have been granted direct access both to corporate bonds and the negotiated dealing platform for government securities, so that dis-intermediation can reduce costs and boost yields for FPIs.
3. To eliminate settlement risks, the Delivery versus Payment (DvP) mechanism has been introduced.
4. To enhance market sophistication, zero coupon bonds, inflation indexed bonds and capital indexed bonds have been introduced.
5. To promote the secondary bond market, the RBI initiated more primary dealers to enter the market.

Despite these and other reforms, the penetration of the corporate bond market is marginal. While the ratio of bank deposits to GDP in 2014 stood at 64%, the corporate bonds to GDP ratio was merely 14%. The following year it rose to 17% while in countries like Malaysia and South Korea it was 45 and 70% respectively. This indicates the tremendous growth potential the Indian bond market has and the strategic role it can play in financing the massive infrastructure needs of the country.

5.4. THE BOND MARKET: THE INTEREST–QUANTITY DIAGRAM

It is more interesting to observe a diagram with the interest rate on the vertical axis, as we are more concerned about the interest rate and not the price of bonds. But the problem is that the demand curve for bonds would slope uncharacteristically up in such a diagram. However, this can be handled by having the demand for and the supply of loans in the diagram with the interest rate on the vertical axis.

We can obtain the same results for the various shocks, as observed using the price–quantity diagram. Take, for instance, a rise in expected inflation. The fall in the real interest rate makes borrowings more attractive, increasing the demand for loans and so the demand curve shifts right in the interest–quantity Figure 5.3a. Lenders find the prospects less attractive, so that the supply of loans shifts left. Hence, we get a rise in the interest rate, just as was observed from the price–quantity diagram.

In Figure 5.3b, as the interest rate rises, the demand for bonds rises—this means that the supply of loans increases. So, the supply curve slopes up in the interest rate–quantity diagram. We can also observe that, when the interest rate rises, the supply of bonds reduces—which means that the demand for loans by firms falls. So, the demand curve slopes down in the interest rate–quantity diagram.

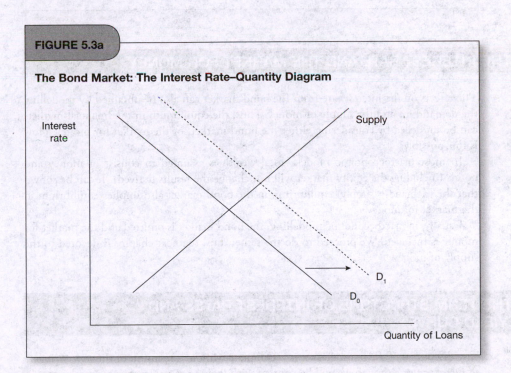

FIGURE 5.3a

The Bond Market: The Interest Rate–Quantity Diagram

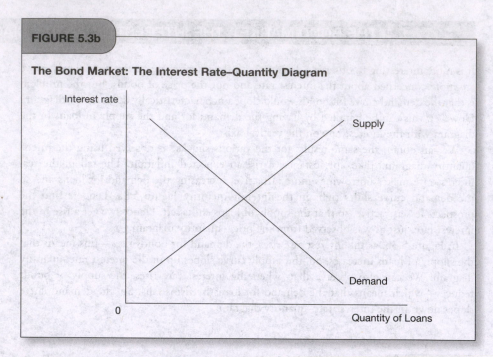

FIGURE 5.3b

The Bond Market: The Interest Rate–Quantity Diagram

5.5. THE INTEREST RATE AND THE MARKET FOR MONEY

The effects on the interest rate from the bond market can also be obtained by modelling the demand for and the supply of money. Thus, the equilibrium in the financial markets can be modelled by considering either the bond market, or the market for money. How is this possible?

In most macroeconomic models, total wealth is assumed to consist of money and bonds (including the equity market will not change the results derived). It can be shown that the (demand = supply) equilibrium in the bond market also implies equilibrium in the market for money.

Usually, in macroeconomic modelling, the bond market is omitted and the market for money is included. We proceed to do the same; thus, the next chapter is devoted to the supply of money.

5.6. THE TERM STRUCTURE OF INTEREST RATES AND THE YIELD CURVE

The term structure of interest rates refers to the relationship between bonds of different terms.

Any discussion of the bond market is incomplete without a mention of the *term structure of interest rates,* although we will be content with looking at one aggregate interest rate in the rest of the book.

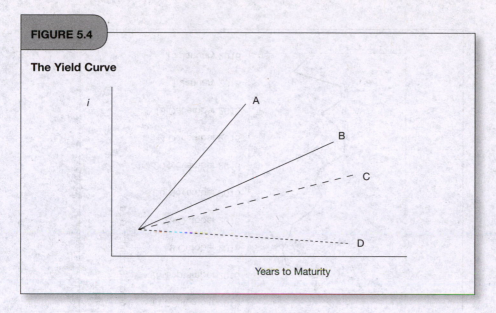

FIGURE 5.4

The Yield Curve

From the price–quantity diagram (see Figure 5.1), we can see that increases in risk, less favourable tax treatments or a decrease in liquidity will all tend to reduce the demand for bonds, shifting the demand curve left and reducing the price—and increasing the interest rate. It is therefore easy to see that bonds will have different associated interest rates, depending on their relative risk, liquidity and tax treatment.

The term to maturity will also differentiate the interest rates between bonds, as this has implications for the riskiness of bonds (has been discussed earlier in this chapter). *The Yield Curve* plots interest rates against maturity and is usually upward sloping, showing higher interest rates for the more risky, longer-term bonds. But sometimes the yield curve can be flat, or even downward sloping (see Figure 5.4). Figure 5.2 shows the yields of government of India securities.

> The yield curve plots the interest rates, at a set point in time, of bonds having same credit quality, but differing maturity dates.

In Figure 5.4, the yield curve A slopes up, as short-run interest rates are expected to rise. The thick curve B and dashed yield curve C rise less sharply, as short-run rates are expected to rise less or even very little. The dotted yield curve D slopes down, as short-run interest rates are expected to fall during the life of the bond.

The yield curve is one of the strongest indicators of the level and changes in the interest rate in the economy. The government yield rates, form the basis of the structure of yield rates in the economy and this is because government securities are risk free, that is, there are no credit risks or default risks. Therefore, they serve as the benchmark for setting yields in other segments of the debt market. Moreover, usually government securities are the largest and most liquid segment in the economy. Figure 5.5 shows the shape of the 10 year government security also called the 'G-Sec' yield curves, between April 2015 and January 2016.

The yield curve's importance is not limited to setting benchmarks for other debt segments and its usefulness can be understood from its large number of applications.

FIGURE 5.5

Yield in the Government Securities Market

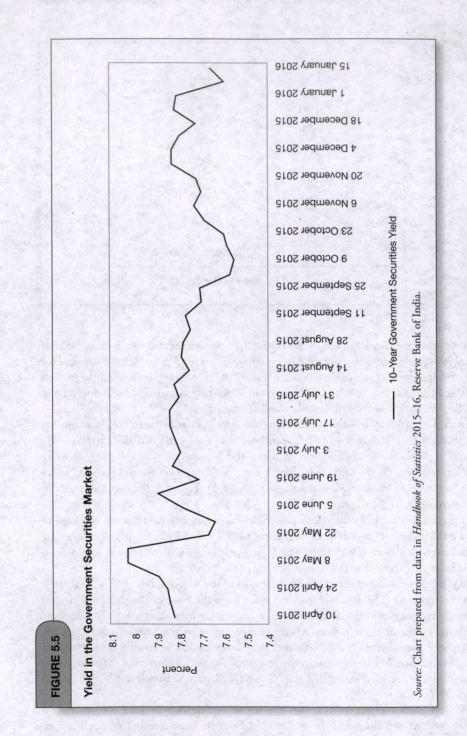

Source: Chart prepared from data in *Handbook of Statistics 2015–16*, Reserve Bank of India.

Primarily, it is used for formulating monetary policies as it gives the market expectation about future movements in the inflation rates and may also contain information about the real growth rate of the economy. Secondly, it is a measure of market risk, that is, the interest rate risk and foreign exchange risk and finally it is a tool used for the pricing of bonds.

The shape of the yield curve depends on expectations about future short-term interest rates, since the long-run rate is based on an average of expected short-run rates over the life of a bond. However, there are premiums associated with certain holding periods when investors show preference for short-term bonds more than longer term ones. This premium is added to the average of short-run interest rates. The yield curve determines the value that investors place today on nominal payments at all future dates—a fundamental determinant of almost all asset prices and economic decisions. The yield curve can also be used as a predictor of economic activity, since it reflects the movement of interest rates. This is presented in Box 5.1 that shows the different term structures of interest rates and government policy stances.

BOX 5.2	The Yield Curve and the State of the Economy

In September 2008, Lehman Brothers, one of the largest investment banks in the USA collapsed. This triggered the global meltdown that shook the world economy and governments across the world initiated stimulus packages to shield their countries against the impact of the global financial crisis. Their major concern was the cascading effect of this crisis leading to a recession. The Indian government launched a slew of measures to protect the economy from recession. The government of India announced three stimulus packages, the first one in December 2008 followed by one in January and February the following year.

The first package was to the tune of $4 billion. A number of incentives were announced. These were drawn up to infuse a sense of optimism in the minds of investors and industrialists. Incentive schemes in the Indian economic stimulus amounting to $70 million were allocated to boost exports. Lending rates on housing loans for low and middle income segments were reduced. Medium and small businesses were offered tax exemptions and tax holidays. Value added tax was cut at different levels to increase spending. The Reserve Bank of India reduced its lending rate to 6.5% and its borrowing rate to 5%.

In January 2009, a second stimulus package was launched. Some of the key measures included the government's plan to recapitalize state-run banks to the tune of 200 billion rupees ($4.1 billion). This was to take place over the next two years to ensure that the banking system did not suffer from capital adequacy constraints. Moreover, the government announced an additional plan expenditure of up to ₹200 billion primarily for critical rural, infrastructure and social security schemes. Indirect tax cuts of 4% ad-valorem across the board, except for petroleum products was also declared. To give a boost to the corporate bond market, the Foreign Institutional Investment (FII) investment limit in rupee denominated corporate bonds in India were raised from US$6 billion to US$15 billion.

The third tranche of the stimulus package was announced in February 2009 by the government through a 2% cut in excise duty and service tax. These tax concessions would lead to a revenue shortfall of about ₹300 billion. The finance minister stated, 'It will have its desired impact because we have given some concessions to the export sector, particularly those which are employment-generating ones, like gems and jewellery, garments and handicraft'.

These strong monetary and fiscal measures were to influence the money market and future expectations. The shape of the yield curve reflects the market's future expectation for interest rates and the conditions for monetary policy (see the yield curves of July, September and December 2008 and March 2009 in Figure 5.6). We look at how these policies are reflected by observing the yield curve of zero-coupon bonds[3] (ZCB for the months of July 2008 (before the Lehman incident), September 2008 (the month of the event) and December 2008 (when the first stimulus package was introduced), subsequently the curve for March after the three packages were launched and their impact on the expectations in the economy, in Figure 5.6. The shape of the curves reveal the changing perception of the market about the future.

FIGURE 5.6

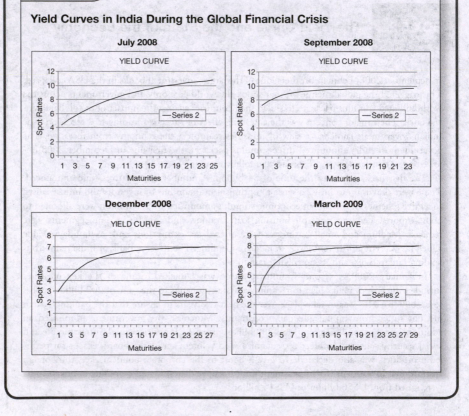

Yield Curves in India During the Global Financial Crisis

---

[3] The zero-coupon bond is the simplest fixed income security in which a single payment is made on the date of maturity.

5.7. CONCLUSION

This chapter has introduced the reader to the basic concepts relating to interest rates and financial returns. The treatment is couched in terms of bond market relationships, as opposed to the usual treatment in macroeconomic textbooks, which only present the concepts from the viewpoint of the market for money. We thought it necessary to bring the bond market in from the shadows, as it helps in understanding the effects of government budgetary policies, etc. (even though formal results can be derived using the money market only).

However, we now proceed to present the money market (strictly speaking, 'the market for money', to distinguish it from the very short-term financial markets, also called 'the money market'). The next chapter we define money supply and discuss the money multiplier, the banking system and other concepts important for obtaining the effects of central bank monetary policies to stimulate the economy and control inflation.

SUMMARY

- Financial markets equilibrium can be modelled by considering either the bond market or the market for money. The aggregate interest rate can be obtained from either of these markets.
- The supply and the demand for bonds and the aggregate interest rate to be used in macroeconomic models can be derived from the bond market.
- The concepts of yield, interest rate and rate of return are related—and need not always be equal to one another.
- The yield to maturity is the interest rate that equates the present value, of all future payments with the current price of the bond (as the face value of the bond). Consider a bond with face value of ₹1,000 and annual coupon of 10%. Here the interest rate is the coupon rate of 10% and the calculated yield will also equal this. So, yield = interest rate.
- However, when that bond is bought in the secondary market at a price of 1,100, the yield for the buyer from holding the bond will be different from the interest rate. The price of the bond = 1,100, equal to the present value PV, but greater than the face value. So, as the price of the bond goes up, the yield goes down. And if the price goes down, the yield goes up.
- This inverse relationship explains the impact of an expansionary monetary policy. Bonds are purchased by the central bank, driving up bond prices and lowering actual market interest rates. The actual rate of return obtained by holding a bond can differ from the yield to maturity, if the final price received is not equal to the face value.
- If the final price received is greater than the face value, there are capital gains. Then, the rate of return from holding the bond = current yield + capital gain.

- The seller of a bond after the interest rate rises, suffers a greater loss with a longer-term bond, than if it is a medium-term one. Hence, the interest rate risk is clearly higher for longer-term bonds.
- According to the theory of asset demand, the demand for an asset rises with its return and with an increase in total wealth. Thus, for a bond, a rise in the interest rate increases bond demand; a rise in wealth and liquidity also increases demand.
- Demand for the bond also rises if it becomes less risky compared to other assets. The expected return, which is the associated probability multiplied by the return then rises relative to other assets.
- The supply curve for bonds slopes up in the demand–supply diagram—which means that the supply increases as the interest falls, given the negative relation between price and interest. A rise in expected inflation reduces the real interest rate and increases the demand for investment funds, increasing the supply of bonds issued for borrowing funds. The supply of bonds increases when the Government finances its budget deficits.
- The yield curve plots interest rates against maturity and is usually upward sloping, with higher interest rates for the more risky, longer-term bonds. Sometimes the yield curve can be flat, or even downward sloping.
- The shape of the yield curve depends on expectations about future short-term interest rates, since the long-run rate is based on an average of expected short-run rates over the life of a bond.
- The yield curve is one of the strongest indicators of the level and changes in the interest rate in the economy. The government yield rates form the basis of the structure of yield rates in the economy.
- The yield curve is a significant element in formulating monetary policies as it gives market expectations about future movements in the inflation rates and may also contain information about the real growth rate of the economy.
- Secondly the yield curve is a measure of market risk, that is, interest rate risk and foreign exchange risk and is a tool for bond pricing.

CASE STUDY

Bond Prices and Yield

The central bank announced that it would purchase ₹48,000 crore of government securities through open market operations, and as this news was reported bond prices gained. Dealers said that bond yields fell to the lowest level in over a month. Treasury Head, of a well-known private bank, remarked, 'The yields have fallen substantially. We can attribute this to the positive factors like the Open Market Operations—the central bank's announcement to buy bonds, because it injects liquidity and it is an opportunity to unload stocks'.[4]

---

[4] Anup Roy, *RBI Opens Up Bond Market*, (26 August 2016): http://www.business-standard.com/article/finance/rbi-opens-up-bond-market-116082501380_1.html

TABLE CS 5.1

Bond Prices and Yields

	Most Highly Traded *8.08% 12-year bond 2022*	*2nd Most Highly Traded* *8.13% 12-year bond 2022*
Previous Closing Price	₹99.90 (8.09% YTM)	₹100.46 (8.06% YTM)
Opening Price	₹99.92 (8.09% YTM)	₹100.4 (8.07% YTM)
Closing Price	₹100.43 (8.02% YTM)	₹101.04 (7.99% YTM)

Source: Authors.

The Chief Investment Officer of a public sector bank said, 'We are expecting further softening in G-sec yields. Despite the cautious outlook from a medium term perspective, we anticipate the yield to decline in the near term'.

After reading the text given in the case study, answer the following questions:

1. Why do you think the bond prices rose in the bond market?
2. What in your view is the reason that the Chief Investment Officer said he anticipated a softening of yields?
3. Do the price of bonds in the table and the YTM values match the expectations based on what you have learned in this chapter?

KEYWORDS

Interest rate
Yield to maturity
Government securities
Bond
Bond market

Interest rate risk
Real interest rate
Term structure of interest rate
Yield curve

CONCEPT CHECK

State whether the following statements are true or false:

1. The yield to maturity is the interest rate that equates the present value, of all future payments with the current price of the bond, as the face value of the bond.
2. A bond is a long-term debt instrument issued by the government to finance its deficit that has a life of just three months.

3. The actual rate of return obtained by holding a bond can differ from the yield to maturity, if the final price received is not equal to the face value.

4. The yield curve plots interest rates against maturity and is usually downward sloping, with higher interest rates for the more risky, longer-term bonds.

5. The supply curve for bonds slopes up in the demand–supply diagram, the supply increasing with the price—which in turn means that the supply increases as the interest falls.

6. The real interest rate is the nominal rate of interest plus the inflation rate.

DISCUSSION QUESTIONS

1. Show that in an economy with wealth consisting of only bonds and money, equilibrium in the money market implies equilibrium in the bond market.

2. A bond with a face value of ₹5,000 and a coupon rate of 10% is bought for a price of ₹5,500. Is the yield to maturity equal to the interest rate? If the bond is sold next year for a price of ₹6,000, is the rate of return equal to the yield?

3. Explain why longer-term bonds carry more risk premiums.

4. Analyse the effects of a government budget deficit financed by issuing bonds

    i. In the interest rate–quantity diagram
    ii. In the price–quantity diagram. What is the effect on the interest rate?

5. Would you expect the yield curve to be relatively flat or relatively vertical during continuing boom conditions? Why?

6

CHAPTER

Money, Money Supply and the Banking System

LEARNING OBJECTIVES

Upon completion of this chapter, the reader will be able to:

- Know how money and banking evolved in a historical perspective.
- Understand the role and functions of money in the economy.
- Explain the role of the central bank and the components of its balance sheet.
- Differentiate between the various definitions of money supply and the factors that determine it.
- Understand how commercial banks create credit by advancing loans, making deposits and operating in the money market using the money multiplier approach.
- Know how the central bank manages liquidity, money supply and inflation through repo and reverse repo rates.
- Understand government behaviour with regard to the budget deficit and money supply.

6.1. INTRODUCTION

Money drives the modern economy, as a medium of transactions, store of wealth and unit of value. In Chapter 5, we introduced the financial system and discussed how bonds are valued and traded in the market for money, driven by changes in the interest rate. In this chapter, we will first look at how money has evolved in the past and then study its functions. We will then examine the different measures of money

Money functions as a means of transacting, as a store of wealth or savings and as a measure of value.

supply following which we will derive the money multiplier. Before that, we will discuss the role of the central bank and take a look at a simplified format of the balance sheet of the Reserve Bank of India and commercial banks.

6.1.1. What is Money?

How did money evolve?

Throughout history, exchange has taken various forms. Without money, all transactions were through the barter system where commodities were directly exchanged for each other. Money as we know today has evolved through several stages[1]:

1. Commodity money
2. Metallic money
3. Paper money
4. Credit money or plastic money and
5. Cyber money

In the early days of human civilization, any commodity that was generally demanded by common consent was used as money. For instance, leather or fur would be exchanged for salt or sheep for wheat. Then goods like fur, skins, salt, rice, wheat, utensils, weapons, tools etc. were commonly used as money. This exchange of goods for goods was known as 'barter exchange'. In barter system, people traded the things they had for what they needed. But this was very inconvenient, as it was dependent on the 'double coincidence of wants'. So in the barter system, commodities played the role of money and so commodity money evolved. Wherever trade flourished, certain goods were assigned the property of money, as it was used as a medium of exchange.

One of the most important improvements over the simplest forms of early barter was the selection one or two items in preference to others because of their qualities as mediums of exchange. The preferred items for barter had to be conveniently stored, with high value densities, be easily portable and durable and thus they came to be accepted as money.

In the distant past, some societies had laws that required compensation for crimes of violence and payment for brides to compensate the head of the family for loss of a daughter's services. Just as rulers imposed taxes, citizens were obliged to pay religious tributes. The compensation towards blood money, bride money and taxed entailed some payment in kind. Objects originally accepted for one purpose were often found to be useful for other non-economic purposes, their growing acceptability leading them to be used for trading, thereby replacing barter. Thus, money evolved out of deeply rooted customs with the clumsiness of barter providing an economic impulse albeit not as the primary factor. Money originated largely from non-economic causes like social and religious rites as much as from barter.[2]

---

[1] The text in this section is based on Glyn Davies, *A History of Money from Ancient Times to the Present Day*, 3rd ed. (Cardiff: University of Wales Press, 2002).

[2] Ibid.

The existence of banking preceded coinage. It is believed that banking originated in ancient Mesopotamia (today's Iraq), where grains were stored for safekeeping in royal palaces and temples. Receipts were used for transfers not only to the original depositors but also to third parties. In Mesopotamia, the rules of banking operations were encoded in the Laws of Hammurabi. In Egypt, the centralization of harvests in state warehouses led to development of the banking system. Written orders for withdrawal of lots of grain by owners, whose crops were deposited or compulsorily deposited to the credit of the king, came to be used for payment of debts, taxes and to priests. Even when coins began to be minted, Egyptian grain banks served to reduce the need for precious metals that were reserved for the purchase of military supplies.

When Egypt fell to the rule of the Greek dynasty, the Ptolemy's (323–30 BC) old system of warehouse banking became more sophisticated. The numerous scattered government granaries were transformed into a network of grain banks. The central bank in Alexandria kept the records from all the state granary banks. In the Hellenic world, Greek banks were involved in money changing and they also financed freight by ships, mining and construction.

The Babylonian banking system was well developed because their banks had to carry out the monetary functions of coinage (since coins had not been invented). The Ptolemaic Egyptians segregated their limited coinage system from their state banking system to economize on the use of precious metals. The Romans preferred coins for many kinds of services. After the fall of the Roman Empire, banking was forgotten in Europe but re-emerged during the Crusades. The need for funding of long-drawn battles revived banking. In the Italian city-states of Rome, Venice and Genoa and in medieval France, the need to transfer sums of money for trade led to the development of financial services like bills of exchange. The nomenclature for bank comes from the Italian word *banca* for bench or counter.

In the 1600s, the goldsmiths in Britain were entrusted with the deposit of gold bullion jewels and coins for safekeeping. Instructions to goldsmiths to pay a customer led to the use of *cheques*. Similarly goldsmiths' receipts were used for withdrawing deposits and as evidence of the ability to pay, by 1660 these developed into the *banknote*.

Cowrie shells, off coastal regions of the Indian Ocean, were widely used from as early as 1200 AD. This primitive form of money continued even in the 19th century in Ghana, India and Nigeria. The cowrie played such a significant role in ancient China that its pictograph is the Chinese language for money. China is known to have used coins as early as 400 BC but in the West, the first known coin was minted by King Alyattes in Lydia, (today's Turkey), between 640–630 BC. The Lydians stamped small round pieces of precious metals as a guarantee of their purity. Later, with improved metallurgical skills, coins had seals as a symbol of their purity and weight. Afterwards, the use of coins spread to Ionia, mainland Greece and Persia.

As humanity progressed, man discovered metals and saw the advantage of using pieces of metal in place of commodities. Recorded history as well as archaeological evidence shows that metal coins had wide acceptance and was the main form of money. Gold coins were issued by several Italian states. Under the influence of Byzantine and Arab coinage, Florence (1252) and Genoa (1253) issued gold coins.

Fiat money is money that is decreed as such by the government. It has no intrinsic value, but is mandated to be accepted as medium of exchange since it is backed by the government.

Although metallic coins were popular, especially gold coins, they were replaced by paper money. As early as 1000 BC, the Chinese were known to be using paper money. To avoid the inconvenience of carrying coins, traders entrusted their precious coins to goldsmiths in exchange for a paper receipt. In Britain, the origin of paper money can be traced to goldsmiths who wrote receipts against deposits. The cost of producing paper notes was negligible and they provided the depositors the advantage of writing cheques of different denominations for liquidating debt and trade transactions. At the beginning of the 20th century, these receipts gained credibility and were widely accepted as money. So, the invention of paper money marked a significant stage in the evolution of money. Ultimately, *fiat money* replaced paper receipts also known as legal tender money. Since fiat paper money had no intrinsic value, it was universally accepted as a means of payment, as every government defended its sovereign value. Paper money is seen to be regulated and controlled by the central bank of a country.

In 1860, the Western Union in the USA pioneered money transfers through telegraphs. John Biggins developed the first credit card in 1946 which is a card issued as a method of payment, allowing the cardholder to pay for goods and services, for which he is expected to pay later and hence enjoy a line of credit. The card issuer, usually a bank, creates revolving accounts and grants line of credit. The card owner has to pay an interest charge until the entire amount of credit is repaid. The Diners Card was the first one to get universal acceptance in 1950 pioneered by Robert Schneider.

The 21st century is abuzz with the Bitcoin, what is also called cyber money. It is a crypto currency or a form of money that uses cryptography to control its creation. It was supposedly envisioned and developed by Satoshi Nakamoto. However, bitcoins are not accepted in many countries although it has large digitally cognizant groups of people who follow it. It can also be referred to as intangible money.

What are the functions of money?

The central bank is the bank that has control over the money supply. In India it is the Reserve Bank of India, in the USA it is the Federal Reserve System.

Money is defined as any medium that facilitates the exchange of goods and services. It is round since it circulates as a medium of exchange and it is flat because it is stored one on top of another. Money has three crucial functions: it acts as medium of exchange for transactions, as a store of value and as a unit of value. Money is sometimes defined as anything that is acceptable as a medium of exchange and as a settlement of a debt.

The primary characteristic of money is liquidity. It is the lubricant that lets the economy function in all its diverse facets. This property of liquidity that money possesses makes other assets less liquid. Money is, therefore, not wealth but wealth can be money. Money is not income; it is a flow of income. Money in itself is a stock. Next, we observe how the Reserve Bank of India acts as the country's *central bank* in managing the money supply and the way banks create credit.

Money supply is determined by the central bank of a country exogenously, which is the key player in money supply. An important part of the money supply is the banking system.

The central bank has the mandate for formulating monetary policy by directly influencing the volume and composition of the money supply, the size and distribution of credit, the level and structure of interest rates and the direct and indirect effects of these monetary variables upon related factors such as savings and investment as well as the determination of output, income and prices in the economy.

6.2. MONEY SUPPLY

The official money supply statistics, that is, the amount of central bank money (currency) that exists in the economy, is determined by the fractional reserve. The central bank indirectly influences the issue of money through monetary transmissions, by raising or lowering interest rates and the *reserve ratios*. However, depending on the circumstances the central bank can adjust the banking regulations to influence money supply. This has been demonstrated by the way demonetization in India of the ₹500 and ₹1000 currency notes was carried out. Box 6.1 discusses demonetization.

There is no universally accepted definition of money supply. Money has varying degrees of liquidity or 'moneyness'. Thus, liquidity of an asset depends on how easily it can be converted into cash. The most liquid assets are notes and coins established by legal fiat. As an asset becomes less liquid, the distinction between monetary assets and other assets become blurred.

The items that are included in money supply are related to the level of financial liberalization, or sophistication in a country. With greater sophistication, an increasing range of monetary and other financial instruments appear and it becomes increasingly difficult to distinguish between them. Therefore, periodic revisions are needed to compile monetary statistics.

The First Working Group (1961)[3] of the RBI defined money supply to consist of government's liability to the public and the monetary liabilities of the banking sector to the

> Reserve ratio is the ratio of bank reserves to bank deposits maintained by banks mandated by the central bank.

BOX 6.1	**What and Why of Demonetization and Its Impact in India[4]**

What: Demonetization occurs in a country when its currency loses its status as a legal tender[5], so that it is no longer valid as a medium of exchange or a store of value nor accepted for settling past debts. The policy to declare a currency as invalid stems from the economic or political environment of that country.

Historical Perspective: In 1853, the East India Company was authorized to issue one-rupee coins and at the same time, the silver one-rupee coin became legal tender money. By 1870, the currency of most of China, Japan and the countries of South East Asia was silver due to the large supply of silver from many newly discovered mines. But in Germany and Scandinavia, silver was demonetized and they moved to the gold standard. In 1873, the Coinage Act was passed in the USA with silver being demonetized and the gold standard adopted.

---

[3] Rituparna Das, 'Definitions and Measures of Money Supply in India', *Munich Personal RePEc Archive* Paper no. 21391, 2010.

[4] The content of the Box 6.1 has been drawn heavily from the *Economic Survey 2016–17*, supported by news from *The Hindu*, 10 November 2016 and 1 March 2017 and *The Economic Times*, 9–15 April, 2017. The history section has been taken from Glyn, *History of Money*.

[5] A legal tender is any official medium of payment recognized by law that can be used to clear a public or private debt or to meet a financial obligation.

In the late 20th century, some countries that demonetized their currency were Brazil in 1990 and again in 1993, the Soviet Union in 1991, Russia in 1991, Iraq in 1993, North Korea in 2009, Cyprus in 2013, Greece in 2015 and Venezuela in 2016. Broadly, all these countries took this policy to fight hyperinflation, organized crime, profiteering and counterfeiting.

On the other hand, in 2002, many European countries demonetized their domestic currency as they adopted the single currency Euro. But this was pre-planned whereby domestic currency was eased out and replaced with the Euro. In 1988 and 2005, Australia demonetized its pound to prevent counterfeiting while in the 21st century, Denmark and Sweden also demonetized their currencies to prevent counterfeiting and issued new currencies with better security features.

On 8 November 2016, the Indian government announced that the high denomination currencies of ₹1,000 and ₹500 were no longer legal tender by midnight and through this dramatic move, 86% of the country's currency became invalid. India being a cash driven economy, this policy had a profound shock impact. Overnight, money in safes to pay for an imminent wedding or medical treatment or buy a property etc., became worthless. It led to severe hardships, woefully more for the law-abiding taxpayers and of course the poor daily wage earners. But they all stood stoically in long queues at the banks, converting their old currency for the new. This is not the first time as in 1946 and then in 1978, the Indian rupee was demonetized, but then it had no significant effect.

Why Demonetization? The objective of the demonetization was four fold; a) to curb corruption b) to prevent counterfeiting c) to stop terror activities that were being financed through high denomination notes and d) to control black money. When demonetization happened, the country's GDP growth was steadily moving at 7.4%. There was widespread belief that this drastic step would bring down the growth rate by 2%, leading to overall distress with huge job losses in both the organized and unorganized sectors with resultant fall in output. The agricultural sector was expected to be particularly vulnerable being largely unorganized and cash driven.

The Short-term Impact: Not surprisingly, stone throwing in Kashmir actually stopped in the immediate aftermath of the demonetization as the sponsors of these activities ran out of money. In a thrust to promote cashless transactions the BHIM (Bharat Interface for Money) was launched and till January 2017, 10 crore transactions have been done. It is expected that digitalization will curtail cash to the extent of reducing tax evasion and promote financial savings. On the black money front, the Revenue Department on 7 April 2017 announced it had detected evasion of more than ₹1.37 lakh crore in both direct and indirect taxes and identified over 1,000 shell companies which indulged in bogus transactions worth ₹13,300 crore in the last three financial years. Assets worth 1,416 crore were seized in 2016–17 compared to 712 crore in 2015–16. Banks became flush with new deposits, but the decline in interest rates triggered a large outflow of foreign portfolio investment, amounting to US$9.8 billion in November and December 2016.[6]

From the economic growth perspective, demonetization is potentially an aggregate *demand* shock because it reduces the supply of money and affects private wealth, especially of those holding unaccounted money. It is also an aggregate *supply* shock to the extent that economic activity rely on cash as an input. For instance, agricultural production could be affected since sowing requires the use of labour that traditionally paid in cash.

Five months later, in April 2017 the GDP growth rate is pegged at 7.1% (CSO).[7] The services, industry and agriculture sectors grew at 7.9%, 5.8% and 4.4% in 2017 as against 8.8%, 5.2% and 4.1% in the previous quarter belying the fears. Surprisingly, even foreign trade is showing a healthy uptrend. *The Economic Survey* writes that demonetization can have long-term benefits. These may not necessarily be visible in the next six months but evidence should start trickling in over a one-year horizon and beyond.

[6] *Economic Times*, 9–15 April 2017.
[7] *Economic Survey*, 2016–17.

public. Variations in the monetary liabilities of the banking sector were expected to reflect corresponding changes in financial assets and net-nonmonetary liabilities. Deposits with banks comprised demand liabilities of banks excluding interbank demand deposits, deposits of state governments and other deposits with the RBI. In 1977, the Second Working Group developed the four measures of money supply for annual compilation in India as:

M1 = currency with public + demand deposits with the banking system + other deposits with RBI
M2 = M1 + saving deposits with post office savings banks
M3 = M1 + time deposits with the banking system
M4 = M1 + all deposits with post office savings banks excluding National Saving Certificates

The money stocks M1, M2, M3 and M4 of India from 2001 to 2016 are shown in Figure 6.1.

There are broadly four players who influence the money supply:

1. The central bank is the monitoring, supervisory body and the regulatory authority of the banking system, responsible for conducting monetary policy which is carried out by *open market operations*. The RBI acts as the clearing agency for cheques and transfers funds between banks. It acts as the lender of the last resort (read about this in Box 6.3) for all banks and the banker to the government. Surely, playing such a wide spectrum of roles the makes the RBI the key player in the financial system.

Open Market Operations refers to central bank purchase or sale of government securities through transactions in the open market.

FIGURE 6.1

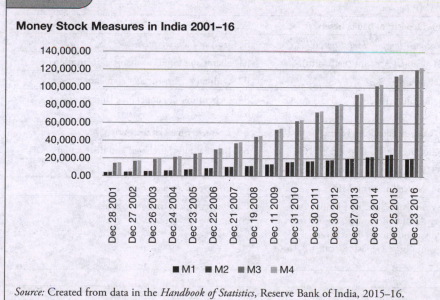

Money Stock Measures in India 2001–16

Source: Created from data in the *Handbook of Statistics*, Reserve Bank of India, 2015–16.

2. Banks, which are depository institutions that accept deposits from individuals as well as corporations and advance loans, including scheduled commercial banks, private, public cooperative and foreign.
3. Depositors are those individuals and corporations that hold deposits in banks, that is, who entrust their savings and earn interest from their deposits.
4. Borrowers can be Individuals or corporations that borrow from banks or State and Local governments like municipal bodies that issue bonds.

Of these four players, the central bank of India, that is, the Reserve Bank of India, is the most important one. It will be useful to examine a simplified format of the central banks' *balance sheet* shown in Table 6.1.

The Balance Sheet is an accounting statement that lists of the value of all the assets and liabilities and net worth of the firm or bank.

TABLE 6.1

Format of the Balance Sheet of the Reserve Bank of India

Liabilities *Monetary Liabilities (ML)*	*Assets* *Financial Assets (FA)*
A1. Notes in circulation	A. Credit to the Government
A2. Other deposits	A1. RBI credit to the centre
a. Deposits of quasi-government	a. Loans and Advances from the RBI to the Centre
b. Balances in the accounts of foreign central banks and governments	b. RBI holdings of Treasury Bills, dated securities and rupee coins and small coins
c. Accounts of international agencies such as IMF etc.	A2. RBI credit to state governments
A3. Deposits of banks (reserves)	Loans and advances to state governments
B. *Non-Monetary Liabilities (NML)*	B. *Credit to Commercial Sector*
B1. Capital Account (net worth)	B1. Shares and bonds of financial institutions
a. Paid up Capital	B2. Ordinary debentures of cooperative sectors
b. Statutory Reserve	B3. Debentures of cooperative land mortgage banks
c. Contingency Reserve, etc.	B4. Loans to financial institutions
B2. Government Deposits	B5. Internal bills purchased and discounted
B3. IMF a/c no. 1 (since 1948)	
B4. Miscellaneous NMLS	C. *RBI's gross claims on Banks*
e.g., Bills Payable, RBI Employees' Pension Fund, Cooperative Guarantee/ Provident Funds (since 1964) Compulsory Deposit Schemes Balance etc.	C1. Refinance of RBI to the banks

Liabilities	Assets
Monetary Liabilities (ML)	Financial Assets (FA)
	C2. Fixed investments in commercial banks' shares/bonds/debentures, e.g., Holding of shares of the SBI
	D. *Net Foreign Assets*
	D1. Gold coins and bullion
	D2. Eligible foreign securities
	D3. Balances held abroad netted for balance in IMF account no.1 minus India's quota subscription in rupees
	Other Assets
	a. Physical assets
	b. Others

Source: Authors.

Assets: Are those items of value that are owned by the organization, for example a loan is an asset for a bank.

6.3. THE MONEY MULTIPLIER APPROACH

The central bank's *liabilities* play a key role in the money supply process. Liabilities are currency in circulation and reserves. Reserves refer to the accounts (deposits, currency in bank vaults) held by commercial banks at the central bank.

Central bank *assets* = government securities, discount loans to banks, gold and foreign currency assets. We can see how the money supply process is generated by analysing the monetary liabilities and the matching assets in the central bank's balance sheet.

Liabilities: are those items of value that an organization owes to others for example a loan taken from a bank.

6.3.1. The Balance Sheet of the Central Bank

In the balance sheet of the central bank, the dated securities of the Central Government include marketable securities, special non-interest bearing securities and gold bonds. The provisions governing loans and advances to the centre are changed time to time. According to the agreement between the Government of India and the Reserve Bank of India, the latter is authorized to purchase and sell government securities.

As a monitoring and controlling body, the RBI mandates commercial banks to maintain deposits with it to ensure that they are able to meet all demands for withdrawal from their depositors. The banks also retain reserves with the RBI over and above the statutory minimum, which are known as the 'excess reserves', discussed later in the chapter.

Commercial banks have to maintain a minimum *cash reserve ratio* (CRR) of 6% on a fortnightly basis of their net demand and time liabilities (NDTL), the maximum rate of the CRR being 20%.

Cash reserve ratio (CRR) is the amount of funds that the banks have to keep with the RBI in relation to their deposits.

The RBI functions as the agent of the government currency, it is responsible for issuing government debt, distribution and handling of the coins and notes to the public.

Therefore, the monetary liabilities of the RBI consist of

1. currency issued by the RBI—notes of rupee two and above
2. reserves held with the RBI by commercial banks
3. other deposits with the RBI

The government of India also issues one-rupee notes, coins and small coins that are part of the currency in the hands of the public. This along with the government money with commercial banks is called *vault cash*.

High-powered money is the RBI's currency along with government money (GM) which forms the monetary base.

$$\text{High-powered money (H)} = \text{Monetary liabilities} + \text{Government money}$$
$$= \text{Currency with public (C)} + \text{Reserves (R)} + \text{Other deposits}$$
$$= C + R \text{ (ignoring other deposits)} \tag{6.1}$$

$$\text{Where R} = \text{Vault cash} + \text{Bank deposits}$$
$$= \text{Statutory reserves} + \text{Excess reserves} \tag{6.2}$$

Most of the high-powered money consists of monetary liabilities (ML) because government money is negligible. Now, let us look at the fundamental identity of the RBI's balance sheet:

Assets = Liabilities

$$\text{Or} \quad FA + OA = ML + NML \tag{6.3}$$

$$\text{Or} \quad FA + OA - NML = ML \tag{6.4}$$

If the net non-monetary liabilities (NNML) of the central bank is defined as non-monetary liabilities (NML) less other assets (A) we get

$$NNML = NML - OA \tag{6.5}$$

Rearranging Equations (6.3) and (6.5) we get monetary liabilities equal to the sum of financial assets less NNML, that is,

$$ML = FA - NNML \tag{6.6}$$

Now, if there is change in high-powered money ΔH, then there will be a change in monetary liabilities and government money, since we are assuming government money to be insignificant, thus

$$\Delta H = \Delta ML = \Delta FA - \Delta NNML \tag{6.7}$$

The money multiplier is defined by the equation

$$M^s = mH \tag{6.8}$$

Where m is the multiplier, M^s is the broad money M_3 and H is high-powered money.

To determine the value of the multiplier m from the point of view of broad money M_3 is used, later if the narrow money is considered then M_1 is used. Broad money supply can be expressed in terms of its components as

$$M_3 = C + DD + TD \qquad (6.9)$$

If r is the reserve ratio then

$$r = R/(DD + TD), \text{ then } R = r(DD + TD)$$

Then from Equations (6.1) and (6.9) we can write the multiplier as

$$m = \frac{C + DD + TD}{C + R}$$

If cu = C/DD and t = TD/DD then we can rewrite the multiplier as

$$m = \frac{1 + C/DD + TD/DD}{C/DD + r(1 + TD/DD)}$$

$$\text{Or}$$

$$= \frac{1 + cu + t}{cu + r(1 + t)} \qquad (6.10)$$

Suppose we consider narrow money then we use M_1, in that case r will be R/DD and hence the multiplier will be

$$m = \frac{cu + 1}{cu + r} \qquad (6.11)$$

If the effect of TD in both the above situations is ignored, then the money multiplier is influenced by three key ratios, namely, cu, t and r. These ratios are behavioural in nature, namely, cu represents the currency ratio, t is TD/DD, r the reserve requirement. Is the money multiplier effective as a determinant of the money supply? This question is explored later in this chapter.

6.4. CREDIT CREATION BY COMMERCIAL BANKS

In the process of credit creation, it may appear that banks have an ability to 'create' unlimited money. But actually, there is a limit and the money multiplier plays a role.

6.4.1. Balance Sheet

The simplified version of a commercial banks' balance sheet (Table 6.2) shows how a bank raises funds and invests them in different types of assets. The liabilities of the bank

---

TABLE 6.2

Format of the Balance Sheet of a Commercial Bank

Liabilities	Assets
1. Share capital	1. Cash in hand
	Cash with the central bank
	Cash with other banks
2. Reserve funds	2. Money at call and short notice
a. Deposits	3. Bills discounted including treasury bills
(i) Time deposits	
(ii) Demand deposits	
b. Savings deposits	
3. Borrowings	4. Investments
4. Other items	5. Advances
	6. Other items

Source: Authors.

---

are its outflow to its shareholders or depositors. The assets are those items from which it expects to receive income.

A bank liabilities are its source of funds including share capital, reserve fund and deposits. Share capital and reserves together constitute the *net worth*. The reserve fund is the amount accumulated over years of undistributed profits. Deposits form the bank's biggest proportion of working capital. Banks also borrow from other banks that lead to miscellaneous liabilities apart from bills of exchange and business bills endorsed on behalf of customers.

Net worth is the value of all assets minus the value of all the liabilities.

The assets side are deployment of funds and a small portion of total deposits is held as cash reserves. Cash reserves include cash with the bank and cash held with other commercial banks or with the RBI. Money at call and short notice are short-term loans that can be called back at a very short notice of 1–7 days. These are highly liquid assets and are low interest earning.

Investments, refers to the part of funds invested in government treasury bill (T-bills) and shares. Banks advance loans to retail customers and corporate bodies, which are their primary earnings. A bank creates credit in three ways; these are as follows:

1. by accepting deposits and issuing cheques
2. by advancing loans and giving promissory notes
3. by buying and selling government bills and bonds

6.4.2. Accepting Deposits

Accepting Deposits: Suppose Ajmer Bank starts operation with a capital of ₹5 lakh and their first customer Mr Aveek deposits ₹300,000 to the bank (for the bank balance sheet, see Table 6.3). Commercial banks have to maintain liquidity through prudential reserve requirements stipulated by the RBI and need to earn profits through loans and advances.

Maintaining Reserves: Commercial banks have to fulfil two legal requirements, namely,

1. the cash reserve requirement and
2. the statutory liquid requirement

What is the logic for maintaining the CRR and the statutory liquidity ratio (SLR)? It is basically to enhance the liquidity of the bank and thereby protect the depositors from losses. In case of a *run on banks,* the depositors can demand the withdrawal of all their funds if they fear the bank is going to go into liquidation. But in an emergency, the cash reserves are not available to the bank as liquid funds. Even if the funds were legally available and accessible, they would be absolutely inadequate to meet serious any 'run' on the bank. Then why have reserves? It is clearly for the RBI to maintain control. *Required reserves* are the tools through which the RBI influences the lending ability of commercial banks. It can announce policies that either increase or decrease commercial banks' reserves and thereby affect their ability to create credit.

Suppose the Ajmer Bank accepts ₹300,000 as a deposit from Mr Aveek. If the CRR is 10%, then the bank has to keep ₹30,000. If the *Statutory Liquidity Ratio* (SLR) is 25%, then for the SLR the bank has to set aside (25 × 300,000/100) = ₹75,000 (see Tables 6.3 and 6.4, respectively).

Banks are also allowed to maintain additional reserves with the RBI, apart from the CRR and the SLR and these form the *excess reserves.* To avoid unanticipated requirements, banks prefer to maintain additional reserves whenever their deposits increase. The Ajmer Bank now maintains a reserve of ₹675,000 (645,000 + 30,000) (Table 6.5).

> A run on banks is a situation when all depositors want to withdraw their funds from their bank accounts because of lack of confidence in their bank.

> Required reserves are the minimum amount of reserves (in cash or the equivalent) required by the central bank of the country as a proportion of bank deposits.

> Statutory Liquidity Ratio (SLR) is the minimum amount of liquid assets to be maintained by commercial banks with RBI which is a specified percentage of outstanding deposit liabilities.

> Excess reserves are any reserves held by the bank in excess of the required minimum stipulated by the central bank.

TABLE 6.3

Balance Sheet of Ajmer Bank

Liabilities	₹	Assets	₹
Capital	500,000	Cash	800,000
Demand Deposits	300,000		

Source: Authors.

TABLE 6.4

Balance Sheet of Ajmer Bank

Liabilities	₹	Assets	₹
Capital	500,000	Cash	695,000
Demand Deposits	300,000	Reserves with RBI	30,000
		Required Liquid Assets	75,000
		Excess Reserves	0

Source: Authors.

TABLE 6.5

Balance Sheet of Ajmer Bank with Excess Reserves

Liabilities	₹	Assets	₹
Capital	500,000	Cash	50,000
Demand Deposits	300,000	Actual Reserves with RBI	675,000
		Required Liquid Assets	75,000
		Excess Reserves	645,000

Source: Authors.

6.4.3. Advancing Loans

Suppose that the Pioneer Industrial Corporation approaches Ajmer Bank for a loan of ₹195,000, which is granted (Table 6.6). This loan amount can be now deposited by the Corporation in its own bank, say the Baroda Bank (Table 6.7). Even before the loan amount of ₹195,000 is deposited, the Ajmer Bank has ₹300,000 still with it, so ₹195,000 is in circulation and new credit has been created. So, the bank, after receiving the cash deposit of ₹300,000 from Mr Aveek, retains the legal minimum of 35% and lends out the remaining amount ₹195,000, and it now has zero excess reserves. Baroda Bank now has a deposit of ₹195,000 of which it retains reserves of ₹19,500 + ₹48,750, the residue is in cash with Baroda Bank. But retaining cash is not profitable so Baroda Bank grants a loan of ₹126,750 when approached by the Delhi Textile Company (Table 6.8).

TABLE 6.6

Balance Sheet of Ajmer Bank after Loan Granted

Liabilities	₹	Assets	₹
Demand Deposits	300,000	Loan	195,000
		Reserves with RBI	30,000
		Required Liquid Assets	75,000
		Excess Reserves	0

Source: Authors.

TABLE 6.7

Balance Sheet of Baroda Bank after Loan Cheque Deposited

Liabilities	₹	Assets	₹
Demand Deposits	195,000	Cash	126,750
		Reserves with RBI	19,500
		Required Liquid Assets	48,750
		Excess Reserves	0

Source: Authors.

TABLE 6.8

Balance Sheet of Baroda Bank after Loan Cheque Deposited

Liabilities	₹	Assets	₹
Demand Deposits	195,000	Loan	126,750
		Reserves with RBI	19,500
		Required Liquid Assets	487,500
		Excess Reserves	0

Source: Authors.

In this way a chain reaction takes place, as a series of banks keep advancing loans and new deposits are made and keeping the required reserves the banks can create credit and the money supply in the economy grows subject to the reserve requirement by RBI.

6.4.4. Purchasing Government Securities

When banks purchase government bonds, new money is created (see Table 6.9).

Suppose Ajmer Bank increases its reserves by depositing cash worth ₹800,000 and it buys ₹755,000 worth of interest bearing bonds from a broker. Then its balance sheet will be as in Table 6.10.

Note that in the balance sheet, the demand deposits or the supply of money has increased to ₹1,055,000 (by ₹755,000). In this way by accepting government bonds the bank has created a demand deposit in favour of the broker which in effect is new money. Thus, the purchase of government bonds has created money. If the broker withdraws by cheque ₹755,000 from the bank, the demand deposit of the bank will be reduced and the balance sheet will appear as in Table 6.11.

Now the banks reserves barely meet the 15% cash reserves, but it will have ₹755,000 worth of government Securities, an excess amount to meet its liquidity requirements.

TABLE 6.9

Balance Sheet of Ajmer Bank

Liabilities	₹	Assets	₹
Capital	500,000	Cash	50,000
Demand Deposit	300,000	Reserves with RBI	645,000
		Required Liquid Assets	105,000

Source: Authors.

TABLE 6.10

Balance Sheet of Ajmer Bank

Liabilities	₹	Assets	₹
Capital	500,000	Cash	–
Demand Deposit	1,055,000	Reserves with RBI	800,000
		Required Liquid Assets	755,000

Source: Authors.

TABLE 6.11

Balance Sheet of Ajmer Bank

Liabilities	₹.	Assets	₹
Capital	500,000	Cash	–
Demand Deposit	300,000	Reserves with RBI	45,000
		Required Liquid Assets	755,000

Source: Authors.

The chain of deposit creation ends only when excess reserves are completely exhausted so there are no excess resources that can be loaned.

$$I + R + R^2 + R^3 + \ldots\ldots = 1/(1 - R)$$

Or

$$₹300,000 \times (1/1 - 0.65) = ₹300,000\ (1/0.35) = ₹857,143$$

And so on, till we arrive at ₹857,134.

Figure 6.2 shows how the deposit creation process and advance of loans by banks through the banking system spreads and the chain of deposits reserves and loans lead to a growth in money caused by an initial deposit of ₹300,000.

6.5. THE DETERMINANTS OF MONEY SUPPLY

In Box 6.2 we read about the RBI's monetary policy announcement that the SLR had been brought down to 24% for reducing the liquidity pressure on banks. From the money multiplier, we observe the factors that influence the money supply. Is the money multiplier as sharp a method for creating money as it looks? So far, it seems that commercial banks can easily create and destroy deposits by purchasing and selling assets of various kinds. The net effect of the multiplier formula can be summarized as:

$$\Delta M = [1 + cu/r + cu]\Delta H \qquad (6.12)$$

Where ΔM is the change in money stock, ΔH is the change in high-powered money, r is the reserve requirements and cu is the factor relating to currency.

Equation 6.12 explains that the change in money stock ΔM is a function of the change in reserves (ΔH), the reserve requirements (r) and the parameter relating to currency (cu). One drawback of the multiplier approach is that it gives the impression that changes in the quantity of money are brought about in a mechanical way. For instance, the formula

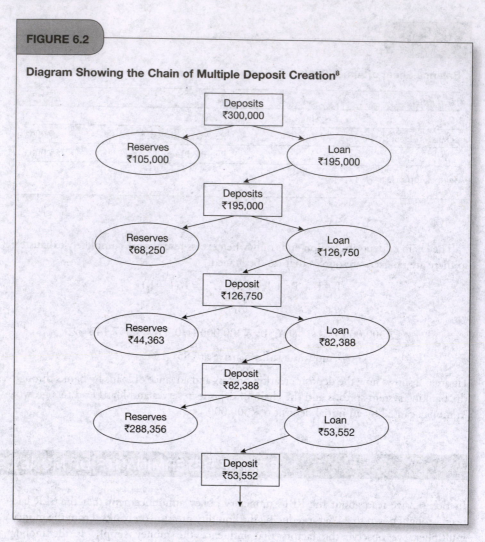

FIGURE 6.2

Diagram Showing the Chain of Multiple Deposit Creation[8]

suggests that given the reserve requirement ratios, the RBI simply picks ΔH and automatically the change in the money supply ΔM takes place. However, for a variety of reasons this is ambiguous and in the next section, we see why it is so.

6.5.1. Behaviour of the Public

The apparent simplicity of the multiplier lies in the way currency affects the money supply, which is captured in 'cu' implying that these are institutionally determined.

[8] The schematic chart has been adapted from W. J. Baumol and A. S. Blinder 's "Economics: Principles and Policy," Dryden Press (1998).

BOX 6.2	'Monetary Review: RBI to Buy Back Government Securities from Banks'[9]

Liquidity alleviation measures took the centre stage in the mid-quarter monetary policy review on 16 December 2010, Thursday with the Reserve Bank of India announcing that it will buy back Government securities from banks. With banks reeling under a persistent liquidity deficit averaging over ₹1 lakh crore daily for the last couple of months, the RBI also permanently reduced the quantum of Government securities that they must mandatorily hold (statutory liquidity ratio or SLR) by one percentage point to 24% of their deposits.

The RBI, however, left key policy rates—the repo rate (interest rate of 6.25% at which banks borrow from the RBI to tide over temporary liquidity mismatches) and the reverse repo rate (the interest rate of 5.25% that banks earn for deploying their surplus with RBI)—unchanged. This is despite the 'upside risk' to its projections of 5.5% inflation by March 2011.

The amount of cash that banks have to park with the RBI (the CRR) has also been retained at 6% of the total deposits. With the liquidity situation appearing to worsen and with the prospect of the government's credit balance with the RBI swelling by about ₹50,000 crore (due to advance tax payments by India Inc.) to ₹1.40 lakh crore by 20 December 2010, the RBI has decided to conduct open market operation auctions for purchase of Government securities for an aggregate amount of ₹48,000 crore in the next one month to help banks tide over the liquidity crunch.

'While the liquidity deficit improved transmission of monetary policy signals with several banks raising deposit and lending interest rates, excessive deficits induce unpredictability in both availability and cost of funds, making it difficult for the banking system to sustain credit delivery', said the RBI in a statement. The RBI, however, cautioned that such provision of liquidity should not be construed as a change in the monetary policy stance since inflation continues to remain a major concern.

Actually, this is not so, the quantities of currency the public chooses to hold depends on the economic factors that change over time.

The demand for currency, demand deposits and other financial assets are determined by the public's perceptions of liquidity and the safety of their relative yields. Consequently, a change in any of these factors can alter the willingness of the public to hold currency vis-à-vis demand deposits (i.e., the parameter 'cu'). So the parameter 'cu' is an economically determined variable and cannot be expected to be constant over time.

6.5.2. Commercial Bank Behaviour

In deriving the multiplier, we have assumed that commercial banks are able and willing to exercise maximum lending power so that they do not add to the excess reserves. However, it has been observed that they do, mainly because the excess reserve serves in maintaining its liquidity and in meeting adverse clearing balances of loan demands of its customers.

---

[9] Readers wanting to know more about the Reserve Bank of India's credit policy can visit http://www.thehindubusinessline.com/2010/12/17/stories/2010121753620100.htm

However, the desire to hold such reserves is dependent on the cost or the interest income foregone from holding non-income earning assets. We can expect that the lower the interest on relatively liquid assets, the lower the opportunity cost on holding such reserves and hence more excess reserves will be held by commercial banks. Evidently, the implicit assumption of the maximum expansion of earning assets will not always be met.

Banks hold excess reserves that increase the 'r' ratio in the expression for the money multiplier. The reserve ratio is affected by market interest rates. When the interest rates are higher, it induces banks to reduce their excess reserves, as banks find it more profitable to advance loans to clients instead of retaining higher reserves with the RBI. On the flip side, lower interest rates cause a counter behaviour and a fall in excess reserves. On the other hand, if banks expect higher deposit outflows or more withdrawals, it will tend to increase the excess reserves kept by them.

6.5.3. Influence of the Central Bank

Finally, the third way in which the multiplier oversimplifies reality is ΔH, which has been defined as the quantity of new reserves. It implies that the central bank has *a reserve dial* that allows it to control the volume of reserves. But reserves are influenced by various factors like the gold stock, borrowing of reserves by commercial banks, volume of foreign owned reserves by the RBI etc. Each of these factors, if imperfectly anticipated, makes the task of regulating the volume of reserves far more complex and not a mechanical one. For instance, discount loans, that is, loans from the central bank at a discount rate are a part of the monetary base, but it is difficult for the central bank to control these while it is easier to control the money supply by bond purchases/sales. In effect, the amount of discount loans that the banks take are positively related to market interest rates and negatively related to the discount rate from the central bank.

Another factor that indicates that the money multiplier oversimplifies the problem are the ways money stock is defined. More importantly, till now we have not yet looked at the government and its behaviour with regard to the money supply and we consider this in the next section.

6.6. GOVERNMENT BEHAVIOUR: BUDGET DEFICIT AND THE MONEY SUPPLY

The central bank influences the money supply but the government's fiscal policy, that is, government expenditure and revenue from tax also have a role. The government budget deficit occurs when its spending exceeds its tax revenues; it can be derived by the following formula:

$$Deficit = spending - tax\ revenue$$

The repo rate is the rate at which the RBI lends short-term money to commercial banks.

When the government runs a deficit budget, then it finances its expenditure by borrowing from the central bank, or borrowing (selling/issuing bonds).

$$Deficit = change\ in\ monetary\ base + sale\ of\ bonds$$

Alternatively,

$$\text{Deficit} = \Delta MB + \Delta Bonds \text{ (sale value of bonds sold)}$$

The change in the monetary base occurs because the government's T-bills and G-securities are bought by the central bank in open market operations. When the central bank pursues defensive open market operations, it is done to offset changes in the monetary base caused by other factors. The rate at which the RBI lends short-term money to commercial banks is called the *repo rate*. Whenever banks have a shortage of funds, they can borrow from the RBI. A reduction in the repo rate helps banks get money at a cheaper rate, so it is a monetary policy instrument.

If the central bank purchases bonds with the agreement that the seller will repurchase them in a short period of time, this is called the *reverse repo*. In the case of reverse repo, the central bank sells government securities to a buyer, which is a commercial bank, that agrees to buy the securities back later, thus it's called a reverse repo (repurchase). An increase in the reverse repo rate can prompt banks to park more funds with the RBI to earn higher returns on idle cash. It is a tool that the RBI uses to drain excess liquidity from the banking system. See the changes in the repo and reverse repo rate in India in 2009–10 presented in Figure 6.3.

We find that the monetary base increases with bank reserves credited by the RBI. In actual practice, the government may sell bonds to the public, which are then purchased by the central bank. Anyway, the monetary base increases and has to be multiplied by 'm' to get the increase in the money supply. In some countries, the government Treasury has the right to issue currency and may finance spending by printing money, this is called deficit financing. Figure 6.4 shows the repo rate and monetary policy instruments such as the base rate and the term deposit rate in 2014–16. Figure 6.5 shows the movements of repo rate, base rate and term deposit rates for 2014–16.

> Reverse Repo is the rate at which the RBI borrows money from commercial banks for a short-term. Banks lend money to the RBI with minimum risk yet earning good interest rate.

FIGURE 6.3

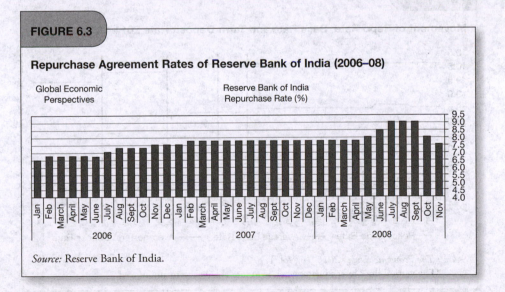

Repurchase Agreement Rates of Reserve Bank of India (2006–08)

Source: Reserve Bank of India.

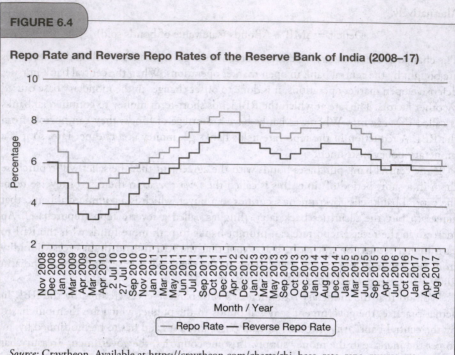

FIGURE 6.4

Repo Rate and Reverse Repo Rates of the Reserve Bank of India (2008–17)

Source: Craytheon. Available at https://craytheon.com/charts/rbi_base_rate_repo_reverse_rate_crr_slr.php Accessed on 24 October 2017.

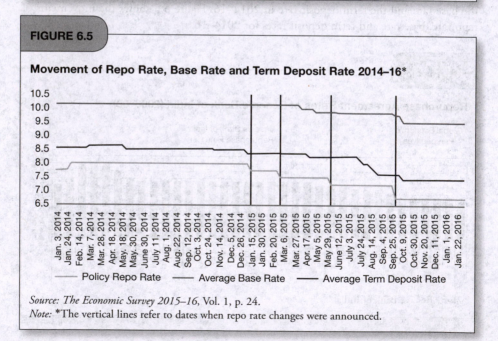

FIGURE 6.5

Movement of Repo Rate, Base Rate and Term Deposit Rate 2014–16*

Source: The Economic Survey 2015–16, Vol. 1, p. 24.
Note: *The vertical lines refer to dates when repo rate changes were announced.

Another way of looking at this is in terms of the monetization of government debt. Suppose the government sells bonds to finance its deficit expenditures. In this case, the monetary base is unaffected, which means that government is borrowing from the public. Consequently, the public's deposits or currency holdings reduce as bonds, but this increases by the same amount when the government makes payments (spends).

The foreign exchange market in an open economy influences the money supply and the central bank's intervention in the foreign exchange market affects the monetary base. When foreign currency is bought, bank deposits at the central bank (reserves) increase, thus increasing the monetary base.

6.6.1. The Central Bank's Targets

The central bank's ultimate targets are to manage inflation, employment and output levels and growth. To achieve these targets the bank has to manoeuvre 'intermediate targets' like the rate of interest and the growth of money supply. To attain these intermediate targets it uses the reserve ratio, open market operations and the discount rate.

It is obvious that managing the money supply target requires monitoring and adjusting the interest rate, which has been discussed at length in Chapter five. But, the RBI can target either a particular rate of interest, or a specific rate of growth of money supply, but not both. In the money market, the demand for money is exogenous, so the money supply has to be appropriately managed for maintaining a particular interest rate. Targeting the interest rate is relatively easy as the central bank announces the interest rate as a signal for other market participants to react. For instance, the interest rates can be manipulated by open market operations in the short-run. To lower the interest rate, the RBI can buy enough bonds set at a higher price to get the lower interest rate. Similarly, to raise the interest rate, it can sell enough volumes of bonds at a set lower price to raise the interest to that level. As explained in the light of the repo and reverse repo instruments.

BOX 6.3	Lender of Last Resort[10]

The central bank of a country acts as the lender of last resort for the commercial banks. So what does that mean? Quite simply put it means that if a bank experiences liquidity problems and is not able to honour its commitments, then it approaches the central bank of the country (in India the Reserve Bank of India). Then the RBI purchases the government securities and bonds from the bank and provides it liquidity. The rate at which this transaction is made is the *repo rate*. Therefore, the rate at which the RBI lends money to commercial banks in their time of crisis is the repo rate. It is a powerful tool in the hands of the central bank to control liquidity, money supply and inflation. If a bank requires ₹10 lakh and the repo rate is 8% then the bank has to pay ₹80,000 to the RBI. So, to curb inflation, the central bank can raise the repo rate to

[10] The content of the Box 6.3 has been supported by news from *The Hindu*, http://www.thehindubusinessline.com/todays-paper/tp-money-banking/article1004293.ece

discourage excessive credit creation and encourage savings, since all the interest rates in the banking system are linked to the repo rate.

Now on the other hand, if a bank has excess liquidity and wishes to deposit the same with the RBI, then the rate at which it lends to the RBI is the *reverse repo rate*. So, when a commercial bank lends to the Central Bank, the interest rate it earns is the reverse repo rate. When the RBI needs to increase its liquidity, it offers attractive reverse repo rates so that banks and financial institutions deposit their excess funds and earn better returns. Thus, the reverse repo is also a strong monetary policy instrument in the hands of the central bank.

Some key points:

- A high repo rate drains excess liquidity from the money market because banks have to pay a high interest rate to get loans from the RBI, whereas a high reverse repo rate injects liquidity into the system.
- Repo rates are always higher than reverse repo rates.
- The repo rate is used to control inflation.
- A reverse repo transaction involves the transfer of funds from the bank to the central bank and repo involves selling securities to the RBI with the intention of repurchasing them at a fixed rate in the future.

6.7. CONCLUSION

In this chapter, money has been introduced to observe its role in the economy. Money facilitates the exchange of goods and services and has three crucial functions: as medium of exchange, as a store of value and as a unit of value. The primary characteristic of money is liquidity and that is its universal acceptability as a means of payment. Though money and income are related, they are not the same and they should not be used interchangeably, because money is stock and income is a flow.

The banking system forms an integral part of the money supply, with the RBI as the supervisory and regulatory authority, having the sole mandate of carrying out monetary policy through open market operations. A substantial part of the money supply is bank deposits with commercial banks. Currency, government debt commercial loans and bank deposits are other major components of money supply in hands of the public.

In the official money supply statistics, the amount of central bank money is determined by the fractional reserve. Banks create credit by accepting deposits and issuing cheques, by advancing loans and giving promissory notes and by buying and selling government bills and bonds. The CRR and SLR reserves control a banks' ability to create credit and increase the money supply through the deposit multiplier.

Although it appears that the banking system drives money supply, it is not entirely true. The central bank manages the government's expenditures; hence, fiscal policy plays a critical role in influencing money supply. If the government runs into a deficit, it has to be financed by borrowings. Therefore, the monetary base changes because the central bank purchases treasury bills and G-securities. Another important function of the central bank is maintaining price stability. To pursue these goals, the central bank uses monetary policy instruments, namely, the reserve ratio, open market operations and the discount rate. In the next chapter, the demand for money, and what influences it, is explored.

SUMMARY

- In pre-modern times, prior to the advent of money, the barter system of trade gave way to commodity money. In the early 20th century, fiat money, which is paper money, became widely acceptable.
- Money functions as a means of transactions as a store of wealth or savings and as a measure of value.
- The primary characteristic of money is its liquidity, the lubricant that makes any economy move.
- The banking system forms an integral part of the money supply process. Money supply is determined by the central bank.
- Currency in the hands of the public, government debt, commercial loans and bank deposits are major components of the money supply.
- There are varying degrees of liquidity or 'moneyness'. M1 and M3 are more widely used by central banks.
- The amount of central bank money in the official money supply statistics is determined by the fractional reserve, which involves the creation of credit through deposits by commercial bank which, in turn, increases the money supply through the deposit creation multiplier.
- A commercial bank can create credit in three ways: by accepting deposits and issuing cheques, by advancing loans and giving promissory notes and by buying and selling government debt.
- The money multiplier m is given by the formula $m = cu + 1/cu + r$, where cu is the currency ratio and r the reserve ratio.
- The money multiplier can be used to control the money supply by contracting or expanding the reserve ratio.
- The central bank indirectly influences the issue of money by the banking system through monetary transmissions. It does so by raising or lowering interest rates and the reserve ratios.
- When the government runs a deficit, it finances its expenditure by borrowing from the central bank.
- A drawback of the multiplier approach is that it gives the impression that changes in the quantity of money happen in a mechanical process. However, this is ambiguous, because the 'cu' the currency ratio reflects the qualities of currency the public choose to hold which is abehavioural factor that is beyond the central bank's control.

- The quantities of currency the public chooses to hold depend on the economic factors that change over time.
- The rate at which the RBI borrows money from commercial banks for a short term is the repo rate. If the central bank purchases bonds with the agreement that the seller will repurchase them in a short period of time it is the reverse repo.
- The central bank is responsible for maintaining stability in the economy. It manages inflation, employment and growth. To achieve these targets, it controls the rate of interest and the growth of money supply by using monetary policy instruments such as the reserve ratio, open market operations and the discount rate.

CASE STUDY

The Central Bank's Policy Announcement[11]

The dynamics of liquidity over the past nine months, since March 2010, has been very challenging for the market. The central bank of the country has decided to conduct open market auctions for the purchase of government securities for an aggregate amount of ₹50,000 crore to help banks tide over the liquidity crunch. As the prospect of the government's credit balance with the central bank rose to ₹1.50 lakh crore due to advance tax payments by the business sector, the liquidity situation appears to be worsening.

However, the midterm monetary policy announcement has left key policy rates; the repo rate (interest rate of 6.25% at which banks borrow from the RBI to tide over temporary liquidity mismatches) and the reverse repo rate (interest rate of 5.25% that the banks earn for deploying their surplus with the RBI) unchanged. The RBI also permanently reduced the quantum of government securities that they must mandatorily hold (statutory liquidity ratio or SLR) by one percentage point to 24% of their deposits. The amount of cash that the banks have to park with the RBI (the CRR) has also been retained at 6% of total deposits.

This policy announcement is unexpected, given the projection of a rise of 6.7% in inflation. A central bank statement said, 'At present several banks have raised deposit and lending interest rates that conveys unpredictability in both availability and cost of funds, making it difficult for the banking system to sustain credit delivery'.

After reading the text given in the case study, answer the following questions:

1. Will the central bank's policy decision to reduce the SLR to 24% cause a decrease in the commercial bank's credit creation capacity? Will this impact inflation levels in the country?
2. 'The midterm policy report by the central bank of the country has left the repo and reverse repo rates unchanged yet it has decided to conduct open market operations'. Why?
3. Do you think the policy announcement is unexpected? If so why?

[11] Case study prepared using material from 'Monetary review: RBI to Buy Back Government Securities from Banks' published in *The Hindu Business Line*, 7 December 2010.

KEYWORDS

Money
Fiat Money
Legal Tender
Demonetization
Central Bank
Open Market Operations
Balance Sheet
Liabilities
Assets

Required Reserves
Net Worth
Reserve Ratio
Cash Reserve Ratio
Statutory Liquidity Ratio
Excess Reserves
Run on Banks
Repo Rate
Reverse Repo Rate

CONCEPT CHECK

State if the following statements are true or false:

1. Money is wealth, which is a stock, it cannot be considered as income because income is a flow.
2. The central bank indirectly influences the issue of money by the banking system through monetary transmissions by raising or lowering interest rates and the reserve ratios.
3. The cash reserve ratio is the amount of funds that the banks have to keep with the RBI in relation to their deposits.
4. High-powered money is the central bank's currency along with government money which forms the monetary base.
5. M3 = currency with public + demand deposits with the banking system + other deposits with RBI + time deposits with the banking system.
6. The rate at which the RBI borrows short-term money from commercial banks is called the repo rate.
7. When a government finances its expenditure by printing money it is also called deficit financing.
8. When the central bank purchases bonds with the agreement that the seller will repurchase them in a short period of time, it is called the reverse repo.
9. The Statutory Liquidity Ratio is a specified percentage of a commercial bank's outstanding deposit or liabilities of liquid assets that they have to maintain with the RBI.
10. In order to lower interest, the RBI can buy enough bonds set at a higher price which will cause interest rates to fall.

DISCUSSION QUESTIONS

1. What is the need for a central bank in a modern economy?
2. What are the functions of money? Is money the same as wealth or is it same as income? If not why?

3. If, in an economy, the currency deposit ratio (cu) and high-powered money (H) are constant and we assume that the money multiplier holds what would happen to the money supply if the reserve ratio increased?

4. In an economy, the currency with the public is ₹4,000 crore and the bank's reserves are ₹1,000 crore. The currency deposit ratio is 0.4 and the central bank imposes a reserve ratio of 0.10. If we assume that the money multiplier holds, what will be the money supply of that country?

5. The following is an extract from the balance sheet of the Central Bank of Alarek. It is assumed that government money is negligible and can be ignored. If the central bank imposes a reserve ratio of 5% and if the money supply is Alarek $ 1957 million, calculate the currency deposit ratio of Alarek.

	Million Alarek $
Credit to government	500
Credit to bank	200
Government deposits	10
Other non-monetary liabilities	5
Net Worth	250
Credit to commercial sector	50
Foreign exchange assets	7
Other assets	35

CHAPTER

The Demand for Money

LEARNING OBJECTIVES

Upon completion of this chapter, the reader will be able to:

- Find the answer to the question why people demand money and the different motives for holding money.
- Understand Keynes Liquidity Preference Theory and its connection to the different motives for money demand.
- Comprehend the concept of the Classical Quantity Theory of Money and the role of the velocity of money.
- Find how the monetarists led by Freidman redefined the classical quantity theory of money and revived it.
- Know how the Portfolio Theory explains the demand for money in the risk–return consideration of a risk-averse investor.

7.1. INTRODUCTION: THE DEMAND FOR MONEY

In the previous chapter, we have discussed the definition of money, its functions and the definition of money supply. In this chapter, we look at the demand side of money. Why do people demand money and what influences their decision. In modern macroeconomic theory, money is of paramount significance. The classical economists believed that money had only two functions, namely, a medium of exchange and a unit of account. In Chapter 3, you read about Keynes' famous *The General Theory* and now you will see how he explained the demand for money. Keynes originally introduced the term 'liquidity preference' with regard to the demand for money. Liquidity refers to the ability to convert

The transaction demand for money arises out of the use of money for making regular payments and purchases.

The precautionary demand for money comes from the need to meet unexpected events.

a financial asset into cash and the term is connected to the LM curve. Keynes explained the importance of money demand and its role in macroeconomic fluctuations. He said that there were three reasons why people wanted money, namely, the transaction demand, the precautionary demand and the speculative demand, and these three motives were influenced by income and the interest rate.

The speculative demand for money evolves from the uncertainties about the value of the assets an individual holds.

The Classical school economists believed that people did not hold money for its sake and there existed a money illusion. Later, the neoclassical economists particularly Milton Freidman developed the Modern Quantity Theory of money, where he linked transactions and money on one side and the price and velocity on the other. First, we discuss the Keynesian explanation for the demand for money and later we look at the Classical view.

In Section 7.1, Keynes' proposals of analysing the demand for money are discussed and along with the opportunity cost of money. In Section 7.2, the classical Quantity Theory of Money is explored along with the role of the velocity of money and its importance in monetary policy. In Section 7.3, Tobin's Portfolio Theory of Demand for money is explained followed by the conclusion.

Keynes' proposed that there were following three main motives for holding money:

1. The *transaction motive* for money that arises from the use of money for making payments and purchases.
2. The *precautionary motive* for money that is driven by the desire to safeguard against unexpected events.
3. The *speculative motive* for money that comes from the uncertainties about the value of the assets an individual holds.

The theories of the demand for money are structured around the trade-offs between the advantage of holding money vis-à-vis earning interest on the cash or the cost of foregoing the earning.

7.1.1. The Transaction Demand

People hold money to buy goods and services, so the more the goods and services to be purchased, the greater is the demand to hold money. How much a person can spend will depend on his nominal income, the price of the commodity as well as one's spending habit. Keynes proposed that people held money for transactions.

The transaction demand happens due to the mismatch between receipts and payments, since not all payments occur at the same time. So money is held for future expenditure, but the amount of money to be held depends upon the trade-off between the loss of interest earned and the inconvenience of holding small amounts of cash.

Suppose a person's salary is ₹6000 per month and, on an average, he spends ₹200 per day. So, if he keeps all the money in the bank, on the second day, he would have ₹5800 on which he can earn interest until the third day when he withdraws another 200 leaving ₹5600 to earn a daily interest. In this case, he would earn interest for the days the money is retained in the bank, that would be the benefit, but the inconvenience of visiting the bank to withdraw money would be a transaction cost. On the other hand, he can withdraw his entire salary at the beginning of the month and lose the interest. In between these two extreme situations is one where the householder can withdraw every fortnight, or ever week. These alternative situations are illustrated in the Figures 7.1a to 7.1c.

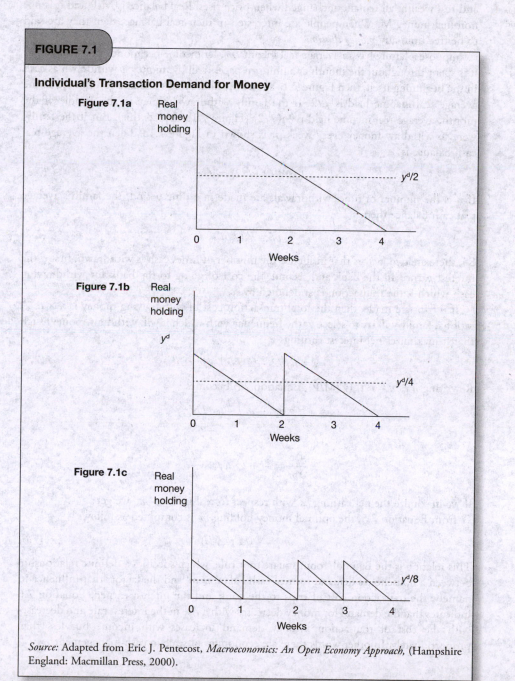

FIGURE 7.1

Individual's Transaction Demand for Money

Figure 7.1a

Figure 7.1b

Figure 7.1c

Source: Adapted from Eric J. Pentecost, *Macroeconomics: An Open Economy Approach,* (Hampshire England: Macmillan Press, 2000).

Money illusion; when
people believe that
nominal wages and
nominal prices increase
ignoring the effect of
inflation they are said to
have money illusion.

We have so far looked at *nominal* money but people are really interested in *real* money. The purchasing power of real money does not change when prices rise. Demand for *real* money does not change when the price level goes up, like the real interest rate, real income and real wealth, all remain unchanged when price rises. Real balance is M/P and it is not nominal money M. When people are interested in their real balance, then they are said to be free from any *money illusion*.

Suppose a family has an average real income m^r, let income per month be y^d, and all of it is spent throughout the month at a uniform pace. If all the money is withdrawn as cash in the beginning itself, then Figure 7.1a shows the household's demand for money. So the average real income held is $y^d/2$. If the family withdraws money in the middle of the month, average real income held is $\frac{1}{2}(y^d/2)$ (Figure 7.1b depicts this). But if the family were to withdraw money every week, it is shown in Figure 7.1c. Then the average real cash balance is

$$(\tfrac{1}{2})\,(\tfrac{1}{2})\,(y^d/2) = y^d/8 \tag{7.1}$$

If n is the number of times withdrawals are made in a time period, the family's average real cash balance then is

$$m^r = \tfrac{1}{2}(y^d/n) \tag{7.2}$$

So, there are two factors that influence the number of times cash is withdrawn, first, i the interest earned in the bank and second, the cost of going to the bank for withdrawing cash which is the transaction cost denoted by tc.

If n trips are made, then the total transaction cost of withdrawing money is $n \times tc$. A rational family will try to select n (the frequency with which it will withdraw money) such that it maximizes net interest earnings z.

$$z = i(y^d/2 - \tfrac{1}{2}\,y^d/n) - tc \times n \tag{7.3}$$

Rewriting n as $n = (\tfrac{1}{2})\,(y^d/M/P)$, Equation 7.3 becomes

$$z = \frac{i(y^d - m^r)}{2} - tc\,\frac{(1)y^d}{2m^r} \tag{7.4}$$

$$\frac{\delta z}{\delta m^r} = -i + \tfrac{1}{2}\,tcy^d \times \frac{1}{m^2} \tag{7.5}$$

If we maximize the net earning 'z' with respect to real income 'm^r' we get from Equation 7.5, the optimal money holding m^r is computed as follows

$$m^r = \sqrt{(\tfrac{1}{2}\,tc\,y^d/i)} \tag{7.6}$$

This relation is the Baumol Tobin square root rule, which specifies a definite relationship between a household's demand for real cash balances m^r and the factors that influence it, namely, the transaction cost of trips to the bank and the interest earned. Equation 7.6 indicates that the demand for money decreases with a rise in the interest rate and decreases with the cost of transaction. Money demand increases with income but less than proportionately. In other words there are economies of scale in cash management.

Two strong propositions emerge from the Baumol Tobin rule: first, if the *income elasticity of money demand* is ½, then the interest elasticity of money is –½. Empirical evidence however supports an income elasticity that is closer to one and that of the interest is closer to zero, although the signs remain the same. So this means that if income increases by 1%, money demand should go up by 1.2 percentage points. If on the other hand, the interest rates fall from 10.5 to 10%, it implies that it has fallen by 5% therefore the demand for money should go down by 2.5%, as people now prefer to hold less cash.

The income elasticity of money demand is the responsiveness of the household's demand for money to changes in income.

7.1.2. The Precautionary Demand

There is no issue of uncertainty per se in the transaction motive for holding money. But if individuals are not sure about the amount of payments to be made and the frequency with which it will be required, they are constrained to keep aside some money for unforeseeable events. Which is what is referred to in the phrase 'setting aside something for a rainy day'. The precautionary motive for holding money comes under this category. Keynes' theory of the precautionary demand for money implies that people save some wealth in the form of cash in case of an emergency need for funds. This motive is connected to money's function as a store of wealth. Moreover, households keep money aside when future income streams are uncertain.

The need to hold cash balances for unexpected events has come down considerably after the technological revolution with the proliferation of credit cards, debit cards and online payment facilities. In the developed or even in today's emerging economies, the financial sector has evolved and people do not have to hold cash. But in the less developed and unstable economies experiencing political disturbances, the precautionary demand for money is high. In times of natural calamities or in anticipation of emergencies, households retain cash balances. The precautionary demand for money is related positively to the number of transactions expected in the future. But if the income level is high, the number of transactions is likely to be greater and in that case, the precautionary demand for money is positively related to income Y.

However, even if one were to keep aside a sum of money for avoiding the inconvenience of illiquidity, there is a trade-off like in the case of the transaction demand for money. Cash holdings do not earn interest as Tobin argued, since the return on money is zero, but it is also a riskless asset, without the prospect of gain or loss.[1] But when interest rates rise, the price of bonds falls and here we are assuming that the alternative to keeping money as cash is holding bonds. Interest rates and existing bonds have an inverse relation which we have seen in chapter five.

Keynes proposed that when interest rates were high, more people would expect it to fall or bond prices to rise and would therefore want to hold bonds and less money. Thus, the demand for money declines as interest rates go up. Changes in bond prices also add a risk to holding bonds. In general, people can be assumed to be risk averse and so they

---

[1] J. Tobin, 'Liquidity Preference as Behaviour towards Risk', *Review of Economics Studies* 25, no. 2, (1958): 65–86.

do not put all their wealth into risky bonds and prefer to hold the relatively less risky asset cash. The third motive for holding money is *speculative* demand.

7.1.3. The Speculative Demand

The third motive for holding money that Keynes proposed was the speculative demand for money. He argued that individuals do not hold money merely for transactions only because there is no reward for holding cash. If a person bought a bond and earned interest he would prefer to do that. In other words the demand for money is interest sensitive.

When Keynes introduced the speculative demand for money, it was a clear departure from the earlier view of the need to hold money. Keynes argued that people held money not only for transactions and for unexpected expenditures, but also to avoid expected capital losses. Investments in bonds gave people an opportunity to earn capital gains, because if they perceived that the bond prices would go up, they would buy them and sell them later. However, if they thought that bond prices would fall, they would prefer to keep the cash and wait instead of suffering capital losses.

In this discussion, we are clearly not defining a specific maturity date for bond redemption and an interest quoted on the bond is simply the ratio of the annual coupon to the price of the bond p_b. If we set the coupon to one for simplicity, that gives the rate of interest 'i' as $I = 1/p_b$, and then the gross expected gain from investing in the bond for a certain time period, say one year would be

$$R = I + g = 1/p_b + (p_b^e - p_b)/p_b \tag{7.7}$$

$$= (1 + p_b^e - p_b)/p_b \tag{7.8}$$

R is the holding period to return that is widely used in finance comprising of yield, g is capital gains and p_b^e is the price of the bond expected at the end of the year. The anticipated capital gain is $(p_b^e - p_b)$, since there is no financial gain from holding cash, that is, the gain from keeping money is zero and so an investor will assess the advantage of holding money with that of holding a bond during the same time period. Speculators who expect the interest rate to fall would expect a capital gain, whereas other investors who expect the rate of interest to rise, will apprehend a capital loss. This uncertainty about the future course of interest is crucial in Keynes' speculative demand for money.

Now the speculator, who thinks that the rate of interest will fall with certainty, will buy bonds to reduce his money balance as long as R > 0, and he will sell them if R < 0. Remember, the relationship between bond prices and the rate of interest we saw in chapter five, the speculator will be indifferent between bonds and money when R = 0. So when

$$R = \frac{1 + (1/\tilde{i}) - (1/i)}{(1/i)} = 0 \tag{7.9}$$

Multiplying both sides by *1/I*, replacing one by $\tilde{i}/\tilde{i}$ and with some algebraic steps we get

$$i = \frac{\tilde{i}}{(1 + \tilde{i})} = \tilde{i} \tag{7.10}$$

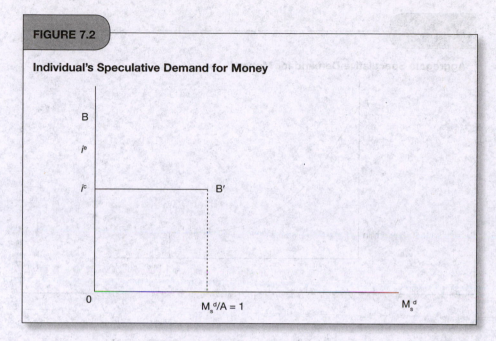

FIGURE 7.2

Individual's Speculative Demand for Money

This equation depicts the value of the rate of interest at which prospective gains from holding bonds is zero and is less than the value of the expected rate of interest itself. This rate of interest is called the critical rate of interest i^c. This denotes the point when people switch their *portfolio* from bonds to money. So if the current rate of interest is below i^c speculators will simply hold their entire portfolio in the form of cash. But if the rate of interest rises above this critical rate, speculators will hold all their wealth in bonds.

Portfolio is a collection of assets like bonds, stock cash owned by individual or firm.

Figure 7.2 shows an individual's speculative demand for money. It is a right-angled curve that is kinked at the critical level of the rate of interest.

$$M_s^d/A = 1$$

It can be argued that at any rate of interest below that of the critical level, capital losses can occur because the interest rate is expected to go back to i^e and bond prices move inversely with the interest rate. But at i^e the critical rate, the prospect of the bond coupon is just about enough to offset the capital loss. This is the reason for the box type curve. If all the individuals in the economy were to agree about the expected interest rate, then small movements around the critical level would create a step like aggregate speculative demand curve.

On the other hand, if speculators differed greatly in their view about the critical rate, the movement of the curve would be smoother as shown in Figure 7.3. Consequently, when the current rate of interest were to fall (or rise), only some investors would change their portfolio from bonds to money (or money to bonds).

Therefore, the aggregate demand for the speculative motive for money would resemble the downward sloping curve depicted in the Figure 7.3. One plausible rationale for this

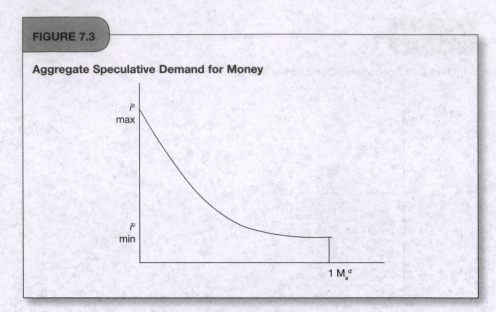

FIGURE 7.3

Aggregate Speculative Demand for Money

could be that the expectations of the interest rate are greatly influenced by current events and news, so it is unlikely that investors would continue to retain the same expectations. In this case, it becomes obvious that the speculative demand for money is a short-term phenomenon, as a change in the rate of interest may lead to large scale switching between bonds and money.

7.1.4. Opportunity Cost

We have seen in the discussions so far that the theories of demand for money are based on the fact that there is a trade-off between the benefits of holding cash versus the cost of doing so. M1, which is money currency, and current account in banks generally earn no interest or less interest than other assets. The higher the interest rate, the less likely is an individual going to retain cash holdings. In practice, the cost of holding can be measured by the difference between the interest rate paid on money (zero) and the interest rate paid on holding a comparable asset such as a savings account or certificate of deposit for corporations. The interest rate on money is referred to as the own rate of interest and the *opportunity cost* of holding money is equal to the difference between the yield on other assets and the own rate of interest.

> The opportunity cost of holding money is the difference between interest on money and the yield on any other asset.

Individual investors retain a portfolio of assets. It is not unreasonable to think that he/she would like to hold those assets that have the highest returns. Sometimes that could be based on recommendations of a certain stock being a hot favourite with a chance of becoming double in value in one year. But many investors are wary of hot tips and recognize the possibility of huge capital losses if the entire investment is made in a single risky asset, whose prices change in an unpredictable manner.

Money is safe as its nominal value is certain and hence predictable. Of course, when the rate of inflation is uncertain, the real value of money is also uncertain and money is no longer a safe asset. Even so, the uncertainties about the value of equity shares is so much larger than the uncertainty about the rate of inflation, that money can be treated as a relatively safe asset with the exception of say countries who are in the grip of hyperinflation.

Tobin argued in an explanation of money as a safe asset in the essential notion of the framework of demand for money with reference to individual's attitude to risk.[2] In his article, 'Liquidity Preference as a Behaviour Towards Risk', he has shown that an increase in the expected return on other assets—an increase in the opportunity cost of holding money implying the loss of return for holding money—lowers money demand. In contrast, an increase in the riskiness of the return on other assets increases the demand for money.

The demand for a safe asset is generated by the degree of *risk aversion* of an investor. However, that asset is not likely to be M1. From the yield and risk point of view, it is obvious that savings deposits or time deposits have the same risk as currency, yet the former have a higher yield. Given the same level of risk, and with the yields of savings deposits or fixed deposits being higher than currency or demand deposits, in the portfolio diversification angle, the demand for money will be M2 in which the former is included rather than M1 or the latter. The classical school's quantity theory of money is explored next.

> Risk aversion is an investor's reluctance to hold risky assets in his/her investment portfolio and to prefer assets with lower returns.

7.2. THE QUANTITY THEORY OF MONEY

The quantity of money in an economy is closely related to the number of times rupees are exchanged in each transaction. More transactions mean more money is in demand. There is a link between transactions and money on the one side and the price and velocity of money on the other (the speed of the movement of money).

$$\text{Money} \times \text{Velocity} = \text{Price} \times \text{Transactions}$$

$$M \times V = P \times T \tag{7.11}$$

This is the *quantity equation* as an identity.

The right hand side of Equation 7.11 shows T, the total number of transactions during one year multiplied by the price 'P'. 'T' represents how many times the goods and services are exchanged for money in a particular period of time. So the product of P with T indicates the number of rupees that change hands in say one year. V is the velocity of money going from one person to another and to another and so on. M is the quantity of money.

---

[2] Tobin, 'Liquidity Preference as Behaviour Towards Risk', 65–86.

Suppose in one year 100 bags of one kg of rice are sold and the price of one kg is ₹25, which is P, T equals 100 bags per year, hence the total number of rupees exchanged is

$$PT = ₹25 \times 100 = ₹2,500 \text{ per year}$$

$$V = PT/M = 250 \text{ times per year}$$

The right hand side of the equation is ₹2,500 and if the total money supply is ₹10, then we can calculate the velocity of money in the country as ₹2,500/10 = 250. The left hand side of the equation shows the money used to make the transactions.

Suppose the money supply is ₹12.50, then the velocity of money in the country will be ₹2,500/12.5 = 200. In this situation, the velocity is lower.

Therefore, for ₹2,500 of transactions per year with a money supply of ₹10, the money will change hands 250 times in a year. When the money supply increases to 12.5, the velocity falls to 200. The four variables *money supply, transaction, price* and *velocity* are interlinked so that if one changes, the other must also change to maintain the identity. On the other hand, if the quantity of money goes up, then the prices will also go up, providing the velocity of money and the number of transaction remains the same.

The Velocity of Money is the speed with which money circulates in the economy. It significantly influences monetary policy and the money supply. If people were to hold money in their wallets after receiving their salary cheques and spent it throughout the month, then money would move slowly from one person to another. On the other hand if people needed to go to the bank to withdraw money every week or every fortnight, the speed of money changing hands would be more and so the velocity of money would be faster. In a metropolitan city, money changes hands quickly, as the same amount of money (money supply) is able to support more transactions. Formally, velocity is defined as the ratio of GDP to the money supply.

The left-hand side of Equation 7.11 shows money used for making transactions. V is the transactions velocity of money. Since the quantity equation is an identity, its usefulness is that if one of the variables changes, the other must also change to maintain the identity. However, when economists observe the role of money in the economy, they find that measuring the number of transactions is difficult, so instead of the total output of the economy Y is used. This is simply because as more goods and services are produced, more goods and services are also purchased and sold.

If Y represents the total amount of output in the economy and P is the price of one unit of output, then the rupee value of output is PY. This concept was discussed in chapter two in the national income accounts. Then Y is the real GDP and P is the deflator and hence PY is the nominal GDP.

The *Quantity Theory of Money* provides a simple way to organize our thoughts linking the relationship between money, price and output. The real output is taken to be fixed because the economy is in full equilibrium and velocity is assumed to be more or less constant. Neither of these premises holds in reality, but it is interesting to see where these arguments lead us. If both velocity and income are fixed, then it follows that the price

Velocity of money is the ratio of GDP to the money supply in an economy.

The Quantity Theory of Money states that the price level is directly related to the quantity of money in an economy MV = PQ with V is the velocity is the real GDP.

level is proportional to the money stock. Hence the relation between price level and the other factors is:

$$P = (V \times M)/Y$$

If V is constant, changes in money supply translate into proportional changes in nominal GDP, that is, P × Y. In effect, the Classical Quantity Theory is nothing but a theory of inflation. So when Y is fixed, changes in money cause changes in the overall price level.

The Classical Quantity Theory of Money had proposed that the nominal interest rate is the opportunity cost of holding money, so it follows from the premise that the demand for money falls as the rate of interest rises. It is the interest rate that enables the demand for and supply of money to be in equilibrium. In this context, inflation implies that money loses its purchasing power, which creates the cost of holding money. The higher the rate of inflation, the lower the amount of real balances a household will keep.

7.2.1. Monetarism

The monetarists, whose leading thinker was Milton Friedman, evolved a different approach called the Modern Quantity Theory of Money. At the heart of monetarism is the quantity theory of money. Friedman after examining the historical relationship between money supply and prices concluded that inflation was always a monetary phenomenon[3]. If money supply were to rise in the long-run, faster than the potential output of the economy, inflation was to be the inevitable outcome.

In the long-run, the Monetarists claim that in the equation MV = PY, both velocity (V) and output (Y) are independently determined. They are not affected by changes in the money supply M, so it only impacts prices P.

Two important conclusions drawn by them are: First, if the money supply rises, then the resulting rise in aggregate demand will lead not only to rising prices but also, for a few months, to higher output and employment. Soon people's expectations will adjust, workers and firms would expect higher wages and prices and thus, after a while, the extra demand would be fully absorbed by inflation while output and employment will fall back again.

Second, reducing the rate of growth of the money supply would cause inflation to come down without leading to any long-run increases in unemployment. Though it would lead to higher unemployment temporarily, as the demand for goods and labour fall. However, once the wage and inflation have adjusted downwards, unemployment would be eliminated.

The Monetarists believe that inflation is damaging to the economy because it leads to uncertainty for firms and industry who then bring down their investments. They further argue that inflation reduces the country's competitiveness in international trade. We will discuss these issues in chapter thirteen. The Monetarist prescription was the government

[3] Milton Friedman, 'The Demand for Money: Some Theoretical and Empirical Results', *Journal of Political Economy* 67, no. 4, (1959): 327–51.

should keep a tight control over the money supply and advocate targets for money supply, something that is a contrast to the Classical school's prescription of complete non-intervention of the government that is *laissez faire*.

The Monetarists went back to the Classical theory as the basis of their analysis and extended it to explain the phenomenon of stagflation that has plagued both developed countries and developing ones like India. *Stagflation* is a combination of low economic growth and hence combines stagnation and inflation. This characteristic feature was visible in different parts of the world during the decade of the 1970s. Does risk influence the demand for money? This question is examined next.

BOX 7.1   Trends in the Velocity of Money in India[4]

In 1987, two economists Bordo and Jonung analysed the predictability of the velocity of money for five countries, namely, USA, UK, Canada, Sweden and Norway and found that the velocity followed a random walk, which means that it could not be predicted. This contradicted the earlier belief of a predictable velocity of money. In India Kamiah and Paul (1987) found that the velocity behaviour of narrow money did not follow the random walk. Rather their findings supported the monetarist argument that velocity can be a behavioural function, so changes in the stock of money lead to predictable changes in the nominal income.

In India, soon after the nationalization of banks, commercial banks rapidly expanded their branches. A decline in the population per bank branch implied greater spread of banking and more monetization which was expected to be negatively correlated with the velocity of money. While, a decline in the share of monetary assets in gross household savings in financial assets indicated more financial sophistication, which was supposed to be positively correlated with the velocity of money. These are called 'institutional variables' and Rami[5] used these 'institutional variables' along with real income and interest rates to create a velocity function. He tested the Monetarist hypothesis of predictability of velocity through past accelerations in money growth. The velocity function was estimated using annual data for broad money of velocity covering the period 1972–2004.

Money supply aggregates, namely, narrow money (M1) and broad money (M3) were used reflecting the velocity of narrow money (V1) and the velocity of broad money (V3). The study was for the period 1950–51 to 2004–05 and was based on income measured by the nominal GDP. For analysing the trends in the velocity of money, the time was divided into 5 periods.

Rami concluded first that the velocity of M3 was consistently lower than that of M1, and this gap between them widened (see Figure 7.4). Second, the relative variation in the velocity of M3 was higher than that of M1 (see CV values Table 7.1). This was mainly because of the heterogeneous composition of broad money relative to narrow money. The fall in the income velocity occurred due to the faster growth of the money supply as compared to the growth of

---

[4] The text in the Box 7.1 has been drawn from Gaurang Rami, 'Velocity of Money Function for India: Analysis and Interpretations', *TIMS QUEST* 1, no. 1 (2010). Available at: http://ssrn.com/abstract=1783473

[5] G. Rami, 'Velocity of Money Function for India: Analysis and Interpretation', *TIMS Quest* 1, no. 1 (2010): 15–26.

TABLE 7.1

Trends in the Velocity of Money in the Indian Economy (from 1950–51 to 2004–05)

		@Variability as Measured by Coefficient of Variation (C.V.)			
Year	*Narrow Money*		*Broad Money*		*Gap*
Period	*Average*	*Variability@*	*Average*	*Variability@*	*V1 & V3*
1951–60	5.5505	0.0609	4.4607	0.06777	1.089
1961–70	6.2589	0.0595	4.4490	0.05008	1.809
1971–80	5.9149	0.0452	3.4088	1.5036	2.506
1981–90	6.1604	0.0351	2.2967	0.08848	3.863
1991–2005	5.4234	0.0600	1.7421	1.5018	3.681
		Over All Time Period			
1951–2005	5.8218	0.769	3.1326	3.804	2.689

Source: Gaurang Rami, 'Velocity of Money Function for India: Analysis and Interpretations', 2010.

FIGURE 7.4

Trends in the Average Velocity of Narrow Money (V1) and Broad Money (V3) in India during 1950–51 to 2004–05

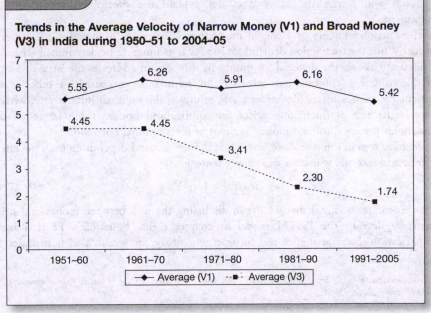

GDP at current market prices. The fall in the income velocity of broad money was due to the faster growth of broad money in comparison to narrow money (Omkarnath and Srutikantha).[6]

Interestingly, the velocity of broad money [V3] in India turns out to be highly predictable, which corroborates the Monetarist proposition. Prior knowledge of a set of explanatory variables such as real income, interest rates, the spread of commercial bank branch networks and past monetary expansions together can explain more than 98% of the variation in the velocity of broad money. Comparing the estimated velocity functions, with and without the 'institutional' variables, showed that the long-run real income elasticity of money demand was significantly reduced when 'institutional' variables were added to the conventional explanatory variables such as real income and the interest rate. These are interesting findings for policy-makers in RBI.

7.3. THE DEMAND FOR MONEY AS BEHAVIOUR TOWARDS RISK**

Keynes' theory of demand for money centres on the assumption that investors expect the interest rates to return to a normal level. The premise was that individuals would hold all their wealth in bonds, besides their requirement for transactions, as long as the interest rate was above the critical level. Once the interest were to fall below that, they would shift all their wealth to money and this assumption would have been valid in the early 20th century when Keynes wrote his treatise. It has become increasingly obvious that investors hold a variety of assets in their portfolio and interest rates in general have been increasing steadily in throughout the last century. Today, investors hold both cash balances as well as bonds and Keynesian theory does not explain the portfolio diversification of investment.

The Portfolio Theory of Demand for Money is based on its function as a store of wealth. While the transaction demand for money is assumed to be determined separately as discussed above, the demand for money in this section addresses the issue of money offering different combinations of risk and returns as compared to other assets. Particularly, money offers the holder a safe return as the nominal interest rate, whereas there is the risk of fluctuating prices for equities and bonds. Tobin suggested that households preferred to hold money as a part of their optimal portfolio.[7]

We have seen in our discussion so far that money demand depends on both the rate of interest and income, which we can simply write as

$$(M/P)^d = L\,(i, Y) \tag{7.12}$$

It is this money demand that we use in discussing the link between money and prices when we develop the IS–LM model in chapter eight. Equation 7.12 is a useful simplification, because it uses real income as a proxy for wealth and it includes the

---

[6] G. Omkarnath and P. Srutikantha, 'Velocity Circulation of Money: A Case of India', *Applied Finance ICFAI University Press* (2006): 52–64.
[7] Tobin, 'Liquidity Preference as Behaviour towards Risk', 65–86.

nominal interest rate as the only return variable. Note that i is the sum of real returns on bonds and the expected rate of inflation that you see in the next equation.

The Portfolio Theory of Demand for Money predicts that money demand depends on the risks and returns associated with money and the various types of assets that households hold instead of money. Moreover, money demand should depend on total wealth, since wealth is reflected in the size of the portfolio to be allocated between money and other assets. The function of money demand for instance can be written as

$$(M/P)^d = L(r_s, r_b, \Pi^e, W) \tag{7.13}$$

where r_s and r_b are the expected real returns on stocks and bonds respectively, Π^e is the expected inflation rate and W is real wealth. If r_b or r_s increases, then the demand for money falls, as other assets become more attractive. Similarly, a rise in Π^e reduces the demand for money because money becomes less attractive as a vehicle of investment. On the other hand, a rise in W increases the demand for money simply because higher wealth means the ability to possess larger portfolios.

To understand whether the portfolio theories of money are useful in explaining, we have to see if we are considering narrow money M1 or broad money M3. M1 includes currency and bank deposits like the current account. Other assets such as Treasury Bills, Certificates of Deposit (CD) and Money Market Mutual Funds (MMMF) earn higher rates of interest and yet have the same risk characteristics as cash. So, according to the portfolio theory, M1 is a dominated asset that has lower returns with the same levels of risk. That is, if side-by-side, we consider aforementioned treasury bills and similar assets mentioned. The Portfolio Theory cannot explain why people demand money or cash.

But if we look at M3 for instance which include the savings account and MMMF, that are relatively less risky than equity shares or bonds, then we can easily understand how the Portfolio Theory of Money Demand can be plausible in explaining broad money. So the theory helps to explain why households prefer to hold M3 assets instead of risky assets like equity shares or bonds simply because of the risk–return consideration.

Let us examine this: money is a safe asset but its nominal return is zero and there is no capital gain or loss if we hold money. If an investor is risk averse, he would prefer to sacrifice higher return for bonds and hold money for a reduction of risk. This is explained in Figure 7.5. The risk–return plane is represented in the upper quadrant where the expected return to the portfolio is measured on the vertical axis and its riskiness in the horizontal axis. The lower quadrant represents the allocation of the portfolio between bonds and money which results in each risk–return combination. If the investor holds only money, then his portfolio will be at point O. As the holdings of bonds (B) increases, the portfolio moves downwards until point W which represents the maximum wealth the investor may have. The schedule B in the lower quadrant shows the relationship between total risk of the portfolio and the proportion held in bonds.

U_1, U_2 and U_3 are indifference curves indicating the level of utility the investor gets. The curves are upward sloping to demonstrate the risk-averse investor. As the investor moves upwards from U_1 to U_3 he enjoys higher utility.

The steepness of the curve on the right hand side shows the rising aversion to risk. The line OT, tangent to the indifference curve U_2 at E represents a portfolio OB_e amount of

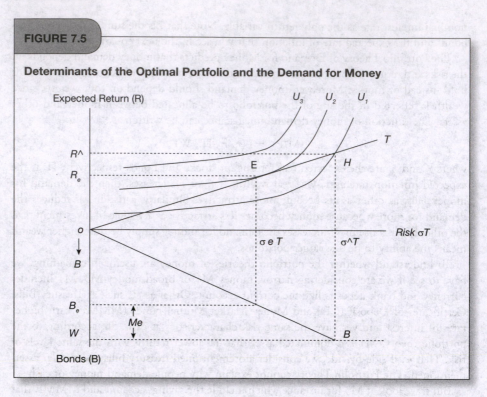

FIGURE 7.5

Determinants of the Optimal Portfolio and the Demand for Money

bonds and WB$_e$ of money shown by M$_e$ where total wealth is OW. So the level of risk tolerance of the investor and the size of wealth will determine his demand for money and bonds in his portfolio. This explanation is the demand for money theory developed by Tobin in his words 'behaviour towards risk'.

7.4. CONCLUSION

In this chapter, we have looked at why households want to hold money? What motivates them to keep cash in hand? Keynes had explained the demand for money from the point of view of what function money plays in our lives. Is it a medium of exchange or a store of wealth? Keynes said both these as well as the possibility of facing uncertainties drive individuals to keep cash. They need to hold money for their day to day purchases and payments and that was the transaction demand for money. The question of how much is demanded was answered by simply three things the disposable real income, interest earned in savings bank or a bond and the cost of visiting the bank to withdraw cash. The precautionary motive was simply driven by uncertainties or unanticipated expenditures.

But households were also concerned about capital losses from their investments and this was the speculative demand for money. The opportunity cost of keeping cash in hand also was an important factor. The Classical economists however, believed in the two functions of money: as a medium of exchange and as a unit of account. They proposed that the product of money supply with velocity or the speed with which money changes hands was equal to the price level multiplied by the number of transactions or MV = PT. But, as we progress new technology and new innovations evolve. A discussion on the velocity of money in India is given in Box 7.1.

Households are also driven by their attitude towards risk and from this, we find the portfolio theory of money demand. The wealth of an individual household can be in the form of cash, or financial or real assets. The traditional definition of money is transforming as credit cards, debit cards and online shopping become increasingly popular. So, the transactions demand for money is not for cash but for card and internet access. We now see there is a need to review how money should be defined.

Let us proceed to understand how the investment–savings schedule and the liquidity of money interact to portray the macroeconomic structure of a country with the help of the IS–LM curves in the next chapter.

SUMMARY

- The Classical economists believed that money had two functions, namely, as a medium of exchange and a unit of account.
- Keynes' theory of money demand was based on money being a medium of exchange and a store of wealth.
- The theories of demand for money are structured around the trade-off between the advantages of holding money vis-à-vis earning interest on the cash.
- The *transaction motive* for the demand for money comes from the use of money for payments and purchases.
- The demand for *real m*oney does not change when the price level goes up. If people are interested in real balances then they are said to be free from *money illusion*.
- The number of times cash is withdrawn and the interest earned in the bank, influences cash withdrawals.
- The Baumol Tobin square root rule specifies a precise relation between a household's demand for real cash balances with the transaction cost of trips to the bank and interest earned.
- The *precautionary motive* for money demand is driven by the need to meet unexpected expenditures. It is related positively to income levels and the number of transactions anticipated.
- The *speculative motive* for the for demand money is due to uncertainties of the asset *value* of households.

- Keynes argued that households invested in bonds to earn capital gains. If they expected bond prices to increase, they would buy bonds and vice versa.
- At a critical rate of interest $\tilde{r}$ the prospect of the bond coupon is just enough to offset the capital loss.
- The cost of holding can be measured by the difference between the interest rate paid on money (zero) and the interest rate paid on having a savings account.
- The interest rate on money is referred to as the own rate of interest and the opportunity cost of holding money is equal to the difference between the yield on other assets and the own rate.
- The Classical Quantity Theory of Money states that the quantity of money is closely related to the number of times it changes hands. Greater the transaction, higher is the money demanded.
- There is a link between transactions and money on the one side and price and velocity (speed of movement of money). Money × Velocity = Price × Transactions.
- The Monetarists, led by Milton Friedman, claimed that in the equation MV = PY, both V velocity and Y output are independently determined and are unaffected by changes in the money supply M.
- The Monetarists argued that if the money supply rises, aggregate demand also rises in the short-run, leading to higher output, employment and inflation as well.
- In the short-run, lower money supply will cause inflation to fall without any long-run rise in unemployment.
- The Portfolio Theory of Demand for Money is based on its function as a store of wealth. Money offers a safe return, whereas equities and bonds are risky. The level of an investor's risk tolerance and the size of his wealth determine his demand for money and the financial assets in his portfolio.

CASE STUDY

Is the Money Supply More than the Demand for Money?[8]

The Annual Report of the Reserve Bank of India (RBI) is perhaps the most authentic statement on the state of the economy and the possible solutions to its various problems. A. Seshan, an eminent economic consultant says two outstanding features of the report are the high standard of analysis diagnosing the economy and transparency in advising the Government. About transparency, he quotes, 'The Reserve Bank conducted the market borrowing programme with the objective of *minimizing the cost of borrowing* for the government

[8] The case study is compiled from A. Seshan, 'RBI Allows Too Much Money Supply', *The Hindu Business Line* (4 September 2012). Available at http://www.thehindubusinessline.com/todays-paper/tp-opinion/article3859852.ece

while pursuing debt maturity profiles that posed a low rollover risk'. The debt buybacks under the Open Market Operations (OMO) are really Debt Management Operations (DMO). OMO has a monetary objective, while the DMO a fiscal one. After all, as a banker to the government, it has the duty of getting the best terms. But looking at the money supply, the basic question is whether the estimated demand for money is effective in ensuring price stability.

He believes that the rising inflationary pressure in India is partly contributed by the RBI's overestimation of the demand for money in the economy. The Central Bank may need to focus on the factors that determine the demand for money in the economy so that it can estimate the required money supply more effectively to maintain stability in the market.

Money demand is defined as the average M(3) for the year and is influenced by real income (nominal income minus inflation) in terms of GDP at constant market prices and the price level as captured by the WPI. Every percentage change in the WPI results in a change in demand for money by almost the same percentage point. It means the absence of 'money illusion'. Keynesian macroeconomic literature has dealt with money illusion or its absence among the public as one of the determinants for policy-making in such areas as wages. Money illusion implies that people are concerned more with their nominal incomes, than their real incomes, which is the purchasing power of money.

According to Wassily Leontief, Keynes assumes that workers suffered from money illusions.[9] So they did not understand the effect of prices on real wages and thus willingly supplies labour when real wages fell. But that does not seem to be the case for the organized sector in India, where workers are aware of the significance of real wages, looking at the contracts relating dearness allowances to price changes. In the agricultural sector too, farmers agitate increasing minimum support prices for their crops whenever the costs of inputs go up. It is obvious therefore that there is no money illusion in India.

The income elasticity of demand for money (IEDM) is estimated to be 1.3. It means that for every percentage increase in real GDP, the demand for money rises by 1.3%. In estimating the growth in money supply required vis-à-vis demand in recent years, to preserve equilibrium in the markets, the RBI has been utilizing the IEDM as an input in recent times at a level above 1.3, resulting in excess money supply.

After reading the case study answer the following questions:

1. Is there a contradiction in the Reserve Bank of India's role in open market operations and debt management operations?
2. The Classical Quantity Theory of Money proposes that people have money illusion. Was the same view held by J. M. Keynes? If people in India had money illusion then would there be a large number of unemployed in the labour market?
3. According to the writer what is one of the important factors causing inflation in India?

---

[9] Wassily W. Leontief, 'The Fundamental Assumptions of Mr Keynes in his Monetary Theory of Unemployment', *The Quarterly Journal of Economics* 5, no. 1, (1936): 192–97.

KEYWORDS

Transaction demand

Precautionary demand

Speculative demand

income elasticity of money demand

Money illusion

Portfolio

Opportunity cost

Own rate of interest

Risk aversion

Velocity of money

Quantity theory of money

Stagflation

CONCEPT CHECK

State whether the following statements are true or false:

1. The Classical economists believed that money had three functions namely as a medium of exchange, as a unit of account and as a store of wealth.
2. For transaction demand for money, the trade-off is between the loss of interest earned by holding cash and the inconvenience of holding small amounts of cash.
3. The velocity of money does not significantly influence monetary policy and money supply.
4. Money is safe because its nominal value is known and predictable, but, when the rate of inflation is uncertain, the real value of money is also uncertain, then money is not a safe asset.
5. The Monetarists like the Classical economists prescribed the government to keep a tight control over money supply and advocated targets for money supply.
6. The Portfolio Theory of the Demand for Money is based on its function as a medium of exchange and a unit of account.
7. Keynes argued that people held money not only for transactions and for unexpected expenditures, but also to avoid expected capital losses and this is called the precautionary demand for money.

DISCUSSION QUESTIONS

1. Discuss the factors that influence a family's decision to hold a real balance. What are the key factors that govern a household's demand for money?
2. If the rate of inflation goes up, how will it affect the demand for money? Will households demand more real balances? Explain this in the context of money illusion.

3. Using the Baumol Tobin model,
   i.   Given your disposable income and the
   ii. Amount of purchases you make with cash as against use of cheques and credit cards annually

   What factors do you need to take into account for estimating how many times you visit the bank to withdraw money? Can you calculate your transaction cost?

4. How do you define the opportunity cost of holding money? Explain with reference to the transaction demand for money.

5. Why do people invest in bonds? What influences their decision to buy bonds or sell them?

6. Do individuals have the same attitude towards risk? If not, why not? What factors impact an investor's investment decisions? When does an investor prefer to hold cash instead of bonds?

7. What does the Classical Quantity Theory of Money propose? How is it different form Friedman's Quantity Theory?

8. Is the velocity of money high or low during a recession? Why?

9. Can the Reserve Bank of India influence the velocity of money?

10. How does Tobin's Portfolio Theory of Demand for Money explain an individual's behaviour in holding money?

8
CHAPTER

The IS–LM Model: The Demand Side of the Economy

8.1. INTRODUCTION TO THE IS–LM MODEL

In this chapter, the financial sector is introduced into the simple Keynesian model that we discussed in Chapter 3. Since the financial sector was excluded from the model, we did not observe the interplay between the real and the financial sides of the economy. This is a lacuna that needs to be filled, since, all policy-making by the central bank uses the links between the real or the goods market and the financial sector. We will see how the government's *fiscal policies* and the central bank's monetary policies interact and influence the macroeconomy in this and the following chapters. The IS–LM model that will be described here essentially adds the financial sector to the simple Keynesian model.

The basic IS–LM model, however, still retains some of the important characteristics of the simple Keynesian model. The price level is kept constant, so that the *aggregate supply curve* is horizontal implying that the costs are not rising in the price–output space. Equilibrium output is again where the demand curve cuts the horizontal supply curve in the price–income space. An *expansionary fiscal policy* through increased government spending shifts the demand curve rightwards, thereby increasing output. The government's increased spending causes an increase in the demand for goods and services and leads to more output and employment.

However, the construction of the demand curve in the IS–LM model is more intricate than the simple Keynesian model we encountered earlier. The characteristics and the conditions of the goods market and the money market enter into the creation of demand and the construction of the demand curve. The demand curve can be shifted by government spending as well as by changes in the money supply, and in the former case, the multiplier effect will not be the same as in the simple Keynesian model.

The name or title IS–LM refers to two curves, the IS investment savings curve which represents equilibrium in the goods market and the LM liquidity of money curve which represents equilibrium in the money market. In this chapter, we develop the IS–LM framework which lies at the foundation of macroeconomics today. The groundwork for this was already laid in Chapter 3, now the financial sector represented by the money market, the influence of the interest rate on investment as well as consumption and the effect of price are all incorporated to demonstrate how the demand side of the macro economy works. In Section 8.2, the nature and slope of IS and LM curves is discussed. Section 8.3 explores the way interest and output are determined in the model followed by the construction of the *aggregate demand curve* in Section 8.4. The adjustment to the balance of payment over time in the LM curve is explained with the conclusion in Sections 8.5 and 8.6, respectively. In the next section, the aggregate demand curve is built-up using the IS–LM curves.

> Fiscal policy is government policy with respect to government purchases, transfer payments and the tax structure.

> Aggregate supply curve represents the relationship between the amount of final goods and services produced in an economy and the price level.

> Expansionary fiscal policy is government's expenditure that induces demand for goods and services and creates jobs, this stimulates the economy to grow or expand.

> The aggregate demand curve measures the demand for total output of the economy at each value of the aggregate price level.

8.2. ELEMENTS OF THE IS–LM MODEL

8.2.1. What is the IS–LM Model?

The IS–LM model consists of equilibrium conditions for the goods market and the money market. The IS curve represents equilibrium in the goods market, while the LM curve represents equilibrium in the money market. We need to combine the *asset market* equilibrium with the goods market equilibrium. The model can be in full equilibrium only when the supply of the stocks of money and bonds match the demand for assets. The assets markets however will be in equilibrium only when the goods market is in

> Assets market is where financial assets like stocks bonds, government treasury bills are bought and sold.

equilibrium that is, when the supply of goods matches the expenditure on goods so that there are no additions or declines in stock by the firms.

It is obvious then, that the intersection of the IS and the LM curves, which is shown in Figure 8.1, in the interest rate–output (r–Y) space, represents simultaneous equilibrium in the goods and the money markets. From the IS–LM diagram, we obtain the levels of the interest rate and output, which are consistent with the simultaneous equilibrium in the goods and the money markets. The equilibrium output 'Y', obtained from the IS–LM diagram, can be also shown to coincide with the equilibrium output in the aggregate demand and aggregate supply diagram drawn in the price–output (P–Y) space.

To give a taste of things to come, we briefly describe now how the IS–LM apparatus relates to the usual demand–supply diagram. The exact nature of the slopes of the curves and of their shifts with policies and so on will be derived later. Here we take these aspects of the IS and LM curves for granted.

FIGURE 8.1

The IS–LM Apparatus and the Aggregate Demand–Supply Diagram

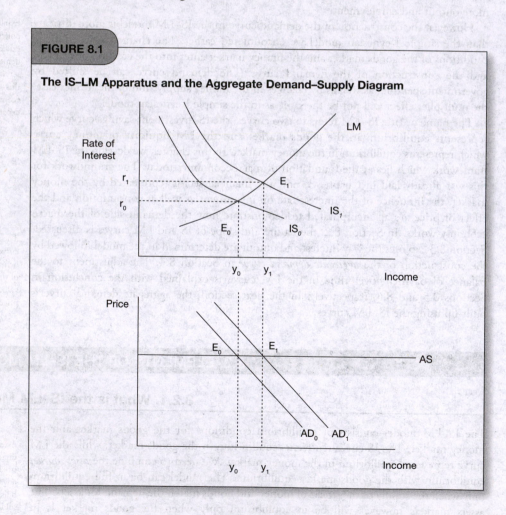

In Figure 8.1, the goods market equilibrium curve (IS) is drawn with a negative slope, and the money market equilibrium curve (LM) is drawn with a positive slope in the rate of interest and income (r–Y) space. We will derive the slopes of these curves below. The intersection of these curves gives the equilibrium output Y_0 and the equilibrium interest rate r_0 (at which equilibrium prevails in both these markets). This output Y_0 is also the equilibrium output level in the AD–AS diagram drawn directly below the IS–LM diagram in Figure 8.1.

Notice that the aggregate demand curve AD has been drawn with a negative slope. The reason for such a slope for the AD curve, which is quite different from that underlying the microeconomic demand curve for an individual commodity, will be discussed later. We can state now that the AD curve is constructed and its slope derived from both the IS and the LM curves, something which was not possible in the simple Keynesian model without the market for money.

Now, consider a policy which shifts the IS curve to the right. We will see later that an expansionary fiscal policy will achieve this, as well as other developments such as an increase in *net exports*. The new equilibrium is E_1 in the IS–LM as well as the demand–supply diagram in the upper and lower blocks of Figure 8.1. The new equilibrium output level is Y_1.

The shift of the IS curve also leads to a shift of the aggregate demand curve, the extent of the shift corresponding to the new multiplier in this model. We will see that the multiplier in this model is less than in the basic model of Chapter 3. The reason for this is that as income rises following government expansionary policies, the interest rate also rises (from r_0 to r_1 in Figure 8.1), reducing investments and (the increase in) output.

> Net export is the difference between the country's exports and imports.

8.2.2. The IS–LM Model, and the Macro-Demand Curve vs the Micro-Demand Curve

Let us clarify the difference between the basic Keynesian model of Chapter 3 and the IS–LM model. When doing so, remember that we are dealing with only one aggregate good. If there were two goods, the demand curve for one of the goods could be shown to be downward sloping, based on the price substitution effect in demand. But when there is only one good, as in Chapter 3, and the only market considered is the goods market, there is no price effect on demand and there is no downward slope for the macro-demand curve as well.

However, now, in this chapter, the money market is added to the model of Chapter 3. We will see later that this addition (of the financial side in the form of the money market) gives the macro-demand curve whose slope we could intuitively expect to be downward from the left to the right in the price–output diagram.

The supply side in the basic IS–LM model is no different from that in the simple Keynesian model. But the demand side is more complex. The demand curve is built up from the IS curve representing goods market equilibrium and the LM curve representing money market equilibrium. We now discuss the IS and the LM curves in detail, in turn.

8.2.3. Goods Market Equilibrium: The IS Curve

The goods market equilibrium condition equates aggregate demand, as set out in Chapter 3, to total output or national income 'Y' (note that after clarifying national accounting concepts in Chapter 2, we do not differentiate between GDP and national income).

$$Y = C + I + G + NX \tag{8.1}$$

The difference here, compared to the basic Keynesian model of Chapter 3 is that investment 'I' is not exogenous here. Rather, investment is modelled as a function of the interest rate. When the interest rate rises, it will be costlier for firms to access funds for investment. So, we can write

$$I = I_0 - br \tag{8.2}$$

where I_0 is autonomous investment not related to the interest rate 'r' and b measures the responsiveness of investment spending to the interest rate, with b > 0. If it is relatively large, then a small increase in the interest rate will lead to a substantial fall in investment. We omit for the moment the responsiveness of investment to income for simplification.

Then, we can write the goods market equilibrium condition from Chapter 3 as

$$Y = A_0 + c(1 - t)Y - br \tag{8.3}$$

where A_0 is autonomous spending not related to output (total national income) Y or the interest rate 'r'

$$A_0 = C_0 + cTR + I_0 + G + NX \tag{8.4}$$

We are using the same notation as in Chapter 3. So, Y stands for real GDP or national income, 'r' stands for the interest rate, C_0 is autonomous consumption spending (not related to income), 'c' is the marginal propensity to consume out of income, 't' is the income tax rate, 'G' is government spending and 'NX' is net exports (exports – imports). So now, we are assuming an open economy, a detailed discussion of which will be done in Chapters 15–17.

8.2.4. The Equation for the IS Curve

The Equation for the IS curve is reflected in the Equation 8.3. Since it represents equilibrium in the goods market, it may be rewritten, using (8.4), as

$$Y = \alpha(A_0 - br) \tag{8.5}$$

where 'α' is the multiplier of the basic Keynesian model. We know that the value of this multiplier is given as $\alpha = 1/[1 - c(1 - t)]$.

But note that the multiplier appears here only for the demand expansion effect and the final output expansion will be less than the multiplier effect given by α, as investment falls with a rise in the interest rate. So the interaction of the market for money is incorporated with the interest rate r.

In the IS–LM model, investment is a function of the interest rate. A rise in the interest rate reduces investment demand, while a fall in the interest rate increases investment demand.

The equation for the IS curve is nothing but the goods market equilibrium condition, adding the endogenous part of investment demand to the simple Keynesian model.

8.2.5. The Slope of the IS Curve

The intuition behind the nature of the slope of the IS curve is simple. If the interest rate rises, investments fall, reducing the demand for goods. We see from Equation 8.5 that if 'r' rises, 'Y' falls. So, the IS curve, along which the goods market is in equilibrium, slopes down and to the right in the interest rate and output/income space, as shown in Figure 8.2.

Now, to maintain equilibrium in the goods market, 'Y', the output level also has to fall and remember that we are considering only one aggregate good!

Another way of looking at the slope is to say that since investment falls as the interest rate 'r' rises, a fall in income 'Y' is needed to reduce savings towards the reduced investment level (in a closed economy, savings always equals investment, though the two are not identical in an open economy, as we will see in the chapters on the open economy). The IS curve is drawn in the interest rate–output space, with the interest rate on the vertical axis and income or output on the horizontal axis.

The IS curve has a negative slope, sloping down from the left to the right in the interest rate–output space. The reason for this slope is that a rise in the interest rate reduces investment demand and hence total demand for output.

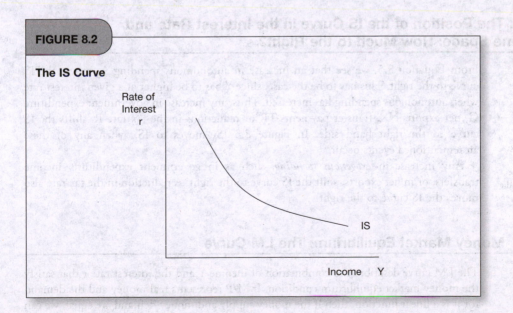

FIGURE 8.2

The IS Curve

8.2.5.1. Factors Affecting the Slope of the IS Curve

Let us now look at the factors which influence the goods market and hence the slope of the IS curve.

From Equation 8.5, $dY/dr = -b\alpha$. So, the decrease in Y is more and the IS curve is more flat if

- 'b' is large, so that a small fall in the interest rate produces a large rise in investments and in total output or national income 'Y'.
- α, the income multiplier, is large.
- So, the IS curve is more steep when 'b' and 'α' are small in value.
- A fall in the tax rate 't' makes the IS curve flatter. So fiscal policy, reflected in the value of the tax rate, affects the slope of the IS curve. This is clear, since the multiplier is given as $\alpha = 1/1 - c(1 - t)$. A fall in 't' increases α, increasing the response of 'y' to a change in 'r'. If the tax rate is lower, the value of the multiplier will be larger; it will increase the change in output following the initial response of investment demand.
- Similarly, from the expression for the multiplier, it can be noted that a rise in the marginal propensity to consume, c, makes the IS curve more flat.

The IS curve is more flat, reflecting a large response in output to an interest rate change, when the response of investment to a change in the interest rate is large (this response is measured by the interest rate elasticity of investment demand).

The IS curve is also more flat when the income multiplier is large. The multiplier is larger for smaller values of the tax rate and for larger values of the marginal propensity to consume.

8.2.6. The Position of the IS Curve in the Interest Rate and Income Space: How Much to the Right?

From Equation 8.5, we see that an increase in autonomous spending A_0 moves the IS curve to the right. This has to be the case, since Y has to be higher at a given interest rate when autonomous spending has increased. Thus, any increase in government expenditure G, net exports NX, transfer payments TR or reductions in the tax rate R, shifts the IS curve to the right hand side. In Figure 8.3 IS_0 moves to IS_1 when any of these aforementioned events occur.

Exogenous spending concerns those expenditures that are determined outside the model.

Any increase in *exogenous spending*, such as in government expenditure, income transfers, or in net exports, shift the IS curve to the right. A reduction in the tax rate also moves the IS curve to the right.

8.2.7. Money Market Equilibrium: The LM Curve

The LM curve describes the combination of income Y and the interest rate r that satisfy the money market equilibrium condition. If M/P represents real money and the demand for it is a linear function, then if the money supply and money demand are equal, we can

FIGURE 8.3

The IS Curve Shifts to the Right When Government Spending Increases or Income Transfers Rise or Tax Rates Fall or Net Exports Go Up

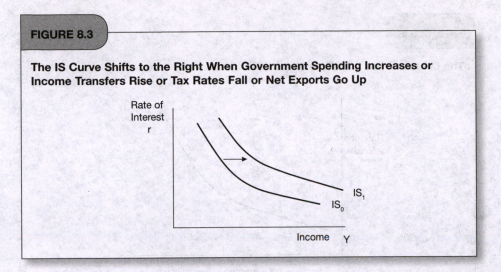

write M/P is = L(r, Y) and then we can say L(r, Y) = KY – hr. We saw in Chapter 7 that the real money demand is positively related to output or income Y and negatively to the interest rate 'r'. Hence, we can write real money demand as

$$L = kY - hr \qquad (8.6)$$

where 'k', is the elasticity of demand for money with respect to income and 'h' the elasticity of money demand with respect to the interest rate; 'k' and 'h' are coefficients with a positive sign such that h > 0 and k > 0.

Real money supply, M/P is controlled by the central bank. The money market is in equilibrium, with money supply equal to money demand, when

$$M/P = kY - hr \qquad (8.7)$$

The equilibrium condition for the money market is given in Equation 8.6. If the conditions of Equation 8.6 are satisfied on all points along the LM curve then, the LM curve represents all combinations of the interest rate and income which keep the money market in equilibrium.

The LM curve is drawn in the interest rate–output space. The money market is in equilibrium on all points on the LM curve, for different combinations of the interest rate and output. So, the LM curve equation is nothing but the money market equilibrium condition.

8.2.8. The Slope of the LM Curve in the Interest Rate and Income Space

So at what rate of interest *r* does the money market equilibrate for any values of income and real money balances? We can find that by rearranging the terms of the equation for the LM curve given in Equation 8.6 and solving for r

$$r = (1/h) (kY - M/P) \qquad (8.8)$$

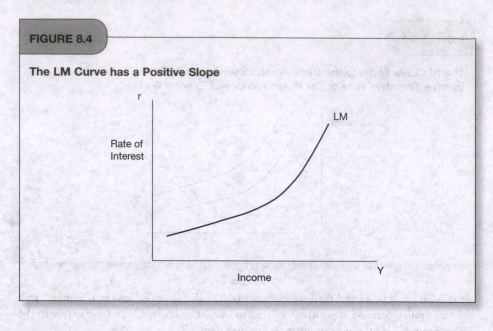

FIGURE 8.4

The LM Curve has a Positive Slope

we now have

$$dr/dY = k/h \qquad (8.9)$$

Thus, from Equation 8.9 we can see that the slope of the LM curve is positive and the LM curve slopes upwards and to the right as shown in Figure 8.4.

8.2.8.1. Factors Affecting the Slope of the LM Curve

The LM curve is upward sloping, but why? What affects its slope? We see that the two parameters, namely, the elasticity of demand for real money with respect to income and with respect to the interest rate are crucial.

- If 'k', representing the elasticity of demand for money with respect to income, has a high value, the LM curve will be steeper.
- If 'h', the elasticity of money demand with respect to the interest rate is low, the LM curve will tend to be steeper.
- Conversely, low values of 'k' and high values of 'h' make the LM curve more flat.

8.2.8.2. Why do the Values of 'k' and 'h' Play Such a Role in the Determination of LM's Slope?

First of all, observe that we are not changing the money supply in these exercises and this implies that the central bank is not active at present. We encountered the income elasticity of money demand in the previous chapter, so when the income elasticity of the demand for money is large, there is a large increase in money demand as income increases. Now, since money supply is not changing, the money demand has to return to its original level to balance the money market. A rise in the interest rate will have to accomplish this reduction in money demand. A large rise in the interest rate is needed for this since the money demand has increased a lot, given the large income elasticity of money demand. Thus, the LM will have to be steep.

When 'h' is small, as income increases and money demand increases, pushing up the interest rate, the interest rate increase does not reduce money demand much. Hence, a large rise in the interest rate is required to reduce money demand back to balance with the unchanged money supply. Hence, the LM curve will tend to be steeper. The LM curve will be steeper for high values of the income elasticity of money demand and for low values of the interest rate elasticity of money demand.

8.2.9. The Position of the LM Curve and Monetary Policy

Now what causes the LM curve to shift? We can see from Equation 8.8 that an increase in the nominal money supply at a given price, or a fall in the price level at a given nominal money supply (M), shifts the LM curve to the right as depicted in Figure 8.5b, since the interest rate 'r' is lower at the same level of Y.

Thus, an expansionary monetary policy by the central bank such as open market operations where the bank purchases securities and increases the money supply M, could cause the LM curve shift to the right as can be seen in Figure 8.5a.

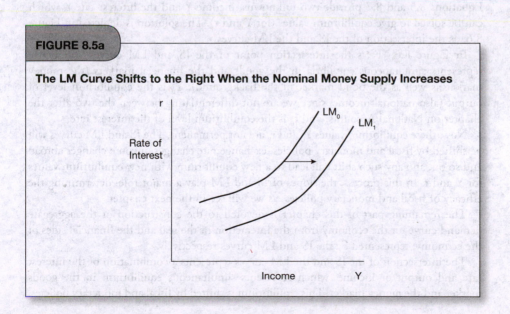

FIGURE 8.5a

The LM Curve Shifts to the Right When the Nominal Money Supply Increases

r

Rate of
Interest

LM_0

LM_1

Income   Y

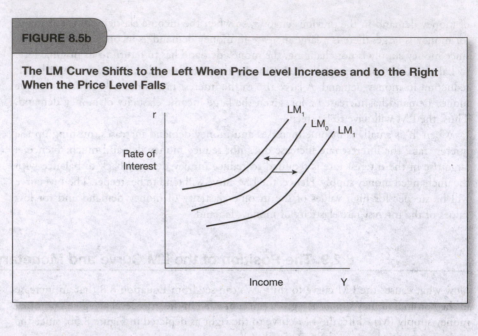

FIGURE 8.5b

The LM Curve Shifts to the Left When Price Level Increases and to the Right When the Price Level Falls

8.3. OUTPUT AND INTEREST RATE DETERMINATION IN THE IS–LM MODEL

Equations 8.5 and 8.7 provide two unknowns, income Y and the interest rate r, which can be solved to give equilibrium values (for Y and r). The solution is depicted in Figure 8.6, as the intersection of the IS and the LM curves.

In Figure 8.6, 'E' is the intersection point of the IS and LM curves and hence represents simultaneous equilibria in the goods and the financial markets (the money market as well as the bond market in the background). Y_0 is the equilibrium level of output (also national income, since we are not differentiating between the two after the chapter on National Accounts) and r_0 is the equilibrium level of the interest rate.

Now, these equilibrium values Y_0 and r_0 are not permanent. The IS and LM curves will be shifted by fiscal and monetary policies, exchange rate changes, income changes abroad and so on, and any such shift will lead to a new equilibrium with new equilibrium values for Y and r. In this process, the slopes of IS and LM play a major role, determining the efficacy of fiscal and monetary policies, as we will see in the next chapter.

The remaining part of this chapter is devoted to the construction of the aggregate demand curve for the economy from the interaction of the real and the financial sides of the economy, represented by the IS and LM curves respectively.

The intersection of the IS and the LM curves represents a combination of the interest rate and output or income, which represents simultaneous equilibrium in the goods market and the money market. This equilibrium is shifted by fiscal and monetary policies.

FIGURE 8.6

Output and Interest Rate Determination in the IS–LM Model

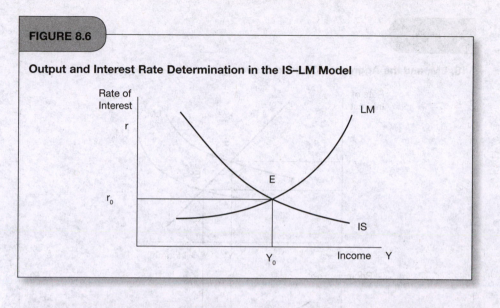

8.4. CONSTRUCTION OF THE AGGREGATE DEMAND CURVE FROM THE IS–LM CURVES

To construct the aggregate demand curve which we encountered first in Chapter 3, we now introduce price level P. The aggregate demand curve has a negative slope in the price–income space. It can be derived by looking at the effects of a price change in the IS–LM model as depicted in Figure 8.7.

In Figure 8.7, E_0 is the initial equilibrium in the IS–LM model, with both the goods and the money market clearing. Y_0 and r_0 are the income and interest rate in the initial equilibrium levels of output and interest rate, respectively. P_0 is the initial price level. Consider now an increase in the price level from P_0 to P_1. The economy experiences a rise in the inflation level; consequently, this increase in the price level causes a reduction in the real money supply M/P. We saw in Figure 8.5a how an increase in the real money supply shifts the LM curve. Here we have a decrease in the real money supply. Hence, the LM curve shifts left due to the rise in the price level. The new equilibrium point is E_1. The new equilibrium level of output is Y_1 and that of the interest rate is r_1.

What has happened is that the reduction in the real money supply requires a rise in the interest rate to maintain money market equilibrium. The higher interest rate reduces investment demand, which, from the goods market equilibrium condition, translates into a reduced output level.

Now, consider the panel below, with the price level on the vertical axis and output on the horizontal axis. The initial combination of the price and output levels corresponds to the equilibrium E_0 in the IS–LM diagram in the upper part of Figure 8.2 is (P_0, Y_0). The rise in the price level has, as seen in this diagram, reduced the equilibrium output to Y_1. Thus, the

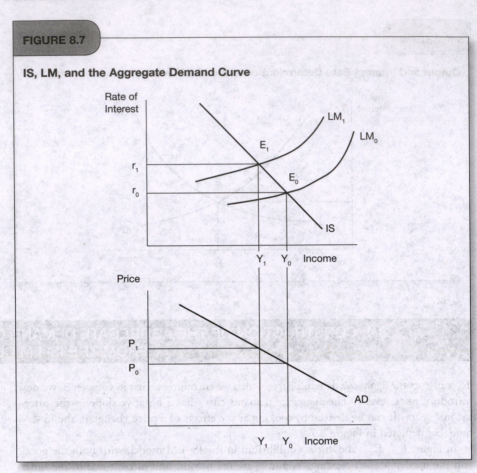

FIGURE 8.7

IS, LM, and the Aggregate Demand Curve

new (P, Y) combination in the panel below is (P_1, Y_1). Connecting (P_0, Y_0) with (P_1, Y_1), we get an upward sloping curve and generating more such combinations gives the aggregate demand curve AD, which slopes down from left to right. This is, indeed, the demand curve, since it shows what happens to output demand when the price level changes.

Thus, moving the LM curve along the IS curve as a result of price changes (which alter the real money supply) to get new equilibrium values of Y for the new price levels, generates the aggregate demand curve in the price–output space. The aggregate demand curve is obtained by combining the IS and the LM curve.

8.4.1. Mathematical Derivation for the Aggregate Demand Curve

The aggregate demand schedule can be mathematically derived from the IS and LM equations, that is, from the goods and money market equilibrium conditions, which are reproduced here for convenience:

$$\text{IS:} \quad Y = \alpha(A_0 - br) \tag{8.10}$$

$$\text{LM:} \quad M/P = kY - hr \tag{8.11}$$

Solving for the interest rate from Equation 8.11, as

$$r = 1/h(kY - M/P),$$

and substituting into Equation (8.10), to get

$$Y = \alpha[A_0 - b/h(kY - M/P)] \tag{8.12}$$

Rearranging,

$$Y = \{h\alpha/(h + kb\alpha)\} A_0 + \{b\alpha/(h + kb\alpha)\}(M/P) \tag{8.13}$$

The expression for the aggregate demand schedule is Equation (8.13) which relates income Y to the price level P. The other variables are the money supply, M and the autonomous expenditure level, A_0, which are both exogenous, thereby determining the positions of the IS and LM curves.

Observe that in Equation (8.13) which represents aggregate demand, the price level 'P' appears in the denominator of the right hand side, while income 'Y' is in the numerator of the left hand side. So, it is clear that dY/dP has a negative sign.

Thus, income Y and price level P are negatively related and the demand curve has a negative slope.

The aggregate demand schedule shows that increases in exogenous spending A_0 and in the nominal money supply, increase demand at a given price by shifting AD in the price–output space. The aggregate demand schedule will be discussed more in detail in the next two chapters dealing with the impacts of fiscal and monetary policies and their multiplier effects in the IS–LM framework.

The aggregate demand curve AD can be derived by solving out for 'Y' from the IS and LM equations. From the solution for 'Y', the negative slope of AD is clear. The aggregate demand curve is shifted by changes in exogenous spending (as happens with fiscal policy) and by money supply changes.

8.5. THE LM CURVE: THE BALANCE OF PAYMENTS AND ADJUSTMENTS OVER TIME

We have not yet discussed the external sector, where goods and capital movements across national borders enter the picture. We need to mention here that the balance of payments (BOP) of a country, which is the sum of the current and capital accounts, influences the money supply. A positive BOP account increases the money supply. This is easy to visualize as when an exporting firm receives payments in a foreign currency, the cheque is deposited by the firm's bank with the central bank, which credits the bank's account, thus increasing the money supply.

The increase in the money supply, as seen here, moves out the LM curve and the aggregate demand curve as well. A new equilibrium is reached in the goods market, at a higher price and output, as can be seen if we draw in an upward sloping supply curve in

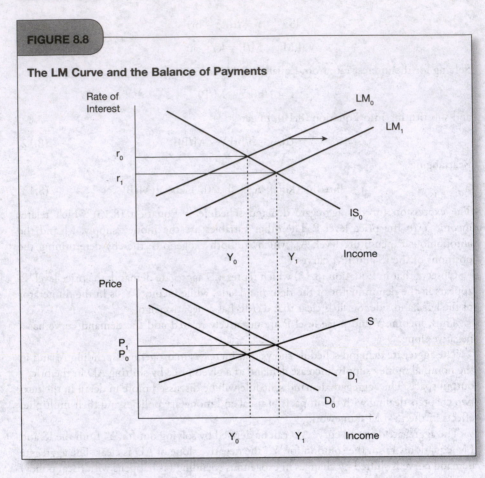

FIGURE 8.8

The LM Curve and the Balance of Payments

Figure 8.7 and shift out the demand curve. In the IS–LM Figure 8.8, the interest rate has fallen, while output has increased.

However, the new equilibrium is a short-run situation, as the BOP is not zero (there is no external balance). The adjustment to a longer-run equilibrium, where the BOP is also in equilibrium will take place as net exports fall because of the higher home goods export prices, the country losing international competitiveness. The adjustment process will be prevented if the central bank sterilizes (neutralizes) the positive BOP effect on money supply by open market operations and by selling bonds to absorb additional money supply.

The IS–LM figure also exhibits changes to the longer run during the adjustment process, with the LM curve moving back up partly and the interest rate also rising. This process is described in more detail at the end of Chapter 10. The position of the LM curve shown in Figure 8.8 is that after the adjustment process has been completed.

It may be added that the change in the money supply occurring through the balance of payments of the external sector affects the goods market also, thus constituting a link between the real and the financial sectors of the economy.

8.6. CONCLUSION

This chapter has extended the basic Keynesian model of Chapter 3 by adding the financial sector of the economy. The goods and the money market are explicitly modelled, with the bond market in the background. Such an extension allows the inclusion of the real economy (the financial economy links) to facilitate further discussions and analysis in the chapters that follow.

The IS–LM framework is, indeed, necessary to model the demand side of the economy in a more realistic and comprehensive fashion. It has been shown here that the aggregate demand curve of the economy is derived from the equilibrium conditions in both the goods and the money market. The IS curve equation is nothing but the goods market equilibrium condition, while the LM curve equation is the money market equilibrium condition. The intersection of the IS and the LM curves represents simultaneous equilibrium in the goods and the money markets, providing the equilibrium values for income and the interest rate.

Considerable efforts have been devoted in the analysis in this chapter, to lay bare the factors affecting the slopes of the IS and the LM curves. These efforts will bear fruit in the next chapter, where the relative efficacies of fiscal and monetary policies in affecting output are discussed.

In the next chapter, we see how the simultaneous equilibrium in the goods and the money markets is changed by fiscal policy, which shifts the IS curve and the monetary policy which moves the LM curve. It may be already seen from the expression for the aggregate demand curve schedule that the aggregate demand curve is also shifted by both fiscal and monetary policies.

SUMMARY

- The term or title 'IS–LM' refers to the combination of the IS curve which represents the investment–savings matching as well as equilibrium in the goods market and the LM curve which represents equilibrium in the market for money, with the demand for money matching the supply of money.
- For the model to be in a stable equilibrium, without any tendency for variables to change, there must be simultaneous equilibrium in the goods market and the money market, which is the asset market.
- The aggregate demand curve is built up from both the IS curve and the LM curve and is different from the demand curve in microeconomic theory.

- The aggregate demand curve, AD plots the demand for output at each price level of the economy. The IS curve and the LM curve are drawn in the interest rate–output space, the term 'output' also representing total income.
- The IS curve slopes down in the r–Y space. The slope of the IS curve is determined by the value of the income multiplier as well as by the factors affecting the multiplier. The interest rate elasticity Z of investment demand also affects the slope of the IS curve.
- The LM curve slopes up in the r–Y space.
- The slope of the LM curve is affected by the elasticities of demand for money with respect to income and the interest rate.
- The IS curve is shifted to the right by expansionary fiscal policies and in the open economy, by increases in net exports.
- The LM curve shifts to the right when real money supply increases. If the price level rises, it reduces the real money supply and moves the curve left.
- When the IS and the LM curves intersect, a pair of equilibrium values for the interest rate and total national income or output is obtained. Fiscal and monetary policies change the equilibrium, causing new equilibrium.
- The aggregate demand curve is derived from the IS and the LM curves, by changing the price level and moving the LM curve along the IS curve. Thus, the IS and the LM curves describe the demand side of the economy, combining the real and financial markets.

KEYWORDS

Fiscal policy	Market for money
Aggregate supply curve	Net exports
Expansionary fiscal policy	Exogenous spending
Aggregate demand curve	Autonomous spending
Assets market	

CONCEPT CHECK

State whether the following statements are true or false:

1. In the IS–LM model, the aggregate demand curve is built up from the IS curve representing the goods market equilibrium and the LM curve representing the money market equilibrium.
2. Investment is a function of the interest rate so that a rise in the interest rate increases investment demand, while a fall in the interest rate reduces investment demand.
3. The IS curve has a negative slope, sloping down from the left to the right and the reason for this slope is that a rise in the interest rate reduces investment demand.

4. The IS curve is flatter when the income multiplier is large and this happens when the tax rates are low and the marginal propensity to consume is high.

5. Suppose the government announces new schemes to provide old age pension to all citizens above sixty five years of age, then the IS curve shifts to the right.

6. The LM curve is steeper when the income elasticity of money demand is high and the interest rate elasticity of money demand is low.

7. The central bank of a country launches open market operations and begins to buy government debt instruments in the money market and this causes the money supply to increase this causes the LM curve to shift out to the right.

8. Is it true that the aggregate demand curve is negatively slopped because demand for output and the price level are related directly?

DISCUSSION QUESTIONS

1. How does the IS–LM model differ from the basic Keynesian model of Chapter 3?

2. Which is the link between the real and the financial sectors of the economy in the IS–LM model?

3. Why can it be stated that this model 'comprehensively' models the demand side of the economy?

4. How does the interest rate elasticity of investment demand affect the slope of the IS curve? Does this elasticity affect the slope of the LM curve?

5. What happens to (a) the slope of the IS curve and (b) the slope of the LM curve, with a rise in the tax rate?

6. Will the income multiplier (the final effect on output and income of an increase in government spending) in the IS–LM model be identical with that in the model of Chapter 3? Explain.

7. Why is the interest rate elasticity of money demand important in determining the slope of the LM curve? Why is the income elasticity of money demand important?

8. How does an increase in the real money supply shift the LM curve? What happens to the LM curve if the nominal money supply and the price level increase at the same rate?

9. Can the AD curve be constructed by combining the IS and the LM curve and changing the real money supply?

10. Will a fall in the real money supply because of a fall in the price level shift the AD curve?

11. Will an increase in income transfers TR shift the IS curve? Will the AD curve be shifted as well?

9

CHAPTER

The IS–LM Model: Fiscal Policies and Compatibility with the Keynesian Model

LEARNING OBJECTIVES

Upon completion of this chapter, the reader will be able to:

- Understand how expansionary fiscal policies adopted by the government in a country can influence economic growth through the IS–LM framework.
- Comprehend the significance of the crowding-out effect and how it impedes the growth process.
- Appreciate the role of monetary accommodation and fiscal policies and their combined effect.
- Be able to compare the simple Keynesian model and the IS–LM framework's interlinkages, similarities and differences.
- Be able to consider the depth and power of the IS–LM model in assessing the effectiveness of government fiscal and monetary policies in the context of the crowding out of private investment.

9.1. INTRODUCTION: THE IS–LM MODEL AND FISCAL POLICY

In the previous chapter, the elements of the IS–LM model, an important workhorse in macroeconomic theory, were laid out. It was seen that the model gives a complete description of the demand side of the economy, handling the real and financial sides separately and building up the aggregate demand curve by combining the real and monetary elements. You will appreciate after going through the contents of this chapter, how such a disaggregation of the demand side gives important insights.

What are these additional insights made possible by the IS–LM approach? These are discussed in the concluding section. Here we may just note briefly that the same amount of output expansion by two different macroeconomic policies may mask considerable differences in their impacts on the relative sizes of sectors, the relationship between variables which may move together or in opposite directions and so on. The IS–LM model is better equipped than the basic Keynesian model by virtue of the addition of the financial side, which enables the tracking of differences in the impacts of various policies on the economy.

Now, we proceed to examine the effects of government fiscal policies and different types of autonomous spending on an economy in initial equilibrium with no tendency for changes in the equilibrium output and interest rate levels. The effects of monetary policies on the economy will be discussed in the next chapter.

9.1.1. Expansionary Fiscal Policies: Effects of an Increase in Government Spending from the IS–LM and Demand–Supply Configurations

Let us revisit the equation of the IS curve, which represents equilibrium in the goods market:

$$Y = \alpha (A_0 - br) \qquad (9.1)$$

where A_0 is autonomous spending which is not influenced by changes in income Y, given as

$$A_0 = C_0 + cTR + G + I_0 + NX \qquad (9.2)$$

Now, in the IS–LM diagram, drawn in the income and interest space, a change in any variable other than income Y or the interest rate r will mean a shift in the IS curve (rather than a movement along the curve). An increase in government expenditure 'G', means that the government is adopting an expansionary policy, which is a part of autonomous spending. This will mean an increase in Y at every given r, that is, an increase in G shifts the IS curve right in the IS–LM Figure 9.1. This is because the increased government expenditure for creating new infrastructure like schools, hospitals, road, bridges or even a sports stadium for instance as the British government did for the Olympics, leads to the

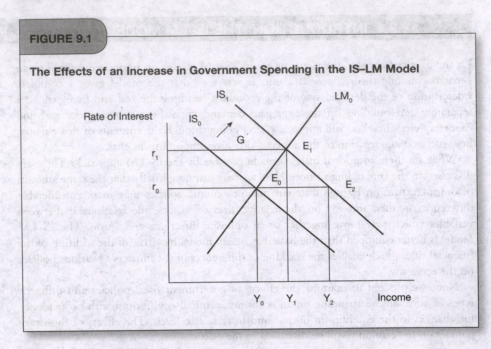

FIGURE 9.1

The Effects of an Increase in Government Spending in the IS–LM Model

demand for raw materials like cement, steel, electricity and transportation and also stimulates the demand for labour and generates employment. Naturally, these actions push up the income to a higher level, which is demonstrated by Y_1 in the figure after the impact of the financial sector on the real sector.

From Figure 9.1, we can see that output would rise to Y_2 that corresponds to equilibrium E_2 when the interest rates remain unchanged. In fact, this would be the outcome if we had used the Keynesian model in Chapter 3. But here what happens is that the rise in income and money demand following government spending, pushes up the interest rate, reducing investment demand. Thus, while consumption demand increases through the multiplier effect that we discussed in the Keynesian model, investment demand falls due to increased cost of higher interest rates, curtailing the increase in aggregate demand and output. So a higher interest rate increases the cost of borrowing for the business sector which in turn curtails new investments. In the final equilibrium, E_1, reached after successive adjustments, the interest rate has risen to r_1 and output has increased to Y_1 only. E_1 is the only equilibrium point now consistent with equilibrium in both the goods and the money markets.

An increase in government spending pushes out the IS curve as output and income rise at a given interest rate, according to the multiplier effect. But the increase is cut back partially due to the crowding out of investment at the higher interest rate and hence an increased cost of borrowing.

The aggregate demand–supply diagram corresponding to Figure 9.1 is provided in Figure 9.2, which builds upon the earlier figure, incorporating the IS–LM representation as well at the top.

FIGURE 9.2

Fiscal Expansion in the IS–LM Model: Aggregate Demand and Supply

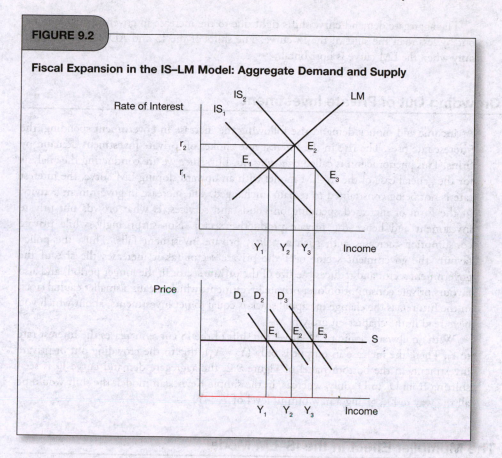

In Figure 9.2, an increase in government spending 'G' shifts the IS curve outwards to the right in the top panel. At unchanged interest rates, output Y would have increased to Y_3, corresponding to the new, hypothetical equilibrium point E_3. Y_3 would be the output level reached by such a policy in the basic Keynesian model, without a financial sector (or, with a constant interest rate, corresponding to a horizontal LM line, as shown at the end of this chapter). Therefore, the increase in output from Y_1 to Y_3 will take place as shown by the Keynesian multiplier α.

It is important to observe that the shifts of the IS curve and the aggregate demand curve differ, unless the LM curve is perfectly horizontal. It is seen that at unchanged interest rate (about which you will read later and which corresponds to the simple Keynesian model in Chapter 3), the shift of the IS curve leads to an increase in the output level, since the horizontal shift of the IS curve is the same as that of the aggregate demand curve, that is, the shift of IS = the shift of the demand curve.

But when the interest rate is allowed to change, as can be seen from Figure 9.2, the shift in the IS curve is less than the shift in the demand curve. The demand curve shifts less than the IS curve and hence the change in output is less than the shift in the IS curve.

The aggregate demand curve shifts right due to the increase in government spending, but by less than the shift of the IS curve. The shifts of the IS and AD curves are equal only when the LM curve is horizontal.

9.1.2. Crowding Out of Private Investment

Crowding out is the reduction in private investment demand due to the interest rate rise caused by an expansionary fiscal policy of higher investments by government fiscal expansion.

As income and money demand rise following the increase in government spending, the interest rate rises. The rise in the interest rate chokes off private investment demand by firms. This phenomenon is called *crowding out*. But, since we are conducting the analysis for the general case of the IS–LM model with an upward sloping LM curve, the interest rate is not being constrained to remain unchanged. The increase in government activity, in the form of increased spending on goods and services, is what crowds out private investment and hence the private productive sector. Not surprisingly, while private consumption increases with such a policy, private investment falls. Thus, the policy favours the government sector over the private sector (as it increases the size of the government sector and reduces the size of the private sector in the longer period) and also favours private consumption over private investment (which means a smaller capital stock in the future), as the change in capital stock is equal to net investments, about which you have read in the chapter on growth.

With an upward sloping LM curve, the shift of the IS curve increases the interest rate to r_2. Then, the increase in output is only $(Y_2 - Y_1)$, due to the crowding out of private investment. In the bottom panel of Figure 9.2, the aggregate demand curve D is seen shifting from D_1 to D_2 only, whereas, in the simple Keynesian model, the shift would be all the way to D_3, giving a new output level of $Y_3 > Y_2$.

9.1.3. The Multiplier Effect in the IS–LM Model

So, let us see what will be the size of the fiscal policy multiplier in the IS–LM model in comparison to the basic Keynesian model. It is fairly obvious by now that it will be lower than the latter, since the rise in the interest rate and the resulting fall in investment curtails increases in output. To see this clearly, consider again the equation for the aggregate demand curve (and the goods market equilibrium) derived in Chapter 8. The equation is reproduced here.

$$Y = \{h\alpha/(h + kb\alpha)\} \, A_0 + \{b\alpha/(h + kb\alpha)\} \, (M/P) \tag{9.3}$$

Or

$$Y = [\alpha/1 + (kb\alpha/h)] \, A_0 + \{b\alpha/(h + kb\alpha)\} \, (M/P) \tag{9.3'}$$

Observe that the solution for the equilibrium interest rate, which can be obtained by substituting (9.3), the solution for the equilibrium income level, into the LM curve equation.

$$r = \{k\alpha/(h + kb\alpha)\} \, A_0 - \{1/(h + kb\alpha)\} \, (M/P) \tag{9.4}$$

Since the government expenditure G is a part of the autonomous investment A_0, the fiscal policy multiplier in the IS–LM model from (9.3) is as follows

$$\Delta Y/\Delta A_0 = \alpha/1 + (kb\alpha/h) \tag{9.5}$$

Comparing this multiplier with the simple Keynesian multiplier α, the IS–LM multiplier is clearly smaller, since $h/(h + kb\alpha) < 1$. It is the fall in investment demand due to the interest rate rise caused by fiscal expansion which reduces the IS–LM fiscal policy multiplier below the level of the basic Keynesian income multiplier.

9.1.4. Fiscal Policy Effectiveness and the Degree of Crowding Out

The question is 'which are the factors that make fiscal policy highly effective in influencing the output and income level "Y"?' This question can be easily answered by looking at the solutions for the income level Y, for the interest rate 'r' as well as the expression for the fiscal policy multiplier.

From Equation 9.5, the fiscal policy multiplier in the IS–LM model is larger when

1. 'h', the interest rate sensitivity of money demand is large. When 'h' is large, as the money demand rises with increasing income, only a small rise in the interest rate is required to keep the money market in equilibrium. This implies a rather 'flat' LM curve.

   In fact, when 'h' tends to infinity', that is, when the LM curve becomes horizontal, the multiplier becomes identical to that in the basic Keynesian model.
2. 'k', the income elasticity of demand for money is small. When 'k' is small, the rise in the interest rate will be less as income rises. Again, this would imply a rather flat LM curve.
3. 'b', the interest sensitivity of investment demand is small. When 'b' is small, investment demand does not fall much as the interest rate rises. Note that a smaller 'b' implies a more vertical (steeper) IS curve.

Thus, the conditions (1) to (3) lead to an IS–LM diagram with definite characteristics, as in Figure 9.3.

Since the IS curve is perfectly vertical, its rightward shift from IS_0 to IS_1, equal to the distance 'ab', is the same as the increase in output $(Y_1 - Y_0)$. When fiscal policy is highly effective, the vertical shape of the IS implies that there is no cut back in investments $(b = 0)$ as the interest rate rises. In fact, the increase in output due to the increase in 'G' will be the same as that which occurred in the Keynesian model of Chapter 3.

Consider now a situation where the IS curve is flatter. The IS curve now shifts from IS_0, to IS_2, equal again, to the distance 'ab'. The new IS curve, IS_2, cuts the LM curve now more to the left, so that the new output level is only Y_2, less than Y_1, which would have been the new output level if the IS curve were perfectly vertical.

Thus, it is clear that a more vertical the IS curve, signifying a smaller response of investment to interest rate increase, the more effective the fiscal policy will be in increasing

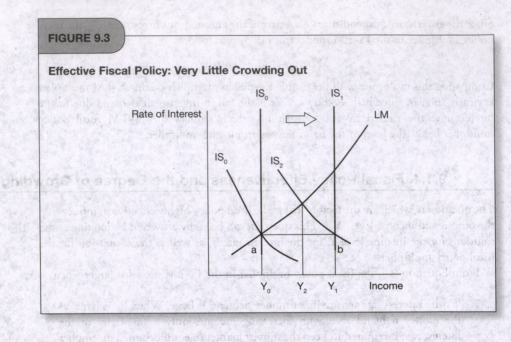

FIGURE 9.3

Effective Fiscal Policy: Very Little Crowding Out

output. Now, we proceed to illustrate the significance of the slope of the LM curve in a similar diagram. We draw an important insight into the effectiveness of the government's fiscal policy which is that fiscal policy is more effective when the IS curve is relatively steep, so that the crowding out of investment demand is less. Now let us see how effective the fiscal policy will be with regard to the slope of the LM curve.

In Figure 9.4, a shift in the IS curve by the distance 'ab', gives an equivalent increase in output, marked as $Y_1 - Y_0$, when the LM curve is horizontal. This increase in output corresponds to that stemming from the multiplier effect in the basic Keynesian model. The interest rate is constant at the initial value and so there is no crowding out of private investment. Take note that a very high value of 'h', the interest rate elasticity of money demand, tending to infinity, will make the LM curve horizontal.

But consider the case where the LM curve slopes upwards (LM′ in the figure). The LM curve now cuts the IS curve more to the left, providing the new equilibrium following an expansionary fiscal policy. The implication is clear: as income rises, money demand also rises, pushing up the interest rate. In turn, the higher interest rate crowds out private investment, so that the increase in output is less, only $(Y_2 - Y_0)$. The output increase will be even less if the LM curve is drawn steeper than LM′.

Thus, the diagrammatic analyses reaffirm what has been seen by an examination of the fiscal policy multiplier, namely, fiscal policy is more effective in affecting output when the IS curve is quite steep and the LM curve is quite flat. So higher the value of 'h' (the interest sensitivity of money demand), flatter the LM curve will be. So, here, we conclude that fiscal policy is more effective in influencing output when the LM curve is relatively flat, so that the interest rate does not change much.

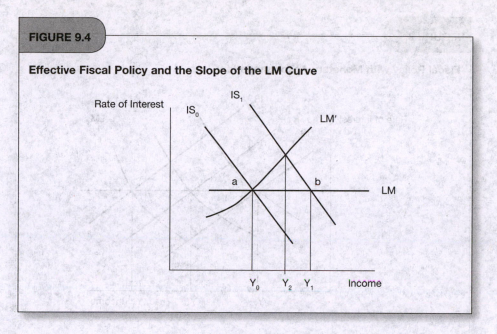

FIGURE 9.4

Effective Fiscal Policy and the Slope of the LM Curve

9.1.5. Fiscal Policy with Monetary Accommodation (as in the Basic Keynesian Model)

In the previous section, we have seen that fiscal policy is most effective, corresponding to a similar result obtained in the Keynesian model, when the LM curve is horizontal as illustrated in Figure 9.4. We also observed that an infinite value of the interest rate elasticity of money demand will make the LM horizontal. So it may be added now that such an infinite value of 'h' is required when the money supply remains constant, as money demand increases with rising incomes.

But the government can also act to ensure that the interest rate remains unchanged by an accommodating monetary policy, which increases money supply in tandem with increasing money demand. Basically, this implies that the increase in government spending will be financed by money supply increases, resulting from the government's borrowing from the central bank. Later, in the chapter on the government budget we will discuss these issues more in detail, but here it may be just noted that any increases in government spending, that lead to a budget deficit, has to be financed either by government borrowing or by money creation. Financing spending by money creation is termed as the '*monetization of the deficit*'.

The monetization of deficit is when the excess of government expenditure over revenue is financed through money creation.

Figure 9.5 depicts the policy of a fiscal expansion with complete *monetary accommodation* to keep the interest rate unchanged.

When the government adopts a policy of complete monetary accommodation, it will prevent the crowding out of investment, because money supply increases as a consequence of the government deficit spending. Figure 9.5 shows how the increases in government

Monetary accommodation is a monetary policy that increases the money supply to offset an increased interest rate due to the rising demand for money.

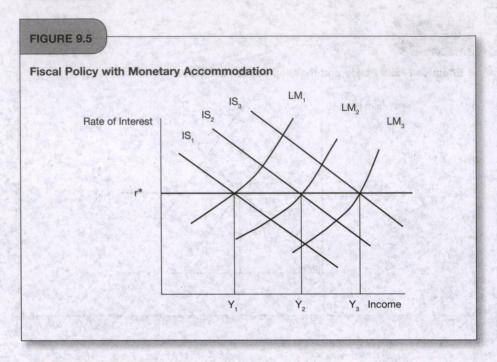

FIGURE 9.5

Fiscal Policy with Monetary Accommodation

spending pushes out the IS curve successively to IS_2 and IS_3 push out the LM curve successively to LM_2 and LM_3. With a policy monetary accommodation, the interest rate is prevented from rising above the level of r^*, which is the unchanged interest rate that the government wishes to maintain (see Figure 9.5). Output increases of Y_2 and Y_3 are more than that which would be forthcoming if there was no policy of monetary accommodation.

The fiscal expansion in the Keynesian model, where no monetary sector is specified, will correspond to a fiscal expansion with monetary accommodation in the IS–LM framework, which keeps the interest rate unchanged. This point is discussed in Section 9.3, where we derive the Keynesian model from the IS–LM framework. Fiscal expansion combined with monetary accommodation to restrain an interest rate rise has the maximum effect on output, identical to that in the basic Keynesian model.

9.1.6. Complete Crowding Out: The Classical Case

If the interest elasticity of money demand, 'h', is zero, then the LM curve is perfectly vertical, as drawn in Figure 9.6. With h = 0, an increase in income which increases money demand, requires a very high (infinitely) rise in the interest rate to reduce money demand back to the original level, to balance the money market again. Thus, the LM curve will be vertical. Essentially, with h = 0, the money market equilibrium can be written as

$$M/P = kY \tag{9.6}$$

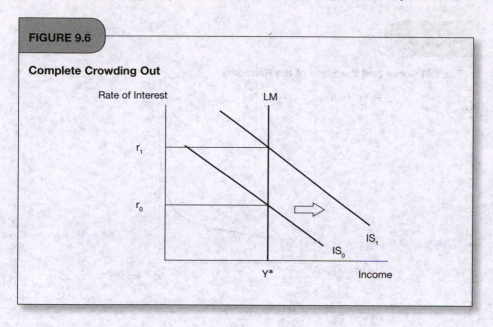

FIGURE 9.6

Complete Crowding Out

From Equation 9.6, the level of nominal income, PY, is seen to depend purely on the quantity of money. This is the Quantity Theory of Money that we have discussed in Chapter 7 and will discuss in more detain Chapter 19 on the different schools of macroeconomic thought.

In Figure 9.6, the LM curve is drawn as perfectly vertical. An increase in government spending shifts the IS curve to IS_1, but output remains unaffected. The rise in the interest rate as income increases leads to a cut back in investment demand that fully offsets the increase in consumption spending.

This case of complete crowding out is referred to as the 'Classical' case, which, strictly speaking, takes into account price developments as well. The Classical model is described in detail in Chapter 20 on schools of macroeconomic thought. Here we may note that a price rise, due to increase in demand, will reduce real money balances (M/P), moving the LM curve up and thereby increasing the interest rate and reducing investment further, leading to complete crowding out.

There is complete crowding out of private investment by government spending increases when the LM curve is perfectly vertical. The increase in consumption is offset fully by investment reductions and there is zero effect on the output.

9.1.7. Crowding Out and the State of the Economy

The previous section depicted a vertical money demand LM curve, which led to the complete crowding out of private investment by increased government spending. How did this happen? When the economy is in a state of full employment, which is always

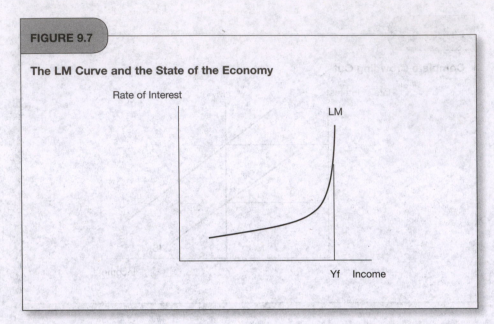

FIGURE 9.7

The LM Curve and the State of the Economy

the case in the Classical model, increased government demand for goods does not create additional jobs and incomes. Hence, even additional saving is not forthcoming to finance a government budget deficit. There are no idle funds for investing in bonds (the vertical shape of the LM curve indicates that very large increases in interest rates are needed to induce money holdings to be channelled into bonds). Hence, increased government demand for borrowing to finance the deficit drives up the interest rates sharply, crowding out private investment demand. Thus, the LM curve will be more vertical as full employment is approached (at full employment output level Yf) in the economy, as seen in Figure 9.7.

On the other hand, when there is unemployment, increased government spending creates jobs, incomes and additional savings, which could finance deficits without pushing up interest rates much. Idle funds for investing in bonds may also be available, as investment opportunities are less at lower output levels. Hence, the LM curve will tend to be more horizontal at lower output and employment levels.

So, for the same economy, the LM curve will be relatively horizontal at low output and employment levels and more vertical at high employment and output levels. With the finding in earlier sections that fiscal policy is more effective when the LM curve is relatively more horizontal, it also implies that fiscal expansion is more effective in increasing output and employment at low output levels, such as that which prevailed in the 1930s, when Keynes wrote his celebrated work.

This may be a good point to pause in the exposition of the IS–LM model and show how the Keynesian model can be derived as a special case of the general version of the IS–LM model. The next section is devoted to this task.

The LM curve will tend to be relatively horizontal at low levels of employment and output so that fiscal policy will be very effective in such a state of the economy. The LM curve will be rather vertical at output levels approaching the full employment level.

BOX 9.1	Concerns About Whether Government Spending will Crowd Out Private Investment are Real but is such Crowding Out Likely to Happen?[1]

The crowding-out effect can theoretically occur when increased government borrowings put upward pressure on interest rates and leave minimal opportunities for the private sector to borrow at viable rates to ensure profitable investments. In 10 October 2008, the Indian government raised ₹106,000 crore and it was expected to exceed its target borrowings of ₹145,000 crore prescribed in the Union Budget 2008–09.

The rise in government borrowings, however, may not lead to crowding out of private investments presently. According to the RBI, the year-on-year net bank credit to government increased by 10.3% as on 26 September 2008 as compared to a year-on-year increase of 23.2% in net bank credit to the commercial sector during the same period. Therefore, the flow of credit to the commercial sector has been fairly robust.

The Indian economy has been adversely affected by the global financial crisis, causing the withdrawal of $4.9 billion from equity markets during 1 September 2008 to 23 October 2008 by Foreign Institutional Investors (FIIs). Cumulatively, the FIIs pulled out about $12 billion from January to 23 October 2008, this being one of the key factors that led to a liquidity crunch in the economy. As a monetary accommodation tool to ease credit availability, the RBI reduced the CRR and repo rate to facilitate recovery across sectors in India. There existed enough liquidity within the banking system in this period to enable lending. Therefore, there is sufficient counter pressure on interest rates to not rise even in the face of additional government borrowing. Hence, we may not witness a crowding-out effect on private investments. Undoubtedly, concerns will remain on the fiscal deficit front, given the increased borrowing.

The only area where it would have some crowding-out effect is in the infrastructure projects. The Eleventh Plan aims at having public–private partnerships (PPP) in many of these projects. As public resources are diverted to populist policies, there could be delays in these projects and private investments would also be restrained. Monetization of fiscal deficit is a cause for concern.

After a long pause, the RBI has started directly supporting government borrowing programmes. This is expected to raise the real interest rates and, hence have a financial crowd-out impact on the private sector. But these concerns are valid only in the short-run (until the financial markets stabilise and up to the completion of elections). Later, there could be a pick-up in proposed PPP projects. To sum up, excess government expenditure might not hamper private investments.

---

[1] The content of the Box 9.1 is compiled from N. R. Bhanumurthy and Kaushal Sampat, 'Is Government Crowding Out Pvt Sector?', *The Economic Time* (24 October 2008). Available at http://economictimes.indiatimes.com/articleshow/3635160.cms

9.2. DERIVING THE BASIC KEYNESIAN MODEL AS A SPECIAL CASE OF THE IS–LM MODEL**

The equation of the aggregate demand curve in the IS–LM model is (reproducing the same from Chapter 8)

$$Y = \{h\alpha/(h + kb\alpha)\}\, A_0 + \{b\alpha/(h + kb\alpha)\}(M/P) \tag{9.7}$$

or

$$Y = [\alpha/1 + (kb\alpha/h)]\, A_0 + \{b\alpha/(h + kb\alpha)\}(M/P) \tag{9.8}$$

From Equation (9.8), the IS–LM multiplier will be identical to the Keynesian multiplier α when 'h', the interest sensitivity of money demand tends to infinity. That is, the IS–LM model will be identical to the Keynesian model, when the LM curve is horizontal, which indicates a constant interest rate.

Thus, the basic Keynesian model, which is represented with a constant price level, also has, implicitly, a constant rate of interest, being consistent with an IS–LM model with a horizontal LM curve.

Also, as noted earlier, fiscal expansion along with complete monetary accommodation will keep the interest rate constant. Thus, it may be stated that government spending increase in the simple Keynesian model is equivalent to fiscal expansion with complete monetary accommodation in the IS–LM framework.

Now, when the interest rate is constant, the endogenous part of investment demand, which depends on the interest rate, does not change and can be added on to the exogenous part I_0. The result will be a goods market equilibrium equation identical to that in the basic Keynesian model. So, what is being clarified is that the IS–LM model, with a horizontal LM curve as shown in Figure 9.8, replicates the policy results from the basic Keynesian model of Chapter 3.

We can verify this further by examining the slopes of the aggregate demand curves in the two models.

We saw in the last chapter that the slope of the aggregate demand curve in the IS–LM model is negative. This is easily obtained by differentiating Equation (9.9) with respect to the price level:

$$dY/dP = -\{b\alpha/(h + kb\alpha)\}MP^{-2} < 0 \tag{9.9}$$

Now, we see that for the IS–LM model to melt into the basic Keynesian model, 'h' should tend towards infinity. Applying this limit to the equation of the slope of the demand curve mentioned earlier, we have

$$dY/dP = 0 \tag{9.10}$$

that is, the aggregate demand curve is vertical in the basic Keynesian model, as was stated in Chapter 3.

Thus, the aggregate demand curve is vertical in the demand–supply diagram of the basic Keynesian model, the Keynesian Cross that we encountered in Chapter 3 is reproduced in Figure 9.9.

FIGURE 9.8

IS–LM Model Consistent with the Keynesian Model

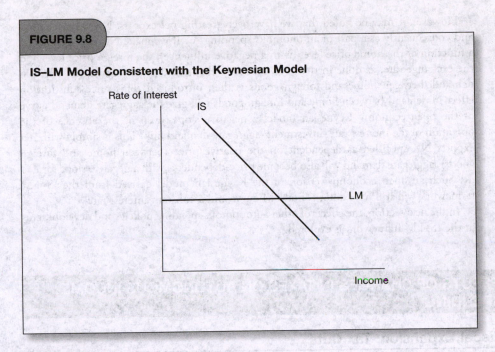

FIGURE 9.9

The Aggregate Demand–Supply Diagram as a Cross: The Simple Keynesian Model

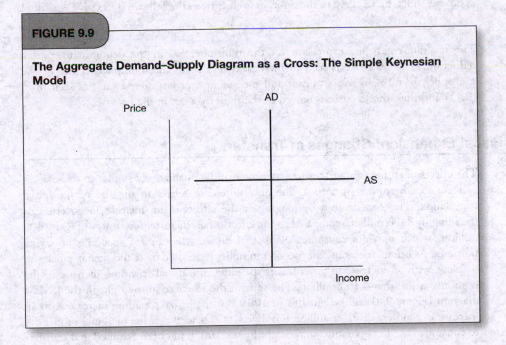

However, it may be noted that we have been treating net exports, NX, as exogenous and consequently as a part of autonomous spending A_0. If we make NX endogenous, as a function of the home price level (with a negative influence), the foreign price level and the exchange rate, as done in the open economy chapters, a price substitution effect in demand, between home and foreign goods is then introduced. This price substitution effect in demand between home and foreign goods will give the aggregate demand curve of the open economy Keynesian model a negative slope, even in the absence of the operation of the interest rate–investment–aggregate demand link. This is simply with net exports NX specified as dependent on the relative price (between home and foreign goods), aggregate demand will also become price-dependent, with a negative slope for dY/dP. Such an open economy version of the Keynesian model derived from the IS–LM framework will still have a horizontal LM curve and a constant interest rate.

In the next section, the effects of other autonomous spending policies and developments in the IS–LM framework is explored.

9.3. EFFECTS OF CHANGES IN TAXES ON AUTONOMOUS INCOME AND SPENDING

9.3.1. Fiscal Expansion: Tax Cuts

A tax cut shifts the IS curve to the right, as is clear from the following IS curve equation:

$$Y = \alpha (A_0 - br) \tag{9.11}$$

The tax rate enters the expression for the multiplier 'α' in the denominator and a reduction in the tax rate is seen to increase the value of the multiplier. A rise in the multiplier, in turn, increases output and income at a given interest rate, as seen from (9.11) and thus, the IS curve is moved to the right by a cut in the tax rate.

9.3.2. Fiscal Expansion: Changes in Transfers

The effects of an increase in transfer payments will be qualitatively similar to those of an increase in government spending. The only difference relates to the size of the initial stimulation. This can be seen by looking at the effects of an increase in government spending by ₹100 million, compared to the effects of an increase in transfers (TR) by 100 million, which provides consumers with an identical amount for spending or saving purposes. As before, the simple Keynesian multiplier is denoted by α and the tax rate by 't'.

Now, with an increase in government spending, the initial spending increase in the economy is just that—100 million. The shift of the IS curve to the right in the IS–LM diagram (Figure 9.8) will be equal to (α.100). But the initial spending increase with an increase in transfers of ₹100 million is only c.(100), where 'c' is the marginal propensity to consume. The IS curve shifts to the right by α.c.100. It has been assumed that transfers

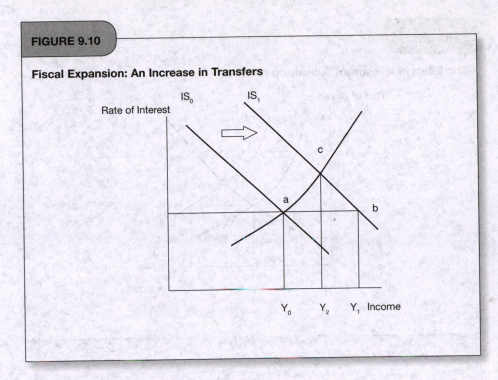

FIGURE 9.10

Fiscal Expansion: An Increase in Transfers

are not taxed, but it may be noted in passing that in some countries even unemployment benefits carry an income tax.

In Figure 9.10, 'ab' is the shift of the IS curve with an increase in transfers of ₹100 million, given as ab = α.c.100. Again, why is the shift of the IS curve equal to α'.c.100? To see this, look again at the following equation of the IS curve:

$$Y = \alpha \ (A_0 - br) \tag{9.12}$$

At a constant 'r', the change in A_0, equal to (c.100) will increase output by α.c.100, which should give the shift of the IS at any given interest rate. But, as described earlier, for the policy of an increase in 'G', the interest rate rises with higher income and money demand, crowding out private investment, so that the final increase in output is less than the shift of the IS curve, only to Y_2.

9.3.3. Changes in Exogenous Investments and Net Exports

Changes in investment demand could occur even when the interest rate is unchanged. The reason could be general market sentiments or government policy in the form of an investment subsidy such as tax credit to companies. Such changes would affect the I_0 in the expression for investment demand written as $I = I_0 + I(r)$.

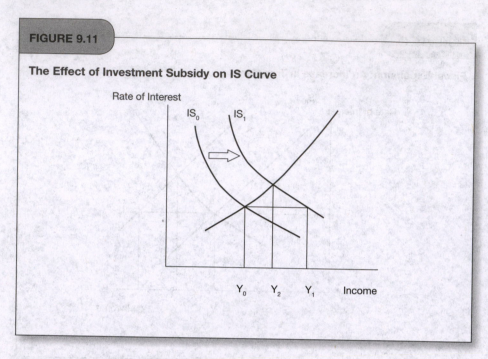

FIGURE 9.11

The Effect of Investment Subsidy on IS Curve

An investment subsidy is government support to partly bear the cost of private investment.

An *investment subsidy* of 100 million INR shifts the IS curve to the right by 'α.100' in Figure 9.11. There is no leakage through savings as is the case with an increase in transfers. The initial spurt to output given by the investment increase is multiplied through consumption spending, as captured by the multiplier α.

But, though the government has initiated an investment of ₹100 million through the subsidy, the economy ends up getting less. This is because, as seen on Figure 9.8, the interest rate rises, crowding-out part of the additional investment demand created by the government policy.

Exogenous investment is investment that is not influenced by changes in the interest rate or government policy.

Increases in net exports NX have the same effect as increases in *exogenous investment* or, for that matter, in *government spending, 'G'*. The initial impulse to the economy is undiluted by leakages through savings, as is the case with transfers. Thus, for an initial increase in net exports of 100 million, the rightward shift of the IS curve is, as in Figure 9.9, given by 'α.100'. The final output level is Y_2, after some crowding out of investment due to the higher interest rate that has occurred.

Later, in Chapters 15 and 16 on the open economy, we will see that a devaluation of the exchange rate will shift the IS curve to the right. There, the change in net exports is not exogenous and is caused by the policy of devaluation (or by market forces leading to depreciation, in the case of flexible exchange rates).

Increases in transfers, net exports and investment subsidies, all have the same qualitative effect on output as an increase in government spending. The effect will be less, quantitatively, with transfers, as there some leakage occurs through savings.

9.4. CONCLUSION

This chapter discussed the effects of fiscal policies in the IS–LM framework by introducing the financial side of the economy into the basic Keynesian model of Chapter 3. With this addition, the demand side of the economy stands complete and the reader is in a position to analyse the effects of fiscal as well as monetary policies, a topic left for the next chapter.

The discussion presented has narrowed in on what makes fiscal policy effective in influencing output. The slopes of the IS and the LM curves were seen to play a crucial role, as specified by the various elasticities carving out these slopes. In particular, it is seen that the closer the IS–LM model comes to the basic Keynesian model, the more effective fiscal policies become.

Moreover, in this chapter, we discussed the derivation of the Keynesian model as a special case of the IS–LM model with a constant interest rate (which can be maintained by a policy of monetary accommodation accompanying a fiscal expansion). The IS–LM specifications which make this compatibility with the Keynesian model possible were seen to be more applicable when the economy was in a state of unemployment with low output levels.

The next chapter takes up the effects and effectiveness of monetary policies in the IS–LM framework. It also considers the additional impacts created by changes in goods prices, though the formal modelling of the supply side, with upward-sloping supply specifications is left for later chapters.

SUMMARY

- An expansionary fiscal policy, as with an increase in government spending, increases output in the IS–LM model, by moving the IS curve to the right.
- The increase in output of an expansionary fiscal policy is less than that which is obtained in the basic Keynesian model. The reason is that the interest rate rises, thereby reducing private investment. This can be seen from the fact that the shift of the aggregate demand curve to the right is less than the shift of the IS curve to the right.
- An expansionary fiscal policy 'crowds' out private investment by raising the interest rate. Private consumption increases, but private investment falls.
- The multiplier in the IS–LM model is smaller than that in the basic Keynesian model because of the crowding-out effect on private investment.
- Increases in transfers, net exports and investment subsidies, all have the same qualitative effect on output as does an increase in government spending. The effect will be less quantitatively with transfers as there is some leakage through savings.
- Fiscal policy (expansive) is more effective in increasing output when the IS curve is quite vertical as then a rise in the interest rate has only a small

negative effect on investment as the interest rate elasticity of investment demand is very small.

- Fiscal policy is also more effective in increasing output when the LM curve is quite horizontal. Then the rise in the interest rate is very small as the IS curve moves rightwards. This will be the case when the income elasticity of money demand is very small.

- A horizontal LM curve, which makes fiscal policy very effective, will correspond to a situation where the central bank follows a policy of complete monetary accommodation to a fiscal expansion, increasing the money supply so that the interest rate does not rise at all. The multiplier in such a case will correspond to that in the basic Keynesian model.

- Thus, the Keynesian model will give identical results to that of an IS–LM model with complete monetary accommodation.

CASE STUDY

Has India Experienced Crowding Out of Private Investment?[2]

Economic theory suggests that government investment, financed by borrowings, reduces the loanable funds available for private investment, thereby driving up interest rates and reducing the level of private investment. If, as the Keynesians argue, the positive impact of increased government investment outweighs the negative impact of reduced private investment, then economic growth will increase. In India, the relationship between government investment and private investment is a controversial issue.

It is proposed that resources consumed by the government are not as effective as they would be in private hands. For India, this means too much government investment is obstructing India's economic growth. Kulkarni and Erickson apply a vector auto regression (VAR) model to Indian budget deficits, interest rates, price level and the exchange rates and find no statistically significant evidence of crowding out.[3] In India, it is not surprising to find no relationship between government deficit and interest rates since the latter has been controlled by the Reserve Bank of India until the mid-1990s. Serven found that in the Indian government's investment in non-infrastructure projects crowded out private investment.[4]

Post-Independence, India focused on stimulating growth through a centrally planned strategy of rapid industrialization through capital-intensive industries. Along with public investments in infrastructure, the government was also competing with the private sector in commercial and industrial activities. The private sector faced complex regulatory barriers, the

[2] The context of the case study has been drawn from an IMF research paper, Pritha Mitra, 'Has Government Investment Crowded out Private Investment in India?', *American Economic Review* 96, no. 2 (2006): 337–41. Available at http://aeaweb.org/assa/2006/0108_1015_0102.pdf

[3] Kishore K. Kulkarni, and Erick Lee Erickson, 'Is Crowding Out Hypothesis Evident in LDCs?: A Case of India', *Indian Economic Journal* 43, no. 1 (1995): 116–26.

[4] Luis Serven, 'Does Public Capital Crowd Out Private Capital?: Evidence from India'. (1996).

license raj and credit allocation by banks. The reforms in 1991 reduced public sector involvement in commercial and industrial activities but continued to play a role.

As a result of this strategy, India's economy has grown impressively: real per capita GDP increased from 1.26% in the 1960s to an average of 3.70% in the 1990s and 4.04% till 2005. This public sector led-growth came at the cost of a large budget deficit financed by domestic borrowing. India's budget deficit has grown from 4.01% in 1960, culminating to 9.28% in 1986 and returning back to the range of 5.00% during the first decade of the 21st century. The persistence of the deficit reflects heavy domestic borrowing by the government.

Over the last 45 years, government investment undertaken by the Indian authorities had a positive impact on the economy in the long-run. For example, infrastructure such as roads and power, have tremendously supported private sector development. The short-run impact of government investment in India has been less positive. Empirical evidence suggests that government investment has been crowding out private investment. Perhaps, India may have had a higher pace of growth with a little less government investment.

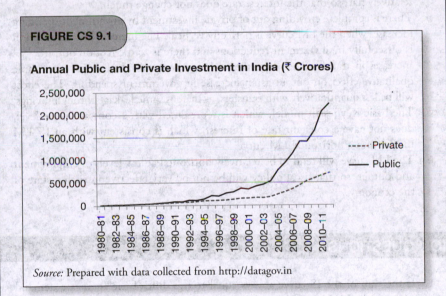

FIGURE CS 9.1

Annual Public and Private Investment in India (₹ Crores)

Source: Prepared with data collected from http://datagov.in

After reading the text given in the case study answer the following questions:

1. Do the findings of the research paper support the Keynesian view that government investment does not impede growth and adversely impacts private investment in the case of India?

2. Discuss the view with that of the figure depicting annual government and private investment. Does it support the view that private investment was crowded out in India? Do you agree with this opinion? If not why not?

KEYWORDS

Monetization of government deficit
Monetary accommodation
Crowding out

Exogenous investment
Investment subsidy

CONCEPT CHECK

State whether the following statements are true or false:

1. Fiscal policy is more effective when the IS curve is relatively steep, so that the crowding out of investment demand is less.
2. Fiscal policy is more effective in affecting output when the LM curve is relatively flat, so that the interest rate does not change much.
3. There is complete crowding out of private investment by government spending increases when the LM curve is perfectly vertical. The increase in consumption is offset fully by investment reductions and there is zero effect on output.
4. Increases in transfers, net exports and investment subsidies all have the same qualitative effect on output as an increase in government spending. The effect will be less quantitatively with transfers, as there is some leakage through savings.
5. The basic Keynesian model, which is represented with a constant price level, does not have a constant rate of interest, which is consistent with an IS–LM model with a horizontal LM curve.
6. The LM curve will tend to be relatively horizontal at low levels of employment and output, so that fiscal policy will be not be very effective in such a state of the economy.

DISCUSSION QUESTIONS

1. Is the shift of the IS curve always equal to the shift of the aggregate demand curve in the IS–LM model with (a) an increase in government spending (b) a cut in the tax rate and (c) an increase in transfers?
2. Going back to question 1 and the three policies considered there, will the shift in the IS curve equal that of the aggregate demand curve under some special conditions, with any of those policies? If so, what are those conditions and policies?
3. Will an increase in net exports give the same increase in output as that of an increase in government transfers of an identical amount?
4. The increase in government spending is ₹1,500 million. The tax rate is 25%. The marginal propensity to consume is 0.8. The interest rate elasticity of

money demand is extremely high, close to infinity. What is the output effect of the policy?

5. Will a fiscal expansion at full employment levels have a strong effect on output? Why? Discuss in the IS–LM framework.

6. A high value of the elasticity 'b' means that investment can increase a lot when the interest rate falls. Will such a value for 'b' tend to increase the effectiveness of an expansionary fiscal policy of increasing transfers?

7. Which particular specification of the IS–LM model that has a financial sector make it possible to make the model compatible with the Keynesian model, which has only a real, goods sector?

10
CHAPTER

Monetary Policy, the Policy Mix and Constraints on Policy-making

---

LEARNING OBJECTIVES

Upon completion of this chapter, the reader will be able to:

- Comprehend the links between the real and the financial sides of the economy.
- Trace the impact of monetary policy and specify the factors that are conducive to effective monetary policy.
- Be able to identify situations in the economy when monetary policy is completely ineffective.
- Appreciate the effect of political ideology on policy-making.
- Comprehend the working of the monetary policy transmission mechanism.
- Understand the ways in which a combination or mix of monetary and fiscal policies can be used to meet targets and the nature of the different constraints on government policy.

10.1. INTRODUCTION

In Chapter 9, we discussed the interest rate and output effects of fiscal policies in the IS–LM framework. This chapter considers the effects of Central Bank monetary policies taken with the explicit intention of influencing output and employment in the economy. As was done in the case of fiscal policy, we will also try to identify the conditions and the states of the economy which are conducive for monetary policy to succeed in impacting output.

Let us recapitulate briefly about monetary and fiscal policy instruments and their nature. Fiscal policy consists of changes in government purchases of goods and services, transfer payments or taxes. Changes in these factors affect aggregate demand. While a rise in government expenditure directly adds to demand, transfer payments and tax cuts increases indirectly demand through the consumption function. An expansionary fiscal policy includes increases in government purchases, increases in transfers and decreases in taxes. A contractionary policy would be just the opposite. An *expansionary monetary policy* would mean an increase in the money supply through open market operations or reduced interest rates, while a contractionary policy or tight money policy would cause a decline in money supply.

Analysing monetary policy makes it possible to get a stronger handle on the link between the real and the financial sides of the economy, although such a link is present in the case of fiscal policy also. It is seen that the speed of reaction of real and financial variables vary, with the financial ones responding faster. The *transmission* from the financial to the real side of the economy takes place through bank lending, interest rates and investments; but, as we will see later in Section 10.4, the successful completion of the process, with all its links functioning smoothly, cannot be taken for granted as an inevitable, foregone conclusion. From this point of view, a *fiscal expansion* in the form of increased government spending may be a more certain, dependable expansionary force on the economy.

After analysing the effects of monetary policy on financial and real variables, the policy implications for the composition of output are also taken up. Will the policy under consideration promote private consumption? Or is it investment that is being favoured? Will the policy contribute to increasing the importance and size of the public sector? These questions are also tinged with political colour, as the conservatives and socialists or social democrats may like different answers to such queries! The possibilities of having a policy mix, such as a combination of different types of fiscal policies (or of fiscal and monetary policies) to reach one objective without sacrificing another desirable outcome, such as increased or stable investment levels, are also taken up.

This chapter also considers the effects of price flexibility in the model, presenting policy multipliers when the prices of goods are not fixed, making for a further degree of crowding out. However, a formal modelling of the supply side, including the derivation of an upward-sloping supply curve, is left for Chapter 13 devoted specifically to the supply side of the economy.

The next section describes the effects of a monetary expansion in the general IS–LM framework, identifying the channels of influence and transmission on to the real economy.

> An expansionary monetary policy is a policy that increases the money supply.

> The transmission mechanism is the path the economy traverses as it responds to changes in monetary policy instruments.

> Fiscal expansion is an increase in government purchases, transfers or/ and a decrease in taxes.

10.2. MONETARY EXPANSION IN THE IS–LM MODEL

As we observed in Chapter 8, an increase in the money supply will shift the LM curve to the right. This ought to be clear from an examination of the equilibrium condition in the money market, reproduced here.

$$M/P = kY - br \tag{10.1}$$

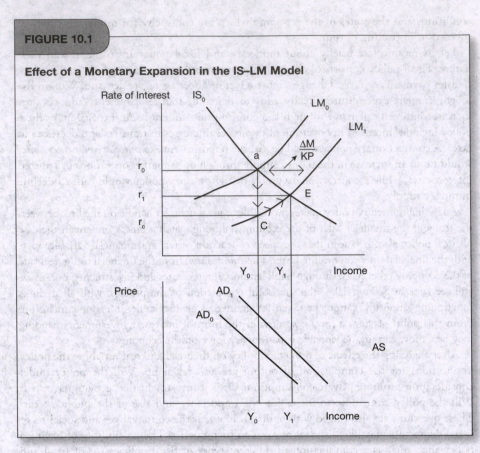

FIGURE 10.1

Effect of a Monetary Expansion in the IS–LM Model

From Equation 10.1, the change in Y for a change in the money supply, at a given 'r', is given as

$$\Delta Y = (1/k).(\Delta M/P) \tag{10.2}$$

According to Equation 10.2, an increase of ΔM in the nominal money supply increases output by $(\Delta M/Pk)$ when the interest rate is held constant; that is to say, the LM curve shifts right by the horizontal distance $(\Delta M/kP)$, as shown in Figure 10.1.

In Figure 10.1, the Central Bank is depicted as undertaking an expansionary monetary policy thereby increasing the nominal money supply by ΔM.

An expansion in the money supply is usually carried out by an open market operation, of the type described in Chapter 7. The Central Bank buys bonds in the open market, crediting the accounts of banks for payment for this purpose, which, in turn, increases the money supply. Other ways to increase the money supply would be to reduce the bank rates (Repo, Reverse Repo), or to lower the statutory liquidity holdings ratio, but these steps are resorted to rarely as one-shot strategies unlike open market operations that carried out routinely to influence the supply of money.

The open market purchase of bonds raises the bond price, which is tantamount to a reduction in the interest rate, as seen in Chapter 5 (the bond price and the market interest rate having an inverse or negative relationship).

In Figure 10.1, the increase in the money supply by ΔM moves the LM curve to the right by $(\Delta M/kP)$. Asset markets adjust faster than the real markets, so that the first impact of the money supply increase is on the interest rate. The additional real balances are spent on buying bonds, as the demand for money is unchanged at unchanged income and interest rates. Hence, at an unchanged income, as the demand for bonds rises, the interest rate falls sharply from r_0 to r_c. The fall in the interest rate also tends to balance the money market (a lower interest rate will increase money demand, to equal the higher money supply).

At 'c', while the money market is still in equilibrium, the goods market is off equilibrium. Investment demand increases at the lower interest rate, but with incomes unchanged, savings do not increase concomitantly. But now, with the multiplier process operating on the additional investment elicited by the lower interest rate, private consumption demand and output 'Y' start rising. The economy moves from 'c' to 'E', the new equilibrium point. Saving rises along with income, satisfying the additional investment demand. But more income also means more money demand, and, so, as the economy moves to the higher output and income level Y_1 and the interest rate rises to r_1. Hence the interest rate in the new equilibrium point is higher than r_c, the instantaneously lowered rate from r_0 due to the money supply increase, and works to curtail the rise in investment.

The bottom panel of Figure 10.1 shows the aggregate demand–supply relation. The increased money supply shifts the demand curve AD towards the right, along the horizontal AS curve, raising the output level from Y_0 to Y_1.

Comparing the aforementioned outcomes with fiscal policy effects, it can be easily understood that while a fiscal expansion raises output as well as interest rates, thereby lowering investment demand, a monetary expansion increases output and reduces the interest rate, bringing forth additional private investment. We will add on more such comparisons later, while discussing the policy mix and the composition of output.

Summing up the effects of monetary expansion, a money supply increase first leads to a portfolio adjustment process, with more bonds being demanded due to higher real balances. This drives up bond prices and lowers the interest rate. The lowered interest rate raises investment demand and income through the multiplier process. At the higher income level, money demand rises, partly raising the interest rate back and curtailing the rise in investment and output to some extent.

The link from the financial side of the economy to the real side, finally affecting the goods market, is depicted in the monetary policy transmission mechanism sketched here in Figure 10.2.

10.2.1. The Monetary Policy Transmission Mechanism: Not a 'Direct Hit'

There is no guarantee that monetary expansion will affect output, as there are a number of links which have to function. Expectations about the future, based on business sentiments, play an important role in getting these links to function so that output is influenced.

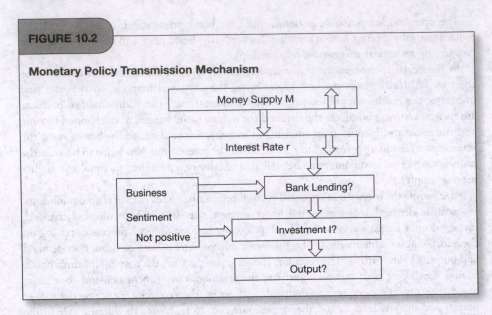

FIGURE 10.2

Monetary Policy Transmission Mechanism

A fiscal expansion, in the form of increased government spending, gives a 'direct' stimulus to the economy; since total spending in the economy increases at once by the amount spent, which is then further increased through the multiplier effect. A money supply increase is, in contrast, not a 'direct hit' on the economy as it needs a number of links to be well oiled and functional, for an expansionary force to be unleashed with certainty on the economy. These links, which ought to be self-evident after the material presented so far in this chapter, are, anyhow, presented schematically in Figure 10.6.

In Figure 10.2, the channels through which a monetary expansion increases output is shown, step by step. The first link in the chain runs from the expansion of money supply to the interest rate, lowering the rate. The increase in real balances at unchanged interest rates will cause holders to buy bonds (unloading excess real balances), raising bond prices and lowering the interest rate. So, this is the first link in the transmission mechanism, a portfolio adjustment effect.

The next link ought to be, from the earlier analysis in this chapter of monetary policy effects, the interest rate to investment demand link. The final link will then be the link between aggregate demand (which has increased) and the output level.

But the problem is that, a rise in investment demand with a fall in the interest rate may not be an automatically given outcome. Banks have to be willing to lend to firms and they may not be willing to lend if expectations about the future state of the economy including business sentiments, are depressing. Then banks would be worried also about defaults by borrowers and would prefer to buy safe government securities rather than lend to private firms. This is what has been happening in the last few years after the global financial crisis imploded.

With business sentiments none too rosy, firms, for their part, may not be willing to borrow and invest. Thus, for a couple of reasons, a fall in the interest rate may not bring forth increased investment and output. If this happens, quite simply, the transmission mechanism of monetary policy fails.

It is to guard against such policy failures that economic policy-making often adopts a combination of policies to achieve desired targets. In the IS–LM model, fiscal expansion together with monetary accommodation is a policy mix involving both fiscal and monetary policies (even if the latter is merely accommodating). We provide further examples of a policy mix to reach desired policy results later in Section 10.4.1. We now turn to another important topic, namely, the identification of factors that increase the effectiveness of monetary policy.

10.3. WHAT DECIDES THE EFFECTIVENESS OF MONETARY POLICY?

In the last chapter, the factors contributing to greater effectiveness of fiscal policy were identified. Here, we proceed to conduct the same type of analysis for monetary policy effectiveness.

It will be useful to have the equation for the aggregate demand curve before us when we analyse the impacts of monetary policy on the economy. The equation is reproduced here:

$$Y = \{h\alpha/(h + kb\alpha)\}\, A_0 + \{b\alpha/(h + kb\alpha)\}\, (M/P) \qquad (9.3)$$

From Equation 9.3, the multiplier for monetary expansion is given as

$$\Delta Y/\Delta M = (1/P)\, \{\alpha/(h/b) + k\alpha\} \qquad (10.3)$$

From the expression for monetary policy multiplier in Equation 10.3, it can be seen that

1. A large value of 'b', the interest rate elasticity of investment demand, makes the impact of money expansion on output larger.

   This result is quite self-explanatory, as when the interest rate falls in the wake of a money supply expansion, investment demand by business increases, causing output to rise. This happens more when investment is more responsive to changes in the interest rate. Translated in terms of the slope of the IS curve, *a large 'b' represents a rather flat IS curve.*

2. A small value of 'h', the interest rate elasticity of money demand, makes monetary policy more effective in influencing output.

   With a small value for 'h', as the interest rate falls following a money supply expansion, money demand does not rise much, arresting or curtailing the fall in the interest rate. Thus, the impact of an expansionary policy is not reduced. *A small value of 'h' translates as a rather vertical LM curve.*

3. A small value of 'k', the income elasticity of money demand is seen to increase the effectiveness of monetary policy. When 'k' is small, as income rises with increased investment and the multiplier effect brought forth by the increase in 'M', money demand rises only little, so that the upward pressure (acting against the initial fall) on the interest rate is limited.

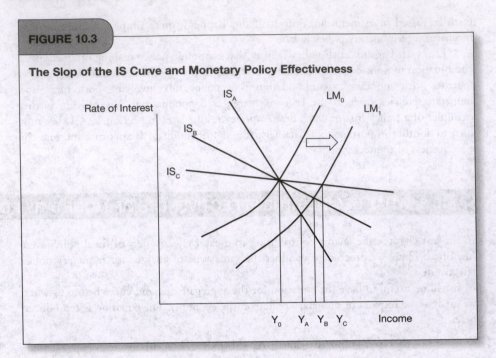

FIGURE 10.3

The Slop of the IS Curve and Monetary Policy Effectiveness

A small value for 'k' also implies a rather vertical LM curve. To see this, think of a fall in the money supply. Then income falls via the falling investment and the multiplier effect. But, while the money supply has fallen, the fall in income does not reduce money demand, as 'k' is very small. So, a large rise in the interest rate, implying a steep LM curve is needed for money demand to fall to balance the reduced money supply.

The conditions 1 to 3, mentioned here, thus state that a flat IS curve and a steep LM curve will make monetary policy more effective in affecting output. These conclusions are forthcoming even by a close scrutiny of the IS–LM diagram for monetary policy effects.

Figure 10.3 shows how *differing slopes of the IS curve* affect the outcome of monetary policy.

In Figure 10.3, the LM curve moves from LM_0 to LM_1 by an open market operation of the purchase of bonds. The output level in the new, common equilibrium for the goods and the money market is read off from the new LM curve's intersection point with the unchanged IS curve. The change in the output level depends on the shape of the IS curve, more specifically, on how flat the curve is.

In Figure 10.3, the new output level after the monetary expansion is Y_A for the IS curve IS_A, which is rather steep. The policy effect is stronger, showing the larger output level Y_B for the flatter IS curve IS_B. Lastly, the effect on the output is strongest at Y_C in the figure, when the IS curve is perfectly elastic (horizontal) as IS_C. *Thus, a flatter IS curve clearly serves the cause of an effective monetary policy.*

Figure 10.4 shows how differing slopes of the LM curve affect the impact of monetary policy on the economy.

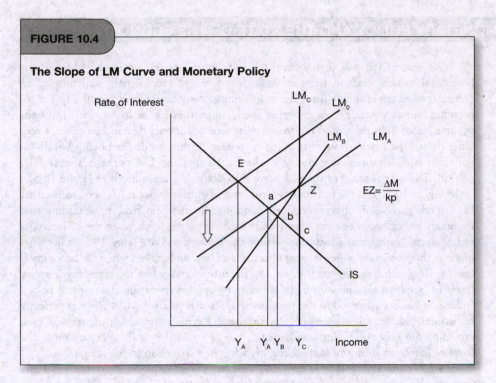

FIGURE 10.4

The Slope of LM Curve and Monetary Policy

In Figure 10.4, the LM curve shifts from the LM_0 position to LM_A through an expansionary monetary policy. The new equilibrium point, common for both the money and the goods markets, is 'a', at a reduced interest rate level and higher output Y_A.

Here the curves LM_0 and LM_A have been drawn quite flat. Consider the case when they are a little steeper (the first steeper curve is left out so as not to clutter the figure and only the new curve LM_B after the shift is shown), using the same horizontal shift (EZ in the figure) for the curve. It is easily seen that the new output level is larger, at Y_B. The steeper LM curve contributes to a larger fall in the interest rate, a larger increase in investment demand, and hence to a larger increase in output.

The increase in output is largest for the same amount of money supply increase when the LM curve is perfectly vertical, as LM_C (the initial vertical LM curve before the shift has been omitted). The new equilibrium point is at 'c', to the right of the equilibrium points 'a' and 'b' with the earlier slopes of the LM curve. The new output level Y_C, is greater than both Y_B and Y_A. *Thus, it is clearly seen that a steeper LM curve increases the effectiveness of monetary policy.*

While a steep LM curve is seen to increase the effectiveness of monetary policy in affecting output, a rather flat IS curve is better than a steep one for the purpose at hand, since the increase in investment demand due to a fall in the interest rate caused by monetary expansion will be greater. The slopes of these curves are dependent on the state of the economy, as discussed in Sections 10.1.3 and 10.1.4.

10.4. MONETARY POLICY AND THE STATE OF THE ECONOMY

We have seen in Chapter 9 that fiscal policy is more effective when the LM curve is horizontal, which tends to be the case at low levels of employment and output. In contrast, when the economy gets close to full employment level of outputs, the LM curve becomes almost vertical. At high output levels, opportunities for investments in bonds become almost fully exhausted and so, when income and money demand increases, a very large rise in the interest rate is required to release further funds for buying bonds (to maintain equilibrium in the money market) such that the LM curve is almost fully vertical. The typical shape of the LM curve thus derived, is reproduced in Figure 10.5.

In Figure 10.5, Y_f is the full employment level of output. Now, it has been seen earlier in this chapter, both diagrammatically and in the mathematical presentation that monetary policy becomes more effective in changing output levels when the LM curve is rather steep. Noting this conclusion against the background of Figure 10.5, it becomes obvious that monetary policy is more effective and best undertaken when the economy is heated, close to full employment levels. On the other hand, when the economy is at low levels of employment and output, it is better to opt for an expansionary fiscal policy. Indeed, it has been stressed in the previous chapter that when the LM curve is perfectly horizontal, the full multiplier effect of the basic Keynesian model, unrestrained by a crowding out-effect on investment demand, can be attained by a fiscal expansion in the form of increased government spending, transfers or a reduction in the tax rate.

The LM curve will tend to be very flat when output and employment levels are low and becomes very steep as full employment output levels are approached.

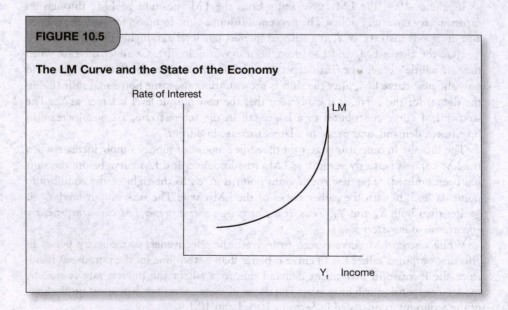

FIGURE 10.5

The LM Curve and the State of the Economy

When the LM curve becomes very flat at very low levels of economic activity, a situation aptly described as the 'liquidity trap', posing a dilemma to central bankers, may become a reality.

10.4.1. The Liquidity Trap

At such a low interest rate, no further fall in the interest rate can motivate agents to hold additional real balances and there is also no incentive to shift portfolios into interest bearing bonds. Thus, monetary police becomes ineffective and the LM curve is horizontal, as in Figure 10.6, at an interest rate close to zero. All investors hold on to cash in expectation of the interest rate to go up as they see it has fallen to the lowest possible rate and this situation is like a trap.

In Figure 10.6, with an expansionary monetary policy the LM moves out, but with the LM curve horizontal at the existing state of the economy, there is no effect on the interest rate. At the very low level of the interest rate prevailing, holders of real balances are indifferent between money and interest bearing assets and there is no portfolio adjustment bringing about a further fall in the interest rate. The interest rate and output levels remain unchanged at r_0 and Y_0 respectively, despite the Central Bank's attempts at stimulating the economy with money supply increases.

The Japanese economy may have been in the liquidity trap for most of the 1990s and the Japanese Central Bank's efforts to revive the sagging economy did not bear fruit at all. Otherwise there are not many instances of an economy being in this unenviable state for any length of time.

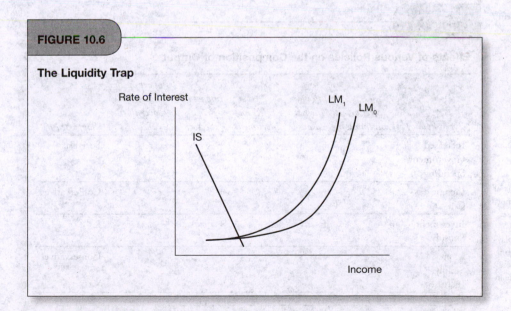

FIGURE 10.6

The Liquidity Trap

Liquidity trap is a situation when the LM curve is horizontal at an interest rate close to zero.

The liquidity trap is a situation when the LM curve is horizontal at an interest rate close to zero. Monetary policy is quite ineffective in such a state of the economy, as portfolio adjustments do not take place in response to such policies.

Before moving on to a discussion of the policy mix options available to and exercised in differing type of economic scenarios by governments, it may be appropriate to compare the effects of monetary and fiscal policies on various macroeconomic variables. In this context, it would be interesting to distinguish the kinds of policies that would normally be chosen by governments of different political leanings or colour.

10.5. POLICIES, POLICY EFFECTS AND POLITICAL COLOUR

Fiscal and monetary policies differ markedly in the effect that they have on the composition of output in an economy. Nor are the different types of fiscal policies themselves similar with regard to their on output composition. Table 10.1 charts out these differences.

The effects shown in Table 10.1 require some explanation.

1. *Increased government spending*: As seen in Chapter 9, consumption spending increases through the multiplier effect, but private investment gets crowded out as the interest rate rises. The government sector can grow over time if such a policy is consistently followed. So, *conservatives* usually do not support increases

Conservatives, also termed as followers of right wing political views, advocate minimum government intervention and expenditure.

Socialists are followers of leftist thoughts, but not necessarily communists, who believe that the government should play an active role in creating jobs and advocate more public sector presence in the economy.

TABLE 10.1

Effects of Various Policies on the Composition of Output

Type of policy	Effect on Consumption	Effect on Interest Rate	Effect on Investment	Impact on Private Sector	Impact on the Size of the Government Sector	Supported by
Increased Government Spending	+	+	–	+	+	Socialists
Income Tax Cut	+	+	–	+	–	Conservatives
Investment Subsidy	+	+	+	+	+	?
Money Supply Increase	+	–	+	+		Conservatives

in government spending, while *socialists* would normally demand such increases in government spending, or in transfers.

2. *A tax cut*: Both government expenditure increases and tax cuts stimulate the economy and are expansionary. The difference is that the expenditure increase tends to increase the size of the public sector.

3. An *investment subsidy* is an *incentive* given to affect the location of investment with the objective of attracting new investment or to retain an existing facility. See Box 10.1 for a description of the investment subsidies offered by the Government of Kerala. The intention of the government to encourage the reduction of industrial pollution is also seen in this listing of subsidies. The *subsidy* can be as money given to a firm, grants and tax measures, loans at below-market interest rates, loan guarantees, capital injections, guaranteed excessive rates of profit, below-cost or free inputs, such as land and power, as well as purchasing goods from firms at inflated prices.

Tax cut, a reduction in government taxes to raise the purchasing power of tax payers, leads to a deficit in the government budget.

| BOX 10.1 | State Investment Subsidies in Kerala[1] |

In the light of the Industrial Policy 1998 and the Information Policy 1998, the Government of Kerala issued necessary orders streamlining the State Investment Subsidy Manual.

1. An investment subsidy of 10% limited to ₹5 lakh will be payable on fixed capital investment of all industrial units set up in the State except those industries included in the negative list and notified from time to time in Government controlled industries, public sector undertakings, units started by Government controlled agencies, units financed by KVIC/KVIB and so on shall not be eligible for investment subsidy under these rules. For the purpose of this scheme, an industrial unit eligible for State Investment Subsidy shall be an independent legal entity.

2. The following have been declared as thrust industries and all new units, tiny, small, medium or large included under thrust sector shall be eligible for investment subsidy at the rate of 15% of fixed capital investment subject to a ceiling of ₹15 lakh or as notified in the specific incentives announced for the sector from time to time.
   - Rubber based industries
   - Information technology
   - Agro based business including food processing.
   - Readymade garments
   - Ayurvedic medicines
   - Mining
   - Marine products
   - Light engineering
   - Bio technology
   - 100% Export Oriented Units.

[1] The source of the contents of the Box 10.1 is taken from http://www.keralaindustry.org/index.php/state-investment-subsidy

The investment subsidy for information technology industries will be 20% of fixed capital investment subject to a maximum of ₹25 lakh.

3. In the case of Industrial Units set up in Idukki, Wayanad and notified industrial areas like industrial growth centres and industrial parks the eligible subsidy shall be 10% of fixed capital investment subject to a ceiling of ₹10 lakh and all thrust sector units mentioned above set up in Idukki and Wayanad districts shall be paid investment subsidy of 25% of fixed capital investment subject to a maximum of ₹25 lakh.

4. An additional investment subsidy of 5% of the value of fixed capital investment subject to a ceiling of ₹1 lakh will be payable for tiny and small scale industries (SSI) units established by entrepreneurs belonging to any one of the following categories provided the proprietor/proprietress, all the partners or Directors must belong to the respective category.

5. Industrial Units both new and existing in the tiny and SSI sectors that install equipment for renewable sources of energy shall be eligible for an additional investment subsidy at 15% on such investment subject to a maximum of ₹5 lakh per unit over and above the normal subsidies. Additional subsidy of 10% subject to maximum of ₹25,000 will be provided for installation of pollution control devices in diesel generators.

An *investment subsidy* gives an impetus to private investment and then to consumption through the multiplier effect. Being expansionary for the private sector, such a policy, one may feel, ought to be popular with the conservatives. However, politicians to the right of centre are usually suspicious of any type of subsidy, as these subsidies, even if meant to be transient, have a habit of staying on permanently. Also, the administration of subsidies may enlarge the size of government departments. For all these reasons, investment subsidies do not usually get the support of the conservatives.

> An investment subsidy is an incentive given in terms of cash or tax benefits, or cheap loans, or even guaranteed purchases to stimulate growth.

An expansionary monetary policy lowers interest rates and expands private investment. Hence, it is expansionary for the private sector, increasing investment as well as consumption. Socialists, while not against the public sector employment creation potential of expansionary monetary policies, would normally prefer the expansion to come from the fiscal side as that may increase employment in the government sectors. Conservative politicians and analysts would prefer a monetary expansion that encouraged private investment to a fiscal expansion which crowds out private investment. *However, they would strongly oppose a government deficit financing monetary expansion.*

It ought to be mentioned here that governments are not always true to colour when in power! While the Thatcher government in Britain certainly pushed privatization hard, more government enterprises were privatized or shut down during the Social Democratic rule in Sweden, than under the Conservative rule.

Now, fiscal expansion tends to encourage consumption at the expense of investment and expand the public sector at the expense of the private sector (with consistent application of such policies). In contrast, monetary expansion is expansionary for both consumption and investment and tends to increase the size of the private sector.

Table 10.1 does not chart out the impacts on inflation, but expansionary polices invariably fuel inflation, though the inflationary impacts of these polices will not be identical. Before discussing the constraints on policy-making faced by the government and the possible policy mix options, it is necessary to understand that when price changes are incorporated into the IS–LM of this chapter, without a fully-fledged supply side, the multiplier effect of expansionary policies will be reduced. That is the task of the next section.

10.6. THE MULTIPLIER WITH PRICE CHANGES

As seen in this chapter and in the previous one, the multiplier in the general IS–LM model, with an upward sloping LM curve is smaller than the Keynesian multiplier of Chapter 3, the reason being the crowding out of investment demand, which curtails the rise in output. Now we proceed to show that the multiplier will be further reduced from its maximum Keynesian model value when price changes are allowed in the model. Figures 10.7a and 10.7b (the lower panels of Figure 10.7) show the effects of fiscal expansion in the IS–LM model with price flexibility, with an upward sloping aggregate supply curve, which is formally derived later in Chapter 13.

In Figure 10.7a, a fiscal expansion moves the IS curve to IS_1. The new equilibrium output, after some crowding out of investment demand due to the interest rate increase from r_0 to r_1 is Y_1. In the aggregate demand–supply diagram of Figure 10.6a, the demand curve shifts right, and the new output level of Y_1 is reached along a horizontal supply curve, drawn for a no-price change scenario.

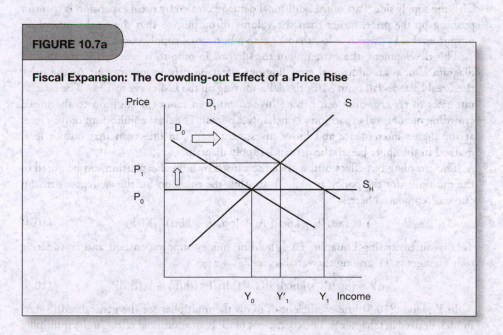

FIGURE 10.7a

Fiscal Expansion: The Crowding-out Effect of a Price Rise

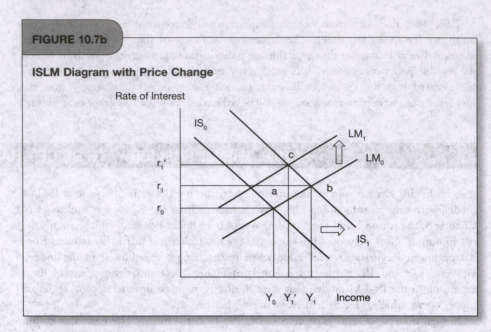

FIGURE 10.7b

ISLM Diagram with Price Change

However, the horizontal supply curve is valid only for the short-run, before the factor costs, especially wages change. Over time, the excess demand in the goods market pushes up the price, so that the supply curve is upward sloping, as derived in the chapters dealing with the supply side. Part of the additional demand created by fiscal expansion is spent in pushing up the price, rather than the volume of output, so that the final equilibrium output level is Y_1', which is less than Y_1 with a horizontal supply curve.

This development, the curtailing of the increase in output, is reflected in the IS–LM diagram also, as an additional crowding-out effect on private investment. As the price rises, real balances fall from M/P_0 to M/P_1, moving up the LM curve to LM_1. The interest rate rises to r_1', crowding out private investment even more (in addition to the initial crowding out of fiscal expansion at unchanged prices). The final equilibrium output level at the higher interest rate and lower investment is Y_1', in line with that output level marked in the upper panel, the demand–supply diagram.

The crowding-out effect of the price rise caused by a fiscal expansion can be noted in the multiplier for the policy as well. To see this, the equation for the aggregate demand curve is reproduced here:

$$Y = \{h\alpha/(h + kb\alpha)\}\, A_0 + \{b\alpha/(h + kb\alpha)\}\, (M/P) \qquad (10.4)$$

Totally differentiating Equation 10.4, holding money supply constant and considering only changes in 'G' among the variables in 'A_0', we get

$$dY = \{h\alpha/(h + kb\alpha)\}\, dG - \{M\alpha/P^2\, [(h/b) + k\alpha]\}\, dP \qquad (10.5)$$

In Equation (10.5), the coefficient of dG is the multiplier for the generalized IS–LM model, derived in Chapter 9. The coefficient of dP is an additional effect in the multiplier for the IS–LM model with flexible prices. It is clear that the price rises with an increase in dG and we do not derive separately the expression for (dP/dG); to obtain the change in the price level, an additional equation for the supply of output has to be added and the system has to be solved simultaneously for Y, r and P.

Examining the coefficient of dP in Equation 10.5, it is straightaway noted that a price rise reduces the multiplier, since the coefficient is negative. Thus, the IS–LM multiplier for fiscal policy is smaller when the price is flexible.

Also, the coefficient for dP is larger when 'b', the interest rate elasticity of investment is smaller, that is, when the IS curve is steep. Then, there is lesser crowding out of private investment with an interest rate rise. This is consistent with the observation that a steep IS curve makes fiscal policy more effective.

The next two sections deal with the policy dilemmas faced by the government in terms of macroeconomic trade-offs offering a positive result only at the expense of some negative outcome(s). Section 10.6 discusses some policy mix options to tackle such trade-offs. The subsequent section specifies the constraints under which the policy-maker operates and describes supply side developments, which could even be policy induced, to ease such constraints.

10.7. THE POLICY MIX IN ACTION

A full-fledged discussion of policy combinations to achieve a desired target or targets needs to bring in price flexibility and openness into the model. In a closed economy, a major issue is the *trade-off* between output and inflation (as one cannot have more output without sacrificing price stability), as will be seen in the Chapters 13 and 14 where the supply side of the economy is fully incorporated. When the economy is opened up, the effort to reach internal as well as external balance also necessitates the adoption of a combination of policy instruments available to the government and the Central Bank.

> A trade-off is a problem confronted in decision-making such that, in obtaining an outcome or result, one aspect is lost for the gaining of another.

Even with our discussion so far, it is clear that a policy mix can often achieve what a single policy cannot, in isolation. Consider the desired outcome of expanding employment and output by fiscal expansion without crowding out private investment. One choice would be to combine fiscal expansion with monetary accommodation, as has been discussed. But if a money supply increase is off the menu card (perhaps due to inflation threats), one possibility would be to combine a spending increase with an investment subsidy, which would prop up private investment.

An easy fiscal policy (a fiscal expansion) combined with a tight monetary policy has been often adopted by cautious governments that are wary of inflation impulses. One famous example, often quoted, is the German policy during the time of the East–West unification. The German Central Bank, traditionally inclined towards anti-inflationary policies (inherited from the hyperinflation post-war period) stepped in to crush any inflationary impulses due to the heavy government spending in the Eastern parts, with a tight monetary policy.

Such a German policy during the unification of the country is discussed further in the chapters related to open economy. Normally, any fiscal expansion creating a government budget deficit would also create a current account deficit, financed by capital inflows (a tight money policy would also drive up the interest rate, attracting capital from abroad). Countries linked to Germany by the European exchange rate cooperation mechanism had to adjust also with a tight money policy to raise interest rates in order to maintain the fixed exchange rate with the German mark. But all this is best left for further explanation in the chapters on open economy.

10.8. CONSTRAINTS ON GOVERNMENT POLICY

Starting in Chapter 3 and elaborating more in Chapters 8–10, we have discussed government policies that affect the economy, usually with the goal of expanding employment and output. But it needs to be made clear here that there are a number of constraints faced by government policy-makers when undertaking such policies. We now proceed to discuss these constraints, using the model structures developed in the book up to the present chapter. These constraints will become evident when the various trade-offs associated with expansionary government policies are described. These trade-offs may be considered to be the costs associated with economic expansion brought about by government policies.

10.8.1. The Consumption–Investment Trade-Off

The model in Chapter 3 did not have a financial sector and interest rate movements did not enter the picture. But, when the financial sector was introduced in the IS–LM model, it was seen that an expansionary fiscal policy which stimulated employment and output via consumption expansion had a cost, that of reduced private sector investment, which also led to reduced growth, due to a smaller future capital stock. A policy mix which involves an investment subsidy (as discussed in the previous section) can arrest the fall in investment, but has negative consequences for the government budget.

10.8.2. The Output–Inflation Trade-Off

This trade-off is discussed in detail in later chapters dealing with the supply side of the economy. Expanding output and employment via expansionary monetary or fiscal policies drives up the inflation rate in the economy, with various negative consequences. Such a trade-off also represents a constraint on possible government policy-making to reduce unemployment.

10.8.3. Government Deficits and the Government Debt

When the government increases spending or cuts taxes to stimulate the economy, such policies generally lead to a government budget deficit that has to be financed either by borrowing or by money creation (i.e., government borrowing from the Central Bank, which credits the government's accounts). Formally,

$$BD = \Delta B + \Delta M \qquad (10.6)$$

where 'BD' is the government budget deficit, 'ΔB' is the value of additional government bonds issued in borrowing to cover the deficit (partially or fully) and 'ΔM' is additional money creation by borrowing from the Central Bank to cover the deficit (partially of fully).

In most countries, including India, various laws have been passed to prevent *deficit financing* by money creation, since it drives up the inflation rate (remember the Quantity Theory!). But financing the deficit through government borrowing is also fraught with problems as the government debt rises. A spiralling of the government debt due to deficits is an unsustainable situation, for many reasons (including that of investment freezing due to large expected future tax increases to reduce the deficit). Thus, the government budget balance itself represents a constraint on expansionary fiscal policies.

> Deficit finance is a practice of a government spending more money than it earns in revenue, covering the resource gap by borrowing or minting new funds.

10.8.4. Government Deficits, External Deficits and the External Debt

In an open economy, running a government budget deficit has important implications for the external balance of the economy, as has been pointed out in the chapter on national accounts and as will also be emphasized again in the chapters dealing with the open economy. Essentially, the following relationship captures the link between the government deficit and the external accounts:

$$BD - (S - I) = TD \qquad (10.7)$$

Where 'S' and 'I' are private sector saving and investment and 'TD' is the trade deficit (exports–imports).

From Equation 10.8, if the private sector does not throw up savings in excess of the sector's own investment needs, the government budget deficit spills over to the external sector, creating a trade deficit. It will be seen later, in the open economy chapters, that such an external sector deficit would result in an increase in the external debt of the country.

Thus, when private sector savings are insufficient to accommodate government borrowings (which result from a government budget deficit, in turn resulting from expansionary fiscal policies to increase output and employment), there will be international borrowing, adding to the country's external debt. Such a relationship could be considered to be an added constraint on government policy-making.

10.8.5. Improving Trade-offs Facing Government Policy-making: Supply Side Policies

The trade-offs discussed in Sections 10.8.1 through 10.8.5, all arise from the demand side of the economy. It can be shown that appropriate supply side policies and developments can affect these trade-offs favourably. Let us consider two such developments, which may well be brought about by judicious government policies targeting the supply side.

10.8.5.1. Technological Advancements

Technical change, which actually accounts for around 65% of the output increase in the Indian industry in the last decade, shifts the aggregate supply curve to the right, as shown in Figure 10.8.

Positive technical changes shift the supply curve rightwards. The result is increased output at Y_1 (an increase from Y_0) and a fall in the price level from P_0 to P_1. Thus, technical change affects the output–inflation trade-off positively. It can be shown that technological progress will also affect the labour market favourably, with employment increases accompanying real wage increases.

10.8.5.2. Increases in Labour Productivity

Figure 10.8 is applicable to the case of labour productivity increases as well. The supply curve shifts right and in the new equilibrium situation, output is higher and the price level lower. Thus, the output–inflation trade-off is affected favourably. The increase in labour productivity leads to an increase in employment also, as firms hire additional labour to the point where productivity matches real wages again.

It has to be pointed out that *a time lag* is involved in government supply side policies. These are not short-run macroeconomic stabilization policies in the same way that, for instance, expansionary fiscal policies are. The results of these policies appear with a time lag. It takes time to develop workers' skills and the investment in research and development also reaps the benefits with a time lag, as technical developments happen over time. Thus,

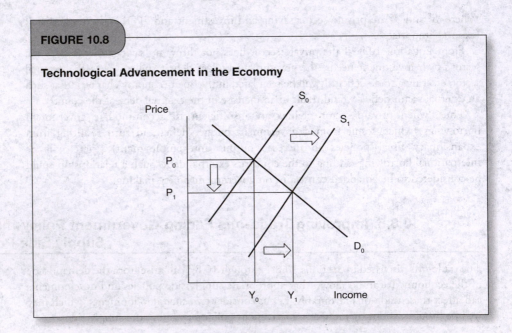

FIGURE 10.8

Technological Advancement in the Economy

the effects of government spending on education and research will not be felt in the same fiscal year, the supply curve shifts happening over a longer period of time.

An example of government spending on skill development producing benefits in the long-run is the success of the Indian information technology (IT) sector in the competitive global arena. The expansion in the IT sector was made possible because of the creation of technical institutions and colleges decades ago. The recent acceleration in technical change in the Indian economy is also due to the investments in education and research made in the past, which have produced the third largest technical personnel supply in the world in this country.

In this vein, the far-sighted policies adopted by Prime Minister Nehru may be recalled. He had set up the prestigious Indian Institutes of Technologies and several other colleges and research institutions in the country. Such a policy, of investing in higher, as opposed to primary education has been criticized. But the benefits reaped over a longer period of time have justified the investments made in higher education in the past. It seems to be the case that to succeed in the present era of globalization, secondary and tertiary education plays an important role.

But the fact remains that the relative neglect of primary education is one of the main reasons for the high levels of poverty and inequality, which could be even proving a constraint in reaching higher levels of aggregate growth. In this context, it may be recalled that Japan had achieved the coveted 100% literacy rate several decades before it became a successful industrial nation. Thus, a fully literate labour force could be one of the initial conditions needed for a successful 'take-off' towards the status of a developed industrial nation.

10.9. CONCLUSION

This chapter focused on the effects of monetary policy and derived the conditions under which such a policy would be effective in affecting output. Interestingly enough, the conditions under which monetary policy is effective are also those which make fiscal policy ineffective.

Thus, the choice of policy seems rather obvious, when the conditions for effectiveness are so clearly spelt out. However, often a combination of policies are required to reach desired policy outcomes, which are often only at a trade-off with each other, such as, increases in output and price stability. This chapter has discussed a few policy mixes to clarify the issues and the choices available. A fuller treatment will have to await extensions of the model to include inflation and the external sector. Still, though the supply side was not introduced fully in this chapter, the multiplier-reducing effect of introducing price flexibility has been presented in some detail.

A comparison of policies with respect to their effect on the mixture of output in the economy was also made in this chapter. Policy choices, often made in response to downturns, do have an effect on the structure of the economy over a longer period of time. Thus, if the government acts as the employer of last resort, increasing spending to absorb unemployed workers, the government sector grows over time. Later, in the chapter devoted to disaggregated models, it is seen that such a policy can affect the competitiveness of the private sector, tending to contract it. In this chapter itself, the crowding-out effect on investment of fiscal expansion could be noted.

In the chapters to follow, the model presented in this chapter is extended and modified to include the external sector, with both trade and capital movements and with different types of exchange rate arrangements. The supply side will be also then brought in, in its full-fledged form. These extensions will enable discussions on policy trade-offs in an open economy as well as when the spectre of inflation is very much a reality.

SUMMARY

- Analysing monetary policy shows the link between the real and the financial sides of the economy.
- The transmission from the financial to the real side of the economy takes place through bank lending, interest rates and investments.
- The money supply expands when the central bank buys bonds in the open market, thereby reducing the interest rate. The lower interest rate raises investment demand and income through the multiplier process.
- At a higher income level, money demand rises, raising the interest rate back partly along with curtailing the rise in investment and output to some extent.
- If the LM curve is steep, it increases the effectiveness of monetary policy in influencing output. Combined with a flat IS curve, when investment demand is more sensitive to the interest rate, the effectiveness of a monetary expansion is more pronounced.
- The LM curve will tend to be very flat when the output and employment levels are low and becomes very steep as full employment output levels are approached.
- An extremely difficult scenario for undertaking monetary policy is when the LM curve is fully horizontal at a very low close to zero interest rate, a situation called 'the liquidity trap'.
- Socialists, favouring employment creation potential of expansionary monetary policies, would normally prefer the expansion to come from the fiscal side.
- Conservative politicians prefer a monetary expansion that encourages private investment to a fiscal expansion which crowds out private investment. However, they strongly oppose any government deficit financing monetary expansion.
- Fiscal expansion tends to encourage consumption at the expense of investments and expand the public sector at the expense of the private sector.
- In contrast, monetary expansion is expansionary for both consumption and investments and tends to increase the size of the private sector.
- A rise in investment demand with a fall in the interest rate may not happen automatically. Banks may be reluctant to lend to firms if expectations about the future state of the economy are depressing.

- The multiplier in the general IS–LM model, with an upward sloping LM curve is smaller than the Keynesian multiplier because the crowding out of investment demand curtails increases in output.
- There are a number of constraints faced by government policy-makers in undertaking fiscal and monetary expansionary policies. These are the various trade-offs associated with expansionary government policies.
- Trade-offs are the costs associated with expansionary policies, for instance the increased inflation as output rises with an increase in government expenditure.

CASE STUDY

Industry Houses Seek Economic Revival Package

The corporate sector in India once again approached the government for an 'economic revival package'. However, the Prime Minister's Economic Advisory Council (PMEAC) chairman has ruled out a booster dose on line of a stimulus package. He remarked that 'there is no scope for the kind of fiscal stimulus we provided in 2008'. The situation in India is different from that of other countries. In other countries, the growth rates are low, but at the same time the inflation is also low. In our country, while growth is slowing, inflation remains at a high level'. In 2008–09, the government had provided a stimulus package of ₹1.78 lakh crore. At present, the fiscal deficit is high so reduction in policy interest rates to supporting growth could exacerbate inflationary pressure.

India's GDP grew by 5.4% in the first half of the FY 2012–13, it would be a 10 year low. Economic growth has fallen below that of the 2008–09 financial crisis when the GDP growth dropped to 5.8%. Gross fixed capital formation decreased to 11.95% in FY 2012 from 14.18% in FY 2011. Private final consumption expenditure fell to 15.83% in FY 2012 from 16.99% in FY[2] 2011. Fiscal deficit to GDP ratio in the 3rd quarter of 2011 stood at 4.3% just below the target of 4.6%. Expenditure over revenue touched 6.75 of GDP in the first half of the current FY 2012–13. Fiscal deficit touched 71.6% of the budget estimate in the first seven months of the FY 2012–13.

Economists do not expect the RBI to cut the repo rate in December as inflation is above the regulator's comfort zone. Ratings agency Standard and Poor (S&P) has suggested that India rein in its fiscal deficit to boost investor confidence. Various business confidence surveys portray weak sentiment about business prospects. The CII Business Confidence Index and the Dun and Bradstreet Business Optimism Index show negative movement –4.3 and –2.0 respectively in year on year basis.

India Inc. often blames the RBI's refusal to lower key interest rates for the current slowdown in industrial growth. But, in its annual report for 2011–12, the Central Bank has clearly stated that the real effective lending rates of banks are relatively lower than their pre-crisis levels. The RBI indicated that monetary policy can have a strong impact on inflation, but its influence on output is more limited to nudging growth toward its potential. It cannot bring about permanent or long-term changes in the levels of output, which are mainly driven by technology, productivity changes and fiscal policy.

[2] The contents of the case study has been prepared from *Business Standard*, 12 February 2012 and 1 December 2012; Arvind Jayaram, 'Real Interest Rate have Declined', *The Hindu Business Line*, September 2012; and RBI, 'Macroeconomic Outlook', In *RBI Macroeconomic Development and Monetary Policy 2nd Quarter Review* (n.d.). http://rbidocs.rbi.org.in/rdocs/Publications/PDFs/07MDMO291012F.pdf

The RBI also underlined that its primary concern will always be the adverse impact of high and persistent inflation, even though a slowdown raises unemployment and lowers income and consumption. The Central Bank said that interest rates are only one of many factors in investment decisions, which in any case depend on the rates over several cycles. While the higher interest rates in 2011–12 may have affected investment, they are clearly not the primary reason for the downturn. Rather, the decline in investment was linked to global and domestic uncertainty, structural constraints, loss of pro-reform policy momentum and persistent inflation.

After reading the text given in the case study answer the following questions:

1. What is the economic environment discussed in the text?
2. Is business confidence optimistic or does the industrial sector need fiscal support from the government?
3. If you answer to the first part of the above question is positive then is there a need for fiscal expansion? If not, why not?
4. What monetary policy stance is being proposed by the Central Bank of the country? Is the position conducive to effective monetary policy? Explain.
5. Is there a cause for concern in the rate at which the GDP is growing? What are the other factors contributing to the overall economic scenario?

KEYWORDS

Fiscal expansion   Socialists
Monetary expansion   Tax cut
Liquidity trap   Trade-off
Conservatives   Deficit finance
Investment subsidy   Transmission mechanism

CONCEPT CHECK

State whether the following statements are true or false:

1. Fiscal expansion raises output as well as interest rates, thereby lowering investment demand.
2. Open market operations by the Central Bank drive up bond prices and increase the interest rate. The higher interest rate reduces investment demand and income through the multiplier process.
3. Fiscal expansion tends to encourage consumption at the expense of investment and expand the public sector at the expense of the private sector and this is also called crowding out.
4. In an open economy, running a government budget deficit has important implications for the external balance of the economy, in other words it leads to a balance of payments deficit.

5. There is no guarantee that monetary expansion will affect output, as there are a number of links which have to function, for instance expectations about the future based on business sentiments, influences the links between employment and output.

6. The liquidity trap is a situation when the LM curve is horizontal at an interest rate close to zero. Monetary policy is quite effective in such a state of the economy, as portfolio adjustments take place in response to such policies.

7. When the economy is in a low level of employment and output, it is better to opt for an expansionary monetary policy.

8. If part of the additional demand created by fiscal expansion is spent in pushing up prices, rather than the volume of output, the final equilibrium output level is below that which can happen when the supply curve is horizontal.

9. Deficit financing is a practice where the government spends more money than it earns in revenues and covers the gap by borrowing or minting new funds. This is a method of financing government expenditure that is widely accepted as it does not have any inflationary implications.

10. When private sector savings are insufficient to accommodate government borrowings, the government will be constrained to borrow from abroad. This adds to the country's external debt.

DISCUSSION QUESTIONS

1. A fiscal expansion was seen to increase private consumption and reduce investment demand due to the upward pressure created on the interest rate. What will be the effect of a monetary contraction on the interest rate? Are the effects of a monetary contraction similar to that of a fiscal expansion?

2. Is it possible to affect output at all, when the economy is in a liquidity trap? Explain your answer.

3. Compare the effects of the following policies on the composition of output: an increase in government spending, an investment subsidy, a money supply increase, and, a monetary contraction.

4. With a monetary expansion, as output increases due to a multiplier effect, the interest rate is seen to rise. So, will a low interest rate elasticity of investment demand increase the effectiveness of monetary policy?

5. Explain why there is a crowding-out effect with (a) a fiscal expansion and (b) with a price increase. Is the crowding-out effect with a price increase due to a substitution in demand because of a downward sloping demand curve?

6. The government wants to increase output by a fiscal expansion, but does not want to discourage private investment. What options does the government have?

7. A monetary expansion creates a link between the financial markets and the real economy (the goods market) via the transmission mechanism discussed in this chapter. Can you think of a link from the real economy to the financial markets, drawing from the material presented in this chapter?

11

CHAPTER

Consumption and Investment Demand

LEARNING OBJECTIVES

Upon completion of this chapter, the reader will be able to:

- Understand the limitations of the simple Keynesian consumption function in explaining observed consumption patterns.
- Explain the requirements of a satisfactory consumption demand function.
- Specify the Life Cycle and Permanent Income theories of consumption fully and explain how the theories fit empirically observed consumption trends, noting also how these new theories affect results of policies derived in the IS–LM framework of the previous chapters.
- Explain the deficiencies of the theory of investment demand based solely on the nominal interest rate and present an advanced theory that captures important output and user cost effects on investment.
- Understand the implication of the significant contribution of Tobin's 'q' that connects the real sector to the stock market.

11.1. INTRODUCTION TO CONSUMPTION AND INVESTMENT

In the macroeconomic models presented so far, private consumption and investment demand have occupied a pivotal role. This is indeed, the way it should be as private consumption accounts for usually around 70% of GDP in most countries and investment demand holds the key to an economy's future production potential. So if a country consumes more and therefore has lower savings for investments, it means that there is a trade-off between these two key macroeconomic variables in the current period. Thus, having lower investment will lead to lower GDP and hence lower consumption and vice versa. In Chapter 4, where economic growth is discussed, we observed that it is possible to find an optimum trade-off between consumption and investment such that the long-run welfare of the country's residents can be maximized.

Having thus lauded the roles of consumption and investment in the economy, it may now come as a bit of a let-down when we state that the treatment of these macro-variables in the models presented so far has been quite rudimentary. The Keynesian consumption function of Chapter 3 and later chapters cannot incorporate the impacts on private consumption of a stock market downturn or changes in other asset holdings and also misses out the important element of consumption smoothing over the years which is noticeable in actual household consumption savings behaviour. Similarly, the simple investment demand function used in the IS–LM model ignores the key influences on the actual user cost of capital and lacks the important link from output developments to the demand for capital.

In this chapter, we present these more modern theories of consumption and investment demand and also indicate the implications of incorporating these in place of the simpler specifications. This is particularly relevant for the policy implications that were derived for the IS–LM model in Chapters 8–10. This chapter is structured as follows: the next section presents Keynes' aggregate consumption function in greater detail and notes empirical evidence that necessitated further theorizing on consumption behaviour to explain the observed trends. We go on to present the modern Life Cycle theory and then the Permanent Income theory of consumption in Sections 11.3 and 11.4 before taking up the extensions of the theory of investment demand. There is also a final section with appropriate concluding comments.

11.1.1. Limitations of the 'Absolute Income' Hypothesis on Consumption

The Keynesian consumption function used in the basic model of Chapter 3 uses the so-called *'absolute income' hypothesis*, in which consumption is solely influenced by current disposable income:

$$C = a + bY_D \qquad (11.1)$$

> The absolute income hypothesis states that consumption is solely based on current disposable income.

where Y_D is disposable income and the parameter 'b' is the marginal propensity to consume (MPC) out of income. Figure 11.1 gives a pictorial representation.

In Figure 11.1, the intercept 'a' indicates that there is a certain subsistence level of consumption even at zero income. This also implies that consumption is not a constant proportion of income, to be read off the 45° line from the origin.

Now, the MPC is the slope of the consumption function (11.1), while the average propensity to consume (APC) is the slope of a line from the origin to the consumption function. We can see that MPC < APC.

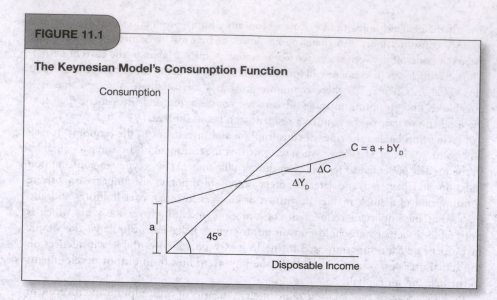

FIGURE 11.1

The Keynesian Model's Consumption Function

Also, writing the expression for APC,

$$APC = C/Y_D = a/Y_D + b \tag{11.2}$$

So we see from (11.2) that as income rises, the APC falls. This can be confirmed from the expression of the average propensity to save, APS (= 1 − APC), which is seen to rise as income rises.

The *short-run consumption function* proposes an MPC (out of income less than the APC (out of income). This implies a falling consumption–income (C/Y) ratio as income increases.

The short-run consumption function proposes MPC < APC which implies a falling consumption–income ratio as income increases.

Keynes explained the changes in the APC as income changes by noting that as income falls, people may try to maintain their consumption levels, which will show up as an increase in the C/Y ratio, while they may not increase consumption in step with income increases, which will lower the APC. Such a difference can be observed even in cross-sections of the population, with rich people tending to save a larger proportion of their incomes, while at the other end poorer people borrowing for subsistence.

Soon after Keynes wrote his seminal contribution on the consumption function that postulates that the MPC is between zero and one, there has been considerable empirical research done by various economists to test his hypothesis that for every extra unit of money earned by people, they spend some and save some. He wrote, 'Men are disposed, as a rule and on the average, to increase their consumption as their income increases, but not as much the increase in their income'.[1] Remember the Keynesian cross of Chapter 3 which was critical to Keynes' policy prescription of the fiscal policy multiplier.

[1] John Maynard Keynes, "The General Theory of Employment," *The Quarterly Journal of Economics* 51, no. 2 (1937): 209–23.

Second, Keynes presumed that the APC falls as income rises. So he conjectured that the rich saved a higher proportion of their income than the poor and this postulate has been a key factor in early Keynesian economics.

Third, Keynes believed that income was the primary determinant of consumption, so he did not attribute much significance to the interest rate. But this contradicts the classical school of thought that people are encouraged to save when interest rates increase, so that consequently consumption comes down. In fact Keynes agreed that interest did influence consumption only theoretically so he wrote, 'The rate of interest on individual spending out of a given income is secondary and relatively unimportant'.[2]

The research carried out by many economists during the interim period between the two World Wars supported Keynes' theory that the MPC lies between 0 and 1 and that households having higher incomes saved more than others. In the years of low income, especially during the Depression years, there was a strong correlation between income and consumption, supporting Keynes' third proposal. So the years following the World Wars with low incomes, households' consumption appeared to be determined by income alone.

But there were puzzles, when Simon Kuznets (1966)[3] checked for consumption for a long period of time. In his study, Kuznets found that the consumption–income ratio had remained almost constant, at around 0.87, between 1869 and 1928 in time series data for the USA. So there was the need for a complete theory of consumption demand behaviour that would be able to account for differences in the short- and long-term patterns. Contrasting this observation with the result of a short-run consumption function, which shows this ratio to be falling over time. Over a long period, the C/Y ratio, the APC, is observed to remain fairly constant. Such an observation stands in contrasts with the result from a short-run Keynesian consumption function which would show this ratio to be falling over time—since MPC < APC.

Finally, as pointed out already in the introduction, any theory of consumption needs to incorporate the impacts of changes in asset holdings, since these have been observed to be important even in demolishing the '*stagnation thesis*' in consumption behaviour, which states that as an economy matures, opportunities for productive investment decline, leading to a decrease in the country's growth rate.

11.1.2. The Stagnation Hypothesis

Economic *stagnation* is a prolonged period of slow growth, usually accompanied by high unemployment. A GDP growth rate of 2–3% is considered to be a sign of stagnation. In the late 1930s, Alvin H. Hansen argued that 'secular stagnation' had set in, so that the American economy would not be able to grow rapidly again because all the growth ingredients had played out, namely technological innovation and population growth. His argument for the secular stagnation theory was that (a) falling population growth and (b) slow technological innovation would lead to the slow growth of 'the economy'. Based on the Keynesian consumption function, as economies grew, households would consume a

Stagnation is a prolonged period of low economic growth and high unemployment.

---

[2] Ibid.
[3] Simon Kuznets, *National Product since 1869* (New York, NY: National Bureau of Economic Research, 1966).

smaller and smaller fraction of their growing incomes. This would result in lower aggregate demand and hence inadequate investment opportunities would not be able to absorb the growing savings. Moreover, there would be a depression, as the wartime demand from the government would stop.

The stagnation thesis ran as follows:

From the basic national income identity,

$$1 = C/Y + I/Y + G/Y \tag{11.3}$$

In Equation (11.3), if consumption falls as a proportion of income, the G/Y or the government expenditure to GDP ratio has to rise to keep up full employment demand, in the absence of a compensating rise in the investment ratio.

Fortunately Hansen's prediction did not become true. The post-War baby boomers, who are currently in their 60s, provided enough stimulus to sustain the aggregate demand. Meanwhile, the technological explosion with automobiles and electricity-powered domestic appliances gave a major thrust to economic growth. Also, the pent up consumption during the War ballooned demand, so although income grew much more than what it was before the War, the rate of savings did not rise as Hansen had predicted, consequently Keynes' conjecture that the APC would decline as income rose did not hold.

Hansen's solution was constant, large-scale deficit spending by the federal government. Despite widespread debate on the stagnation thesis, the outcome in the USA was contrary to the post-war era fear that the demand stimulation subsidized by government spending—would prove to be insufficient to stimulate growth. However, such fears were unfounded as private consumption got a spurt from liquid asset holdings accumulated due to forced savings during the war years.

Economists today ask whether the sub-prime mortgage crisis of 2007–08 was due to secular stagnation. Gordon writes:

> Even if innovation were to continue into the future at the rate of the two decades before 2007, the U.S. faces six headwinds that are in the process of dragging long-term growth to half or less of the 1.9 percent annual rate experienced between 1860 and 2007. These include demography, education, inequality, globalization, energy/environment and the overhang of consumer and government debt. A provocative exercise in subtraction suggests that future growth in consumption per capita for the bottom 99 percent of the income distribution could fall below 0.5 percent per year for an extended period of decades.[4]

Coming back to our discussion of the consumption function, we now focus on those theories that explain long-run consumption behaviour.

There is substantial evidence for a satisfactory theory of consumption which should be able to account for the following:

1. The observed short-run differences between the MPC and APC, in a boom as well as in a recession

---

[4] Robert J. Gordon, 'Is U.S. Economic Growth Over? Faltering Innovation Confronts the Six Headwinds' (working paper, no. 18315, National Bureau of Economic Research, August 2012).

2. The cross-sectional observation that as income rises the C/Y ratio falls
3. The long-run stability of the C/Y ratio
4. The impact of asset holdings

The theories developed independently by Franco Modigliani (1963)[5] and Milton Friedman (1957)[6] were successful in meeting these criteria for a satisfactory theory of consumption behaviour. We will first present Modigliani's Life Cycle theory. But before doing so, let us first present a basic element common both to the Life Cycle theory and Friedman's Permanent Income Hypothesis.

BOX 11.1	Is Europe Following Japan? Is China Also Heading for Stagnation?[7]

Japan's outstanding story of success rising from isolation in the 19th century to be a world leader in the 20th century is a fairy tale that's gone wrong. Having blazed a stellar path to industrialization recovering from the devastation of the Second World War, Japan was the economic powerhouse pioneering robotics and bullet trains. Western business leaders craved to understand the magic of Japan's success. But its fortune has reversed, undergoing no real growth in the last 30 years, its low-cost imports and robotics have slashed the demand for wage–labour. Since the 1990s, the country has faced a serious economic decline. Its aging population with median age of 45 suffers from a lack of economic dynamism burdened by a rigidly hostile immigration policy.

Since 2012, the Japanese government has launched structural reforms to stimulate growth that continues to elude. The zero interest policy (ZIRP) has now turned into negative interest. The quantitative easing policy of the Bank of Japan will make the bank's debts greater than that of Japan's economy by 2018. The Central Bank holds virtually all the debt the government issues and holds roughly 60% of the equity market's exchange-traded funds. Japan's fiscal deficit is nearly 8% of GDP, and the gross government debt will be 260% of GDP by the end of fiscal 2016.

The post-industrialized countries of Europe could take a page out of Japan's experience. Low trade barriers and non-competitive wages indicate that only highly skilled and non-tradable jobs as in health care, education, construction and retail were relatively secure. Not unlike Japan, Europe's immigration, education and employment policies curtail competitiveness and innovation. Entrepreneurs and researches are drawn towards the US. In Europe, the median age is as

[5] Albert Ando and Franco Modigliani, 'The "Life Cycle" Hypothesis of Saving: Aggregate Implications and Tests', *The American Economic Review* 53, no. 1 (1963): 55–84.

[6] Milton Friedman, *A Theory of the Consumption Function: A Study by the National Bureau of Economic Research*, (New Jersey: Princeton University Press, 1957).

[7] The text for the Box 11.1 was prepared based on inputs from Bill Powell, 'Will China Follow Japan into Economic Stagnation'. Available at: http://europe.newsweek.com/china-japan-renminbi-economy-426747?rm=eu and Jai Shankar's blog to be found in the following link http://www.usnews.com/opinion/blogs/world-report/2015/02/19/japans-economic-stagnation-is-a-cautionary-tale-for-europe (accessed on 17 July 2017).

high as 42. Although Europe has the common market for sustenance, it also has a larger pool of talent and a more heterogeneous society than Japan, its existing problems could be aggravated from technological advances and rising unemployment and disillusion among its youth leading to social instability and stagnation. The European economies have to deal with the vicious cycle of burdensome entitlements, spiralling debts, high unemployment and slow growth. But their calls for austerity or stimulus packages offer only near-term fixes.

The miracle economies of East Asia, Japan, South Korea, Taiwan, had led the way and China was gearing up to follow. Japan headed downhill in the early 1990s and has not recovered in the second decade of the 21st century. China seemed to fulfil the prophecies, racing ahead with year after year of rapid growth, which makes the current economic plight of both countries all the more stunning.

China is not nearly in the downward spiral like Japan, at least not yet. The country is growing at a healthy 6 to 7% per year. However, the growth rate is decelerating. The Chinese growth model is based on heavy capital expenditures and is export driven like Japan. Analysts believe that debt growth needs to be curtailed as an additional $1.7 trillion is necessary just to retain the 6.5% growth target in China. The distressing news is that an increasing amount of new debt is being used to service existing debt, a sure sign of a looming debt crisis.

Moreover, capital flight is accelerating. In 2015 China's official foreign exchange reserves fell by nearly $100 billion to $3.2 trillion, the lowest level since 2012. This is surprising when we can recall that China was one of the only economies that was unscathed by the global financial crisis of 2008–09. 'Are Japan and China now the sick men of East Asia?'

11.2. CONSUMPTION BASED ON THE PRESENT VALUE OF INCOME

Both the modern theories of consumption that we are about to discuss take off from the precept that current as well as all future consumption is based on the present value of all current and future incomes, rather than only on current income levels, that is,

$$C_t = f(PV_t) \tag{11.4}$$

where PV_t is the present value income, from all present and future income streams, given as

$$PV_t = \sum Y_t/(1 + r)^t \tag{11.5}$$

An implication of such a representation is that an increase in current income, say, due to a temporary tax cut, will affect consumption in all periods, so that the impact on current consumption may be small.

While both Modigliani and Friedman use the concept of the present value of income, the exact treatment of the relevant income term differs in their theories.

Consumption is related to what kind of income? The concept that consumption is influenced by the present value of life-long income, from all sources, rather than just current or a temporary surge in income, underlies the treatment of consumption behaviour in both the important modern theories of consumption.

11.3. THE MODIGLIANI LIFE CYCLE THEORY

11.3.1. Outline of the Theory

The Life Cycle theory was developed by Franco Modigliani, Albert Ando and Richard Brumberg.[8] The point of departure of this theory was the hypothesis that the consumption and savings decisions of households at each period of time reflected a conscious attempt to achieve their preferred distribution of consumption over their life cycles, subject to the constraints imposed by the resources accruing to them over the entire life cycle.

On an average, peoples' income changes over their life time in the course of their career, business or livelihood. They usually start at an entry level and work to reach a higher level of income. For some there may be bouts of unemployment or being between jobs, sometimes they may even enjoy an unanticipated bonus, but needless to say towards the end of their working life people retire and do not have a steady source of earnings and thus they need to plan for their retirement. Hence, individuals are assumed to plan their current consumption based not just on their current income, but on long-run expected earnings. Such a pattern is even obvious from the consumption pattern of students admitted to prestigious MBA programs. They are often observed to step up luxury consumption, based on the high future incomes assured by their degrees in the near future.

The Life Cycle theory assumes that the consumer tries to smoothen his/her income stream over her lifetime, basing consumption decisions on long-run expected earnings, rather than on current income.

We can illustrate this with a simple example, where it is assumed that the households desire a constant level of consumption over their lifetimes. If the life expectancy is T years, working life N years, yearly labour income Y_L, current income and asset holdings Y_t and A_t respectively, then that constant level of consumption is

$$C_t = 1/T \{Y_t + (N-1) Y_L + A_t\} \tag{11.6}$$

From (11.6), it can be easily seen that a permanent income increase in the form of an increase in labour income Y_L has more impact on current consumption than a one shot increase in current income Y_t.

For instance, if T = 50 and N = 40 and current income increases by ₹400, then the increase in current consumption would be only 400/50 = 8. On the other hand, if yearly labour income Y_L also goes up by 400, the increase in current consumption would equal

$$\Delta C_t = 400 \{1/T + (N-1)/T\} = 400 \times N/T = 400 \times 40/50 = 320.$$

The consumption pattern deriving from the Life Cycle specification is depicted in Figure 11.2.

Figure 11.2 shows that there is *dissaving* at the beginning and end of a life cycle, when income is absent or meagre and saving in the middle part of human life when earnings

The Life Cycle theory proposes that individuals plan their current consumption based on their long-run expected earnings.

Dissaving is spending of income saved in the past or expected income of the future.

---

[8] Franco Modigalni, Albert Ando, and Richard Brumberg, 'The Life Cycle Hypothesis of Saving the Demand for Wealth and the Supply of Capital', *Social Research* 33, no. 2 (1966): 160–217.

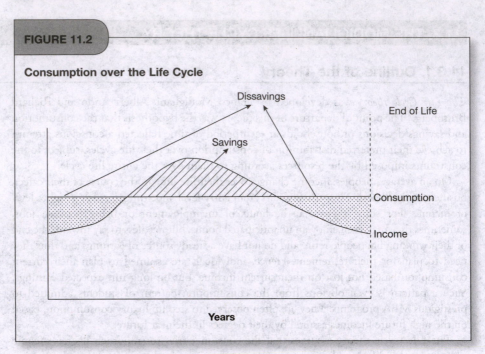

FIGURE 11.2

Consumption over the Life Cycle

are high. The individual or the household is seen to smooth consumption expenditure over the life cycle.

The representative consumer will be consuming as depicted in Figure 11.2 over a life cycle, subject to the constraint that the present value of consumption expenditure will be equal to the present value of all income flows, including that from human capital and physical and financial assets. Current consumption can be then written as a function of the present value of all incomes:

$$C_t = f(PV_t) \tag{11.7}$$

with

$$PV_t = \{\textstyle\sum_0^T Y_t^L/(1 + r)^t + \sum_0^T Y_t^A/(1 + r)^t\} \tag{11.8}$$

In (11.8), Y^L is labour income and Y^A is earnings from assets. With efficient capital markets, the current market value A_0 of assets can replace the second term:

$$PV_t = \{\textstyle\sum_0^T Y_t^L/(1 + r)^t + A_0\} \tag{11.9}$$

So let us re-capitulate: The Life Cycle model produces a smooth consumption pattern over the consumer's lifetime, with dissaving in the beginning and towards the end and saving in the middle part.

Equation (11.9) may be further simplified as follows

$$PV_t = Y_0^L + (T - 1) Y_0^e + A_0 \tag{11.10}$$

Where Y_0^e is the average expected income over the remaining years of life. If current income gives a fair indication of the future average expected income, then we can write

$$Y_0^e = \beta Y_0^L \text{ and}$$

$$PV_0 = [1 + \beta(T - 1)]Y_0^L + A_0 \qquad (11.11)$$

We can illustrate this with the help of a common econometric estimation of consumption spending, such as

$$C_t = 0.72\, Y_t^L + 0.06\, A_0 \qquad (11.12)$$

which gives an MPC from income of 0.72 and an MPC from asset value of 0.06.

11.3.2. Does the Life Cycle Theory Meet the Requirements of a Satisfactory Consumption Function?

Equation (11.12) implies a general consumption function of the form

$$C_t = \alpha Y_t^L + \beta A_t \qquad (11.13)$$

Such a function is represented in Figure 11.3, drawn with an intercept equal to βA_t.

In the short-run, with assets not changing, consumption varies along the short-run function. The short-run function shifts up over time as assets are accumulated.

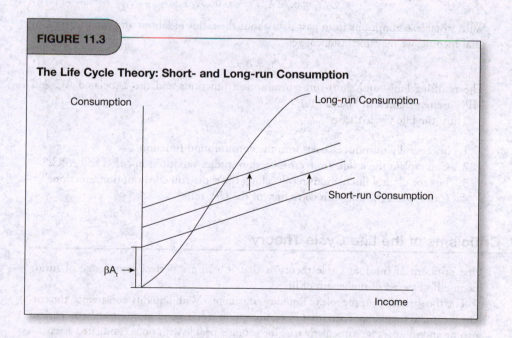

FIGURE 11.3

The Life Cycle Theory: Short- and Long-run Consumption

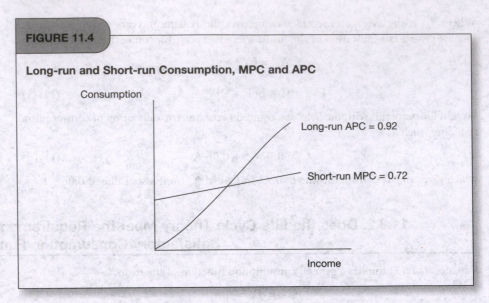

FIGURE 11.4

Long-run and Short-run Consumption, MPC and APC

Consumption

Long-run APC = 0.92

Short-run MPC = 0.72

Income

The *average propensity to consume (APC)* is the slope of the long-run consumption function passing through the origin. To take an example, divide the estimated function (11.12) by Y_t:

The average propensity to consume is the ratio of consumption to income C/Y.

$$C_t/Y_t = 0.72\ Y_t^L/Y_t + 0.06\ A_t/Y_t \tag{11.14}$$

With suitable assumptions from past data about the ratios of labour and asset income to total income, we may, for instance, get

$$C_t/Y_t = 0.92.$$

The resulting long- and short-run consumption functions and the associated AC and MPC are represented in Figure 11.4.

Thus, the Life Cycle theory:

1. Successfully introduces assets into the consumption function.
2. Can explain the results from cross-section studies variations in MPC and APC.
3. Fits the cyclical fluctuations results along the short-run consumption function.
4. Can explain the long-run constancy of the C/Y ratio.

11.3.3. Criticisms of the Life Cycle Theory

One criticism of the Life Cycle theory is that it assumes perfect knowledge of future income flows, even of the length of life.

The theory leaves out the role of liquidity constraints. With liquidity constraints, the current income is more important, that is, consumption will depend more strongly on current income and this may be particularly true for younger people with no accumulated assets.

11.3.4. Incorporating the Life Cycle Hypothesis into the IS–LM Framework

The consumption function of the earlier chapters is now modified as

$$C_t = C_t\,(Y_t,\, TW_t/P) \tag{11.15}$$

where 'P' is the price level and TW_t is total nominal wealth given as

$$TW_t = K_t + B_t + M_t \tag{11.16}$$

'K', 'B' and 'M' represent the stock of physical capital, bond holdings and the money supply respectively.

An implication of (11.15) is that the money supply will now have a direct effect on aggregate demand through the consumption channel, whereas earlier the influence was only via the interest rate and investment demand.

An increase in the money supply will now shift the IS curve out because of the following reasons:

1. The interest rate has been lowered, which raises the market value of bonds and hence total wealth, affecting private consumption demand positively.
2. If the increase in 'M' is due to a reduction in the bank reserve ratio, the increase in total wealth due to the rise in 'M' will affect consumption demand through the wealth effect. But if the rise in the money supply is due to a government budget deficit financed by selling bonds, the wealth effect does not materialize, as the *wealth effect* of an increase in bond holdings is offset by the reduction in commercial bank reserves at the central bank.

Wealth effect is the increase or decrease in consumption due to a rise in relative wealth due to an increase or decrease in bond prices and other real or financial assets.

Total wealth is affected by an expansionary monetary policy, as the market value of bonds rises with a fall in the interest rate. The wealth effect arising from increased money supply due to an expansionary monetary policy positively affects consumption, increasing the potency of monetary policy is the IS–LM framework. To summarize, the wealth effect in consumption, captured by the Life Cycle theory, increases the potency of monetary policy in the IS–LM model framework. In the long-run, price increases tend to reverse the wealth effects.

11.4. THE PERMANENT INCOME HYPOTHESIS

11.4.1. Outline of the Theory

Friedman's approach is based on the presumption that individuals wish to smoothen their income streams into a more or less uniform consumption pattern across time. The level of permanent consumption is proportional to the level of *permanent income*:

$$C_{pt} = \phi Y_{pt} \tag{11.17}$$

Permanent income is the normal income that households expect will remain at the same level in the future.

Permanent income Y_{pt} depends both on human capital income and income from asset accumulation. This permanent income concept is similar to Modigliani's present value of income concept, with an additional distinction between *transitory* and permanent incomes.

Transitory income is that component of income that households do not expect to be stable or persist in the future, so it is current income less permanent income.

Now, in any period, total income is made up of permanent income and transitory income, which is a random fluctuation:

$$Y_t = Y_{pt} + Y_{Tt} \qquad (11.18)$$

A similar distinction is postulated between permanent and transitory consumption:

$$C_t = C_{pt} + C_{Tt} \qquad (11.19)$$

These assumptions can generate the result MPC < APC. This is possible from Friedman's assumptions that

1. Transitory and permanent incomes are uncorrelated.
2. Transitory consumption is not correlated with transitory income or permanent consumption.

In the short-run, years of high incomes imply a positive transitory income component. But since permanent consumption only rises with permanent income, the C/Y ratio will be low in years of high incomes. Cross-section studies show that high-income families have a lower C/Y ratio than low-income families, which is consistent with the Permanent Income hypothesis. Low-income families will tend to have a negative transitory income component and the C/Y ratio will be high since consumption is based on permanent income.

In the Permanent Income hypothesis, consumption is based on permanent income only. There could be a transitory consumption component in any period, but that is unrelated to transitory income, so that observed consumption may be low in n year of high temporary or transitory income, lowering the C/Y ratio.

Figure 11.5 depicts these relationships and their implications.

Figure 11.5 can be also interpreted as drawn for time series data for the same household. Then C_1 is consumption for an above average earning year, while C_2 is consumption for a below average income year, when the household cannot reduce its consumption proportional to the new, lower income level.

Friedman assumed that individuals revised their estimates of permanent income from year to year in the following manner:

$$Y_{pt} = Y_{p(t-1)} + j(Y_t - Y_{p(t-1)}) \quad o < j < 1 \qquad (11.20)$$

If the estimate of permanent income currently is 550,000 and the increase in income in the current period is 20,000 above this level, then the new level of permanent income will be $Y_{pt} = 50,000 + 0.2 \times 20,000 = 54,000$ only, when the adjustment coefficient 'j' is 0.2. Thus, of the increase in income of 20,000 in the current period, only 4,000 is reckoned as the increase in permanent income.

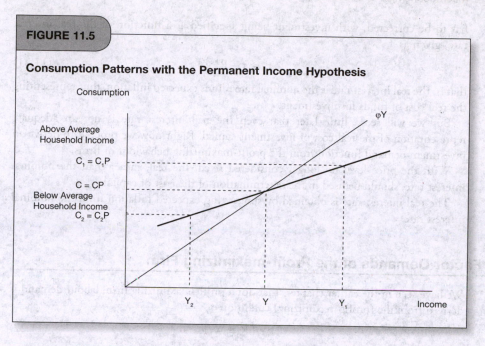

FIGURE 11.5

Consumption Patterns with the Permanent Income Hypothesis

11.4.2. Policy Implications of Friedman's Hypothesis

Consider a tax increase, designed to cool down the economy. With the Keynesian consumption function prevailing, consumption will adjust according to the long-run MPC value. But with the permanent income hypothesis in operation, the long-run MPC is out of permanent income. Hence, the tax change will affect consumption only if it is perceived to be permanent and not just limited to the current period.

A temporary tax cut that affects transitory income will not affect consumption when the Permanent Income theory is applied. In contrast, consumption gets a boost with a temporary tax cut in the short-run Keynesian consumption framework.

11.5. INVESTMENT DEMAND

11.5.1. Modifications to the Simple Investment Function of the IS–LM Model

In the previous chapter, we had specified investment demand as a function of the nominal interest rate. This representation was acceptable in a world without inflation, with constancy in the price levels. But when we allow for inflation, such a representation has to be corrected, with investment being specified as a function of the real interest rate, given as

$$r^* = r - P^{*e} \qquad (11.21)$$

that is, the real interest rate is the nominal rate minus expected inflation, thus representing the real cost of funds for investment.

But we will see a little later that even the real interest rate is not an adequate representation of the real cost of investment capital. Right now we proceed to derive an investment demand function from the profit-maximizing behaviour of firms.

With the price level no longer considered fixed, the real, rather than the nominal interest rate, should be used in the determination of the cost of capital.

The real interest rate is obtained by subtracting expected inflation from the nominal interest rate.

11.5.2. Factor Demands of the Profit-maximizing Firm

We have seen in the earlier chapters that, for a profit-maximizing firm, labour demand is derived from the (profit-maximizing) condition

$$\delta Y / \delta K = W/P \qquad (11.22)$$

that is, the real wage has to be equal to the marginal product of labour. By the same token, demand for the production factor, capital, is derived from the condition

User cost of capital is the overall cost of capital for a firm that uses an additional unit of capital for a period.

$$P \, \delta Y / \delta K = CC \qquad (11.23)$$

where 'CC' is the *user cost of capital*.

11.5.3. The Accelerator Model of Investment Demand

To make these concepts more clear, consider now the following Cobb-Douglas production function with two production factors, capital and labour:

$$Y = \alpha K^{\alpha} L^{(1-\alpha)} \qquad (11.24)$$

where the exponents of the inputs add up to 1.

Differentiating,

$$\delta Y / \delta K = \alpha \, (\alpha K^{\alpha}/K) \, N^{(1-\alpha)} = \alpha Y/K \qquad (11.25)$$

Then, from Equation (11.23),

$$\alpha Y/K = CC/P \qquad (11.26)$$

From Equation (11.25), the equilibrium level of capital stock demanded can be written as

$$K = K \, (Y, \, CC/P\alpha) \qquad (11.27)$$

Note that if the price level P rises because of an increase in the wage rate, the cost of the other production factor, the real cost of capital (CC/P) is lowered, raising the demand for capital. *Thus, changes in relative factor costs induce factor substitution.* To illustrate this, let us say that due to a shortage of skilled labour, an industry faces rising wages. This can be easily seen in the construction industry, the firms involved in real estate development and property promotion then will be constrained to use more capital intensive methods of production. For instance, the widespread use of mechanical concrete mixers in construction of multi-storied buildings is a case in point. The demand for capital will naturally rise leading to an increase in P.

Gross investment is the sum of net investment and depreciation or replacement investment, i_r or δK:

$$i_g = i_n + i_r \tag{11.28}$$

Net investment is just the change in the equilibrium level of capital stock, so that

$$i_g = \Delta K \left[Y, \alpha/(CC/P) \right] + i_r \tag{11.29}$$

If we assume that the real cost of capital, CC/P, which we may now denote as 'CCR', remains constant, which will be the case if the wage rate is stable, then we can write

$$i_g = (\alpha/CCR) \Delta Y + \delta K \tag{11.30}$$

Equation (11.30) is the '*accelerator model*' of investment demand, with investment driven by changes in total output.

The accelerator model of investment demand links investment demand to changes in output.

An investment demand function, which incorporates the accelerator principle as well as the real user cost of capital as the other determinant, can be derived as the factor demand for capital. It can also be interpreted as a production factor in a profit-maximizing firm.

The 'flexible accelerator' model will allow for a partial adjustment of the capital stock to the desired level, implying a slower response of investment to changes in income:

$$I_n = \lambda \left(\alpha Y_t - K_{t-1} \right) \tag{11.31}$$

The flexible accelerator model seems to fit observed facts better. The rate of adjustment may depend on factors such as the user cost of capital.

> The accelerator model is business investment model that relates the level of investment to the rate of change of output.

11.6. THE USER COST OF CAPITAL

11.6.1. The Interest Rate and the User Cost of Capital

When the user cost of capital is not constant, the accelerator model has to be augmented to the form

$$I_{n,t} = I_{n,t} (Y, CCR, K_{t-1}) \tag{11.32}$$

where CCR is the real user cost of capital, a rise in which will lower investment demand, as is clear from (11.26). But now we proceed to examine the concept of the user cost of capital in more detail, going beyond its representation merely as the real interest rate.

If the price of the capital good is P_t at time t, the user cost of capital can be written, for a start, as

$$CC_t = rP_t + \delta P_t - dP_t \qquad (11.33)$$

The first term in (11.33) is the interest cost, the second term is depreciation and the third capital gain. The real user cost is, then

$$CCR_t = C_t/P_t = (r - P_t^{e\wedge}) + \delta \qquad (11.34)$$

where the hat represents rate of change. The term within brackets is the real interest rate, assuming that the expected rate of inflation is captured by the current inflation and the last term on the right hand side is the depreciation rate.

However, the tax policy of the government will also affect the cost of capital. The government may often subsidize, rather than tax investments, particularly in developing countries. If τ (>0 and <1) is the rate of capital subsidy, then the real user cost of capital (CCR) is (dropping the time subscript for convenience)

$$CCR = (1 - \tau) (r - P^{e\wedge} + \delta) \qquad (11.35)$$

The real cost of capital is affected by changes in the real interest rate. A rise in the nominal interest rate, or a fall in the (expected) inflation rate, both of which increase the real interest rate, raises the real cost of capital.

A rise in the depreciation rate, will increase the real cost of capital. On the other hand, a rise in the tax on capital will increase the real cost of capital. Finally a fall in government subsidy for capital will raise the real cost of capital. Thus, there are a number of factors that need to be considered when the real cost of capital is likely to go up when it is computed from the government's policy intervention: (a) rise in depreciation rates, (b) increase in tax rates and (c) fall in subsidy.

Hence, a general investment function, which incorporates the accelerator principle, will be of the form:

$$i - i (Y, CCR) \qquad (11.36)$$

with the real user cost CCR given by (11.35). This may be contrasted with the simple investment function $I = i(r)$ used in the IS–LM model.

11.6.2. Profits and the User Cost of Capital

One final point on user cost that needs to be made on the interest rate to be used in (11.35) is not, strictly speaking, the bond market interest, since investments can be also financed by equity issues and internal funds. The interest rate to be used ought to be a weighted sum of the bond market rate, returns on equities and the rate imputed to internal funds. Now, if the imputed rate for internal funds is less than the market interest rate, a rise in profits which increases internal funds for investments will lower the weighted interest rate and thereby, the user cost of capital.

11.7. THE EXTENDED INVESTMENT FUNCTION AND THE IS–LM MODEL RESULTS

What are the modifications implied for the fiscal and monetary policy analyses for the IS–LM model as a result of the extensions made to the theory of investment demand in this chapter?

In the IS–LM model, an expansion in government spending increases output by the multiplier effect. But, such an increase is curtailed by the rise in the interest rate that leads to a contraction in investment demand. However, when the accelerator principle comes into play, with an increase in output creating additional investment demand, the depressing effect on investment of the interest rate rise is neutralized to some extent. The accelerator effect serves to create additional investments even with monetary expansion. But a monetary contraction which raises interest rates and reduces investment and output will see a further reduction in investment due to output contraction.

The expanded concept of the user cost of capital also offers additional policy options for affecting investment demand, such as investment tax credits or subsidies, embedded in the parameter 'τ'. Consider an expansionary fiscal policy that meets policy-makers' expectations with regard to an increase in output, but is accompanied by an unwelcome reduction in private investment. *The government could combine such an expansionary policy with an investment subsidy which reduces the cost of capital, thus providing a stimulus for investment that counteracts the rise in the market interest rate.*

The accelerator relationship serves to curtail the crowding-out effect on investment of a fiscal expansion and investments get a boost by the increase in output.

A fuller treatment of the cost of capital reveals the possibility of a government intervention through a capital subsidy to counteract the negative investment effects of a fiscal expansion.

11.8. TOBIN'S 'q'

It is readily observed that healthy stock market developments encourage physical investments by firms. The 'q' theory of investment emphasizes this link.

The 'q' ratio is the ratio of the market value of a firm to the replacement cost of capital. When the stock market rises and the firm's share price also rises, 'q' also rises, encouraging the firm to undertake additional investments.

> Tobin's q is the ratio of the market value of a firm to the replacement cost of capital.

$$q = \frac{\text{Market value of installed capital}}{\text{Replacement cost of installed capital}}$$

The numerator in Tobin's q is the value of the economy's capital as determined by the stock market and the denominator is the current market price of the capital. Essentially, when q > 1, the firm adds physical capital, since for each rupee worth of new equipment, the firm can sell a stock for 'q' and gain the difference (q − 1). Thus, the investment function is written as a positive function of 'q'. In other words, Tobin argued that net investment depends on whether q is greater or less than one. So if 'q' is greater than one then, the stock market values the installed capital of firms more than the replacement cost of capital. Then managers can raise the market value of their firm's shares by buying more capital. The converse is true if 'q' is less than one.

The Tobin's 'q' is a clever tool that connects the real sector to the stock market that is generally perceived to be a gambler's stronghold! If the marginal product of capital is greater than the cost of capital, then firms are supposed to be earning profits on their existing installed capital. These profits make the firms desirable for investors consequently raise the market value of shares. The opposite will be true if the marginal product falls short of the cost of capital. The benefit of Tobin's 'q' as a measure of the incentive to invest is that it reveals expected future profitability as well as current profitability. So higher expected profits increase the current share price of a company, raising Tobin's 'q' and thus stimulating investments today.

11.9. CONCLUSION

In this chapter we have presented the modern theories of consumption and investment demand as well as key elements of the economy's macroeconomic model. The Life Cycle and Permanent Income theories of consumption behaviour were noted to capture observed consumption patterns, time series as well as cross-sectional, better than the simple consumption function that is solely based on current incomes. The extended investment demand function derived and detailed in this chapter also goes well beyond the simple investment function of the IS–LM model which is based only on the nominal interest rate and incorporates the important impulses from output changes and other influences on the real user cost of capital.

The extended consumption and investment functions presented here were also shown to offer additional policy possibilities, while still remaining within the realm of the IS–LM model, for affecting output development in a positive manner.

SUMMARY

- The simple consumption function used in earlier chapters used the 'absolute income hypothesis', relating current consumption only to current income. Such a treatment gave current income excessive importance in consumption determination, which is not supported by empirical observation. The role of assets in influencing in consumption, clearly observable in times of real estate or stock market booms, was thus ignored.
- The simple consumption function could also not reconcile observed short and long-term consumption patterns, or differences in cross-sectional behaviour across different income groups.
- The modern theories of consumption, the Life Cycle and the Permanent Income theories, assume that households smoothen out consumption over a

lifetime, basing decisions on the net present value of income, or permanent income, which is a similar concept.

- The Life Cycle theory considers income from asset returns also.
- In the Permanent Income hypothesis, consumption depends only on permanent income and not on transitory or temporary income.
- Both the modern theories of consumption are capable of explaining short-run and long-run consumption patterns as well as the differences between the two.
- In the Permanent Income theory, the assumption that permanent consumption is only correlated to permanent income means that consumption will not rise in times of high transitory income for high-income households, so that the C/Y ratio falls as income rises. But for low-income households experiencing transitory income falls, consumption will not be reduced, which means that the C/Y ratio rises as income falls. Thus, both the time series and the cross-section patterns of consumption can be explained.
- Incorporation of the Life Cycle theory into the IS–LM model increases the potency of monetary policy which affects the value of asset holdings.
- The Permanent Income hypothesis implies that government policies affecting transitory incomes, such as a temporary tax cut, would not affect consumption, so that the intended effect may be absent.
- An expanded investment function will have output (the acceleration principle) and the real cost of capital (which is composed of the real interest rate, the depreciation rate and tax or subsidy rate on capital), as the determinants. Such a function offers the policy-maker some possibility of curtailing the crowding-out effect of a fiscal expansion.

CASE STUDY[9]

Savings Behaviour and the Permanent Income Model in Low-income Rural Households

The Permanent Income model is widely used to explain how individuals save or borrow to smooth their consumption. A key implication is that purely transitory fluctuations in income should not significantly affect consumption compared to changes in permanent income, that is, in the persistent components of income. For example, if rural households in the agricultural sector in low-income countries exhibit the same pattern of behaviour, then it would indicate that such households are able to cope well with the vagaries of weather and other sources of income variability that are associated with agricultural activities. Whatever the cause, the primary challenge facing populations in low-income countries is maintaining consumption when incomes are both low and highly variable. This would also question the demand for better

[9] The text for this case study has been adapted from Mark Rosenzweig, 'Savings Behaviour in Low Income Countries', *Oxford Review of Economic Policy* 17, no. 1 (2001): 40–54, Oxford University Press; Shubhashree Naik, 'Determinants and Pattern of Saving Behaviour in Rural Households of Western Odisha' (unpublished master's thesis, Department of Humanities and Social Sciences, National Institute of Technology Rourkela, 2016).

credit facilities for the rural poor across different regions across the world. Some researchers have used differences in the mean rainfall distribution to estimate the permanent income effect for rural farmers in India and applied contemporary village level indicators of rainfall deviations from mean rainfall to estimate the transitory component of income.

Rosenzweig and Wolpin have found that consumption was unresponsive to transitory changes in income using the estimates of rainfall. Farm income was stochastic and solely a function of rainfall.[10] Farmers can save and borrow, but they cannot purchase insurance or make bequests. This study ignores the role of labour particularly in low-income economies where families contribute the labour. Kochar, based on data from the International Crop Research Institute of Semi-Arid Tropics (ICRISAT) in India, focuses explicitly on how labour supply by family members is a choice and can serve as a consumption smoothing mechanism.[11] In Kochar's model, family members do not work in the wage–labour market. But hired labour is not a perfect substitute for family labour. In fact, Rosenzweig and Wolpin find that family members act as supervisors to avoid the moral hazard problem and that at least one family member functions as a supervisor in 12% of the families in the data base for India.[12]

A low-income environment is characterized by the absence of well-developed insurance and credit markets, particularly in the agricultural sector, where risk is associated with the standard problems of moral hazards and adverse selection. The Indian ICRISAT data indicate that approximately 85% of the value of total assets held by farm households is in the form of land and buildings. However, farmers in India rarely sell or buy land, nor use it as a buffer stock. Rather, 10 year data indicates that bullock sales were significantly higher when incomes were lower and purchases were high when incomes were high. This provides evidence that bullocks are used as a buffer stock. Naik's study of villages in the Sundergarh district of Odisha with a large tribal population finds that rural households prefer to save in the form of cash or paddy (near cash) instead of livestock, indicating the greater vulnerability of such families.[13]

Behrman, Foster and Rosenzweig use data from farm households in Pakistan to assess the role of banks in affecting savings compositions.[14] They show that the net-indebtedness of farm households' proximity to banks is positively related to harvest income. So, the seasonal nature of agricultural income influences savings behaviour. They also find that a 20% rise in harvest profits increases net savings by 9% for farms located within a 5 km radius of banks, thereby demonstrating that the introduction of formal credit agencies shifts the households away from informal smoothing mechanisms.

After reading the text in the text in the case study answer the following questions:

1. In low-income countries, does the consumption pattern rural households' follow the changes in the permanent component of their income?
2. Is rainfall the only source of variation in the income of farm households?
3. Is the absence of formal credit facilities likely to benefit farmers in the rural areas of low-income countries?

---

[10] Mark R. Rosenzweig and Kenneth I. Wolpin, 'Natural "Natural Experiments" in Economics', *Journal of Economic Literature* 38, no. 4 (2000): 827–74.

[11] Anjini Kochar, 'Smoothing Consumption by Smoothing Income: Hours-of-work Responses to Idiosyncratic Agricultural Shocks in Rural India', *The Review of Economics and Statistics* 81, no. 1 (1999): 50–61.

[12] Rosenzweig and Wolpin, 'Natural "Natural Experiments" in Economics', 827–74.

[13] Naik, 'Determinants and Pattern of Saving Behaviour in Rural Households of Western Odisha', 2016.

[14] Jere R. Behrman, Andrew D. Foster, and Mark R. Rosenzweig, 'The Dynamics of Agricultural Production and the Calorie-income Relationship: Evidence from Pakistan'. *Journal of Econometrics* 77, no. 1 (1997): 187–207.

Absolute income hypothesis

Short-term consumption function

Stagnation

The Life Cycle theory

Dissaving

Average propensity to consume

Wealth effect

Permanent income

Transitory income

User cost of capital

Accelerator model

Tobin's q

CONCEPT CHECK

State whether the following statements are true or false:

1. In the Life Cycle model, consumption demand is based on the present value of labour income as well as the current market value of asset holdings. The present value of asset income is captured by current asset values.

2. Total wealth is affected by an expansionary monetary policy, as the market value of bonds falls, the interest rate rises.

3. In the Permanent Income hypothesis, consumption is based on permanent income only, although there could be a transitory consumption component in any period, but that is unrelated to transitory income.

4. A temporary tax cut that affects transitory income will not affect consumption when the Permanent Income theory is applied. In contrast, consumption gets a boost with a temporary tax cut in the short-run Keynesian consumption framework.

5. When the price level is not considered to be fixed, then the real interest rate itself should be used in determining the cost of capital, instead of the nominal interest rate.

6. The accelerator model of investment demand links investment demand to changes in consumption.

7. The real cost of capital is not affected by changes in the real interest rate.

8. A rise in the nominal interest rate, or a fall in the (expected) inflation rate, both of which increase the real interest rate, raises the real cost of capital.

9. The accelerator relationship serves to curtail the crowding-out effect on investment of a fiscal expansion and investment gets a boost by the increase in output.

10. There is a possibility of a government intervention by way of a capital subsidy to counteract the negative investment effects of a fiscal expansion when cost of capital rises.

DISCUSSION QUESTIONS

1. What is the 'absolute income hypothesis' in relation to the theory of consumption demand?

2. What constitutes the common ground for both the modern theories of consumption?

3. What are the empirically observed consumption patterns that have to be captured by any satisfactory theory of consumption demand?

4. How do the Life Cycle and the Permanent Income theories reconcile the short- and long-term observed relationships between consumption and income?

5. What are the important elements of the user cost of capital that have not been taken into account in the IS–LM model of the previous chapters?

6. In the light of the existing theories of investment demand, is the government always powerless to prevent the crowding-out effects of a fiscal expansion? Substantiate your answer.

7. What do the modern theories of consumption behaviour imply for the effects of government tax policies?

8. Will the effectiveness of fiscal policy be affected when the IS–LM model is endowed with the Life Cycle theory?

9. In the same vein, what are the implications for fiscal policy of extending the investment demand function in the IS–LM model as portrayed in this chapter?

10. Does the incorporation of the Life Cycle theory in the IS–LM model have any implications for the effectiveness of monetary policy?

11. Does the presence of liquidity constraints have any impact on the interpretation of consumption demand patterns suggested by the Life Cycle model?

12

CHAPTER

The Role of the Government and the Government Budget Balance

| LEARNING OBJECTIVES |

Upon completion of this chapter, the reader will be able to:

- Get an idea of the scope of government activity under different types of economic systems.
- Understand the necessity for government interventions in the market economy and see how such interventions and participation expands the public sector of the economy.
- Appreciate the implications of the definitions of different types of budget deficits and calculate these with given budget data.
- Evaluate the relevance of the different budget deficit formulations for budgetary policy reforms and policy-making in the Indian context.

12.1. INTRODUCTION

12.1.1. The Role of the Government

In the discussion of fiscal and monetary policy, in the closed as well as an open economy, the role of the government has been of macroeconomic stabilization, in influencing output and increasing employment. This role is, indeed a major one and has important implications for the relative size of the public sector and for the structure of the economy itself, particularly in the welfare states of Europe as has been pointed out by Soderstrom and Viotti.[1] These authors show that with the government acting as the 'employer of last resort', absorbing all unemployed labour, the wage rates could keep rising with the assurance of full employment in the kitty, but that the expansion of the public sector had a flip side in the contraction of the competitive sectors of the economy.

However, the role of the government is not limited to macroeconomic stabilization. In this chapter we describe briefly the important roles of the government, some of which may not be well understood by the layman on the street! The implications of these roles for the government budget are also discussed, leaving the topic of the impact of government budget deficits on the macro-economy to the Chapter 14.

The chapter is structured as follows: in Section 12.2, we make a comparison across different countries and economic systems, with the objective of obtaining insights on how the fundamental characteristics of an economy influence the size and reach of the public sector. Sections 12.3–12.5 focus on the major roles of the government, the rationale for these and their execution. The remaining sections are devoted to the analysis of the government budget. There is a final, concluding section.

12.2. THE SIZE AND REACH OF THE PUBLIC SECTOR IN DIFFERENT TYPES OF NATIONAL ECONOMIES

12.2.1. Pure Socialist Economies

A purely socialist economy is one where the entire economy is the public sector. The private sector is almost absent.

We start this section by observing that the People's Republic of China, with its vibrant private sector, does not fall into the category of a *purely socialist economy*! However, the 'late' Soviet Union would have fitted this bill. In such an economy, the public sector is synonymous or identical with the entire economy, sector outputs are all centrally planned and there is no market mechanism, the famous *'invisible hand'* of Adam Smith in operation. Instead, *'the long arm of the government'* is there in every nook and corner of the economy, leaving no room for any other organized force. There is 100% ownership of the factors of production by the government in the economy.

12.2.2. Pure Capitalist or Market Economies

A purely market economy is one where the role of the government is negligible, present only in the defence and social sectors.

Pure market economies, with allowance for a government role in defence and foreign affairs, are also very rare. Perhaps Hong Kong, before its take-over by China, was one. In such economies, the government's role is very limited, not visible, perhaps, even in education and health.

[1] Hans Soderstrom and Staffan Viotti, 'Money Wage Disturbance and the Endogeneity of the Public Sector in an Open Economy', in *Inflation and Employment in Open Economies*, ed. A. Lindbeck (Amsterdam: North-Holland Publishing Co., 1978).

And now we turn to the most important type of economy, with different shades even within a broad categorization, namely, the 'mixed economy'.

12.3. THE MIXED ECONOMY

12.3.1. The Indian Economy

The expression that the public sector rules over '*the commanding heights*' of the economy may not be entirely true now (any more), but India remains very much a mixed economy, with an important role for the government in the economy.

In India, unlike in the Western market, *mixed economies*, there is considerable government production of goods and not just of services. Thus, one finds some state governments even undertaking the production of consumer items like soaps and toothpastes. The rationale for undertaking such production, which is better left to the competitive private sector and market forces of demand, may be that such items now constitute 'basic necessities'. But, there is an anomaly in this position that these items are not rationed, so that even the rich can buy such government-produced necessities.

The Indian economy differs from the welfare market economies of Europe also with regard to the heavy involvement in the production of metals, minerals, defence equipment, etc., all of which belong to the commanding heights of the economy. The Indian government is also involved in providing health services and educational facilities to the population and in this respect it does not differ from the Western economies, which also devote a greater percentage of their total national outputs to efforts directed towards human capital formation and sustainment.

In fact, the Indian government has been criticized for lagging behind many other countries, even in the developing world, such as Costa Rica, in increasing the reach primary education. The policy-makers have been also criticized for investing too much in higher education, at the expense of primary education, which has been starved of funds. Yet, it has to be pointed out that it was the far-sightedness of the planners in setting up world-renowned institutions like the Indian Institutes of Technology, that has enabled India to emerge as a leader in the information technology area, though it took many years for that concept to materialize—which is always the case with returns to investments in human capital formation.

Mixed economies have both public and private sectors participating in all economic activities. The government is the main provider of public goods and is involved in some market-oriented areas as well.

In welfare states, the government is the key provider of health services, most of which are available free to the citizens of the country. The private holdings of resources are high in these countries, but the government is the key employer.

12.3.2. The Welfare States of Europe

In the *welfare states* of Europe like Sweden, Norway, Holland, etc. (and, perhaps, even England, the oldest welfare state), there is heavy involvement of the government in the provision of services. Health facilities and medical treatment used to be entirely free, until the conditions of the European Union membership changed the situation, now requiring the residents to meet a part of the medical costs themselves.

The contrast to a mixed economy like India lies in the fact that these welfare states do not undertake government production of goods that can be produced gainfully in the competitive private sector. Thus, private ownership of factors of production in the Swedish economy is close to 90%. But the public sector of these welfare states are large, as percentages of the total national output, due to the large output of government services and the large number of public sector employees. These nations have also had a heavy tax burden with high marginal tax rates considered necessary for financing public services, in some cases the marginal taxes reaching 90%. But tax reforms, mostly in the 1990s, have reduced the marginal tax rates to around 50–60% at the maximum.

Other market, mixed economies like the United States, Singapore, etc. have a smaller public sector. See Table 12.1 for an international comparison in this regard. While countries like Denmark and Sweden have almost 50% of GDP in their total

TABLE 12.1

The Size of the Public Sector: An International Comparison

Country	Size of the Public Sector: % of GDP
Australia	37.48
Canada	40.41
Denmark	55.67
Germany	43.98
Japan	39.27
Singapore	19.01
Sweden	48.93
UK	40.00
USA	35.04
Australia	37.48
Bangladesh	13.80
Brazil	42.03
China	31.34
India	28.00
Kenya	27.78
Malaysia	25.24
Pakistan	19.74
South Africa	33.51
Russia	36.27

Source: Table created using data from World Economic Outlook; data presented is for the year 2015.

FIGURE 12.1

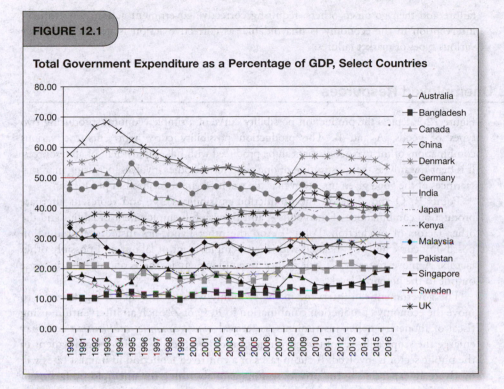

Total Government Expenditure as a Percentage of GDP, Select Countries

government expenditure representing the size of the sector, countries like Bangladesh and Pakistan have less than 20% of GDP of the public sector. The data is for the year 2015. Socialist countries like China or Russia have more than 30% size of public sector. Figure 12.1 provides a diagrammatic comparison of the importance of the public sector in a number of countries.

The next section analyses the reasons which necessitate government intervention in the national economy. Let us conclude this section by noting again that the scope and reach of the public sector varies between countries. While in India, the government is active in providing services as well as in production, in the welfare states of Europe, the government is active only in providing services.

12.4. MARKET FAILURES AND CORRECTIVE GOVERNMENT ACTION

Government intervention is essential in any economy of any type, because of the presence of *market failures*. In this book, we have already discussed one such failure, the inability of the market to guarantee full employment. We start with a discussion of such a market

Market failure occurs when the market is unable to guarantee full employment.

failure and then go on to others, requiring corrective government action. Government intervention in the economy is unavoidable, as corrective action is needed to handle various types of market failures.

12.4.1. Unemployed Resources

Figure 12.2 depicts the production possibility curve of a simple economy, producing two types of goods, A and B. The production possibility curve represents the various combinations of the two goods that can be produced with full employment of all resources. It is bent inwards, as the substitution of one good for the other involves increasing marginal sacrifices of the good given up, given that the resources are specialized in production.

Points R, Q and Z lie on the production possibility curve and represent alternate production combinations of the goods A and B, with full employment of labour and the other factors of production. Point 'F', on the other hand, lies inside the production possibility curve and is associated with the unemployment of labour and possibly other factors. A move to, say, 'R', will reduce unemployment in the economy and increase output to the potential level.

Macroeconomic stabilization is countercyclical policies of the government to contain inflation and promote growth.

The government can intervene in the economy with fiscal policies, for instance, to move the economy's production combination to R, Q or Z. Such an intervention, using fiscal or monetary policy instruments, is termed *macroeconomic stabilization* and may enlarge the scope and size of the government sector, especially if direct employment in the public sector is involved. A cut in taxes or a contrived reduction in interest rates will motivate an expansion in the private sector, again absorbing the unemployed factors of production.

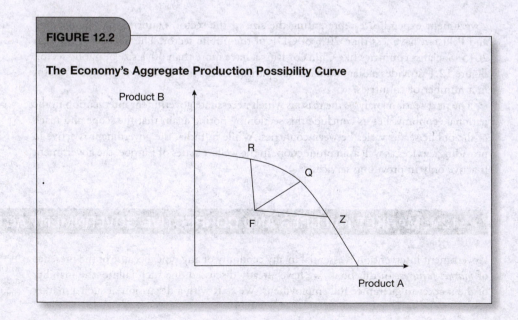

FIGURE 12.2

The Economy's Aggregate Production Possibility Curve

12.4.2. Public Goods

Public goods, as the term indicates, are goods which are consumed by all. To understand this, think of a person eating an apple, a private good. His/her consumption of the apple implies that no one else can consume that apple. If you buy a cinema ticket to see a movie, that ticket is not available to anyone else.

In contrast to the consumption of a private good, individual consumption of a public good does not prevent anyone else from also consuming it. Examples of public goods are crime-free streets, national defence, clean air, etc.

Public goods cannot be produced by the private sector, at least to any large extent, because it does not pay the private sector to do so. To get paid for the activity, the person consuming it has to be identified and charged, which is impossible in the case of public goods.

Hence, the production public goods falls in the domain of the government, which devotes substantial resources to producing these goods. Typically, the production of public goods increases with the level of development of a country, as the country devotes more attention to foreign affairs, the quality of life, etc. The private sector cannot provide public goods to any large extent as it is not profitable. The government is the most important and often the sole provider of public goods like regional and national security, clean environment, central parks, etc.

12.4.3. Externalities

Externalities, positive as well as negative, arise because the market pricing mechanism is not comprehensive enough to take into account social costs and benefits. Externalities exist for many production activities and are not priced by the market for individual firms creating the externalities. Government action is needed to correct the impact of both positive and negative externalities on the economy.

Let us start by looking at externalities of the negative kind and possible government action to remove or reduce the *externality*.

> Externality is the cost or benefit arising of out of the market pricing mechanism, which requires government intervention.

12.4.4. Negative Externalities

Consider a factory producing leather and emitting effluents into the adjoining river, polluting the water. Alternatively, think of a chemical firm discharging effluents into the air.

Now, these firms do not directly take into account the costs of such pollution as it is not something they have to bear, such as the wages paid to employees, unless they are forced to do so by the government.

When the costs to the environment and to society of such pollution are not taken into account, the firms will be producing at too high a level to be socially optimal. What can the government do to force these firms to lower their production to a socially optimum level?

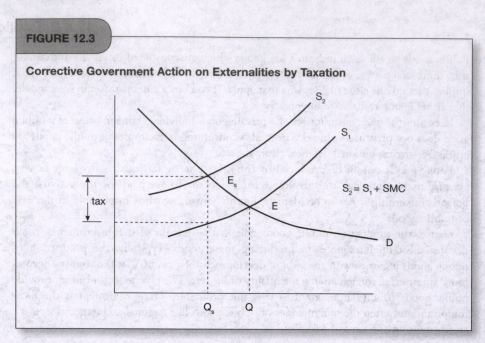

FIGURE 12.3

Corrective Government Action on Externalities by Taxation

All the possibilities of correcting externalities will not be taken up here, since such details belong to a course in environmental economics (with river pollution by firms which impose a cost on fishermen, there is even a possibility of arriving at a socially optimum level of firm production by bargaining between the two private parties). Here we will take up one course of action that the government can resort to that is, the imposition of a tax on the polluting producer. Figure 12.3 portrays the effect of such a tax.

In Figure 12.3, the firm's output is at 'Q' without taxation. S_1 is the supply curve of the firm, which is nothing but the (upward-sloping part of the) marginal cost curve. Curve S_2 is drawn, adding the social marginal cost on to the private marginal cost of the firm. So,

$$S_2 = \text{Total marginal cost} = S_1 + \text{Social marginal cost of pollution (SMC)}.$$

Assume that the government considers the output level Q_s to be socially optimal. Then, a tax can be imposed such that the tax equals the social marginal cost at output level Q_s. Such a policy moves the equilibrium from E to E_s and the output level to Q_s.

Such a policy is also effective in reducing cigarette consumption, etc. Note from Figure 12.2 that the price level also increases, but that the price increase is less than the tax imposed. This has happened because the seller passes on a part of the tax to the consumer. But a detailed analysis of these issues lies more in the realm of a course in public finance.

Tax administration, monitoring of firms and pollution levels, and so on involve an increase in the size of the public sector. Monitoring costs will be higher with a policy of fixing a pollution limit on firms by decree.

The policy just discussed will also involve a change in the goods combination represented in a simple fashion in Figure 12.2, in the production possibilities curve. If 'B' is the polluting sector, the government corrective policy may change the combination from 'Z' to 'Q', or even 'R', with more production by the non-polluting sector.

12.4.5. Positive Externalities

Education is sometimes taken to be a public good, but is treated more properly as a good or service with a positive externality. Research and development is, similarly, a good with a positive externality. A private firm undertaking research and development may reach and stop at a certain level of activity which is profit-maximizing, not taking into account the positive externality to society through the generation of knowledge.

The government may motivate the scientific, knowledge producing firm, to expand its activities by giving a subsidy (see Figure 12.4).

In Figure 12.4, S_2 is the marginal cost line, drawn adjusting for the negative social marginal cost associated with the social marginal productivity of the research output. Remember from microeconomics that, with labour as the only variable factor, marginal cost is given as W/MP, where MP is marginal productivity. Now S_2 will be the marginal cost line with the social marginal productivity added to private marginal productivity.

The government can make an estimate of the level of research output that is socially optimal and allow a subsidy to the firm to generate that level of output.

We now turn to another type of market failure which justifies a huge amount of government activity, namely, economies of scale.

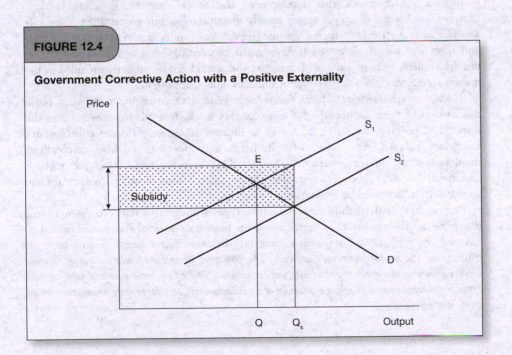

FIGURE 12.4

Government Corrective Action with a Positive Externality

12.5. THE ECONOMIES OF SCALE

Some activities like electricity generation and other utilities exhibit increasing returns to scale over a large level of output range, which requires a very large level of production capacity. If left to the private sector, the production scenario would involve an unacceptable level of market power to an individual private company. Such a scenario necessitates government production in the utilities sector, in most countries. In countries like India, the utilities sector is also considered a sensitive sector, almost part of the commanding heights group of sectors, that is, best left to the public sector. Although now a certain level of private sector participation is also encouraged and even considered desirable, since the government is unable to 'deliver the goods'.

12.6. MARKET POWER

Market power is the ability of a firm or a group of firms as in oligopolistic collusion or monopoly to maintain a price above that which would exist if there was competition.

Unacceptable levels of *market power*, sometimes with market ownership ratios of over 80%, or collusion between firms in price fixing in an oligopoly industry structure, inevitably lead to government intervention in most countries (the recent developments with Microsoft in the USA is an example). Again, the administrative apparatus required for such interventions has steadily grown over the years and is another reason for the expansion of public sector in scope and size.

This chapter has so far dealt with the rationale for the existence and expansion of the public sector. Obviously, this development has to be financed in some fashion. Government budget financing comes mostly from taxation, but government revenue is also forthcoming from net interest income (if positive), profits of government enterprises and from the sale of assets and disinvestment proceedings. But non-tax revenues are usually available only in some financial years and should not be properly included in the budget statements to show government finances in a positive light.

There are various kinds of taxes available for generating government revenues, but a description of these lie outside the scope of this book. Instead, we now turn to the impacts of government activities as well as independent events on the government's budgetary balance. Any policy of subsidizing activities with positive externalities involves a drain on the government budget. On the other hand, taxing a negative externality provides revenues, even though the main objective was to reduce private sector output, not revenue generation.

Before taking up the definitions of the various types of budgetary balance representations, it may be desirable to say a few words about the impact of external events, not related to government actions, on government budgetary balance. These events usually have an impact on the macro-economy as well. *The structure of industry often requires market interventions by the government. This happens when a single firm or a group of firms possess excessive market power, or when economies of scale necessitate very large scale production by an individual producer.*

12.7. AUTOMATIC STABILIZERS

Automatic stabilizers have an impact on the economy, without any particular step or policy taken to initiate such an impact. Examples of automatic stabilizers appear in the government budget balance itself, as will be seen in the next section.

Unemployment benefits: Consider the payment of benefits to unemployed people. More people become unemployed when the economy contracts, perhaps due to lack of aggregate demand. The payment of unemployment benefits acts the same way as fiscal expansion by the government. As the unemployed persons receive benefit payments, they spend the amount on goods and services, according to their marginal propensity to consume out of disposable income, serving to create additional demand.

Thus, the automatic release of unemployment benefits—as more people become unemployed—works as an automatic stabilizer, since it counteracts the recessionary trend in the national economy.

Income taxes: The marginal tax schedule guiding income taxation also works as an automatic stabilizer. As people become richer in an expansionary phase of the economy, they move into higher income brackets, having to pay higher tax rates, which take away more of their earned incomes, reducing their levels of disposable income, thus providing a brake on the heating-up economy. Automatic stabilizers are triggered off as an automatic response (without any deliberate policy change) when the economy becomes heated or contracts reducing the extent of overheating or contraction of the economy. We now turn to the various representations of the government budgetary balance.

12.8. THE GOVERNMENT BUDGET BALANCE

12.8.1. The Overall Budget Balance

The overall *government budget balance* is the difference between government revenues and expenditures. Assuming for simplicity that the only tax is the income tax and including unemployment benefits in the general transfer term, the budget balance 'GB' is given by

> The government budget balance is the difference between government revenues and expenditure.

$$GB = Yt - G - TR \qquad (12.1)$$

Here 'TR' includes pensions, unemployment benefits and other income transfers.

From Figure 12.2, it is clear that automatic stabilizers affect the overall budget balance. Increased unemployment benefit payments deteriorate the budget balance, while increased tax revenues lead to an improvement.

In fact, the relationship between the cyclical developments in output and the budget can be represented in a simple diagram.

In Figure 12.5, increases in output are seen to improve the budget balance, while a deep recession drives the balance to negative. The reasons for this relationship are obvious:

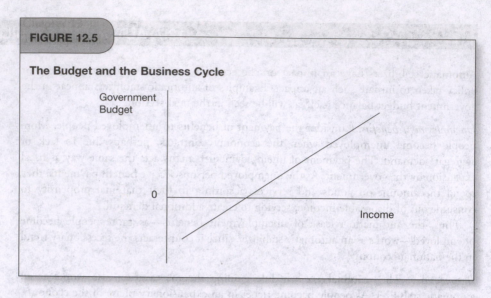

FIGURE 12.5

The Budget and the Business Cycle

increased output brings in more tax revenues and reduces unemployment benefits payments, while a downward spiral in output will reduce tax revenues and release a larger stream of unemployment benefit payments.

The overall budgetary balance is the difference between total revenues, including capital and current account (or revenue account) incomes and total expenditures, including current and capital account expenditures. Increases in output and employment improve the overall budgetary balance due to higher tax revenues and reduced unemployment benefit payments.

12.8.2. Structural and Cyclical Budget Balances

It is fruitful to differentiate between 'structural' and 'cyclical' budget balances, as it provides a pointer to some steps that may have to be undertaken by the government, in the overall context of budgetary policies.

The cyclical budget balance is simply the difference between the actual budget balance and the budget balance that would exist at the full employment level of output. Thus, the cyclical budget balance is given as

$$GCB = GB - GBF \qquad (12.2)$$

In (12.2), GCB is the cyclical budget balance and GB_F is the budget balance consistent with the full employment level of output.

A cyclical budget deficit can be eliminated by expansionary fiscal or monetary polices which lead to the full employment level of output, giving the government increased tax revenues.

The structural budget balance is the budget balance (GB_F) that would prevail at the full employment level of output. The structural budget balance is unresponsive to government policies designed to affect output. Factors that could influence the structural balance include increased productivity in the government sectors, changes in the budget structure such as a cut-back in subsidies, or in defence spending due to reduced threat perceptions, increased tax collections due to better governance, etc.

12.8.3. Ex-ante and Ex-post Budget Balance

The terms ex-ante and ex-post refer to the economic scenario before and after government policies affect output. This distinction is important, since the government may be undertaking a policy, such as a tax increase and targeting a certain level of budgetary balance. But, the change in output and the resulting impact on tax revenues can cause the government projections of the budgetary balance to go haywire.

To understand this issue better, refer again to Equation (12.1). Assume that the government increases the tax rate (t) to obtain an increase in tax revenues by (Y.dt). The equation will give the new (ex-ante) budgetary balance if the new tax rate is used instead of the old tax rate.

However, subsequent developments could deteriorate the budget balance. The tax increase reduces disposable income and depresses output through the income multiplier effect, as seen in Chapters 3 and 8–10. Thus, 'Y' becomes endogenous in Equation (12.1). The ex-post budgetary balance is the final level of the budget balance after all such adjustments have taken place. The ex-post balance will be less than the ex-ante balance in the case of a tax increase, though larger than the original budget balance before the policy was undertaken.

A numerical example to illustrate the difference between the ex-ante and the ex-post budget balances is given as a discussion question at the end of this chapter.

12.8.4. Fiscal, Revenue and Primary Budget Balances

The budget balance or rather budget deficit targets in India are usually stated in terms of the fiscal deficit (whereas the overall budget deficit figures in discussions in the European Union). But there are compelling reasons for concentrating on the revenue and primary deficits, rather than on the fiscal deficit. We may be jumping the gun a bit here as the definitions of these budget deficits are yet to be given.

12.9. THE FISCAL DEFICIT

The *fiscal deficit* is the *total revenue in the revenue account minus total expenditure*. Thus, capital income is excluded, which is where it differs from the overall budget deficit.

But note that capital expenditure is included in the calculation of the fiscal deficit. So, investment enters the fiscal deficit account with a negative connotation, despite the fact that such investment bodes well for the future, increasing the productive capital stock in

Fiscal deficit is the total revenue less the total expenditure.

Revenue deficit is the total revenue in the revenue account minus total expenditure in the revenue account.

the economy. From this perspective, the *revenue deficit* should to be considered to be an improvement over the fiscal deficit in judging government budgetary policies.

Table 12.2 shows the mode of calculation of the fiscal deficit and the development of the deficit over a few financial years. The revenue and primary deficits are also presented in the table.

12.9.1. The Revenue Deficit

The revenue deficit is equal to the *total revenue in the revenue account minus total expenditure in the revenue account*. Thus, capital expenditure is not included here, which means that the revenue deficit will be always less than the fiscal deficit.

It would be better for the central as well as the state governments to narrow down the revenue deficit, rather than the fiscal deficit. Relying too much on the fiscal deficit to evaluate budgetary policy effectiveness may mean that important, productive investment opportunities go begging. The effect would be similar to that deriving from the imposition of stringent demands on the budget and current account deficit positions of heavily indebted countries by multinational organizations to grant debt relief. Such demands end up by diminishing the future production potential of those poor nations and consigning them to poverty for a longer period of time.

The primary deficit could be deemed to be an improvement over the revenue deficit concept, in the sense that the importance of controlling the burgeoning public debt of the country is highlighted by the former, that is, by the primary deficit concept.

Refer now to Table 12.2. Examining the developments of the fiscal and revenue deficits over time, it can be seen that while the fiscal deficit reduced between the years 2009–10 to 2010–11 and again between 2012–13 and 2013–14, the revenue deficit increased. The reason for this is also clear from the table: the fiscal deficit was reduced by cutting down on capital expenditures, not a welcome development! The fiscal deficit and the revenue deficit in the years of the first decade and half of the 21st century in India is shown in Figure 12.6.

12.9.2. The Primary Deficit

Primary deficit is revenue deficit minus interest payment on government debt.

The *primary deficit* is a concept that is important for both a country's external, balance of payments accounts as well as the government's budget accounts. The reason for this is that narrowing in on this definition of the budget deficit enables a budget analyst to note whether the government's budgetary policies are causing an increase in the public debt burden.

How are the primary deficit and the level of government debt related? The relationship is clear from the very definition of the primary deficit. The primary deficit is just *the revenue deficit minus the interest payments on government*. So, if the primary deficit is in the red, it means that the revenue or the current (as opposed to the capital account) budgetary position is creating a deficit, one which is amenable to reductions through current expenditure reductions or revenue generation. This is because the interest payments on past debt cannot be reduced and have to run their life through.

TABLE 12.2

Government Budget Accounts and Budget Deficits (Select Years)

	2008–09	2009–10	2010–11	2011–12	2012–13	2013–14 (BE)	2013–14 (RE)	2014–15 (BE)
1. Revenue receipts (a + b)	540,259	572,811	788,471	751,437	8,776,330	1,056,330	1,029,251	1,189,763
(a) Tax revenue (net of States' share)	443,319	456,536	569,869	629,765	740,256	884,078	836,025	977,258
(b) Non-tax revenue	96,940	116,275	218,602	121,672	137,357	172,252	193,226	212,505
2. Revenue expenditure	796,798	911,809	1,040,723	1,145,786	1,243,509	1,436,168	1,399,539	1,568,112
(a) Interest payment	192,204	213,093	234,022	273,150	313,169	370,684	380,066	427,011
(b) Major subsidies	123,206	134,658	164,516	211,319	247,493	220,972	245,451	251,397
(c) Defence expenditures	73,305	90,669	92,061	103,011	111,277	11,693	124,800	134,412
3. Revenue deficit	253,539	338,998	252,252	394,349	365,896	379,838	370,288	378,349
4. Capital receipts	343,697	451,676	408,857	552,928	532,754	608,967	561,183	605,129
(a) Recovery of loans	6,139	8,613	12,420	18,850	16,268	10,654	10,803	10,527
(b) Other receipts	566	24,581	22,846	18,088	25,890	55,814	25,841	63,425
(c) Borrowings and other liabilities	336,992	418,482	373,591	515,990	490,596	542,499	524,539	531,177
5. Capital expenditure	90,158	112,678	156,604	158,579	166,858	229,129	190,895	226,780
6. Non-debt receipts [1 + 4(a) + 4(b)]	546,964	606,005	823,737	738,375	919,771	1,122,798	1,065,895	1,263,715
7. Total expenditure [2 + 5 = 7(a) + 7(b)]	883,956	1,024,487	1,197,327	1,304,365	1,410,367	1,665,297	1,590,434	1,794,892
(a) Plan expenditure	275,235	303,391	379,029	412,375	413,625	555,322	475,532	575,000
(b) Non-plan expenditure	608,721	721,096	818,298	891,990	996,742	1,109,975	1,114,902	1,219,892
8. Fiscal deficit [7 − 1 − 4(a) − 4(b)]	336,992	418,482	373,590	515,990	490,596	542,499	524,539	531,177
9. Primary deficit [8 − 2(a)]	144,788	205,389	139,568	242,840	177,427	171,815	144,473	104,166

Source: Handbook of Statistics 2015–16, RBI publication under DBIE.

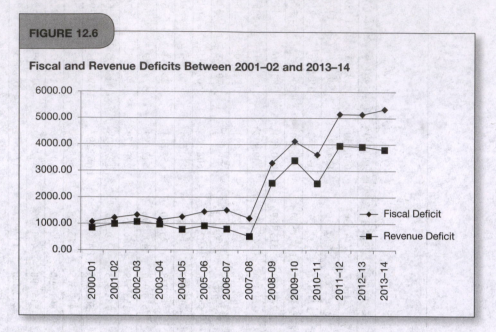

FIGURE 12.6

Fiscal and Revenue Deficits Between 2001–02 and 2013–14

An increase in the primary deficit might also mean that the government has to resort to additional borrowings to cover the increased deficit, an action that will push up the interest payments in the future, increasing the revenue deficits in the coming years.

Thus, a reduction in the debt burden, or a non-increasing debt burden of the government, requires a reduction in the primary deficit while a stable debt burden, derived later in Chapter 14, presupposes a balanced primary account.

As an exercise, the reader might go back to Table 12.2 and see if the government has been on the right track to a stabilization of the debt burden, by examining the development of the primary deficit. Let us re-capitulate:

The Fiscal Deficit = Total expenditure (including capital account expenditure) – Income in the revenue account. Capital income is not included.

The Revenue Deficit = Expenditure in the revenue account – Income in then revenue account. Capital expenditure and income are not included.

The Primary Budget Deficit = (Expenditure on the revenue account – Net interest payments on debt) – Income on the revenue account.

12.10. CONCLUSION

In this chapter, the spotlight has been on the scope of government actions in a mixed economy and the implications of being at the helm of the country's economic affairs on government finances. The macroeconomic impacts of the government's budgetary imbalances are taken up in Chapter 14.

The differences between the various concepts of the budget deficit noted in this chapter assume considerable importance in the Indian context. It does seem to be the case that undue attention is being given to the fiscal deficit, both in the central and the state budgets. From the point of view of minimizing government financial imbalances with the least harm done to the long-run prospects of the economy, a close watch should be kept, instead, on both the revenue and the primary deficits.

Macroeconomic stabilization is only one reason, even if one of the most important ones, for the existence and expansion of the public sector in an economy. Providing a stable environment for growth and development with equity, of which the physical environment is only one element, is something which only the national government can orchestrate.

Much of this chapter has dealt with the quantitative aspects of government: the size of the government, the level of the budget deficit, etc. But the qualitative aspects of government are equally important. It is often said and is probably true, that an effective and small public sector is better for an economy than a large and inefficient public sector. In this context, the goal of governance, often stated by Indian leaders (but, unfortunately, not put into actual practice), that every rupee spent should count (in poverty reduction) assumes great significance. Also, it has to be pointed out that government intervention need not necessarily correct a market failure and can even move the economy from a point on the production possibility curve to a point inside the curve.

Normally, the scope of government activity in the economy is larger when a country is struggling to get on to a high growth path. The government is then active even in the production area and not engaged only or mostly in the public services sector, as in the European welfare states. Low levels of development necessitate government production as well as 'infant industry' protection for setting up industries. But as important as this 'engagement' in the economy is the required policy decision to 'disengage' from sectors that would be run more efficiently by the private sector. In this sense, government strategy in India has not been optimal, despite various disinvestment initiatives.

In conclusion, it may be pointed out that the role of the government is a key one, even in countries like the USA and Korea, considered to be bastions of free market capitalism. The US government's industrial policy has not just been limited to controlling market power as the government has actively helped American firms to win competitive bids in key technological areas worldwide. The contribution of the US public sector is also very visible in the area of education. Similarly, the Korean government has been very active in industrial policy, selecting areas with possible Korean international competitive advantage and then assisting Korean firms in those sectors to gain worldwide prominence and success.

The natural corollary to the discussion of government budget deficits presented in this chapter is an analysis of the macroeconomic impacts of these deficits. This topic is taken up in Chapter 14.

SUMMARY

- The government has to necessarily intervene in the market economy due to various types of market failures, to correct such failures.

- Macroeconomic stabilization to reduce unemployment is a major reason for government activity and for the gradual increase of the public sector.
- Public goods are goods whose consumption by an individual does not preclude consumption by another individual. Safe neighbourhoods, clean air, national defence, the legal system, etc. are all examples of public goods. Since the private sector produces these only to a small extent, or not at all, the government has the responsibility to provide these.
- The government has to intervene in the economy also due to the existence of externalities in production by the private sector. Externalities arise because the private sector is not confronted with the full marginal cost or benefit of their production. There can be both positive and negative externalities.
- Market power (too much of it!) in various sectors of industry and services and the existence of economies of scale in the production of utilities, also require corrective action or participation in production by the government.
- Government intervention and participation in economic activities require financing, which is mostly through tax revenues. Government budgets may sometimes show a deficit.
- Automatic stabilizers are triggered off when the economy expands or contracts and affects the government's budgetary balance also. The payment of unemployment benefits and the automatic movement of economic actors into different income tax brackets during the business cycle, are all examples of the working of automatic stabilizers.
- The various definitions of the government budget balance include that of the overall budget balance, the fiscal deficit, the revenue deficit and the primary deficit.
- To evaluate budgetary policies, it may be better to focus on the revenue deficit, which excludes productive capital expenditures and the primary deficit, which excludes interest payments on debt from the fiscal deficit, rather than on the fiscal deficit itself.

CASE STUDY

How to Avoid a Fiscal Debacle?

Like in 2012–13, when the Centre's fiscal deficit was kept below 5% of GDP, it is a reduction in plan expenditure that has helped Finance Minister achieve the fiscal target in the year 2014.[2] Containing the deficit to 4.6% in 2013–14 is a result of the combination of cuts and savings from the low utilization of allocated funds. The Centre's total plan spending this year

[2] 'Averting a Fiscal Wreck', *The Hindu Business Line*, 17 February 2014, http://www.thehindubusinessline.com/opinion/editorial/averting-a-fiscal-wreck/article5699599.ece

according to the revised estimates is expected to be ₹79,790 crore lower than the budgeted amount. It was a whopping ₹107,400 crore below the budget estimate in the previous fiscal. It is such compression, as well as the rolling over of ₹35,000 crore of the fuel subsidy payments to the next fiscal year and making state-owned enterprises cough up around ₹14,300 crore of more-than-budgeted dividends, that has enabled the fiscal deficit to be contained below the 'red line' of 4.8%.

But did the Finance Minister have an alternative in a scenario where the Centre's gross tax revenues and mop-up from disinvestment were slated to fall short of the budget estimates by almost ₹107,000 crore? Cutting Plan Spending isn't desirable in the midst of a slowdown, but the cost of not adhering to fiscal targets and the negative perception it could trigger among global investors in these difficult times for emerging economies is far worse. Moreover, by steering the economy back on the path of fiscal consolidation, the government has created some elbow room for the RBI to cut interest rates. Easing inflationary pressures and a stable rupee makes this more feasible. Lower interest rates in tandem with excise duty reductions can provide a much-needed boost to investor and consumer sentiments.

Going forward though, both growth as well as fiscal consolidation require more enduring policy interventions. This can be possible by generating greater revenue buoyancy and cutting wasteful non-Plan expenditures. More public resources will be released for highways, railways, irrigation and other productive infrastructure investments. The economy-wide stimulus from this will bring more revenue for the government, resulting in a virtuous cycle of higher growth and fiscal consolidation.

After reading the text given in the case study, answer the following questions:

1. Do you think containing the fiscal deficit is the primary objective of a government?
2. What are the key goals of any macroeconomic stabilization policy?
3. What is the policy prescription suggested by the author for fiscal consolidation?

KEYWORDS

Purely socialist economies	Macroeconomic stabilization
Purely market economies	Externality
Mixed economies	Government budget balance
Welfare states	Fiscal deficit
Market failure	Revenue deficit
Market power	Primary deficit

CONCEPT CHECK

State whether the following statements are true or false:

1. The scope and reach of the public sector varies between countries; in the welfare states of Europe, the government is active only in providing services.

2. Government intervention in the economy is avoidable and its corrective action sometimes leads to various types of market failures.

3. An important intervention by the government in the economy is to reduce unemployment and act as the employer of last resort which enlarges the public sector to unwieldy proportions like the Indian Railways.

4. The government is the most important, often the sole provider of public goods like regional and national security, law and order.

5. Government action is needed to correct the impact of both positive and negative externalities on the economy.

6. When a single firm or a group of firms possesses excessive market power, or when economies of scale necessitate a very large scale of production by an individual producer, there is a need for governments to intervene and prevent the exploitation of market power.

7. The overall budget balance is the difference between total revenues, including capital and current account income and total expenditure, including current and capital account expenditures.

DISCUSSION QUESTIONS

1. Compare the role of the government sector in the SA, in a welfare state like Sweden or Holland as well as in India.

2. Do you think the public sector in India should 'disengage' from some activity in India? Give reasons.

3. How will increased investments by private firms affect the government's budgetary balance? How will a global economic crisis, transmitted to India, affect the Indian government's budgetary balance?

4. Can you motivate the necessity for the government to be active in the education sector?

5. Take any state government's budget positions for four years. Analyse the budgetary performance using the various definitions of the budget deficit given in this chapter.

6. The total national income 'Y' of a country is 1,000 million dollars in a financial year. The tax rate is 10%, and total government spending, including transfers, is 200 million dollars. The marginal propensity to consume is 0.8.

   Seeking to balance the budget, the government raises the tax rate to 20%. Calculate the current, ex-ante after the tax change and the ex-post government budget balance. State whether the government eventually succeeds in balancing the budget.

7. Evaluate the performance of the government from the budgetary accounts presented above, from the fiscal, revenue and primary deficits for the two consecutive years. Budget account data for a state in the union is as follows (in 1,000 millions):

	Year 1	Year 2
GDP	100,000	100,000
Revenue account expenditure On goods, salaries, pensions, etc. Excluding interest payments	4,000	4,500
Net interest payments	1,000	200
Tax revenues	3,500	3,500
Capital expenditure	1,500	500
Capital income	0	0

Note: Interest payments in year 2 were reduced because of the central bank writing off outstanding debt.

13
CHAPTER

The Supply Side: A Complete Macroeconomic Model of the Economy

LEARNING OBJECTIVES

Upon completion of this chapter, the reader will be able to:

- Understand why the supply curve for a period longer than contemplated in Chapter 3 has an upward slope.
- Derive the upward slope of the supply curve.
- Understand the relationship between the wage formation process, price-setting and the slope of the supply curve.
- Perceive that, with price variability, there is another type of crowding out which diminishes the size of the Keynesian income multiplier.
- Explain the concept of the Phillips Curve and represent it in a diagram.
- Distinguish between demand-pull inflation and cost-push inflation and note which of these can be represented by the Phillips Curve.
- Accommodate inflationary expectations into the Phillips Curve relationship and explain what this means for policy trade-offs facing the government.
- Understand how the supply side relationships developed in this chapter fit into a comprehensive macroeconomic model.

13.1. INTRODUCTION

This chapter provides a detailed analysis of the supply side of the economy. The supply side is, of course, very much present in the Keynesian model of Chapter 3 and in the IS–LM model of Chapters 8–10. Yet, the demand side plays a more prominent role in demand-determined models. It is aggregate demand that decides the level of output in the economy. Why is that the case?

It may be worthwhile repeating here what we have stressed earlier in Chapters 3 and 8 that the models studied so far are 'demand-determined' ones because the supply side is horizontal. The horizontal supply curve is realistic only for the short-run, when labour costs do not rise, or when there is large scale unemployment so that increases in labour demand do not drive up wages.

Now we proceed to present a more general version of the supply curve: one derived for a scenario where both the price and the wage level can change and is consistent with profit-maximization behaviour by producers.

With the supply side not constrained to be horizontal, price effects of government policies also enter the picture and the policy-maker now has to consider the inflationary impacts pf expansionary policies. This chapter also discusses the inflationary consequences of monetary and fiscal policies and the trade-off between output and price increases.

13.2. THE SLOPE OF THE SUPPLY CURVE

13.2.1. Profit-maximization and the Slope of the Supply Curve

When studying firm behaviour in microeconomics we find that profit-maximizing behaviour by producers implies the following optimum condition:

$$W = \partial Y/\partial L. \, P \qquad (13.1)$$

where 'W' is the wage rate, 'P' the price level and 'Y' is output. In other words, the wage rate is determined by the marginal product of labour multiplies by the price. The supply is given by the production function

$$Y = Y(L, K), \qquad (13.2)$$

where 'L' and 'K' represent the labour and capital used in production.

Condition (13.1) says that labour is hired to the point where extra revenue (given as price times the marginal product of labour) from using one more unit of labour equals the cost (the wage) of that input.

Rewriting (13.1) as

$$W/P = \partial Y/\partial L, \qquad (13.1')$$

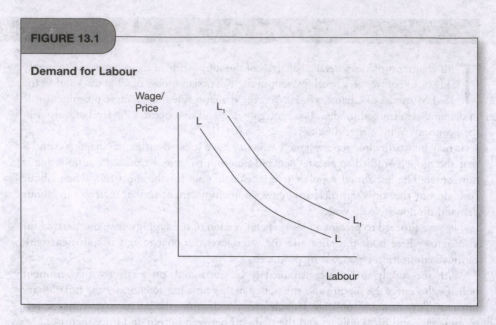

FIGURE 13.1

Demand for Labour

We get the optimum hiring condition which is the real wage should equal the marginal productivity of labour. Real wage is wage divided by the price W/P. So, if the real wage rises, labour demand falls and the labour demand function can be written as

$$L_d = L \ (W/P), \tag{13.3}$$

where L_d is the demand for labour.

Provided that the capital stock remains unchanged, taking the form given in Figure 13.1.

Thus, keeping capital constant, the actual employment is determined on the labour demand curve. Here, the labour supply curve has not been drawn to retain the simplicity of our exposition. When labour demand falls short of labour supply (due to too high a wage rate), there will be unemployment. So given the wage rate which is relatively high, the number of persons willing to work will exceed the number of jobs available.

Now if the capital stock increases, then labour productivity will go up, the use of smarter technology will render existing labour to be more efficient and hence more productive. In that case employment will increase in order to reduce the marginal product of labour if the condition in Equation (13.1') has to be true. The increased capital stock will shift the labour demand curve to the right from LL to L_1L_1 in Figure 13.1.

We see, from the production function (13.2) and the labour demand (and actual employment) function (13.1'), that output can be represented as a negative function of the real wage, or as a positive function of (P/W). In other words, output and real wage are inversely related, whereas output is positively related to the ratio of price to wages.

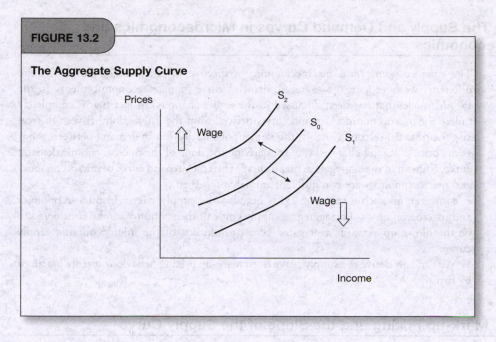

FIGURE 13.2

The Aggregate Supply Curve

Output can be also represented as a positively sloped function of the price, P, shifting up with a rise in the wage rate W and moving down when W falls. Such a function is nothing but the aggregate supply curve of the economy, aggregated across all producers, given in Figure 13.2.

The supply curve will shift to the right with an increase in the capital stock. This could imply the introduction of new technology, new machinery, or an innovative method of production that requires investment of capital. Better methods of producing the same output faster or producing the same thing in a newer version like a newer model of an automobile, a mobile phone, a computer, etc. are improvements actually cause labour productivity to increase and therefore employment, as indicated by condition (13.1′).

Thus, we have derived the positive relation from the supply side between price and output. The supply curve in the price – output/income space, in Figure 13.1, slopes upwards and to the right. Such a curve is realistic when the time period considered is longer as compared to the model in Chapter 3. In the specification of the latter model, the marginal cost does not rise in the short-run, nor does large-scale unemployment keep the wage rate from falling.

Profit-maximizing producers equate the marginal revenue from one more unit of labour (given by price times the marginal product of labour), to the wage rate. This profit-maximizing condition implies an upward-sloping supply curve.

In Section 13.7, a formal derivation of the slope of the supply curve is discussed. Being an advanced topic, it presents the complete macroeconomic model, inclusive of the supply side.

13.2.2. The Supply and Demand Curves in Microeconomics and Macroeconomics

The microeconomic and macroeconomic perspective of the demand curve is quite different. We have seen the aggregate demand curve in macroeconomic theory in the IS–LM model that has been discussed in the earlier chapters. In fact that is completely unlike the microeconomic demand curve, derived from the interaction between the real and the financial sectors. Notably, the element of substitution in demand between goods as the price of a good changes, vital for deriving the slope of the microeconomic demand curve, is absent in the aggregate demand curve. Thus the demand curve of microeconomics and macroeconomics are two different animals altogether.

However, no such distinction exists between the supply curves in microeconomics and macroeconomics. The aggregate supply curve of the economy can be considered to be the blown-up version, aggregated across producers, of the microeconomic supply curve.

We can now derive the supply curve from mark-up pricing behaviour usually practiced by firms.

13.2.3. Mark-up Pricing and the Slope of the Supply Curve

We now introduce the concept of mark-up pricing, where the managers of the firm price their product through adding a mark-up above the cost of production.

The mark-up pricing relation can be written as

$$P = (1 + z).\ ULC \tag{13.4}$$

The Unit Labour Cost (ULC) is the labour cost of one unit of the good produced.

where 'z' is the price mark-up factor and ULC is *Unit Labour Cost*, defined as

$$ULC = W/q \tag{13.5}$$

where 'q' is the number of units of output produced by one unit of labour. In fact 'q' is the average productivity of labour that most students of microeconomics are familiar with.

Why does Equation (13.5) give the labour cost of one unit of the good?

Now, one unit of labour produces q units of the good. The cost of one unit of labour (one labour hour) is W. So, since the cost of q units of the good is W, the labour cost of one unit of the good is W/q. Equation (13.3) says that the price of the good is a mark-up 'z' on this labour cost of one unit of the good. In mark-up pricing, the product price will be a mark-up on ULC, the unit labour cost. The ULC rises with the wage rate and falls with increasing labour productivity.

The supply curve can be now derived. Look at the P–Y space of Figure 13.3.

Starting at point 'a' in Figure 13.3, consider an increase in Y. When Y increases, more labour is hired, which pushes up the wage rate W. From (13.5), the rise in W will raise the price through the mark-up relation. Also, the additional labour, from the law of decreasing returns, will lead to a fall in the marginal productivity of labour and hence in

FIGURE 13.3

Derivation of the Aggregate Supply Curve

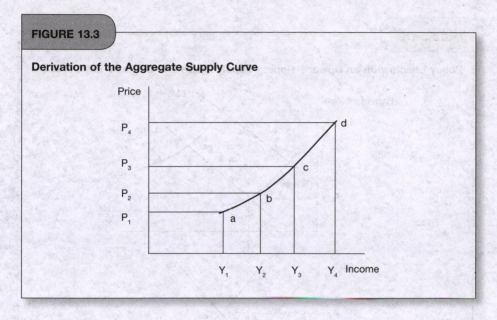

'q', which is the average labour productivity (output divided by labour input). From (13.5) and (13.4), a fall in 'q' will raise ULC and hence the price.

Thus, an increase in Y leads to a rise in the price level in Figure 13.3. As Y rises from Y_1 to Y_2, the price level rises from P_1 to P_2. Point 'b' represents the price-output coordinate at output level Y_2.

Similarly, points 'c' and 'd' represent the price-output coordinates at the higher output levels of Y_3 and Y_4. Connecting all these P–Y combinations, that is, points a, b, c and d, gives the upward sloping supply curve in Figure 13.3.

When output increases, the higher demand for labour raises the wage rate. Increased labour usage lowers labour productivity. Therefore the price level has to be increased to supply the increased output, since the price mark-up is on a higher unit labour cost.

13.3. POLICY EFFECTS

In the discussion of policy effects using the IS–LM model, the supply curve was implicitly assumed to be horizontal. With the realistic upward slope of the curve introduced in this chapter, policy results will be somewhat modified, quantitatively, if not qualitatively, an outcome that was indicated at the end of Chapter 10.

See Figure 13.4. As in the discussion of the IS–LM model in Chapters 8–10, a fiscal expansion shifts out the IS curve to IS_2, raises the interest rate (from r_1 to r_2) and also output as before, in the analysis of the IS–LM model. The crowding out of investment due to the interest rate rise means that the output increase is less than in the basic

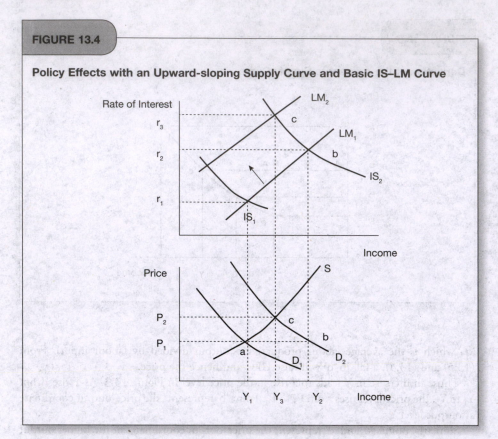

FIGURE 13.4

Policy Effects with an Upward-sloping Supply Curve and Basic IS–LM Curve

Keynesian model of Chapter 3. The output increases from Y_1 to Y_2, in the upper panel of the figure, which is simply the IS–LM diagram.

But, in contrast to the analysis in the IS–LM model chapters, we now have an upward-sloping supply curve to reckon with. In the diagram in the lower panel of Figure 13.4, as the demand curve shifts out to the left to D_2, it intersects with the upward-sloping supply curve at a higher price level, P_2. So, fiscal expansion has led to an increase in output as well as an increase in price.

The price rise feeds back into the IS–LM framework in the upper panel of Figure 13.4. As the price level rises, real money balances, M/P, fall, pushing up the LM_1 curve to the left to LM_2. The upward shift of the LM curve causes the interest rate to rise still more, from r_2 to r_3, reducing the output level from Y_2 to Y_3, which is the output level corresponding to the intersection of the aggregate demand curve and the upward-sloping aggregate supply curve. (Note that the output level Y_2 corresponds to the intersection of the aggregate demand curve with a horizontal supply curve).

With an upward-sloping supply curve, an expansionary demand policy raises the price and hence the interest rate, thereby reducing private investment demand.

13.4. THE KEYNESIAN INCOME MULTIPLIER WITH AN UPWARD-SLOPING SUPPLY CURVE: THE CROWDING-OUT EFFECT OF A PRICE RISE

Introducing an upward slope to the supply curve reduces the multiplier, as compared to the IS–LM model without price changes. Given the relative sizes of the multiplier effects in the various models that we have discussed the outcome can be summed up as follows:

- Compared to the basic Keynesian model, the multiplier is *lower* in the IS–LM model because the rise in the interest rate as a result of a fiscal expansion reduces investment demand. This is because the higher cost of borrowing for producers dampens investment.
- Compared to the IS–LM model with a flat supply curve, the model with a supply side (with an upward-sloping supply curve) can exhibit price changes and a trade-off between output increases and inflation (price rise). With a price rise, the interest rate moves up still more with a fiscal expansion (than if the price was fixed) and consequently, the fall in investment is also more. This means that the output increase and hence, the income multiplier, will be smaller than in the basic IS–LM model of Chapters 8–10.

It may be stated that with an upward-sloping supply curve, there is a crowding-out effect on investment from the price rise (of course, acting through an interest rate increase).

The basic Keynesian multiplier is greater than the multiplier in an IS–LM model with a financial sector which is in turn greater than the multiplier in an IS–LM type model allowing price changes.

The price rise with an expansion in demand creates an additional crowding-out effect on investment, as the interest rate rise is more than when the price is constant.

13.5. INFLATION AND OUTPUT

13.5.1. The Demand Policy Trade-Off

The foregoing section has shown that an expansionary fiscal policy raises output and also increases the price level.

The same result is forthcoming even with an expansionary monetary policy though the crowding out of private investment does not occur. But, the final interest rate level, with an expansionary monetary policy, would be higher than that in the basic IS–LM model with a horizontal supply specification, as the price rise would push up the LM curve back up to some extent, raising the interest rate also, after the initial fall due to a monetary expansion. The diagram depicting the effects of monetary policy with an upward-sloping supply curve is not shown here, rather, it is left as an exercise for the reader (see questions at the end of the chapter).

Then, what transpires from the previous discussion is that an expansionary demand policy by the government or the central bank involves a trade-off between a beneficial expansion in output and employment and an unwelcome increase in prices. In other words, there is an inflation-output trade-off associated with aggregate demand policies. *The Phillips Curve depicts this trade-off.*

An expansionary fiscal or monetary policy has an associated trade-off, with the upward-sloping supply curve specification. An output increase comes at the cost of a price increase.

The Phillips Curve shows the relationship between inflation, employment and output.

13.5.2. The Phillips Curve

The Phillips curve is a heart-warming example of an economic theory developing from the observation of actual developments in the economy, a good example of empirical observations leading to theoretical formulation. William Phillips, a British economist in 1958[1] had noted the relationship between inflation, employment and output in the UK economy and set out the original version of the Phillips curve, as represented here.

In formulating the Phillips Curve relationship, the change in the wage rate is modelled as being driven by the excess of unemployment over the natural rate of unemployment. The natural rate of unemployment is discussed in more detail later in Chapter 19. Here we may just note that the natural rate of unemployment will not mean full, 100% employment of the labour force; there will be some unemployment due to *frictional* and *structural* unemployment—the former existing due to the time spent on searching for new jobs and the latter due to the time required to acquire new skills. While workers devoting time to search jobs that match their skills is called *frictional unemployment*, it not very much different to *structural unemployment* although the latter is considered to be for the longer run. The replacement of bullock drawn ploughs by tractors, for example. Frictional unemployment therefore can be associated with a mismatch between the skills required for jobs and existing skill levels. Structural unemployment too is similar, but the time to eliminate it through developing newer skills takes longer and is therefore sometimes thought to be permanent.

Frictional unemployment is the result of workers taking time to search for jobs which suit their skills. It can be associated with job searches.

Structural unemployment arises out of loss of jobs in a particular industry or region.

The natural rate of unemployment is also interpreted sometimes as the unemployment rate at which inflation is not rising, the so-called NAIRU, the 'non-accelerating inflation rate of unemployment'.

Thus, the change in the wage rate 'W' is given as

$$w = -\varepsilon (u - u^*) \tag{13.6}$$

where 'w' (in small letters) is the rate of change of 'W', 'u' is the actual unemployment rate and u* is the natural rate of unemployment. 'ε' is a parameter taking a positive value.

What (13.6) states is that if the actual unemployment rate is lower than the natural rate, the wage rate will rise. An unemployment rate higher than the natural rate will put downward pressure on the wage rate (but, note that downward wage rigidity is present very often in most economies).

---

[1] A. W. Phillips, 'The Relationship Between Unemployment and the Rate of Change of Money Wages in the United Kingdom 1861–1957', *Economica* 25, no. 100 (1958): 283–99.

Equation (13.6) can be derived explicitly by relating changes in the wage rate to the excess demand condition characterized by deviations in the output level from the output level corresponding to full employment, or the level of employment corresponding to the natural rate of unemployment:

$$w = -\varepsilon \, (Y^* - Y) \tag{13.6'}$$

When the actual output level Y is above the full employment output level Y*, the excess demand for output will translate into excess demand for labour and the wage rate will rise. Equation (13.6) follows from Equation (13.6'), since employment and output are related by the production function and the level of unemployment is the difference between the labour force and the employment level. To relate unemployment levels to the inflation level, we can use the price mark-up Equation (13.4) to write

$$\Pi = -\varepsilon \, (u - u^*) \tag{13.7}$$

Equation (13.7) shows the Phillips Curve relationship which is the negative relation between inflation (price) and the unemployment level, shown in Figure 13.5.

In the Phillips Curve specification, wage inflation (the rate of change in the wage rate), is a function of the difference between the actual unemployment rate and the full or natural rate of unemployment. Wage inflation is alternately expressed, in drawing the Phillips Curve, as a function of the difference between the full employment level of output and actual output.

The shape of the Phillips Curve reflects the policy dilemma facing any government, attempting to reduce the unemployment rate. In the economy represented in the Figure 13.6, an expansionary fiscal policy can reduce the unemployment rate from 5% to 4%, but at a perceptible cost, namely the inflation rate rises from 2 to 3% due to the demand expansion.

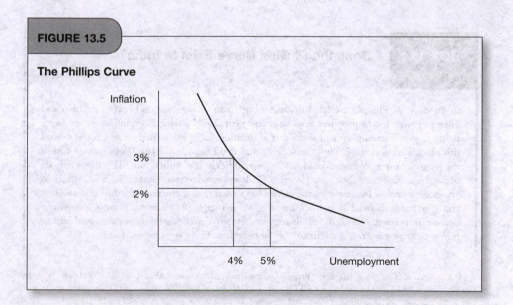

FIGURE 13.5

The Phillips Curve

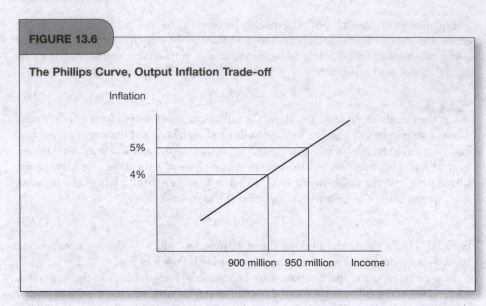

FIGURE 13.6

The Phillips Curve, Output Inflation Trade-off

The Phillips Curve can also be represented with the output level, instead of the unemployment rate, on the X-axis, as in Figure 13.6.

In the example shown in Figure 13.6, an increase in the output level from 900 to 950 million requires an acceleration of inflation from 4% to 5%. The Phillips Curve is drawn so that a fall in the unemployment rate combines with a rise in the inflation rate, by moving up the curve.

BOX 13.1	Does the Phillips Curve Exist in India?[2]

In 1958, A. W. Philips postulated that there existed an inverse relation between inflation and unemployment and he proposed that the government should pursue an expansionary monetary policy to reduce unemployment at the cost of inflation. In 1960, Samuelson and Solow termed this phenomenon as the Phillips Curve. Freidman and Phelps in the late 1960s showed that in the long-run, unemployment could not be lowered below the 'natural rate'. The 1970s episode of stagflation vindicated their view. However if inflation could be controlled through a contractionary monetary policy by decreasing the money supply and raising interest rates, then consumption and investment demand would fall, leading to lower aggregate demand, causing inflation to decline. If therefore real GDP fell, firms would employ fewer employees which would lead to higher unemployment, while inflation would fall due to lower aggregate demand.

[2] The text of Box 13.1 has been prepared using information from Ananya Kotia, 'Trade-off Between Unemployment and Inflation in India' (NIPFP and Government of India Database, 2013). Available at: https://community.data.gov.in/trade-off-between-unemployment-and-inflation-in-india/ (accessed on 18 July 2017).

In the case of India, all studies on the Indian Phillips Curve proclaim that without controlling for supply shocks, a Phillips Curve cannot be estimated. One of the strongest oppositions to the Phillips Curve for India has been by Dholakia, who said that, a serious trade-off between inflation and unemployment in India is '*imaginary*', implying a horizontal Phillips Curve with Keynesian-type short-run price rigidities.[3] Supply-side shocks have played an important role in the inflation-output dynamics of the Indian economy. However, Kotia, using quarterly data for GDP and inflation (WPI) (1996 Q1–2013 Q3), estimates a robust Phillips curve for India. She shows for the first time that even without controlling for supply shocks, there exists a trade-off between these two variables in India, providing perhaps the strongest support in favour of a Phillips Curve for India.[4]

Supply side shocks to the economy come from (a) food price, (b) global commodity prices such as crude oil and (c) exchange rate fluctuations. India continues to have 60% of it labour force occupied in agriculture such that food forms a major component of the consumption basket. As a largely oil importing country, commodity price volatility triggers domestic inflation. After 1993, the Indian rupee has been gradually liberalized and a dynamic exchange rate has significantly influenced the import bill thereby triggering inflation. Such supply side shocks from food and commodity price fluctuations and exchange rate movements need to be controlled.

Kotia uses the Kalman filter in place of the Hodrick Prescott (HP) filter which has been found to be inadequate in the earlier works.

Figure 13.7 clearly demonstrates the lag between the output gap and the inflation level persistently from the first quarter of 1996. Different robustness test shows that Kotia's (2013)

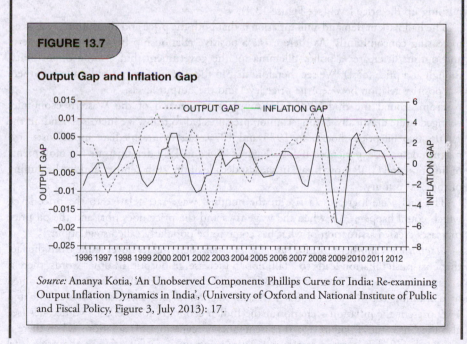

FIGURE 13.7

Output Gap and Inflation Gap

Source: Ananya Kotia, 'An Unobserved Components Phillips Curve for India: Re-examining Output Inflation Dynamics in India', (University of Oxford and National Institute of Public and Fiscal Policy, Figure 3, July 2013): 17.

---

[3] Ravindra H. Dholakia, 'Extended Phillips Curve for the Indian Economy', *Indian Economic Journal* 38, no. 1, (1990): 69.

[4] Kotia, 'Trade-off Between Unemployment and Inflation in India'.

model is stable and has good predictive power. The paper finds that in the pure Phillips Curve, without controlling for supply shocks, a 1% rise in the output gap (i.e., a 1% rise in deviation of actual GDP above the trend) raises inflation by 1.73 percentage points. The second model, which has control for supply shocks reveals that a 1% rise in the output gap (i.e., a 1% rise in the deviation of actual GDP above its trend) raises inflation by 2.49 percentage points. This demonstrates that the Phillips Curve indeed exists for India negating the findings of many eminent economists earlier.

13.5.3. Demand-pull Inflation, Stagflation or Cost-push Inflation, and the Phillips Curve

Demand-pull inflation is an expansion in demand due to government spending and private consumption and investment expenditure that pushes up the price level.

The Phillips Curve captured, almost perfectly, the policy dilemma facing the Western economies up to the mid-1960s or so, when the inflation being experienced was due to aggregate demand pressures, termed 'demand-pull' inflation. The phenomenon of demand-pull inflation refers to the forces leading to a price rise, discussed so far in the book; an expansion in demand, due to government spending, consumer spending or private investment demand increases, pushes up the aggregate demand to the right, pushing up the price level (see Figure 13.4).

The hallmark of demand-pull inflation is that both the price and the output levels keep increasing concomitantly. As there exists a positive relationship between the price level and output, it creates a policy-dilemma for the government, but also an opportunity, though at a price (cost). We see therefore that in the case of demand-pull inflation, there is a positive relation between the price level and the output levels.

From around the mid-1960s, the supply side scenario of the Western economies changed quite drastically. Stronger union pressures led to real wage increases. And, in the 1970s, two oil price shocks, in 1973 and 1979, raised intermediate input costs at a magnitude never experienced before. Figures 13.8 and 13.9 demonstrate the movements of inflation and GDP growth rate in the last decade of the 20th century and the beginning of the 21st century.

The real wage increases (a rise in the nominal wage rate relative to the price level, which could happen even when the wage rises and the price does not) and the oil price increases created a situation of what has come to be popularly called stagflation.

Stagflation is a situation when output stagnates yet prices rise.

Stagflation is another term for *cost-push inflation*, deriving its novel name from the fact that cost-push inflation leads to a fall, not an increase, in output. In other words, there is a stagnation in output even as inflation rises. The term 'stagflation', was, in fact, coined by combining the first and last few letters of 'stagnation' and 'inflation'! Figures 13.8 and 13.9 present the inflation scenario for the Indian economy for the last two decades (see also the Case Study). Figure 13.10 presents such a scenario, of stagflation. When there is cost-push inflation, termed stagflation, output continues to fall, even as the price level rises, the worst of both worlds, so to say.

FIGURE 13.8

Inflation (1997–2016)

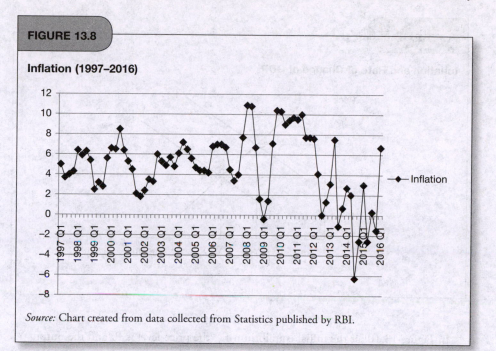

Source: Chart created from data collected from Statistics published by RBI.

FIGURE 13.9

Rate of Change of Inflation and GDP (1997–2012)

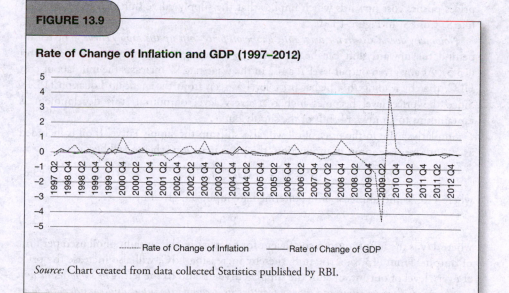

Source: Chart created from data collected Statistics published by RBI.

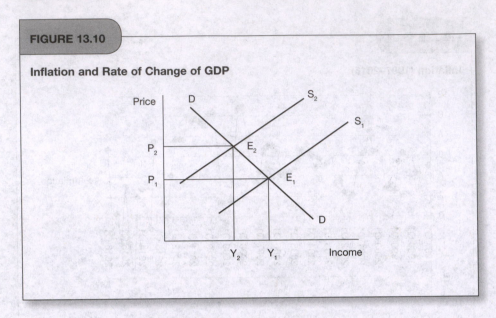

FIGURE 13.10

Inflation and Rate of Change of GDP

In Figure 13.10, at the initial equilibrium E_1, the price level is P_1 and the output Y_1. This equilibrium is disturbed by a rise in the wage rate and/or a rise in raw material prices like the crude oil price. The critical role that crude oil plays as the primary source of energy throughout the globe can hardly be over emphasized. Increase in wages and or oil prices pushes cost upwards which implies that the supply curve shifts up and to the left like S_2 from S_1 in Figure 13.10.

Now, why does a rise in the wage rate, or the oil price shift up the supply curve? The reason behind the upward shift can be explained by referring back to Equations (13.4) and (13.5). At any given output level Y, a rise in the wage rate W increases the unit labour cost ULC, thereby leading to a higher price level as seen from the mark-up Equation (13.4). Since the price level becomes higher at every level of output, this development is tantamount to an upward shift of the supply curve.

Similarly, a rise in the price of oil will also shift up the supply curve. If oil is included as an intermediate input in production, the price mark-up scheme will become

$$P_o = (1 + z) \, (ULC + UIC) \qquad (13.8)$$

where UIC is the unit cost of the intermediate input oil, given by

$$UIC = P_o/v \qquad (13.9)$$

where $1/v$ is the input–output coefficient for oil, that is, the amount of oil used per unit of output. From (13.8), a rise in P_o thereby increasing UIC, will also increase the price at every level of output, or shift the supply curve up and to the left. *The same result will be obtained if we treat oil and labour together as a composite input and consider the joint unit cost of such a composite input in production.* When there is a rise in the wage rate, or in the price of an intermediate input in production, such as oil, the supply curve shifts upwards, such that a decline in output is accompanied by a rise in price, creating stagflation.

For the sake of completeness of this discussion about the shift of the aggregate supply curve, it may be stated that an increase in capital stock, or technical progress, will shift the supply curve down and to the right in Figure 13.10 (this has not been shown in the figure). The reason for such a shift is, again, clear from Equations (13.4) and (13.5). The increase in the capital stock, or technical progress, increases the productivity of labour (due to increases in the stock of complimentary factors of production, or improvements in the complementary factors), increasing 'q' and thereby lowering ULC. The fall in the ULC means, from Equation 13.4, that the price level will be lower at every output level, that is, the supply curve will shift down and to the right.

It is obvious that the simple Phillips Curve does not capture the inflationary scenario represented by Figure 13.11, depicting stagflation. In Figure 13.11, when the price level rises from P_1 to P_2, output falls from Y_1 to Y_2. According to the tenets of the Phillips Curve, output should have risen when the price level rose to P_2.

However, bringing in inflationary expectations into the picture makes it possible to capture the phenomenon of stagflation in the Phillips Curve diagram, transforming it into the 'expectations-augmented Phillips Curve'.

The Phillips Curve represents the scenario of demand-pull inflation, but cannot capture the phenomenon of stagflation. But stagflation can be explained or captured with an 'expectations-augmented Phillips Curve' specification.

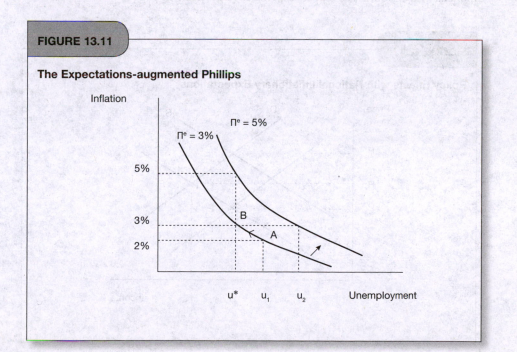

FIGURE 13.11

The Expectations-augmented Phillips

13.5.4. The Expectations-augmented Phillips Curve

The Augmented Phillips Curve is specified as

$$\prod = \prod^e - \varepsilon \, (u - u^*) \qquad\qquad (13.10)$$

where $\prod^e$ is expected inflation, passed on fully to actual inflation.

It can be seen from (13.10) that when actual unemployment is at the *natural rate of unemployment*, actual inflation becomes equal to expected inflation, $\prod = \prod^e$.

Changes in expected inflation move the Phillips Curve up and down, posing a major problem for the policy-maker, attempting to stabilize the economy (see Figure 13.11).

Changes in expected inflation move the Phillips Curve up and down in Figure 13.12. When expected inflation rises from 3 to 5%, the Phillips Curve moves up; for the same 'u', actual inflation is now higher. This can be seen by noting that the natural rate of unemployment was at 3% to begin with, which also meant that actual inflation was 3% (since $\pi = \pi^*$ at the natural rate of unemployment, from Equation 13.10, for the augmented curve).

Consider the rate of unemployment marked as u_1. The economy was moving along the bottom Phillips Curve, from A to B, towards the targeted natural rate of unemployment, reducing unemployment and increasing inflation, perhaps due to an expansionary monetary policy.

But, then, expected inflation rose, as depicted in Figure 13.11, from 3 to 5%. The rise in inflationary expectations could have been due to the anticipation of continued monetary expansion, based on past experience of government policy.

FIGURE 13.12

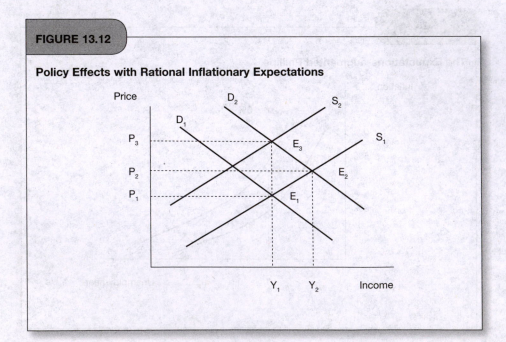

Policy Effects with Rational Inflationary Expectations

When augmented with inflationary expectations, a rise in inflationary expectations moves up the Phillips Curve, so that at an unchanged output level, the inflation level rises. Policy-makers targeting a certain inflation-output combination will be now able to reach only a worse combination, due to such a shift of the Phillips Curve. In other words we are looking at a stagflation type of situation!

The move from the higher unemployment rate of u_1 to the natural rate $u*$ could have been possible earlier with a rise in actual inflation from 2 to 3%. But the upward shift of the Phillips Curve, due to the rise in expected inflation from 3 to 5%, now implies that a move from 2 to 3% inflation will not reduce the unemployment rate and the unemployment rate observed will be higher at u_2, higher than u_1. Thus, due to rising inflationary expectations, actual inflation and the rate of unemployment rise together with a fall in output even as inflation rises.

Thus, the expectations-augmented Phillips Curve can capture the phenomenon of stagflation, defined as a fall in output combined with a rise in inflation, which has been the bane of Western economies since the 1960s and is now afflicting even emerging market economies like India.

Stabilizing and lowering inflation levels in the scenario described above requires the dampening of inflationary expectations, something that can be achieved only by a demonstrated will on the part of the policy-makers to control inflation. Some possible steps that could be taken to bring down inflationary expectations include removing the possibility of deficit financing (that of printing money by government borrowing from the central bank), reduction of fiscal deficits and the curtailment of government expenditure over several consecutive quarters, etc.

13.5.5. Expectations, Wage Responsiveness and Policy Effectiveness

The expectations-augmented Phillips Curve of Equation 13.10, if written in output terms (using Y and Y* instead of u and u*), gives the relation between the output level and the percentage change in the price level. Therefore, the upward move of the Phillips Curve has a counterpart in the supply–demand diagram, shown on the P–Y axis.

In the aggregate demand–aggregate supply figure, the demand curve can be moved out by say, an expansionary monetary policy to increase employment. But if workers expect higher inflation, that is, if inflationary expectations rise, they will demand higher wages, thereby shifting up the supply curve. With *rational expectations*, the supply curve shift with rising inflationary expectations can neutralize the effect on output of an expansionary monetary policy.

Rational expectation is an approach which assumes that people behave logically by optimally making decisions based on all the available information on current and future policies.

An upward shift of the Phillips Curve due to rising inflationary expectations, which affects workers' wage demands and price mark-ups, has a counterpart in an upward shift of the supply curve. With perfect or rational expectations on the part of the workers, demand management policies can be rendered ineffective.

Economic policy with rational expectations is discussed in detail in Chapter 19 on the schools of macroeconomic thought. Here we briefly indicate the mechanisms operating with such a scenario in place.

In Figure 13.12, the aggregate demand curve shifts up due to a monetary expansion and in the new temporary equilibrium E_2, both the price and output increase to P_2 and Y_2 respectively.

However, workers with rational expectations foresee the impact on inflation and adjust their wage demands to compensate for the price rise. The wage increase shifts the supply curve up (in the Phillips Curve diagram, an increase in inflationary expectations by workers shifts up the Phillips Curve) until in the new, stable equilibrium, the price increases further to P_3, while output is back at the original level. Thus, demand policy becomes ineffective with rational inflationary expectations by the workers. As discussed further in Chapter 19 on the macroeconomic schools of thought, long wage contracts can prevent such neutralization of policy, even when there is perfect information about future inflation. Then, since information about inflation does not translate into actual wage increases and price mark-ups, the Phillips Curve does not shift up.

Again, it is possible to move the Phillips Curve down, with suitably demonstrated commitment on the part of the government to control and reduce inflation. A downward movement of the Phillips Curve will make it possible to reach the full employment level at a lower inflation rate than before. A wage fall due to lowered inflationary expectations will shift the supply curve down in the aggregate demand–supply diagram as well. However, the problem is that there may be downward wage stickiness (which could be due to current employees organizing to keep the wages up, to prevent 'outsider' entry). With such downward stickiness of the wage rate, the Phillips Curve does not move down to enhance the inflation-unemployment trade-off facing the policy-maker.

13.6. THE AGGREGATE SUPPLY CURVE IN THE LONG-RUN

If the supply curve underlying the basic Keynesian model of Chapter 3 could be called as 'short-term', the supply curve presented in this chapter is appropriately termed as a 'medium-term' curve, when prices are allowed to vary. In contrast, the Classical theorists, whose approach is discussed in more detail in Chapter 19, discussed a long-term supply curve, representing the output level when all the factors of production are fully employed. In this approach, wages adjust to ensure full employment. As pointed out in that chapter, the long-run version of the Monetarist approach also conforms to such a specification of the supply side. The Keynesian approach, in contrast, does not reach out to the very long-run horizon, remember Keynes' famous statement that, 'in the long-run, we are all dead!'

The 'long-run' supply curve is vertical at the full employment or maximum, potential output, as shown in Figure 13.13.

In Figure 13.13, the supply curve S_1 is vertical at the full employment level of output Y^*. An expansionary fiscal or monetary policy, shifting the demand curve up to D_2, only serves to raise the price level from P_1 to P_2.

The only way output can increase above Y^*, is if the capital stock 'K' increases (or, if technical progress occurs), which will also increase labour productivity. The increase in the capital stock can shift out the supply curve to S_2, increasing output above Y^* without pushing up the inflation rate.

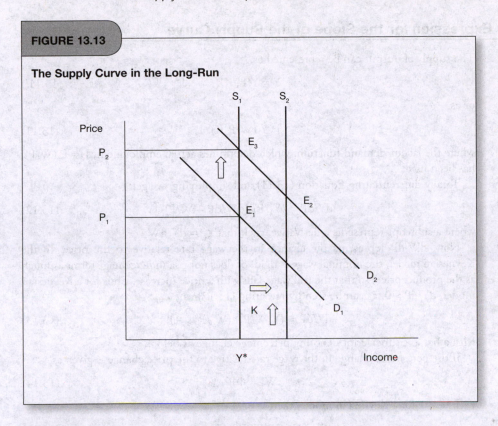

FIGURE 13.13

The Supply Curve in the Long-Run

The long-run supply curve is vertical at the full employment level or potential level of output, with all capital and labour fully employed. Expansionary demand policies cannot increase output in the long-run while supply side policies, such as those increasing productivity, are required to achieve a long-run increase in output.

The full employment level of output can actually figure even in the presentation of the medium-term supply curve of Figure 13.3. The curve is then drawn with a vertical section to the right, at the full employment level of output, following the same reasoning that underlies Figure 13.12. Such a supply curve, sloping up to the right and becoming vertical at the extreme right end is not shown here and it is left as an exercise for the student.

13.7. THE COMPLETE IS–LM MODEL WITH THE SUPPLY SIDE INCLUDED

In this section, a complete macroeconomic model, with the supply side added to the IS–LM model system, is presented. It will be useful, when doing the formal solutions for policy effects, to have a formal expression for the slope of the supply curve, which we now proceed to provide.

13.7.1. Expression for the Slope of the Supply Curve

The supply of output can be represented as

$$Y = Y(L, K), \qquad (13.11')$$

or as

$$Y = Y(W/P, K). \qquad (13.11)$$

where the labour demand function, which determines actual employment, $L = L(W/P)$, has been used.

Totally differentiating Equation (13.11) and simplifying, we get

$$dY/dP = (Y_w/P)(dW/dP - W/P) \qquad (13.12)$$

where a subscript represents a derivative, such that $Y_w = dY/dW$

Now, dW/dP represents the change in the wage rate relative to the price. In the Keynesian model, the nominal wage is rigid, or does not rise in percentage terms as much as the product price, so that the real wage falls with a price increase. Thus for a Keynesian model, $dY/dP > 0$, as can be seen by rewriting (13.12) as

$$dY/dP = (Y_w W/P^2)(W^{\wedge}/P^{\wedge} - 1), \qquad (13.13)$$

with a hat as a superscript denoting percentage change as before.

If the percentage change in the wage rate relative to the price change is given as

$$W^{\wedge} = \Phi P^{\wedge}, \qquad (13.14)$$

with $\Phi < 1$ for a Keynesian model, then

$$dY/dP = (Y_w W/P^2)(\Phi - 1) > 0 \qquad (13.15)$$

(Note that $Y_w < 0$; output falls with an increase in the real wage W/P, which reduces labour demand and actual employment).

From (13.15), the aggregate supply curve in the Keynesian model slopes up. In contrast in the classical and the long-run monetary models, the wage rate rises in tandem with a price rise, to keep the real wage unchanged so that $\alpha = 1$ and $dY/dP = 0$. The supply curve is thus vertical in the classical and the (long-run) monetary models. The differences between the various types of macroeconomic models and approaches are taken up in detail in Chapter 19.

13.7.2. A Complete Macroeconomic Model with a Supply Side

13.7.2.1. Specification of the Model

We are now in a position to view the complete IS–LM (closed economy) model, with the supply side added in. The following system of equations represents the complete model.

Demand for output, the IS equation:

$$Y = C_0 + cY + I_0 - br + G \qquad (13.16)$$

Money market equilibrium, the LM equation:

$$M/P = kY - hr \tag{13.17}$$

Supply of (output) the good:

$$Y = Y(L, K) \tag{13.18}$$

Labour demand and employment:

$$L = L(W/P) \tag{13.19}$$

Wage formation:

$$W^\wedge = \Phi P^\wedge \tag{13.20}$$

In the aforementioned equation system, 'K' (in capital letters) is the capital stock and is fixed and exogenous, but investment demand, which adds to capital stock in the long-run, is changing as the interest rate 'r' adjusts. 'c' is the marginal propensity to consume, equal to C_y.

The Equations (13.16) and (13.17) represent the demand side of the economy, while Equation (13.18) represents the supply side, with Equations (13.19) and (13.20) substituted in to it. Equation (13.20), specifying the change in the wage rate as dependent on 'dY', the difference between actual output and the exogenous full employment level of output, is substituted in when differentiating the system.

Equation (13.19) captures actual employment formation (the labour market equilibrium is characterized by unemployment, since the wage is not completely flexible).

The wage formation equation is equivalent to wage formation from a Phillips Curve relation, $W^\wedge = P^{\wedge e} - \varepsilon (Y^* - Y)$, when actual output $Y < Y^*$ and expected inflation equals actual inflation, since then the rate of change of the wage will be less than inflation (the rate of change of the goods price).

13.7.2.1. Equilibrium Conditions in the Model

Goods market equilibrium: Demand for output in (13.16) = Supply in (13.18)

Money market equilibrium: Equation (13.17)

Labour market: $L_s(.) = L_d(W/P) + U$

The labour market equilibrium is an unemployment equilibrium, with labour supply L_s equal to labour demand plus the level of unemployment, 'U'. Labour supply can be assumed to be fixed at full employment here. The different labour supply specifications for the Keynesian and Monetary models are discussed in Chapter 19 and also alluded to later in this chapter.

13.7.2.2. Solving the Model: Effects of an Expansionary Fiscal Policy (dG)

The system of Equations can be solved from (13.16), (13.17) and (13.18) for the price level, output and the interest rate, when Equations (13.19) and (13.20) are substituted in.

The supply of output is written in a different functional form, using (13.19), as $Y = Y(W/P, K)$. Totally differentiated, the system will solve for changes in P, Y and r, for fiscal or monetary policy changes. The solution can be done recursively, but it is convenient to use matrix algebra. The notation of using a subscript to denote a derivative is used here so that $Y_w = dY/d(W/P)$ etc. Thus, Y_w is the partial derivative of the supply of output with respect to the real wage W/P.

After total derivation, the system in matrix form is as follows:

The determinant is

$$\Delta = (1 - c) \, [hY_w \, (1 - \Phi)/P^2] - b \, [M/P^2 - kY_wW(1 - \Phi)/P^2] < 0.$$

$$
\begin{vmatrix}
(1 - c) & B & 0 \\
1 & 0 & Y_w \, W(1 - \Phi)/P^2 \\
k & -h & M/P^2
\end{vmatrix}
\quad
\begin{vmatrix}
dY & = & 1 \\
Dr & = & 0 \\
dP & = & 0
\end{vmatrix}
\; dG \qquad (13.21)
$$

and (simplifying after entering the determinant in the denominator of the expression for dY/dG),

$$dY/dG = \{1/[(1 - c) + b \, (k/h) - (b/h).M/Y_w(1 - \Phi)]\} > 0, \qquad (13.22)$$

Or, using the expression for the slope of the supply curve in (13.15),

$$dY/dG = \{1/[(1 - c) + b \, (k/h) + (b/h). \, (M/P^2). \, dP/dY]\} > 0 \qquad (13.23)$$

Or

$$dY/dG = (1/\Delta). \, \{1/[(1/\alpha) + b \, (k/h) + (b/h). \, (M/P^2). \, dP/dY]\} > 0, \qquad (13.24)$$

where 'α' is the Keynesian income multiplier of Chapter 3. Comparing (13.24) with the fiscal policy multiplier derived in Chapter 9 (presented in Equation 9.5) it can be seen that the only difference is the additional last term in (13.24). This last term represents the effect on output of the reduction in investment due to the price increase, with flexible prices (as opposed to the fixed price model of Chapter 9).

You may also take note from Equation (13.24) that when the supply curve is horizontal, with $dP/dY = 0$, as in the IS–LM model, the expression for the multiplier reduces to that derived in Chapter 9.

It is easy to show that the price rises as a result of the fiscal expansion.

Solving from the matrix system,

$$dP/dG = -h/\Delta > 0.$$

Thus, expansionary policies, whether fiscal or monetary, increase the output level, but only at the cost of higher inflation. A fiscal expansion raises the interest rate, while a monetary expansion lowers the interest rate. And, as already pointed out in Chapter 10, the Keynesian income and output multiplier is reduced with price variability, as the amount of investment crowding out is more.

13.8. THE COMPLETE MACROECONOMIC MODEL WITH LABOUR MARKET CLEARING**

The macroeconomic model presented in Section 13.7.2 is one with unemployment and wage rigidity that is, the wage rate does not adjust to maintain full employment. How will a model with flexible wages and no unemployment look like? It depends on whether the model is of the Keynesian or the Monetarist type. The difference between these models is discussed in detail in Chapter 20. Here we will just indicate the changes to be made in the model in Section 13.7.2.

13.8.1. A Keynesian Type Model

In the Keynesian model, the labour supply is a function of the nominal or money wage, while labour demand is, as in the model with unemployment, a function of the real wage. So, in the equation system in Section 13.7.2, the wage formation Equation (13.20) will be replaced with the following labour market equilibrium condition that provides the solution for the market-clearing wage:

$$L_s(W) = L_d(W/P) \qquad (13.25)$$

Actual employment is decided by firms' labour demand. An expansionary fiscal policy that raises the price will increase labour demand and also employment as labour supply, a function of the nominal or money wage, is not cut back due to a fall in real wages. The model solutions can be obtained after replacing Equation 13.20 of the model in Section 13.7.2 by Equation (13.25).

13.8.2. A Monetarist Model

In the Monetarist model, labour supply will (like labour demand) be a function of the real wage and the labour market equilibrium condition, replacing (13.20) in the model system, will be

$$L_s(W/P) = L_d(W/P) \qquad (13.26)$$

An expansionary policy that raises the price and initially lowers the real wage, will have no effect on employment and output. Labour supply is reduced at the existing wage level, leading to an equilibrium wage rate that is stable and unaffected by the policy. With the real wage thus held rigid, employment and output cannot be affected by the policy.

13.9. CONCLUSION

The demand side of the economy, characterized and affected crucially by the all-important interaction between the goods and the financial markets, had been the focus of this book, up to the present chapter. In this chapter, the supply side was introduced in a comprehensive way and shown to be crucially dependent on developments in the labour market, that is, the wage formation process and also on the raw material or intermediate good markets.

A major insight obtained in this chapter is that with the supply curve derived as upward-sloping, expansionary demand policies by the government or the central bank meet up with a constraint (not seen in the basic Keynesian model of Chapter 3 and the basic IS–LM model of Chapters 8–10, also characterized by price inflexibility), namely a trade-off between output expansion and (higher) inflation.

What's worse, as described in some detail in the earlier sections, even the output-inflation trade-off became inoperable in the 1970s, due to certain supply side developments such as real wage increases and oil price shocks. These developments meant that a higher inflation level did need not be accompanied by a higher output level. It was also shown in this chapter that inflationary expectations, introduced to augment the Phillips Curve, could give rise to stagflation and sabotage the attempts of policy-makers to raise output, even at the cost of higher inflation.

This chapter has also seen the formulation of the complete macroeconomic model, with the supply side added to the closed economy IDS–LM model of Chapters 8–10. Adding the relationships characterizing the open economy, as seen in Chapters 11 and 12, will easily extend the model developed in this chapter to a full-fledged macroeconomic model of the open economy.

We will see in Chapter 19 that it is the supply side and the labour market in particular, that accounts for differences in policy results thrown up by the models espoused by the various schools of macroeconomic thought. The present chapter lays the ground for the arguments and discussions put forward and portrayed in the concluding chapter of this book devoted to macroeconomic theory.

SUMMARY

- The models analysed until this chapter did not incorporate variability in the price level. The present chapter introduced this important characteristic of economic models. A variable price implies an upward sloping supply curve.
- With variables price and wages, as output rises, there is more demand for labour, which drives up the wage rate. Profit-maximizing firms have to then increase the price.
- An upward slope for the supply curve can be derived from the profit-maximization hiring condition facing firms, a condition that equates the real wage rate to the marginal product of labour.
- Firms practice mark-up pricing, the price being marked up over the unit labour cost (ULC). The ULC rises with the wage rate and falls with increasing labour productivity.
- The aggregate supply curve is a summation of the supply curves of individual firms. The underlying logic in deriving the aggregate supply curve is therefore the same as that for the microeconomic supply curve, which contrasts with the

marked difference between the microeconomic demand curve and the aggregate macroeconomic demand curve.

- The supply curve shifts up with a rise in the wage rate and shifts down with an increase in capital stock, or technical progress.

- With an upward-sloping supply curve, the policy-maker faces a trade-off between additional output (and employment) and higher price inflation.

- The Phillips Curve portrays the macroeconomic trade-off between higher output and inflation, or between the unemployment rate (i.e., a lower unemployment rate) and inflation.

- The trade-off referred to is present with demand-pull inflation, arising with expansionary demand policies. Cost-push inflation, or stagflation, is a different animal altogether. In stagflation, output and employment are seen to fall, even while inflation rises.

- The simple Phillips Curve cannot characterize the scenario of stagflation. The 'expectations-augmented Phillips Curve' can explain stagflation.

- Inflationary expectations pose an additional dilemma for the policy-maker. A rise in inflationary expectations shift up the Phillips Curve, so that, even as the government is raising inflation by added expenditures to create employment, the Phillips Curve moves up, thereby the possible unemployment inflation combination changes for the worse, to a mix of a higher level of inflation for the same (unchanged) level of unemployment.

- The presence of rational expectations about future price levels makes aggregate demand management impotent. But, even with rational expectations, some institutional features can make demand management policies effective.

- Some institutional features may also make it difficult to lower inflationary expectations, a necessary step in the fight to reduce actual inflation to a desirable or targeted level.

CASE STUDY[5]

Is India in the Throes of Stagflation?

There is a view that India is in the midst of stagflation. The weak productivity and loss of production with a sliding IIP are clearly indications of stagflation. The fiscal deficit, rural wages and National Rural Employment Guarantee Act (NREGA), low capital expenditure (Capex) and negative real rates are the four issues that are causing serious concern.

[5] The case study has been prepared from inputs of the following articles: Moneylife Digital Team, 'Morgan Stanley: India Still Stuck in Stagflation-type Environment', 2014. Available at: http://www.moneylife.in/article/stagflation-in-india-says-morgan-stanley/36114.html (accessed on 18 July 2017); M. C. Govardhana Rangan and Gayatri Nayak, 'India in Stagflation, Not Crisis: Kenneth Rogoff, Harvard Economist', 2013. Available at: http://articles.economictimes.indiatimes.com/2013-12-23/news/45510274_1_janet-yellen-global-interest-rates-kenneth-rogoff (accessed on 18 July 2017).

Firstly, India's fiscal deficit remains in grave danger of breaching the double digit mark. If it does, it will put a severe dent on India's growth prospects. The fiscal deficit rose from 4.8% of GDP in F2008 to 9.9% in F2009 and remains above 7.5%. Perhaps fiscal deficit will touch double digits if the National Food Security Bill is implemented.

Secondly, there is a mismatch between rural wages and productivity. While rural wages have shot up, productivity hasn't, thanks to the poorly implemented NREGA. It is believed that the NREGA has been mainly responsible for pushing up rural wages without commensurate rise in productivity.

Thirdly, global factors entwined with declining corporate confidence have reduced investments and deteriorated corporate productivity. The Capex to GDP ratio has reached a nine year low.

Lastly, the negative real interest rate is discouraging financial saving, exacerbating the macro stability risks and further widening the current account deficit. When households expect inflation to be 12%, they will see a 4% interest rate paid by the bank as yielding –8%. Consequently on the one hand, households and firms expend excessive effort on minimizing their holdings of low-yield cash. On the other, households tend to shift away from fixed income, contracting with the formal financial system towards investments in gold.

It is widely debated that the high interest rate is hurting growth; thus everyone wants to keep rates low to revive growth. But growth does not come from low interest rates. Growth requires structural reforms that enable building infrastructure like airports, reducing transport costs, finding ways to allow rural–urban migration without crowding and choking the cities. If India has to get a good decade, it is not going to come from fiscal or monetary

FIGURE CS 13.1

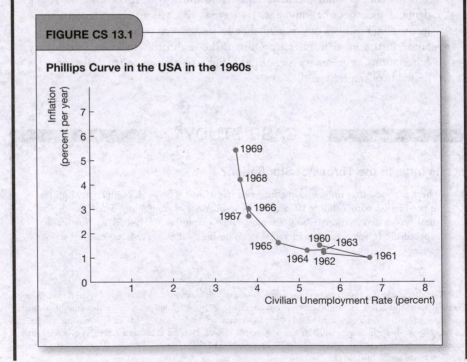

Phillips Curve in the USA in the 1960s

stimulus. You don't produce lasting growth from monetary policy. Eventually, it just produces inflation.

Why is low inflation valuable?

For a brief period, empirical evidence in the USA suggested that there was a trade-off between inflation and unemployment. Here's the classic picture for the 1960s in the USA which shows a nice relationship where higher inflation has gone with lower unemployment. This evidence has led many people, particularly those concerned with the plight of the unemployed, to advocate higher inflation. A look at the same evidence for the USA, over a longer time period, shows no such trade-off.

Empirical literature quite clearly shows that double digit inflation has a discernible and negative impact on growth. If we look at the target inflation rate set in the numerous countries which have setup either *de facto* or *de jure* inflation targeting, we find that typically, the inflation target is 2%. This underlines the universal consensus in favour of targeting low inflation—more like 2% and far below the 10% that India is experiencing. In the West, there are some who are weak in economics, but with strong sympathy for the unemployed and have argued that high inflation is a good thing because it helps reduce unemployment. In contrast, in India, economists have consistently found that the poor are adversely affected by inflation.

After reading the text given in the case study, answer the following questions:

1. What signs indicate that India is in stagflation?
2. Explain the factors that are cause for concern.
3. Why is it believed that there is a trade-off of between inflation and growth?
4. Is India suffering from an inflation crisis? What needs to be done to emerge from the crisis?

KEYWORDS

Upward-sloping supply curve

Unit labour cost

Phillips Curve

Frictional unemployment

Structural unemployment

Demand-pull inflation

Cost-push inflation

Stagflation

Rational expectations

CONCEPT CHECK

State whether the following statements are true or false:

1. The demand curve derived in microeconomics is very similar to the aggregate demand curve in macroeconomics.
2. When output increases, the higher demand for labour raises the wage rate. Increased labour usage lowers labour productivity.

3. With an upward-sloping supply curve, an expansionary demand policy reduces the price and hence the interest rate, thereby increasing private investment demand.

4. There is a crowding-out effect on investment when the supply curve is upward-sloping, from the price rise which acts through an interest rate increase.

5. An expansionary fiscal or monetary policy has an associated trade-off, with an upward-sloping supply curve specification. An output increase comes at the cost of a price increase.

6. In the Phillips Curve specification, wage inflation, or the rate of change in the wage rate, is a function of the difference between the actual unemployment rate and the full or natural rate of unemployment.

7. The hallmark of demand-pull inflation is that both the price and the output levels keep increasing intermittently, always moving in the opposite direction

8. Stagflation can be explained or captured with an 'expectations-augmented Phillips Curve' specification.

9. The long-run supply curve is vertical at the full employment level or potential level of output, with all capital and labour fully employed. Expansionary demand policies cannot increase output in the long-run.

10. With perfect or rational expectations on the part of workers, demand management policies can be rendered ineffective.

DISCUSSION QUESTIONS

1. Why does the profit-maximizing condition for producers imply an upward-sloping supply curve?

2. Is the production function a relation between the price level and the output level?

3. When there is unemployment, is the actual employment level determined by labour supply at a given wage rate?

4. What are the factors influencing the unit cost of labour? Lay down a scenario in which a country which has a higher wage rate than its neighbour, manages to keep a lower unit cost of labour.

5. Discuss the factors that can shift the aggregate supply curve up or down.

6. Are fiscal and monetary policies usually associated with demand-pull inflation? Can you think of any government policy that can create cost-push inflation?

7. How can a government policy of expanding employment, even at the cost of inflation, fail to reach its objective? Explain using appropriate diagrams.

8. Discuss the applicability of the original Phillips Curve and the expectations-augmented Phillips Curve to explain economic developments in various periods, in India and in OECD countries.

9. What type of policies would you recommend to bring down inflation, when inflationary expectations are held? Is the success of such policies dependent on any labour market or institutional conditions or arrangements?

CHAPTER

The Budget: Links to Unemployment, Inflation and the Debt Burden

> ### LEARNING OBJECTIVES

> Upon completion of this chapter, the reader will be able to:
>
> - Explain what is meant by the labour force, employment rate, unemployment rate as well as the links between these macroeconomic variables.
> - Understand what constitutes the full employment level of an economy and explain the presence of a certain amount of unemployment at the full employment level.
> - Understand the possibilities and limitations of government action to influence unemployment levels in the short and long-run.
> - Understand the role of the government budget balance as a link between the real and the financial sectors of the economy.
> - Understand the macroeconomic impacts of financing the government budget, particularly on the inflation rate and the level of government debt.

14.1. INTRODUCTION

In this chapter, some important issues concerning the government budget deficit are discussed, namely the consequences of a *budget deficit* on inflation and the government *debt burden*. The role of the government and the concepts relating to the government budgetary processes were explained to some extent in Chapter 12.

The government budget deficit is the excess of government expenditure over the revenue that it receives in taxes.

It will be seen that the macroeconomic costs of government deficits depend on the way the deficit is financed. But it will be also revealed that, regardless of the way the deficit is financed, there are undesirable effects on the economy with the trade-off between a reduction in unemployment and inflation not the only difficult choices confronting the government.

The public debt burden is measured as the ratio of total public debt to GDP. The cost of debt servicing is also important. In the case of external debt, the ratio of debt servicing payments to export earnings is a measure of the external debt burden.

But, before a discussion of the consequences, the stage for the discussion is set by defining the concepts relating to unemployment, because government deficits emerge primarily via the process of employment creation. It will be also seen that the causation is not one way. With government deficits formed by increases in spending or cuts in taxes increasing employment, the unemployment rate can change without any change in government policy, and this change can affect the budgetary balance of the government. To understand such impacts, the exact definition and treatment of unemployment in the national accounts has to be understood first.

This chapter is structured as follows. Section 14.2 is devoted to the explanation of concepts relating to the unemployment rate and clarifies the two-way link between unemployment and the government budget—the budget, thus, serving a link between the real and financial sectors. Section 14.3 discusses different types of unemployment, and the government's ability to influence these in the short- and long-run. Section 14.4 points out the individual and social costs of prolonged unemployment. Section 14.5 analyses the implications of budget deficits for the public debt burden. Section 14.6 analyses the macroeconomic effects of budget deficit, and is followed by Section 14.7 that discusses the possibility of tackling inflation, and the costs of inflation. Section 14.8 lays bare the link between budget deficits and the public debt, the next Section 14.9 provides the derivation of the stability condition for a non-increasing public debt burden. There is a final, concluding section, which is Section 10.10.

14.2. UNEMPLOYMENT AND THE GOVERNMENT BUDGET

14.2.1. Measuring Unemployment

For measuring unemployment let us first define the unemployment rate. The unemployment rate is the ratio of number of unemployed persons to the total labour force. This is expressed mathematically as follows:

$$u = UL/TLF \tag{14.1}$$

where u is the unemployment rate, UL is the number of unemployed persons and TLF is the total labour force.

A number of points have to be noted about (14.1). First of all, the total labour force includes only those who are of employable age and does not include old people above the statutory retirement age and the very young (usually below 16 years of age although this threshold can vary between countries). The labour force does not include full time students and housewives who are not looking for work.

Also, UL, the number of unemployed, includes only those who are actively looking for work (usually in the last four weeks or so, before the reckoning), as confirmed by their registration in unemployment exchanges. Thus, even one hour of work per reference week will normally mean that the person falls out of the unemployed group UL.

Now, the level of unemployment, UL, can be written as

$$UL = (TLF - L), \tag{14.2}$$

where 'L' is the level of employment. It follows that the unemployment rate can be stated as:

$$u = 1 - (L/TLF) \tag{14.3}$$

where (L/TLF) is the employment rate. Thus, the unemployment rate equals (1 – the employment rate).

From (14.3), we can make some interesting observations.

Suppose that a large number of persons reaches the retirement age. This reduces the denominator of the second term in (14.3). So, the effect of the assumed demographic trend is to lower the unemployment rate.

Suppose there is net migration into the country, without the new migrants having the required skills to get jobs. Such a development, which increases the denominator in the second term of (14.3), without increasing the numerator, increases the unemployment rate.

The unemployment rate is the ratio of the number of persons seeking jobs actively to the total labour force, which does not include children below the working age and retired persons.

The labour market and demographic developments discussed above have implications also for the government budget balance. We now turn to the relationship between the unemployment level and the government budget.

14.2.2. Unemployment and the Government Budget: A Two-way Link

In the previous chapters, we have observed that an increase in government spending or a cut in taxes, which obviously increases the government budget deficit, will increase output and employment. Here we will see how changes in the unemployment rate with no changes in government policies, can affect the government budget.

To initiate this discussion, the government budget balance can be set down, assuming an initial deficit, as

$$BD = Y.t - G - TR - b.UL \tag{14.4}$$

where BD is budget deficit, Y.t is the tax revenue since t is the average income tax rate, TR represents *transfer payments*, b is the benefit per unemployed person and UL is the total number of unemployed persons.

Equation (14.4) is written in real terms, with the same price deflator for all terms. The equation states that the government budget deficit BD equals tax revenue is Y.t minus total government spending G (which includes salary payments to government employees) and transfers minus unemployment benefits. Assume now that the private sector, with rosy expectations about the future, undertakes large investment in firms, increasing employment and output. This affects the budget deficit BD in two ways.

Transfer payments is money transferred to individuals by the government for welfare benefits, such as unemployment, disability or old age pensions, etc.

Firstly, the increase in income also increases tax revenues, improving the budget balance and hence reducing the deficit.

Secondly, the increase in employment 'L', reduces the unemployment level UL and the unemployment rate, as seen from (14.2) and (14.3), reducing the amount of unemployment benefits (b.UL) paid out. This naturally also acts to reduce the budget deficit.

Demographic trends seen in India and in advanced industrial nations (especially in Europe, more than in the USA) also have marked effects on the government budget balance. We turn to that discussion now.

Increased unemployment affects the government budget negatively because unemployment benefits increase and tax revenues fall due to the reduction in output produced. Thus, there is a two-way link between unemployment and the government budget deficit.

14.2.3. The Goldilocks Effect

India now has a major share of the world's population of young people (those below 14 years of age and even of those below 25 years of age). Such a position in the history of the country offers great demographic dividends, termed the 'Goldilocks Effect'.

With a very large entry of young people into the workforce, the country's total output, which is a function of the employed labour force, will also register a huge increase. Investments by firms will rise, anticipating the huge consumer market that is looming ahead. Such a Goldilocks Effect is awaiting India, something like what happened in Europe after the Second World War. This is expected to make the economy buoyant all the way to 2050, unlike China, whose economic growth is expected to taper off by 2030 due to the exactly opposite demographic trend with an ageing population.

However, for the Goldilocks Effect to be functional, the new young entrants to the labour force have to be provided employment, as Raghuram Rajan, the Governor of the Reserve Bank of India, pointed out when he took charge.

What does the Goldilocks Effect imply for the government budget? From (14.4), tax revenues will rise as the new entrants join the employed labour force. But if they become unemployed, the unemployment benefits term (b.UL) will rise. But, almost by definition, the Goldilocks Effect is supposed to be positive, with the new labour force entrants driving up economic growth for an extended period of time.

Thus, the 'Goldilocks Effect' refers to the demographic dividend on national output of a sharp increase in the working age population due to an influx of the young into the working age group. This effect is projected to help the Indian economy to grow well into the middle of the current century.

14.2.4. The Opposite of the Goldilocks Effect: A Rising 'Dependency Burden' in Europe

In the case of European countries, the demographic transition threatens the living standards as the number of aged, pension-eligible citizens is rising relative to the active labour force. In other words, the *dependency ratio* or dependency burden, which relates pension-receiving to wage earning residents is increasing.

The effect of such a demographic trend is clear from Equation (14.4). An increase in the number of pensioners increases transfer payments TR. At the same time, output Y falls because the number of persons in the workforce has gone down. This creates a serious problem for public finances, which has been sought to be overcome by pension reforms which reduce transfer payments TR, despite the increase in the number of beneficiaries.

Countries like Sweden have managed to combine pension reforms with tax reforms which have sharply brought down the maximum marginal tax rates. But it seems clear that, for the European countries to tackle the long-run public finances problem, the flood gates have to be opened to allow immigration from lands outside the European Union given that even the new Eastern members face the same problem of an ageing population. The injection of fresh blood in the form of young, working age immigrants from outside Europe will ensure that living standards are maintained for an ageing native European population, by expanding output and tax revenues.

Before moving on to an analysis of the effects of budget deficits, we take a look at the costs of unemployment which would justify policies to reduce unemployment, even when such polices involve trade-offs with other undesirable economic outcomes. But first, some other concepts relating to the topic of unemployment have to be clarified.

> The dependency ratio is the ratio of old people to those of working age.

BOX 14.1	**The Goldilocks Scenario in India[1]**

In 2016, foreign fund flows seem to have picked up into emerging markets. Fund flows are always difficult to predict, but currently the spate of recovery in emerging markets fund flows are likely to continue for some more time. If you look back at the reasons why the fund flows recovered and accelerated, there were possibly two key factors, namely

1. First, global central banks turned significantly more dovish than what the markets expected them to be. The Bank of Japan set the tone in this regard, the Bank of England and the European Central Bank followed suit, the process reached its peak in the Fed's announcement in mid-March of abstaining from an interest rate hike.
2. Secondly there has been a glimmer of hope about the recovery in demand globally and in emerging markets, which has been demonstrated by the slight recovery of commodity prices. But it is not likely to be sustained for a while because China still consumes 50–55% of most of the hard commodities.

This current stabilization of commodity prices and mild recovery could sustain in the medium term. So based on these factors, it would be correct to conclude that the flows into emerging markets may sustain for some more time. The biggest beneficiaries have been Taiwan, Korea

---

[1] The text in the Box 14.1 is prepared with inputs from Abha Bakaya and Ashu Dutt, 'India's Goldilocks Economic Scenario Can Be a Strong Influence on Investors', *The Hindu Business Line*, 27 March 2016. Available at: http://www.thehindubusinessline.com/markets/indias-goldilocks-economic-scenario-can-be-a-strong-influence-on-investors/article8402386.ece (accessed on 19 July 2017).

and India, in that order, but we can also see a trend change in favour of India at least in the near future. We are seeing some kind of economic Goldilocks scenario for India, which could actually sustain a strong influence in the medium term. India is in a Goldilocks period of low inflation combined with a gradual output recovery, with GDP growth rate forecasts for the fiscal year of 2015–16 touching 7.6%. Even industrial output has risen to 6.4%, a three-year high due to improvements in the manufacturing and capital goods industries. These data strengthen the view that India is in a Goldilocks period of low stable inflation superimposed with a gradual growth recovery.

14.3. UNEMPLOYMENT AND FULL EMPLOYMENT: FRICTIONAL, STRUCTURAL AND CYCLICAL UNEMPLOYMENT

Frictional unemployment is a result of workers taking time to search for jobs which suit their skills.

Structural unemployment arises out of loss of jobs in a particular industry or region.

The full employment level is the output level when all factors of production are fully employed.

Full employment does not mean that all members of the labour force are gainfully employed. At the full employment level, the so-called 'natural rate of unemployment' (discussed in more detail in Chapter 19) exists, due to *frictional unemployment* and *structural unemployment*, arising from job searches and retraining necessities.

Frictional unemployment exists due to the time spent on searching for jobs and shifting between jobs and some 'structural unemployment' exists because of the need to retrain for new jobs. Hence, the *full employment level* in a country could be, for instance, construed as 2%, whereas in some other country, the figure may be close to 4%.

In the long-run, the government can reduce frictional and structural unemployment by more effective training and re-training programmes that enhance skill development and human capital formation and by providing better market information and labour market support of various types. However, in the short-run, the frictional and structural unemployment rates cannot be affected in any noticeable way.

Cyclical unemployment is unemployment caused by fluctuations in business cycles.

The short-run labour market aims of the government, will, therefore be, limited to reductions in *cyclical unemployment* (the unemployment level in excess of the full employment level or the natural rate of employment), due to lack of sufficient aggregate demand. Running a budget deficit will therefore be targeting a reduction in cyclical unemployment and not in frictional or structural unemployment.

There can be a certain level of unemployment even at the full employment level due to frictional and structural unemployment.

14.4. THE COSTS OF UNEMPLOYMENT

The costs of unemployment *at the individual and the family level* are obvious. Unemployment has very serious negative physical and psychological impacts, with poor health and malady afflictions and can even lead to individual and group suicides. Such negative impacts at the individual level are enough to warrant a commitment on the part of the government to assure high levels of employment. Remember that it was after seeing a single woman staggering along under a heavy burden on her head, while he was traveling through the countryside, that Jawaharlal Nehru wrote in his book *Discovery of India* that he would like to wipe the tears off every (suffering) face.

Having noted the individual costs of unemployment, let us now turn to the *costs to society* of persisting high unemployment levels.

- An obvious social cost of unemployment is the *loss of output due to unemployment*. The unemployed persons would have produced a certain amount of output if gainfully employed, which is now lost to society. The quantitative impact of unemployment on output reduction can be noted by referring to Okun's law which states that every percent of added (additional) unemployment causes a loss of GDP of 2%.
- The loss of output also causes a loss of tax revenues to the government, which can negatively affect various welfare programs of the government.
- There is also a strong distributional element that is manifested when unemployment increases. Unfortunately, it is usually the disadvantaged sections of society, including women and young entrants in their first forays to the labour market, that are laid off first. Since the reduction of inequalities in society is an important goal in nations aspiring for inclusive development, reducing unemployment has to be a major priority for their governments.
- Finally, ill health and psychological problems, almost invariably seen at the individual level as a result of unemployment, also have a negative impact on government finances. Thus, unemployment is really a cost for the society as a whole, considering the costs of the medical facilities, which have to be allocated to treat these illnesses.

Hence, there are serious costs associated with unemployment at the individual as well as macro-level for society as a whole. At the macro-level, lost output and tax revenues are some of the costs as are medical costs and rising crime rates.

Now we proceed to take up the macroeconomic effects of government deficits.

14.5. GOVERNMENT BUDGET BALANCE AND ITS MACROECONOMIC IMPACTS

14.5.1. Government Budget and Deficit Financing: A Link Between the Real and Financial Sectors

A government's expenditure is funded through a number of ways. The primary source, non-debt creating and non-inflationary, but with a dampening impact on private activity, is the revenue the government gets from taxes and excise duties. The government also funds its spending by borrowing from the public by issuing government debt (also called treasury bills which you would have read about in Chapter 5), or by borrowing from the central bank, which is the sole prerogative of a sovereign government, but is normally frowned upon as being inflationary. When the government is unable to meet all its expenses from tax revenues, it has a deficit budget. The budget deficit, which is government spending not covered by tax revenues, is financed in two ways: by borrowing from the market through bond issues or by borrowing from the central bank, which increases the monetary base and the money supply and this is termed 'printing of money'. Thus,

$$BD = \Delta B + \Delta M, \tag{14.5}$$

where 'BD' is the government budget deficit (see Equation 14.1), ΔB is the value of bonds issued to cover the deficit and ΔM is the increase in money supply through central bank borrowing by the government for the same purpose. Note that the increase in money supply referred to here is only in the domestic monetary base and does not include the foreign component through the balance of payments. (so one could write ΔH instead of ΔM in (14.5), representing the domestic base by 'H').

These two methods, both borrowing and deficit financing by increasing the money supply, to cover the government's deficit, have serious implications on the financial sector of the economy. Thus, the government budget functions as a link between the real and the financial sectors of the economy.

To recapitulate, budget deficits can be financed in two ways: by borrowing from the market or by borrowing from the central bank and thereby increasing the money supply.

14.5.2. The Budget Deficit and Inflation

In Chapter 13, we have discussed inflation, which can be of two types, namely demand-pull and cost-push. In the former situation, demand pulls stimulate more output but rising demand raises prices. This is represented by the aggregate demand curve which shifts out, increasing both output and the price level. In the cost-push type of inflation, the increase in supply-side cost due to the increase in wages, oil prices and so on; increases the market price while reduces the output. This type of development is also referred to as 'stagflation'. Cost-push inflation is represented by the supply curve shifting up due to increases in the wage rate or in intermediate input prices (such as oil), with a reduction in output even as the price level increases.

Running a government budget deficit creates inflation of the demand-pull type, when increases in government spending are financed by borrowing or by money supply increases. But money financing of the deficit is more inflationary than bond financing, as will be seen in the next section. We will start by looking at the inflationary impact of an expansionary fiscal policy which creates a budget deficit that is financed by borrowings.

14.5.3. Deficit Financing by Borrowing

We now examine the effect of borrowings to meet deficit finance requirements. Figure 14.1 illustrates the effects of financing the budget deficit by borrowing through the issue of government debt or bonds, also known as T-Bills.

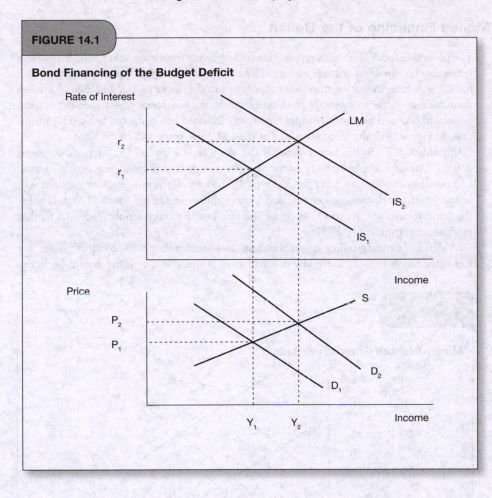

FIGURE 14.1

Bond Financing of the Budget Deficit

The increased spending moves out the IS curve, as seen in Chapter 8. In the bottom panel, the aggregate demand curve shifts out. In the new equilibrium E_2, output increases and so does the interest rate. The price also increases, as seen in the bottom panel.

In this situation you can notice that the LM curve does not move up, though the government is borrowing money from the private sector, with a bond issue. The money borrowed by the government is deposited in active expenditure accounts (as the purpose of borrowing is to spend more) and is not retired from the economy; therefore, there is no reduction in the money supply. *This scenario may be contrasted with an open market operation by the central bank, involving the sale of bonds, which reduces the money supply.* With the central bank operation, as seen in Chapters 8–10, there is a reduction in the money supply as the accounts of commercial banks with the central bank are debited.

Again, in contrast to a central bank, open market operation involving the sale of bonds, government fiscal expansion by borrowing increases the stock of public debt. We will return to this topic a little later in this chapter.

14.5.4. Money Financing of the Deficit

The government can finance its expenditure by borrowing from the market, but alternatively it can also borrow from the central bank. When the government borrows from the central bank it is de facto increasing the money supply by printing more money and thereby leading to an increase in the money supply. In other words, the composite policy followed is fiscal expansion financed by a money supply increase, facilitated by the central bank. This means that, in Figure 14.2, the IS curve as well as the LM curve move out to the right.

Equilibrium E_2 in the upper panel is the same as in Figure 14.1 for bond-financed deficits. But now, the increase in money supply due to money financing pushes out the LM curve to the right to LM_2 and the new IS–LM equilibrium is E_3. Correspondingly, in the lower panel, the aggregate demand curve shifts out further, from D_2, relevant for the bond-financing case, to D_3 since the increase in the money supply leads to a further increase in output.

A deficit financing policy is not the same as a fiscal policy with complete monetary accommodation (which, as we saw in Chapter 8, is equivalent to fiscal expansion in the

FIGURE 14.2

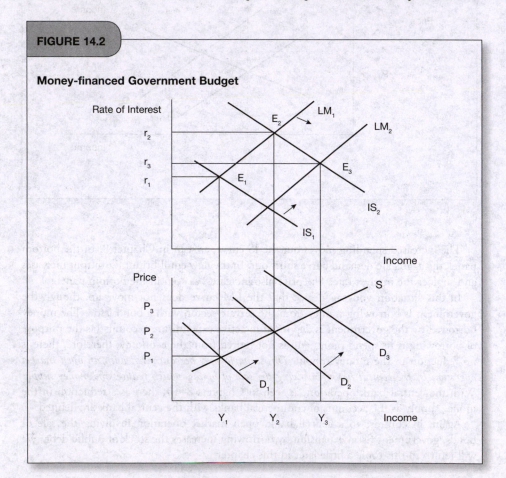

Money-financed Government Budget

basic Keynesian model of Chapter 3). This is because the money supply increase is only to finance the initial increase in government spending and does not cover the subsequent demand expansion due to the multiplier effect. Hence, there will be some increase in the interest rate, but not as much as it would have been when the deficit budget is financed through bond issue.

In the final equilibrium, the increase in the interest rate is less than in the bond-financing case and there is no increase in government debt. But the price level increases more than what would have been the case with government borrowing to finance the deficit to $P_3 > P_2$.

Hence, money-financing of the budget deficit is more inflationary than bond financing, as aggregate demand increases with the associated increase in the money supply, in addition to the expansionary effect from the increase in government spending (or cut in taxes).

14.5.5. Money-financing of Deficits and Inflation

Money financing of government deficits is more inflationary than financing by borrowing as discussed in the previous section. Clearly, this looks like a straightforward situation but wait, sometimes money financing follows bond financing with a lag, to obtain further increases in output and in this scenario, the original advantage claimed for bond-financing is lost. Indeed, the Monetarist school keeps insisting on the inflation-creating aspects of money supply increases which will be discussed in detail in Chapter 19. In their view, money has a direct effect on aggregate demand through a 'real balance' expenditure effect on consumption, so that consumption is modelled as

$$C = C\,(Y, M/P) \tag{14.6}$$

where C, Y, M and P are the usual notations of consumption, income, money supply and price. Equation 14.6 therefore indicates that consumption is positively influenced by income and increases as the *real money supply* (M/P) goes up. Thus, increases in the real money supply increase investment demand through a fall in the interest rate and consumption through a 'real money balances' effect.

The real money supply is the nominal money supply divided by the price level.

The Quantity Theory embodies the Monetarist view that expansionary monetary policies have no effect on real output, serving only to increase inflation. The theory is stated in Chapter 6, but is always worth repeating:

$$MV = PY \tag{14.7}$$

In (14.7), 'Y' is real output and 'V' is the velocity of circulation of money. Writing in percentage terms, the inflation rate is given by (π is the rate of change of the price level 'P')

$$\pi = M^\wedge + V^\wedge - Y^\wedge \tag{14.8}$$

In the long-run, output is fixed at the full-employment level and the velocity of circulation of money is assumed to be stable. Then inflation is equal to the rate of change of the money supply:

$$\pi = M^\wedge \tag{14.9}$$

Thus, money financing of the government budget deficit directly feeds into inflation. This raises the question about what the appropriate policies are to combat inflation.

14.6. STOPPING HIGH INFLATION

Inflation is defined as a continuously rising price level, at the aggregate level and not just for a single product. While supply shortages can create price jumps, a process of continuously rising prices can be caused by continuous monetary expansions.

Hyperinflation is an increase in the price level at a very high rate, sometimes as high as 1000% annually.

In some countries like India, the facility open to the government of borrowing from the central bank has been revoked. But countries like Zimbabwe continue to finance exorbitant government expenditures by money printing, causing runaway inflation, also called *hyperinflation*.

Monetary expansion creates expectations about future price increases, which, as we saw in the discussion of the Phillips Curve, leads to a more difficult inflation–output trade-off. In the context of the Quantity Theory equation, rising inflationary expectations raise the velocity of circulation of money, V since people become averse to holding real balances: why hold real balances when it is better to spend now, before prices shoot up even by the next hour! Such a phenomenon was seen in Germany after World War II, in late 1940s, when people withdrew their salaries immediately on receipt into their bank accounts, and pushed around ready cash in wagons for purchases before prices shot up further.

It is clear, then, that to halt the process of continuously and steeply rising prices, the policy-makers have to bring down inflationary expectations. This can be achieved by signalling a policy of very strict and continuing curtailment of monetary expansion. Such a policy can eventually win the confidence of the economic actors in the belief that the government intends to adhere to a policy of controlling expenditure and monetary expansion and bring down inflationary expectations. *Winning public confidence about continued control of money expansion will require adhering to pre-announced money supply targets.*

In short, the only way to stop high inflation is to bring down inflationary expectations.

How can any government achieve that?

Disinflation is a phenomenon in which price levels decline or inflation reduces substantially.

The government has to announce a strict policy of controlling the money supply followed up with building confidence among the citizens about the authenticity of the stated intentions and adhering rigidly to pre-announced money supply targets, come what may.

14.7. THE COSTS OF INFLATION AND DISINFLATION

14.7.1. The Cost of Disinflation

Sacrifice ratio is the amount of aggregate real output (or employment) foregone per unit of lower inflation.

The cost of disinflation, or of fighting inflation, is the loss in output and employment. This cost can be expressed as a 'sacrifice ratio'.

The *Sacrifice Ratio* in inflation control = (% loss in GDP)/(% reduction in inflation).

However, while such a sacrifice is indeed involved in inflation control, it has to be noted that bringing down inflation by reducing inflationary expectations improves the inflation–output trade-off to be faced with any subsequent policy. This issue considerably concerns central bank credibility. Following rational expectations and the expectations-augmented Phillips curve reasoning, if central banks could make a credible commitment to reduce inflation, expectations would accordingly adjust to leave output unchanged. The issue is that monetary authorities are tempted to renege in favour of a temporary boost in output, so that they would be much more willing to tolerate inflation if the loss in output is minimal. Therefore, expectations incorporate such 'time inconsistency' and do not adjust.

But the question is, 'Can a policy to curb inflation through a strong disinflationary policy lead to large output losses? Or can favourable circumstances and wise policies reduce or even eliminate these costs?' Different economists suggest different answers to this question.

A prevailing traditional view (that can be termed 'gradualism') is that disinflation is less expensive if it occurs slowly, so that wages and prices have time to adjust to tighter policy. On the other hand, a contrasting opinion is that quick disinflation can be inexpensive, because expectations adjust sharply. Yet another group of economists argue that disinflation is less costly if tight monetary policy is accompanied by incomes policies or other efforts to coordinate wage and price adjustments. Whatever, the outcome of the debate may be, the social cost of disinflation will be high. It is possible that the cost or sacrifice will be higher, the higher the inflation rate. We now turn to the cost of inflation.

14.7.2. The Cost of Inflation

With 'imperfectly anticipated inflation', there are substantial income and wealth redistribution effects. Fixed income earners, such as pensioners tend to lose out (but they lose even if inflation is perfectly anticipated). There is wealth redistribution between borrowers, who gain and creditors who lose (unless creditors have protected themselves with inflation and interest rate dependent clauses in loan terms). Persons holding real assets such as houses gain. Stock holders may lose as empirical evidence seems to show. Tax payers lose as they move to higher income brackets. Investments may be curtailed or held back, because of uncertainties regarding the future.

But, even with perfectly anticipated inflation, there are costs involved like those in mark-ups. And, with high inflation, even if perfectly anticipated, cost and competitive advantage considerations may hold back investments by firms.

However, zero inflation is not something that is normally held desirable by policy-makers or firms. A low inflation rate, around 2–3% for high inflation countries like India may be desirable to keep profit possibilities alive and bring forth increased investments and output. Although in the current scenario of soaring prices the sacrifice ratio for India may be substantial, but somehow the government has to bite the bullet.

Both anticipated and imperfectly anticipated inflation have economic costs and distributional impacts. Disinflation too has associated economic costs for which unemployment looms large as the most disturbing one.

14.8. GOVERNMENT BUDGET DEFICITS AND THE PUBLIC DEBT BURDEN

14.8.1. The Public Debt Burden

Now we return to the topic of government deficits financed by borrowing. It is time to look at the long-run implications for the level of government debt, because, additional borrowing adds to the debt burden of the government and it may get into a trajectory that becomes unsustainable.

First of all, we may define the public debt burden of the economy, namely the government's debt burden, as the ratio of the stock of government debt to GDP. It is more meaningful to look at such a ratio, rather than at the absolute level of government debt, since, for example, a large country like China would be able cope up with a larger debt than a small country like Mauritius.

The public debt burden is written as

$$DB = PD/Y \qquad (14.10)$$

where 'DB' is the debt burden, 'PD' is the stock of government public debt and 'Y' is the economy's GDP.

It is possible to derive a condition for the stability of the debt burden, that is, a condition which ensures that the debt burden is not increasing. The condition states that, for the debt burden to be stable and non-increasing,

$$g = r_d \qquad (14.11)$$

where 'g' is the growth rate of (real) GDP and r_d is the interest rate on government debt. It follows that when $g > r_d$, the debt burden will fall and when $g < r_d$, the debt burden will burgeon. The derivation of the condition is given in Section 14.9.

Condition (14.11) implies that it is not always a bad thing for the government to borrow, particularly when there are good public investment opportunities, or employment creation is high on the public agenda. It is advantageous, obviously, to borrow at low interest rates as many of the present-day industrialized countries have done for purposes like building the national railways. But the condition also points out that when the country is on a high growth path, it will be possible for the government to borrow without increasing its debt burden. Debt burdens above 50% are generally considered to be too high, at least in the Indian scenario, requiring corrective action.

To recapitulate, budget deficits financed by borrowings increase the government's debt burden. High economic growth and/or reduced interest rates on debt are required to stabilize and lower the public debt burden.

14.9. DERIVATION OF THE DEBT BURDEN STABILITY CONDITION**

A formal condition for a stable public debt burden is easily derived, working with the chosen measure, the total government debt to GDP ratio.

The total public debt to GDP ratio, $DB = PD/Y$, where 'PD' is the level of government debt, 'Y' is GDP and 'r_d' is the interest rate on debt. The change in the external debt burden can be written as

$$\Delta(PD/Y) = (PD/Y) - (PD_{-1}/Y_{-1}) = \{(PD_{-1} + PD_{-1}.r_d)/Y\} - PD_{-1}/Y_{-1} \quad (14.12)$$

The assumption of a balanced budget, excluding interest payments, has been adopted for Equation (14.12). Thus, the primary part of the budget is in balance and the budget deteriorates only due to the interest payments on debt, causing the government to borrow to cover these payments.

In Equation (14.12), PD_{-1} is the stock of government debt (PD) lagged by one period. Rewriting (13.4) as

$$\Delta(PD/Y) = (PD_{-1}/Y)(1 + r_d) - (PD_{-1}/Y) . (Y/Y_{-1}) \quad (14.13)$$

that is,

$$\Delta(PD/Y) = (PD_{-1}/Y)(1 + r_d) - (PD_{-1}/Y)(1 + g) \quad (14.14)$$

where g is the GDP growth rate.

From (14.14),

$$\Delta(PD/Y) = (PD_{-1}/Y)(r_d - g) \quad (14.15)$$

For a stable or non-increasing debt-burden, that is, for a zero growth rate of the public debt to GDP ratio, the economy's growth rate should be at least equal to the interest rate on public debt that the government has to reckon with.

Moreover, when the GDP growth rate exceeds the rate of interest on government debt, the public debt burden will fall if the non-interest part of the budget is not in deficit.

To be more specific, the following may be stated (assuming that the non-interest rate part of the budget is in balance):

- When $r_d = g$, the public debt burden is stable (unchanging).
- When $g > r_d$, the government debt burden reduces.
- When $r_d > g$, the public debt burden keeps increasing.

Although this analysis of the stability condition for public debt burden appears simple enough, there are operational issues when we consider the interest rate. Interest rates vary across the maturity of the debt as well as its date of issue. Thus a detailed description of this condition has to factor in such issues.

14.9.1. Setting Limits on Government Deficits

Given the negative macroeconomic consequences of government budget deficits, not only governments, but even international bodies have been active in trying to set a limit on public deficits. A 4% fiscal deficit has been long a target for Indian policy-makers, one that has proved to be quite elusive. Multinational cooperation agencies like the IMF and the World Bank have also harped on the Indian economy keeping to such a limit on government deficits. And, as is well-known, the recent downgrading of the Indian economy by credit rating agencies (which can be contended on many fronts) has been to a large part due to the high level of government deficits.

The European Monetary Union had also set up stringent demands on government finances, to be fulfilled before acceptance into the fraternity. The so-called Maastricht criteria specified limits on government deficits and on other macroeconomic variables that are affected at least partly by deficits (see Box 14.2).

BOX 14.2   **The Maastricht Criteria for Entry into the European Monetary Union**

The European countries' aspiration to form a Common Market can be traced back to the post Second World War and the Brussels Treaty in 1948. However, achieving the reality to become a part of a single currency union or the Euro zone came in much later after the signing of The Maastricht Treaty in 1992. The aim of forming a united economic entity was embedded in the convergence criteria also called the Maastricht criteria. The membership in the European Union

FIGURE 14.3

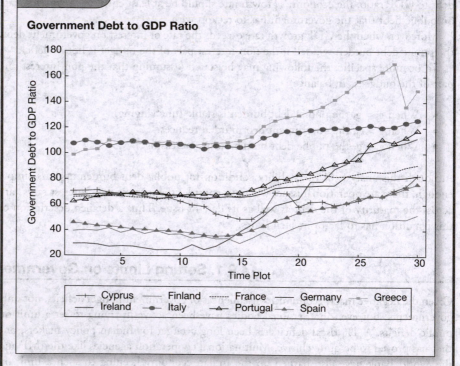

Government Debt to GDP Ratio

and to enter the European Economic and Monetary Union (EMU) to adopt the euro as the currency involved compliance with certain conditions of controlled inflation, public debt and the public deficit, exchange rate stability and the convergence of interest rates.

The five main criteria consist of a 'fiscal criterion', a 'debt criterion' and a 'deficit criterion'. They are as follows:

- Inflation in the aspiring nation to be not more than 1.5% higher than the average of the best performing three European Union nations. Maximum of 3% as of 31 March 2012.
- Government budget deficit to be less than 3% of GDP, the fiscal year prior to the proposed entry into the EMU.
- Government debt burden to be less than 60%, or declining fast towards that level.
- Long-term interest rate maximum of 5.8% as of 31 March 2012 and not more than 2% higher than in the lowest inflation-manifesting three EU nations.
- Exchange rate cooperation in the ERMII mechanism for two consecutive years prior to entry, without devaluation during that period.

As early as 2001, the unemployment level in many European member countries was high which combined with a high debt to GDP ratio, stagnating GDP growth and plummeting yield rates

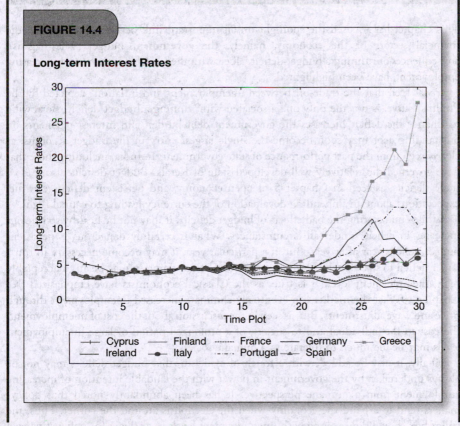

FIGURE 14.4

Long-term Interest Rates

of bonds issued by central banks of these countries, all of which were clear signals of an impending disaster that remained ignored by the regulatory and political authorities. Quarterly data from 2005 to 2012 of public debt to GDP ratio and the long-term interest rate for the nine European Union (EU) member countries including PIIGS (Portugal, Ireland, Italy Greece and Spain) shows that many of these criteria were largely violated. (*Source:* World Bank Data)

See Figures 14.3 and 14.4 depicting the debt to GDP ratio and the long-term interest rate.

As can be seen, the criteria for EMU entry have set limits on government deficits as well as on inflation and the government debt burden. The problems arising for cooperation in the common currency area have been clearly highlighted by the economic performance in the weaker peripheral nations of the EMU, the so-called PIIGS nations of Portugal, Ireland, Italy, Greece and Spain.

Indeed, queries about the level of government budget deficit when judging economic performance and soundness of policy-making in a country are now as mandatory as queries about the mileage performance of a car to be purchased!

14.10. CONCLUSION

This chapter has focused the spotlight on an important link between the real and the financial sectors of the economy, namely, the government budget. The negative consequences of running a budget deficit, albeit with the laudable intention of increasing employment, have been highlighted.

It was seen that the trade-off between unemployment and inflation, depicted by the Phillips Curve, is not the only one associated with running a budget deficit. Borrowing to finance the deficit increases the government debt burden and interest payments on outstanding debt may soon become the single largest entry in the budget accounts, as clearly seen from the past performance of state governments in India, including those that have governed the relatively well-developed state of Kerala. Budget deficits also lead to trade deficits, as seen in Chapter 5 of open economy, and persistent deficits can fuel expectations about an impending devaluation of the currency leading to capital flight.

While enumerating the bad effects of budget deficits, it may not be healthy to rule out increases in deficits under all circumstances. What is certainly dangerous is persistent budget deficits year after year. But in a particular year, it may become necessary to run a larger deficit to stabilize the economy as the cost of not doing so may be an unacceptably high unemployment level. It is true, as the Classical economists have emphasized (see Chapter 19) that the market can eventually eliminate increased unemployment through price and wage adjustments. But, as seen in the discussion about the cost of unemployment, the cost to the individual and to society, of a prolonged period of large unemployment levels may be too much to tolerate in a humane society.

Finally, it may be added, with a touch of cynicism, that budget deficits may not be always undertaken by the government in power with the laudable intention of increasing employment from a humane perspective. It has been abundantly noted that policy-makers tend to expand the economy when the election is around the corner. Thus, the ballot box should figure along with unemployment levels as a trigger for deficit-financed operations. In fact, there have been serious discussions about staggering the elections in the three largest economies of the world, the USA, Japan and Germany, so that election fervour does not spin the global economy into an inflationary spiral.

SUMMARY

- The unemployment rate relates the number of actively job-seeking persons of working age to the total labour force.
- Full employment does not mean 100% employment. At the defined full employment or the natural rate of unemployment level, there could be frictional and structural unemployment. The former could be due to the time taken to relocate and search for jobs and the latter due to the need for retraining and acquiring new skills.
- Budget deficits affect the unemployment rate, tending to increase employment; but there is a reverse link from unemployment to the government budget also.
- The government budget balance constitutes an important link between the real and the financial sectors of the economy.
- Budget deficits are financed in two ways: by borrowing from the market (by issuing bonds) and by borrowing from the central bank which amounts to an increase in the money supply, a policy that is referred to also as printing money.
- Money financing is more inflationary than bond financing of the budget deficit.
- However, government borrowing to finance budget deficits increases the debt burden of the government, that is, the public debt burden.
- Reduction of the public debt burden depends on the economy's growth rate and the interest rate on government debt.

CASE STUDY[2]

Gujarat's Public Debt Burden Rises as the GDP Growth Dips to 8.5%

Treading the path of fiscal responsibility and stimulating growth with the sword of inflation hanging overhead requires caution and wisdom. The government of Gujarat has a large public debt burden, for the financial year 2013–14, the public debt stood at ₹150,153 crore while it paid ₹11,989 crore as interest on the debt. The Gujarat government announced this in response to a question in the Assembly. The Report said, Gujarat's public debt has been increasing steadily. In 2011–12 it was ₹123,406 crore which rose to ₹136,367 crore in 2012–13. It is forecasted that the debt will escalate to ₹169,538 crore in 2014–15, ₹184,538 crore in 2015–16 and ₹200,538 crore in 2016–17.

The weighted average interest on these borrowings is expected to be 8.79%. During 2008–09 and 2013–14, a total of ₹62,745 crore was paid as interest. On 31 May 2014,

---

[2] The text for the case study was adapted from the following three sources: http://www.bbc.com/news/world-asia-india-17919364; http://timesofindia.indiatimes.com/toireporter/author-Kapil-Dave.cms; http://www.dnaindia.com/ahmedabad/report-gujarats-gdp-growth-dips-to-85-from-10-1802446

Gujarat's gross public debt was 19.4% of the gross state domestic product (GSDP) standing at ₹150,153 crore. Despite the enormous increase in its debt burden, the government claims that it was well within the approved limits of the Gujarat Fiscal Responsibility Act, 2005. The average cost of debt for the state was 10.79% in 2004–05 which reduced to 8.82% in 2012–13 and was expected to be 8.79% for 2013–14 (revised estimates). The interest payment on public debt as a percentage of revenue receipt in 2013–14 was 14.10%, which was 14.47% in 2012–13 and 26.82% in 2004–05.

But the spotlight on the economic success of Gujarat is the growth story. Between 2004–05 and 2011–12, the six states that grew at double digit figures were Uttarakhand at 13.2%, followed, by Bihar at 10.9%, Gujarat at 10.08%, Maharashtra at 10.7%, Tamil Nadu at 10.4% and Haryana at 10.1%.

The Socio-Economic Review (2012–13) of the Gujarat government reported that the GSDP at constant prices grew at 8.5% in 2011–12 over the previous financial year 2010–11. This was a substantial dip in growth over the previous years, which saw an increase of 10% in 2010–11 and 11.2% in 2009–10. Gujarat exports much of its produce to the international markets and therefore the state of Gujarat, like rest of the country, cannot be impervious to international economic forces. Agriculture growth has remained robust and the performance of the manufacturing sector has improved. The number of tourists travelling to Gujarat is expected to grow 20% during 2013–14. This indicates a 13.6% growth in the number of tourists visiting Gujarat during 2011–12. The Tourism Corporation of Gujarat Ltd, had targeted a growth rate of 20% in 2013–14. 'Gujarat's story is well-known and shows what sustained growth-oriented policies can do to a state's economic fortunes', reports the Business Standard.[3]

After reading the text given in the case study, answer the following questions:

1. The public debt burden in Gujarat is large according to the Report, yet the government is not concerned. Why?
2. Looking at the numbers given on the public debt and the interest burden, does it appear to be stable, or, rather, likely to increase?
3. If the government expenditure of Gujarat were to be pragmatic in stimulating growth, do you think it could avoid an inflationary spiral? Is the information provided in the text sufficient to answer that question?

KEYWORDS

Budget deficit

Debt burden

Transfer payment

Dependency ratio

Cyclical unemployment

Frictional unemployment

Structural unemployment

Full employment

Real money supply

Disinflation

Sacrifice ratio

Hyperinflation

[3] Soutik Biswas, 'Gujarat is a Red Hot Economy', *Business Standard*, 2 May 2012, http://www.bbc.com/news/world-asia-india-17919364

State whether the following statements are true or false:

1. The unemployment rate is the ratio of the number of persons seeking jobs actively to the total labour force, which does not include children below the working age and retired persons.

2. There is a two-way link between unemployment and the government budget deficit: as unemployment benefits increase and tax revenues fall, the government budget is negatively affected, because of the fall in output produced.

3. The 'Goldilocks Effect' refers to the demographic dividend in national output of a sharp increase in the working age population when younger workers enter the labour force.

4. Budget deficits can be financed in two ways: by borrowing from the market or by borrowing from the central bank and increasing the money supply as a result.

5. Even at the full employment level there can be a certain level of unemployment, due to frictional and structural unemployment, when people search for jobs or are constrained to get retrained.

6. Money-financing of the budget deficit is less inflationary than bond financing, as aggregate demand increases with the associated increase in the money supply, while increase in government spending (or cut in taxes) has an expansionary effect.

7. The sacrifice ratio for curbing inflation is the percentage of GDP reduced divided by the percentage reduction in inflation.

8. The associated cost of disinflation is the potential for an increase in the unemployment level in the economy.

9. Budget deficits financed by borrowing increase the government debt burden. High economic growth and/or reduced interest rates on debt are required to stabilize and lower the public debt burden.

1. How is the unemployment rate related to the employment rate?

2. Are school boys taking up summer vacation jobs considered as part of the labour force?

3. The population of an Eastern European country is ageing, while, at the same time, there is emigration to the richer parts of the European Union. (a) How is the unemployment rate affected in the country? (b) How is the unemployment rate affected in the countries to which the young Eastern Europeans emigrate? Do you need any more information to answer (b)?

4. Which of the following can be affected in the short-run by expansionary fiscal policies: (a) frictional unemployment, (b) cyclical unemployment and

(c) structural unemployment. Which of these can be affected by government policies in the long-run? What kind of long-run policies would accomplish that?

5. Explain in words, without diagrams or mathematics, how money-financing of a budget deficit is more inflationary than bond-financing.

6. Is a policy of government borrowing by issuing bonds identical to a central bank open market operation involving the sale of bonds?

7. What is meant by the printing of money?

8. Which trade-offs are presented by a fiscal expansion creating government budget deficits?

9. How is the government debt burden affected by budget deficits? How can a reduction in the debt burden come about by market developments, without government efforts?

10. Is tax-financing of government expenditure a part of the deficit-financing choices available to the government?

11. Will increased employment have an impact on the government budget? Explain.

12. Would you recommend stricter laws in the European Union to control immigration from non-European areas? Explain your stand.

15

CHAPTER

The Open Economy

LEARNING OBJECTIVES

Upon completion of this chapter, the reader will be able to:

- Understand how trade and financial relations with the outside world distinguish an open economy from a closed one.
- Analyse the different components of the balance of payments accounts that record a country's economic interaction with the rest of the world's current account and capital account.
- Explain how the openness of an economy can be measured, and evaluate the advantages of the different methods of measuring openness.
- Understand the definition and the role of the exchange rate of a country and the differences between the various types of exchange rate regimes.

15.1. INTRODUCTION TO THE OPEN ECONOMY

What is an *open economy*? It is one where citizens of a country can consume goods made by those of another without leaving the borders of the home country. For instance, we can go to our local grocery shop and buy apples grown in New Zealand and dates from Muscat easily as they have been imported. Similarly, a Kuwaiti can watch a Hindi movie and a Malaysian national can drink tea from Sri Lanka. So in an open economy, citizens of a country can spend on goods and services beyond what is produced in the country. They can also spend more than the country produces by borrowing from another country. A country can spend less than its output by lending to other countries. If all countries in the world were using the same currency, the concept of an exchange rate

An open economy is one in which the citizens are actively involved in international trade and financial transactions with other countries of the world.

would be superfluous. However, in the current scenario, barring groups of countries in a monetary union, such as the European Monetary Union (EMU), trade and other international transactions between countries are governed by the exchange rates.

Thus, when an importer in India pays for imported goods, the payment is not made in rupees. It has to be made in the currency of the exporting country or in a globally accepted hard currency such as the dollar or the euro. For example, at an exchange rate of 60 rupees to the dollar, if the imported good is quoted at 100 dollars, the importer in India has to buy dollars, paying 100×60 rupees, from an authorized foreign exchange dealer.

> The exchange rate of a country's currency is the number of units of the home currency that can be exchanged for one unit of the foreign currency.

It is now easy to see that when the *exchange rate* of the rupee goes up (weakens) from 60 to 65 rupees to the dollar, it becomes more expensive for the Indian importer, as he now has to pay 100×65 rupees for the same good. On the other hand, the foreign importer of goods from India has to pay less for a given rupee price of an Indian good. Thus, changes in the exchange rate affect the volume of exports and imports, with a weakening of the rupee increasing exports and reducing imports (more on this under the concept of the *'real'* exchange rate that will be discussed later in this chapter).

> The BOP is a statistical record of the flow of external receipts and payments of a country in a year.

The rest of this chapter goes as follows: in Section 15.2, we look at the components of the *balance of payments (BOP)* of a country: the trade balance, the current account, the capital account and the official settlement balance. After that, we discuss issues of openness or the degree of integration of an economy with the rest of the world. In the last section, the definitions and the different exchange rate regimes are discussed.

15.2. THE BALANCE OF PAYMENTS

> The current account is the sum of net exports of goods and services and net interest, aid and transfer and royalty payments.

The BOP account records the flow of payments between the residents of a country and the rest of the world during a year or a quarter. Since the BOP records the flow of payments, it is dimensionally the same as the national income accounts. Actually, the part of the BOP accounts that records the values of exports and imports also appears in the national income accounts.

> The capital account records the net inflow into the country BOP resulting from the acquisition of domestic assets by foreigners and foreign assets by home residents.

But why do we need a BOP account? Simply because it records the statistics of the inflow and outflow of payments of a country during a year or any interval of time and thereby provides a record of the sources of supply and demand for a country's currency. The trade relations of a country with the rest of the world are maintained in the external sector accounts that consist of:

1. *The current account* (that includes net exports)
2. *The capital account*

The BOP is simply a sum of the current and the capital accounts:

BOP = Current account + Capital account

The BOP accounts follow the double entry system, which simply implies that every debit or credit in the account is also represented by a corresponding credit and debit somewhere else. So there is the need for a rule to identify which transactions are debits and which are credits. Now for debits, the rule is that when any transaction leads to a demand for the home currency (say INR) in the Indian foreign exchange market, it is recorded as a positive entry. Whereas the transaction that gives rise to a supply of the home currency is recorded as a debit, so that it has a minus sign in the accounts. In other words, a country's BOP accounts always balance. This is key in double entry bookkeeping.

The sub-accounts of the BOP are as follows:

1. The trade balance
2. The current account
3. The capital account

15.2.1. The Trade Balance

The *trade balance*, also called the visible balance, accounts for all the different receipts for the exports of goods and payments or expenditures for the imports of goods that 'visibly' cross borders. The receipts for exports are recorded as credit and payments for imports as debits. When the receipts for exports exceed the payments for imports, the trade balance is in surplus. In Table 15.1, it is also called the 'merchandise' balance. For India, the trade balance has been chronically in deficit due to the country's massive dependence on imported oil and petroleum products to meet escalating energy needs. The inescapable need to import capital goods has also contributed to the run on the trade balance. One silver lining in this scenario has been the considerable export earnings from the information technology services sector (in the aftermath of the economic reforms), appearing under 'invisibles' in the Indian balance of payments statistics, which have served to keep the current account deficit down.

> Trade balance is the receipt from exports minus the payments from imports.

15.2.2. The Current Account

The current account is the sum of the visible trade balance and the invisible balance. The latter is the record of the difference between revenue earned for export of services such as shipping, insurance, banking, tourism, education and other services and, in the case of India, software services. Moreover it also includes receipts and payments of interest, dividends and profits of companies that operate across different countries, that is, multinationals, for their debt and equity transactions.

Another item we find in the current account is 'unilateral transfers'. Foreign aid, non-military grants, gifts, donations, repatriation from emigrants, are all part of unilateral transfers. They are called unilateral because unlike other items in the account, they are one-sided. But to retain the format of double entry bookkeeping, unilateral transfers are matched with an opposing entry called 'goodwill'. So, gifts or aid given to citizens of another country are recorded as an import of goodwill. Emerging countries like India, Pakistan, Sri Lanka and the Philippines, for instance, are major receivers of transfer payments from the relatives of residents working abroad. The sum of the sub-totals of the trade balance, invisibles and unilateral transfers is the current account balance of the BOP.

TABLE 15.1

Balance of Payments Accounts (1970–71 to 1979–80)

(1970–1971 to 1979–1980) (US$ Million)

Item	1970–71	1971–72	1972–73	1973–74	1974–75	1975–76	1976–77	1977–78	1978–79	1979–80
I. Merchandise										
A) Exports FOB	1,890	2,122	2,579	2,997	4,006	4,830	5,750	6,354	6,817	7,817
B) Imports CIF	2,435	2,759	2,796	3,646	5,620	6,197	6,097	7,051	9,512	12,076
Trade Balance (A − B)	−545	−637	−217	−649	−1,614	−1,367	−347	−698	−2,696	−4,259
II. Invisibles, Net	−49	−32	−186	2,093	415	1,161	1,347	2,011	2,406	3,574
III. Current Account (I + II)	−594	−669	−403	1,444	−1,198	−206	1,001	1,313	−290	−685
IV. Capital Account (A to F)	580	697	360	−1,416	600	913	905	828	1,597	1,090
A) Foreign Investment	48	58	40	67	87	−9	−29	−12	30	86
B) External Assistance, Net	672	682	488	−1,525	1,071	1,409	1,421	1,030	555	813
C) Commercial Borrowings, Net	22	13	70	92	195	267	183	39	200	55
D) Rupee Debt Service	—	—	—	—	—	—	—	—	—	—
E) NRI Deposits, Net	0	0	0	0	0	42	187	234	190	201
F) Other Capital	−162	−56	−238	−50	−753	−796	−857	−463	622	−65
V. Overall Balance (III + IV)	−14	28	−43	28	−599	707	1,905	2,141	1,308	405
VI. Monetary Movements (VII + VIII + IX)	14	−28	43	−28	599	−707	−1,905	−2,141	−1,308	−405
VII. Reserves (Increase −, Decrease +)	118	−128	43	−107	−9	−959	−1,562	−1,805	−1,218	−457
VIII. IMF, Net	−205	0	0	79	608	252	−343	−336	−244	−102
IX. SDR Allocation	101	100	0	0	0	0	0	0	154	154

Source: Handbook of Statistics on Indian Economy, RBI.

15.2.3. The Capital Account

The capital account records the transactions relating to the inflow and outflow of capital in a country. When citizens or firms borrow from abroad or sell foreign assets, these lead to the inflow of capital, which is a credit post in the capital account. Capital inflows are in effect a reduction in a country's holding of foreign assets or a rise in liabilities to foreigners. On the other hand, capital leaves the country when citizens or firms lend/buy assets overseas and these transactions are capital outflows. Therefore, capital outflows are, in effect, an increase in a country's holdings of foreign assets and a decrease in liabilities to foreigners.

The main components of the capital account are foreign investment, loans and banking capital. Foreign investment comprises of foreign direct investment (FDI), portfolio investment, consisting of foreign institutional investors' (FIIs) investment and American Depository Receipts/Global Depository Receipts, as well as banking capital, which includes non-resident Indian (NRI) deposits.

A surplus or deficit in the BOP is reflected in the change in the official foreign exchange reserves (see Table 15.1). For data pertaining to 2014–15, refer to the BOP Table 15A.1 in the appendix.

Let us consider the current account first. The current account includes net exports of goods and services. It also includes net interest flows and other flows where there is no two-way exchange taking place.

The trade balance = Net exports, goods + Net exports, services (excluding IT services)

The current account balance = Trade balance + Net interest payments + Net transfers, including NRI transfers + Aid flows + Net royalty payments

In Table 15.2, note that items b and c are one-way flows, that is, there is no two-way transaction with a payment being made in exchange for the receipt of a good or a service. Such transactions have been very important in the case of India. In the past, during the oil price shocks of the 1970s, India ran a huge *trade deficit*, but burgeoning NRI transfers helped in keeping the current account deficit down to a reasonable level, within a couple of percentage points of the GDP. In recent years, software service exports have become as important as NRI transfers. In Indian BOP accounts, they are included along with transfers and interest payments, separated from net service exports. See Tables 15.1 and 15.2 which give the BOP accounts for the 10 years between 1970 and 1980 and for 2008 accompanied by Figures 15.1 and 15.2.

The country experienced a current account deficit perpetually except in certain years like 1973, 1976, 1977 and again in the year 2003. Notice how the current account surplus in 2003 of $14,083 million deteriorated to a deficit of $27,915 million.

The key role played by NRI transfers, from the 1970s to the current day and in recent years by IT service exports, in keeping the current account deficit down to an acceptable level (usually considered as below 3% of GDP) can be seen from Tables 15.1 and 15.2.

Note the post 'changes in official reserves' in these tables. For the double entry bookkeeping purpose in the BOP accounts, this is entered with the opposite sign for the surplus or deficit (i.e., a negative sign if there is a surplus, a positive sign if there is a deficit), as seen in Table 15.2.

> The trade deficit is the excess of imports over exports in the BOP accounts.

TABLE 15.2

Balance of Payment Accounts (2003–04 to 2008–09)

(US$ Million)

Items	2003–04	2004–05	2005–06	2006–07	2007–08	2008–09
A. Current Account						
I. Merchandise	−13,718	−33,702	−51,904	−61,782	−91,467	−1E + 05
II. Invisibles (a + b + c)	27,801	31,232	42,002	52,217	75,731	91,605
a) Services	10,144	15,426	23,170	29,469	38,853	53,916
i) Travel	1,435	1,417	1,215	2,439	2,091	1,469
ii) Transportation	879	144	−2,012	−94	−1,500	−1,509
iii) Insurance	56	148	−54	553	595	292
iv) GNIE	28	−10	−215	−150	−45	−404
v) Miscellaneous of Which:	7,746	13,727	24,236	26,721	37,712	54,070
Software Services	12,324	16,900	22,262	29,033	36,942	43,736
Business Services	—	−2,151	1,559	−1,322	219	3,286
Financial Services	—	−320	244	115	84	1,470
Communication Services	—	646	1,286	1,466	1,548	1,211
b) Transfers	22,162	20,785	24,687	30,079	41,945	44,798
i) Official	554	260	194	254	239	232
ii) Private	21,608	20,525	24,493	29,825	41,706	44,567
c) Income	−4,505	−4,979	−5,855	−7,331	−5,068	−7,110
i) Investment Income	−3,757	−4,095	−5,262	−6,762	−4,433	−6,626
ii) Compensation of Employees	−748	−884	−593	−569	−635	−484
Total Current Account (I + II)	**14,083**	**−2,470**	**−9,902**	**−9,565**	**−15,737**	**−27,915**

B. Capital Account

1. Foreign Investment (a + b)	13,744	13,000	15,528	14,753	43,326	5,785
a) Foreign Direct Investment (i + ii)	2,388	3,713	3,034	7,693	15,893	19,816
i) In India	4,322	5,987	8,901	22,739	34,728	37,672
Equity	2,229	3,714	5,915	16,394	26,757	27,863
Reinvested Earnings	1,460	1,904	2,760	5,828	7,679	9,032
Other Capital	633	369	226	517	292	776
ii) Abroad	-1,934	-2,274	-5,867	-15,046	-18,835	-17,855
Equity	-1,122	-1,637	-3,766	-12,604	-14,422	-13,688
Reinvested Earnings	-552	-248	-1,092	-1,076	-1,084	-1,084
Other Capital	-260	-389	-1,009	-1,366	-3,330	-3,083
Portfolio Investment	11,356	9,287	12,494	7,060	27,433	-14,031
In India	11,356	9,311	12,494	7,004	27,270	-13,854
FIIs	—	—	9,926	3,226	20,327	-15,017
GDRs/ADRs	—	—	2,552	3,776	6,645	1,162
Abroad	—	-24	—	56	163	-177
2. Loans (a + b + c)	-4,364	10,909	7,909	24,490	40,653	8,318
a) External Assistance	-2,858	1,923	1,702	1,775	2,114	2,441
i) By India	-104	-104	-64	-12	-4	-344
ii) To India	-2,754	2,027	1,766	1,787	2,119	2,785
b) Commercial Borrowings (MT and LT)	-2,925	5,194	2,508	16,103	22,609	7,862
i) By India	3	-232	-251	-340	-31	1,214
ii) To India	-2,928	5,426	2,759	16,443	22,640	6,648
c) Short Term to India	1,419	3,792	3,699	6,612	15,930	-1,985
i) Suppliers Credit >180 Days and Buyers Credit	—	—	1,725	3,307	10,913	463
ii) Suppliers Credit up to 180 Days	—	—	1,974	3,305	5,017	-2,448

(Continued)

Items	2003–04	2004–05	2005–06	2006–07	2007–08	2008–09
			(US$ Million)			
3. Banking Capital (a + b)	**6,033**	**3,874**	**1,373**	**1,913**	**11,759**	**–3,246**
a) Commercial Banks	6,501	3,979	442	1,581	12,112	–2,774
i) Assets	789	–47	–3,175	–3,494	6,894	–2,902
ii) Liabilities	5,712	4,026	3,617	5,075	5,217	128
of which: Non-resident Deposits	3,642	–964	2,789	4,321	179	4,290
Others	–468	–105	931	332	–353	–472
4. Rupee Debt Service	**–376**	**–417**	**–572**	**–162**	**–122**	**–100**
5. Other Capital	**1,699**	**656**	**1,232**	**4,209**	**10,969**	**–3,990**
Total Capital Account (1 to 5)	**16,736**	**28,022**	**25,470**	**45,203**	**106,585**	**6,768**
C. Errors and Omissions	**602**	**607**	**–516**	**968**	**1,316**	**1,067**
D. Overall Balance (Total Capital Account, Current Account and Errors and Omissions (A + B + C))	**31,421**	**26,159**	**15,052**	**36,606**	**92,164**	**–20,080**
E. Monetary Movements (i + ii)	**–31,421**	**–26,159**	**–15,052**	**–36,606**	**–92,164**	**20,080**
i) IMF	–	–	–	–	–	–
ii) Foreign Exchange Reserves (Increase –/Decrease +)	–31,421	–26,159	–15,052	–36,606	–92,164	20,080

Source: Table 142 : India's Overall Balance of Payments – US Dollars, *Handbook of Statistics on Indian Economy.* Available at: https://www.rbi.org.in/scripts/PublicationsView.aspx?id=11727

FIGURE 15.1

Current Account and Capital Account (1970–71 to 1979–80)

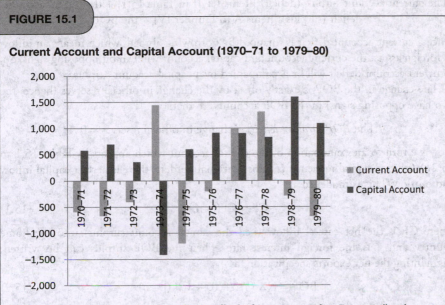

Source: Chart prepared with data from the *Handbook of Statistics on Indian Economy*, dbie.rbi.org.in. Available at: https://rbidocs.rbi.org.in/rdocs/Publications/PDFs/19385.pdf

FIGURE 15.2

India's Current Account and Capital Account Balance (2003–04 to 2014–15)

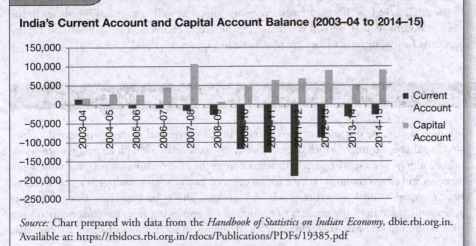

Source: Chart prepared with data from the *Handbook of Statistics on Indian Economy*, dbie.rbi.org.in. Available at: https://rbidocs.rbi.org.in/rdocs/Publications/PDFs/19385.pdf

The current account surplus (deficit) {items I + II in Table 15.1} + the capital account deficit (surplus) {items A to F under IV} = the BOP

Since a current account deficit is financed by borrowing abroad, which means an inflow of foreign assets, the current account and capital account will exhibit opposing signs. So, a current account deficit will be accompanied by a capital account surplus.

The change in the BOP is exactly offset by the change in official reserves (hence, the two have opposing signs) in the BOP accounts, so that:

> The *BOP surplus (deficit)* + change in official reserves = 0

The BOP surplus (deficit) = current account surplus (deficit) + capital account (surplus).

Now we turn to an examination of the capital account which appears in Tables 15.1 to 15.2. With free capital movements across national borders, there is perfect capital inflow and outflow. This is modelled as

$$CF = CF(i - i_f) \qquad (15.1)$$

where CF is the net capital inflow (i.e., the capital account surplus) into the home country and i_f is the foreign interest rate. Then the BOP surplus can be written, augmenting the net exports specification, as

$$BOP = NX\,(Y, Yf, R) + CF\,(i - i_f) \qquad (15.2)$$

However, note that certain other entries in the current account part of the BOP, such as aid flows and transfers have not been modelled here.

Foreign direct investment is investment in a foreign firm in which the investor has a measure of control, usually taken to be 10% or more of the voting rights of a company.

You can observe that this specification of the capital account, treating capital flows as depending on interest rate differentials, is largely true only of foreign institutional inflows (portfolio investments). FDI, *foreign direct investment*, is influenced by a number of other factors such as the availability of skills in the host country, political scenarios, growth prospects, host country income, etc.

This response of capital flows to international interest differentials plays a major role in the analysis of the effects of macroeconomic (fiscal as well as monetary) policies in the open economy, which we will discuss in the next two chapters. The current and capital accounts for the different years are presented in Figures 15.1 and 15.2.

15.3. TRADE AND CAPITAL FLOWS IN AN OPEN ECONOMY

A closed economy does not have trade relations with other countries, they consume the output produced domestically only.

We now discuss the openness of an economy. In the previous chapters we observed a *closed economy* that is a country which does not have any trade relations with its neighbours or any other country. The most important difference from the macroeconomic perspective between an open and closed economy is that, for an open economy, total spending in a year does not have to equal its total output of goods and services. This is because the residents can buy and spend more than the country's production by borrowing from abroad, or spend less than its output and export. A closed economy like Albania or North Korea,[1] for instance,

---

[1] However, North Korea engages in trade with the Russian Federation, the People's Republic of China and Syria.

cannot do that. Any country that does not have any trade relations is called an autarky. It is a policy pursued with the intention of self-sufficiency that maintains a domestic localized economy even if it faces isolation.

But an open economy has the freedom to spend more than its produces or spend less than its output. In a closed economy, all output is sold domestically and expenditure is divided between consumption, investment and government purchases. On the other hand, in an open economy, while some output is sold domestically, some of it is also exported abroad. Let us re-visit the national income accounts equation of Chapter 2.

$$Y = C_d + I_d + G_d + X \qquad (15.3)$$

where

C_d = Consumption of domestic goods and services

I_d = Investment in of domestic goods and services

G_d = Government purchases in of domestic goods and services

X = Exports of domestic goods and services

The sum of the first three terms on the right hand side of the Equation 15.3 represents expenditure on the domestic production of goods and services and the last term X is the foreign consumption of domestic output.

In a closed economy $C_d + I_d + G_d$ represents consumption, investment and savings and the last term exports X would be equal to zero. But in an open economy, total consumption includes foreign goods and services as well as domestically produced goods and services. The same applies to investments and government purchases. So

$$C = C_d + C_f$$
$$I = I_d + I_f$$
$$G = G_d + G_f$$

We substitute these three equations in the identity of Equation (15.3) to get

$$Y = (C - C_f) + (I - I_f) + (G - G_f) + X$$

Or we can write

$$Y = C + I + G + X - (C_f + I_f + G_f)$$

In other words, the sum of domestic expenditure on consumption investment and government purchases of foreign goods and services is nothing but imports and can be represented by M. Hence the national income account identity is

$$Y = C + I + G + (X - M) \text{ or}$$
$$Y = C + I + G + NX \text{ where } (X - M) \text{ is net exports NX.} \qquad (15.4)$$
$$\text{So } NX = Y - (C + I + G)$$

Thus, in an open economy, domestic expenditure need not equal domestic output. If a country produces in excess of its domestic expenditure, it has positive net exports and if not, the trade balance is negative. Hence, just as in a closed economy, the goods markets are closely related to the financial markets, but with links to international asset markets as well.

15.3.1. Trade Balance and Net Foreign Investment

If we write the national income accounts from the savings investment angle we get

$$Y = C + I + G + (X - M)$$

Re-visiting Chapter 2, the national income identity, we know that

$$S = Y - C - G = I + (X - M)$$

The aggregate of private savings and public savings is $S = I + (X - M)$.

Replacing $(X - M)$ with NX, we see

$$S - I = NX \tag{15.5}$$

NX is the trade balance, but the left side of Equation (15.5), $S - I$ is the net foreign investment which represents the amount of money that citizens and residents are lending abroad or borrowing, depending upon whether the trade balance is a surplus or a deficit. When $S - I$ and NX are exactly zero, the country has a balanced trade.

The national income accounts identity demonstrates that the flow of funds from across borders to finance capital accumulation and the international flow of goods and services are really mirror images. So in the open economy scenario, how open is an economy? There are many degrees of openness. Some countries maintain a certain level of protectionist trade policies while others do not. In the next section we explore the issue of openness.

15.4. THE OPENNESS OF AN ECONOMY

An open economy is characterized by the absence of man-made barriers against cross-border flows of productive factors such as goods, services, capital and ideally, but not always labour. To measure the degree of openness, the trade–GDP ratio is a widely used as the indicator. It is computed by dividing the (nominal) value of exports and imports of goods and services to the (gross) value added of domestic output. Broadly this ratio reflects the relative importance of international trade for an economy. In terms of interpretation, small economies typically depend more on international trade than large economies (with the same level of import barriers). In addition, economies like Singapore and Hong Kong that have acquired roles as trade hubs record very large trade–GDP ratios due to the importance of transit trade.

The trade–GDP ratio is usually biased in favour of low-income countries, when measured at market exchange rates. The reason is that, the GDP of low- and middle-income countries valued at international prices (or at purchasing power parities) is generally two–three times larger than that valued at current market exchange rates. Hence, comparing imports and GDP valued at current prices and market exchange rates tends to overstate the relative importance of trade to output in many developing countries.

The debate on the measurement of openness continues, especially since it is a vital issue in today's world of globalization and integration. Adam Smith was perhaps the first to contemplate the effects of market size on specialization and hence on volumes exchanged. The Theory of Commercial Policy establishes the relation between protection and the volume of trade. Rodriguez[2] writes,

> [V]ariability of openness ratios is quite evident (see Table 15.3). While Malaysia exports 93% of her GDP, Myanmar's exports are just 1.5%. Of course, commercial policy is one determining factor in explaining some of these observed differences: Myanmar is more protectionist than Malaysia. However, we observe that the US, India and Argentina have similar exports to GDP ratios (around 11%) while the first country is relatively non-protectionist and the last two are very protectionists. So it can be concluded that protectionism alone cannot explain openness.

TABLE 15.3

The Most Open and Closed Economies in 1996

	Country	GDP US$ billion	GDP pc US$	(X + M)/GDP	X/GDP
1	Myanmar	101.0	2,199	0.035	0.01
2	Brazil	749.3	4,746	0.160	0.07
3	Argentina	272.3 s	7,731	0.215	0.10
4	Japan	4,186.7	33,291	0.218	0.11
5	Burundi	0.8	135	0.230	0.06
6	USA	7,674.0	28,928	0.235	0.11
7	India	392.4	418	0.244	0.10
8	Peru	57.5	2,401	0.301	0.13
9	Iran	134.5	2,200	0.307	0.17
	WORLD	**27,678.9**	**5,514**	**0.436**	**0.22**

(Continued)

[2] Carlos Alfredo Rodriguez, 'On the Degree of Openness of an Open Economy' (Universidad del CEMA, Buenos Aires, Argentina, 2000), Available at www.ucema.edu.ar/~car/Advantage.PDF

	Country	GDP US$ billion	GDP pc US$	(X + M)/GDP	X/GDP
97	Estonia	4.2	2,868	1.504	0.69
98	The Republic of Congo	2.4	883	1.581	0.70
99	Antigua	0.5	7,759	1.644	0.78
100	Bahrain	5.8	9,679	1.725	0.92
101	Panama	8.2	3,053	1.824	0.90
102	Malaysia	98.7	4,801	1.842	0.93
103	Malta	3.3	9,028	1.870	0.87
104	Swaziland	1.1	1,191	1.998	0.85
105	Equatorial Guinea	0.3	642	2.495	0.68
106	Singapore	100.9	27,955	2.967	1.55

Source: Carlos Alfredo Rodriguez, 'On the Degree of Openness of an Open Economy'.

What, then, can be the appropriate measure for openness?

The merchandise ratio of trade volume to GDP can be computed in two ways: one is from the World Bank and the other is from the Penn World Tables (Version 6.1). One advantage of World Bank data is that they are published in terms of exports and imports, which enables investigations into the export-growth connection and the import-growth connection separately. On the other hand, the trade ratio of the Penn World Tables is published only as a sum of exports and imports at current prices (usually referred to as 'current openness'). But this data is better in the sense that it is available for a larger number of countries. The simple correlation between these two trade ratios is almost one.

Commercial policy has an important impact on the degree of openness, which is not limited to the relationship between trade and GDP only. While trade or real openness relates to the degree of substitutability of goods across borders and the efficiency advantages to be reaped from reducing interventions in the free flow of real trade, financial openness has to do with the substitutability of foreign and domestic financial assets and the extent of interference with free capital mobility.[3]

The International Chambers of Commerce (ICC) has developed the Open Market Index (OMI) with a range of criteria to capture this critical component in international economics. Some of the rankings are reported in Table 15.4.

[3] Michael Bruno, 'Real Versus Financial Openness Under Alternative Exchange Rate Regimes', (working paper no. 785, National Bureau of Economic Research 1050, Massachusetts Avenue, Cambridge MA 02138, October 1981).

TABLE 15.4

Country Scores and Ranking as per the OMI of ICC 2011

Country	Rank	Score	Country	Rank	Score
Hong Kong	1	5.4	USA	39	3.6
Singapore	2	5.3	Spain	40	3.6
Luxembourg	3	4.8	Portugal	41	3.5
UAE	4	4.7	Italy	42	3.5
Belgium	5	4.7	Japan	43	3.5
Netherlands	6	4.6	Thailand	44	3.4
Ireland	7	4.5	Ukraine	45	3.4
Switzerland	8	4.4	Korea	46	3.4
Estonia	9	4.4			
Denmark	10	4.3	China	57	2.8
			Mexico	58	2.8
UK	26	3.9			
Saudi Arabia	27	3.9	India	66	2.4
France	28	3.9	Uganda	67	2.3
Australia	29	3.8	Brazil	68	2.3
Canada	30	3.8	Venezuela	69	2.2
Malaysia	31	3.8	Pakistan	70	2.2

Source: Table prepared from the International Chamber of Commerce, Open Market Index, 2011. Available at: www.iccwbo.org

The Open Markets Index (OMI) comprises of four key components:

• Observed trade openness
• Trade policy
• Openness to capital flows
• Trade-enabling infrastructure

In this measure, both real openness and financial openness have been incorporated to prepare the scores. A more comprehensive methodology has been applied in computing the OMI so that trade tariff barriers, anti-dumping laws, non-tariff barriers, agricultural and non-agricultural most favoured nation (MFN) policies have been included. Note how small countries like Luxembourg, Belgium, Estonia and Denmark appear in the top ten list. The USA ranks 39 followed by Spain, Portugal and Italy. China ranks 57th followed by Mexico and India stands at the 67th position with Pakistan in the 70th.

While the debate on measuring openness rages on, a more attention-grabbing issue is the exchange rate and openness connection. Meanwhile, there is also considerable concern about the openness and growth nexus. As we have discussed economic growth and associated theories already in Chapter 4, we shall only look here at the implications of exchange rate regimes and openness.

Some eminent researchers have proposed that there exists a negative correlation between the *real effective exchange rate* (REER) volatility and openness, where the REER takes into account price differentials between countries also. They argue that REER volatility and trade openness which are the outcomes of a policy measure, are negatively correlated. This is true for industrial and developing countries. This implies that the higher the degree of openness to international trade in goods and services (and the longer the existence of an open trade regime in a country), the lower the volatility of *real exchange rate* fluctuations. So, trade openness helps in reducing the effects of volatility in some fundamentals (such as output growth, money growth, the terms of trade or government consumption) on the real exchange rate. A more detailed discussion on this will be found in Chapter 17. We now proceed to discuss the different definitions and concepts associated with exchange rate regimes.

The real effective exchange rate (REER) is the weighted average of nominal exchange rates adjusted for the relative price differential between the domestic and foreign countries. It relates to the purchasing power parity (PPP) hypothesis.

The real exchange rate is the relative price of the basket of foreign goods in terms of the basket of home goods.

BOX 15.1	Trade Openness in India and the Growth Nexus[4]

In the 21st century as much as in the past, trade opened doors for growth, thereby increasing job creation and improvements in the quality of life, with citizens consuming goods that could not be produced domestically. Traditionally, developing trade relations with neighbours and the rest of the world led to openness, which was measured by the ratio of the trade balance to the GDP as a percentage. But there are other important benchmarks for measuring openness; in today's globalized and integrated world, financial openness is a critical aspect that influences a country's ability to reap gains from engaging in interactions with other nations. Chatterji, Mohan and Dastidar applying the Vector Auto Regression (VAR) approach have found that trade openness (proxied by trade volumes) is good for growth in India's case.[5] Also, an increase in the import penetration ratio share leads to an increase in GDP growth rate for India. The import penetration ratio is a measure of trade intensity computed by taking total imports as percentage of GDP and total trade.

In the 1980s, the precursor to the economic reforms of the 1990s, the effect of the trade volume on growth became significant. India gradually started to shift from a state-led growth model towards a market-oriented regime by undertaking various industrial reforms. Indian industries started importing superior intermediate and capital goods in spite of high tariffs, which increased labour productivity and consequently led to faster economic growth.[6]

---

[4] The Box 15.1 is prepared with inputs from Monojit Chatterji, Sushil Mohan, and Sayantan Ghosh Dastidar, 'Relationship Between Trade Openness and Economic Growth of India: A Time Series Analysis', *Journal of Academic Research in Economics* (2014). Available at: http://eprints.brighton.ac.uk/13863/1/openness%20%26%20growth_JARE.pdf (accessed on 19 July 2017).

[5] Chatterji, Mohan, and Dastidar, 'Relationship Between Trade Openness and Economic Growth of India'.

[6] Ajit Sinha and Shirin Tejani, 'Trend Break in India's GDP Growth Rate: Some Comments', *Economic and Political Weekly* 39, no. 52, (2004): 5634–639.

Interestingly, they did not find evidence of any empirical relationship between trade barriers and growth. This is because the data on trade barriers was perhaps unreliable. Surprisingly they observed that there was actually some reverse causality from growth towards trade barriers. This might imply that as the Indian economy was growing as a result of increasing its trade openness, its export and imports were increasing and as a result, the total taxes collected on trade were also rising. See Figure 15.3.

FIGURE 15.3

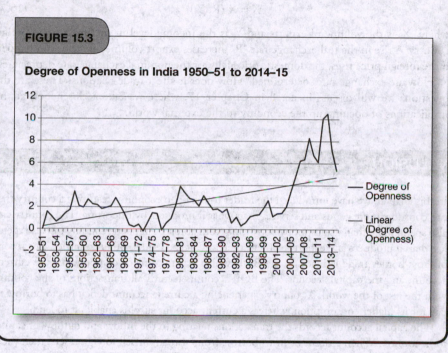

15.4.1. The Spot and Forward Exchange Rates

The spot exchange rate is the current exchange rate, for current transactions. The *forward rate* is the rate (e.g., three months forward rate) fixed now for the exchange of bank deposits at a future date.

> The forward rate is an agreement to exchange currencies at a specified exchange rate at a future date.

15.4.2. The Real Exchange Rate

The real exchange rate is a measure of a country's competitiveness in trade, giving the country's aggregate price level relative to the foreign country, measured in the same currency. Thus, the real exchange rate 'R' is given as

$$R = P_f \times e/P \qquad (15.6)$$

P is the home aggregate price level, P_f is the foreign aggregate price level and 'e' is the nominal exchange rate.

The real exchange rate is, in fact, the relative price of the basket of foreign goods in terms of the basket of home goods. When the real exchange rate falls, our consumers will opt to buy more of foreign goods, while when the real exchange rate rises, foreigners will buy more of our goods along with our imports of the more expensive foreign good being reduced.

The relevance of the real exchange rate for competitiveness can be seen from the usual specification for the export function:

$$X = X\ (R,\ Y_f),\ (15.7)$$

where 'X' is the volume of exports and Y_f is the income level in the importing, foreign country. A rise in the real exchange rate 'R' increases export volumes and this can happen if the foreign price rises, the domestic price falls, or the nominal exchange rate depreciates.

How are exchange rates determined? How does it affect trade relations? These are the questions we will discuss in detail in Chapter 17, where we take a closer look at the implications of opening up the economy to the external world.

15.5. CONCLUSION

In this chapter, we have introduced the reader to the open economy, featuring a country that can consume more goods and services than what it produces by importing. The country can also spend more than its output by borrowing from abroad. An open economy can also spend less than it produces and export to others; therefore, it can lend to other countries. The record of cross-border trade is made in the BOP, which has two major components: the current account and the capital account. The BOP accounts records all transactions of the country with the rest of the world. A country experiencing a current account deficit has to borrow to pay for its higher consumption, whereas a current account surplus enables it to lend.

The capital account records the transactions relating to the inflow and outflow of capital for a country. When citizens or firms borrow from abroad, or sell foreign assets, then there is an inflow of capital that is recorded as a credit. The main components of the capital account are foreign investments, loans and banking capital. A surplus or deficit in the BOP is reflected in the change in the official foreign exchange reserves. Capital flows across borders are driven by the interest rate differentials between countries. When capital flows in or out freely, it is called perfect capital mobility or complete financial openness.

Trade without man-made barriers against cross-border flows of goods and services and of the productive factors, that is, capital and labour, are characteristics of an open economy. Openness of a market is sometimes measured by the trade–GDP ratio. This captures the impact of a protectionist policy that a country pursues. Apart from the choice of commercial policy, the geographical size, level of economic development, availability of natural resources, skill endowments of residents and technology levels also affect the degree of measured openness.

This chapter has also introduced the student to the different exchange rate regimes and the role of the exchange rate in determining BOP outcomes. The intriguing topic of exchange rate determination is explored in Chapter 17. The factors driving inter-country capital movements and their implications for macroeconomic policy effectiveness, are discussed in Chapter 16.

- Residents of an open economy can spend more than the total domestic production of goods and services by importing. Also, they can spend more than their total earnings by borrowing from other countries. Similarly, they can consume less than the national output and export and lend to others.
- The trade balance is the sum of the net exports of goods and services:
  Net exports, goods + net exports, services (excluding IT services) = the trade balance for goods and services.

  The current account balance = trade balance + net interest payments + net transfers, including NRI transfers + aid flows + net royalty payments
- The BOP is the sum of the current and the capital accounts:

  BOP = Current account + Capital account.
- The exchange rate of a country's currency is the number of units of the home currency that can be exchanged for one unit of the foreign currency. Devaluation occurs when the central bank of a country reduces the value of the home currency.
- In an open economy there are no barriers to cross-border flows of goods, services, capital and ideally, labour. To measure the degree of openness, the trade–GDP ratio is sometimes used.
- Protectionism through tariffs, quotas and anti-dumping laws is the hallmark of a closed economy. Financial openness exists when capital flows freely across national borders.
- Revaluation occurs when the central bank raises the value of the home currency under a system of fixed exchange rates.
- The real exchange rate is a measure of a country's competitiveness in trade, giving the county's aggregate price level relative to that in the foreign country, both expressed in the same currency.
- A fall in the real exchange rate makes foreign goods cheaper relative to home goods, so that imports increase and net exports fall. When the real exchange rate rises, foreigners prefer to buy more of the now cheaper home goods, while home imports are cut back, so that there is an increase in the country's net exports.

CASE STUDY

Why Exports Need to Be Robust[7]

The robust exports performance in India during February 2011 is attributed to the rebound in the USA and other advanced economies. According to figures released by the Commerce Ministry, exports grew by nearly 50% over February 2010 to 23.6 billion dollars. Between

[7] The inputs of this case study has been drawn from editorial title: 'Why Exports Must Be Robust', *The Hindu*, 16 March 2011, Available at: http://www.thehindu.com/opinion/editorial/Why-exports-need-to-be-robust/article 14949729.ece

April 2010 and February 2011, exports grew to over $208 billion, crossing the annual target of $200 billion. The government's strategy of encouraging diversification into newer markets and the focus on non-traditional exports as the cornerstones of the country's foreign trade policy paid off. The government was encouraged by strong export performance and optimistically proposed a doubling of exports to $450 billion by 2014 in a strategy paper, something that could happen if exports grew at an annual rate of 26% over the next three years. The strategy was based on a visionary approach on 4 pillars: product strategy that would build on the intrinsic strength of some industries, market diversification, incentivizing research and development and building a Brand India.

However, while such a visionary approach was necessary, the limitations of the Ministry of Commerce should not be overlooked. While considerable success has been achieved in fine-tuning procedures and building an impressive technology backbone, the ministry depends on the other arms of the government to attain some of the basic goals of reducing transaction costs. Despite the adverse impact of rupee appreciation on export competitiveness, it has not always been possible to counter it just for the benefit of exports. On the external front, the recessionary conditions persisting in Japan call into question the assumption of the world trade bouncing back to the pre-crisis levels. Obviously Indian exports ought to be encouraged to maintain the momentum, but trade policy is also about imports and what matters most in the prevailing macroeconomic calculations is the level of the merchandise trade deficit and its implications for the current account of the BOP. To a large extent the growth in imports has been due to the buoyant economic conditions at home, but the spikes in petroleum prices are a big cause for concern as energy imports are bound to expand in the coming years.

After reading the text given in the case study, answer the following questions:

1. What were the suggestions announced by the Commerce Ministry to increase the competitiveness of Indian exports in 2011?
2. Does the growth of exports depend only on trade policy? If not, what are the factors that need to be considered for raising export performance?
3. What are the key, critical issues mentioned in the case study concerning the overall scheme of international trade policy in India?

KEYWORDS

Open economy	International capital flows
Exchange rate	Devaluation
Balance of payments	Spot rate
Current account	Forward rate
Capital account	Real exchange rate
Trade deficit	Fixed exchange rates
Foreign direct investment	Flexible exchange rates

CONCEPT CHECK

State whether the following statements are true or false:

1. The current account is the sum of net exports of goods and services and net interest, aid and transfers and royalty payments.
2. The BOP surplus (deficit) = Current account surplus (deficit) – Capital account deficit (surplus)
3. Capital inflows depend positively on the difference between the home interest rate and the foreign interest rate.
4. Under a fixed exchange rate system, the central banks of countries do not intervene in the foreign exchange market to keep the exchange rates at the announced levels.
5. When a country follows a policy of managed float, the exchange rate is allowed to vary within a band, which could sometimes be as wide as plus or minus 15% from the central value of the band.
6. The real exchange rate is the ratio of the price of the foreign good multiplied by the nominal exchange rate (to get it in home currency terms), divided by the home good price.
7. The export volume is a function of the nominal exchange rate and income in the importing (foreign) country.

DISCUSSION QUESTIONS

1. What economic variables might affect the value of a country's merchandise exports?
2. What is a current account surplus?
3. What is a capital account deficit?
4. Check out the movement of the rupee–dollar rates in the 1970s and the 1980s. Draw a graph using this time series. Note down also the inflation rates in India and the USA during this period. Did the exchange rate movement maintain Indian export competitiveness?
5. In Bravadia, a country in the southern hemisphere, the BOP accounts for the year 2009 show that its export of goods was US$176 million, export of services including royalties, license fees and travel was US$74 million and income receipts were US$63 million. The imports of goods stood at US$ 299 million, services at US$61 and income payments at US$61 million. If the country received unilateral transfers of US$13 million, what was its trade balance and current account balance in that year? If it had a deficit current account balance how did the country balance its BOP?

6. The data for the BOP accounts of a country for the year 2002–03 are given in the table below. Calculate the

   a. The trade balance
   b. The current account balance
   c. The capital account balance
   d. The overall BOP

Data on Balance of Payments Accounts

		US$ (In Million)
1	External assistance to the country	36
2	External assistance by the country	82
3	Transfers (debit)	170
4	Transfer (credit)	248
5	Merchandise exports	34,954
6	Merchandise imports	36,984
7	Exports of service	31,944
8	Import of services	24,928
9	Earnings of loans and investment to abroad	858
10	Earnings of loans and investment from abroad	2,108
11	Short-term loans and investment to abroad	576
12	Short-term loans and investment from abroad	84
13	Foreign direct investments to abroad	70
14	Foreign direct investments from abroad	200

TABLE 15A.1

Balance of Payment Accounts (2012–13 to 2014–15)

Item/Year	2012-13			2013-14			2014-15		
	Credit	Debit	Net	Credit	Debit	Net	Credit	Debit	Net
1	2	3	4	5	6	7	8	9	10
A. Current account									
1. Merchandise	306,581	502,237	–195,656	318,607	466,216	–147,609	316,741	460,920	–144,179
2. Invisibles (a+b+c)	224,044	116,551	107,493	233,231	118,019	115,212	237,083	120,841	116,242
a) Services	145,678	80,763	64,915	151,475	78,510	72,965	155,448	79,765	75,683
i) Travel	17,999	11,823	6,176	17,922	11,810	6,112	20,334	15,306	5,028
ii) Transportation	17,334	14,806	2,528	17,380	14,792	2,588	17,476	16,177	1,299
iii) Insurance	2,227	1,409	818	2,121	1,116	1,005	2,201	1,119	1,083
iv) G.n.i.e.	574	813	–239	488	979	–490	543	961	–418
v) Miscellaneous	107,544	51,912	55,632	113,564	49,814	63,750	114,894	46,203	68,691
of which: Software services	65,887	2,363	63,504	69,439	2,481	66,958	73,108	2,708	70,400
Business services	28,447	30,349	–1,902	28,482	27,189	1,293	28,422	27,644	778
Financial services	4,949	4,633	316	6,650	5,814	835	5,661	3,580	2,081
Communication services	1,686	741	945	2,410	1,063	1,347	1,997	1,023	975
b) Transfers	68,090	4,057	64,034	70,405	5,129	65,276	70,152	4,610	65,542
i) Official	463	772	–309	767	972	–205	322	1,055	–733
ii) Private	67,627	3,285	64,342	69,638	4,157	65,481	69,831	3,555	66,275

(Continued)

Item/Year	2012-13			2013-14			2014-15		
	Credit	Debit	Net	Credit	Debit	Net	Credit	Debit	Net
1	2	3	4	5	6	7	8	9	10
c) Income	10,276	31,731	-21,455	11,352	34,380	-23,028	11,483	36,466	-24,983
i) Investment income	7,202	29,572	-22,370	8,062	31,583	-23,521	7,925	33,720	-25,805
ii) Compensation of employees	3,074	2,159	914	3,290	2,797	493	3,558	2,737	821
Total Current account (1+2)	530,625	618,788	-88,163	551,838	584,235	-32,397	553,824	581,761	-27,937
B. Capital account									
1. Foreign investment (a+b)	215,027	168,316	46,711	246,766	220,380	26,386	306,429	232,868	73,561
a) Foreign direct investment (i+ii)	39,786	19,967	19,819	43,582	22,018	21,564	50,939	18,312	32,627
i) In India	34,298	7,345	26,953	36,047	5,284	30,763	44,290	9,864	34,426
Equity	22,885	6,853	16,032	25,275	4,786	20,489	31,884	9,612	22,272
Reinvested earnings	9,880	–	9,880	8,978	0	8,978	8,983	0	8,983
Other Capital	1,534	493	1,041	1,794	498	1,296	3,423	252	3,171
ii) Abroad	5,488	12,622	-7,134	7,535	16,734	-9,199	6,649	8,448	-1,799
Equity	5,488	7,101	-1,614	7,535	12,420	-4,884	6,649	4,075	2,573
Reinvested earnings	0	1,189	-1,189	0	1,167	-1,167	0	1,092	-1,092
Other capital	0	4,331	-4,331	0	3,148	-3,148	0	3,280	-3,280
b) Portfolio investment	175,241	148,349	26,891	203,184	198,362	4,822	255,490	214,556	40,934
i) In India	173,762	145,992	27,770	202,332	197,304	5,029	254,777	213,854	40,923
of which: FIIs	173,575	145,992	27,582	202,312	197,304	5,009	254,777	213,854	40,923
GDRs/ADRs	187	0	187	20	0	20	0	0	0
ii) Abroad	1,479	2,357	-878	851	1,058	-207	713	702	11

2. Loans (a+b+c)	155,085	123,961	31,124	134,836	127,071	7,765	123,877	120,442	3,435
a) External assistance	4,735	3,752	982	4,659	3,627	1,032	5,781	4,151	1,630
i) By India	52	338	-286	45	244	-199	61	484	-423
ii) To India	4,683	3,415	1,268	4,614	3,383	1,231	5,719	3,667	2,053
b) Commercial borrowings	27,617	19,132	8,485	30,060	18,283	11,777	28,368	25,638	2,729
i) By India	2,120	2,217	-97	1,642	581	1,061	1,611	273	1,338
ii) To India	25,497	16,915	8,582	28,418	17,702	10,716	26,757	25,366	1,391
c) Short term to India	122,734	101,077	21,657	100,117	105,161	-5,044	89,729	90,653	-924
i) Suppliers' Credit > 180 days & Buyers' Credit	119,236	99,397	19,839	99,832	103,861	-4,029	87,643	90,043	-2,399
ii) Suppliers' credit up to 180 days	3,498	1,680	1,818	285	1,300	-1,015	2,086	610	1,476
3. Banking capital (a+b)	83,727	67,157	16,570	108,049	82,601	25,449	90,094	78,476	11,618
a) Commercial Banks	83,086	66,985	16,101	107,556	82,601	24,955	88,361	78,476	9,885
i) Assets	12,033	13,382	-1,349	14,601	21,224	-6,623	17,031	18,546	-1,515
ii) Liabilities	71,052	53,603	17,450	92,955	61,377	31,578	71,329	59,930	11,399
of which: Non-Resident Deposits	65,309	50,466	14,842	87,750	48,858	38,892	63,262	49,205	14,057
b) Others	641	172	469	494	0	494	1,733	0	1,733
4. Rupee debt service	0	58	-58	0	52	-52	0	81	-81
5. Other capital	17,861	22,908	-5,047	22,171	32,932	-10,761	27,869	26,443	1,426
Total capital account (1 to 5)	471,701	382,401	89,300	511,823	463,035	48,787	548,269	458,310	89,959
C. Errors & omissions	2,689	0	2,589	887	1,769	-882	1,470	2,086	-616
D. Overall balance (A+B+C)	1,005,015	1,001,189	3,826	1,064,548	1,049,040	15,508	1,103,563	1,042,157	61,406
E. Monetary movements (i+ii)	0	3,826	-3,826	0	15,508	-15,508	0	61,406	-61,406
i) I.M.F.	0	0	0	–	–	–	0	0	0
ii) Foreign exchange reserves (Increase-/Decrease+)	0	3,826	-3,826	0	15,508	-15,508	0	61,406	-61,406
of which: SDR Allocation									

Source: Handbook of Statistics on Indian Economy, Table 139, page 220. Available at: https://www.rbi.org.in/scripts/PublicationsView.aspx?id=16583

16
CHAPTER

Capital Mobility

LEARNING OBJECTIVES

Upon completion of this chapter, the reader will be able to:

- Understand the effects of additional factors, relative to a closed economy, influencing policy outcomes in an open economy.
- Appreciate why policy-makers have to take into account the impact of capital mobility when making policy choices.
- Evaluate the impact of monetary and fiscal policies under a fixed exchange rate regime with perfect capital mobility.
- Understand the impact of an exchange rate devaluation on the trade balance in the short and long-run, relating outcomes to export and import price elasticities, as put forth in the Marshall–Lerner condition.
- Explain the impact of macroeconomic policies under a flexible exchange rate regime and appreciate that the effectiveness of macroeconomic policies in an open economy hinges on the degree of international capital mobility.

16.1. INTRODUCTION

In the previous chapter, we have studied the forces underlying the movement of exchange rates. A more detailed treatment awaits in Chapter 17. This leads us to the next logical sequential step, the analysis of macroeconomic policies in an open economy. The movement of exchange rates feeds into developments in the aggregate

TABLE 16.1

Trade Shares in GDP and Country Growth Performance

Country	Exports + Imports (% of GDP)	GDP Growth (%), in 2007
Armenia	55.97	13.4
China	68.71	12
Georgia	82.26	11.6
Ethiopia	46.95	11.0
Mongolia	99.72	10.0

Source: Table prepared from World Development Indicators 2009 and Penn World Table 7.1.

economy, while macro-stabilization policies, both fiscal and monetary, influence the exchange rate.

In this chapter, the open economy IS–LM model includes not only exports and imports but also international capital flows. This is an important step, since no country in the world today, even Albania, is really totally isolated from the rest of the world. Of course, some countries are more open than others and this is often reflected in their aggregate economic growth performance. Available evidence seems to indicate that the more open countries have grown faster. Table 16.1 provides data on the trade share of GDP for selected countries[1] and their growth in percentage terms during 2007.

The data in Table 16.1 does give some support for the view that open economies grow faster. This hypothesis is also supported if you look at the experience of individual countries who undertook economic reforms, opening up the economy, cutting tariffs and non-tariff restrictions and promoting exports. Figure 16.1, taken from *The Economist*, October 2010, shows a remarkable congruence between the experiences of China and India after undertaking reforms. In both countries, in the first few years of reforms, both exports as a percentage of GDP and the GDP growth itself rose rapidly.

Notice that the growth in GDP also picked up in a similar fashion in these two Asian giants after reforms were initiated in them. China's early head start meant that it would take India a few decades to catch up, if at all possible, to China's per capita income levels. We must remember, however, how the recent financial crises have reawakened to life the discussion about the superior economic performance of an open economy compared to a relatively closed one. We will have more to say about this in the concluding section of this chapter. Now, in the next section, we proceed to present the formal model of the open economy.

[1] As per the World Development Indicators 2009, all the countries are in the middle income with growth a rate above 10%.

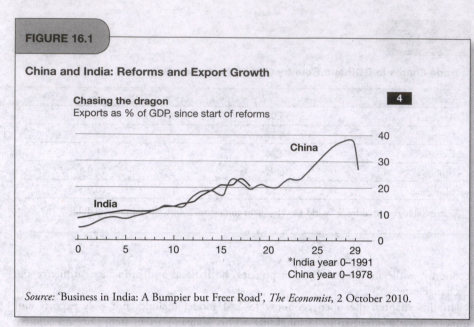

Source: 'Business in India: A Bumpier but Freer Road', *The Economist*, 2 October 2010.

16.2. THE OPEN ECONOMY MODEL

16.2.1. The IS Curve for an Open Economy

We now refer back to the fundamental national income identity that we discussed in Chapter 2.

$$Y = C + I + G + NX$$

While net exports (NX), was included in this identity in the basic model of Chapter 3, it was really exogenous there. Now, with the opening up the economy, it becomes necessary to specify the determinants of net exports in an open economy.

Net exports depend on home income, foreign income and the real exchange rate:

$$NX = X(Y_f, R) - M(Y, R) \qquad (16.1)$$

In an open economy, net exports NX, are an addition to total expenditure on goods and services. Net exports are equal to home country exports minus imports, which reduces the total home demand being spent on foreign goods.

In Equation 16.1, exports are written as a function of foreign income Y_f and the real exchange rate 'R'. Exports clearly rise as foreigners become richer and demand more of home goods. The real exchange rate is defined as

$$R = e \times P_f/P \qquad (16.2)$$

where P_f is the foreign price level, 'P' is the home price level and 'e' is the nominal exchange rate in the home currency per unit of foreign currency. The real exchange rate is the relative price between foreign and home goods expressed in a common currency, here in terms of the home currency, so that the nominal exchange rate enters the expression.

As the real exchange rate R rises, foreign goods become expensive relative to home goods; this can happen if 'e' rises with a home *currency depreciation*, or if the foreign price rises, or if the home price falls. With an increase in R, home goods become relatively cheaper and foreigners demand more of these thereby increasing home exports.

If the real exchange rate rises, it follows that imports 'M' will be curtailed by the home country, as foreign goods have become relatively more expensive. On the other hand, if home income 'Y' rises, more imported goods will be demanded.

Thus, net exports may be specified as depending on home and foreign income levels and the real exchange rate (which includes the nominal exchange rate as well as home and foreign price levels).

These effects can be incorporated into the IS curve of the closed economy IS–LM model as follows. The IS curve equation for the open economy can be written as

$$Y = C(Y) + I\,(i) + G + NX\,(Y, Y_f, R) \tag{16.3}$$

The LM curve equation is unchanged and is the same as for the closed economy IS–LM model.

> Currency depreciation is the decrease in the value of the domestic currency relative to the currencies of other countries, when exchange rates are flexible.

16.2.2. The Effects of External Sector Developments

We are now in a position to analyse the effects of external sector developments (barring those in the foreign interest rates and capital flows, which will be taken up shortly) on home output. In Figure 16.2, a depreciation that raises the real exchange rate 'R', or an increase in foreign incomes, shift the IS curve outwards, by increasing net exports. This is clear from Equation (16.3) as well.

In Figure 16.2, a real depreciation, with 'R' rising, or an increase in foreign income, increases net exports NX. This increases aggregate demand at the unchanged interest rate 'i' which means that the IS curve shifts to the right. The new equilibrium is at E_2, where the new IS curve cuts the LM curve and output has risen to Y_2.

Correspondingly, in the bottom panel, the AD curve shifts to the right, giving the new output level Y_2. A devaluation shifts IS to the right, increasing output y. In the aggregate demand–supply figure in the bottom of Figure 16.2, the demand curve AD shifts to the right.

> External balance in an open economy means a balance in the external payments accounts, with the balance of payments nearly zero with no large balance of payments surplus or deficit.

16.3. INTERNAL AND EXTERNAL BALANCE IN AN OPEN ECONOMY

The basic macroeconomic objective of the government in a closed economy is of maintaining full employment with price stability and it needs to be augmented by external sector considerations in an open economy. An *external balance* requires the

FIGURE 16.2

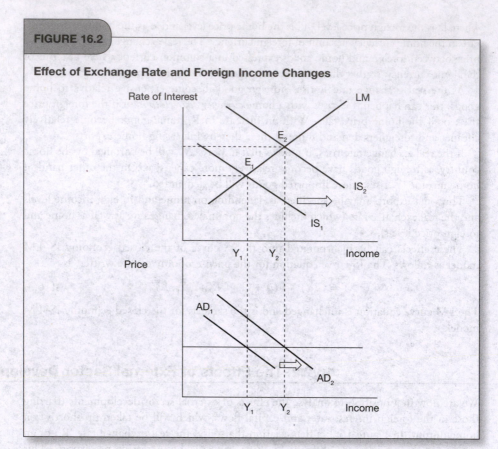

Effect of Exchange Rate and Foreign Income Changes

balance of payments to be in equilibrium, with no persistent deficits or surpluses. With surpluses for example, a situation such as now reigning with the threat of a currency war between the USA and China will arise, while with deficits, the balance of payments crisis with continuing reserve losses will lead to a breakdown of the country's exchange rate system, perhaps requiring major rearrangements in the currency value. Let us consider these internal and external policy objectives and related policy dilemmas with fixed exchange rates. The *internal balance* in an economy pertains to maintaining full employment with low, stable inflation, whereas external balance in an open economy means a balance in the external payments accounting, with the balance of payments nearly zero (with no large balance of payments surpluses or deficits).

Figure 16.3 depicts policy choices with perfect international *capital mobility*. With free capital flows, the balance of payments equilibrium, with BOP = 0 occurs only at the home interest rate that is exactly equal to the foreign interest rate. At all other home interest rates, vast capital inflows and outflows will create BOP surpluses and deficits.

Internal balance in an economy pertains to full employment mainte-nance with low, stable inflation.

Capital mobility implies that investors in different countries can alter their portfolios by buying and selling securities denomi-nated in different curren-cies across borders.

FIGURE 16.3

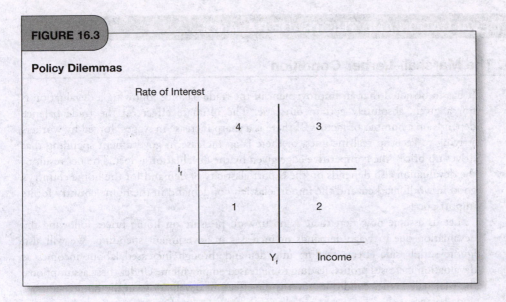

Policy Dilemmas

Y_f in the figure represents the full employment level of output. The regions marked as 1, 2, 3 and 4 represent vastly differing policy problems facing national policy-makers.

In region 1, there is a BOP deficit (since the home interest rate is less than the foreign rate, capital outflows create the deficit) and unemployment (since output is less than Y_f). In region 2, there is a BOP deficit and overemployment (with inflation which is not depicted in the figure). In region 4, there is a BOP surplus existing together with unemployment.

How can policy-makers respond to these situations, in a regime of fixed exchange rates? The situations in regions 2 and 4 are easier to tackle. With a BOP surplus and unemployment, expansionary policies will reduce unemployment and worsen the BOP, which is fine, since there is a BOP surplus to begin with. Similarly, the policy response is straightforward with a BOP deficit and excess employment, that is, a contraction will improve the BOP and reduce employment (and inflation pressures).

Now consider the problem posed in region 3. Monetary contraction can be used to reduce excess employment and inflation pressures, but then the interest rate would rise, bringing in capital flows and increasing the BOP surplus yet more. So, combinations of monetary and fiscal policies may have to be resorted to.

'Beggar-thy-neighbour' policies: Exchange rate changes can also be used for achieving the internal and external balance simultaneously. For instance, in a recession with a BOP deficit, a devaluation can expand output, while contributing to the expansion of exports and an improvement in the BOP deficit. But, a country cannot resort to such policies often, as it is a 'beggar-thy-neighbour' policy which means that you improve your *trade balance*, but the trading partner loses exports, faces an output contraction and may devalue in turn. This can lead to devaluation wars. Thus, devaluation by a country will be acceptable to the trading partner only if that country is facing overheated conditions and a BOP surplus.

'Beggar-thy-neighbour policy' is a strategy which attempts to increase domestic output at the expense of the output of other countries.

Trade balance is the difference between receipts for exports of goods and services and the expenditure on imports of goods and services. It is also called the 'visible balance'.

16.4. DEVALUATION AND THE TRADE BALANCE

16.4.1. The Marshall–Lerner Condition

It has to be noted that an improvement in the trade balance following a devaluation is not a given, absolutely certain outcome. The ultimate effect on the trade balance depends on a number of factors. If there is a sharp increase in wages, forced by workers striving to keep up real incomes, or there is an increase in government spending that drives up prices, the competitive edge given by the devaluation is lost. The net result of the devaluation also depends on the export elasticity of demand for the home country's good in world markets and the import elasticity of demand in the home country for its import goods.

Let us assume now that there is no upward pressure on home prices following the devaluation due to wage demands or increases in government spending. We will also ignore supply side effects feeding into demand through increased labour incomes as devaluation increases profits, leading to increased employment. Under these assumptions, the Marshall–Lerner condition governs the effects of devaluation on the home country's trade balance.

The Marshall–Lerner condition states that for devaluation to improve the trade balance,

The price elasticity of demand for exports is defined as the percentage change in the volume of exports divided by the percentage change in the export price, perhaps due to a devaluation.

$$\acute{\varepsilon}_x + \acute{\varepsilon}_m > 1 \tag{16.4}$$

where $\acute{\varepsilon}_x$ is the *price elasticity of export demand* for home exports in the foreign markets and $\acute{\varepsilon}_m$ is the *price elasticity of import demand* for imports in the devaluing (home) country. The condition is explicitly derived in the appendix to this chapter.

Why are these export and import elasticities important?

The price elasticity of demand for imports is defined as the percentage change in import volume divided by the percentage change in the import price exchange rate.

Look at the expression for the trade balance, which is nothing but net exports NX, expressed in home currency units.

$$TB = NX = P_x . x\, (p_m.e/P_x) - P_m.e.\, m\, (P_m.e/P_x) \tag{16.5}$$

where TB is the trade balance, P_x is the price of exports in home currency units, P_m is the price of imports in dollars (foreign currency units), s is the volume of exports, m is the volume of imports, and e is the exchange rate in units of the home currency per dollar (foreign currency unit). Foreign and home incomes are assumed to be constant, so that exports 'x' and imports 'm' depend only on the real exchange rate (the relative price) $R = P_m.e/P_x$. Note that here the foreign price in dollar terms is P_m (this price is expressed as P_f, the foreign price, in Equations (16.1) and (16.2) for net exports and the real exchange rate).

It is clear from the aforementioned expression that devaluation has a volume as well as a price effect. When the home currency is devalued (e is written up to a higher value, with more home currency units per dollar), there is a price effect because each unit of imports costs more in home currency terms. This effect deteriorates the trade balance. Offsetting this price effect are the volume effects as the devaluation reduces imports, which become more costly in home currency terms and increases home exports, which become cheaper in foreign markets as at the same home currency price, home exports are cheaper in foreign currency terms.

Then it is also clear that larger the volume effects, with export and import volumes responding strongly to the relative price change caused by the devaluation, the greater the positive impact on the trade balance. When $\acute{\varepsilon}_x$ is large, home exports increase substantially following a devaluation and when $\acute{\varepsilon}_m$ is large, home import volumes fall substantially following a devaluation. The combined volume effects are likely to outweigh the negative price effect of an increased cost of import per unit of imports. The required condition, for the strength of the price elasticity effects on volumes, is given by the Marshall–Lerner condition, which may be formally derived by totally differentiating Equation (16.5) for the trade balance, assuming initially balanced trade. The effect of a devaluation on the trade balance depends on the price elasticities of exports and imports. The Marshall–Lerner condition states that the effect is positive only if the sum of these elasticities is greater than one.

16.4.2. Devaluation, the Trade Balance and the J Curve: The Short-run versus the Long-run Effect

The discussion in the previous section has clarified that the trade balance effects of devaluation depend on the price elasticities of demand for exports and imports. The larger these are, the stronger the positive effect on the trade balance.

Now, the elasticities $\acute{\varepsilon}_x$ and $\acute{\varepsilon}_m$ are not invariant but are typically much lower in the short-run. For a hypothetical country which exports only textiles and imports only machinery, the short- and long-run price elasticities of demand for exports and imports may well look like the figures given in Table 16.2. In the short-run, the effect of a devaluation on the trade balance may not be positive because short-run price elasticities of export and import demand tend to be small. However, long-run elasticities are larger, so that the trade balance may be improved in the longer run.

Will the country under the microscope succeed in improving its trade balance by devaluing its currency? Table 16.3 provides the answer. In the short-run, the devaluation

TABLE 16.2

Short- and Long-run Price Elasticities of Demand for Exports and Imports

Goods	Short-Run $\acute{\varepsilon}_x$ (for a period < one year)	Long-Run $\acute{\varepsilon}_x$	Short-Run $\acute{\varepsilon}_m$	Long-Run $\acute{\varepsilon}_m$
Textiles	0.4	1.1		
Machinery			0.25	0.9

actually deteriorates the trade balance, since the Marshall–Lerner condition is not satisfied. The price elasticities of exports and imports add up only to 0.65. The foreign country does not switch in a big way to home exports, which have become cheaper and the home country is unable to cut back in a big way on imports of machinery, which have become more expensive with the devaluation. A main reason for the low short-run elasticities is that contracts for exports and imports may have been already entered into for the short-run period and therefore cannot be revoked.

However, the picture is rosier for the long-run. The long-run elasticities for the country's exports and imports add up to 2.0, well above the required sum of 1.0 specified under the Marshall–Lerner condition. Hence, the country's trade balance improves in the long-run after a short-run setback.

Table 16.3 shows the elasticities of demand for export and import for six developed and five emerging countries. The elasticities have been computed for periods of one to one and half years or more, that is, the long-run. Since, for all of them, the sum of the elasticities is more than one, the Marshall–Lerner condition is satisfied. If that does not happen, we observe the 'J curve' effect discussed here.

> The 'J curve' effect indicates that in the short-run, export and import volumes do not change much so that the price effect outweighs the volume effect leading to a deterioration in the trade balance after devaluation.

TABLE 16.3

The Elasticity of Exports and Imports of Select Developed and Emerging Countries

Developed Countries	Elasticity of Export Demand	Elasticity of Import Demand	Sum
Canada	0.68	1.28	1.96
France	1.28	0.93	2.21
Germany	1.02	0.79	1.81
Japan	1.40	0.95	2.35
UK	0.86	0.65	1.51
USA	1.19	1.24	2.43
Average	1.1	0.97	2.05
Emerging Countries			
Brazil	0.4	1.7	2.1
India	0.5	2.2	2.7
Pakistan	1.8	0.8	2.6
Philippines	0.9	2.7	3.6
Turkey	1.4	2.7	4.1
Average	1	2.02	3.02

Source: Table created from Gylfason, Thorvaldur, and Ole Risager, 'Does Devaluation Improve the Current Account?', *European Economic Journal* 25, no. 1 (1984): 37–64.

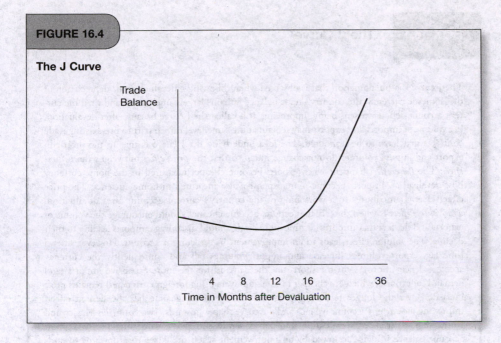

FIGURE 16.4

The J Curve

The J curve captures the contrast between the short and long-run effects of a devaluation on the trade balance (see Figure 16.4).

What is seen from Figure 16.4 is that the trade balance deteriorates for a number of months before it starts turning up. The effect is seen to resemble a 'falling down' 'J' shape and hence the name 'J curve' for the relationship between the time period after devaluation and the trade balance (see Box 16.1). The precise shape of the curve, including the point at which the effect on the trade balance turns positive will vary from country to country. The J curve depicts the short and long-run effects of devaluation on the trade balance where the trade balance is on the vertical axis and time is on the horizontal axis. The implication here is that the Marshall–Lerner condition does not hold in the short-run.

We will now turn to the most important subject of this chapter in open economy macroeconomic analysis, namely, the effectiveness of fiscal and monetary policies in open economies. This was first laid out in Robert Mundell's famous article in the *Journal of Political Economy* in 1961[2] and for this seminal contribution, he was awarded the Nobel Prize in Economics by the Swedish Academy in 1999.

---

[2] Robert Mundell, 'Capital Mobility and Stabilization Policy under Fixed and Flexible Exchange Rates', *The Canadian Journal of Economics and Political Science* 30, no. 3 (1964): 413–21.

BOX 16.1   The J Curve

The J curve is a phenomenon that is observed when following a devaluation or depreciation of the domestic currency, the country's trade balance remains largely unchanged and then the current account deficit worsens before improving. It is called the J curve because after devaluation, the volume of imports and exports may remain at the same level due in part to pre-existing trade contracts that have to be honoured. The idea underlying the J curve is that in the short-run export and import volumes do not change much so that the *price effect* outweighs the *volume effect*. The *Price effect* happens when exports become cheaper measured in the home currency post devaluation. Imports become more expensive also measured in home currency. The price effect clearly contributes to a worsening of the country's current account after devaluation. *The Volume effect* is when the fact that exports become cheaper should encourage the volume of exports and the fact that imports become more costly should discourage imports leading to their decline. The volume effect leads to an improvement in the current account. However, after a time lag, export volumes increase and import volumes fall and consequently the currency account deficit improves. In the short-run, the demand for the more expensive imports (and demand for exports, which are cheaper to foreign buyers using foreign currencies) remains price inelastic. Over the longer term, a depreciation in the exchange rate has the desired effect, improving the current account balance and the curve shapes upwards. Two countries Mexico and Korea that experienced devaluation and subsequently suffered a worsening of the current account balance initially, followed by an improvement when the curve rose upwards towards elimination of the deficit demonstrated the 'J curve' phenomenon as illustrated in the Figures 16.5a and 16.5b.

FIGURE 16.5a

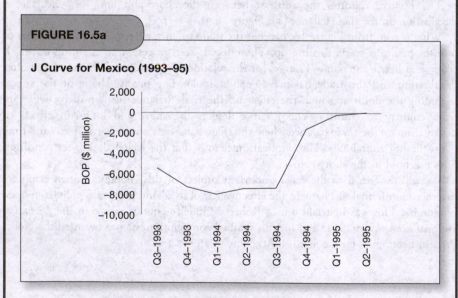

J Curve for Mexico (1993–95)

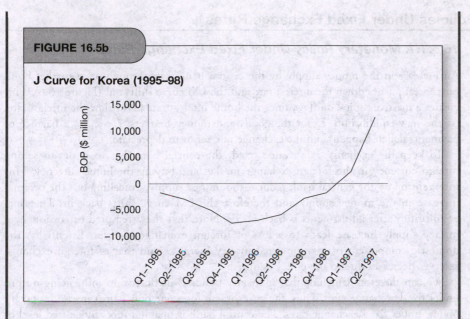

FIGURE 16.5b

J Curve for Korea (1995–98)

Mexico is the tenth largest oil producer and the largest silver producer in the world. It is considered to be an upper middle-income country by the World Bank. It has been the first Latin American member of the OECD since 1994. Mexico is considered to be a newly industrialized country and an emerging power, having the tenth largest GDP in PPP terms.

Peso, the Mexican currency depreciated in 1993 from 3.1156 pesos/$ to 11.29 pesos/$. Figure 16.5a plots the BOP of Mexico against time for this time period to illustrate the 'J curve' effect. The BOP initially worsened before starting to increase around the fourth quarter of 1994.

South Korea is Asia's fourth largest economy and the worlds' 12th in PPP terms. The economy is export driven and it produces electronics, automobiles ships, petrochemicals and robotics. It is a G20, OECD and member of the ASEAN group of countries. Being heavily dependent on exports, it is the tenth largest importer in the world. The country experienced depreciation of its currency during the Asian crisis. Between 1995 and 1998 the Korean currency the Won witnessed a depreciation from 771.27W/$ to 1401.44W/$. Note how the current account deficit began to improve after the second quarter of 1996.

16.5. MONETARY AND FISCAL POLICIES IN OPEN ECONOMIES

Let us now look at the relative effectiveness of monetary and fiscal policies with perfect capital mobility, under fixed as well as flexible exchange rate regimes.

16.5.1. Policies Under Fixed Exchange Rates

16.5.1.1. Monetary Policy Under Fixed Exchange Rates

An increase in the money supply by the central bank (say, through open market bond purchases) pushes down the interest rate and the LM curve shifts out (Figure 16.6). This creates a massive capital outflow, since the home interest rate falls below the foreign rate. At the new equilibrium 'E' for the goods and money markets, $i < _f$. So, a balance of payments deficit happens and the exchange rate tends to depreciate.

To keep the exchange rate's value fixed, the central bank has to resort to selling foreign currency in the foreign exchange market and buying the home currency. This intervention by the central bank reduces the money supply, cancelling out the original increase in the money supply and therefore the LM curve shifts back in. The final equilibrium after adjustments is back at 'E'. Note that the attempted expansion by a money supply increase leads to a loss of foreign exchange reserves. Essentially, the domestic component of high-powered money increases and that of foreign exchange reserves decreases due to the policy adopted.

We can therefore conclude that monetary policy is ineffective in influencing output under fixed exchange rates. Thus, the government loses one policy instrument, monetary policy, under fixed exchange rates. The central bank is unable to fix any desired level of money supply, as there are deviations from the targeted money supply due to (the maintenance of) the fixed exchange rate. An expansionary monetary policy does not affect output under fixed exchange rates. The need to fix the exchange rate takes away the ability of the central bank to choose any level for the money supply and monetary policy is no longer a viable policy instrument.

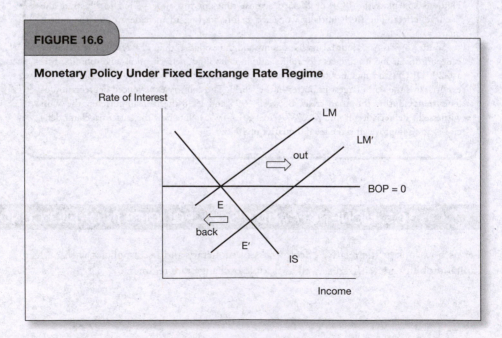

FIGURE 16.6

Monetary Policy Under Fixed Exchange Rate Regime

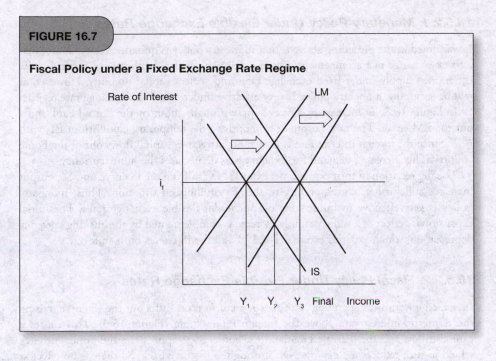

FIGURE 16.7

Fiscal Policy under a Fixed Exchange Rate Regime

16.5.1.2. Fiscal Policy Under Fixed Exchange Rates

An increase in government spending, or a cut in the tax rate moves the IS curve out (Figure 16.7). This shift will equal the multiplier in the basic Keynesian model. Output 'Y' rises. Now, the home interest rate rises above the foreign rate and $i >_f$. So, capital flows in, creating a BOP surplus, which tends to appreciate the exchange rate.

To maintain the fixed exchange rate, the central bank has to sell home currency and buy foreign currency. This naturally increases the money supply and the LM curve shifts out, like the IS curve did when the policy was initiated. The increase in 'M' and the rightward shift of the LM curve increases output still further.

Thus, fiscal policy is very effective under fixed exchange rates, the fiscal expansion effect on output being complemented by the subsequent monetary expansion that it gives rise to. The central bank intervention required to maintain the fixed exchange rate complements the fiscal policy effect on output. Both the IS and LM curves shift out.

> A central bank intervention is the purchase or sale of domestic or foreign currency in the exchange market by the monetary authority, to influence the value of the domestic currency.

16.5.2. Policies Under a Flexible Exchange Rate Regime

We now turn to the effects of fiscal and monetary policies under a flexible exchange rate regime. Let us start again with a monetary policy and then a fiscal policy.

1. Monetary policy under flexible exchange rates.
2. Fiscal policy under flexible exchange rates.

16.5.2.1. Monetary Policy Under Flexible Exchange Rates

It was noted in the preceding sections that monetary policy is quite ineffective under that a fixed exchange rate arrangement. Quite simply, the central bank cannot control or fix the money supply under fixed exchange rates and perfect capital mobility. However, as will be seen now, monetary policy is very effective under a flexible exchange rate regime.

In Figure 16.8, an increase in money supply brought about by the central bank shifts out the LM curve. The new output corresponds to the temporary equilibrium E1, with $i < _f$. Since the foreign interest rate is now more attractive, capital flows out of the home country. This increased demand for foreign assets depreciates the home currency.

The depreciation in turn expands net exports NX, shifting the IS curve out. So, output increases still further, corresponding to the 'E' equilibrium situation. Thus, monetary policy is very effective in influencing output under flexible exchange rates. The initial expansionary effect of a money supply increase is complemented by the ensuing currency depreciation, which expands exports. The LM and the IS curves both shift out.

16.5.2.2. Fiscal Policy Under Flexible Exchange Rates

Increased government spending, transfers or a cut in taxes shifts out the IS curve, raising the domestic interest rate above the foreign interest rate (Figure 16.9). This causes a capital inflow and the increased demand for home assets appreciates the home currency which in turn reduces net exports NX, shifting the IS curve back. So there is no effect at all on output and fiscal policy is ineffective under flexible exchange rates.

FIGURE 16.8

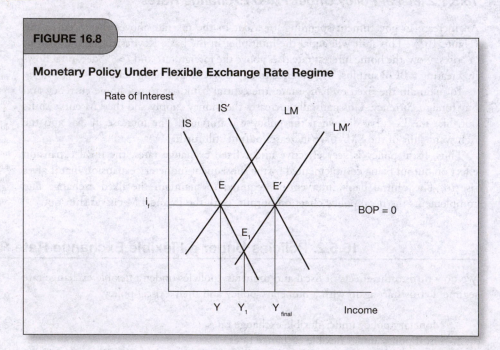

Monetary Policy Under Flexible Exchange Rate Regime

FIGURE 16.9

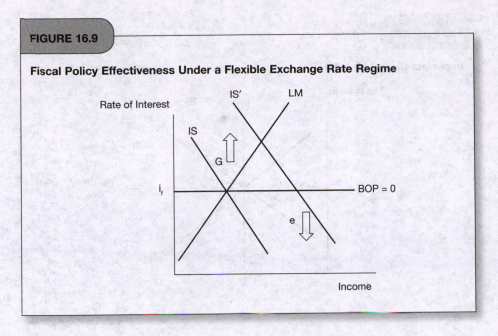

Fiscal Policy Effectiveness Under a Flexible Exchange Rate Regime

Note that under a flexible exchange rate regime, the current account deficit (surplus) is exactly matched by a capital account surplus (deficit), making the BOP = 0. There is no central bank intervention and no change in reserves. The exchange rate does all the adjustment. Fiscal policy fails under flexible rates because the initial expansion is offset by a contraction in net exports due to the ensuing currency appreciation.

Currency appreciation is the increase in the value of the domestic currency relative to the currencies of other countries when the exchange rates are flexible.

16.6. MACROECONOMIC POLICY WITH IMPERFECT CAPITAL MOBILITY

The results derived in the previous section hinge upon the assumption of perfect capital mobility. The results will not hold with complete absence of capital flows (capital mobility), but may hold for a certain level of capital mobility. We turn to a discussion of this issue, restricting ourselves to the case of fixed exchange rates, since imperfect capital mobility goes hand-in-hand with fixed and, not flexible exchange rates. In what follows, we will analyse the output effects of a fiscal expansion under different degrees of international capital mobility.

In Figure 16.10, the complete absence of capital mobility is represented by the vertical BOP = 0 line. This is because if output Y increases and net exports NX fall due to the ensuing rise in imports, an infinite rise in interest rates is needed to balance the BOP. The horizontal BOP = 0 line represents perfect capital mobility, since the slightest deviation in home interest rates from the given foreign rate produces capital flows that could balance the trade deficit due to lower net exports. The sloping BOP = 0 line represents

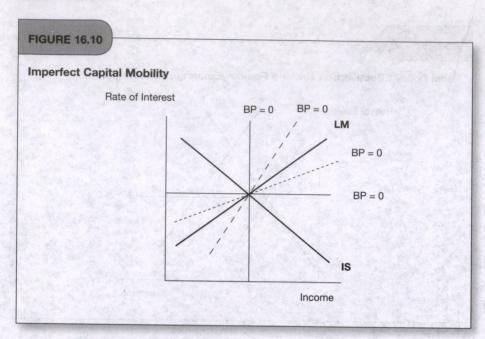

FIGURE 16.10

Imperfect Capital Mobility

the balance in external payments. It slopes up in general, since more home output means more imports and that needs capital inflows, requiring higher interest rates for balance. As already pointed out, a horizontal BOP = 0 line represents perfect capital mobility. Indeed, as should have become clear by now, the slope of the BOP = 0 line represents the degree of capital mobility.

The region between the vertical and the horizontal BOP = 0 lines represents varying degrees of capital mobility. The BOP line has to slope up, not down, since a rise in Y which leads to a fall in NX has to be balanced by capital inflows, which require a higher interest rate (given that Y increases along the x-axis). So, the points on the BOP = 0 line represent the rates of interest needed to bring in sufficient capital flows to balance the external account.

The BOP dashed line with a slope higher than that of the LM curve represents a level of capital mobility where fiscal policy will not be effective under fixed exchange rates. However, the dotted BOP line, flatter than the LM curve, represents sufficient mobility of international capital for fiscal policy to be fully effective under fixed exchange rates. These policy effects can be studied using Figure 16.11.

An expansionary fiscal policy (such as an increase in government spending) shifts the IS curve to the right. When the BOP balance (BOP = 0) line is the vertical line, indicating no capital mobility at all, it is seen from the figure that the IS curve, after shifting, cuts the LM curve to the right of the points 'F' and 'G'. These points, 'F' and 'G' are the points where the IS curve cuts the BOP lines with very little capital mobility. Since the IS curve cuts the LM curve to the right of these points, the resulting interest

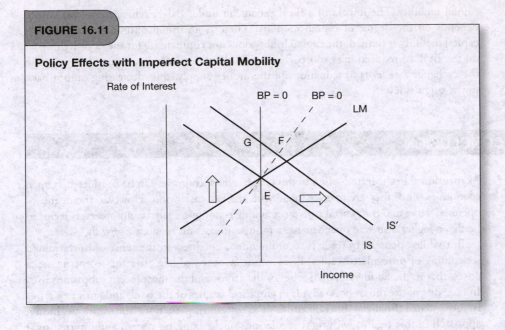

FIGURE 16.11

Policy Effects with Imperfect Capital Mobility

rate in the new equilibrium is not high enough for the balance of payments to balance (BOP = 0).

Hence a balance of payments deficit develops, since the amount of capital flows with such limited capital mobility are not enough to balance the BOP and match the fall in net exports. This leads to a fall in the money supply M, since the deficit will lead to a depreciation unless the central bank intervenes in the foreign exchange market to buy the home currency.

With a fall in M, the LM curve shifts back (not shown in the figure to avoid cluttering) until it cuts the IS curve at the old output level. Thus, there is no fiscal policy effect on output even under a fixed exchange rate regime. Even if the BOP = 0 line is not vertical, that is, there is some degree of capital mobility, the same story will be repeated if the BOP line is steeper than the LM curve because, as a BOP deficit develops, the LM curve shifts left as the money supply falls.

But if the BOP = 0 line is flatter than the LM curve, the new IS curve (after shifting right with a fiscal expansion) will cut the LM curve to the left of the BOP line. Then the resulting interest rate is higher than what is needed for balancing the fall in net exports by capital inflows. Then a BOP surplus will develop due to the excess capital inflows. To prevent the currency from appreciating, the central bank has to sell home currency, which increases the money supply thereby shifting the LM curve to the right.

With both the IS curve and the LM curves shifting to the right, fiscal policy is now (at this level of capital mobility) very effective in expanding output. Thus, the effectiveness of macroeconomic policies in an open economy hinges on the degree of international capital mobility. The impact of a fiscal expansion under fixed exchange rates on output depends on the degree of capital mobility. There is an initial output increase. But, if capital mobility is limited, the capital inflow does not compensate for the negative impact on the BOP of reduced net exports. The central bank intervention required to maintain the exchange rate leads to reductions in the money supply, thus decreasing output back to the original level.

16.7. CONCLUSION

As mentioned in the introduction to this chapter, most countries can be considered as open economies, since they are open to trade with the external world. However, the degree of openness varies and the general consensus among economic analysts and observers seems to be that a higher degree of openness has a positive impact on economic growth.

But while openness to trade is recommended, openness in the sense of unrestrained welcoming of unregulated capital flows is not favoured of late after the recent financial crises, that is, the Southeast Asian crises of the 1990s and the most recent subprime crisis. In fact, one of the causes pointed out in empirical studies of the bank and currency crises is unregulated financial liberalization. It is interesting to note the cautious Indian approach in this regard, with tight regulations of the banking system and international capital flows which won acclaim even from the IMF in the aftermath of the crisis of the 1990s.

Still, developing countries and emerging market nations do tend to actively encourage longer-term foreign direct investment flows. These are not 'footloose' and don't create financial instabilities and do not contribute to the worsening of an incipient financial crisis. But all capital flows have implications for the relative effectiveness of different macroeconomic policies as we have seen in this chapter. There are instances when Indian policy-makers have put the brakes on capital inflows because of the pressure on the rupee to appreciate, which then has a detrimental effect on exports.

But the type of capital flows discussed in this chapter, which are responsive to interest rate differentials, are of the short-term nature. FDI inflows have a number of other determinants, such as growth prospects, skill availability in the host nation, the choice of base for exports, and so on. So, strictly speaking, while FDI inflows do appear in the capital account of the balance of payments, they have not been included in the standard model of policy effectiveness under fixed and flexible exchange rates.

SUMMARY

- The IS–LM framework of the closed economy is expanded to include trade and capital flows characterizing an open economy interacting with the rest of the world. Net exports are specified to depend on home and foreign incomes. Net exports are also affected by the real exchange rate, composed of the nominal exchange rate and home and foreign price levels. Net capital inflows rise when the home interest rate shows a positive differential against the foreign interest rate.

- The internal balance in an economy pertains to maintaining full employment with low, stable inflation, whereas the external balance in an open economy means a balance in the external payments accounting, with the balance of payments nearly zero.

- Exchange rate changes can be used for achieving internal and external balance simultaneously. In a recession with a BOP deficit, devaluation can expand output, contributing to expansion of exports and improvements in the BOP deficit. But, a country cannot resort to such policies, as it is a 'beggar-thy-neighbour' policy since as the trading partner loses exports and faces an output contraction.

- However, devaluation does not necessarily lead to improvements in the trade balance, because that depends on the increase in wages, government spending raising prices, which erode the benefits of devaluation. Ultimately, devaluation depends on the export elasticity of demand for the home country's goods in the world markets and the import elasticity of demand in the home country for its import goods.

- The Marshall–Lerner condition states that the effect of a devaluation is positive only if the sum of the trade elasticities is greater than one. But short-term elasticities are small, so that the Marshall–Lerner condition can be satisfied only in the long-run.

- The J curve captures the contrast between the short and long-run effects of a devaluation on the trade balance. The implication of the J curve effect is that the Marshall–Lerner condition does not hold in the short-run.

- Under the fixed exchange rate regime, when the exchange rate tends to depreciate, the central bank resorts to selling and buying foreign currency and/or home currency, leading to a reduction in the money supply and a loss of foreign exchange reserves. Hence an expansionary monetary policy that lowers the domestic interest rate and tends to depreciate the currency, does not affect the money supply and output.

- But an expansionary fiscal policy (an increase in government spending or a tax rate cut) moves the IS curve out, raising the home interest rate above the foreign rate. The interest differential attracts capital inflows, creating a BOP surplus, tending to appreciate the currency.

- To maintain a fixed exchange rate, the central bank intervenes, shifting the LM curve out to the right, which increases output still further. Thus, fiscal policy is very effective under fixed exchange rates.

- Under a flexible exchange rate regime, the current account deficit (surplus) is exactly matched by a capital account surplus (deficit), maintaining BOP = 0. There is no central bank intervention and no change in reserves. Fiscal policy fails under flexible exchange rates because the initial expansion is offset by a contraction in net exports due to the ensuing currency appreciation.

CASE STUDY

Continuing Challenges in the External Sector: The Effectiveness of Policy Prescriptions[3]

The current account deficit (CAD), which rose from 2.7% of GDP in 2010–11 to 4.2% of GDP in 2011–12, went on to reach an alarming level of more than 4.5% in 2013–14. The RBI Governor was clearly apprehensive, because he said, 'It's going to be historically the highest CAD measured as a proportion of GDP'. The basis for his apprehensions lay in the fact that since 1980, only once in 2010 did the current account deficit exceed 3% of GDP. So 4.2% in 2011–12 was a 30-year high. Year-on-year, it rose from 3.2% in the first quarter of 2011–12 to 3.9% in the corresponding quarter of 2012–13 and from 4.8% to 5.4% between the second quarters of those two years. Ironically, in the three years preceding the balance of payments crisis of 1991, the current account deficit had touched only 2.4%, 2.3% and 2.2% respectively.

In the light of this, the improvement in the balance of payments data during the second quarter of 2013 looked spectacular. According to the RBI, India's current account deficit (CAD) narrowed sharply to $5.2 billion (1.2% of GDP) in the second quarter from $21 billion (5.0%) during the corresponding period in 2012. It was also much lower than the 4.9% noted in the first quarter. The sharp fall was attributed to a contraction in the trade deficit to $33.3 billion from $47.8 billion a year ago. Merchandise exports picked up, while imports, especially of gold, moderated. Exports increased by 11.9% to $81.2 billion on the back of significant growth in leather and textile exports. On the other hand, merchandise imports at $114.5 billion recorded a steeper decline of 4.8% on a year-to-year basis. Gold imports fell steeply to $3.9 billion compared to $16.4 billion in the preceding quarter and $11.1 billion a year ago.

The free fall of the rupee in August 2013 was both the cause and the consequence of the prevailing macroeconomic uncertainty. It exposed in no uncertain terms the perils of over-dependence on short-term capital flows to fund the current account. This is amply reflected in the latest BOP data: net portfolio investment outflows were of the order of $6.6 billion, almost matching the inflows under foreign direct investment.

Altogether, in the first half of 2013, reserves were down by more than $10 billion, despite the vast improvements in the CAD. The rupee's path towards relative stability since then reflects, above all, a considerable improvement in the external economy. The RBI's unconventional measures to shore up the rupee, such as opening a separate window for oil companies, also helped. Exports received a major fillip in the wake of the rupee's depreciation. But the narrowing of the CAD was also due to continued weakness in non-gold and non-oil imports. Any acceleration in growth would push up the import bill of such items. Finally, government policies might have sharply curtailed gold imports but the underlying demand for gold remained.

After reading the text given in the case study answer the following questions:

1. Why was the Current Account Deficit (CAD) considered to be alarming? Based on the theoretical analysis presented in this chapter, explain the adverse effects of a ballooning CAD.

---

[3] Text for this Case Study was drawn from: Jayati Ghosh and C. P. Chandrashekhar, *The Hindu Business Line*, 18 February 2013, Available at: http://www.thehindubusinessline.com/opinion/columns/c-p-chandrasekhar/disquieting-imbalance/article4428567.ece Accessed on 30 October 2017.

2. Did the currency depreciation improved the balance of payments situation?
3. What policy measures by the RBI helped to narrow the CAD? Are such policies sustainable in the long-run? If not, why not?
4. Is the capital mobility presently observed beneficial to the economy?

KEYWORDS

Trade balance
Internal balance
External balance
Price elasticity of export demand
Price elasticity of import demand
Currency appreciation

J curve
Central bank intervention
Capital mobility
Beggar-thy-neighbour policy
Currency depreciation

CONCEPT CHECK

State whether the following statements are true or false:

1. In an open economy, the net export is equal to home country exports plus imports.
2. A devaluation of the home currency shifts the IS curve to the right, increasing output y and consequently the aggregate demand curve AD shifts to the right.
3. The Marshall–Lerner condition states that the current account deficit will decline after a devaluation of the home currency only if the sum of the elasticities of demand for exports and imports is greater than one.
4. The J curve depicts only the short-run effects of devaluation on the trade balance, namely, the trade balance rapidly falls and reaches a balance as soon as the country devalues its currency.
5. An expansionary monetary policy does not affect output under fixed exchange rates.
6. Monetary policy is very effective in influencing output under flexible exchange rates as the initial expansionary effect of a money supply increase is complemented by the ensuing currency depreciation, which expands exports.
7. Fiscal policy succeeds under flexible rates because the initial expansion is offset by a contraction in net exports due to the ensuing currency appreciation.
8. A horizontal BOP = 0 line represents perfect capital mobility, hence the slope of the BOP = 0 line represents the degree of capital mobility.
9. The impact of a fiscal expansion under fixed exchange rates on output depends on the degree of capital mobility.

DISCUSSION QUESTIONS

1. How is an open economy's IS curve different from the closed economy's IS curve?
2. Are international capital flows a relatively minor effect on the balance of payments?
3. Explain the role of a central bank in the outcomes of the policies followed under fixed exchange rates.
4. Discuss the limits on capital mobility that have a bearing on the outcome of fiscal policy under flexible exchange rates.
5. What is the difference between flexible and fixed exchange rate regimes with regard to possible BOP surpluses and deficits?
6. Why are the price elasticities of demand for exports and imports important in trying to forecast the effects of a devaluation on the trade balance?
7. Which factors give the J curve its shape? Will the J curve for a developing country and for an industrial nation tend to have the same shape and position in the figure?

APPENDIX

Here we derive the Marshall–Lerner condition, presented as Equation (16.4) in the chapter. The trade balance, which is also net exports, NX, is given as

$$TB = P_x . x \ (P_m . e / P_x) - P_m . e . m(P_m . e. / P_x . x) \qquad (16A.1)$$

'TB' is the trade balance, P_m is the foreign price, which is also the import price, in dollars, 'e' is the exchange rate in rupees per dollar and 'P' is the home good price in rupees. 'x' and 'm' are export and import volumes respectively, which are assumed to depend only on the real exchange rate, 'R', which is the relative price $P_m . e / P_x$, since foreign and home incomes are held constant in this derivation.

Totally differentiating Equation 16A.1 and representing the rates of change by the superscript hat ^ (so that, for example, $e^{\wedge} = de/e$), we get

$$d(TB) = P_x . (dx/dR) . R . e^{\wedge} - Pm . m . e . e^{\wedge} - Pm . e . (dm/dR), R . e^{\wedge} \qquad (16A.2)$$

where,

$$R = P_m e / P_x. \qquad (16A.1')$$

Note, that the changes in P_m and P_x are put to zero, so that the real exchange rate changes only due to a change in 'e', that is, by a devaluation of the nominal exchange rate.

Rewrite Equation (16A.2) as

$$d(TB) = P_x . (dx/dR) . (x/x) . R . e^{\wedge} - P_m . m . e . e^{\wedge} - P_m . e . (dm/dR) (m/m) . R . e^{\wedge} \qquad (16A.3)$$

Now, defining the price elasticities of exports and imports respectively as

$$\acute{\varepsilon}_x = (dx/dR).(R/x) \qquad\qquad (16A.4)$$

and

$$\acute{\varepsilon}_m = -(dm/dR).(R/m) \qquad\qquad (16A.5)$$

Note that the elasticities are written as absolute numbers and relate export and import demands to the relative price R, the constituents of which are the individual foreign and home good prices and the nominal exchange rate. Note also that $(dm/dr).(m/R)$ is a negative number, so that $\acute{\varepsilon}m$ is represented as a positive number.

Using these definitions, rewrite Equation (16 A.3) as

$$d(TB) = P_x.x.\acute{\varepsilon}_x.\, e\hat{\ } - P_m.e.m.e\hat{\ } + P_m.e.\acute{\varepsilon}_m.m.e\hat{\ } \qquad\qquad (16A.6)$$

We will assume initially balanced trade, so that

$$P_x.x = P_m.m.c \qquad\qquad (16A.7)$$

Using Equations (16 A.7) in (16 A.6), we have

$$d(TB) = P_x.x.e\hat{\ }\, (\acute{\varepsilon}_x - 1 + \acute{\varepsilon}_m.) \qquad\qquad (16A.8)$$

From Equation (16 A.8), we get the Marshall–Lerner condition, which states that the trade balance 'TB' improves following a devaluation, if

$$\acute{\varepsilon}_x + \acute{\varepsilon}_m > 1 \qquad\qquad (16A.9)$$

17
CHAPTER

The Determination of Exchange Rates in an Open Economy

LEARNING OBJECTIVES

Upon completion of this chapter, the reader will be able to:

- Have a grasp of the historical background as well as the evolution of the different exchange rate regimes during the last century.
- List all the factors that influence exchange rates.
- Explain and distinguish between the factors that affect exchange rates in the short-term and long-term perspectives.
- Comprehend why exchange rates overshoot and relate the phenomenon to differences in the speed of adjustment in the goods and the asset markets.
- Discuss the relative advantages and disadvantages of fixed and flexible exchange rate regimes.

17.1. INTRODUCTION TO EXCHANGE RATES

In an open economy, the foreign exchange rate is the crucial link between the domestic economy and the rest of the world. As long as we are within the borders of the home country, we have almost no interaction with matters relating to foreign exchange. But when we go abroad, be it for work, study or for holidaying, we have to deal with foreign currencies. The rates of exchange of the domestic currency for the foreign currency for traveller's cheques or currency are posted in banks, at the offices of foreign exchange dealers and at tourist centres. You may have noticed that there are buying and selling prices and the difference between the buying and selling prices is called the spread. The prices are usually unfavourable for the tourist, but that rate is not universal. However, an exporter or an importer may not pay the same high rate as charged to foreign tourists, as they acquire the foreign exchange (which is usually the US dollar) from the wholesale forex market. The determination of the foreign exchange rate is a complex process involving importers, exporters, banks, foreign exchange dealers and the central banks. The trading of currencies and bank deposits denominated in various currencies takes place in the foreign exchange market, large banks being the main actors while individuals are not important participants in the foreign exchange market.

In Chapter 15, we had introduced the concept of fixed and flexible exchange rates. Here, in this chapter, we discuss the various theories of exchange rate determination. The chapter contents are as follows: after the introduction, in Section 17.2, we meander through the historical background of the exchange rates regimes of the Gold Standard and the Bretton Woods system and their eventual collapse in the 1970s. Sections 17.3 and 17.4 are devoted to the short-term determination of exchange rates, the long-term theories of purchasing power parity (PPP), Dornbusch's Sticky Price model and other monetary models. The last section deliberates on the advantages and disadvantages of the different exchange rate regimes.

17.2. THE GOLD STANDARD, BRETTON WOODS AND AFTER: A BRIEF HISTORY OF THE EXCHANGE RATE REGIMES

Before World War II, the exchange rates were not always specified in terms of other currencies. The currency values were fixed in terms of gold, and they were convertible to gold and this was the Gold Standard. After the war, a new system emerged at the Bretton Woods conference in 1944. In a small town in New Hampshire, a path-breaking agreement was signed by 44 nations. India was a signatory too. At that historic moment two major financial bodies, the International Monetary Fund (IMF) and the International Bank for Reconstruction and Development (later known as the World Bank) were established.

Under the Bretton Woods system, the dollar was the kingpin as after all it was the currency of the leading economy. The US dollar's value was fixed in terms of gold, with all other currencies linked to the dollar at fixed rates. The Bretton Woods System was a fixed exchange rate system, but an adjustable one. The dollar was fixed at a parity of $35 per ounce of gold, but was allowed to fluctuate by 1% above or below this rate. All currencies that were pegged to the dollar could be converted into gold, thus providing confidence in the dollar. It is of interest to note that, in 1945, the USA held around 70% of the total gold reserves in the world.

In the early 1970s, with the Vietnam War at its zenith, the US current deficits expanded, flooding the world markets with dollar holdings. Attempting to defend an overvalued exchange rate, which tended to depreciate, involved continuing losses in international reserves. At some stage, this became unsustainable and the exchange rate had to be freed and allowed to depreciate. But this was not possible under the existing exchange rate system thereby marking its imminent collapse.

In 1973, Richard Nixon, the then American President, declared that the convertibility of the dollar to gold would be suspended. The Bretton Woods System of fixed exchange rates finally collapsed because countries with balance of payments surpluses were not willing to take on more expansionary policies and let their currencies appreciate. This put an untenable pressure on the deficit countries which had to defend overvalued exchange rates. Most importantly, the dollar became overvalued without corrective measures being possible since it was the reserve currency with a fixed parity to gold.

With the breakdown of the Bretton Woods system, the fixed exchange rate system was replaced by a flexible rate system where currency values could change continuously in response to market forces. There are variations of this flexible rate system, such as the *managed float*, where the central bank intervenes to keep the currency values within a broad band.

Many countries, especially in the developing world, moved, post-Bretton Woods, to a system of fixed rates, with the currency value being fixed in terms of a basket of currencies, rather than the dollar. The weights of the foreign currencies in the basket were usually in accordance with the weight of those countries in the international trade of the home country. However, the dollar was usually given a larger weight than would have been dictated by the importance of the US in the total trade of that country. India too, had such a system for many years until 1993, when the country adopted current account convertibility as a move towards a flexible exchange rate system with government intervention, which was essentially a managed float.

The European Monetary System (EMS) came into being in 1979, with member countries requiring to manage their exchange rates with a fellow member within a 2.25% plus or minus band which was later revised upwards to a plus or minus 15% band. When currencies tended to move outside this band, both countries were required to take corrective measures, intervening in the foreign exchange market. But speculative attacks on currencies did take place, making successful central bank interventions difficult.

> Managed float is a flexible exchange rate regime where the central government intervenes to maintain the currency within a prescribed band.

17.3. DETERMINANTS OF THE EXCHANGE RATE

The forces that determine the exchange rate in the short-run are different from the predominant long-run forces. However, we ignore this time dimension to begin with and in Figure 17.1, gather together all the relevant determinants.

Figure 17.1 is a simple supply and demand diagram for foreign currency in the foreign exchange market. The nominal exchange rate 'e' is along the vertical axis, while the quantity of foreign currency is along the horizontal axis.

The demand curve for foreign currency slopes down as a lower value of 'e', indicating more units of foreign currency per unit of home currency will mean more import demand for foreign goods and hence for foreign currency. The supply curve slopes up since a

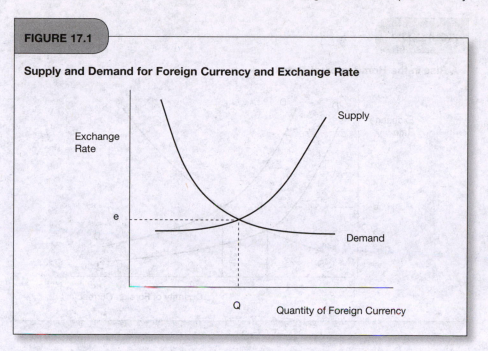

FIGURE 17.1

Supply and Demand for Foreign Currency and Exchange Rate

higher value of '*e*' will mean more demand for home exports which in turn implies that more foreign currency is supplied to buy home currency.

It will be more interesting to discuss here what causes changes in the exchange rate rather than the equilibrium level obtained from the intersection of the demand and supply schedules. The arrows indicate the directions in which the respective variables represented in the figure shift the schedules.

17.3.1. A Rise in the Home Interest Rate

If the domestic interest rate increases, it will lead to capital inflows, because foreign institutional investors are always seeking opportunities to benefit from interest differentials across borders. This will cause the demand for home currency-denominated assets to increase, shifting the demand schedule for foreign currency to the left from DD to D'D' and consequently '*e*' falls, which means that the home currency appreciates (see Figure 17.2).

17.3.2. A Rise in the Foreign Interest Rate

A rise in the foreign interest rate increases the demand for foreign currency-denominated assets, shifting the demand curve for foreign currency to the right, thereby leading to capital outflows and depreciating the home currency ('*e*' rises; see Figure 17.3).

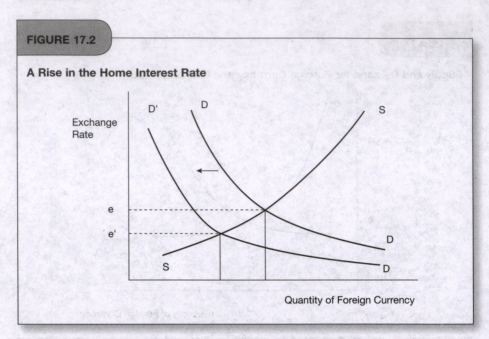

FIGURE 17.2

A Rise in the Home Interest Rate

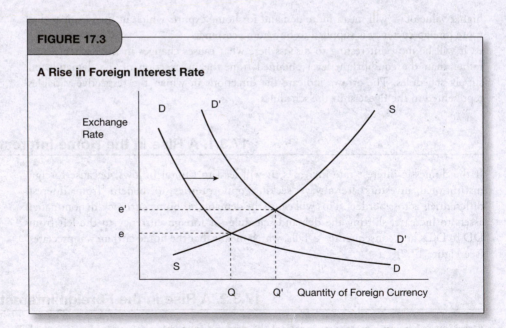

FIGURE 17.3

A Rise in Foreign Interest Rate

FIGURE 17.4

A Rise in Home Inflation

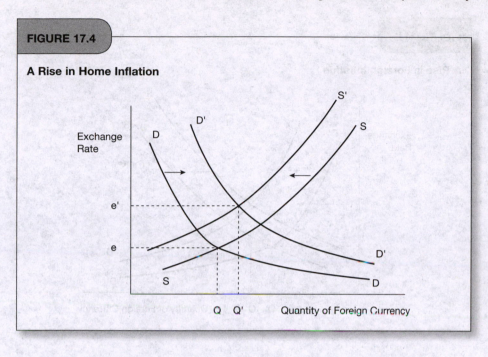

17.3.3. A Rise in Home Inflation

A rise in the home price level means the country becomes less competitive and the demand for home goods and home currency reduces. So the demand for foreign goods and foreign currency rises, shifting the demand curve right. Also, since less foreign money is supplied to buy home goods, the supply curve shifts left. Clearly then, the home currency depreciates ('*e*' rises) (see Figure 17.4).

17.3.4. A Rise in Foreign Inflation

The demand for home goods and home currency increases leading to a shift in the demand curve in Figure 17.5 to the left. Also, since more foreign currency is supplied to buy the home currency, the supply curve shifts right. Clearly, the home currency appreciates ('*e*' falls).

17.3.5. Expectations: An Expected Depreciation of the Home Currency

An expected (future) depreciation of the home currency causes capital flights now, reducing demand for the home currency-denominated assets. So, the demand curve for foreign currency shifts right, the home currency depreciates today and '*e*' rises (see Figure 17.6).

FIGURE 17.5

A Rise in Foreign Inflation

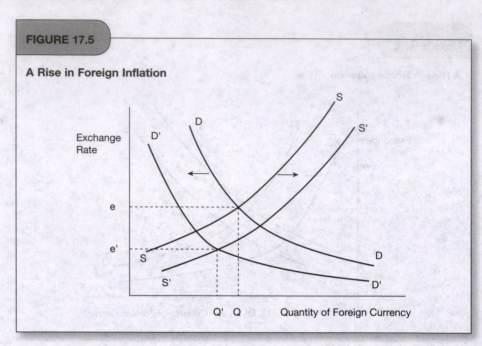

FIGURE 17.6

An Expected Depreciation of the Home Currency

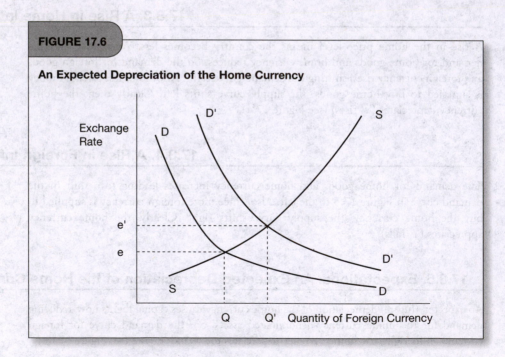

17.4. THE TIME FRAME

While Figure 17.1 captures in summary form the various forces influencing the exchange rate, the timeframe is missing. Some of the forces depicted in this figure may be more potent now, in the short-run, while others may be more potent in the longer run. It is therefore imperative to consider the short-run and long-run determination of the exchange rate separately.

17.4.1. The Long-run: The Purchasing Power Parity Theory

The PPP theory rests on the principle of one price for the same good, with no restrictions on trade in the good. But this is considered to hold only in the long-run, since goods prices take time to adjust, compared to the returns on financial assets. Thus, if a good is lower priced in a market, the shift in demand towards that market should push up prices there and lower the price in the higher-priced market from which the demand has shifted. But this is a time-consuming process.

The law of one price states that

$$eP_f = P \tag{17.1}$$

Here the price levels represented are the aggregate economy-wide price levels. So it is easy to see that with **non-traded goods** in the picture, the law of one price, which is the same as the *purchasing power parity (PPP) theory*, will not hold.

From Equation (17.1), if the foreign price rises or the home price falls, the exchange rate depreciates to satisfy the law of one price across markets. The mechanism underlying this development is easily outlined, namely, with higher inflation in the home country and in the absence of obstructions to free trade between countries and transport costs, the shift in demand towards the less expensive good in the foreign country will drive up demand for the foreign currency, depreciating the home exchange rate

The PPP is a long-run theory because good prices adjust slowly compared to asset prices and there may be other forces at work that may drive the exchange rate independently. The usual caveat 'other things equal' applies very much with regard to exchange rate adjustments also. Other factors such as changes in tastes, incomes and so on, will slow down the materialization of the PPP relationship. The presence of non-traded goods, the prices of which enter the aggregate price index, also prevents the strict adherence to PPP.

> The purchasing power parity (PPP) theory states that a good has the same price in all markets, when there are no impediments to trade.

Relative PPP: While the absolute version of PPP, (Equation 17.1), does not usually hold, a weaker version, the relative PPP, may hold at any point in time. The relative version of PPP states that

$$\hat{e} = \hat{P} - \hat{P_f} \tag{17.2}$$

In Equation 17.2, hats denote rates of change. The equation states that the rate of depreciation in the exchange rate equals the excess in the inflation rate of the home country over inflation in the foreign country. This is often true, even if the exchange rate changes do not fully reflect inflation differentials; for instance, in India the rupee exchange rate steadily and slowly depreciated against the dollar through much of the 1970s and early 1980s. This was largely due to the Reserve Bank of India's policy to retain export competitiveness in the face of higher inflation in India relative to international levels. When the relative PPP holds, there is also a gradual correction towards absolute PPP in the long-run.

The PPP theory states that a good has the same price in all markets when there are no impediments to trade. This means that the nominal exchange rate will be the home price divided by the foreign price.

This 'absolute PPP' is a long-run condition. Relative PPP, with the exchange rate adjusting according to inflation differentials between countries is what is observed in practice.

17.4.2. The Monetary Model of Exchange Rate Determination: A Long-Run Theory

The monetary model of exchange rate determination, one of the earliest approaches to this issue, has the PPP theory as an underlying factor. It also assumes a vertical supply curve, so that output is treated as fixed. The model may be described concisely by the following system of equations:

$$P = eP_f \tag{17.3}$$

$$M_d = kPy \tag{17.4}$$

$$M_d = M_s \tag{17.5}$$

Equation 17.3 is the PPP condition, while (17.4) specifies nominal money demand as dependent on nominal income only ('k' is a constant). Equation 17.5 is the equilibrium condition in the money market. 'e' is the nominal exchange rate as before (in units of the home currency per foreign currency unit) and 'y' is real home income.

Now, substituting from Equations 17.3 and 17.4 into Equation 17.5, we get

$$keP_f y = M_s, \tag{17.6}$$

and

$$e = M_s/kP_f y \tag{17.7}$$

From Equation (17.7), it is seen that an increase in the domestic money supply depreciates the home currency, while a contraction in money supply appreciates the exchange rate.

These results are consistent with the monetary school of macroeconomics, discussed in detail later, in Chapter 20. In the Monetary approach, money supply expansion increases the domestic price level, without having any effect on output or employment in the long-run. Combining this result with the PPP theory, a depreciation of the home currency is a bygone conclusion.

In actual estimation, a two-country framework is usually adopted to forecast bilateral exchange rates. Real incomes are allowed to change and the interest rates are added separately, so that the estimation is done using the log form of the expression

$$e = e\,(m,\, m_f,\, y,\, y_f,\, r,\, r_f) \tag{17.8}$$

with '*m*' and '*m_f*' representing the real money supplies and '*y*' and '*y_f*' real incomes at home and in the foreign country.

It has to be mentioned that the monetary model, despite the role played by the interest rate in determining the exchange rate, does not adequately capture the role of capital mobility and asset markets in explaining exchange rate movements. The interest rate movements in this model only work through the money market equilibrium condition, by affecting changes in the price which are needed to balance this market. The impact on the exchange rate then runs through the PPP condition, which is solely related to the trade in goods, not in financial assets.

17.4.3. Exchange Rate Determination in the Short-run

In the short-run, financial flows, which can be quite immense, decide the fate of the exchange rate. Hence, in the short-run, the exchange rate is determined by developments in the asset markets.

With perfect mobility of capital, rates of interest will be equalized across countries under fixed exchange rates. But under flexible exchange rates and with perfect capital mobility, investors will also consider future scenarios for the exchange rate, requiring an additional return if depreciation in the currency they hold is expected. Thus,

$$r = r^f + e^{\wedge e}, \tag{17.9}$$

where r^f is the foreign interest rate, '*r*' is the home interest rate and $e^{\wedge e}$ is the expected depreciation of the home currency. The returns to holding home currency-denominated assets have to be the returns to holding domestic currency plus the expected depreciation of the home currency. Equation 17.9 is the '*uncovered interest rate parity* condition (UIP)', a well-known result in international finance. It is this condition that drives the movement of the exchange rate in the short-run. It is usually referred to as the uncovered interest rate parity condition because it is assumed that the exchange rate risk is not being covered using future markets.

The interest rate parity condition basically implies that the rates of return on comparable assets should be equalized across the world, with the perfect international mobility of capital. Perfect capital mobility means that there are no barriers to the movement of capital. If interest rates are higher abroad, the movement of capital in search of higher returns will lower the rate of return abroad and raise them at home until the rates are equalized.

Rewriting (17.4) as[1]

$$r = r_f + (e^\varepsilon_{t+1} - e)/e \tag{17.10}$$

where e^ε_{t+1} is the expected exchange rate in the next period. We can draw the following conclusions about the movements in the current (also called 'spot' exchange rate) exchange rate '*e*'.

> The uncovered interest rate parity condition implies that the difference in interest rates between two countries is approximately equal to the difference in their expected exchange rates.

---

[1] The 'covered interest rate parity' condition is represented as $F/S = (1 + r)/(1 + r_f)$, where 'F' and 'S' are forward and spot rates respectively.

17.4.3.1. The Effect of a Rise in the Foreign Interest Rate

From Equation 17.10, we can write the solution for 'e' as

$$e = e^e_{t+1}/(1 + r - r_f) \tag{17.11}$$

From Equation 17.11, a rise in the foreign interest rate raises 'e', that is, the spot (current) exchange rate depreciates. A rise in the foreign interest rate makes foreign currency-denominated assets attractive, increasing demand for the foreign currency and depreciating the home currency exchange rate.

1. *A Rise in the Home Interest Rate:* From Equation (17.11), a rise in 'r' lowers 'e', that is, the spot exchange rate appreciates. Higher home interest rates increase the demand for home currency and appreciate the current exchange rate.

2. *An Expected Future Depreciation:* Again, from Equation (17.11), let us look at the situation when there is a rise in e^e_{t+1}, then 'e' also rises. So, an expected future depreciation channels demand away from the home currency-denominated assets, thereby depreciating the spot exchange rate.

3. *A Rise in the Home Money Supply:* If there is an increase in the money supply in the domestic economy, it lowers 'r', the home interest rate. Consequently, it depreciates the home spot exchange rate, as seen previously. In addition, the larger money supply leads to a higher expected price level and hence a higher expected 'e' in the future (higher e^e_{t+1}), which also causes the spot exchange rate to depreciate, as also seen here.

Thus, as seen from the aforementioned exercises, the interest parity condition can be used to trace short-run movements in the exchange rate. However, for exchange rate forecasting, the movements in the interest rates themselves have to be modelled and for this purpose, a larger, more general equilibrium kind of framework is required. Such a framework is provided by the most influential asset market-based theories of exchange rate determination, that is, by the monetary model (which has only domestic assets) itself, and the portfolio balance approach, which will be discussed later in this chapter. These popular theories also provide a bridge from the short-run to the long-run, but these have not been really successful in empirical works.

17.5. EXCHANGE RATE DYNAMICS: THE SHORT-RUN TO THE LONG-RUN IN DORNBUSCH'S 'OVERSHOOTING MODEL'

The distinction between the short and the long-run, as can be seen from the discussions in the previous two sections, is based on the fact that financial variables adjust much faster than real variables and good prices. Indeed, a simple version of Dornbusch's famous exchange rate overshooting model, dating back to 1976, can be presented using just the uncovered interest rate parity (UIP) condition, an assumption of sticky good prices in the short-run, the LM curve and the long-run PPP condition.

We start by writing down the LM curve equation:

$$M/P = L(r, y) \qquad (17.12)$$

Equation 17.12 is just the conventional LM equation, with the money demand (on the right side) depending on the interest rate and real income. The UIP condition is

$$r = r_f + e^{\wedge c} \qquad (17.13)$$

The PPP condition is

$$P = e.P_f \qquad (17.14)$$

Now, consider an expansion in the money supply, which raises the LHS of Equation 17.12. Money demand should rise to balance the market and this is achieved by a fall in the interest rate 'r'. But while the interest rate falls instantaneously, the price level is fixed in the short-run. The foreign interest rate 'r_f' is also fixed. Then, clearly, '$e^{\wedge c}$' has to fall as there has to be a decrease in the expected depreciation of the home currency, which is tantamount to an expected appreciation of the home currency.

But over time, the price level rises as a result of the monetary expansion. This result can be solved out in a more complete system of equations, but this is omitted here for the sake of brevity. From the PPP condition, this will lead to a depreciation.

Thus, while a monetary expansion creates an expected appreciation immediately, it also leads to a long-run depreciation, which clearly indicates an overshooting initially of the long-run equilibrium exchange rate. From the LM curve equation, we can also see that as the price rises over time, with an assumption of fixed incomes and a vertical supply curve (Monetarist assumptions!), the interest rate will rise over time after an initial sharp fall.

The Dornbusch's *overshooting* model complements the long-run monetary model with the interest rate parity condition and a sticky goods price assumption to obtain an adjustment path from the short to the long-run. The model generates an expected appreciation in the short-run, which, combined with long-run depreciation, gives it the exchange rate overshooting characteristic.

These adjustment patterns are presented in Figure 17.7, the most interesting part of the figure being the overshooting pattern described by the exchange rate.

The overshooting phenomenon is represented also in the price-exchange rate diagram in the upper right-side block of Figure 17.7. To do this, we write the equations of the model in log terms. For convenience, the log form is represented by the small letter, except for the exchange rate, interest rate and real income, for which a subscript of 'g' is used to represent the log form.

$$m - p = \eta y_g - \sigma r_g \qquad (17.15)$$

$$e^*_g = p - p_f \qquad (17.16)$$

$$r = r_f + e^{\wedge c} \qquad (17.17)$$

$$e^{\wedge c} = \Phi (e^*_g - e_g) \qquad (17.18)$$

Here, η, σ and Φ are parameters. Equation (17.18) specifies an adjustment pattern for the exchange rate, based on the difference between the long-run equilibrium exchange rate and the short-run rate.

'Overshooting' here refers to the phenomenon when a country's exchange rate depreciates beyond the eventual equilibrium rate and then returns to that level.

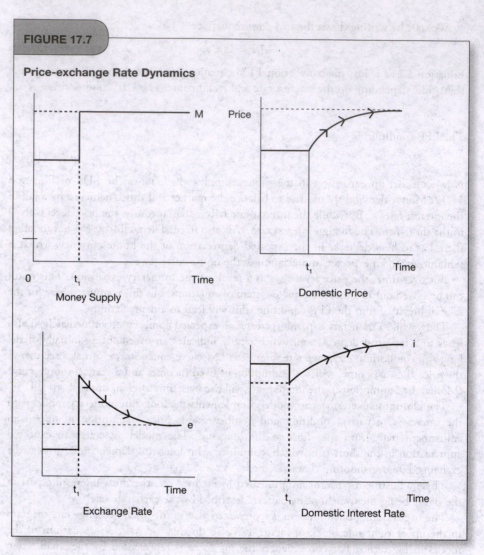

FIGURE 17.7

Price-exchange Rate Dynamics

Substituting from the other Equations into (17.15), we get

$$\sigma \Phi e_g = \sigma \Phi e^*_g - p + m - \eta y_g + \sigma r_f \tag{17.19}$$

From Equation (17.19), it is clear that 'e' and 'P' have to be negatively related to maintain equilibrium in the money market. This relationship is represented by the negatively sloping curve 'MM' in Figure 17.8.

The goods market equilibrium is (ignoring government spending)

$$C(y, M/P) + I(r) + NX (eP_f/P) = y \tag{17.20}$$

Output is assumed to be constant, so that $y = y^*$, the long-run output with full employment of the factors of production, in the Monetarist tradition (see Chapter 20). From Equation (17.18), we can derive a positive relation between 'e' and 'P', which is required to keep the goods market in equilibrium. (We do not derive this here, but leave it as an exercise for the reader).

The negative relationship between the price level and the exchange rate to keep the goods market in equilibrium is obvious. Depreciation increases the demand for home goods while output is constant and thus a rise in the price level is needed to reduce output to the equilibrium level. This relationship is represented as the curve 'GG' in Figure 17.8. Also, since there is more than one avenue through which a rise in prices reduces demand (through a rise in interest rates leading to a fall in investment demand that is needed to keep the money market in equilibrium, through a fall in real balances which reduces consumption), the rise in the price level required will be less than that required to keep net exports unchanged. Thus, GG will have a smaller slope than the line marked 'PPP' which represents the long-run purchasing parity relationship between the price level and the exchange rate. Figure 17.8 can be used to illustrate the dynamics of exchange rate adjustments from the short to the long-run.

BOX 17.1	**Will the Currency War Looming Large Impact Corporate Profitability?[2]**

The decline in the rupee dollar exchange rate nearing 66 is likely to influence the profitability of the corporate sector in India. The Peoples Bank of China changed the way it calculated the reference rate of the yuan in January 2016, which led to a fall of more than 4% in the Chinese currency against the US$.[3] In retaliation, other countries devalued their currency to retain their global competitive position. The devaluation of the yuan reflects the market concerns of the slowing down of the Chinese economy and flagging exports reports the ICRA. Unless the Chinese economy shows signs of recovery and improvements in its macroeconomic fundamentals, there may be further devaluation of the yuan prompting a currency war. The RBI Governor, Raghuram Rajan, said that the Chinese move of depreciation of their currency raises questions about the strength of their economy. If they continue to devalue their currency, there will be a tit for tat action by other countries.

In India, the sectors to be directly impacted by the devaluation of yuan include steel, tyre and automobile components as these have a large overhang of Chinese capacity in the global market. Apart from these, the power and telecom sectors would also be impacted indirectly by the devaluation of the INR against the US$. This is because of a combination of input costs and foreign currency borrowings.

[2] Source of text in Box 17.1 is Oommen A. Ninan, 'Exchange Rate to Determine Corporate Profitability', *The Hindu* (Monday, 23 August 2015). Available at: http://www.thehindu.com/business/Economy/the-impact-of-corporate-earnings-exchange-rate-to-determine-corporate-profitability/article7572165.ece

[3] *Source:* Chinese Yuan: Here's what's happening to the currency Everett Rosenfeld CNBC updated 7 January 2016. https://www.cnbc.com/2016/01/07/chinese-yuan-heres-whats-happening-to-the-currency.html

In an RBI working paper, it was reported that the rupee exchange rate against the US$ would be the most important risk component for Indian corporate profitability. It says that during the period 2002–07, corporate profitability was mostly influenced by firm specific indicators such as firm size, leverage, liquidity, and so on[4]. However, since 2009, the domestic economy has become more integrated with the global economy and has, therefore, become more sensitive to external shocks. The manufacturing and infrastructure sectors have been saddled with high interest rates and are also facing a demand slowdown with resulting excess capacity. So this would be a time for a real test of managing the rupee.

The importance of macroeconomic factors such as the exchange rate, the interest rate and the WPI inflation rate to determine corporate profitability is therefore amplified. In fact, the importance of exchange rate has increased manifold. There is a negative association between corporate profitability and the exchange rate, implying that a depreciation of the Indian rupee is likely to give a boost to profitability as these firms are carrying out more imports than exports. But in the long-run, the impact would depend on the import and export elasticities.

In Figure 17.8, the initial exchange rate is e_0, which is consistent with equilibrium in the money and goods markets. M_0M_0 is the money market equilibrium schedule and G_0G_0 is the initial goods market equilibrium schedule.

An increase in the money supply pushes out the MM schedule (since, at a given 'e', the price level should be higher to balance the money market or, at a given 'P', 'e' should be higher to balance the money market). Financial markets adjust faster, while the goods market prices could be sticky and slow to adjust. So, the short-run equilibrium is on the new M_1M_1 schedule at the unchanged price P_1. The short-run exchange rate is then 'e_2'.

As already pointed out, at 'e_2', an expected appreciation of the exchange rate is the market sentiment, as seen from the uncovered interest rate parity condition. This expectation is indeed fulfilled over a period of time. As the price begins to adjust, with the GG schedule moving up (since, with an increase in the money supply, the goods market equilibrium requires a higher price at each exchange rate), the exchange rate

[4] Shaoni Nandi, Debasish Majumder and Anujit Mitra, 'Is Exchange Rate the Dominant Factor Influencing Corporate Profitability in India?' (working paper no. 4, Reserve Bank of India, 2015).

FIGURE 17.8

Dornbusch's Overshooting Model

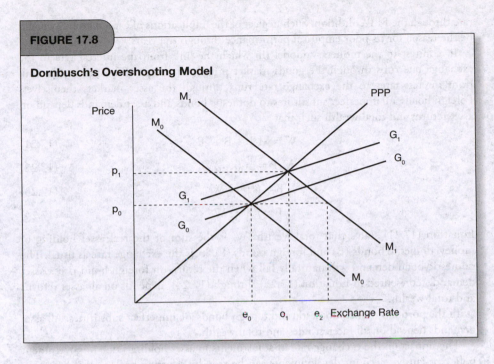

begins to appreciate towards its long-run value on the PPP line. This appreciation from e_2 to e_1 is consistent with the rise in the interest rate due to a rise in the price, needed to balance the money market.

The long-run equilibrium, simultaneously in the money and goods markets, at the new intersection of G_1G_1 and M_1M_1, gives an exchange rate value of e_1. This long-run value of the exchange rate represents a depreciation from the initial level e_0 before the money supply expansion, but is an appreciation from the short-run value of e_2. Thus, the exchange rate shows an overshooting pattern on the way to long-run PPP equilibrium.

17.6. THE PORTFOLIO BALANCE MODEL: SHORT-RUN EXCHANGE RATE DETERMINATION AND OVERSHOOTING

The portfolio balance model does not have the assumption of perfect substitutability between domestic and foreign assets that is present in the monetary approach. Both have something in common namely, that the exchange rate adjusts to changes in asset supplies and demands and not to equilibrate international trade in goods, as is the case in the PPP model.

However, as already mentioned, the monetary model does not really invoke the impact of *capital mobility* and interest rate differentials in explaining exchange rate movements. Rather, when there is a change in the domestic interest rate, it also has an impact on the price through the money market equilibrium condition, which then affects the exchange

Capital mobility is the ability of private funds to move across national boundaries in pursuit of higher returns, through cross border investments. This mobility depends on the degree of financial openness, manifested in restrictions on the currency and the inflows and outflows of capital.

rate through the PPP condition. Such neglect of the implications of capital mobility could be the reason for its poor empirical performance through the years.

In contrast to the monetary model (in which the link from the interest rate to the exchange rate runs through the goods market prices), in the portfolio model, the link from interest rates to the exchange rate runs through the asset markets themselves. Foreign bonds are imperfect substitutes to domestic bonds and asset demands depend on asset returns and total wealth such that

$$W = M/P + B + eF \tag{17.21}$$

$$M/P = m \ (r, r_f)W \tag{17.22}$$

$$B = b(r, r_f) \ W \tag{17.23}$$

$$F = f(r, r_f) \ W \tag{17.24}$$

Equation (17.21) states that total wealth 'W' is the sum of the real asset holding of money, domestic bonds (B) and foreign bonds (F). 'e' is the exchange rate as usual. The domestic bond demand will naturally fall when the return on foreign bond rises. Asset demand, represented in Equation (17.22) through (17.24), depends on all asset returns and total wealth.

In the portfolio model, domestic and foreign bonds are imperfect substitutes. All asset demands depend on all interest rates and total wealth.

The impact on the exchange rate of adjustments in asset holdings due to government policy or current account developments can be seen by referring back to the discussion around Figures 15.1 to 15.4 in Chapter 15. Consider an expansion of the money supply by the central bank. The domestic interest rate falls, causing the demand for foreign bonds to increase (and that for domestic bonds to fall). There is an increase in demand for foreign currency to pay for foreign bonds, driving up the price of foreign currency; that is to say, the exchange rate 'e' depreciates.

If there is a current account surplus, the country is accumulating foreign bonds, which increase in supply. This should, by similar reasoning, lead to an appreciation of the home currency. This can explain the experience of some newly industrialized countries, which expanded exports by currency depreciation and then over time, saw a currency appreciation as their current account showed a steady surplus.

The current account movement is the factor that provides *overshooting* in the portfolio model. The current account surplus creates an exchange rate appreciation, but in the long-run, the requirement of a reasonable balance in the current account requires a further adjustment in the exchange rate. Expectations play no role in this exchange rate dynamics, in contrast to the dynamic process in the model.

As already indicated, the portfolio model is an improvement over the monetary model in the theoretical sense, since the interest rate impact on the exchange rate leads through asset portfolio adjustments, rather than through the goods market (price). Yet, the empirical performance of the portfolio model in tracking exchange rates has been disappointing. In actual empirical estimation, the model encompasses the rest of the world (ROW) and asset holdings of the foreign country are also modelled, as in the estimation of the two-country monetary model mentioned in Section 17.4.2.

In the portfolio model, the assumption of capital mobility plays a key role in exchange rate determination, with asset substitution due to interest rate changes influencing the exchange rate. In contrast, in the monetary model, the interest rate effects on the exchange rate work through the money market equilibrium condition and the goods market prices.

The reason for the poor empirical performance of the portfolio model is obvious. In the real world, asset demands change instantaneously due to exchange rate expectations. Expectations are not modelled nor included in the simple version of the portfolio model, in which relative asset demands and supplies change only due to government policies or current account feedbacks on total wealth and asset holdings. In leaving out expectations, a sizeable chunk of the real world is also omitted!

17.7. FIXED EXCHANGE RATES AND MANAGED FLOATS

Under a fixed exchange rate system, the central banks of countries intervene in the foreign exchange market to keep the exchange rates at the announced levels. Thus, when the rupee is fixed at 60 to the dollar, the Reserve Bank intervenes continuously in the foreign exchange market to maintain that rate. The managed float is similar, except that in this case, the exchange rate is allowed to vary within a band, which could be sometimes as wide as plus or minus 15% from the central value of the band.

The following sub-sections discuss how this intervention works in practice.

17.7.1. Strengthening of the Rupee

Consider now an increase in short-run capital inflows. The increased demand for the rupee tends to appreciate the rupee exchange rate. The Reserve Bank intervenes by buying dollars with the home currency, the rupee, which depreciates the rupee back towards the fixed exchange rate of 40 to the dollar.

Such an operation affects the home money supply too and this, in fact, underlies the movement of the exchange rate. The purchase of dollars with rupees increases the domestic money supply, since the RBI releases new money into the financial system.

Thus, if the central bank buys 100 million rupees worth of dollar assets, 100 million rupees are added to the monetary base, with this amount being credited to the bank

RBI Foreign Exchange Market Intervention	
RBI Assets	*RBI Liabilities*
International Reserves + 100 million	Currency in Circulation + 100 million

deposits held at the central bank. The money supply will increase by the money multiplier times 100 million. This increased money supply pushes down the home interest rate. From the interest rate parity condition given in Equation 17.9, which, as we have seen, drives short-run exchange rate determination, the (current) rupee exchange rate will depreciate. Also, the higher money supply signals higher prices (expected prices) in the future and hence a lower rupee rate *under a managed float (i.e., higher e^e_{t+1}, but not under fixed rates, because then the change in the expected rate is zero)*. This also tends to depreciate the current exchange rate. The central bank's intervention continues until the fixed exchange rate is reached and maintained.

17.7.2. The Rupee Tends to Depreciate

In this situation, the Reserve Bank releases dollars into the system, buying up rupees. If 100 million rupees worth of dollars is sold by the central bank, the monetary base and the money in circulation also reduces by that much and the deposits of commercial bank in the central bank are reduced to pay for the foreign currency purchases.

The reduction in the money supply increases the rupee interest rate, which as we see from Equation 17.9, tends to appreciate the rupee. In addition, the money supply reduction lowers the future expected price (*under a managed float, not under completely fixed rates, because then the expected change in the exchange rate is zero*) and also appreciates the expected exchange rate (**lowers** e^e_{t+1}, *under a managed float, not under completely fixed rates, because then the expected change in the exchange rate is zero*), which also tends to appreciate the current, spot exchange rate.

A look at the 1992 exchange rate crisis in Europe helps in illustrating some of the concepts discussed earlier. German inflation accelerated after the German unification, with higher government spending to help East Germany in the integration. The Bundesbank raised interest rates, putting the exchange rates of other EMS members under pressure. Countries like the UK could not raise their interest rates with the threat of a recession at home and other countries like Italy and Sweden were also in trouble with Sweden raising interest rates to 500% to prevent massive capital outflows. Speculative attacks also began with an expectation of devaluation. Eventually the system broke down, with members going in for a free float of the currency.

17.8. THE PROS AND CONS OF FIXED AND FLOATING EXCHANGE RATES

Under fixed exchange rates, the central bank cannot conduct independent monetary policy. In effect, the country loses one instrument of macroeconomic policy. To see this, consider an increase in money supply by the central bank. Let us say that the central bank purchases securities in the open market, which increases the domestic money supply. This reduces the domestic interest rate, leading to capital outflows under perfect capital mobility (with no restrictions on international capital flows), since foreign currency-denominated assets now become more attractive. Essentially, to buy foreign currency assets, payments are made by debiting commercial bank deposits with the central bank, which in turn reduces the monetary base and the money supply. Thus, the original increase in money supply brought about by the central bank is finally completely neutralized.

Imported inflation: Under fixed exchange rates, higher inflation abroad is transmitted fully to the home country when demand shifts to home products. Also, lower interest rates abroad cause capital flows to the home country, increasing home money supply and inflation. Foreign buyers (say, in the US) pay with dollar cheques and when these cheques get cleared in the central bank of the home country (India), the deposit accounts of commercial banks at the central bank are credited with that amount in rupees thereby increasing the money supply at home.

Other international repercussions: The home country is vulnerable to other disturbances emanating from partner countries in the fixed exchange rate system and not just inflation. To see this, we may again consider the problems raised by the German unification for the other members of the EMS.

In Figure 17.9, the interest rate in Germany moved up from r_{old} to r_{new} as the Bundesbank tightened money supply to control inflation brought about by government expenditure on the less developed eastern region of the newly united country. The members of the EMS had two choices, one of which is diagrammatically shown in the Figure 17.9.

If they chose to stay within the EMS, capital flows to Germany would raise home interest rates to the German level. As the home country's central bank would defend the exchange rate by buying up the home currency, the money supply would reduce shown

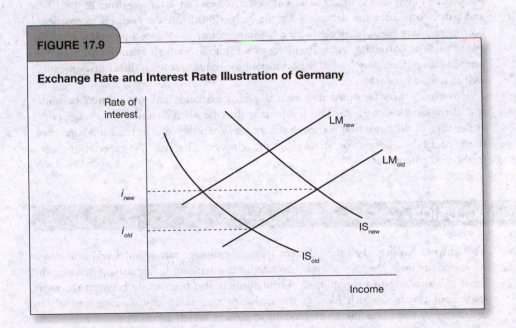

FIGURE 17.9

Exchange Rate and Interest Rate Illustration of Germany

by the upward shift of the LM curve, to the LM$_{new}$ position. This would cause a fall in home country output.

Thus, opting for the fixed exchange rate system would open up the country to the impact of foreign disturbances, which are transmitted freely home. If the members had instead opted out of the system, they could be free of the repercussions of German policies, as clear from the discussion to follow on the response under flexible exchange rates.

Under flexible exchange rates, the domestic money supply is not determined abroad, as seen here in the case of fixed exchange rates. When capital flows abroad (to Germany in this example), the exchange rate takes the burden of adjustment and depreciates, which pushes the IS curve to the right. The interest rate goes up in this case also, but output rises as against the fixed exchange rate case where output falls as a result of the international transmission of disturbances.

Similarly, with higher inflation abroad, as demand shifts to home goods, inflation does not rise at home. Instead, as demand for the home currency rises for payment for home goods (and home currency-denominated assets), the exchange rate appreciates, thus insulating the home country from the inflationary disturbance abroad.

17.8.1. Disadvantages of Flexible Exchange Rates

The insulating property of flexible exchange rates described above are not available fully for managed exchange rates, since these rates are allowed to move only within a band. As for fully flexible exchange rates, they introduce a strong element of uncertainty into international economic transactions which may be only partly offset with forward markets and derivatives. Since the advent of flexible exchange rates regimes in the 1970s and particularly after the debt rises for the early 1980s, interest rates on international borrowings have risen, particularly for developing countries—since a premium is usually added to their borrowing rates. Exchange rate instability, which characterizes a flexible interest rate regime, may lead to export instability, reduced foreign direct investments as well as reduced growth.

However, it may be noted that even the fixed exchange rate regime may be under speculative attack sometimes. This is especially the case when a country's exchange rate is at the edge of the band that it tries to adhere to. When the edge of the band is reached, there could be speculative attacks on the currency, because of expectations of a forthcoming depreciation.

17.9. CONCLUSION

This chapter has described the different types of exchange rate regimes and provided a survey of the main theories of exchange rate determination, distinguishing between the short and the long-run scenarios. A distinction has also been made between the more traditional theories, which look at the exchange rate as an equilibrating variable in international trade and the more modern approach, which focuses on the role of the exchange rate in equilibrating financial asset markets.

The short-run movement of the exchange rate satisfies the interest rate parity condition, which can be used to explain exchange rate movements. But for exchange rate forecasting, the interest rates have to be endogenous to the model, as is the case in the popular asset models such as the monetary model and the portfolio model.

The monetary model, which properly falls into the category of an asset model, may be, nevertheless, called a hybrid model, since the long-run condition in the model is generated by the PPP condition, by the law of one price in international trade in goods. The portfolio model offers a richer menu in asset models, with investors holding both domestic and foreign models. Both the Monetary (the Dornbusch variant) and the portfolio models provide a path, with the exchange rate overshooting the equilibrium rate, from the short to the long-run, provided by the PPP condition in the former model and by current account balancing in the latter.

We have also discussed the advantages and disadvantages of fixed and floating rate regimes. The common currency systems, such as the Euro are of course a larger variant of the single country exchange rate regime. Joining a currency union has been noted to increase total bilateral trade with other members, with estimates ranging from as low as 6%, to as high as 150% in the case of the Euro. Still, non-acceding members in Europe (such as Sweden) have not seen the common currency as providing any unmitigated benefits. Arguments against joining a currency union are often based on perceptions of differences in business cycle patterns and in exchange rate variability with respect to the currency of a major trading partner such as the United States, which could be exploited in downturns and for maintaining competitive advantages in trade.

SUMMARY

- In an open economy, the exchange rate of the domestic currency is the crucial link between the domestic economy and the rest of the world, facilitating exchanges of goods and financial assets without going abroad. Under the Bretton Woods System, set up in 1944, the US dollar's value was fixed in terms of gold, all other currencies being linked to the dollar at fixed rates. The Bretton Woods Agreement collapsed in 1973 because countries with balance of payments surpluses were not willing to take more expansionary policies and let their currency appreciate. Subsequently, this fixed rate system in developed countries was replaced with a flexible rate or a managed exchange rate arrangement.
- Capital inflows depend positively on the difference between the home interest rate and the foreign interest rate.
- Trading of currencies and bank deposits denominated in various currencies take place in the foreign exchange market.
- The forces that determine the exchange rate in the short-run are different from the predominant long-run forces.
- All forces that increase the demand for foreign currency and decrease the demand for the home currency tend to depreciate the exchange rate and vice versa.
- An increase in the home interest rate increases the demand for the home currency and decreases demand for the foreign currency, appreciating the exchange rate.

- The PPP theory rests on the principle of one price for the same good, with no restrictions on trade in the good. But this is considered to hold only in the long-run, since goods prices take time to adjust, compared to returns on financial assets.
- Dornbusch's overshooting model complements the long-run monetary model with the interest rate parity condition and a sticky goods price assumption to obtain an adjustment path from the short to the long-run.
- The Dornbusch model generates an expected appreciation in the short-run, which, combined with long-run depreciation, gives it the exchange rate overshooting characteristic.
- In the portfolio model, domestic and foreign bonds are imperfect substitutes. All asset demands depend on all interest rates and total wealth. The central bank's expansionary policy reduces the domestic interest rate, causing the demand for foreign bonds to rise (and the demand for domestic bonds to fall). The increase in demand for foreign currency to pay for foreign bonds drives up the price of foreign currency, leading to a depreciation of the domestic currency.

CASE STUDY

The Global Financial Crisis and Currency Wars[5]

The global financial crisis might have abated, but certain factors that were responsible for it remain just as potent and need to be tackled. In a recent policy brief, the UNCTAD has said that global imbalances—manifested in a few Asian countries with current account surpluses bridging the large deficits of the United States and other rich countries—continue to be a major cause for worry.[6]

One facet of the problem is reflected in the controversy surrounding the exchange rate policy of China, the country with the largest surplus. Its critics say that, by deliberately keeping the renminbi undervalued in relation to the dollar, China has boosted its exports, augmenting its reserves to record levels. According to this view, the Chinese currency must be allowed to float so that the play of market forces will cause its exports to shrink and stimulate domestic consumption, the two critical steps needed for restoring the balance with debtor countries. The UNCTAD finds both the diagnosis and the prescription too simplistic. It is unreasonable to put the onus of rebalancing the global economy on a single country and its currency. The real problem has to do with systemic failures, which require comprehensive and inclusive multilateral action.

Recent experiences suggest that neither a fully fixed exchange rate system nor a freely floating one can be the optimal solution to the volatility and uncertainty caused by the global

---

[5] The content of the Case Study have been taken from the following sources: http://unctad.org/meetings/en/Presentation/Internationalization%20of%20RMB.Mr.%20X.%20Sun.pdf; http://unctad.org/en/PublicationsLibrary/webditcted2016d5_en.pdf

[6] World Investment Report 2013, UNCTAD, Available at: http://unctad.org/en/pages/PublicationWebflyer.aspx?publicationid=588

imbalance. Multilateralism of the type seen during the height of the crisis in 2008 should guide a new, coherent approach to restoring the balance between trade and non-speculative financial flows. Like the World Trade Organization, which has contributed remarkably to an orderly trade, a new global regulatory body for the monetary system can help substantially in minimizing exchange rate misalignments and preventing external shocks, the two major factors associated with global imbalance. The UNCTAD has proposed a 'constant real exchange rate' rule that will guide the exchange rate policies of countries; the prescription proposed is to ensure that the nominal exchange rates follow the interest rate differentials between two currencies.[7] However, neither the monitoring of the constant exchange rate nor, indeed, the creation of a WTO-type body for the monetary system is going to be easy. However, the UNCTAD's suggestions are worth pursuing over the medium term.

After reading the text given in the case study answer the following questions:

1. According to UNCTAD what is the key source of concern that is leading to the global imbalance?
2. Do you think that China can be persuaded to follow a truly flexible exchange rate? Is that the only problem plaguing the international trade and global capital flows today?
3. What is the key proposal forwarded by the UNCTAD that will address the present concern of all the countries connected by international trade and exchange rates?

KEYWORDS

Managed float
Uncovered Interest Parity
Purchasing Power Parity

Capital mobility
Over shooting

CONCEPT CHECK

State whether the following statements are true or false:

1. Under the Bretton Woods system of fixed rates, the currency values for countries were fixed in terms of a basket of currencies.
2. The monetary model of exchange rate determination combines the money market equilibrium condition with the PPP condition. It is a long-run theory. An increase in the money supply depreciates the exchange rate in the long-run.
3. Dornbusch's overshooting model complements the long-run monetary model with the interest rate parity condition and a sticky goods price assumption to obtain an adjustment path from the short to the long-run.

---

[7] World Investment Report 2013, UNCTAD, Available at: http://unctad.org/en/pages/PublicationWebflyer.aspx?publicationid=588

4. In the portfolio balance model, domestic and foreign bonds are perfect substitutes as in the monetary approach.
5. If there is a current account surplus, the country accumulates foreign bonds, which leads to an appreciation of the home currency.
6. Under fixed exchange rates, a higher inflation abroad is transmitted fully to the home country when demand shifts to home products.

DISCUSSION QUESTIONS

1. Identify the factors that influence the exchange rate of a country in the short-run.
2. Are interest rates key determinants of the exchange rate in the long-run? Is it the Law of One Interest Rate that decides the long-run exchange rate?
3. Are central banks a necessary element for tackling balance of payment imbalances? If so, explain why.
4. Write down a regression equation specification for export demand using the key determinants.
5. Write down the interest rate parity condition using expected appreciation rather than expected depreciation of the home currency.
6. Explain how foreign disturbances are transmitted to the home country under fixed exchange rates. Does this also occur under flexible exchange rates? If not, why is the home country insulated under flexible rates?
7. Suppose the home country's interest rate is 10% and the foreign interest rate is 5%. The expected exchange rate is 50 rupees to the dollar. What is the current rupee rate? What happens to the current exchange rate if the expected rate falls to 48?
8. Explain why a monetary expansion in the home country depreciates the current exchange rate.
9. If India is in recession and you believe that a depreciated exchange rate will stimulate aggregate demand and help the economy out of recession,
   (a) How can the depreciation be triggered?
   (b) What will be the impact on foreign trade?
10. Explain the characteristics of the monetary model that provides an overshooting path from the short to the long-run equilibrium.
11. Which model has some resemblance to the traditional exchange rate models emphasizing the role of the exchange rate in balancing trade? The monetary model or the portfolio model?
12. Are fixed exchange rate regimes totally free of one of the drawbacks of the flexible rate regimes, the uncertainty regarding future paths?
13. Are the roles of capital mobility and interest rate movements identical in the Monetary and the portfolio balance models for exchange rate determination? Explain briefly.

18
CHAPTER

Business Cycle Theory

LEARNING OBJECTIVES

Upon completion of this chapter, the reader will be able to:

- Understand the movement of factors underlying economic fluctuations in the context of macroeconomics.
- Identify the stages of business cycles, which are the patterns of expansion and contraction of an economy.
- Comprehend the Multiplier and Accelerator principles that are widely believed to cause economic fluctuations.
- Explain the different ways business cycles occur and the theoretical logic behind them with the interpretation of Keynesian, Monetary, New Classical and Real Business Cycle (RBC) theories.
- Identify the factors that are included in computing the lead, coincidental and lag indicators (LgIs) of peaks and troughs of business cycles' in the dating of business cycles.

18.1. INTRODUCTION

18.1.1. What is a Business Cycle?

Cyclical movements in the economy have been debated ever since the Biblical times, when they appeared in the Pharaohs' dreams. Today, with globalization, integration and liberalization throughout the world, business cycles have gained immense significance in political and economic discourse. Perhaps the largest thrust to this debate occurred with the Great Depression in the early 20th century. Their initiation into the field of macroeconomics is attributed to John Maynard Keynes, a towering legend in his own lifetime. His path-breaking contributions, the specification of the consumption function and the creation of an analytical apparatus to model economic realities constituting a decisive break from the Classical school of economic thought, has had far-reaching consequences for government policy-making. Most of these have already been discussed in great detail in Chapter 3 and in subsequent chapters. The Keynesian theory of a *business cycle* is ascribed to the consumption function, which is a linear function of disposable income. As mentioned already, Keynes strongly advocated an active role for the government in stabilizing the economy through the use of fiscal and monetary policies, opposing the classical thought of laissez faire.

In Chapter 1, the three perspectives of the timeframe was discussed: the very long-run behaviour of the economy, the domain of growth theory (Chapter 4), the medium-term and the short term. The long-term concentrates on the growth of the economy's capacity to produce goods and services, highlighting historical capital accumulation and technological progress.

In the medium term, a snap shot of the economy is taken, keeping the stock of capital and technology relatively constant while permitting temporary shocks to occur. The productive capacity of the economy with fixed capital and technology is called 'potential output'. In the long-run, the supply of goods and services equals potential output. Fluctuations in demand determine price and inflation over this period. It is however, the short-run fluctuations or the business cycles, which are of key interest in this chapter.

The oscillations in demand in the short-run determine how much of the existing capacity is utilized thereby determining the level of output and employment. This concept of time is similar to what is discussed in microeconomics. We concentrate on the short-run phenomenon of business cycles and the theories that explain them.

When the economy tends to grow and then contract alternatively, that phenomenon is called a business cycle. Business cycles are unpredictable long-term patterns of alternating periods of economic growth (recovery) and decline (recession), characterized by changes in employment, industrial productivity and interest rates. They are periodic in nature, but irregular with the up-and-down movements in economic activity mirrored in fluctuations in the real GDP and other macroeconomic variables (see Figure 18.1). A discussion on whether recession can be predicted is given in Box 18.1.

Business cycles are characterized by a sequence of four phases (see Figure 18.1): '*Contraction*' is the slowdown or down turn in the pace of economic activity. Contraction is the lower turning point of a business cycle, where a contraction turns into an expansion. '*Expansion*' or recovery is the phase when economic activity picks up pace. '*Peak*' or the boom is the highest point in that cycle and is the upper turning point. A '*recession*' occurs if a contraction is severe enough. A deep *trough* is called a slump or a depression. Readers today are familiar with the term recession with the whole world having experienced massive job losses, and hence rising unemployment levels and falling GDP growth rates across the globe after the 2008–09 global financial crisis.

In the next section, the Keynesian theory of business cycles is discussed, followed by a treatment of the Acceleration theory. Section 18.3 contains the Monetarist theory of

---

Margin notes:

... cycles are ... ctable long-term ... s of alternating ... ds of economic ... wth (recovery) and ... cline (recession), ... haracterized by changes in employment, industrial productivity and interest rates.

'Contraction' is the slowdown or down turn in the pace of economic activity; it is the lower turning point of a business cycle.

'Expansion' is the phase when economic activity begins to increase and recovery sets in.

'Peak' is the highest point in that cycle and is the upper turning point.

'Recession' is a period of low output and high unemployment in the economy, also known as 'downturn', when businesses curtail investments, confronted with the spectre of falling profits.

FIGURE 18.1

Business Cycle

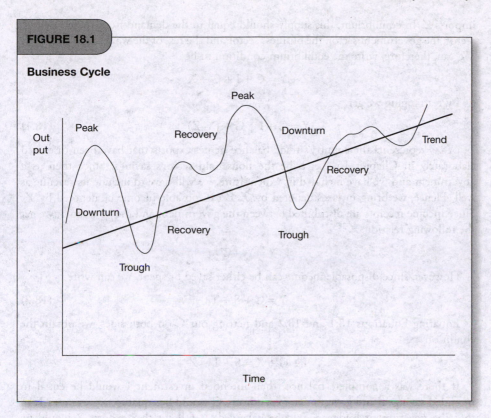

business cycles as proposed by Friedman and the RBC theory is explained in Section 18.4. The National Bureau of Economic Research (NBER) of the USA has developed methods to identify turning points in the economy bolstered by indicators computed by the Bureau of Economic Analysis (BEA). Section 18.5 contains a discussion on the dating techniques of the NBER and BEA. Concluding remarks are in the Section 18.6.

In Figure 18.1, the trend line is the thick straight line going upwards. This represents the long-term growth path of the economy and it is moving upwards, indicating that the economy's potential output is on a rising path contributed by new technology and capital accumulation. In the next section, we revisit the Keynesian model introduced in Chapter 3.

18.2. THE SIMPLE INCOME DETERMINATION MODEL

In the simple Keynesian model, we assume an open economy. Income is Y, consumption expenditure including imports is represented by C, intended investment by I, expenditure by G, exports by X and imports by Z. The aggregate supply of goods and services (total output) available in the economy consists of domestic production plus the level of imports Z. In equilibrium, this supply should equal to the demand from the household sector, the government sector, the business sector and the rest of the world (foreign trade). We can, therefore, write the equilibrium condition to be

$$Z + Y = C + I + G + X$$

By rearranging we get,

$$Y = C + I + G + (X–Z) \tag{18.1}$$

(X–Z) represents the country's trade balance or net exports that have been discussed elaborately in Chapter 15. Let S be the household sector's savings. Since there is a government and we have included its expenditure, we will have to include its revenue as well. Hence, we bring in taxes denoted by T. Let disposable income be denoted by Y_d. Since income receipts are distributed between the government and the household, we get the following relation:

$$Y = Y_d + T$$

However, since disposable income can be either saved or spent, we can write

$$Y = C + S + T \tag{18.2}$$

Equating Equations 18.1 and 18.2 and netting out C on both sides, we obtain the condition

$$I + G + X = S + T + Z$$

If there was a complete balance, then intended investment I would be equal to intended savings S and government expenditure G would be equal to tax revenues T, so that the government budget would be balanced. It follows that exports X would be equal to imports Z and the balance of payments would be balanced. But we know that that does not happen in reality. The imbalances in several of these factors cause changes leading to fluctuations in economic activity. One of the primary sources of imbalance arises from the business sector's investment behaviour, which is driven by business expectations about profit. This in turn is influenced by the household sector's consumption behaviour.

The Consumption Function: The key proposition of the simple income determination analysis is that aggregate real consumption in an economy is determined by the after-tax disposable income Y_d. Keynes asserted that aggregate demand determined the level of economic activity in the economy. In other words, a nation's production and employment depended on the amount of expenditure. Too little spending would cause unemployment, too much would cause firms to produce more than the quantity demanded, causing inflation. However, more demand would persuade business to invest more, creating more jobs and higher levels of national income.

For a simplified analysis, let us assume that we have an economy, which has no government budget, retained business earnings, or foreign trade. Let us also agree that prices remain constant, so that inflation is zero. This will help us to keep all magnitudes in real terms. So GDP represented by *Y* will be:

$$Y = C + I_a$$

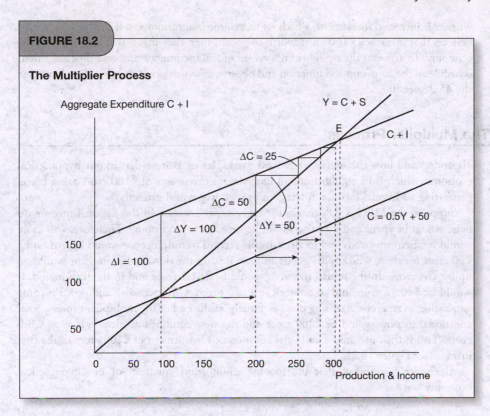

FIGURE 18.2

The Multiplier Process

where I_a is the net realized investment or actual investment and C is consumption. In this model, all income is disposable income. A consumption function for a hypothetical economy is shown in Figure 18.2, where real disposable income is measured on the horizontal axis and real consumption expenditure on the vertical axis. The slope of the consumption function drawn as a straight line is the marginal propensity to consume (MPC), which is the fraction of additional rupee income that will be consumed. Theory and empirical evidence show that it is less than one. It is obvious that people save a part of their new income and spend the rest. So for every additional rupee earned, one part is consumed and the part saved.

However, there are some persons who tend to consume more than their current real incomes, either by dipping into their past savings, or by borrowing. The 45 degree line is a guideline, which denotes that any point on the line is equidistant from both the axes. The point where the consumption function intersects the line is the point where the entire additional income is consumed, that is, the zero savings point.

Suppose we assume that the MPC is 0.5. The point of zero savings is ₹100 crore. When real income reaches ₹200 crore, consumption will be ₹50 crore and savings will be ₹50 crore. If the MPC is 0.5, the marginal propensity to save is 1–0.5 = 0.5. In a closed economy with no government, from Equation 18.1, we get

$$Y = C + I \tag{18.3}$$

where *I* is intended investment, which let us assume is autonomous. If the business sector believes that it can sell ₹100 crore worth of goods, then they invest that amount into the economy. To arrive at the equilibrium level 'E' of real income we now add the investment schedule to the consumption function and observe at which point the C + I line intersects the 45 degree line.

18.2.1. The Multiplier Process

The (income) multiplier is the increase in total output or GDP for each ₹1 increase in autonomous investment or government expenditure.

Autonomous investment is investment expenditure that increases the capital stock and is not induced by any incentive from the government.

To understand how the *multiplier* process works, let us assume that in our hypothetical economy, which is in equilibrium, an *autonomous investment* of ₹100 crore takes place, generating additional income in terms of profits, wages and interests.

Suppose, the MPC is 0.8, that is for every rupee increase in the national income 80 paise would be spent and 20 paise would be saved in this economy. Therefore, ₹80 crore would be spent on goods and services. In the second round, income would have risen by ₹80 crore for those who supply goods and services. In the third round, income would go up by ₹64 crore. In the fourth round, it would be ₹51.2 crore and in the fifth period, it would be ₹40.96 crore and so on until it reaches zero with successive additional income generation in an ever-decreasing process. Finally, at the end of the multiplier process, total additional income would be ₹200 crore and the new equilibrium income level at ₹300 crore. This is the outcome of an initial autonomous investment of ₹100 crore in the first instant (see Figure 18.2).

Algebraically recollect that the income equilibrium equation of our hypothetical economy was

$$Y = C + I \qquad (18.4)$$

If autonomous investment rises by ΔI, then income and consumption increase by ΔY and ΔC:

$$Y + \Delta Y = C + \Delta C + I + \Delta I \qquad (18.5)$$

Subtracting Equation (18.4) from Equation (18.5), we get

$$\Delta Y = \Delta C + \Delta I \qquad (18.6)$$

If the consumption function is denoted as C = a + bY, then

$$\Delta C = b\, \Delta Y \qquad (18.7)$$

Substituting in Equation (18.6), we get

$$\Delta Y = b\, \Delta Y + \Delta I \qquad (18.8)$$

Or

$$\Delta Y\, (1{-}b) = \Delta I \qquad (18.9)$$

That is,

$$\Delta Y = \Delta I\, [1/(1{-}b)] \qquad (18.10)$$

The term [1/(1–b)] is the multiplier '*m*'. So we can easily see that the change in income is equal to the change in autonomous investment times the multiplier. So the consumption function influences income through the multiplier. Since the MPC *b* is less than 1, the Keynesian multiplier will be greater than 1, so that an increase in autonomous spending, such as a change in G or I, has a multiplier effect on income.

18.2.2. The Accelerator Theory

When the economy recovers from a slump, investment grows rapidly, indicating the euphoric expectations of the business sector. But when national income begins to grow slowly and a downturn is in the offing, investment falls dramatically and during a recession, it disappears almost completely. The *Accelerator theory* relates investment to changes in national income. One of the earliest expositions of the accelerator principle was by J. M. Clark.[1] The term accelerator refers to the phenomenon when a relatively modest rise in the GDP can cause a much larger percentage rise in investment.

In times of stability, the only type of investment made by the business sector is replacement investment. Replacement investment happens for replacing worn-out machinery or obsolete equipment, since at that time there is no rise in national income and no rise in consumption. However, when income and consumption increase, there will be a need for new investment to raise production capacity and this is *induced investment*.

Once this has taken place, investment will fall back to only the replacement only, unless there is a further change in national income and consumption. Hence, induced investment depends on changes in income, ΔY, as represented in (18.11)

$$I = \alpha \, \Delta Y \qquad\qquad (18.11)$$

where α is the amount by which induced investment depends on changes in national income. α is known as the accelerator coefficient. So if the national income rises by ₹1,000 crore and causes induced investment to go up to ₹2,000 crore, the accelerator coefficient is 2. The size of α will be dependent on the economy's marginal capital to output ratio $\Delta K/\Delta Y$. This is the cost of extra capital required to produce ₹1 worth of additional national output.

In real life, the accelerator is not so dramatic and clear-cut. The actual effect of the accelerator is very complex and difficult to predict for various reasons. For instance, many firms have excess production capacity or could be carrying inventories. Hence, they could be in a position to meet new demand without making any new investments. Again, some firms' decisions to make new investments will depend upon the specific industry's future prospects.

In a report in *The Economist*,[2] it has been claimed that the demand for exquisite luxury chocolate truffles made by Lindt and Sprungli has fallen so much that the company has closed fifty of its eighty outlets across USA, whereas the lower priced and

The Accelerator theory relates investment to changes in national income. The term accelerator refers to the fact that a relatively modest rise in the GDP can cause a much larger percentage rise in investment.

[1] J. M. Clark, 'Business Accelerator and the Law of Demand', *Journal of Political Economy* 25, no. 3 (1917): 217–35.
[2] 'Trading Down', *The Economist*, 30 May–5 June 2009, 5.

non-luxury chocolates like Hershey's have experienced a sharp rise in their sales in the economic downturn.

There may also be some firms who have long-term investment plans in place and unwilling to make major changes in their investment policies. These factors tend to decrease the extent of the impact of the accelerator, making it extremely difficult to predict. Nevertheless, firms do take note of consumer demand and decide about their investments, so that the accelerator effect does exist. The combination of the multiplier and accelerator has been advanced as a key causal factor for business cycles by Samuelson (1939) and Hicks (1950), discussed in the next section.

18.2.3. The Keynesian Theories of Business Cycles

In the early 20th century, it was believed that ups and downs in economic activity were inevitable and that they occurred fairly regularly. Economists spoke of business cycles, delineating them as waves with different durations. There were long swings of 25-year durations known as the 'Kondatrief waves', eight to ten year swings known as the 'Jugular cycles' and the shorter four year swings called the 'Kitchin cycles'. It was widely believed that what goes up must come down, and that recessions were like a hangover, a price that an economy paid for past excesses.

The currently ongoing global recession, from the first decade of the 21st century, seem to support such a viewpoint! We have pointed out in the previous section that investment could be influenced by expectations of profit and income levels and that the acceleration principle could be a major source of instability. After the Great Depression and the advent of Keynesian economics, the role of the government in stabilizing the economy through monetary and fiscal policies gained wide acceptance.

The Keynesian theories of business cycles operate with the assumption that prices are fixed and the money supply adjusts to the quantity of output. With an increase in expected output, an increase in demand appears for additional capital, causing an increase in investment. Samuelson[3] named it the multiplier–accelerator interaction where output adjusted to demand shocks. Increases in investment led to expansions in output by an amount equal to the rise in investment times the income multiplier. This model was strictly for a closed economy. The investment demand equation lay at the heart of the business cycle. The Samuelson[4] and Hicks[5] model is based on the following three equations:

$$Y_t = C_t + I_t \tag{18.12}$$

$$C_t = a + bY_{t-1} \tag{18.13}$$

$$I_t = v\,(Y_{t-1} - Y_{t-2}) + \beta_t \tag{18.14}$$

[3] P. A. Samuelson, 'Interactions Between Multiplier Analysis and Principle of Acceleration', *Review of Economics and Statistics*, 21, no. 2 (1939): 78–88.

[4] Samuelson, 'Interactions Between Multiplier Analysis and Principle of Acceleration'.

[5] J. R. Hicks, *A Contributions to the Theory of Trade Cycles* (Oxford: The Clarendon Press, 1950).

Equation 18.12 is the goods market equilibrium condition in a closed economy without a government sector. The consumption function that was introduced in the previous section is represented by Equation 18.13, which indicates that consumption is a function of the disposable income of the previous period and the MPC *b* which is assumed to be less than one but greater than zero $(0 > b > 1)$. Finally, the last Equation 18.14 represents investment behaviour, which is an accelerator. Investment is determined by the change in income in the previous periods Y_{t-1} and Y_{t-2}, autonomous investment β and v, the accelerator coefficient.

By substituting the values of the consumption and investment equations in the income equation, we get the following:

$$Y = a + (v + b)\, Y_{t-1} - vY_{t-2} + \beta_t \qquad (18.15)$$

If the expected MPC *b* is less than one and the accelerator coefficient *v* greater than one, it seems likely that the time path of the economy would be like that of A in the Figure 18.3. In other words, suppose the MPC *b* is 0.75 and the accelerator *v* is 1.2, then the cycle is likely to be explosive. We observe therefore that any deviation from the initial level of income would result in an ever increasing or ever decreasing level of income. What about autonomous investment β?

If the autonomous investment grows at the same rate as the economy, then $\beta_t = \beta_0$ $(1 + g)^t$, where 'g' is the natural rate of growth of the economy. The equilibrium time path of the economy is composed of two elements. The first term shows the underlying growth rate of the economy and the second part is the fluctuating component corresponding to the relationship of the income to previous time periods, namely in t–1, t–2, and so on.

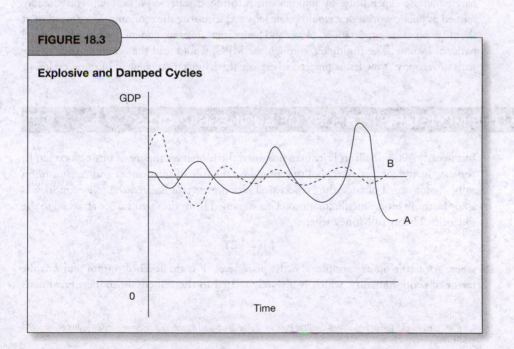

FIGURE 18.3

Explosive and Damped Cycles

Suppose in time t there is a small unforeseen rise in income, which causes an increase in investments over and above what is needed to stay in the steady state. Here the accelerator effect dominates with a greater than usual rise in income, which in turn has a multiplier effect on income. The effect is to push the economy further and further away from the steady state growth path, which is the explosive path. Hick's[6] theory of income fluctuations and business cycles contributed little to policy-makers' intent on adopting counter cyclical measures. He believed that that the accelerator mechanism would not work in a downturn. Hicks explained that the cycle could be unstable, though to some extent self-adjusting.

Baumol[7] introduced the government sector into Hicks' model to incorporate government counter-cyclical policies. It was expected that rather than remaining exogenous, government expenditure would adjust according to the business cycle. So as the output gap increased, government expenditure would be raised. However, when the full employment level of output was crossed, government spending would be reduced to curtail inflationary pressures. Here the fiscal policy would have a stabilizing effect on the economy. Interestingly, Baumol's model showed that countercyclical policies may not always be beneficial and could in fact result in increased instability. This was because even in a simple good—economy—the inability of a government to respond quickly to economic information could destabilize the system.

Keynes in his seminal treatise recommended that the Classical school's notion of a balanced budget should be abandoned in favour of a deficit budget to fight recession. This was to be mostly through discretionary monetary and fiscal policies and most of these ideas have been explored in the previous chapters. The government should, on the one hand bring down taxes to raise disposable income in the hands of the households and on the other hand, increase expenditure by building roads, bridges, waterways, hospitals etc., broadly termed as public works, that would create jobs and stimulate the economy. The government should enter as an important employer and hence increase employment, leading to increased national income. The multiplier, through the MPC, would lead the economy back to the path of recovery. Now let us proceed to explore the Monetarists' view of business cycles.

18.3. THE MONETARIST THEORY OF BUSINESS CYCLES

In the early 1960s, Milton Friedman proposed the monetary theory of business cycles. In contrast to the Keynesian school that proposed the role of investment and consumption to be major causal factors, the Neoclassical economists emphasized the role of money as a key factor in economic fluctuations. This stemmed from the significance attached to the Quantity Theory of Money where:

$$Ms = kPY$$

where M^s is the money supply, P is the price level, Y is the level of output and k is the factor of proportionality, which is inversely related to the velocity of money. Friedman's

[6] Ibid.

[7] W. J. Baumol, 'Pitfall in Contra-Cyclical Policies: Some Tools and Results', *Review of Economic and Statistics* 43 (1961, February): 21–26.

analysis closely followed the Neoclassical view. Monetarists argue that in the long-run, output is determined by the supply side of the economy such that it is consistent with the full employment level. Therefore, changes in the money supply cause changes in the price level via the Quantity Theory.

In the short-run, however, changes in the money supply can cause fluctuations in the output level. In other words, the causality runs from money supply to production and the two are not related to each other in the long-run. Friedman dedicated considerable effort to demonstrating that the money supply was the key to business cycles.

Friedman and Schwarz[8] argued that a contraction of the money supply was the primary cause of the severe recessions the US economy faced in the second half of the 19th century, during the periods 1873 to 1879 and 1892 to 1894 and in the early 20th century, during 1907 to 1908 and 1929 to 1933. They found evidence of a relationship between the rate of change of money supply preceding the reference cycle peak by seven months and the reference trough by four months. Their conclusion was mainly aimed at advocating the need to avoid the discretionary monetary policy proposed by the Keynesian school.

There have been several critiques of to the Monetarists' proposition. Firstly, regarding their contention that changes in M^S preceding the changes in Y do not justify the claim that one causes the other, it has been argued that the changes in M^S and that in Y are due to changes in another variable, say Z. Secondly, economists have had reservations about Friedman's explanation that the money supply is endogenously determined. It is possible that the public's currency to deposit ratio could vary as income changes as may the banks' own reserve ratio. As the demand for money grows less rapidly in relation to its supply, the rate of interest is likely to decline. This could cause the currency to deposit or reserve to deposit ratio to contract. The line of causality therefore would be from income to money supply and not vice versa.

Hawtrey (1913)[9] proposed a similar argument that the money supply was partly driven by endogenous forces. During a slowdown, central banks could pursue an expansionary policy, which would lead to more trade and commerce and related economic activity. This could be re-enforced by distribution in favour of businessmen from fixed income earners and labourers. This could continue until a downward spiral starts and central banks begin to adopt a contractionary policy.

In these Monetarist theories of business cycles, the phenomenon is clearly attributed to banking policies and their interaction with income and the money supply. However, there are economists who consider the Monetarist view as rather 'naïve'. They argue that such a simplistic approach to explain a complex phenomenon has a limited agenda which is only to dissuade policy-makers and thinkers from supporting the strength and feasibility of the discretionary monetary and fiscal policy prescriptions advised by the Keynesians. Recently, another school of thought has evolved the RBC theory, which is discussed in the next section.

---

[8] Milton Friedman and A. Schwarz, 'Money and Business Cycles', *Review of Economics and Statistics* 45 (1963b, supplement): 52–64.

[9] Hawtrey, R. G. 'Good and Bad Trade. London: Constable and Co. 1925. Public Expenditure and the Demand for Labour'. *Economica* 5 (1913): 38–48.

18.4. THE REAL BUSINESS CYCLE THEORY

How do we tackle the problem of short-run fluctuations in output and employment? Most economists today have accepted the position that the aggregate demand and aggregate supply format using monetary and fiscal policies should suffice. However, there exists a small, but significant minority who think otherwise. They are those who espoused the cause of the RBC theory.

According to this theory, short-run oscillations should be explained while maintaining the assumptions of the Classical model, namely that prices are fully flexible even in the short-run. Most microeconomic analysis is built on the premise that prices clear the market. The followers of this theory argue that macroeconomic analysis should be based on the same assumption making it consistent with the classical dichotomy that the money supply and price level do not influence real variables like output or employment. The 'real' in the term RBCs refers to the theory's exclusion of nominal variables in explaining shor-run fluctuations.

Inter-temporal substitution of leisure is the extent to which temporarily high real wages cause workers to work harder today and enjoy more leisure tomorrow.

The RBC emphasizes that the amount of labour supplied at any point of time would be influenced by the incentive to work. Hence, workers, when well rewarded, work for longer hours, but when the compensation is low, they chose to work for lesser hours. The willingness to re-allocate hours of work and leisure is called the *inter-temporal substitution* of leisure. The theory proposes that inter-temporal substitution reflects the change in the amount people want to devote to work and in the enjoyment of leisure. They believe that desired employment is not sensitive to real wages or the real interest rate. The high levels of unemployment in recessions suggest that the labour market does not clear.

Considerable research has been undertaken to examine if such inter-temporal substitution is of significance in the explanation of short-run fluctuations. However, available evidence does not convince everyone and one major stumbling block to these kind of studies is that data is not always perfect.

The second source of fluctuation as per the RBC theory is technological shocks. The theory assumes that the economy experiences technological shocks that determine the way inputs, namely capital and labour, get converted to output. These shocks cause the economy to move in an observed irregular fashion, upwards and downwards. Higher level of productivity induced by superior technology lead to the inter-temporal substitution of labour. Hence, improved technology would lead to more employment. Accordingly, the proponents of the RBC theory have argued that recessions were periods of 'technological regress'. The line of argument was as follows: output and employment would fall during recessions since the available production technology would deteriorate, lowering output and reducing the incentive to work.

Another key factor in the RBC theory has been the neutrality of money. The proponents of the RBC theory assume that money is neutral and hence monetary policy does not have any effect on real variables like output and employment even in the short-run. The advocates of the RBC theory claim that the money supply is endogenous such that fluctuations in output might cause fluctuations in the money supply, but not the other way round. So the debate on business cycles continues unabated, creating fodder for new thoughts and research.

18.5. DATING BUSINESS CYCLES

How does one identify a business cycle? When does a recovery start? When does the decline begin? These are the tough questions that plague policy-makers, businessmen and economists in think tanks, government departments and universities. Over the years, many economists have developed methods to identify turning points with varying degrees of sophistication and technical skills, but a consensus remains elusive. The most well-known methods of dating business cycles are those adopted by the NBER in the USA. The NBER published the first formal list of cyclical indicators in 1938. It then produced revised lists in 1950, 1961, and 1967. To begin with, we will refer to the quote from the Burns and Mitchell (1946)[10] definition of a business cycle, namely:

> Business cycles are a type of fluctuation found in aggregate economic activity of nations that organize their work mainly in business enterprise: a cycle consists of expansion occurring at about the same times in many activities, followed by similarly by general recessions, contractions, and revivals which merge into the expansion phase of the next cycle; this sequence is recurrent but not periodic; in duration, business cycles vary from more than one year to ten to twelve years; they are not divisible into shorter cycles of similar character with amplitudes approximating their own.

This definition itself is subject to controversy in terms of whether a single index should be used or a reference cycle date. While some researchers are of the view that business cycles are symmetric and mirror images of each other so that the peaks and troughs replicate, others do not accept this view. Given the wide variety of business cycles experienced in the last century, the latter view is clearly more plausible. There are several business cycle dating procedures, but here we discuss only three of them briefly, since the others are rather complex and outside the scope of this text. These are:

1. The NBER Business Cycle Dating Committee approach
2. The Gross Domestic Product (GDP) rules of thumb approach
3. Peaks and troughs of the Commerce Department's BEA business cycle indicators

The NBER's approach observes numerous data series that are believed to be coincidental with the aggregate economy, such as the indices of industrial production, employment and the capital market. Clusters of turning points are used to set the reference cycle dates. Their decisions closely track those prescribed by the Burns and Mitchell's concept of business cycles. The criteria include:

1. A full cycle should last for more than one year and not less than 2 years and
2. A later turning point is selected over an earlier one to err on the side of caution.

---

[10] Arthur F. Burns and Wesley C. Mitchell, *Measuring Business Cycles*, (Cambridge, US: NBER, 1946).

A 'coincident' indicator is an index that shows the current state of the economy. It includes personal income, manufacturing and trade sales, residential investments and private fixed investments.

The Boards' decisions are conservative in order to avoid false calls.

The GDP growth rules of thumb affirm that two consecutive quarters of negative output indicate the beginning of an 'official recession'. In this method, peaks and troughs are more difficult to be characterized when there is, for instance, zero growth. While announcing a recession with these criteria seems reasonable, proclaiming the start of a recovery and expansion is unclear. Hence, a 2.5% growth rate over three consecutive quarters as a precursor to an upturn is acceptable. In some instances, as in the 1990s, the NBER dates did coincide with those of the GDP rules. Announcing a peak really implies that a downturn is approaching.

A 'lead' indicator can signal future trends in the economy.

The BEA computes three indices for the analysis of business cycles and for predicting economic trends. These include the *coincident indicator* (CI), the *lead indicator* (LI) and the LgIs. The weighted average growth of individual components is the monthly percentage change in each indicator, while in some cases the quarterly series is utilized. Tables 18.1 to 18.3 report the different items included in the three indicators as per the BEA methodology.

TABLE 18.1

Components Included in the Computation of Coincidental Indicators*

Coincidental Indicator		Peak	Trough
1	Personal income less transfer payments	Monthly	Monthly
2	Manufacturing and trade sales	Monthly	Monthly
3	Gross domestic product	Quarterly	Quarterly
4	Private non-residential fixed investment	Quarterly	Quarterly
5	Private fixed investment in equipment and software	Quarterly	Quarterly

Source: Tables prepared from Carol E. Moylan 'Third International Seminar on Early Warning and Business Cycle Indicators Moscow, Russian Federation, 17–19 November 2010, Cyclical Indicators for the United States' BEA.
*Inflation Adjusted Unless Otherwise Stated.

TABLE 18.2

Components Included in the Computation of Lead Indicators*

Lead Indicator		Peak	Trough
1	Private residential fixed investment	Quarterly	Quarterly
2	Change in private inventories	Quarterly	Quarterly
3	Corporate profits after tax (current dollars)	Quarterly	Quarterly

Source: Tables prepared from Carol E. Moylan 'Third International Seminar on Early Warning and Business Cycle Indicators Moscow, Russian Federation, 17–19 November 2010, Cyclical Indicators for the United States' BEA.
*Inflation Adjusted Unless Otherwise Stated.

A 'lag' indicator shows that an event has already occurred. For instance, a rise in employment shows that the economy is going to recover.

TABLE 18.3

Components Included in the Computation of Lag Indicators*

Lag Indicator		Peak	Trough
1	Ratio, manufacturing and trade inventories to sales	Monthly	Monthly
2	Private fixed investment in non-residential structures	Quarterly	Quarterly
3	Private fixed investment in equipment and software	Quarterly	Quarterly
4	Private non-residential fixed investment	NA	Quarterly

Source: Tables prepared from Carol E. Moylan 'Third International Seminar on Early Warning and Business Cycle Indicators Moscow, Russian Federation, 17–19 November 2010, Cyclical Indicators for the United States' BEA.

**Inflation Adjusted Unless Otherwise Stated.*

BOX 18.1   **What is a Recession? Can it be Predicted?**[11]

A recession happens when a decline occurs in some measure of aggregate economic activity and through a domino effect causes declines in other key measures of activity. If sales come down that causes inventories to build-up which leads to a drop in production, triggering a downward trend in employment and income. This in turn leads back into further falls in sales resulting in a vicious cycle culminating in a recession. At some point, the vicious cycle is broken when a self-reinforcing virtuous cycle begins as sales increase with employment, output and income feed into each other towards an uptrend. The transition points between the vicious and the virtuous cycles signals the start and end date of the recession.

But can recessions be predicted? A simple and popular rule for determining the onset of a recession is two consecutive quarters of declines in the GDP. This may be unreliable; for instance, if a period with rising sales as well as output and employment is followed by a mild decline in two consecutive quarters, then it can be misguiding. It would be difficult to date business cycles on such a rule. In the post-World War II period, Germany and Japan underwent rapid revival, so much so that the Classical business cycle theory seemed to be irrelevant.

USA in the meantime developed a wide range of statistical series ranging from leading indicators, CIs and composite indicators. But could the Subprime Crisis that engulfed the whole world have been predicted? In hindsight it seems it could have been!! Traditional leading indicators show the direction of a business cycle but not its magnitude. These indicators

---

[11] The text in Box 18.1 has been prepared with inputs from Carolyn E. Moylan 'Cyclical Indicators for the United States', *Bureau of Economic Analysis* (2009). Third International Conference on Early Warning and Business Cycle Indicators, Moscow.

have provided analysts' with information about a recession coming in December 2007 but its intensity and severity could not be gauged.

New data series combined with traditional ones showed that the US housing stock annual value relative to personal income between 1970–2009 was significantly much higher and that the housing index rose much more rapidly than personal income and then started to fall in 2006 and more in 2007, with the ratios still very high compared to the historical trends. It did not appear to be important to understand that there was a housing bubble waiting to burst. Data shows that residential investment peaked in the 4th quarter of 2005 and then declined sharply for 14 consecutive quarters. Identifying the bubble before its collapse could have been an early warning signal.

Figure 18.4 clearly demonstrates how housing prices rose rapidly from 2000 onwards to dive down in 2005, while personal income grew at a slow and steady pace through the whole period.

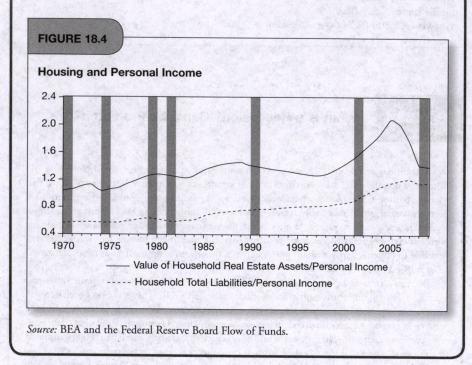

FIGURE 18.4

Housing and Personal Income

——— Value of Household Real Estate Assets/Personal Income

- - - - Household Total Liabilities/Personal Income

Source: BEA and the Federal Reserve Board Flow of Funds.

The Federal Reserve Bank, the central bank of USA, publishes coincident economic indices compiled from a variety of CIs. By compiling several indicators into an index, some of the short-term noise associated with individual indicators can be eliminated, giving a more reliable measure. A CI reflects the current state of the economy. A LI signals likely future trends in the economy. Yield curves are found to be relatively good indicators because bond traders anticipate and speculate trends in the economy (even though they may not be always correct). The importance of a lagging indicator is its ability to confirm that a pattern is occurring or about to occur. Unemployment is one of the most popular LgIs. If the unemployment rate increases, it indicates that the economy has been doing poorly.

The methods of dating business cycles discussed above are not exhaustive and are only indicative. The Bry and Buschan (1971)[12] method mentioned in the case study has gained some popularity, while the Stock and Watson (1999)[13] method remains in the realms of frontier- level research. What is intriguing is that the origins of business cycles, that is, the reasons for their occurrence as well as the frequency and duration with which they prevail continue to be the focus for research and debate. Different business cycles sometimes have different characteristics and the 'one size fits all' approach does not seem to make any sense. In the concluding section, we recapitulate the business cycle theories discussed here.

18.6. CONCLUSION

Business cycles are fluctuations in the total level of output and employment in an economy. They are characterized by a sequence of four phases: contraction, then slowdown and then recovery; or, a period of expansion followed by a peak or boom and then again a downturn in the pace of economic activity. In this chapter, we have explored the theories of business cycles. The Keynesian theory of business cycle attributed the cyclical fluctuations in economic activity to the consumption function, which was a linear function of the disposable income. Keynes asserted that aggregate demand determined the level of economic activity in an economy, so that the nation's production and employment levels depended on the amount of expenditure. Too little spending would cause unemployment and too much would lead firms to produce more than aggregate demand, thereby causing inflation. However, increased demand would persuade businesses to invest more, creating more jobs and leading to higher levels of national income. On the other hand, inadequate investment and downsizing of firms would cause a decline in employment and output, leading to an eventual downturn.

Keynes strongly advocated an active role for the government in stabilizing the economy through the use of discretionary fiscal and monetary policies, thus opposing the Classical school and thought of laissez faire.

Samuelson and Hicks developed this approach further by introducing the accelerator principle of investment, arguing that it was the primary source of instability. Later economists like Milton Friedman proposed the Monetarist approach to business cycles.

---

[12] Gerhard Bry and Charlotte Boschan, 'Programmed Selection of Cyclical Turning Points', in *Cyclical Analysis of Time Series: Selected Procedures and Computer Programs.* (Cambridge: NBER, 1971), 7–63.

[13] James H. Stock and Mark W. Watson, 'Business Cycle Fluctuations in US Macroeconomic Time Series', in *Handbook of Macroeconomics* 1 (1999): 3–64, http://www.sciencedirect.com/science/article/B7P5X-4FD73BS-4/2/0fc60af4adc161ceaae891f83758540e

Friedman explained the phenomenon as purely driven by monetary forces, identifying central banking and monetary policy as key elements for managing trade cycles. A more recent contribution to the business cycle theory, the RBC theory, has gained some currency, but its argument incorporating the inter-temporal substitution of labour, technological shocks and neutrality of money is yet to receive wide acceptance in the academic forum.

To identify when a downturn is going to happen or when a recovery is in the offing is the field of dating business cycles. The NBER in USA is the pioneer in developing methods for predicting and warning against a slowdown. The GDP growth rate is a widely used and easily comprehended technique, but reliable and timely data is the essence for dating business cycles. The BEA in USA has played a prominent role in devising coincidental, lead and LgIs for business cycles.

Today, in the second decade of the 21st century, the world is engulfed in another Great Recession. The proponents of the New Keynesian school continue to vote for a stronger and more active role for the government through quantitative easing and larger government expenditures. In Europe, the mood is in favour of the Classical school with austerity and a balanced budget policy. As can be seen, the question of how business cycles happen and how they can be managed continue to be debated among macroeconomists and policy-makers alike. So as they say, the jury is out there on this one. We conclude this chapter here, to go on to explore how the myriad schools of macroeconomic thought are driven by the labour market, in Chapter 19.

SUMMARY

- Business cycles are characterized by a sequence of four phases: contraction: the slowdown, expansion: recovery in economic activity, peak: the upper turning point and recession: severe contraction. A deep trough is called a depression.

- The equation $I + G + X = S + T + Z$ implies that the economy is in a stable equilibrium, when intended investment I and savings S are equal as well as government expenditure G and tax revenue T are equal, that is, when the government has a balanced budget. Finally, exports X equal imports Z and the balance of payments is in balance. The imbalance in this relation leads to business cycles or fluctuations in economic activity.

- A change in income is caused by a change in autonomous investment times the multiplier $m = 1/(1-b)$. The consumption function influences income through the multiplier.

- The MPC b is less than 1 and hence the Keynesian multiplier will be greater than 1. Thus an increase in autonomous spending, such as a change in G or I, has a multiplier effect on income.

- The term accelerator refers to a phenomenon when a relatively modest rise in the GDP can cause a much larger percentage rise in investment.

- In times of stability, the only type of investment is replacement investment. When income and consumption increase, new investment is required called *induced investment, which* depends on changes in income. $I = \alpha\,\Delta Y$ where α is the accelerator coefficient.

- Samuelson[14] composed the multiplier–accelerator interaction. An increase in investment leads to an expansion in output by an amount equal to the rise in investment times the income multiplier. The investment demand equation lies at the heart of a business cycle.

- Keynes recommended that the Classical school's notion of a balanced budget should be abandoned in favour of a deficit budget to fight recession, through discretionary monetary and fiscal policies.

- The Monetary theory of business cycles proposed by Milton Friedman emphasized the role of money as a key factor in economic fluctuations. This stemmed from the significance attached to the Quantity Theory of Money: $M^s = kPY$.

- The critics of the Monetarist proposition argued that changes in M^s preceding the changes in Y do not justify the claim that one causes the other. Secondly, there were reservations about Friedman's explanation that the money supply was endogenously determined.

- According to the RBCs theory, short-run oscillations need to be explained within the Classical model, namely by the assumption that prices are fully flexible even in the short-run. The 'real' in this refers to the theory's exclusion of nominal variables in explaining short-run fluctuations.

- The RBC emphasizes that the amount of labour supplied at any point of time is influenced by the incentives to work. Hence, workers when well rewarded work for longer hours, but when the compensation is lower, they are willing to work only for lesser hours. The willingness to reallocate hours of work and leisure is termed as the '*inter-temporal substitution* of labour'.

- Secondly, the RBC theory argues that the economy experiences technological shocks that determine the way inputs, capital and labour get converted to output. These shocks cause the economy to move in an observed irregular fashion.

- The most well-known methods of dating business cycles are those adopted by the NBER, in the USA.

- The NBER observes numerous data series that are believed to be coincidental with the aggregate economy, such as the index of industrial production, employment indices, the capital market index etc. The clustering of turning points is used to set the reference cycle dates.

- Secondly, the GDP growth rules affirm that two consecutive quarters of negative output indicate the beginning of an 'official recession'.

- Thirdly, the BEA computes three indices for the analysis of business cycles and for predicting economic trends, namely, CIs, LIs and LgIs).

---

[14] Samuelson, 'Interactions Between Multiplier Analysis and Principle of Acceleration'.

CASE STUDY[15]

Business Cycles or Growth Cycles?

The growth cycle is a relatively recent concept of the business cycles, in which the fluctuation is around the long-run trend (Moore, 1983).[16] This definition portrays periods of accelerating and decelerating rates of economic growth. Identifying business cycles has hardly received academic attention in India. The dilemma lies firstly in identifying business cycles and then creating reliable indicators to predict them as tools for macroeconomic management.

In independent India, data show four episodes since 1950–51 when the growth in GDP fell sharply, followed by 1965–66, 1979–80 and 1991–92 (see Table CS 18.1). In each of these years, the growth rate fell by more than 4% to less than 1%. All of these movements saw a sharp decline in agricultural output, sometimes even negative. In 1957–58, growth in manufacturing became negative while in 1965–66, the severe drought conditions caused agricultural output to decline by over 11%. The year 1979–80 witnessed a fall in agricultural output by over 12%. Manufacturing growth was –3.4%. In 1991–92, the time of the balance of payment crisis, a fall in agricultural and manufacturing growth led to an overall decline in GDP growth.

TABLE CS 18.1

The Chronology of Business Cycles—Peak & Trough Dates

	Peak and Trough	Dates Supported by Studies Using Other Methods
PERIOD I	1956–57, 1957–58	Mall (1999),[17] Chitre (1986)[18]
PERIOD II	1963–64, 1965–66	Mall (1999), Chitre (1986), Dua & Banerji (2000)[19]
PERIOD III	1978–79, 1979–80	Mall (1999), Chitre (1986), Gangopadhyay & Wadhwa (1997)
PERIOD IV	1990–91, 1991–92	Dua & Banerji (2000), Gangopadhyay & Wadhwa (1997)

Source: Ila Patnaik and Rachna Sharma (2002).

[15] The text for the Case study 18.1 was prepared from *Business Cycles in the Indian Economy*; Vasanth Kumar J., *Study of Yield Curve Spread As Predictor of Economic Slowdown* (Madras School of Economics, Unpublished Master's Thesis, Chennai, 2012); Ila Patnaik and Rachna Sharma (2002).

[16] Geoffrey H. Moore, *Business Cycles, Inflation and Forecasting*, (Cambridge, US: NBER, 1983).

[17] O. P. Mall, 'Composite Index of Leading Indicators for Business Cycles in India', *Reserve Bank of India Occasional Papers* 20, no. 3 (1999): 373–414.

[18] Vikas S. Chitre, 'Quarterly Prediction of Reserve Money Multiplier and Money Stock in India', *Journal of the Gokhale Institute of Politics & Economics* (Artha Vijnana, 1986), ISSN: 0004–3559.

[19] Pami Dua and Anirvan Banerji, 'An Index of Coincident Economic Indicators for the Indian Economy', (working paper, no. 73, Centre for Development Economics, 2000): http://www.cdedse.org/pdf/work73.pdf

The concept of business cycles is different from the prevailing perception, as these are not caused by intrinsic market forces, but purely by external factors such as the monsoon. As agriculture contributed to 40% of GDP in the 1970s, the fall in GDP was mainly due to monsoon failure. In the 21st century, focus has shifted to finding coincidental factors or better LIs to predict downturns as the economy has become more market oriented.

Composite Indicator

A CI includes gross national income, disposable personal income, final sales, manufacturing and trades sales, industrial production and employment in real terms. These types of data are unavailable for long time series for India. A composite CI constructed by Patnaik and Sharma (2002)[20] uses (a) non-petroleum imports and exports (in dollars) and (b) the Index of Industrial Production (IIP).

Peaks and troughs are identified using the Bry–Boschan (1971) method, which is a set of decision rules: (a) A peak is followed by a trough and a trough by a peak (b) Each phase (peak to trough or trough to peak) must be for at least six months (c) A business cycle from peak to peak or trough to trough have a duration of at least 15 months to distinguish business cycles from seasonal cycles; (d) Turning points within six months of the beginning or end of the time series are eliminated as these are peaks (troughs) within 24 months of the beginning or end of the series, if any of the points after (before) are higher (lower) than peak (trough).

TABLE CS 18.2

Turning Point Date: Coincident Indicator

Trough	February 1982
Peak	December 1989
Trough	September 1991
Peak	February 1997

Source: Ila Patnaik and Rachna Sharma (2002).

An RBI (2003)[21] study constructs a composite index with: (a) M1 money supply, (b) non-food credit and (c) Nifty Index. Vasanth[22] uses the yield spread (finding it to be superior to the money supply), non-food credit and the stock market index S&P CNX Nifty. He finds that the yield spread between the yield rate of 10-year bond and 15–90 days T-bills in the composite index is a better predictor of a downtrend for the post liberalization period of 1994 to 2012.

---

[20] Ila Patnaik and Rachna Sharma, *Business Cycles in the Indian Economy,* (New Delhi: Margin, 2002): 71–80.

[21] C. Rangarajan and Anoop Singh, 'Reserve Money: Concepts and Policy Implications for India', in *Money and Banking: Select Research Papers by the Economists of Reserve Bank of India,* ed. A. Vasudevan (New Delhi: Academic Foundation, 2003): 61.

[22] Vasanth Kumar J., *Study of Yield Curve Spread as Predictor of Economic Slowdown* (Madras School of Economics, Unpublished Master's Thesis, Chennai, 2012).

Answer the following questions after reading the text given in the case study:

1. Are the business cycles identified in independent India different from those in the post-liberalization regime? If so why?
2. How do you think a good LI would help in macroeconomic management?
3. What are the different factors included to construct a composite index? Explain why in your opinion they have been selected. Do you feel that they can be improved upon?

KEYWORDS

Business cycles
Contraction
Expansion
Recession
Peak

Multiplier
Autonomous investment
Inter-temporal substitution of leisure/labour
Coincidental indicator
Lead indicator
Lag indicator

CONCEPT CHECK

State whether the following statements are true or false:

1. Recovery is the phase in business cycles when economic activity begins to slow down and investment declines due to falling expectations about profits.
2. The consumption function is the quantitative relationship between consumption and disposable income, linked by the propensity to consume.
3. The MPC is the fraction of additional rupee income that will be consumed. Theory and empirical evidence reveal it to be less than one.
4. The term 'accelerator' refers to a phenomenon when a relatively modest rise in the GDP causes a much larger percentage rise in investment.
5. If the MPC b is less than one and the accelerator coefficient v is greater than one, it is likely that the time path of the economy will be explosive.
6. The Monetarist theory clearly points to banking policy and its interactions with income and the money supply, as the cause of business cycles.
7. Monetary policy is a country's central bank's policy, involving the adjustment of money supply and interest rates to manage inflation and support government contra-cyclical policies.
8. The inter-temporal substitution of labour is the extent to which temporarily high real wages cause workers to work harder today, or withhold their labour when wages fall.
9. The NBER is a pioneer in developing methods to date business cycles.

1. After you have read this chapter, do you think the time frame in which we observe an economy is important? If so how? If we were to examine business cycles, what is the time horizon we should be observing?

2. How does a macroeconomic model help in studying business cycles? If the four sectors, namely, households, businesses, government and rest of the world were in balance, then would there be no economic fluctuations? If not, explain your answer through an illustrative simple model.

3. John Maynard Keynes made immense contributions to the understanding of business cycles. The multiplier model proposed by him has substantially helped governments to pursue economic policies to stabilize their economies. Do you think the Accelerator principle suggested by Samuelson is an even better explanation? If so how?

4. What is the role of the price level in the Monetarists' theory of business cycles? Do you think this is useful from a businessman's point of view when he faces lower demand for his products?

5. The proponents of the RBC theory argue that prices are flexible just as the Classical economists believed. Do you find that prices are really as flexible in the real world you live in? Does the phenomenon of rising job losses throughout the world today support the inter-temporal substitution of labour view?

6. What are the difficulties in dating business cycles? What methods can be used to address the issues?

19
CHAPTER

The Labour Market as the Kingpin: The Various Schools of Macroeconomic Thought

LEARNING OBJECTIVES

Upon completion of this chapter, the reader will be able to:

- Perceive how the different schools of macroeconomic theory differ because of the primary role played by the labour market.
- Distinguish the key features of the Classical school in determining the macroeconomic outcome of full employment output, from those of the Keynesian school.
- Explain the differences and similarities between the Monetarist school developed by Milton Friedman and the Classical school in terms of the role played by monetary policy in influencing the macroeconomy.
- Understand the short-run and long-run outcomes emerging in the models of the various schools and the new Keynesian school's rejection of previous conclusions by the promotion of the rational expectations argument.
- Appreciate the synthesis of the Keynesian and the Classical schools, and the policy prescriptions proposed by them.
- Comprehend the nuances emerging out of real wage rigidity, and the role of trade unions in the labour market.
- Understand the meaning of the natural rate of unemployment in the context of macroeconomic policy and the implications of the persistence of unemployment for prolonged periods as observed in the Western world today.

19.1. INTRODUCTION

19.1.1. The Schools of Macroeconomic Thought

Economics is a dynamic discipline. It is a branch of knowledge that evolved as the economic scenario changed over the last century. Keynes published his celebrated 'General Theory', when the world was in the grip of a severe depression. Keynes' policy prescriptions were most appropriate at the time as his work addressed the pressing problems of the times, the most compelling one being the devastating depression and soaring unemployment. In later years too, the task of macroeconomic theory has been to expand the realm of analysis to be able to explain the actual developments in national and global economies. Such an endeavour naturally gave rise to competing schools of thought, which, however, did not make the earlier approaches redundant. Given a certain set of assumptions about the functioning of the various markets and the formation of agents' expectations, every school, including the basic Keynesian approach, could hold its own. It was just that the appropriate set of assumptions and the school which they represented, varied from era to era.

In fact, the key differences between the various schools of macroeconomic thought (and the differences in policy recommendations which these gave rise to) can be traced to the manner in which the *labour market* has been modelled (including the modelling of worker expectations about prices). So, it may be fair to say that the labour market is the kingpin of macroeconomic models. Perhaps this is only appropriate, since the labour share of national income is often in the range of seventy to seventy 5%!

Chronologically, the Classical school of macroeconomics was the first to emerge. This school was, for a while (for many years really), superseded by the Keynesian School of thought. Subsequently, as the global economic environment underwent transformations, the need for newer policy measures gave rise to the Monetarist school. We find, thereafter, the revival of Keynesian thought under the new Keynesian approach as well as the revival of the Classical school as the new Classical school of thought developed. Today, these various strands exist and flourish. The common thread running through them all is the labour market, making a discussion of all the different schools under one umbrella possible, in somewhat of a pioneering fashion as laid out in this chapter.

Thus, the various schools of macroeconomic thought are represented by the Keynesian, Monetary, Classical, the New Keynesian and the Classical models. In what follows, we first present the Classical Model and show how the basic results of the model are derived from the manner in which the labour market is modelled. Then we proceed to present the Monetarist model, the Keynesian approach, the New Classical as well as the New Keynesian schools of thought, clarifying the differences in labour market assumptions which differentiate all these models from one another.

The various schools of macroeconomic thought are represented by the Keynesian, Monetary, Classical, the New Keynesian and the New Classical models.

> The labour market is the countrywide market where workers willing to work supply labour to employers and firms, who wish to employ them at the existing wage rate.

19.2. THE CLASSICAL MODEL

19.2.1. Labour Demand in the Classical Model

Under the assumption that the objective of the firm is to maximize profits, the firm will increase output until the extra revenue, that is, the marginal revenue, from an additional unit of output equals the marginal cost of producing that output, that is,

$$MR = MC \qquad (19.1)$$

For the competitive firm, the marginal revenue is the price of the product, since the demand curve facing the firm is horizontal, which means that none of the firms can influence the price set by the entire industry. The marginal cost is the cost of the additional labour needed for an extra unit of output, since capital stock remains unchanged in the short-run. So, Equation (19.1) can be rewritten as

$$P = (dL/dQ).W \qquad (19.2)$$

The real wage is the money or nominal wage divided by the aggregate product price.

where 'Q' is output, 'W' is the money wage and 'L' is the demand for labour. Equation (19.2) can be rewritten as

$$W/P = MPL \qquad (19.3)$$

where MPL is the marginal productivity (*the marginal physical product*) *of labour* (dQ/dL), and (W/P) is the *real wage*. Note that (W/P), which is the real wage in production, also called the 'product wage', is the same as the real wage in terms of a CPI in the model being discussed here, since there is only one aggregate good. In contrast, in the two sector model discussed later in Chapter 20, the product wage will differ from the real wage defined as the nominal wage divided by the CPI.

The marginal (physical) labour product, also called marginal labour productivity, is the increase in units of output for one additional unit of labour input, holding inputs of other factors of production unchanged.

It is important to understand that in the labour demand function, which is based on decision-making by the producer, it is the real wage defined as the product wage which is considered. If the product wage falls relative to the marginal physical labour product, the producer demands more labour as additional employment would bring down the marginal labour product to equal the product wage again.

The labour demand function derives directly from Equation (19.3) and is shown in Figure 19.1.

In Figure 19.1, if the real wage falls, the MPL will also fall to satisfy the profit maximization choice. This is achieved by increasing labour demand, since additional employment lowers the MPL. This basic labour demand function is also applicable to the other models to be discussed here.

Labour demand is a function of the real wage. The labour demand function slopes down to the right in the real wage–employment diagram. A rise in the real wage reduces labour demand, moving up along this curve. The real wage equals marginal labour product along the labour demand curve.

The labour demand function can be also drawn as a function of the nominal wage (Figure 19.2). Then, there is a separate labour demand function corresponding to each final good price P. If 'P' rises then it will shift the labour demand function to the right, increasing labour demand at a given nominal wage. This effect will correspond to a movement down along the labour demand curve in Figure 19.1.

FIGURE 19.1

Labour Demand as a Function of Real Wage

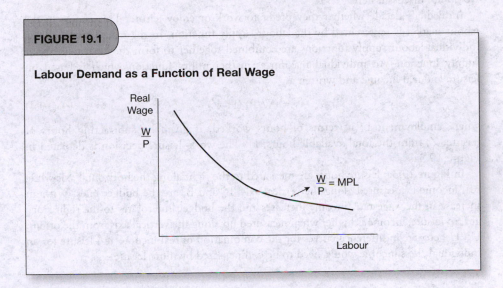

FIGURE 19.2

Labour Demand as a Function of Nominal Wage

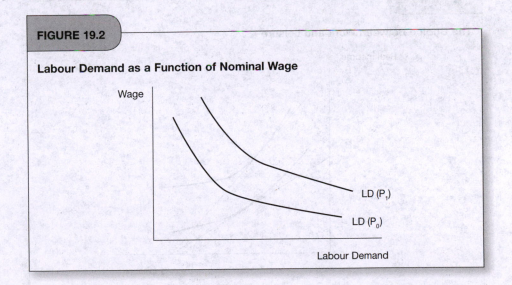

19.2.2. Labour Supply in the Classical Model

The difference between the Classical and the basic Keynesian approaches lies in the labour supply functions used in these models. In the Classical model, labour supply depends on the real wage, while in the Keynesian case, it is the money wage which is assumed to be fixed. Most standard microeconomic textbooks explain the derivation of labour supply, so we do not discuss it here.

Individuals decide whether they prefer to work or enjoy leisure. This choice in the labour market is represented by the labour supply function. In the macro sense, all the individual labour supply functions are combined together to form the aggregate labour supply function. An individual maximizes his/her utility function which is based on leisure and real income and written as

$$y = (W/P)(H-Z) \tag{19.4}$$

where employment L, in terms of hours worked, is given by subtracting hours of leisure, Z, from the total available hours, H. The work–leisure decision is depicted in Figure 19.3a.

In Figure 19.3a, leisure hours are measured to the right along the horizontal axis while real income is measured along the vertical axis. B_0 and B_1 are the budget lines. With an increase in the wage rate, income increases and the budget line rotates to the right since at zero leisure, income is higher when measured up along the vertical axis from the origin. U_0, U_1, etc. are indifference curves for the combination of real income and leisure for an individual. Less income would need to be compensated by more leisure.

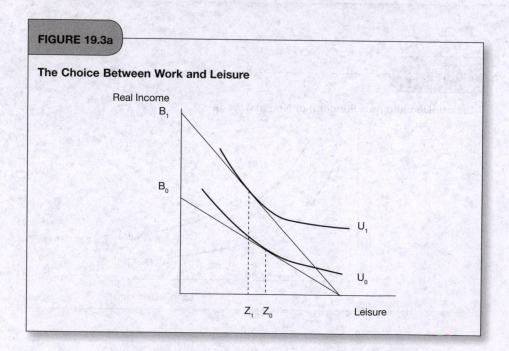

FIGURE 19.3a

The Choice Between Work and Leisure

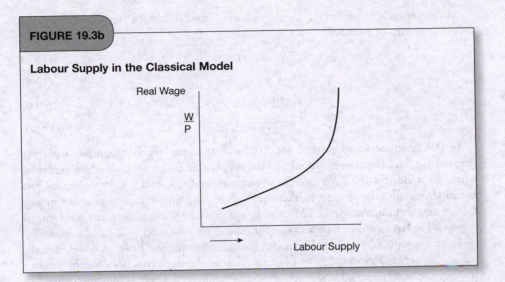

FIGURE 19.3b

Labour Supply in the Classical Model

At the initial real wage level, B_0 is the budget line and its tangential point with the family of indifference curves provides the choice between leisure and work. The chosen hours of leisure are Z_0 on the horizontal axis. The hours of work will be equal to total hours 'H' minus 'Z_0' which has clearly arisen because of the hike in real wage.

Now, with an increase in the real wage rate, the budget line swings clockwise. The new tangential point between the budget line and the family of indifference curves is at a reduced choice of leisure, given by Z_1. The labour supply function is derived from the individual worker's utility maximization. Summing across individuals gives a similar aggregate labour supply function, drawn in Figure 19.3b.

At very high real wages, the labour supply function becomes almost vertical as there is increasing reluctance to sacrifice leisure for income.

Note that just as we did for the labour demand function, the labour supply function can be drawn against the nominal wage. Then, a rise in price (the goods price, P) will shift the function up and consequently less labour will be offered at the unchanged nominal wage as the real wage has fallen due to the price rise.

The labour supply function slopes up to the right in the real wage–labour supply Figure 19.3b, it would slope up to the right even in the money wage–labour supply diagram. A rise in price reduces the real wage and labour supply falls along the labour supply curve in the Figure 19.3b with real wage on the vertical axis. In the Figure using the money wage, the labour supply curve moves up with a rise in the goods price.

Labour market equilibrium in the Classical model is given as

$$Ls\ (W/P) = Ld\ (W/P) \tag{19.5}$$

with both labour supply and labour demand depending on the real wage. This can be expressed as

$$F(W/P) = G(W/P) \tag{19.6}$$

Macroeconomic equilibrium in the Classical model can be represented by the following system of equations:

$$y = C + I + G \tag{19.7}$$

$$y = y \ (L, \ K\text{-}) \tag{19.8}$$

$$M/P = Md \ (r, \ y) \tag{19.9}$$

$$f(W/P) = g \ (W/P) \tag{19.10}$$

In the aforementioned system, the first two equations represent output from the demand (i.e., the IS curve equation) and the supply side (from the production function, where K- stands for the fixed amount of short-run capital stock). Combining the two equations provides the product market equilibrium. The third equation gives the money market equilibrium, that is, the LM curve equation where y is income and r is the rate of interest. The last equation represents labour market equilibrium.

From the reduced form of this model, we can solve for the three variables, namely, wages, 'W', price 'P' and the rate of interest 'r' from the three equations for the product market, the money market and labour market equilibrium. There is full employment in the sense that there is no involuntary employment and the hours offered for work are employed, the wage adjusting to equate the supply and demand for labour. There could be voluntary unemployment in the sense that more hours of work are not offered as labour supply at the prevailing wage.

Demand management policies are fruitless in the Classical model as output is fixed at the level corresponding to full employment. Consider an increase in the money supply, intended to expand output.

In the IS–LM diagram of Figure 19.4a, the LM curve moves out. The new intersection with the IS curve is at a higher output. This corresponds to a shift outward of the aggregate demand curve in Figure 19.4b. At the higher output, there is more labour demand also. This corresponds to a shift outwards of the labour demand curve (drawn against the nominal wage as in Figure 19.1) in Figure 19.4c.

Now, the demand shift, captured in Figure 19.4b, pushes up the price. This causes an upward shift in the labour supply function, which continues until the real wage corresponding to the full employment level is restored. In the money market diagram, Figure 19.4a, the LM curve moves back up due to the price rise (which means a fall in the real money supply) and this continues till the new equilibrium corresponding to full employment output y*. In the supply–demand diagram of Figure 19.5b, the supply curve moves up due to the fall in the real wage (due to the rise and the resulting fall in labour supply), until output is back to y*.

All that finally happens with the *monetary expansion* is that the nominal variables P, W and r rise in value. But the real variables remain unchanged. The real wage returns to the level compatible with full employment, given the level of technology and capital stock and output is also comes back to the full employment level.

In the Classical model, a demand expansion raises the price. The labour supply curve rises until the real wage is restored. There is no increase in output or employment. All nominal variables are higher in value.

Monetary expansion is the increase in the money supply by the central bank's expansionary monetary policy.

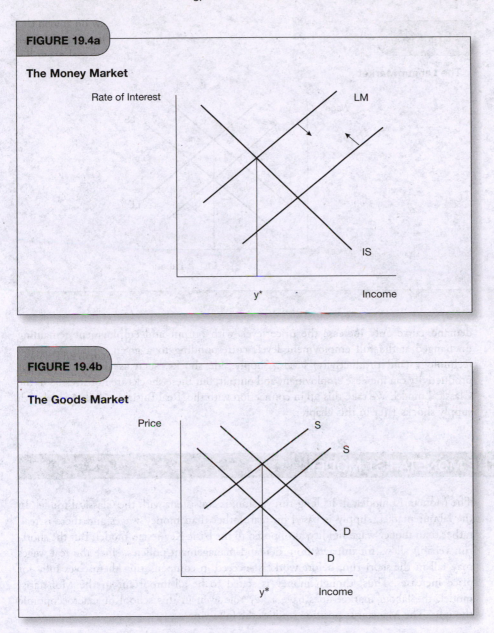

FIGURE 19.4a

The Money Market

FIGURE 19.4b

The Goods Market

Real wage rigidity: When the real wage is rigid, if the price level is increased from an initial equilibrium situation, so that the real wage falls, the money wage rises over time until the real wage is restored to its initial equilibrium value.

What we can see is that the supply curve in the goods market can be considered to be vertical at the full employment level. Expansionary demand policies which shift up the

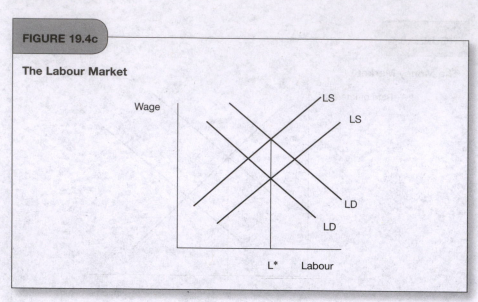

FIGURE 19.4c

The Labour Market

demand curve only increase the price level, with output and employment remaining unchanged at the full employment levels corresponding to a given capital stock and technology (and productivity) levels. Supply side shocks, such as changes in labour productivity can increase employment and output, but these shocks are not stressed in the Classical model. We take this up in connection with the 'Real Business Cycle Model with supply shocks' later in this chapter.

19.3. THE MONETARIST MODEL

The Monetarist model, in its long-run version, is consistent with the Classical model. In the labour market, supply is based on real, rather than money wages and there is real, rather than money wage rigidity, as opposed to the basic Keynesian model. But the short-run version allows for impacts from demand management policies, since the real wages may fall in the short-run, before workers succeed in compensating themselves fully for price increases. Thus, though money is stated to be all-important in the Monetarist model, the labour market does have a key role even in this school of macroeconomic thought. The Monetarist position implies the following:

1. Money is the dominant influence in the economy. It can influence output and employment in the short-run, while fiscal policy is not effective in demand management even in the short-run. In fact, the Monetarists posit a direct relation between money supply and output, working through consumption demand, not merely an indirect link through the interest rate and investment demand.

2. In the long-run, money is the key influence on inflation, but resembles the Classical model in that employment and output are fixed at the full employment levels.
3. Extending the Monetarist arguments to the global economy, domestic money supply expansions can increase inflation levels in the global economy and not just the national economy through balance of payments effects.

In the Monetarist model, money supply expansion is effective in increasing output in the short-run, but fiscal policy is not. Here, money also enters into the consumption function positively. The model gives classical results for the long-run with money being the main determinant of inflation.

The long-run in the discussion in this chapter refers to a time period which is long enough for all actors in the economy to adjust their demands, for workers to revise their age contracts etc. It is still not long enough a period for the accumulation of the economy's capital stock due to investment.

19.3.1. The Monetarist Model in the Short-run

The Monetarist position that monetary policy is effective in affecting output, while fiscal policy is ineffective, can be explained using the IS–LM diagram.

As can be seen from Figure 19.5a, the LM curve has been drawn vertical, indicating that at high interest rate levels almost the entire stock of money holdings is used for transaction purposes and the interest rate elasticity of money demand is close to zero. So, with a small increase in income, a large interest rate rise is needed to maintain equilibrium in the money market, making the LM curve almost vertical. As regards the IS curve, it is drawn almost

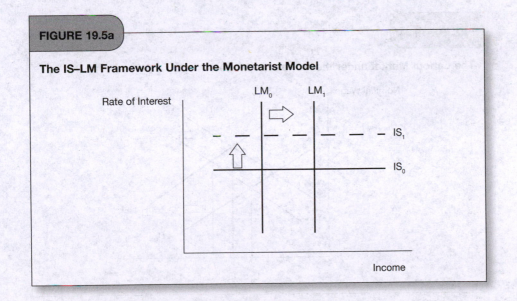

FIGURE 19.5a

The IS–LM Framework Under the Monetarist Model

horizontal, under the assumption that investment responds strongly to interest rate changes (brought about by changes in the all-important variable, money supply).

As can be seen in Figure 19.5a, an increase in the money supply moves the LM curve right and is highly effective in increasing output. A shift of the IS to the right following an expansion in government spending has no effect when the LM curve is vertical.

In the product and labour markets we see these effects in the equilibrium position shown in Figures 19.5b and 19.5c, respectively.

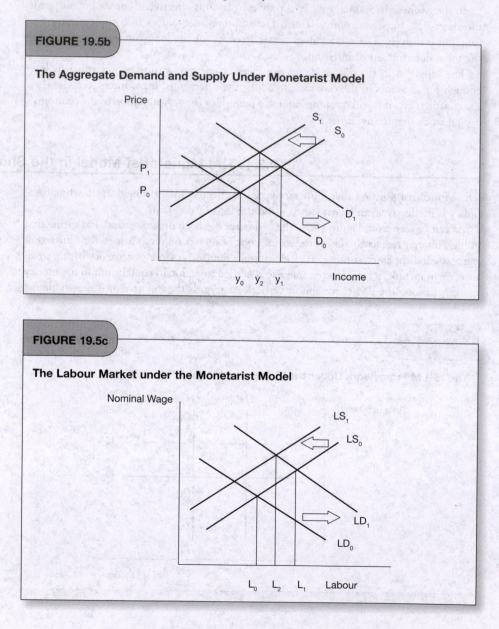

FIGURE 19.5b

The Aggregate Demand and Supply Under Monetarist Model

FIGURE 19.5c

The Labour Market under the Monetarist Model

In Figure 19.5b, the money supply increase causes the aggregate demand curve to shift to the right, increasing output to y_1 and price to P_1.

Note that, in the Monetarist approach, this demand shift is due to a direct effect as well as an indirect effect. The indirect effect is the impact of the money supply increase on the interest rate, pushing it down and causing an increase in investment demand. This is captured by the increase in output at the new intersection of the new LM curve and the old IS curve in Figure 19.5a.

The shift to the right of the aggregate demand curve in the Monetarist model is also due to a direct effect, that on consumption spending of an increase in the money supply. In this model, the aggregate consumption function (with only one final good) may be written as

$$C = C(y, M/P) \qquad (19.11)$$

So, an increase in the money supply has a direct effect on total spending, through consumption, over and above the money $\rightarrow$ interest rate $\rightarrow$ investment $\rightarrow$ aggregate expenditure effect. Actually, the impact is just like that of an increase in government spending wherein the IS curve and the aggregate demand curve shift to the right.

Note that the direct effect of the increase in money supply (with increases in the money supply having a direct expansive effect on consumption expenditure) on aggregate demand is not operational under the Monetarist assumptions about the ineffectiveness of fiscal policy: with the LM curve assumed to be vertical, shifts to the right of the IS curve does not increase aggregate demand in the economy. Thus, the usual Monetarist assumptions themselves rule out this direct effect of monetary policy on aggregate demand!

The shift of the demand curve to the right leads to a price increase, with further developments. See the labour market Figure 19.5c.

The rise in price lowers the real wage and increases labour demand, which shifts the labour demand curve to the right (in this figure with the money wage) and employment rises to L_1.

But now workers start demanding compensation for the price increase and thus the labour supply curve moves up since the real wage has fallen. In the short-run, the fall in the real wage is not totally neutralized and employment rises to L_2 (down from L_1), in the short-run equilibrium situation. (Also, since the price rise reduces real money supply, the direct effect on consumption of the original increase in the money supply is reduced, moving the IS curve—and hence the demand curve back to some extent. This effect has not been included in Figure 19.5b).

Such a development in the labour market is reflected in the goods market, where the supply curve moves up, thereby reducing the equilibrium output from y_1 to y_2. (Note: The LM curve will also shift back, but not all the way, with the price rise, increasing the interest rate (not shown here).

Short-run results for the Monetarist model reveal therefore that a money supply expansion increases aggregate demand, raising the price. The labour supply curve moves up, but not enough to keep real wages constant. Output and employment also rise.

19.3.2. The Monetarist Model in the Long-run

The Monetarist model replicates the effects of the Classical model in the long-run. Essentially, the supply curve becomes vertical at the full employment level, fixed for a given level of capital stock, technology and labour productivity. Short-run increases in output due to the expansionary monetary policy are completely reversed, the mechanism operating as seen in Figures 19.6a, b, c and d. In the long-run, the supply curve becomes vertical in the Monetarist model and thus demand expansion only affects the price.

Consider an expansion of the money supply, which increases aggregate demand by pushing out the LM curve and hence the demand curve (the direct link may also be operational in shifting the demand curve). We do not consider an expansionary fiscal policy, since under Monetarist assumptions it does not increase demand (a shift in the IS curve does not push put the demand curve, under the vertical LM curve assumption).

The excess demand in the goods market raises the price and lowers the real wage, thereby shifting out the labour demand curve.

But the rise in price reduces the real money supply and the LM curve starts shifting back up. In the labour market, workers reduce supply as the real wage has fallen and the labour supply curve shifts up. The upward shift of the labour supply curve stops only when the flexible money wage rate has risen to a level where the real wage is back at the initial level.

Thus, in the long-run equilibrium, employment and output are back to the original levels. These levels correspond to the long-run equilibrium levels consistent with the given

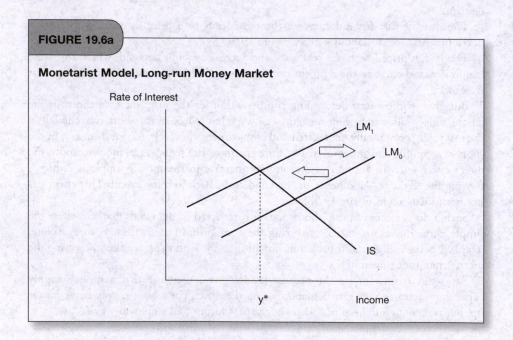

FIGURE 19.6a

Monetarist Model, Long-run Money Market

FIGURE 19.6b

Monetarist Model, Long-run Goods Market

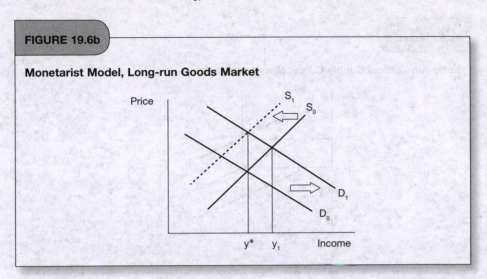

FIGURE 19.6c

Monetarist Model Long-run Labour Market

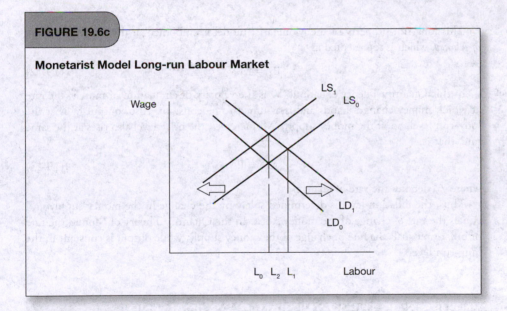

levels of capital stock and technology. All that has been achieved by an expansionary monetary policy is to drive up nominal price and the wage levels.

The long-run for the Monetarist model: A money supply expansion moves the demand curve right, raising price and output initially. But the labour supply curve moves up until the real wage is restored in the labour market. In the new equilibrium, output and the real wage are back to the original levels with higher price and money wage levels.

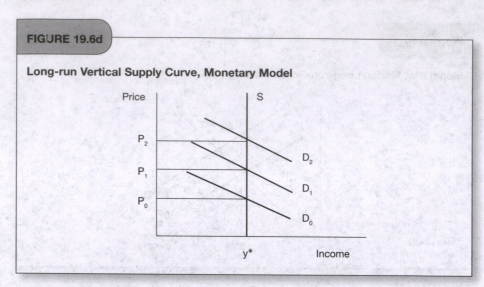

FIGURE 19.6d

Long-run Vertical Supply Curve, Monetary Model

This long-run property of the Monetarist model is embodied in the *Quantity Theory of Money*, which is represented as

$$P.y = M.V \qquad (19.12)$$

The Quantity Theory of Money states that the price level is directly related to the quantity of money in an economy: MV = PQ, where V is the velocity and Y is the real GDP.

In this Quantity Theory equation, 'V' is the velocity of circulation of money, the rate at which money changes hands and is assumed to be constant. Also, output 'y' is at the long-run level. So, if the money supply, 'M' increases, the price level also rises at the same rate, that is,

$$M^{\wedge} = P^{\wedge} \qquad (19.13)$$

where '∧' denotes the rate of change.

Thus, the inflation level is determined solely by the change in the money supply and equals the rate of change of the money stock. In the Quantity Theory of Money, the rate of inflation equals the rate of change of the money supply, while output is constant in the long-run level.

19.4. A SYNTHESIS OF THE KEYNESIAN, CLASSICAL AND MONETARIST APPROACHES

The IS–LM model, supplemented by the supply side with an upward sloping supply curve actually represents a synthesis of the Keynesian and Classical approaches and has retained its popularity despite attacks from new Keynesian and classical approaches. Let us see how such a synthesis works in practice. We will also encompass the monetary model in the synthesis, including a role for fiscal policy and not rejecting it as ineffective as in the monetary approach.

In the synthesis, output is not completely demand-determined as in the basic Keynesian model of Chapter 3, with a horizontal supply curve. Nor is output determined as in the Classical or Monetary model, with a vertical supply curve (in the long-run version), or affected solely by monetary policy, as in the Monetary model, with no role for fiscal policy. Such a supply side formulation implies that the money wage is not fixed as in the Keynesian model, unresponsive to price changes. Also, the real wage can fall as workers are unable to compensate fully for price changes, at least within a short period.

A synthesis of the Keynesian, Monetary and Classical models is when the demand curve is not horizontal and the supply curve is not vertical. Fiscal policy is also effective, not just monetary policy, so that the LM curve is not vertical. The real wages can also fall.

The system of equations representing such a synthesis will be the classical model of Equations 19.7 to 19.10, but with the last Equation 19.10 altered to reflect the assumptions of the present model. Equation 19.10 may be rewritten to represent the labour market equilibrium in this model as

$$f(W/P) = g(W, P) \tag{19.14}$$

In Equation (19.13), labour demand depends only on the real wage while labour supply depends separately on the money wage and the price. Such a representation, in a simple way, can capture the response in labour supply to a price change, namely, the money wage would rise as the goods price rises, but there is no constraint that it would rise so as to compensate fully for the price rise and keep the real wage constant.

Note that keeping the labour supply dependent only on the money wage represents the Keynesian approach. In this case, there will not be any change in labour supply as the price rises. Equations (19.6), (19.7), (19.8) and (19.13) describe the synthesis of the Keynesian and Classical models. Let us now see the effects of an expansionary fiscal policy (which would have had no effect in the monetary model) in this model. The effects are captured in Figures 19.7a, 19.7b and 19.7c.

Consider now an expansionary fiscal policy in the form of an increase in government spending. The IS curve moves out in Figure 19.7a, which is reflected in the outward shift of the aggregate demand curve in Figure 19.7b. The price level rises and output also rises as seen from the new equilibrium at the intersection of the new demand curve and the (old) supply curve.

The rise in the goods price lowers the real wage of workers. Labour supply reduces, with the labour supply curve moving up in the labour market Figure 19.7c, which has money wage on the vertical axis. But, in a short period, workers are unable to compensate fully for the price increase with equivalent rates of increase in wage demands. This could also reflect the aggregated situation with real wage rigidity in some sectors (where wages rise to compensate fully for price rises) and money wage rigidity, or at least some real wage flexibility in some other sectors. Employment, which had risen (or would have risen) to L_1 before the wage responded to the price rise, is now at L_2 and does not fall back to the original level of L_0.

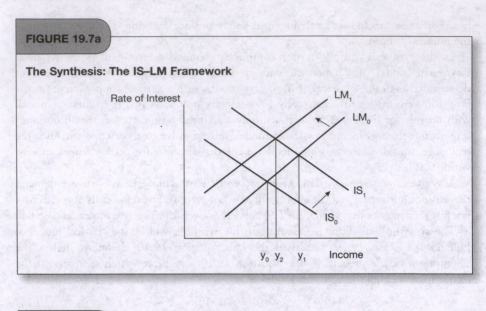

FIGURE 19.7a

The Synthesis: The IS–LM Framework

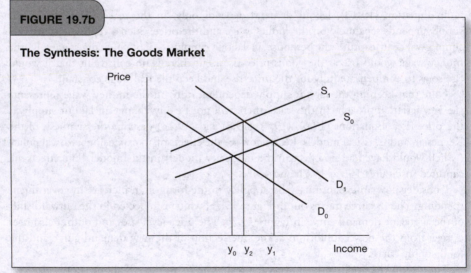

FIGURE 19.7b

The Synthesis: The Goods Market

These developments are reflected in the goods market Figure 19.7b. The reduction in labour supply is seen in the upward shift of the supply curve. Output rises only to y_2, instead of to y_1 (in the absence of the price rise compensating the wage rise). The price rise also causes the LM curve to move up in Figure 19.7a, where it cuts the new IS curve at the output level y_2.

Thus, in this synthesis of the Keynesian, Classical and Monetary approaches, fiscal policy is effective in affecting output as would also be monetary policy. This is in

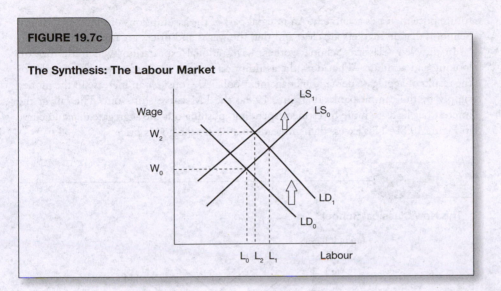

FIGURE 19.7c

The Synthesis: The Labour Market

contrast to the Classical and Monetary (in the long-run) approaches where output could be influenced by demand management policies. This also contrasts with the Monetary approach in which fiscal policy has no effect on output even in the short-run. But, even in such a synthesis, the long-run equilibrium will have to accommodate further labour market demands and will tend to gravitate towards that in the Classical and Monetary approaches.

The synthesis: both fiscal and monetary policies can affect output in the short-run, not just monetary policy as in the Monetarist model. The long-run results resemble those in the Classical and Monetarist models.

19.5. THE FUTURE'S OURS' TO SEE: NEW CLASSICAL ECONOMICS AND RATIONAL EXPECTATIONS BY THE LABOUR MARKET PARTICIPANTS

The economists of the *New Classical School* do not accept the distinction between the short and the long-run which are seen in the synthesis of the Keynesian and Classical approaches and in the monetary model. They argue that such a distinction (between the short and the long-run) is based on the assumption of a flawed expectations formation mechanism. In the New Classical approach, agents will not base their price forecasts on past values, which will in turn lead to wrong forecasts.

In short, the New Classical approach assumes that agents, especially workers, will base their price forecasts on all available information, even about forthcoming monetary and fiscal policies, so that their expectations are rational. Their expectations are forward looking rather than backward looking, taking into account only past values of variables. With such forward-looking rational expectations, workers would then be able to judge

The New Classical School assumes that all markets clear and all wages and prices are flexible.

future price increases accurately. An integral part of the assumptions of the New Classical School is that all markets are clear and that the wages and prices are not sticky.

In the New Classical School, workers have rational expectations which are forward looking and accurate. What does the assumption of such *rational expectations* imply for the results of aggregate demand management policies? Consider an increase in the money supply by the central bank. In Figure 19.8a, the LM curve shifts out. The fall in the interest rate leads to more investment spending, pushing out the aggregate demand curve in Figure 19.8b. This excess demand leads to a rise in the goods price.

Rational expectations are decisions made by agents based on a forward-looking attitude, with the ability to judge future prices accurately.

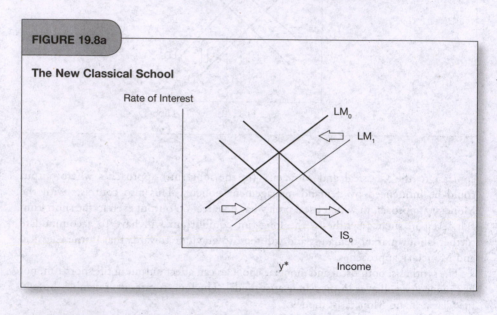

FIGURE 19.8a

The New Classical School

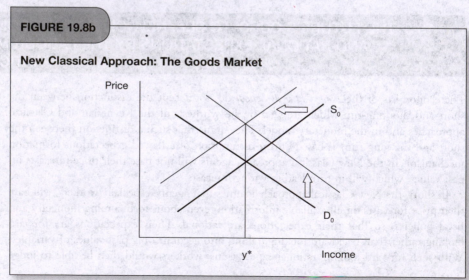

FIGURE 19.8b

New Classical Approach: The Goods Market

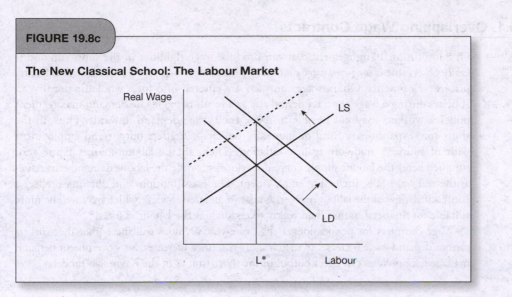

FIGURE 19.8c

The New Classical School: The Labour Market

Here is where rational expectations on the part of the workers comes in. The workers correctly anticipate forthcoming expansionary demand policies and the extent of the price rise. They demand full compensation for the price rise and do not commit themselves to a fixed wage rate for a longer period of time, having anticipated government intentions correctly (the central bank cannot surprise the workers with a sudden decision to increase the money supply and lower real wages).

In the labour market Figure 19.8c, the labour supply curve moves up until the real wage is restored and this happens at the original level of employment. This employment level also corresponds to the original level of output with the supply curve moving back up in the goods market Figure 19.8b (the LM curve also moves back up in response to the price rise). Thus, an expansionary monetary policy is ineffective in expanding output even in the relatively short-run.

Hence, the assumption of rational expectations leads to ineffective aggregate demand management policies in the short as well as the long-run, in contrast to the Keynesian approach and even the monetary approach (in which at least monetary policy can be effective in the short-run). Demand policies cannot affect output even in the short-run in the New Classical Approach.

19.6. NEW KEYNESIAN ECONOMICS AND OTHER LABOUR MARKET THEORIES

The New Keynesians have criticized the New Classical School for ignoring certain aspects of real-life institutional arrangements pertaining to the labour market. They point out that such institutional realities can create wage stickiness even if the assumption of rational expectations is (reluctantly!) accepted.

19.6.1. Overlapping Wage Contracts

One institutional arrangement that can produce wage rigidities in the short-run and is easily observable is *long-run wage contracts* which can overlap across periods with differing price developments. Often, wage contracts are entered into for a whole financial year. If prices during a wage contract period rise as a result of aggregate demand management policies, workers may not be able to revise their wage demand upwards. Thus, in the short-run, expansionary fiscal or monetary policies can affect output and employment with of course a trade-off against inflation. Then, in the labour market figure (not supplied here) the labour supply curve does not rise, while the labour demand curve rises as the real wage falls, increasing employment. These assumptions and outcomes reflect a contractual view of the labour market, as against an auction view, which may well be more suitable for financial, rather than real markets such as the labour market.

Wage contracts for periods longer than one year or more will mean that the workers cannot demand wage increases to match short-run price increases. So, government demand management policies can affect output in the short-run, as in the Keynesian model.

19.6.2. The Efficiency Wage Model

In this model, the efficiency of workers depends on the real wage they earn. Concomitantly, it is the efficient units, rather than mere numbers of labour which enters the production function. Henry Ford, in 1914, is said to have followed the efficiency wage concept and paid his automobile workers above-market level wages.

Formally, efficiency 'Φ' depends on the real wage:

$$\Phi = \Phi \ (W/P) \tag{19.15}$$

The production function then takes the form

$$y = f \ (\Phi L, K) \tag{19.16}$$

Firms are able to pay workers above-market clearing wages because it increases their productivity. The payment of efficiency wages also boosts employee morale and reduces turnover.

The efficiency wage is the real wage which maximizes the efficiency units of labour bought with each rupee of the wage bill. This will be achieved when

$$[\% \text{ change in } \Phi]/[\% \text{ change in } (W/P)] = 1 \tag{19.17}$$

The level of the real wage at which Equation (19.16) is satisfied is the *efficiency wage*.

This model can support the money wage rigidity assumption in the basic Keynesian model when combined with the so-called 'Sticky Price Model of Menu Costs'. In the 'sticky price' model, profit-maximizing firms do not change prices often due to the costs associated with changing price tags often and the risk of alienating customers. This implies that to keep the real wage at the efficiency wage, above the market-clearing level, the money wage also has to remain unchanged. Thus, when aggregate demand falls, the money wage does not adjust down to maintain labour market equilibrium and involuntary employment (is the existence of unemployment even though labour supply is forthcoming) is created.

In the 'Efficiency Wage Model, the wage is set at the *efficiency wage*, higher than the market clearing wage, to maximize the labour efficiency units per rupee of the wage bill. This creates *wage rigidities* in the basic Keynesian model.

Efficient units of labour are those adjusted labour units which enter the production function and are written as the efficiency of labour times the actual physical units of labour used in production.

'Wage rigidity' refers to the downward inflexibility of wages by the application of power to negotiate by unions to retain existing wages.

19.6.3. The Insider–Outsider Models

In insider–outsider models, the labour union members are the 'insiders' who demand real wages above the market-clearing levels to maximize their utility. Employers do not replace insiders with 'outsiders' having no union affiliation due to costs of recruitment and training.

However, all insiders may not remain employed when there is a drop in aggregate demand. So, insiders can become outsiders because lay-offs may become permanent. Also, since outsiders cannot exert downward pressure on the real wages, higher unemployment persists, which is a case of 'hysteresis', a term that is discussed later in this chapter when the concept of the 'natural rate of unemployment' is taken up. It follows that insider–outsider models can also vindicate the non-market clearing wage assumption of the Keynesian models.

'*Insiders*', are union members who keep the wages high and the real wages remain rigid even with higher unemployment. 'Outsiders', are unemployed workers without affiliation to any union. When unemployment increases, their ranks may swell by the newly unemployed workers, who cannot press down wages. Thus, the wage rigidity assumption of Keynesian models is supported.

Insiders are union members who keep wages high and real wages rigid with their power of collective bargaining.

19.7. REAL BUSINESS CYCLE MODELS WITH EXOGENOUS LABOUR PRODUCTIVITY SHOCKS

These models postulate that it is changes in the supply side factors which lie behind fluctuations in employment and output, in contrast to the Classical and traditional Keynesian models where demand shocks (changes in aggregate demand) cause such fluctuations.

Consider the case in which there is an exogenous reduction in labour productivity. This shifts the production function to the left in Figure 19.9a and the labour demand function to the left in Figure 19.9b, since at the same employment level, a lower real wage is needed to equal the lower productivity level, which is the profit-maximizing condition for employment by the firm. The net result is a fall in employment (and

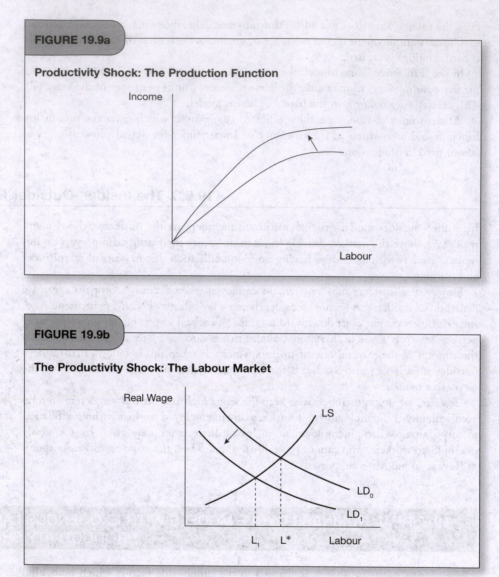

FIGURE 19.9a

Productivity Shock: The Production Function

FIGURE 19.9b

The Productivity Shock: The Labour Market

Supply side shocks are changes in the total stock of labour or capital, or in the productivity of these factors of production, or exogenous technical change.

output) in the new equilibrium situation, caused by a *supply side shock*, namely, a fall in productivity.

However, critics have pointed out that the unemployment which materializes with such shocks is voluntary in nature, when workers remain on their labour supply curves while in the Keynesian models unemployment is involuntary, with the outcome off the labour supply curves, as shown in Figure 19.10.

In Figure 19.10, the money wage is rigid at W_0 (the figure is drawn with money wage on the vertical axis. A fall in productivity will require a fall in the real wage, and at a given

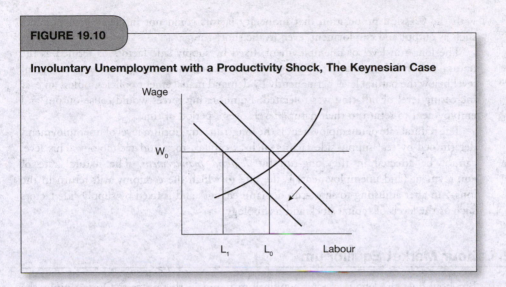

FIGURE 19.10

Involuntary Unemployment with a Productivity Shock, The Keynesian Case

price, this is brought about by a downward shift of the labour demand curve). There is involuntary unemployment, at the employment level L_0, since the outcome on the labour demand curve is off the labour supply curve. A productivity fall moves the labour demand curve down, increasing involuntary unemployment at the lower employment level of L_1.

The real business cycle model depicted in Figures 19.9a and 19.9b has been criticized because the large unemployment levels noted in the downturns would require a very flat labour supply curve, which is empirically not substantiated. Critics say that the Keynesian model with wage rigidity is more likely to explain high unemployment creation in the downturns.

The Real Business Cycle model points to supply side shocks as the main reason for generating unemployment. A fall in labour productivity lowers labour demand thereby causing involuntary unemployment when there is wage rigidity. Supply side shocks are changes in the total stock of labour or capital, or in the productivity of these factors of production, or exogenous technical change, all of which originate on the supply side of the economy. Oil price shocks also fall into this category.

19.8. THE NATURAL RATE OF UNEMPLOYMENT AND LABOUR MARKET EQUILIBRIUM

19.8.1. The Natural Rate of Unemployment

The concept of the *natural rate of unemployment* was developed by Milton Friedman and Edmund Phelps independently. Freidman powerfully stated the monetary proposition that in the long-run, real variables were determined by the real supply side factors such as capital stock and technology and not by monetary factors. But he was not in agreement

The natural rate of employment (and unemployment) is the rate to which the economy will return in the long-run after adjusting to short-run demand changes and is fixed by supply side factors such as the levels of capital stock and technology.

Demand management policies are government policies to stimulate and/or maintain aggregate demand to the full employment level.

with the Classical proposition that monetary factors could not influence real variables such as output and employment, even in the short-run.

The long-run level of unemployment, fixed by supply side factors, is termed as the natural rate. Friedman stated that the government could not maintain an unemployment level below the natural level permanently by demand management policies, unless an ever increasing level of inflation was tolerated. Equilibrating forces would cause output and employment to return to their natural levels over a period of time.

The natural rate of unemployment is the long-run, equilibrium level of unemployment, determined by real supply-side factors such as capital stock and technology. This level cannot be affected in the long-run by *demand management*. The natural rate of employment (and unemployment) is the rate to which the economy will return in the long-run after adjusting to short-run demand changes and is fixed by supply side factors such as the levels of capital stock and technology.

19.8.2. Labour Market Equilibrium

The equilibrium real wage rate is the rate at which labour demand equals labour supply at the natural rate of employment.

But how does the labour market equilibrium figure in this process? Quite simply, the natural rate of employment (and unemployment) has a property that it is consistent with equilibrium in the structure of real wage rates; that is, labour demand equals labour supply at the natural rate of employment, at the *equilibrium real wage rate*. The economy returns to this real wage rate level, as was seen in the discussion of the Classical model, after a sufficiently long period has passed after a monetary or other demand shock. So, in Figure 19.11, $(W/P)^*$ is the equilibrium real wage rate in the long-run and L^* is the natural rate of employment. Again, as seen in the discussion of the Classical and Monetary models, any shock that moves the labour demand curve outwards will be matched in the

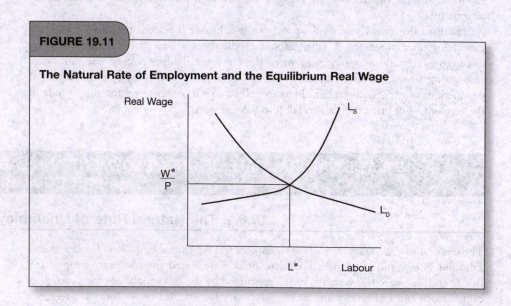

FIGURE 19.11

The Natural Rate of Employment and the Equilibrium Real Wage

long-run by an upward move of the labour supply curve that will restore the equilibrium real wage rate and the equilibrium level of employment.

In Figure 19.11, the real wage equals the MPL along the demand curve, while the labour supply curve is based on W/P_e, where P_e is the expected goods price level. If P_e changes, the labour supply curve shifts so that the real wage is unchanged and this corresponds to the natural level of employment. The natural rate of unemployment is obtained as the difference between the labour force and the natural level of employment, divided by the labour force.

The natural rate of unemployment is not unchanging, even when supply side shocks are absent. Changes in labour mobility, government programs in retraining and skill development, extended periods of higher unemployment levels, the level of unemployment benefits etc., cause the natural rate of unemployment to shift over time, as has been seen in the European countries. High unemployment benefits seem to increase the natural rate, as workers are less prone to seek work actively.

The natural rate of unemployment corresponds to the equilibrium real wage rate in the labour market, with labour supply matching demand.

The equilibrium real wage is the real wage that corresponds to the natural rate of employment and to which the economy returns after changes in the real wages due to demand side shocks and the subsequent adjustments.

19.8.3. Hysteresis

The phenomenon of 'hysteresis' occurs when past unemployment influences current unemployment levels. Workers, who have been unemployed for long, tend to drop away, stop searching and become passive, even though they are formally registered as job seekers. They may also face resistance from the insiders who block their re-entry. The natural rate of unemployment has been increasing in Europe in recent years and this phenomenon, where past unemployment levels influence current levels and tend to become permanent, is very much part of the explanation. Figure 19.12a may help clarify what happens when hysteresis is present.

In Figure 19.12a, a fall in aggregate demand lowers the aggregate product price level. Labour demand falls along the labour demand curve, to L_A, corresponding to the higher real wage (since the money wage does not fall, while the price does). Clearly, at point A, involuntary unemployment would be created, since labour supply is more than labour demand at the higher real wage.

But there is no wage rigidity in the Classical model so as unemployment develops, the real wage falls back along AE on the labour demand curve, until the original labour market equilibrium, 'E', is restored. The real wage also goes back to the original level, corresponding to the natural level of employment L^*.

In Figure 19.12b, labour demand falls along the labour demand curve as the goods price falls (due to a fall in aggregate demand) and the real wage rises at the given money wage. Unlike in the Classical adjustment process in Figure 19.12a, real wages do not fall despite higher unemployment (perhaps due to insider activity) and involuntary unemployment (= AB) is created. If this persists for a long time, some workers become

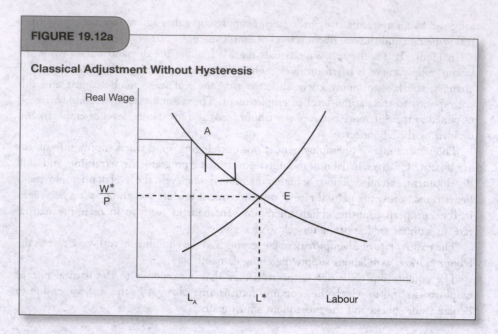

FIGURE 19.12a

Classical Adjustment Without Hysteresis

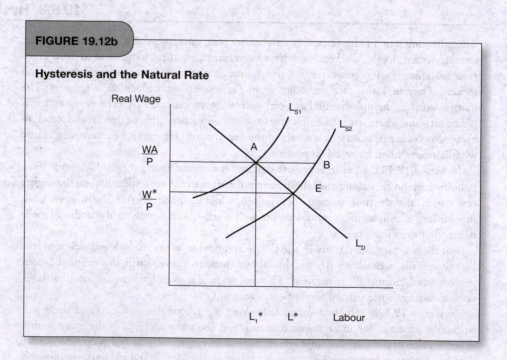

FIGURE 19.12b

Hysteresis and the Natural Rate

inactive and drop out of active search, so that the labour supply curve shifts up (while the labour force does not change). So, the natural rate of employment reduces from L^* to L_1^* and this occurs due to hysteresis.

The phenomenon of '*hysteresis*', can explain the increase in the natural rate of unemployment in the Western economies and refers to the influence of past unemployment levels on current levels. Long unemployed workers become passive and stop searching, effectively reducing the labour supply and thereby increasing the natural rate of unemployment (reducing the natural rate of employment).

> Hysteresis is a phenomenon in which past rates of unemployment, which have existed for long periods of time, affect the current level of unemployment.

19.9. CONCLUSION

This chapter gives a brief overview of the different schools of macroeconomic thought, ranging from the Keynesian and the monetary schools to the New Classical and Keynesian approaches. The assumptions adopted about labour market mechanisms, including the formation of expectations about future price developments, are the key elements which differentiate these schools from one another. Other presumptions such as the overriding role of money also make their presence felt in such contrasts, particularly in the short-run period.

While economists schooled in the macroeconomics of developed nations do not subscribe to the basic Keynesian model of Chapter 3, a synthesis of the Keynesian and Classical (and the related Monetary) approaches is quite acceptable to them. Such a synthesis has been presented in this chapter. Empirical evidence would also reject the die-hard Monetary School with its zero interest rate elasticity of demand for money (and the implied vertical LM curve) the estimates of this elasticity tending to fall around -0.7 for the US economy.

Generally speaking, the Keynesian approach is more favoured in developing countries while the Classical and the Monetarist views that demand expansions only serve to raise prices in the long-run and are ineffective in increasing employment and output, are not seriously taken (perhaps because we are all dead in the long-run, as Keynes once famously said!). But the adoption of expansionary fiscal policies in these countries run up against government budget constraints and monetary policy is toothless as financial markets are undeveloped, so that the money $\rightarrow$ interest rate $\rightarrow$ investment link is not operational.

The Monetary and the Classical approaches have found more adherents among policy-makers and economists in industrialized nations. Hence the emphasis has been on removing labour market rigidities and increasing productivity to arrest a gradual increase in the natural rate of unemployment (though, of course, the aftermath of the financial crisis has seen a revival of support for Keynesian policies, manifested in massive government spending plans as in the United States).

These labour market reforms and policies are essentially supply-side initiatives. It may be noted that supply-side policies are also very important in developing nations, since in these countries, policies have to be growth oriented in contrast to economic scenario in the developed nations where macroeconomic stabilization and the trade-off between employment and inflation are the key concerns. Technical change, an agent of economic growth, as seen in Chapter 4, can bring about concomitant increases in real wages and employment (and output), as can be seen from the Real Business Cycle model subjected to a positive labour productivity shock, which may be due to technical progress. It is interesting to note in this context that the recent growth in India has been overwhelmingly due to technical progress, as was the case in the developed Western economies during the heydays of their economic expansion.

SUMMARY

- The key differences between the various schools, monetary and Classical models etc., is due to the differences in labour market assumptions, particularly in the short-run. The differences of macroeconomic thought and their policy recommendations can be traced to modelling of the labour market. So, we can say that the labour market is the kingpin of macroeconomic models. The various schools of macroeconomic thought are represented by the Keynesian, Monetary, Classical, the New Keynesian and the New Classical schools.

- In the Classical model, labour supply depends on the real wage, while in the Keynesian case, it is the money wage which is assumed to be fixed. In the Classical model, a demand expansion raises price but no increase in output or employment. Supply side shocks, such as changes in labour productivity can increase employment and output, but these shocks are not stressed in the Classical model.

- The Monetarist model, in its long-run version, is consistent with the Classical model. In the labour market, supply is based on real, rather than money wages and there is real money wage rigidity, as opposed to the basic Keynesian model.

- Under the Monetarist assumptions, fiscal policy is ineffective. The rise in price lowers the real wage and increases labour demand, which shifts the labour demand curve to the right. But then workers demand compensation for the price increase. The labour supply curve moves up since the real wage falls. In the short-run, the fall in the real wage is not totally neutralized and employment rises in the short-run equilibrium situation.

- The phenomenon of 'hysteresis' occurs when past unemployment influences current unemployment levels. Workers without jobs for long periods, tend to stop their job search and become passive.

- In the short-run, the Monetarists propose that an expansion of money supply increases aggregate demand, raising the price. The labour supply curve moves up, but not enough to keep the real wages constant. Output and employment rise.

- In the long-run for the Monetarist model: expansion in money supply moves the demand curve right, raising price and output initially. But the labour supply curve moves up until the real wage is restored in the labour market. In the new equilibrium, output and the real wage are back to the original levels and the price and money wage levels are higher. This long-run property of the Monetary model is embodied in the Quantity Theory of Money.

- In the synthesis between the Keynesian and Classical schools, output is not completely demand-determined as in the basic Keynesian model, affected solely by monetary policy, as in the Monetarists argue, with no role for fiscal policy.
- The New Classical School does not distinguish between the short and the long-run, visible in the synthesis of the Keynesian and Classical approaches. In the rational expectations formulation, workers are able to judge future price increases accurately. So in the New Classical School all markets clear and the wages and prices are not sticky.
- In the insider–outsider models, labour union members are the 'insiders' who demand real wages above the market-clearing levels to maximize their utility. Employers do not replace insiders with 'outsiders' with no union affiliation due to the cost of recruitment and training. This model supports the money wage rigidity assumption in the basic Keynesian model when combined with the so-called 'Sticky Price Model'.
- The concept of the natural rate of unemployment is the long-run, equilibrium level of unemployment, determined by real supply-side factors such as capital stock and technology. It is obtained as the difference between the labour force and the natural level of employment, expressed as a proportion of the labour force.
- Generally speaking, the Keynesian approach is more favoured in developing countries while the Classical and Monetarist views that demand expansions only serves to raise prices in the long-run and are ineffective in increasing employment and output, are not seriously taken (perhaps because we are all dead in the long-run, as Keynes once famously said!).

KEYWORDS

Labour market	Wage rigidity
Marginal labour product	Insiders
Real wage	Supply side shock
Monetary expansion	Natural rate of unemployment
Rational expectations	Demand management
New classical school	Equilibrium real wage rate
Long-run wage contracts	Hysteresis
Efficiency wage	

CONCEPT CHECK

State whether the following statements are true or false:

1. The real wage equals the marginal labour product along the labour demand curve.
2. The labour supply function slopes up to the right in the real wage–employment space and a rise in price reduces the real wage and increases the labour supply.

3. At very high real wages, the labour supply function becomes almost vertical as there is increasing reluctance to sacrifice leisure for income.

4. In the Classical model, a demand expansion raises prices and then the labour supply curve rises until the real wage is restored.

5. In the Monetarist model, money supply expansion is ineffective in increasing output in the short-run, but fiscal policy is effective.

6. In the long-run, the supply curve becomes vertical in the Monetarist model. Demand expansion only affects the price.

7. If there is a synthesis of the Keynesian, Monetary and Classical models, the demand curve is not horizontal and the supply curve is not vertical. In such a situation fiscal policy is also effective and not just monetary policy.

8. In the New Classical School, workers are supposed to have rational expectations which are forward looking and accurate.

9. If the unions sign wage contracts for longer periods of one year or more, it means that the workers cannot demand wage increases to match short-run price increases. So, government demand management policies can affect output in the short-run, as in the Keynesian model.

10. The Real Business Cycle model points to supply side shocks as the main reason for generating unemployment.

11. The natural rate of unemployment is the long-run, equilibrium level of unemployment, determined by real supply-side factors such as the capital stock and technology. This level cannot be affected in the long-run by demand management.

12. Hysteresis refers to the influence of past unemployment levels on current levels, as workers without jobs become passive and stop searching, effectively reducing labour supply and thus increasing the natural rate of unemployment.

DISCUSSION QUESTIONS

1. Are the outcomes of aggregate demand policies the same in the Classical and the Monetary Models in the short-run? What is the role of the labour market in any distinction in this respect between the two models?

2. Are the outcomes of expansionary fiscal and monetary policies similar in the Keynesian and Monetary models in the short-run? What are the roles played by money and labour market assumptions in this regard?

3. In the neoclassical synthesis of models presented in this chapter, how is the compromise affected for the short-run between (a) the Keynesian and Monetary models? (b) the Keynesian and Classical models?

4. Discuss the effects of a positive labour productivity shock in the Real Business Cycle model.

5. Consider a scenario where labour market participants engage in long-run contracts of one year or more. They also have perfect, rational, forward-looking

expectations about current and future price developments. Can an aggregate demand management initiative by the government or the central bank increase output in the economy in the short-run (of less than a year's time span)?

6. How is the natural level of unemployment affected, if at all, by (a) generous unemployment benefits (b) shorter skill development training and (c) increased inter-regional labour mobility?

7. Will an increase in labour productivity affect the natural rate of unemployment?

8. Has the monetary model been validated for advanced economies? Which criteria have to be satisfied?

9. How can the insider–outsider model be termed New Keynesian?

CHAPTER

Disaggregated Multi-sector Models for Industrial Nations and Developing Countries

LEARNING OBJECTIVES

Upon completion of this chapter, the reader will be able to:

- Understand the limitations inherent in an aggregated model of the type discussed so far and note how disaggregation widens the horizon and scope of macroeconomic analysis.
- Understand the elements and construct a Small Open Economy model and diagram and see how it can produce the phenomenon of unbalanced growth, that is, expansion in one sector and contraction in another thereby crowding out of the other sector.
- Explain the Dutch disease phenomenon, observed in industrial nations such as the Netherlands and the United Kingdom.
- Understand the elements of the Bose model and note the important role played by demand-induced output expansion in a key sector.
- Discuss the suitability of the various multi-sector models to analyse developments in industrial nations and developing countries/emerging markets.

20.1. INTRODUCTION: MULTI-SECTOR MODELS

The models presented so far in this book are at a much aggregated level, considering only one final good. This treatment follows what is prevalent in virtually all textbooks of macroeconomics. However, while key results for fiscal and monetary policy can be derived in such an aggregated framework, rich insights can further be obtained by disaggregating the economy into more sectors. Such disaggregation also makes it possible to choose the appropriate model structure for the country under scrutiny, depending on whether it is a developed nation, an emerging market or a developing nation. In other words, with more disaggregation, it is easier to choose the model so as to fit the structures of countries at varying stages of development.

In what follows, we first recapitulate the main results from the aggregated one-sector models presented in the earlier chapters, in a very brief fashion, to enable comparisons with the multi-sector models to be discussed in this chapter. Then we proceed to present a popular model of the open economy, used extensively in the analyses of developments in industrial nations. Finally, a two sector model designed exclusively to study the problems of developing economies is presented and the model structure and derived policy results compared with the open economy model for an industrial nation.

20.2. POLICY RESULTS IN THE AGGREGATED MODELS

Before venturing to pinpoint the differences in model structure and policy effects in two sector models applied to the developed and developing nations, let us briefly recapitulate the policy results derived in the aggregated models presented up to now in this book.

Consider first the Keynesian model of Chapter 3. The model assumes nominal wage rigidity and therefore, has a flat supply curve. The model therefore is demand determined. An increase in government spending increases aggregate demand and results in higher output and employment. A simple model, but supremely effective in a recession or depression situation such as that in the 1930s, which provided the fertile ground for this brilliant creation by John Maynard Keynes.

Moving on to the IS–LM model, we bring in the financial sector and the supply side explicitly. With nominal wage rigidity, the model again throws up the result of an increase in output and employment following an increase in government spending which could be even in terms of a pay increase for government workers, or an increase in government sector employment. But there is also a structural effect possible. An increase in the interest rate crowds out private investment and hence private sector output. Thus, an expansionary fiscal policy increases the size of the government sector and *crowds out* the private sector (with an expansionary monetary policy, the fall in interest rates prevents this from happening).

The longer-run effects are also discussed. In the longer run, wage rises may catch up with the rise in the price of the final good following an increase in government spending.

Crowding out is the reduction in private investment demand due to a rise in the interest rate caused by an expansionary fiscal policy.

So, in the long-run, the effect on output and employment may not be there at all (is nil). But, the composition of output changes in favour of the government sector, reducing the size of the private sector since investment is crowded out. But in what follows, we will concentrate on the short-run in making model comparisons.

An expansionary fiscal policy increases output and total employment in the aggregate model. The composition of output changes, private investment falls while the government sector expanding.

We now proceed to introduce more disaggregated models of the economy, where there are two final goods produced and consumed.

20.3. TWO SECTOR MODELS

The relative price is the price of a commodity in terms of another, that is, the ratio of two prices.

As already indicated in this chapter, we look at a couple of important two sector models, one suitable for the analysis of an industrialized nation and the other better suited for an emerging market or developing economy. Important two sector models applied to industrial economies often do not seem to be useful in explaining developments in semi-industrialized, or even emerging market economies. The analysis with these models often brings forth a crowding out, rather than a complimentary relation between the various sectors of the economy, which does not usually hold in the case of industrializing countries. The growth process in these nations seems to be better explained by some specifically designed models.

Traded goods are sold and purchased, or are tradable, in the international markets. Traded goods prices are determined in world markets and are beyond the control of individual nations.

Thus, an important difference that emerges between some two sector models on closer scrutiny is that the model for industrial nations exhibits a crowding-out effect between the two sectors (i.e., when one sector expands, the other tends to contract), while the model for developing nations exhibits a crowding in effect between sectors (with the two sectors tending to expand in unison). We will see later that the development of the *relative price* is a key element that brings about this difference. It may be noted that in the aggregated models with only one good, there is only one final good price, there being no relative price changes between goods. But in models with two final goods, government policies can alter the relative price between goods, with implications for the development of outputs of the sectors as well as sectoral and total employment.

Non-traded goods are those that cannot be supplied from a distance like real estate, haircuts, hot meals and so on, they have to be purchased in the local/domestic markets, where their prices are determined.

In two sector models, the sector effects could differ. The two sectors could expand together, or one sector could contract when the other expands showcasing a crowding-out effect. The relative price between goods is important.

20.4. THE SMALL OPEN ECONOMY MODEL FOR INDUSTRIALIZED NATIONS

One of the most widely used models of developed industrial economies is the Small Open Economy (SOE) Model. It portrays an economy producing *traded goods* (T) and *non-traded goods* (N). Thus, there is one aggregated tradable good and one aggregated non-traded good in the model. The definition of traded goods is that they are traded or tradable in world markets, where the price is determined. So, 'T' is the internationally competitive sector and the country is a price taker in the world market. The non-traded sector consists of utilities and services such as haircuts, which are not tradable across national borders. The price of the non-traded good is determined by its demand and supply in the national market.

Therefore, there are differing price formation mechanisms in the closed and the open sectors. For the traded goods, there is no possibility of a mark-up pricing at home, or of the price moving in tandem with domestic demand. The price is quite simply set in the world market, which the domestic economy, appropriately considered to be a SOE, has no influence worth remarking upon. With profit maximizing behaviour by the domestic firms making tradable goods, with an increase in domestic demand, the trade balance is affected negatively, but there is no change in the output and employment levels in that sector. In contrast, goods produced in the non-traded sector are priced in response to domestic conditions of supply and demand only. Changes in domestic demand can affect output and employment in the sector. Changes in domestic demand also affect the relative price between goods, with important further implications as will be seen in further in the chapter. Traded goods are priced in world markets, while for the non-traded goods, domestic supply and demand determines the price. The relative price between traded and non-traded goods is the key variable.

The two-sector SOE model can be conveniently represented by the following equations (we ignore trade balance equations, concentrating on the results for output and employment):

$$S_T = S_T(P_T/W) \tag{20.1}$$

$$S_N = S_N(P_N/W) = D_N(Y, P_N, P_T) + G_N \tag{20.2}$$

$$Y = P_T S_T + P_N S_N \tag{20.3}$$

$$W^* = aP_T^* + bP_N^* \tag{20.4}$$

$$L = L_T(P_T/W) + L_N(P_N/W) \tag{20.5}$$

Where S_T is supply of traded goods in the economy, S_N is supply of non-traded goods, P_T the prices of traded goods, P_N the price of non-traded goods, W is the wage rate, G_N is government demand, D_N is private demand which is function of total income Y, and L is total employment.

Equation 20.1 specifies output in the traded sector as dependent on the relation between product price and the wage rate (the so-called product wage). This relationship is a reduced form of the supply or production function, derived from the employment function, since labour demand depends on the product wage. Capital is assumed to be fixed in the short-run.

According to Equation 20.1, if the wage rises while the price of the traded goods is unchanged, employment and hence output would fall in the traded goods sector.

Equation 20.2 specifies output in the non-traded sector in a similar way and also states the equilibrium condition as demand = supply for non-traded goods, depending on the total income Y, which is the sum of outputs as indicated in Equation (20.3).

Equation 20.4 represents a wage formation process, the unions pushing up wages with weight 'a' for the traded goods price and weight 'b' for the non-traded goods price. When $a + b = 1$, there is real wage rigidity, with the wage rising by the same percentage as the CPI. In the equation, the asterisk (*) stands for rates of change.

Equation 20.5 shows that total employment is the sum of employment in the traded and non-traded sectors. Employment in sector i ($i = T, N$) rises if the price P_i rises relative to the wage and falls if the product wage (W/P_i) rises. We could add government employment as well.

Let us now trace the developments following an expansionary fiscal policy.

Increased spending by the government on non-traded goods and services (it could be even a pay rise in the government sector, or more government employment) creates excess demand in this sector and thereby raises the price of non-traded goods. This effect can be seen by substituting Equations 20.1, 20.3 and 20.4 into Equation 20.2, which is the equilibrium condition in the non-traded sector and then solving for P_N.

Now, from Equation 20.4, we can see that the wage rate rises by 'b' times the rise in P_N. With P_T unchanged, we have the following effects:

1. The product wage W/P_T rises in the traded sector, that is, P_T/W falls.
2. The product wage W/P_N falls in the non-traded sector, thus P_N/W rise.
3. 1 and 2 imply that employment and output falls in the traded goods sector, while employment and output rises in the non-traded sector.
4. Total employment may rise or fall. It may fall if the traded goods sector is relatively labour intensive in production, compared to the non-traded goods sector (which would then be the relatively capital-intensive sector).

The crux of this analysis is that increased government spending due to an expansionary fiscal policy raises the price of the non-traded goods price. The wage rate rises and the product wage falls in the non-traded sector and rises in the traded sector. Employment rises in the 'N' sector and falls in the 'T' sector. Total employment may rise or fall. These effects in the non-traded and traded goods markets are depicted in Figures 20.1 and 20.2.

The increase in government spending pushes out the aggregate demand curve for non-traded goods 'N' from D_1 to D_2, increasing the equilibrium price. The wage rate rises, trailing the increase in the CPI. Consequently, it results in the supply curve moving up from S_1 to S_2. However, since the rise in wage is less than the percentage rise in P_N, the net result is an increase in the supply of non-traded goods.

Let us now portray the developments in the traded goods market. From the impacts on the non-traded goods market, we have seen that the wage rate rises, trailing the rise in P_N. Now, refer to Figure 20.2. The demand curve for the traded good is horizontal at the fixed price P_T. As mentioned, the price of traded goods is defined in world markets and is given for the economy. The traded goods can be sold only at this price, and the supply by the home country is determined by profit maximization by firms. S_1 is the original supply curve, and the equilibrium output is then Q_1, where supply and demand intersect.

FIGURE 20.1

Fiscal Policy Effects in the Non-traded Goods Market

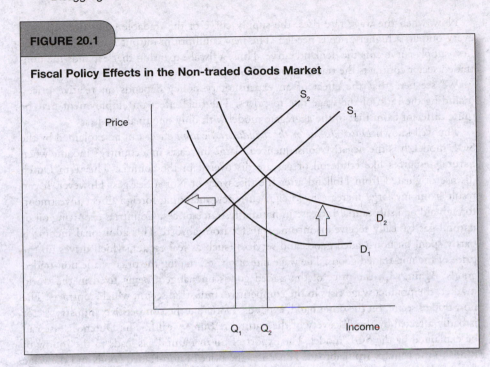

FIGURE 20.2

Fiscal Policy Effects in the Traded Goods Market

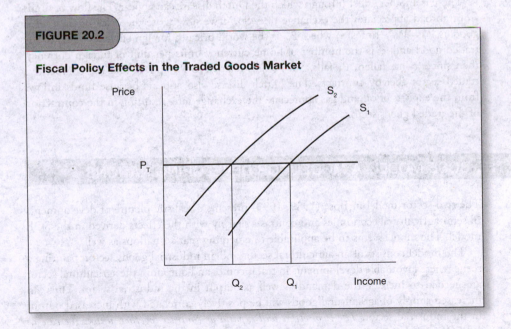

Now, when the wage rate rises, the supply curve of the tradable good rises up as at every output, a higher price is needed. The new equilibrium output is at Q_2, where the new supply curve cuts the demand curve. Thus, a fiscal expansion that expands the non-traded sector contracts the traded goods sector.

We see here that the effect of an expansionary policy depends on relative prices, including the ratio of the wage rate to prices. The final effect on employment may be quite different from that in the aggregate model with only one final good.

The Dutch disease or deindustrialization occurs when the traded manufacturing sector of an open industrial economy becomes less price-competitive following the discovery and international marketing of a natural resource.

The well-known *Dutch disease or the deindustrialization* effect can be explained by the SOE model. It is the negative consequence of large increases in a country's income when natural resources like crude oil or gas are discovered in the country. The term Dutch disease originated from Holland after the discovery of North Sea gas. However, it can result from any large increase in foreign currency, including foreign direct investment, foreign aid or a substantial increase in natural resource prices. Countries exporting oil or natural gas basically receive an income transfer from abroad. This additional income is partly spent on non-traded goods and services (such as real estate), which drives up the price of the non-traded goods. The wage rate also rises, trailing the price of the non-traded goods. Again, with the price of the traded goods unchanged, being fixed in the world market, the product wage rises in the competitive, industrial sector, which contracts. The non-traded sector, on the other hand, expands. Note that the competitive, industry sector is badly affected by the discovery of the natural resource wealth. The Dutch disease can be explained by the SOE model. The export of oil or natural gas leads to the inflow of funds to the country from abroad. This raises the price of non-traded goods and the wage rate, at the expense of the competitive traded goods sector.

There is another effect through which the Dutch disease can appear. The flow of funds from abroad appreciates the exchange rate. So, if we now write the price of the traded good as $P_T = P_W^*$ (times) e, where P_W is the world price in foreign currency units of the traded good and 'e' is the number of home currency units per unit of foreign currency, then since 'e' has fallen, P_T falls. So, P_T falls relative to P_N and W and the competitive traded sector thereby contracts. The Dutch disease also appears because funds inflows from the exports of oil and gas appreciate the exchange rate, resulting in the contraction of the traded goods sector.

20.5. THE BOSE MODEL: A MODEL FOR DEVELOPING NATIONS

The two-sector model in Bose (1989, 1993) presents a realistic picture of developments in semi-agricultural economies and contrasts sharply with the effects derived in the SOE model. The model seems to be applicable to emerging market nations as well.

The model consists of an agricultural sector and an industrial goods sector, painting a scene where favourable developments in real incomes and output in the agricultural sector are needed to increase the demand as well as output in the industrial sector. Thus, an increased supply of agricultural goods will be positively correlated with increased output in the industrial sector. *The two sectors will expand or contract together, unlike the case in the SOE model, wherein when one sector expands, the other tends to contract.*

There is no wage–push or pull mechanism operating, but a poor harvest leading to a rise in the price of the non-industrial (i.e., agricultural sector in this model) sector output will mean less real income for wage earners and hence less demand for industrial goods such as textiles, which are labour intensive in production. It can be observed that increased agricultural productivity will also lead to higher agricultural output and thereby lower food prices and raise real wage incomes, which would in turn hence enhance the output of industrial goods. Thus, ideally, agricultural output growth and industrial growth should show a positive correlation.

The main message of the Bose model can be described by Figures 20.3 and 20.4 but note that the actual model itself is more complex, as it becomes transparent from the equation system of the model presented here later.

With productivity growth in the agricultural sector, there is an increase in the marketed surplus of agricultural products by farmers, and the supply curve shifts to the right, reducing the price from P_1 to P_2. This has important effects on the industrial sector.

The agricultural productivity increase leads to increased supply and thus reduces the price of agricultural goods. This is a *windfall gain* for wage income earners, since their real incomes increase because of the price fall. The increase in real incomes increases the demand for industrial goods.

Now, output is demand determined in the industrial sector, which employs a mark-up above the costs pricing scheme. Thus, the supply curve is horizontal as in the basic Keynes model. The demand curve shifts to the right and output expands in the industrial sector, from Q_1 to Q_2. Thus, agricultural and industrial outputs move in tandem, having a

A windfall gain is an unexpected profit from a business or other source. The term connotes gaining huge profits without working for them either due to unforeseen inheritance or shortage of supply.

FIGURE 20.3

The Bose Model: Agricultural Sector, Productivity Growth

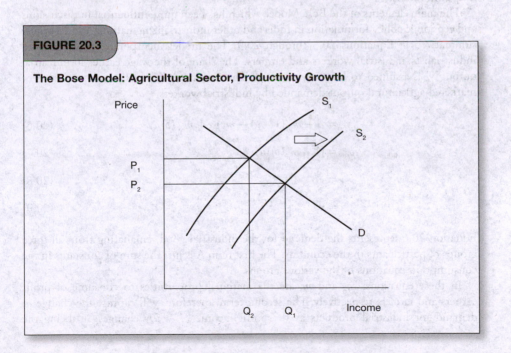

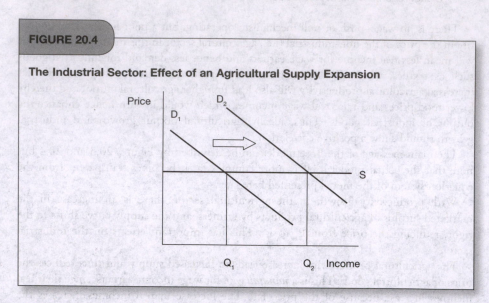

FIGURE 20.4

The Industrial Sector: Effect of an Agricultural Supply Expansion

positive correlation with each other. Output is demand determined in industry and demand depends on real incomes. Real incomes rise when the price of agricultural goods falls due to an agricultural supply increase. So higher output in agriculture leads to higher output in industry.

The main elements of the Bose Model, which has been quite influential in discussions and economic policy formulation in India and other industrializing nations, can be briefly summarized in Equations 20.6 through 20.9. The model incorporates profit earning industrialists, industrial workers and farmers. The share of the wage earner in industrial output 'y' is assumed to be constant at 'u'. The income of farmers equals the value of marketed agricultural output demanded by industrial workers.

$$y^d = A + m_p (1 - u) + m_f px + m_w (p) uy \tag{20.6}$$

$$px^d = [1 - m_w(p)]uy \tag{20.7}$$

$$y = y^d \tag{20.8}$$

$$x = x^d \tag{20.9}$$

Equation 20.6 represents the demand for the industrial good, emanating from all three groups of participants in the economy. The first term A is just the sum of constants in the consumption equations of the various groups.

In these equations, m_p and m_f are the marginal propensities to consume of profit earners and farmers respectively. The second term, therefore, will capture the change in demand for industrial products as the profit income *(1 − u)y* changes, 'u' being the capitalist share. Similarly the third term is the demand arising from farmer income *(px)*, obtained through the sale of the marketable agricultural surplus '*x*', which is held exogenous in the model.

The third term in Equation 20.6 is the demand due to worker incomes *(uy)*, but the marginal propensity to consume from this income, m_w, is modelled to be dependent on the price of the agricultural product (food), '*p*'. The marginal propensity to consume industrial products falls as the price of food rises, since the *demand for food is price inelastic*. For simplicity, we rewrite $m_w(p)$ in what follows as *(a − kp)*, with $k > 0$, so that the marginal propensity of workers to consume the industrial good falls as the price of food, p, rises. The rise in the price of food plays a key role by affecting the real income available for consumption to the workers.

Equilibrium in the system is represented by equilibrium in the industrial and agricultural product markets, that is, Equations (20.8) and (20.9), respectively, equating demand and supply. Substituting these equilibrium conditions into Equations 20.6 and 20.7, we can solve for '*y*' and '*p*'. In fact, we can substitute Equation 20.7 also into Equation 20.6 to solve for '*y*' [also using $m_w(p) = \alpha - kp$, with $k > 0$] as

$$y = A/1 - \varphi \qquad (20.10)$$

where

$$\varphi = [(1 - u)m_p + um_f(1 - \alpha) + u\alpha + puk(m_f - 1)] \qquad (20.11)$$

It can be observed from Equations 20.10 and 20.11 that as long as m_f is less than 1, '*y*' and '*p*' have an inverse relationship. Thus a rise in the price of the marketed agricultural surplus may increase industrial demand from farmers, but the fall in demand from workers whose real incomes have fallen will bring about a reduction in the total demand for industrial goods. Thus, with industrial output being demand determined, an increase in agricultural production (and marketed surplus), which reduces food prices, will also boost industrial production. The model therefore has features that can bring about a complimentary relationship between agricultural and industrial output growth.

The Bose Model has seen further development and applications, but we do not elaborate on these here. We just briefly note that the model generates interesting results with respect to income distribution issues as well. Disaggregating industrial production into luxury goods and wage goods output, with profit earners consuming only the former, it can be shown using reasonable assumptions about the relative marginal propensities to consume that the production of luxury goods may increase even when total industrial output contracts. Also, recognizing the existence of marginal farmers who do not sell any agricultural surplus, it can be shown that their real incomes will fall when agricultural prices and agricultural incomes as a whole rise. This effect also translates into less demand for wage goods and exacerbates the contraction of the aggregate industrial sector. Since such goods like textiles are usually more labour intensive in production than luxury good like automobiles, there are also important implications for the level of employment in the model results.

In the Lewis and Harris-Todaro models of less developed countries also, a complimentary pattern of growth between the rural (agricultural) sector and the urban (manufacturing) sector is shown as possible,[1] provided there are no serious wage shocks or unfavourable productivity developments.

It may be noted that the terms of trade (i.e., the relative price of goods) play an important role in all the models discussed here and are the common strand that binds them together. In the SOE model applications, it is usually increased government demand for non-traded services, often with the intention of propping up employment levels, that turns the terms of trade in favour of the non-industrial sector. In Bose's model[2] too, harvest failures or changes in government procurement policies involving support prices could affect the terms of trade between industry and agriculture. In both cases, turning the terms of trade against the industry led to a reduction in industrial output. Thus, despite considerable differences between the models used for industrial nations and developing economies, similar results could be forthcoming under certain conditions or assumptions.

But, despite these common elements in the SOE and the Bose Model, what has been empirically observed is that the former does well in tracking developments in the industrial nations, while the Bose model is very useful in analysing structural changes and output effects in developing countries. Indeed, the propositions put forth in this chapter can be tested empirically, as seen in the case study provided at the end of the chapter.

20.6. CONCLUSION

This chapter has presented disaggregated models of a market economy, leading to additional, rich insights that are not forthcoming from an aggregated model with only one good. Important structural changes can be captured by such a disaggregation. Also, importantly, the final impacts of government policies could very well depend on the particular structure of the economy in which it is undertaken. For instance, we have seen that the effects on total employment of an expansionary policy could well turn out to be negative in a disaggregated model, which could not be the case in the aggregated model of earlier chapters.

It has been also noted that there are important differences in the economic structures of industrial nations and developing countries, so that different types of disaggregated models, with varying sectoral assumptions about the supply and demand sides are needed to understand policy effects and economic developments in these countries at varying stages of the development process. In other words, disaggregation serves a useful purpose by offering the possibility of formulating models in different ways to suit the actual realities prevailing in the country under the microscope.

---

[1] W. Arthur Lewis, 'A Model of Dualistic Economics', *American Economic Review* 36, no. 1 (1954): 46–51; John R. Harris and Michael P. Todaro, 'Migration, Unemployment and Development: A Two-Sector Analysis', *The American Economic Review* 60, no. 1 (1970): 126–42.

[2] Bose's (1989, 1993).

SUMMARY

- In the aggregate model, an expansionary fiscal policy increased output and total employment. The composition of output also changed with private investment falling and the government sector expanding and this was known as the crowding-out effect.
- The two sector models applied to industrial economies are often incapable of explaining developments in semi-industrialized, or in even emerging market economies. The analysis often comes up with a crowding out, rather than a complimentary relation between the various sectors of the economy, something that is not usually observed for industrializing countries.
- The SOE Model portrays an economy producing *traded goods* (T) and *non-traded goods* (N). Traded goods are those that are traded or are tradable in world markets, where their prices are formed. The non-traded sector consists of utilities and services such as haircuts, which are not tradable across national borders. The price of the non-traded good is determined by the demand and supply in the national market. Therefore, there are differing price formation mechanisms in the closed and the open sectors.
- Increased spending by the government on non-traded goods and services, such as a pay rise for government servants, or an increase in government employment, creates excess demand in this sector and raises the price of non-traded goods. With the rise in wage rate, the product wage falls in the non-traded sector and rises in the traded sector. Employment rises in the 'N' non-traded sector and falls in the 'T' traded sector. Total employment may rise or fall.
- The SOE model can explain the *Dutch disease* or the *deindustrialization* effect. It is the negative consequence of a large increase in a country's income when any natural resource like crude oil or gas is discovered in the country and the consequent impact on demand and relative goods prices. The Dutch disease also appears because the funds inflow from the exports of oil and gas appreciates the exchange rate, resulting in the contraction of the traded goods sector.
- The Bose two-sector model[3] in presents a realistic picture of developments in semi-agricultural economies, which contrasts sharply with effects derived in the SOE model. The model is applicable to emerging market nations too. It consists of an agricultural sector and an industrial goods sector. The two sectors expand or contract together, unlike the case in the SOE model, where when one sector expands, the other tends to contract.
- The agricultural productivity increase leads to increased supply and reduces the price of agricultural goods. This is a windfall gain for wage income earners, since their real incomes increase due to the price fall. The increase in real

[3] Ibid.

incomes increases the demand for industrial goods. Output is demand determined in the industrial sector, which employs a mark-up above the costs pricing scheme. The model has, therefore, features that can bring about a complimentary relationship between agricultural and industrial output growth.

- The terms of trade (i.e., the relative price of goods) plays an important role in all the models discussed here and can be the common strand that binds them together. In the SOE model applications, it is usually increased government demand for non-traded services, often with the intention of propping up employment levels, which turns the terms of trade in favour of the non-industrial sector. In Bose's model[4] too, harvest failures or changes in government procurement policies involving support prices can affect the terms of trade between industry and agriculture. In both cases, turning the terms of trade against industry leads to a reduction in industrial output. Thus, despite considerable differences between the models used for industrial nations and developing economies, similar results can be forthcoming under certain conditions or assumptions.

CASE STUDY

The Two Sector Models for Open Economies

The two sector models applied to industrial economies do not appear to be useful in explaining developments in newly industrialized or even emerging economies. In these models the analysis often brings forth a crowding out, rather than a complimentary relation between the various sectors of the economy.[5] A better explanation of the growth process in emerging economies seems to come from a model specifically designed for them. For instance the two-sector model in Bose shows the industry–agriculture growth correlations to be strong for developing countries as well as emerging markets.[6] However, there are possibilities of synthesis of these different two sector models, theoretically, or empirically, so that the approaches have wider application, to more than a limited group of countries.

A study using a large cross-section sample of developed, developing and emerging market countries[7] tested the propositions put forward in this chapter. Some of the results obtained from this study are presented in the box. The following sample of more than 50 countries, drawn from the developed, developing and emerging market groups was used for the study:

---

[4] Ibid.

[5] Lars Calmfors, 'Real Wages, Inflation and Unemployment in the Open Economy', *Inflation and Employment in Open Economies*, (Amsterdam:North-Holland, 1979); Assar Lindbeck (ed.), *Inflation and Employment in Open Economies: Essays. Vol. 5*, (North Holland, 1979); W. Max Corden, and J. Peter Neary, 'Booming Sector and De-industrialisation in a Small Open Economy', *The Economic Journal* 92, no. 368 (1982): 825–48.

[6] Bose (1989, 1993).

[7] B. Batavia and P. Nandakumar, *Journal of Economic Asymmetries* 8, no. 2 (2011).

TABLE CS 20.1

Fifty Countries Across Developed, Emerging and Developing Countries

Emerging Countries	Developing Countries	Industrialized Countries
1. Argentina	1. Bangladesh	1. Australia
2. Brazil	2. Bolivia	2. Austria
3. Chile	3. Botswana	3. Belgium
4. India	4. Burundi	4. Canada
5. Indonesia	5. Cameroon	5. Denmark
6. Republic of Korea	6. Colombia	6. Finland
7. Malaysia	7. Republic of Congo	7. France
8. Mexico	8. Costa Rica	8. Germany
9. Philippines	9. Dominican Republic	9. Greece
10. Thailand	10. Ecuador	10. Italy
11. Turkey	11. El Salvador	11. Japan
12. Venezuela	12. Gambia	12. Netherlands
13. Vietnam	13. Ghana	13. New Zealand
	14. Guinea-Bissau	14. Portugal
	15. Iran	15. Spain
	16. Jamaica	16. Sweden
	17. Jordan	17. United Kingdom
	18. Kenya	18. United States
	19. Nicaragua	
	20. Niger	
	21. Nigeria	
	22. Pakistan	
	23. Paraguay	
	24. Peru	
	25. Senegal	
	26. Sierra lone	
	27. South Africa	
	28. Sri Lanka	
	29. Trinidad and Tobago	
	30. Tunisia	
	31. Zimbabwe	

Data on aggregate GDP growth, sector-wise growth in manufacturing output, agricultural output and in the output of services was collected for all these countries. The hypothesized relationships were tested using the following multiple regression equation, with a cross-section sample, for different time periods:

$$g_m = \alpha_0 + \alpha_1 g_a + \alpha_2 g_s + \varepsilon,$$

where g_m is the growth rate in the manufacturing sector and g_a and g_s are the growth rates in agricultural and services output respectively ('ε' is the residual).

TABLE CS 20.2

Regressions with Manufacturing Growth as the Dependent Variable (2005–08)

Countries	Coefficient for Service Sector Growth	Coefficient for Agricultural Sector Growth
Emerging markets and developing countries	0.64*	0.12
Developed nations	0.024	0.123

*represents significance at 5% level.

Sector growth rate correlations were also obtained for various time periods. These are given in Tables Case Study 20.3 and 20.4.

TABLE CS 20.3

Sector Correlations, Developing Countries (1990s)

Sector	Industry	Agriculture	Services
Industry	1	0.24	0.62
Agriculture	0.24	1	0.28
Services	0.62	0.28	1

Another result obtained from the study is that total, aggregate growth in the economy is positively related to the high positive correlations between sectoral growths, this being particularly true for the emerging market nations.

TABLE CS 20.4

Sector Growth Correlations, Industrial Countries (1990s)

Sector	Industry	Agriculture	Services
Industry	1	0.28	0.12
Agriculture	0.28	1	0.27
Services	0.12	0.27	1

After examining the results supplied in the tables given in the box, answer the following questions:

1. Is balanced growth (growth across all or at least some of the sectors) taking place in all three groups of countries?
2. If the answer to question 1 is 'no', then identify the (group of) countries in which balanced growth is taking place.
3. What could be the reason(s) for unbalanced growth in some groups of countries?
4. The Bose Model looks at the link between the agricultural and the manufacturing sectors. In this study, which sectors exhibit the strongest positive linkage in sector growth? Which group(s) of countries show such a strong positive inter-sector linkage? Is India a part of this group(s)?

KEYWORDS

Crowding out
Relative price
Traded goods

Non-trade goods
Dutch disease
Windfall gain

CONCEPT CHECK

State whether the following statements are true or false:

1. In the aggregate model, an expansionary fiscal policy increases output and total employment, but the composition of output changes private investment falls and the government sector expands.

2. In the two sector model, unlike in the aggregate model, an expansionary fiscal policy leads to both the sectors expanding together or one sector contracting while the other expands, namely, a crowding-out effect.

3. The price of traded goods is determined by domestic supply and demand in the domestic market, but non-traded goods are priced in the international markets.

4. In the interaction between traded and non-traded goods, the relative price between them is the key variable.

5. Increased government spending due to expansionary fiscal policy raises the price of non-traded goods.

6. The Dutch disease can be explained by the SOE model as follows: the export of oil or natural gas leads to the flow of funds into the country from abroad causing the exchange rate to appreciate, making domestically produced manufactured goods less competitive in the world markets.

7. Output is demand determined in industry. Demand depends on real incomes. Real incomes rise when the price of agricultural goods falls due to an agricultural supply increase. So higher output in agriculture leads to higher output in industry.

8. The Dutch disease also appears because the fund inflows from the exports of oil and gas appreciate the exchange rate resulting in the contraction of the traded goods sector.

DISCUSSION QUESTIONS

1. What do the terms 'traded' and 'non-traded' goods mean?

2. Is output demand determined in the traded goods sector in the SOE model?

3. How is the wage determination process related to the relative prices of goods in the SOE model?

4. What would happen in the SOE model if the government devalued the currency?

5. Are real incomes dependent on industrial goods prices in the Bose model?

6. Is agricultural output demand determined in the Bose model?

7. Compare the employment effects of expansionary policies in the aggregated model and the SOE model.

8. What happens with a harvest failure in the Bose model? Do sector outputs move in tandem?

Index

absolute income
  hypothesis, 243–45
  limitations on consumption, 243–45
accelerator model, 257
accelerator theory, 418
advancing loans, 142
aggregate production possibility curve, 270
aggregate demand curve, 193–94
  mathematical derivation for, 191
aggregate model, 477
aggregate production possibility curve, 270
aggregate supply curve
  long-run, 305
annual public and private investment in India, 215
automatic stabilizers, 70, 282
autonomous income
  spending changes in taxes, effects on, 212

balanced budget, 56
balance of payments (BOP)
  accounts 1970–71 to 1979–80, 340
banking system, 153
Bose model, 477
  model for developing nations, 476
Bretton Woods system, 407
budget deficit, 148
budget government, 35–36, 62–64
business cycles, 428
  chronology of, 430

capital gain
  short- and long-term bonds with, 115
capital inflows, 407
capital–labour ratio, 106
capital mobility, 401
capital stock, 106
case
  business cycles, 430
  continuing challenges in the external sector, 382
  fiscal debacle, 282
  global financial crisis and the currency wars, 408

India experienced crowding out of private
  investment, 214
India in throes of stagflation, 313
industry houses seek economic revival
  package, 240
package in aftermath of the global financial
  crisis in the G20 countries, 71
savings behaviour and the Permanent Income
  model in low income rural households, 261
state of higher education in India, 107
two sector models for open economies, 478
cash reserve ratio (CRR), 137
Central Bank, 154
  balance sheet, 137
  Intervention, 375, 403
  targets of, 151
circular flow of income, 44
closed economy, 347
coincidental indicators
  components of, 424
coincident indicators, 431
complete crowding out, 204
conservatives, 228
Consumer Price Index (CPI), 11–12
consumption function 55, 242–45, 251–52, 414
cost of inflation, 327
credit creation, 139
critical rate of interest, 174
crowding out
  state of the economy and, 205
currency, 153–54
  appreciation, 377
current account deficit (CAD), 381–82
cyclic budget balances
  structural, 65

dating business cycles, 427
debt burden
  stability condition, derivation of, 329
deficit finance, 235
demand
  bonds, 112, 115–19, 221
  side GDP, 34–35, 46, 49
  labour curve, 106

management, 256
money, behaviour towards risk, 17
demonetization, 133–34
devaluation, 381
devaluation and trade balance
Marshall–Lerner condition, 369
divergence between countries across the world, 100
Dornbusch's overshooting model, 397, 408
Dutch disease, 477

economic growth, 104
economy
technological advancements in, 236
European Monetary Union
Maastricht criteria for entry into, 330
elasticity of import, 368, 370
elasticity of exports, 368, 370
excess reserve, 141
exchange rate, 149, 184
country's currency, 163
determinants of, 191–95
Dornbusch's overshooting model, 199–201
dynamics, 201
exogenous spending, 184
expansionary fiscal policies, 213, 381
extended investment function
IS–LM model results and, 259
external debt, 235
external deficits, 235

financial markets equilibrium, 125
fiscal deficit, 70
fiscal expansion, 238
fiscal policy
monetary accommodation with, 204
fixed and floating exchange rates
pros and cons of, 404
fixed exchange rates system, 403
rupee tends to depreciate, 404
strengthening of rupee, 403
foreign direct investment (FDI), 346
Friedman Milton, 167, 247–48, 253–55

GDP deflator, 32–33
golden rule, 105, 106
government budget
accounts and budget deficits, 279
government deficits, 235
setting limits on, 329
government intervention, 282

government policy
constraints on, 237
government policy-making
supply side policies, 237
gross domestic product (GDP), 47
measuring, 31
gross national product (GNP), 26
growth, 19, 105
accounting, 106
diversity of, 81
indicators of Latin American countries, 82
growth in East Asian countries
contribution of TFP in GDP, 86

High-powered money, 138
home interest rate
rise in, 396
human capital accumulation, 106
Indian, 104

imperfect capital mobility
macroeconomic policy with, 380
imported inflation, 405
income
per capita 6–19, 77–78, 87, 98, 100
disposable
personal disposable, 27
Index of Industrial Production (IIP), 31–32, 311, 431
inflation
cost push inflation, 298
demand pull inflation, 298
inflationary expectations, 311
interest rate risk
period to maturity, 114
internal balance, 381
inventory investment, 46
inverse relationship, 125
investment demand
accelerator model of, 257
IS curve, 190, 194
position of, 184
IS–LM curves
construction of aggregate demand curve from, 191
IS–LM framework, 380
IS–LM model
elements of, 189
IS–LM model, 193
output and interest rate determination in, 188–89

J curve, 381
   effect, 370
John Maynard Keynes, 53

Keynesian Hidden Cross, 60
Keynesian model, 69
Keynesian multiplier, 57

labour productivity
   increases in labour productivity, 237
lag indicators
   components of, 425
lead indicators
   components of, 424
legal tender, 132–34
Life Cycle theory, 261
liquidity trap, 228
LM curve, 190, 194
   adjustment over time, 191
   balance of payments, 191–92
   factors affecting, slope of, 187
   position and monetary policy, 187
   shifts, 187–88
   slope in interest rate and income space, 185
long run, 5
   wage contracts, 454

macroeconomic stabilization, 282
Mahatma Gandhi National Rural Employment
   Guarantee Act (MGNREGA), 15
marginal propensity, 428
market power, 282
Marshall–Lerner condition, 381
microeconomics, 2
monetarists, 174
monetary policy
   state of economy, 228
money
   characteristic of, 153
   functions of, 153
   illusion, 173
   multiplier, 153

national income accounts, 23
national income of India, 45
national product
   expenditure method, 30
   final goods and services, 26
   income method, 28
nominal GDP, 46

open economy, 31, 355, 407
   monetary and fiscal policies in, 377
   trade and capital flows in, 348
optimal portfolio
   demand for money, 172
overall unemployment rate in rural and urban
   India, 16

Phillips curve, 311
   expectations-augmented, 303
policies, 228
   effects of on composition of output, 228
   under flexible exchange rates, fiscal policy
     effectiveness, 377
portfolio balance model, 403
portfolio model, 408
portfolio of demand, 174
precautionary motive, 173
price elasticity
   export demand of, 368
   import demand of, 368
primary deficit, 278
private final consumption expenditure (PFCE), 12
problems and issues in GDP measurement
   economic bads and side effects, 39
   environmental costs, 39–40
   imputation of values, 38
   leisure and human costs, 39
   non-market production, 38
   quality of goods, 38
   underground economy, 38
protectionism, 355
public expenditure on higher and technical
   education, 109
public goods, 282

quality of goods, 38
quantity equation, 165
quantity theory of money, 165–67

rate of growth of output, 105
real business cycles, 422
real effective exchange rate (REER), 352
real exchange rate, 355
real GDP, 10–12, 31–33
real interest rate, 37, 116
real money, 173
recession, 425
repo rate, 149
required reserves, 141

Reserve Bank of India
    repo rate and reverse repo rate, 150
revenue deficit, 277
reverse repo, 149
run on banks, 141

short- and long-run price elasticities
    demand for exports and imports of, 369
small open economy model (SOE), 477
socialists, 238
Solow growth model, 105
Solow growth theory, 105
speculative motive, 173
stagflation, 168
Statutory liquidity ratio (SLR), 141

Tobin's q, 259
total factor productivity, 85
trade balance, 355
trade shares in GDP and country growth
    performance, 363
transaction motive, 173
transfer payments, 27
transfers and net exports, 213
trends in velocity of money in India, 168
two sector model, 477

uncovered interest rate parity condition (UIP),
    395
unemployment, 20
    benefits, 70
    frictional, 36, 294, 320
    structural, 36
    seasonal, 36
user cost of capital
    interest rate, 258
    profits and, 258

vault cash, 138
velocity of money
    in Indian, trends in economy, 169

welfare states, 267
wholesale price index (WPI), 12–14
windfall gain, 473

yield
    curve, 102, 106
    government securities market, 103
    interest, 95
    maturity, 105
    rate of return and, 96